THE COMPLETE
GARDENER'S GUIDE

THE COMPLETE GARDENER'S GUIDE

The One-Stop Guide to Plan, Sow, Plant, and Grow Your Garden

CONTENTS

MAKE A START

10 What plants need

*Understanding plants • Garden jargon •
Right plant, right place • Choosing healthy
plants • From the ground up • Enriching
the soil • Basic tool kit*

DESIGN YOUR GARDEN

28 Assess your garden needs
32 A space to entertain
36 The productive garden
40 Family garden
44 A calming retreat
48 Wildlife haven
52 Enthusiast's garden
56 Easy care garden
60 What is achievable?
62 Where to start

*Old garden, new garden • Surveying the site •
Dealing with slopes • Creating boundaries •
Surfaces • Garden buildings • Lighting*

78 Design principles

Drawing simple plans • Creating a design

84 Putting up fence posts
86 How to lay a path

88 How to lay a patio
90 How to install a deck
92 Laying a lawn
94 Making a pergola
96 Making a pond
98 Building a raised bed

PLANT YOUR GARDEN

102 Plant families
104 Designing with plants
106 Create a planting style
110 Introducing color and texture
112 Seasonal effects
114 Maximizing plant power
116 Creating a simple planting plan
118 Introducing trees

*Selecting and planting ornamental trees •
Tree recipes • Ornamental cherries*

126 Styles with shrubs

*Selecting and planting shrubs • Shrub recipes •
Classic roses*

134 Planting with perennials

*Selecting and planting perennials • Perennial
recipes • Perennials for foliage*

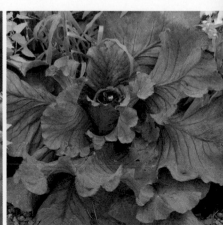

142 Introducing climbers and wall shrubs
*Selecting and planting climbers and wall shrubs •
Climber recipes • Climbing clematis*

150 Bamboo and grass effects
*Selecting and planting bamboos and grasses •
Bamboo and grass recipes • Focus on grasses*

158 Using bulbs effectively
*Selecting and planting bulbs • Bulb recipes •
Dazzling dahlias*

166 Easy-going annuals and biennials
*Selecting and planting annuals and biennials •
Annuals recipes • Striking sunflowers*

174 Water gardening
*Selecting and planting water plants •
Water plant recipes • Perfect water lilies*

GROW YOUR OWN

184 What to grow
186 Where to grow
188 Tools and equipment
*Prepare a site • Sow your own • A year
in the vegetable garden • Healthy crops •
Continuous harvest • Storing vegetables*

202 Vegetable crop planner
206 Lettuce

207 Cut-and-come-again
208 Loose leaf crops
210 Tomatoes
212 Peppers and chiles
213 Eggplants
214 Cucumbers
216 Sweet corn
217 Florence fennel
218 Rhubarb
219 Celery
220 Zucchini and marrows
221 Summer squash
222 Pumpkins
223 Winter squash
224 Radishes
225 Beets
226 Carrots
227 Kohlrabi
228 Potatoes
230 Root and stem crops
232 Onions
233 Shallots
234 Garlic
235 Leeks

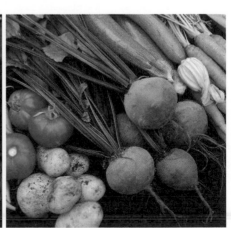

236 Peas
237 Fava beans
238 Green beans
239 Runner beans
240 Cabbages
242 Kale
243 Brussels sprouts
244 Broccoli
245 Cauliflower
246 Globe artichokes
247 Asparagus
248 Annual herbs
250 Hardy border herbs
252 Fruit in the garden
*Buying and planting fruit • A year
in the fruit garden • Managing a glut*
260 Fruit crop planner
262 Apples
264 Pears
266 Plum family
268 Cherries
270 Peaches and nectarines
272 Quinces
273 Figs

274 Grapes
276 Strawberries
278 Raspberries
280 Blackberries and hybrids
282 Black currants
283 Red and white currants
284 Gooseberries
285 Blueberries

CARE FOR YOUR GARDEN

288 The gardening year
298 How to water
300 Saving water
302 How to feed
304 Container growing
306 A good display
308 Tender plants
310 Pruning
*Pruning shrubs • Pruning for a purpose •
Pruning climbers • Pruning roses • Pruning to
renovate • How to cut a hedge • Basic topiary*
326 Propagating plants
*Growing from seed • Taking cuttings •
Layering and dividing*

334 Lawns

Caring for your lawn • Lawn problems •
Mini meadows

342 Ponds and water

Maintaining pond plants • Fish and wildlife

HELP AND ADVICE

350 Controlling weeds
354 Diagnosing problems
356 Controlling pests and diseases
360 A–Z of common pests
364 A–Z of diseases and disorders

PLANT CHOOSER

372 Annuals, biennials, and bedding
374 Plants for summer containers
376 Spring-flowering bulbs
378 Summer and fall bulbs
380 Spring and early summer perennials
383 Summer and fall perennials
386 Perennials for winter interest
388 Water and bog plants
390 Plants for scent
392 Shrubs for walls

394 Climbers for shade
396 Climbers for sun
398 Screening and hedging plants
400 Rock plants
402 Spring-flowering shrubs
405 Summer-flowering shrubs
408 Shrubs for fall interest
410 Shrubs for winter interest
412 Ground-cover plants for sun
414 Ground-cover plants for shade
416 Grasses, sedges, and bamboos
418 Conifers for small gardens
420 Structural plants
422 Trees for small gardens
424 Multi-interest trees
426 Plants for acid soils
428 Plants for chalky and lime-rich soils
430 Plants for heavy clay
432 Plants for hot, dry sites
434 Plants for exposed sites

436 Index

MAKE A START

If you are fairly new to gardening, start here. This chapter
takes you through the basics that will make gardening
easier and you a better gardener from day one. All the key
topics are covered here: how plants grow and reproduce,
how to improve your soil, how to recognize healthy plants,
and how to choose the most suitable ones for your plot.
Plant names and garden jargon are decoded, and there's
a guide to the most useful tools.

WHAT PLANTS NEED

All plants need moisture, nutrients, sunlight, and a suitable temperature for healthy growth and optimal development. However, they will need different levels of each depending on the natural habitats in which they have evolved.

▼ MOISTURE

Water is vital for plants since it is used in photosynthesis (*see facing page*) and to keep leaves and stems firm and upright. Plants have a variety of methods to absorb and store it. Most take up moisture through microscopic root hairs and lose it via the leaves in a process called transpiration. This cycle enables sugars and nutrients to be circulated. Plants from arid regions, such as cacti, often have a reduced leaf area and a waxy coating to control moisture loss.

Water-loving bog plants, such as *Gunnera manicata* and some irises, need moisture-rich sites at the margins of garden ponds and pools.

► TEMPERATURE

Plants are classified according to hardiness: tender specimens tolerate temperatures down to 41°F (5°C), frost-hardy to 23°F (-5°C), and fully hardy to -4°F (-20°C). Every plant has specific temperature requirements; young plants are especially vulnerable and usually need protection to survive. Seedlings that have been raised indoors should be gradually introduced to cooler outdoor temperatures, a process known as "hardening off." Frost-sensitive plants should be wrapped up *in situ* or moved to a frost-free location over winter.

Tender, exotic plants, such as cacti, aloes, and agaves, require a warm, dry site and need protection against frost in cold winter climates.

◄ SUNLIGHT

Sunlight powers plant growth in the process of photosynthesis. The green parts of plants, which contain the pigment chlorophyll, absorb light and use it to convert carbon dioxide and water to sugar and starches. These compounds make cellulose, the building block of plant tissue.

Shoots and leaves will move to trap light as efficiently as possible, but if they receive an insufficient amount or a restricted spectrum, they become pale and drawn, or "etiolated." Plants that are adapted to heat and bright light tend to have small or narrow, even needlelike, leaves and may have various "sunscreens," such as dark masking pigments or silver-gray felting. Shade-adapted plants often have broad leaves or large leaves made up of smaller leaflets, which allow them to absorb as much light as possible. In full sun, shade plants may scorch since they are unaccustomed to the high light levels.

The large surface area of the leaves of the banana plant enable it to absorb light.

▲ NUTRITION

Plants need three key elements and a range of trace elements for healthy growth. Nitrogen (N) governs the growth of leaves and shoots; potassium (K), or potash, is required for flowering and fruiting; and phosphorus (P) promotes strong root growth. Adverse growing conditions, such as incorrect pH or underwatering, can inhibit absorption. When plants run short of these, they show deficiency symptoms including stunted or distorted growth or discolored foliage. High-potassium fertilizers suit most plants.

Fast-growing plants such as *Rosa* 'The Fairy' have greater nutritional demands than plants that are adapted to poor or dry soils.

Seed heads can be an ornamental feature of plants like poppies (*Papaver*), which will quickly populate a wide area if allowed to spread their seeds. For more targeted seedlings, remove the heads, and save the seed.

UNDERSTANDING PLANTS

A basic understanding of plants underpins everything you do in the garden. Are you planting annuals for just one season, or a shrub or perennial that will become permanent? Knowing how plants reproduce also helps you maximize their contribution to your garden.

LIFE CYCLES

Annual plants complete their life cycle in a single growing season: growing from seed, flowering, and then dying. Removing fading flowers before they get a chance to set seed tricks them into producing more and lengthens the floral display.

Hardy annuals, such as pot marigolds, nasturtiums, and candytuft, will germinate outdoors and can be sown in the fall to overwinter as young plants for early summer flowers but are usually sown in the spring as soon as soil conditions allow. Half-hardy annuals require indoor warmth to germinate and are transferred outdoors after the risk of frost has passed. This group includes most traditional bedding plants, such as petunias, salvia, and French marigolds.

Biennials, such as foxgloves and forget-me-nots, usually complete their life cycle in two years. Seedlings appear in summer and then overwinter before producing flowers in spring or early summer, then setting seed and dying.

What is a perennial?

Perennials live on from one year to the next. The term is mainly used to describe nonwoody herbaceous plants like delphiniums and geraniums, which die back in winter and reshoot in the spring. Tender perennials, such as pot geraniums, also survive from year to year if kept in temperatures above freezing.

Annual plants, such as nasturtiums (*Tropaeolum*), reproduce by setting seed before they die at the end of their life cycle. You can collect seed from your annuals to sow for new plants the following year (see pp.326–329).

Biennial plants, including foxgloves (*Digitalis*), set seed before the end of their two-year life cycle. They require two growing seasons before blooming—pinch off any buds that form in the first season to ensure a good display

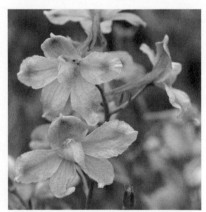

Perennial plants have a root system that lives for three or more years; "herbaceous" explains the fact that the part above the ground dies down each year, although a few perennials are evergreen and provide winter interest.

REPRODUCTION

Pollination leading to setting seed is by far the most common way by which flowering plants reproduce in nature. Most garden flowers, fruits, and vegetables are pollinated by insects, particularly bees, but grasses, conifers, shrubs and trees with catkins, and crops like sweet corn are wind pollinated.

Pollination is a method of sexual reproduction and therefore means that a variety of genetic combinations are possible and the resulting seedlings can vary. Although some flowers are self-pollinating, which means they do not need to receive pollen from another flower to reproduce, cross-pollination or cross-fertilization ensures a good genetic mix, giving plants in the wild a greater chance of adapting to their environment.

In horticulture, variation is what enables plant breeders to select and produce cultivars with new combinations of desirable characteristics. Commercial seed production is carefully controlled to minimize this genetic variation and produce predictable results that retain these characteristics. F1 seed (see pp.328–329) is the most uniform and the most expensive, followed by F2 and the cheaper, open-pollinated strains.

Asexual reproduction

As well as pollination and seeding, plants use a number of other ways to reproduce at ground level and beneath the soil. Runners, rhizomes, bulbils, and offsets (see right) are all "vegetative" or "asexual" means of reproduction that are useful for gardeners, because the plants produced are normally identical to the parent and produce garden-ready specimens quickly and easily.

Runners are stems that grow out from the parent plant. They root where they touch the soil surface and can later be severed and transplanted. Strawberries and spider plants (*Chlorophytum*) reproduce in this way.

Rhizomes are specialized stems that travel through the ground from the parent plant, emerging as a cluster of new shoots a distance away. Perennials that spread via rhizomes can be invasive, especially in light soils.

Bulbils are bulblike growths produced from the stems of some plants, including several ornamental lilies and some members of the onion family. They drop onto the soil and take root or can be pulled off and planted.

Offsets are miniature versions of a parent plant, usually an alpine or succulent, growing in ground-encrusting colonies. They can be pulled away and potted separately and usually root quickly when they make contact with the soil.

Insect pollination relies upon the presence of the right insects. If bees are scarce, perhaps because of cold, wet weather, flowers may not be pollinated, and seeding, fruiting, and cropping will be adversely affected.

Wind pollination occurs mainly in grasses and in cone- and catkin-bearing plants. These don't rely on colored or fragrant blooms to attract insects—their pollen grains are small and light, allowing distribution on the breeze.

GARDEN JARGON

The terminology associated with plants and gardening can seem intimidating if you are new to gardening. However, the Latin name system is used all over the world, and a little knowledge of it goes a long way.

Although many plants have familiar common names such as "rose" or "lavender," not every plant has one. As an added complication, several may share their name with other plants or be named differently in different regions and countries. Botanical names are used universally to avoid this kind of confusion, which makes it useful to know something about them.

Botanical names classify each plant with two Latin words. The first word describes the genus (for example, *Ilex*) and the second, the epithet (for example, *aquifolium*). Together, they make up the name for a particular plant species, such as *Ilex aquifolium* (English holly). Other species in the same genus are given different epithets, such as *Ilex crenata* and *Ilex serrata*. The system has been developed so that the entire plant kingdom is divided into a universally recognized "family tree" (*see facing page*).

A family may contain only one genus (for example, *Eucryphia* is the only genus in the family Eucryphiaceae) or many—the daisy family Compositae has over 1,000 genera. Each genus comprises related plants, such as oaks (genus *Quercus*) or lilies (genus *Lilium*), with several

Plant names may contain useful information about the plant's natural habitat; for instance, *Cryptostegia madagascariensis* (allamanda violet) comes from Madagascar.

BEHIND THE NAME

The two-part Latin name given to each plant can give useful clues to the plant's geographic origins and natural habitat, as well as allowing similar plants to be grouped together.

The second part of the plant's name denotes the species (*see facing page*) and often reflects the physical characteristic of the plant. For example, *cyanus* describes a blue plant, such as *Centaurea cyanus* (right), and *Octopetala* (as in *Dryas octopetala*) means "eight petals." The species name can also reflect the person who discovered the plant (as in *Magnolia wilsonii*); its natural habitat (*pratensis* denotes a meadow-growing plant); or the plant's country of origin (species called *sinensis* are from China).

Centaurea cyanus

Magnolia wilsonii

Cardamine pratensis

Hibiscus rosa-sinensis

Many summer annuals originate from South Africa. Here, the orange-flowered *Ursinia cakilefolia* and blue-flowered herb *Heliophila arenaria* grow wild in the Western Karoo.

features in common, and a genus may contain one or many species. For example, a member of the genus *Lilium* could be any lily, but *Lilium candidum* denotes just one type. A species is a group of plants that consistently and naturally reproduce between themselves, generating plant populations that share similar characteristics.

VISUAL GUIDE TO PLANT CLASSIFICATION

In horticulture, plants are classified according to a hierarchical system and named primarily on the basis of the binomial approach (genus followed by species epithet). As an example, part of the family Rosaceae has been set out below, showing all levels of this system.

Family A group of several genera that share a set of underlying natural characteristics. Family names usually end in -aceae. Family limits are often controversial.

Genus (plural: genera) A group of one or more plants that share a range of distinctive characteristics. Several (rarely one) genera are classified into one family. Each genus contains one or more species, and its name is printed in italic type with an initial capital letter.

Species A group of plants that breeds naturally to produce offspring with similar characteristics; these distinguish it from other populations in nature. Each species has a two-part name, conventionally printed in italic type.

Subspecies A naturally occurring, distinct variant of a species, differing in one or more characteristics. Subspecies are indicated by "subsp." or "ssp." in Roman type and an epithet in italic type.

Varietas and forma A *varietas* (var.) is a minor species subdivision, differing slightly in botanical structure. A *forma* (f.) is a minor variant of a species, often differing in flower color or look from others in the species.

Cultivar Selected or artificially raised, distinct variant of a species, subspecies, *varietas*, *forma*, or hybrid. Cultivars are indicated by a vernacular name printed in Roman type within single quotation marks.

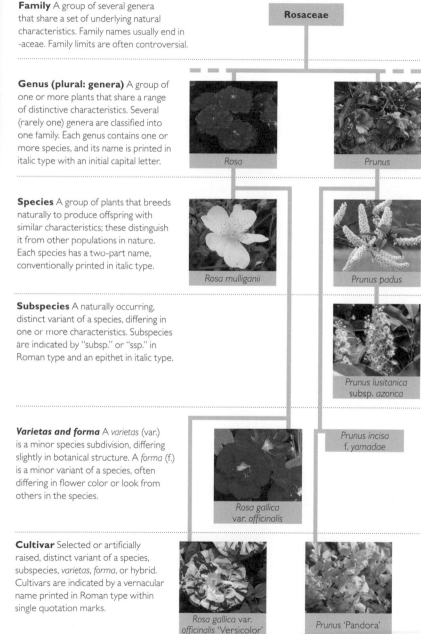

Rosaceae

Rosa

Prunus

Rosa mulliganii

Prunus padus

Prunus lusitanica subsp. *azorica*

Rosa gallica var. *officinalis*

Prunus incisa f. *yamadae*

Rosa gallica var. *officinalis* 'Versicolor'

Prunus 'Pandora'

RIGHT PLANT, RIGHT PLACE

The choice of garden plants is enormous, but the sites you can offer may be more limited. Matching the plants you choose to the varying conditions in your garden, from full sun to damp shade, is the key to success.

Discovering plants' natural habitats is an important part of planning flower displays, helping you place them in their optimal position for health and vitality.

When plants are in the wrong place, they suffer stress, are more vulnerable to damage during adverse weather conditions, and are more susceptible to pests and diseases. Fortunately, there are plants that will thrive in even the most extreme conditions that you might find in your garden. In the wild, plants occupy almost every possible niche in a range of habitats, and there are varieties that will fill the most troublesome areas in the garden: waterlogged soil; dry, shady places; windswept or sun-baked spots.

Wild plant hunters collect plants from a wide variety of natural environments in countries around the world. The species and varieties growing in our gardens today might have originated from places as varied as high alpine slopes, woodland, meadow, marsh, shoreline, or desert.

Hot spots

Plants adapted to full sun and parched soils are useful if you find yourself with an open garden and very free-draining soil. Where winters are relatively mild,

SITING PLANTS

Plants can be used to perform different functions if chosen carefully. An ugly shed could be camouflaged by a vigorous climber, like *Clematis montana* or a rambler rose, but you would be less likely to use the same plant to decorate a small wooden arch. For this, pick a compact-growing, large-flowered clematis hybrid or a modern, repeat-flowering climbing rose.

For ground cover beneath trees, self-seeding perennials, bulbs, and bamboos with a rhizomatous habit would work, but these same plants behave like weeds in a flower border. Check plant dimensions when designing borders to avoid ending up with large, bulky plants at the front, obscuring others (see pp.116–117).

Disguise unsightly structures with climbers.

Naturalize bulbs in a lawn for a woodland effect.

Bamboo screening can hide fences or views.

Train wall shrubs to enhance sheds and fences.

MICROCLIMATES

The area where you live has a
general climate, but every garden
has potential microclimates
created by its exposure and
surroundings. In cold regions, a
sheltered, south-facing plot will
experience higher temperatures
than average for the area; cities
also generate heat, keeping
temperatures high. Even in a
north-facing garden, the area
around a house may remain
frost-free in winter. Walls and
fences cast shade and may trap
cold air, causing frost pockets,
while mature trees may provide
some frost protection.

succulents, silver- and gray-leaved
plants, perennial herbs, and flowering
bulbs adapted to Mediterranean
climates would do well.

Damp shade

You might find damp, shady spots
due to poorly drained clay soils next
to buildings. Plants adapted to this
environment tend to be those that
originated in forests and woodlands.
In warmer, sheltered areas, the only
limiting factors are nutrients and light,
so a range of large-leaf ferns would
do well. For more advice on siting
plants in difficult corners of your
garden refer to the "plant problem
solver" pages in the Plant Chooser
chapter (*pp.370–435*). Here you will
find catalogs and lists of plants that
fit specific conditions well.

The four main conditions found in various
combinations in most gardens are (*clockwise
from top left*): low-lying damp areas where
plants such as *Gunnera* thrive; arid conditions
suitable for drought-tolerant plants; deep
shade beneath tree canopies; and hot, sunny
borders for bursts of exotic blooms.

Compare plants before deciding which to buy, and avoid those in full flower unless you are looking for specific colors.

CHECK PLANT LABELS

It is easy to be tempted into buying attractive-looking plants on impulse at garden centers, but check the label to make sure they are suitable for your soil and site. Check the plant's eventual height and spread, too, to be sure it will fit your space.

Any questions? If you're still not sure about a plant after reading the label, ask an employee for advice.

CHOOSING HEALTHY PLANTS

The starting point to a successful garden is to buy strong, healthy plants that establish quickly and give a good display. Shop around for the best plants, and check them over first to find the healthiest specimens.

WHAT TO LOOK FOR

To find the healthiest specimens, compare several examples of the same plant at garden centers and nurseries. Avoid any with obvious problems, such as broken stems, sparse growth, or signs of pests and disease. Also steer clear of plants that don't appear fresh, with old growth, tired-looking potting mix, and faded or missing labels. Inspect the plants fully, and ease them from their pots to check the condition of the root system (see below right).

The best time to buy and plant perennials, shrubs, and trees is while they are dormant from fall to spring. This does make it hard to check their conditions, however, so you might prefer to wait until spring when new growth shows. Evergreen perennials should be planted in mid- to late spring so that they can toughen up before the following winter. (Container-grown types can be planted at any time, as long as you keep them well watered.)

For healthy perennials, look for plants with plenty of stems emerging from the potting mix. You can plant perennials and shrubs in full flower, but they will be slower to establish. It is preferable to pick plants in bud or those that have finished flowering. When deciding between new trees and shrubs, look out for balanced, well-branched plants with plenty of new growth or buds.

CHECKLIST

When buying any new container-grown plants, it's a good idea to give them a quick check before taking them home. It will only take a few minutes for each plant and is a useful way to avoid potential problems or costly disappointments.

Don't feel awkward doing this in garden centers and nurseries, since they only want to sell healthy plants anyway. Most reputable stores guarantee their plants for at least 12 months, so keep your receipt as proof of purchase in case of any problems.

Signs of care are a good guide to how well a plant has been looked after. Look for plants that have been well supported with neat, tied-in growth and fresh potting mix. Avoid any plants that are tangled, straggly, or scruffy.

▲ **Bare root** plants, such as hedging, can be "heeled in" until ready to plant.

◀ **Container-grown** plants will last a short time in their pots if regularly watered.

STORING PLANTS

It is best to plant new plants within a few days of buying them to help them establish quickly. That might not always be possible however, especially if the weather is wet or you are in the middle of a garden project. Container-grown plants will be fine for a few days if kept well watered. If you need to store them for longer, move them to a sheltered spot so they don't blow over, and keep them out of full sun, or they will dry out too quickly. For longer-term storage, it may be a good idea to repot them into large containers. This will also avoid checking their growth.

Bare root plants sold in fall or winter are at a greater risk of drying out and frost damage than container-grown plants and need protection. As a temporary measure, "heel" plants into the soil, which involves burying the roots in a trench or hole. Choose a sheltered site in free-draining soil, and keep the plants well watered. Plant them out into their final positions before new growth appears in the spring.

If you are unsure when you will be able to plant out bare root plants, consider potting them and standing them in a sheltered spot. Keep well watered and fed, and they will survive into summer.

Reject pots with mature weeds, because this suggests plants have not been well maintained; you will also avoid introducing weed species to your garden. Moss-covered pots should be rejected for the same reason.

Look under the pot to see if there are roots growing through the drainage holes. Just a few suggests a healthy root system; lots of roots indicate the plant is pot-bound and should be avoided. Remove the pot to check.

Check the roots to see if they are healthy. Look for pale, plump roots and clear signs of new growth. Avoid plants with dead, black, or hollow roots that fall away from the potting mix. Also avoid plants with congested roots.

FROM THE GROUND UP

Knowing how to make the best of your garden's conditions by nurturing and improving the soil will help you work wonders on your plot—even with challenging soils, like heavy clay or chalk.

Earthworms save work by incorporating organic matter into the depths of the soil, as well as opening up drainage channels.

WORKING WITH YOUR SOIL

Analyzing the basic structure and drainage of your soil, its pH (see p.66), organic content, and fertility is an important first step. If you dig down into soil, you will eventually see a change from the darker, fertile, topsoil layer to the paler, infertile subsoil layer and rock beneath. Some soils have very little depth, adversely affecting cultivation. On the other hand loams cultivated over many years with regular additions of manure can be very deep.

The color difference between topsoil and subsoil is due to the lack of humus, or organic matter, at depths where earthworms are not active. In clay, the subsoil is orange, but in waterlogged conditions it can be blue-gray due to the lack of oxygen. Never mix subsoil into topsoil; the lower layer can be toxic to plants.

In poor soils the lack of depth can severely affect the growth of both ornamentals and crops. Raised beds allow more topsoil to be added, contained within a frame.

WHAT IS SOIL?

Soil is a mixture of ground-up rock particles, organic matter or humus, and countless microscopic organisms and tiny invertebrates. In healthy, well-drained soil, the particles are clumped together with the spaces in between occupied by water and air. This crumb structure allows earthworms to move through, creating a network of channels that plant roots can make use of. Earthworms are very active "gardeners," pulling leaf litter and other organic debris down into the soil where bacteria and fungi, together with other soil organisms, break it down, releasing and recycling nutrients. Creating conditions that benefit these soil organisms is the best way to maintain fertility.

Sandy soils have coarse grains and lack organic matter, which makes them very free-draining. They are easy to dig, can be cultivated all year, and warm up quickly in spring for early sowings. Self-seeding plants can become a nuisance; they germinate freely, but weeds and unwanted plants can easily be pulled out.

Loam soils are ideal, having a good balance of clay particles to retain moisture and nutrients, and sand grains to improve drainage. Loam usually has a healthy worm population, and most plants thrive with little extra feeding. A clay loam will be slower to warm up in spring than a sandy one.

Improve your soil's structure by working in plenty of bulky, well-rotted organic matter, such as manure (see p.303).

To dig or not to dig?

Soil can be damaged in several ways. Compaction destroys air and rooting channels, impairs drainage, and reduces earthworm activity. Digging is then essential to help loosen up compacted and heavy soil. You will also need to turn over uncultivated soil to prepare it for planting. Some soils are easy to dig and can be cultivated all year, while others, such as heavy, clay soils, may have a relatively narrow window for sowing and planting.

Generally, there is little need for routine digging in a garden that is already cultivated. Worms will do much of the hard work for you, incorporating organic matter added to the surface. Digging shallow soils can be problematic because there is a risk of bringing infertile subsoil to the surface; digging can also disrupt beneficial soil microorganisms. Walking on or digging wet clay also damages its structure. If you need to dig clay, do this in fall when it is softened but not saturated by rain, or in spring when it is not too wet.

COMPARING POTTING MEDIA

Commercial, peat-based media, are the best choice for the long-term health of perennials, climbers, shrubs, and trees grown in containers. Compared with soil-free potting media, they retain their structure better and don't shrink or compact over time.
Peat-free potting media are ideal for short-term planting such as summer patio pots, and retain moisture and nutrients well.
Potting media for acid-loving plants, free of lime, are used for shrubs, such as camellias and rhododendrons, that require acid soil.

Clay soils are some of the most fertile, because clay particles hold on to nutrients. Poor drainage is a common problem with clay soils, and this can be improved by digging in bulky organic matter such as well-rotted manures and composts.

Chalk soils and other limestone soils have a high pH and are unsuitable for acid-loving plants. Because they are peppered with fragments of flint or limestone, they drain freely but are prone to drought. They warm up quickly in spring but can be shallow, overlying solid rock.

PROBLEM SOILS

To improve the texture and drainage of heavy clay soils, work in large amounts of bulky organic matter, about two buckets of organic matter for every 10 square feet. This chemically alters the clay and causes the fine particles to cluster, opening up drainage channels. Avoid digging or walking on clay when it is wet; both activities destroy the structure. When it is dry, it is very hard to dig, but it may be possible with a fork.

Sandy soils are free draining, but this can leach nutrients out of the upper layers and away from the roots of plants, leaving the soil impoverished. They can be improved by the addition of well-rotted organic matter to hold nutrients and moisture in the soil; moisture-loving plants can also be mulched.

ENRICHING THE SOIL

To get the most out of your productive crops and ornamental plants, you may need to improve the fertility or moisture-retaining capacity of your garden soil. There are many ways to go about this, following organic or chemical methods.

Organic manure improves soil structure, promotes soil microbes, and adds plant nutrients, all of which encourage plant health.

IMPROVING FERTILITY

Some plants, such as bush and patio roses and many summer bedding varieties (fuchsias and petunias, for example), are particularly "hungry" and need regular feeding to keep them growing and flowering well, especially on naturally poor ground. You can feed border plants by adding well-rotted manures and garden compost to the soil around them or by applying granular or liquid fertilizers.

Other woodland species, like Japanese maples, ferns, and deciduous azaleas, can survive with less feed, but the soil needs to be enriched with leaf mold or organic matter to create a suitably moisture-retentive rooting environment.

Some plants have evolved to grow in relatively poor soils, and if concentrated granular fertilizers are applied around their shallow root systems, they scorch and suffer shoot die-back. A common example of this is boxwood (*Buxus sempervirens*),

Leaf mold makes an excellent soil conditioner. It does not require any special conditions and can be made by collecting leaves either in a wire cage or in black garbage bags, wetting them, and composting them for two years.

Farmyard and horse manure should be well rotted before use, as fresh manure is liable to scorch roots. Nitrogen can be locked up while soil organisms decompose strawy manure, leading to short-term yellowing of foliage.

Garden compost is ideally made up of 25–50 percent soft, green garden waste (to feed microorganisms) to one part woody waste. (*See p.303 for detailed information on recycling garden and kitchen waste for your own compost.*)

which is best fed with well-rotted manure or diluted liquid fertilizer. Hardy annuals and Mediterranean herbs and shrubs also thrive in nutrient-poor soils, such as sands, gravels, and chalks.

Fertilizer recipes

Unless you enrich the soil organically, you will need to replenish lost nutrients using an appropriate artificial fertilizer, especially around flowering plants and crops. On the labels of most chemical fertilizers you will often see an "NPK" ratio, which shows the relative proportions of nitrogen (N), phosphorus (P), and potassium (K) in the mix. Other micronutrients may also be listed. Feeding with a potassium-rich fertilizer, such as a tomato fertilizer, will suit all plants. High-potassium feeds can help particularly to condition cold-sensitive plants prior to winter and initiate flower bud production in

Mulching with garden compost will improve the soil structure as well as adding plant nutrients to the soil. Don't use a commercially produced soil improver without first checking its pH—most are alkaline.

shy-flowering shrubs and climbers. For a more specific recommendation, send your soil to a laboratory that carries out soil tests.

Getting the balance right

Follow instructions carefully for the amount and frequency of feeding. Too much fertilizer can be just as damaging as too little, and using the wrong type can also cause problems. Feeding flowering and fruiting plants with a high-nitrogen mix encourages leafy growth at the expense of blooms, and the resulting tall stems are more vulnerable to weather damage. Soft, sappy shoots are also more attractive to pests, such as aphids, and overfeeding lawns makes them prone to frost and fungal infection. (*See pp.302–303 for more information on feeding.*)

MULCHING

Covering soil with a layer of organic matter, such as chipped bark, garden compost, manure, or cocoa shells (if a sustainable source can be found), is known as mulching. To be most effective, a layer of organic mulch needs to be 2–3 in (5–8 cm) thick. Materials, such as plastic sheeting, pebbles, or cardboard, can also be used as mulch.

Mulches conserve valuable soil moisture and suppress weeds, and organic mulches also release nutrients as they break down, feeding the surrounding plants. Woody mulches, such as chipped bark or shredded wood, last a long time and do not deplete soil nitrogen.

Mulches are applied to the soil surface, rather than dug in, to minimize root damage, keep light from reaching weeds, and enhance soil microbes and earthworms near the surface where they do the most good. (*See p.350 for more information on using mulches to suppress weeds.*)

GREEN MANURES

A green manure is a crop grown and dug in before it sets seed and is used on vegetable beds to improve the soil. It can also be harvested and soaked in water to produce a liquid feed. Growing green manures improves the soil structure and can be used to help bind light soils or break up heavy clays. They can also draw nutrients from deep down and add atmospheric nitrogen to the soil.

Clover is grown to lock nitrogen into the soil.

Alfalfa roots help break up heavy clay soils.

Grazing rye grass helps to bind light soils.

Secondhand tools can be easy to come by and are proven performers. Choose the best quality tools you can afford, if buying new.

BASIC TOOL KIT

To tend a garden you need tools, and a fairly small selection will cover most routine tasks. Tools are versatile and can be used for more than one purpose, and you can build a more comprehensive kit over time.

TENDING THE SOIL

Caring for your soil is a key task in the garden and plays an important role in keeping plants healthy. Digging prior to planting aerates the soil, mixes in nutrients, and breaks up hard lumps. Either a spade or a fork can be used for digging, but it is worth having one of each. Forks are ideal for working on heavy or stony soils; spades are better for digging holes and for general earth moving. On a smaller scale, hand trowels and forks are indispensable for lighter digging and planting and loosening the soil.

Controlling weeds is another important part of maintaining your plot and is most easily done using a long-handled hoe that cuts weeds off at the base. This tool is ideal for larger beds, because you can easily weed between plants. You can also make seed drills with a hoe.

You will find a garden rake useful for leveling and tilling the soil surface to ready it for seed sowing and for clearing light plant debris.

KEEP TOOLS CLEAN

Cleaning tools after use keeps them in good condition and makes them easier to use. Brush off any soil and debris before putting them away, and clean and sterilize your pruning tools to prevent spreading diseases between plants.

To keep tools sharp, wipe oil onto cutting blades, including spades; this also keeps them rust-free.

Spades and forks are used for cultivating the soil and come in various sizes. Choose one with a long enough handle to suit your height, and that is light enough to manipulate easily.

Hand tools are useful for light tasks and allow you to tend the soil in awkward places. They are ideal for planting out seedlings and young plants and for uprooting small weeds.

Caring for plants

Water is essential to plants, and a watering can is a must. While a hose is useful for watering established borders, a basic can is ideal for new plants, containers and baskets, and greenhouse crops. Fit a fine rose to the spout to water young seedlings, or use the can to apply plant feeds.

Keeping plants to size and shape is important for their health, so you will need pruning tools. Hand pruners are useful for pruning light woody stems; it is worth investing in a good-quality pair. If your garden has large trees or shrubs, consider buying long-handled loppers and a pruning saw. Shears are effective when cutting back leafy growth and for trimming lawn edges.

Like other plants, lawns also need care and maintenance; you will need a mower to use regularly throughout the summer. There are many to choose from, and before you buy the biggest and most powerful, consider the space you have to store it. A manual push-mower may be all you need on a small area. Another worthwhile lawn tool is a leaf rake, used to remove moss and to collect fallen leaves. You can also use it to tidy around the garden in general.

Storing tools

Before buying your tools, make sure you have somewhere to store them under cover. Even if you only have space for a covered tool organizer or a garden cupboard, tools last longer and work better if kept clean and dry. It also helps keep your tools in one place so you know where to find them. If you have space, install a shed to house costly power tools along with the mass of sundries you will gradually acquire over time, and to prevent children or pets accessing garden chemicals.

Weatherproof storage in a shed or tool locker is recommended, because tools last longer when kept under cover. Keep expensive tools under lock and key to safeguard against theft.

Watering cans can be used for carrying water wherever needed. It is worth having a few different sizes to use for various tasks, such as watering hanging baskets and general feeding.

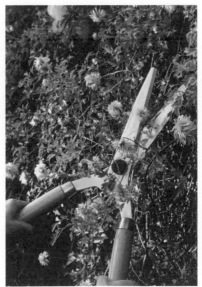

Pruning tools are worth having close at hand throughout the year to keep plant growth in check and to prune out weak or diseased stems whenever you spot them.

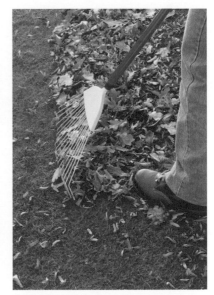

Lawn rakes make quick work of clearing lawns and borders of debris and can be used instead of garden brooms to help tidy up in the fall. Garden rakes are used to cultivate soil.

DESIGN YOUR GARDEN

Before you reach for your spade, think about how you would like your space to look and how you will use it, then create a garden to suit you. Be inspired by the range of styles, layouts, and techniques in this chapter, and use them to make your garden beautiful, practical, or productive—or a combination of all three.

ASSESS YOUR GARDEN NEEDS

Try to visualize your dream garden and the features it might include—take inspiration from designs that excite you. How will it fit in with your lifestyle, and how much time will you have to maintain it? How will you use it? Decide whether plants, people, or wildlife will take precedence.

▶ SPACE TO ENTERTAIN

Transform your garden into a useful, comfortable outdoor space, and use it as an extension of your house for eating, drinking, relaxing, and socializing. Bring the interior outside by adding homey touches, such as colorful cushions, soft lighting, and a fire pit to create an area to lounge. Combined kitchen and dining spaces make open-air cooking and eating easy and enjoyable, and if you grow your own crops, make the journey from plot to plate even shorter. For a touch of luxury, consider adding a hot tub with a sauna and lounge chairs.

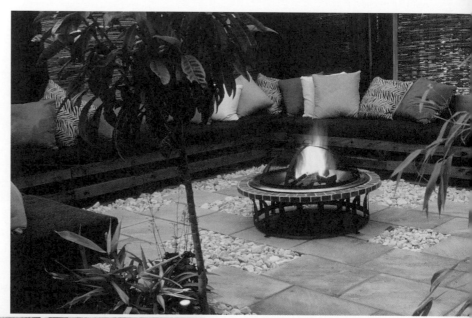

◀ HOMEGROWN PRODUCE

Whether you have the space to create a full-scale garden plot or you simply want to grow a pot of peppers on a sunny windowsill, the rewards will be tasty, wonderfully scented herbs, fruits, and vegetables—an attractive asset to any garden. The best thing about growing your own is that you can select exactly which varieties you want to eat, including unusual types that are not readily available. You will also know exactly what has gone into their cultivation.

► FOR THE WHOLE FAMILY

Maximize outdoor family time by designing the garden so that adults and children can enjoy being outside together. Gardens have more to offer children than just fresh air and exercise—they can create opportunities for wild encounters with nature and encourage imaginative play, so create special areas for these "secret" adventures to occur. Screen these and larger pieces of play equipment from view if necessary, or leave the garden layout open, and construct a relaxing seating area so that you can keep an eye on the activities of younger children.

◄ CALMING RETREAT

Use your garden as a place to escape from everyday stresses and ground yourself in nature. You can experience feelings of real freedom out in the open air surrounded by birdsong and the rustle of leaves, especially when your private sitting area is shielded from the house and overlooking windows. Consider using water to create a sense of tranquility. Feed your senses with the sound of a trickling fountain or the sight of reflections in a still pool of water. A single focal point helps create a perfect space for contemplation.

▲ WILDLIFE HAVEN

Attracting a range of wildlife to your garden is as much about your gardening approach as your plant selection—relaxed and not too tidy works best. Use colorful, highly scented flowers to attract hoverflies, bees, and butterflies. Create a woodland environment for visitors as diverse as beetles, hedgehogs, and wood mice. A pond will be attractive to birds and amphibians, and an eco-pile will provide a welcoming habitat for beneficial insects.

► EASY CARE GARDEN

Even if you do not have a lot of time to dedicate to your garden, there is no reason why it can't still be beautiful. Making life easier does not necessarily mean resorting to expanses of paving: use easy care landscaping solutions, such as gravel and railroad ties and select plants that do not require frequent pruning, feeding, or watering.

◄ A PLACE FOR PLANTS

Some types of plants may interest you more than others, so adapt your garden to suit their needs. With a bit of consideration, fussy plants such as tender types or even exotics can be accommodated if given a warm spot and moved under cover in the winter. There is no need to feel limited by your existing garden: consider adding a pond or bog area, or creating a shaded woodland zone; or build a rock garden.

FINDING INSPIRATION

Initially, let your imagination run wild. Think about what you like rather than your garden's restrictions. You may already have a favorite gardening style or at least a mental list of must-have features. A mood board with magazine images, fabrics, and color swatches can help you focus, or you can scan online sources such as Pinterest or Instagram for ideas and direction.

Formal gardens juxtapose topiary colors and textures to striking effect—apply these principles to your plant choices.

Natural habitats allow you to discover plants in the wild. Where possible, mimic these conditions in your garden.

Show gardens are often made to draw attention to exciting, contemporary plans and interesting planting designs.

Art or mosaics may inspire formal planting schemes or color themes; re-create your favorite mosaics with paving.

Eye-catching plants inspired by a tropical vacation can brighten your garden; make sure you can create the conditions needed.

Sculptures make wonderful focal points—collect them on your travels, or pick up ideas from any you admire.

A SPACE TO ENTERTAIN

Extend your living space into the garden, and create a stylish outdoor kitchen, an intimate dining area for starlit gatherings, or even a relaxation space complete with hammock. Mirror your indoor styles for a seamless transition.

Elements for constructing your al fresco room are readily available, from exterior tiles and decking for barefoot garden access to instant "walls" constructed from decorative screen panels or "hedges" of potted bamboo. Make a "ceiling" using a pergola festooned with night-fragrant jasmine, or fit a sail-like awning for summer shade. Many stylish sofas and armchairs are designed to stay out no matter the weather. Impromptu seating (from raised beds at sitting height) is perfect to encircle a fire pit.

Finish with paints and stains, matching cushion fabrics and china to interior color schemes. Dress your outdoor room with topiaries and sculptural foliage in contemporary containers. Add drama at nightfall with low-voltage lighting.

KEY DESIGN ELEMENTS

All-weather surfaces
Many contemporary doors roll back or fold, blurring the barrier between indoors and out. Mirror your flooring—choose feet-friendly tiles, smooth paving, and decking that repels rain and is frost-proof.

Outdoor lighting
Dramatic choices include recessed neon deck lights and colored floods that turn plain walls into modern art, while candles, oil lamps, and string lights woven through plants create atmosphere.

Dining space
Al fresco summer dinner parties with flickering candelabras, or lunches in the dappled shade of a vine-clad pergola, can be stylish, memorable events. Bring out the best tableware for a dinner party.

Privacy and shelter
Need shade at midday? Try a sail-like awning. Being out of the wind is essential; being beyond the gaze of neighbors is desirable if you want to doze in a hammock or on a sofa.

▼ **Colorful, hard-wearing furniture** creates a versatile outdoor room.

Outdoor furniture

As well as being comfortable and practical, furniture should add to your garden's design. Whether you prefer a traditional feel or modern style, pick furniture and fabrics to mirror interior luxury.

Food preparation area

Cooking and eating outdoors is an epicurean delight. Outfit a kitchen with easy-clean surfaces, a stove, and perhaps a wood-burning oven. Grow a range of herbs close by to enhance your cookouts.

Fire pit

A fire pit will draw people together at social gatherings and makes a captivating focal point, so position soft seating to make the most of it. Some designs have safety guards and some can be used for cooking.

ALSO TRY

Garden art

Turn your garden into a gallery with pieces that enhance the style of the surroundings.

Pools and fountains

Choose a pool with nighttime illumination or a sparkling fountain to add movement.

Soft seating

Convert steps, walls, and raised beds into comfortable perches with outdoor cushions.

SOCIAL STYLE

Extending the house into the garden creates extra living space with a unique backdrop—flowers and foliage; the sights, scents, and sounds of nature; and the open sky—so install a second kitchen, dining room, or lounge.

▼ Fresh and fast

You can be sure of the freshness of your herbs and salads when they are growing within arm's reach. Surrounding an outdoor kitchen with crop-filled raised beds and walls of salad leaves is convenient, attractive, and usually highly aromatic. Plant a variety of colors, shapes, and textures for maximum impact.

▲ Summer house

Garden buildings can make a wonderfully romantic addition to period and English gardens. Here, a curved pathway and deep, well-filled borders help give a feeling of seclusion. Add soft furnishings, lighting, and storage so you don't have to go back to the house too often.

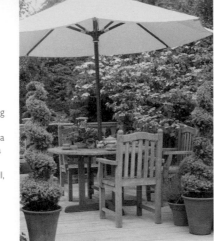

► Café chic

Add a touch of elegance by positioning a small table and oversized umbrella in a quiet corner. Create a sense of privacy by surrounding it with tall, dense plants, and introduce glamour by marking the entrance with a stylish pair of corkscrew topiaries.

▲ Wilderness sanctuary

Glimpsed through diaphanous screens of flowers, this sculptural seating arrangement looks remote and wild. During the day it would be a peaceful sanctuary from modern-day living; at night you could sit and stargaze.

ADAPTING THE STYLE

Careful planning will allow you to make the most of your space. Use the plan below for design inspiration and then customize it to suit your needs. Site dining and cooking areas close to the house for easy access. Create extra seating with wide-edged raised beds. Separate the lawn from the patio with a screen of tall potted plants, to give each area an enclosed feel.

Shaded seating area

Armchairs with cushions

Path to seating area

Screening plants

Outdoor kitchen

Wide raised bed for extra seating

Social garden

▲ Inside out

The open-plan design technique employed in contemporary homes can work particularly well in the garden, too. A covered veranda or canopied terrace creates a useful transition between the house and open-air cooking and dining areas. Use spotlights or strings of twinkling lights to create atmosphere and highlight favorite plants. If the weather gets too chilly, you can move the party under cover and continue to enjoy the outdoor atmosphere.

◄ The green room

In larger gardens it may be possible to create an outdoor seating area well away from the house, creating a peaceful, scenic retreat. An open-sided shelter will protect you from light rain showers, and will provide welcome shade in bright weather. Use pergola posts, climbers, and specimen plants to frame selected specimens. A slightly raised platform gives the area prominence; lead the eye to it with a wide path flanked with colorful flowers and foliage.

THE PRODUCTIVE GARDEN

You might start off with a few potted herbs or an annual crop of greenhouse tomatoes, but "growing your own" soon becomes addictive. Happily, there is a wealth of ingenious options for making even a small plot productive.

Mixing crops into flower borders, English-garden style, is useful if you don't have a dedicated vegetable plot, and certain leafy crops are just as good-looking as they are flavorful. Runner beans produce delicate flowers, and the blooms and fruits of apples, cherries, and strawberries are as attractive as any grown for ornament. Red currants, followed by the fall foliage of blueberries, also create eye-catching displays.

Kitchen and formal knot gardens are dramatic, and even raised beds with decorative edging can make a statement. Maximize your culinary space by training fruit against walls, and by growing vines and climbing vegetables against a trellis. In a courtyard or patio garden many crops can be grown in pots or hanging baskets.

KEY DESIGN ELEMENTS

Crops in containers
Even in the smallest garden, you can grow a variety of crops in pots, growing bags, or window boxes. Choose compact vegetable types and dwarf fruit trees; tender ones in pots can be moved under cover.

Decorative varieties
There are many delicious and ornamental vegetables to choose from, with colorful foliage, fruits, or flowers. Cabbage, kale, and chard are highly ornamental and look striking grown in a kitchen garden.

Chickens
If you have room for a run, hens make excellent pets. It's best to confine them since they produce a lot of waste and will scratch up the garden looking for worms. You don't need a rooster to get eggs.

Wall-trained fruit
Espalier- and fan-trained trees crop better than freestanding types and look beautiful, too. Use any vertical space—varieties are even available for north-facing walls. Also try training fruits such as gooseberries.

▼ **Break up expanses of green** with a line of purple cabbages and a colorful border of flowers.

Productive baskets
Mixed displays of herbs, edible flowers, and trailing strawberries or tomatoes are full of color and are convenient for harvesting if hung by the back door. Try using novel containers, such as an old colander.

Raised beds
On heavy or very stony soils, raised beds can provide you with enough quality topsoil to grow a wide range of crops. Add compost and manure to the surface to develop a healthy, fertile soil full of worms.

Crop covers
Use polytunnels, cloches, or cold frames to extend the growing season and provide vulnerable crops with frost protection and extra warmth. Use barriers like fabric or netting to deter pests.

ALSO TRY

Edible flowers
Try petals of sunflowers, roses, and calendula, or blooms of violas and nasturtiums.

Herb garden
Create a formal herb garden edged with clipped hedging, santolina, or lavender.

Climbing crops
Use trellis, arches, and pergolas to support climbing squash, zucchini, and pole beans.

PRODUCE-FILLED PLOTS

There are many attractive ways to incorporate crops into your garden, whether you want to plant a pot of salad on the patio, grow climbing vegetables up a screen or trellis, or dedicate your entire space to drills and rows.

▶ Recycled containers
You can use virtually any container as long as it will hold potting mix and allow drainage. Ensure that you water smaller pots frequently since the soil may dry out quickly.

▼ Additional lines
Consider turning the whole garden into a productive plot. Use long, straight rows and plant dahlias and sunflowers for color.

▶ Productive patio
You can nurture a surprising range of fruits, vegetables, and herbs on even a tiny patio. Showcase a variety of heights, colors, and textures for maximum contrast and interest. Mix and match your containers to give the patio a rustic feel.

▲ Squashed together
Some crops will take up a lot of space unless confined. Grow sprawling squash and climbing beans up fencing or trellis, and keep them contained within a low raised bed. Many fruits can be wall-trained to save space.

ADAPTING THE STYLE

Before you create a detailed crop plan, position permanent unsightly elements and those that are likely to smell, such as a compost bin or chicken enclosure, at the far end of the garden. Plant a line of raised beds with an array of colorful crops, and flank them with beds filled with ornamental edibles to create a lovely view from a garden bench.

▲ Old-world charm
A potager is a highly structured, decorative planting design and an ideal way to make vegetable and herb areas more attractive, especially in a period setting. Lay out the design, and then edge the segments with gravel boards, dwarf hedging, or an evergreen herb such as cotton lavender. Here, clipped hedges gives the plot definition, and old rhubarb forcers are used as ornaments. Bay and rosemary standards could also be used as attractive centerpieces.

◄ Pretty tasty
Save space by mixing edibles and ornamentals together, English-garden style. Varieties like purple-leaf cabbages, kale, sage, or red-stemmed chard provide a lovely foliage contrast when grown with colorful perennials or gold- or silver-leaf herbs. Crops such as tomatoes, zucchini, and strawberries will add a splash of color, while many ornamental flowers have edible petals that make an attractive and tasty addition to a salad.

Chicken enclosure with run

Compost bins

Greenhouse and cold frame

Raised beds

Wall-trained fruit trees

Decorative edibles

The productive garden

FAMILY GARDEN

A garden can cater to the needs of every family member—there's no reason for play areas to dominate. With an integrated design, grown-ups can enjoy more sophisticated pursuits while still keeping an eye on the children.

First, secure boundaries and deal with potential hazards. Lock away tools and chemicals, and remove poisonous or thorny plants. Children need the freedom to run around or play ball games, so choose a hard-wearing lawn mix. Make pathways smooth and spacious for pedaling tricycles or scooters, and provide "secret" areas where they can build forts, let their imaginations take flight, or lose themselves in nature. Children love water: pebble fountains are a strong but harmless draw, and a bog garden gives the illusion of water but is also very safe.

A raised patio or deck creates a vantage point for adults and doubles as a sanctuary for relaxing or family dining, perhaps given extra protection with a pergola and trellis panels.

KEY DESIGN ELEMENTS

Raised beds
Lifting plants above ground level helps protect them during play and keeps toy trucks and race cars on the right track. If you have dogs, growing vegetables in a raised bed deters trampling or eliminating.

Hard-wearing lawns
Choose durable grass seed or turf mix that contains rye grass. Aerate and resow thin patches, and move play equipment to aid recovery. Mixes are available for problem areas such as shade or poor soils.

Play spaces
Consider children's ages before investing in play equipment—look for adaptability: a sand pit could later be converted to a raised bed or pool. Swings have lasting appeal and can be adjusted over time.

Wide paths
For easy pedaling, keep paths wide with gentle inclines rather than steps. This helps protect plants that cascade over the edge of borders, and reduces the wear on grass pathways.

▼ **Separate the lawn** from the
seating area using a stylish
border of tall, dense plants.

Casual seating
Dot benches around the garden, especially in wilder parts where children can connect with nature. Introduce swings, hammocks, or outdoor bean bags. Keep cushions handy for walls and steps.

Built-in storage
Stow toys and equipment away so that they don't clutter the garden. Keep them within easy reach in waterproof cupboards concealed in purpose-built screened storage areas or fitted under hinged seats.

Private corners
Adults may prefer a gazebo, but for children, any simple shelter will do, whether a tent, a living willow teepee, or an old shed. Raised platforms and tree houses provide an exciting lookout point.

ALSO TRY

Wet-weather play
Include a sheltered area where children can be out of the house no matter the weather.

Nature ramble
Wind narrow paths through wildflowers, or build a zigzag boardwalk over a bog garden.

Kid's blooms
Grow plants that attract butterflies and bees and are fragrant, colorful, or oversized.

SPACE FOR EVERYONE

Creating a garden that is suitable yet enjoyable for the whole family can be easier than you might think, and it shouldn't compromise on design. An imaginative layout can maximize the uses of even the smallest garden.

▶ In the thick of it
Keep little ones close by integrating toys with the productive garden. Use vibrant flowers and decoration to appeal to them.

▼ Free range
Secure your boundaries so that children, pets, and chickens can run around in safety. Use fenced areas to store a compost bin or to create a secret children's hideaway.

▶ All grown up
Choose a secluded corner where you can sit and recharge your batteries but which allows you to observe children's activities. Fill surrounding borders with fragrant plants in gentle colors, and use a bird bath or fountain as a focal point.

▲ Explorer garden

Lay a winding path between borders filled with tall cottage flowers and herbs, and create screened-off, "secret" hideaways so that children can have fun investigating while adults relax and enjoy the scenery.

ADAPTING THE STYLE

Decide which features need to be located furthest from the house, such as the "secret" children's play space. Consider your seating: create an area of raised decking in a position that overlooks the entire garden, and place a bench where you can view a relaxing water feature. Keep useful storage cupboards close to the house for easy access.

▲ Grow and play

In a small plot you'll need imaginative design to make the most of the available space. Create privacy with tall fences rather than borders. Integrate features such as built-in seating with raised beds, and plant them with aromatic herbs to create a scented relaxation area. Use a simple layout to create garden "zones," such as a play area and a vegetable patch. Separating them with a different material, such as decking, creates a clear division between them.

◀ Family room

If you've got space, a gazebo can be an outdoor home away from home. Install a microwave and a fridge to ensure that hot and cold drinks are always on hand. Choose comfortable but portable armchairs and tables that can be lifted in or out depending on the weather. Use soft furnishings such as a rug, which is ideal for babies and toddlers, or a bean bag or two. Fit built-in storage for toys and wet-weather games, and shelves for books and magazines.

"Secret" play space

Raised seating and dining area

Pebble water feature

Large, hard-wearing lawn

Smooth, wide patio

Garden storage

Family garden

A CALMING RETREAT

Even in the heart of the city, a garden can be an oasis of peace and tranquility. Cocooned by lush foliage and soft-colored blooms and soothed by the sounds of nature, you can escape day-to-day pressures and feel rejuvenated.

Blurring garden boundaries is a first step to establishing your own private sanctuary. Create deep, curving borders, and fill them with a number of plants that are head height or taller. Surprisingly, this makes the garden feel larger, while dense planting muffles surrounding noise. Wind chimes, rustling grasses, or a trickling fountain are also pleasingly distracting. Where space is limited, use screening plants like bamboos, strategically placed trees, or a climber-clad pergola to block overlooking windows.

For a contemplative atmosphere, choose muted blues and purples against a green backdrop. Keep lines simple and open spaces uncluttered; try a large, simple container for sculptural contrast or a statue as a point of focus.

KEY DESIGN ELEMENTS

Simple containers
Use large pots with intriguing shapes, colors, or textures as focal points. Weathered terra-cotta, oxidized metal, and partially glazed finishes all work well. Plant simply, using topiary or grasses.

Spiritual features
Sculptures such as a Buddha or an angel provide a good focus for contemplation, as do plaques and paving carrying quotations or symbols. Place in a reflective space in dappled shade or beside a pool.

Gentle sounds
Hang wind chimes, or set up outdoor speakers to pipe soft music into the garden. For sounds of nature, plant whispering grasses and bamboos, and encourage birds and bees into the garden.

Relaxing water
A natural pond or reflecting pool creates a peaceful ambience. Arrange water features to give a gentle trickling sound rather than loud gushing. Adjust the flow to make the sound less hollow.

▼ **Use a curving low wall** as a peaceful seating area in a secluded part of the garden.

Focal points
Natural elements such as a piece of gnarled olive wood or a stone monolith make ideal focal points. A reflective, weathered mirror or metallic orb can add magic, as can a well-sited bubble fountain.

Informal seating
Avoid hi-tech steel and glass, and go for wicker effect and sturdy wooden chairs. A stone or roughly chiseled wooden bench would also work well. Choose sculptural pieces with flowing, organic lines.

Subtle screening
The pattern and color of bamboo stems are a striking feature. Strip the bottom portion of leaves, and thin weak stems to reveal their beauty. Use to create partial screens that rustle in the breeze.

ALSO TRY

Grounding experience
Create a treat for tired feet by designing walkways made of grass, stone, and wood.

Soothing shades
Include soft grays, greens, and pinks for their calming and therapeutic effects.

Heaven scents
Introduce heady rose, jasmine, and honeysuckle scents, as well as aromatic herbs.

PLAN TO RELAX

You can transform a plot of any size into a peaceful oasis using flowing shapes and muted colors, no matter the location. Where space is limited, provide a strong focal point, and use screening to shut out distractions.

▼ Natural haven
In a larger garden you may have space to create a secluded, semi-wild area, such as a wildflower meadow or a wooded thicket. In this environment you can feel closer to nature and enjoy the sound of bees, rustling leaves, and birdsong. It's the ideal spot to string a hammock or to build a shady gazebo.

▲ Simple landscape
It is worth considering a minimalist approach to planting if you are creating a contemplation garden. Here, a threefold color palette is used: white-stemmed birches are underplanted with soft green ferns and feathery pink astilbe.

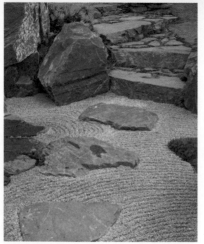

► Zen approach
There's a Japanese saying that states that a garden is only finished when you can take nothing else away. This rock and gravel garden, or *karesansui*, is both simple and stylized. The shapes and textures can create drama in even a tiny space.

▲ Tranquil water
If you have enough space, a pond is a beautiful, calming garden feature and will attract a range of wildlife. Use lush marginal plants in a variety of colors and textures to create an attractive reflection.

▲ Cool seclusion
The use of deep, generously planted borders filled with tall plants can make a garden feel bigger than it really is and seclude it from the rest of the world. Create partially screened-off areas to increase the illusion of space. Choose an organic layout; natural materials, such as stone, gravel, and wood; and a limited palette of greens, browns, and gray-blues to give the garden a soothing feel.

◄ Spirit garden
The color white is associated with purity and the sacred and can be used in a variety of places, most strikingly here, as paving. Create a strong focal point, and direct the garden toward it. Here, the ribbons of green act as markers on the journey. Play with shapes: provide symmetry with the rounded hummocks of greenery and the shapes of the pebble sculptures, and use angular tree branches and swordlike phormium foliage as a contrast. Choose greens, blues, and purples for a soft, gentle color palette.

ADAPTING THE STYLE

Think about the way the eye will be drawn around your garden: choose flowing, circular shapes that lead toward a focal point in the distance. Create deep, curving borders, and plant them with tall trees and shrubs and soft color-themed flowers. Use striking features on a compact scale, such as potted bamboos or a small circular water feature.

Tall plants in deep borders

Informal curved seating

Pebble fountain focal point

Subtle bamboo screening

Still water feature

Seated viewing area

A calming retreat

WILDLIFE HAVEN

Gardens are a prime resource for insects, birds, and amphibians. Whether yours is a city patio or a sprawling rural plot, there are simple ways to create a refuge for native wildlife without compromising on aesthetics or practicality.

Many English-garden perennials attract bees with their pollen- and nectar-rich flowers. Encouraging butterfly breeding is more difficult, but if you include native plants, butterflies are more likely to visit and lay their eggs, as they may find suitable food plants for their caterpillars. Birds will feast enthusiastically on the berries of ornamental shrubs and, in winter, perennial seed heads are appreciated by gardeners and foraging finches alike. Large shrubs and evergreen climbers create safe nesting sites, and small trees offer vantage points for birds checking for predators. Ponds attract a host of creatures from dragonflies to frogs, but if you don't have room, provide water for drinking and bathing. Long grass, compost heaps, and log piles can harbor insects and invertebrates—a crucial food for birds.

KEY DESIGN ELEMENTS

Winter food plants
Plant a range of fruiting shrubs, trees, and climbers to cater to visiting migrants as well as local residents. Plants like holly, mountain ash, and crab apples are also highly ornamental.

Bird feeders
Pick a location that has shelter from airborne predators but that won't encourage cats to wait in ambush. Remove stale or moldy food, which can cause fatal poisoning, and keep feeders clean.

Nooks and crannies
Dry-stone walls and bundles of pruned twigs and branches known as eco-piles provide habitats for a range of creatures. Don't disturb in the winter, when hedgehogs and queen bumblebees hibernate.

Green roofs
Turn a flat roof into prime insect real estate. Ensure that the surface is waterproof and well supported before laying pre-planted sedum matting or buying plug plants and creating your own ground cover.

▼ **Plant a rainbow meadow** of highly decorative, insect-friendly flowers.

Ponds and water

Even tiny pools can accommodate a frog or two and provide drinking and bathing water for birds; larger pools can support many species. Sloping sides allow safe access, and marginals and aquatics offer cover.

Insect nests

Provide a nest site for mason bees or a hibernation station for ladybugs and lacewings by filling pots with hollow bamboo stems, or fit a purpose-built box. Position in a warm, sheltered spot.

Nest boxes

Wild birds often lack nest sites, so position a range of boxes around the garden. Attach to trees or climbers on walls, or affix beneath the eaves of a shed or other garden building in cool shade.

ALSO TRY

Long grass

Allow areas of long grass for the benefit of butterflies, mammals, and amphibians.

Mini woodland

Create a fast-growing, shady woodland habitat with close-planted silver birch.

Bog garden

Attract insects and provide a home for amphibians with moisture-loving bog plants.

NATURAL BY DESIGN

You don't need a large garden, or even one in the country, to foster nature. It's all around you, but the design of your garden and the plants you choose will have an impact on how much wildlife you attract to your yard.

▶ **Suburban bliss**
Hedges, lawns, ornamental shrubs, and trees offer birds food, sites for nesting, and vantage points from which to watch for predators.

▼ **Meadow haven**
Long grass can support many beneficial insects, including butterflies. At night, listen for foraging mice and voles—if you're lucky you may see bats and owls, too.

▶ **Wall habitat**
Rock gardens and raised beds made from loosely arranged stones create nooks and crannies that make perfect homes for beneficial insects, such as ground beetles, queen bumblebees, and centipedes. They may also encourage toads, which kill slugs.

▲ Designer wilderness
Create a stylized meadow or scrub area—birch trees provide sites for nesting and roosting, while the long grass can be sown with insect-friendly daisies and wild-looking perennials like the bee-magnet, *Knautia*.

ADAPTING THE STYLE

Your layout will affect the amount of wildlife you will attract. Features such as a wildlife pond or bird and bat boxes are best at a distance from the house. Let your yard develop its own style: allow the grass to merge into a meadow at the far end of the garden. Place pots of scented flowers around a seating area to attract butterflies near the house.

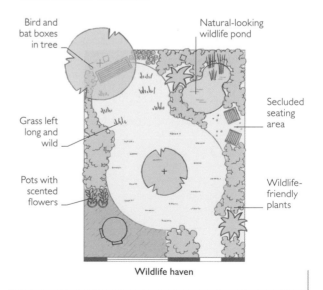

Bird and bat boxes in tree

Natural-looking wildlife pond

Grass left long and wild

Secluded seating area

Pots with scented flowers

Wildlife-friendly plants

Wildlife haven

▲ Aquatic life
A naturalistic pool is a huge draw for insects that attract dragonflies, birds, and even bats; birds will also use the pool to drink and bathe. Provide at least one shallow spot for safe access to the water. Use marginals and submerged aquatics to filter the water and a few floating leaves to reduce the amount of light and heat that reaches the surface. These will also provide shelter and camouflage for amphibians and beneficial insect larvae.

◄ Winter garden glory
Providing an abundance of colorful fruits, berries, and seeds not only enriches views of the garden in the winter, it also means there's a supply of food for birds and mammals, which will feast in the fall to build up fat reserves. There is a range of striking berries in colors as diverse as yellow and purple. Ornamental grasses and other seed heads are also a valuable food source; tree ivy provides late nectar and fruits. Bees will appreciate early heathers.

ENTHUSIAST'S GARDEN

Most gardeners love plants, but for some they are a real passion. Providing conditions for unusual specimens is part of the challenge; so is creating year-round beauty. With research and planning you can adapt your space to suit almost any plant.

Familiarize yourself with microclimates and soil conditions (see pp.66–67) so that you can develop diverse planting situations. Deep borders can offer room for attractive plant arrangements, and even walls and fences can be utilized by attaching supports, pots, and baskets. Favored specimens and collections will look even more striking if mixed with a variety of foliage and flowers.

Squeeze in a sitting area, growing fragrant plants over a pergola, and conceal propagation or maintenance areas behind screening plants or vine-covered trellis panels. Create narrow, foliage-fringed paths leading to open spaces to provide contrast and variety in the garden, and to give additional planting opportunities.

KEY DESIGN ELEMENTS

Vertical planting
Use wires or trellis to create a climbing frame on any vertical surface; grow climbers and wall shrubs over archways or pergolas. In the right conditions, specimens can be combined to great effect.

Unusual varieties
Creating the right environment for a prize plant can be a challenge. It could entail creating a particular microclimate or soil type or, for large, frost-sensitive plants, wrapping them in situ for winter.

Special collections
Once you begin collecting, you may focus on acquiring specific genera or groups, such as succulents. Show these off with an auricula theater or tiered displays on greenhouse or patio staging.

Generous planting
If you have trouble squeezing in new plants, curb over-vigorous types and give away those that no longer interest you. Use potted plants to fill gaps in borders and to invigorate your planting designs.

▼ **Line the banks of a shallow pool** with a mix of plants for color and foliage.

Niche habitats

Some plant groups can't be accommodated in conventional borders so you'll need to create conditions to suit them, such as a water garden, boggy area, or shady woodland.

Plant protection

Exotic and tender plants require a frost-free shelter, ideally a heated greenhouse or sunroom. Some alpines need protection with a cold frame, while ferns and some orchids will thrive in a humid shade house.

Tender specimens

In warmer months, cacti, palms, tender succulents, and citrus may be moved outside to add a Mediterranean feel to patios and decks. Others may be placed in borders for an exotic touch.

ALSO TRY

Behind the scenes

Invest in a greenhouse or cold frame to store any plants that are temporarily off display.

Natural plantings

Create wild-looking groupings of plants from a particular geographic region.

Trained shapes

Show off your skills with clipped topiary shapes, trained fruits, and flowering standards.

PLANT HAVENS

Creating a variety of conditions, such as a bog garden, woodland, or alpine scree, allows you to incorporate diverse, even exotic plants into your collection. Plan your design carefully to feature your favorites.

▶ Tropical paradise
If you can shelter nonhardy plants over the winter, it's possible to create a summer garden with jungle appeal. Use sculptural bananas, tree ferns, and cannas for an exotic flavor.

▼ Topiary theatrics
Even simple clipped shapes, spheres, or pyramids can look striking, especially when arranged as part of an abstract design.

▶ Show time
Put your favorite plants on show using simple displays of pots. Stepped stands or walls are ideal for maximizing the visibility of foliage and flowers. Plants can be changed around throughout the year to make the most of their seasons of interest.

▲ Water world
Creating a pond or bog garden is perhaps the most extreme way to cater to a specific group, but most aquatics and marginals are easy to please and often have sculptural blooms and large, architectural foliage.

ADAPTING THE STYLE

Use trellis or screening to disguise any areas of the garden that you don't want on display, such as a potting shed, greenhouse, or maintenance area. Use a winding path to separate the different planting zones, such as a bog garden and gravel garden. Site your favorite plants as focal features, and position a seating area so that you can fully appreciate them.

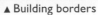

▲ Building borders
Most gardens aren't naturally equipped with the conditions you'll need to support every type of plant. It's easier to control conditions, such as drainage and pH, if you grow plants in raised beds or build up soil behind retaining walls. Mix and match to include as many species as possible, using bulbs like alliums to grow through perennials and alpines. You could also set pots of lilies, dahlias, or other "fillers" in the beds to fill temporary gaps or make the most of your prize specimens by showing them *in situ*.

◄ Drifting with nature
You can mimic the way plants grow in the wild by creating drifts and large blocks of the same species, such as *Kniphofia* or grasses. This organic approach works particularly well in larger, rural gardens. Rather than straight-lined, formal beds or borders, allow the garden's borders to form in organic, flowing shapes. The mixing of perennials with grasses in this way is often referred to as prairie planting.

Specimen tree focal point

Pond and bog garden

Rock and gravel garden

Potting shed and greenhouse, screened with trellis

Seating under scented pergola

Sunny planting

Enthusiast's garden

EASY CARE GARDEN

You can enjoy a beautiful garden even if you can't devote a lot of time and effort to it. There is a wealth of low maintenance plants to choose from, and you can still create dramatic effects without resorting to expensive landscaping.

By adopting a few simple techniques, you can keep your garden looking vibrant and attractive. Choose pest- and disease-resistant plants, and cut down on weeding by using mulches (see p.23). Select drought-tolerant plants where possible, and maintain more demanding types with automatic irrigation. Instead of annual displays of tender bedding, grow permanent, colorful evergreens and long-flowering perennials; select those that do not need support or deadheading. Some shrubs do not require pruning, while others may only need one simple cut per year.

Consider replacing a lawn with a gravel garden or meadow. Adding easy care design features, such as a pebble fountain, helps keep the garden interesting during the winter months.

KEY DESIGN ELEMENTS

Colorful evergreens
Though planting emphasis is often on flowering annuals and perennials, evergreen shrubs, herbs, and grasses have longer lasting displays, and many are equally colorful and attractive.

Drought-proof containers
A row of architectural specimens can make as much impact as a multitude of high maintenance bedding plants. Use automatic irrigation, or plant drought-tolerant herbs, alpines, and succulents.

Raised beds
Easy care raised beds can be filled with alpines, herbs, compact perennials, or even a pond. You can garden at a comfortable height with no digging, and they can also be used for casual seating.

Living carpets
Species adapted to long periods without rain, such as alpines and succulents, are often tough in other ways. Many can withstand harmful insects and don't require regular feeding or pruning.

▼ **Line your floors and walkways** with gravel for an attractive surface that needs minimal upkeep.

Decorative ground cover

Laying colorful pebbles or aggregate on top of a weed-suppressing membrane is an attractive solution to weeds and is striking combined with creative planting.

Hard landscaping

Create clean lines and surfaces with natural stone or manufactured paving. Bricks can be laid in patterns or as edging. Mix materials: try cobblestones with decking, or sandstone with brick.

Ornamental features

Display sculptures or use large, empty containers for architectural effects or as part of a color theme. Use furniture as a focal point, or consider a paving feature, such as a mosaic or circular patio insert.

ALSO TRY

Handy storage

Store soft furnishings, tools, and toys in built-in units so they're within easy reach.

Wild ways

Leave areas wild or convert lawns to meadows (see *p.340*) to free up your spare time.

Simple lighting

Use solar lights—there is a wide range of easy-to-install products available (see *pp.76–77*).

DESIGNED TO BE EASY

Make your garden easier to maintain by reducing the need for ornamental plants with creative landscaping. The textures and colors can create a striking foil for features such as fountains, vases, and sculptural plants.

▼ Water features

Self-contained water features with a reservoir and small submersible pump look and sound good and need very little maintenance compared with pools and ponds; the water is moving, so it doesn't clog with algae and weeds. Surround with foliage that will contrast with the shape of the structure.

▶ Lawn conversion

Large lawns can feel overwhelming if time is limited. You could adopt a more relaxed approach. It's easy to establish drifts of spring bulbs and snowdrops in grass. Just mow paths until September, when you can do an overall mow to prevent tussocks forming.

▲ Sculptural plants

To cut down on work, use easy care, evergreen plants, shrubs, grasses, and compact bamboos, and limit the number of flowering varieties. To compensate, position eye-catching specimens in key spots, such as the corner of a bed next to paving or decking.

▲ Clean sweep
This elegant courtyard with built-in bench seating and slate paving is a useful, stylish outdoor room. With automatic irrigation the bold planting could almost look after itself—it will only need an occasional sweeping.

ADAPTING THE STYLE

Construct a simple design by lining the edges of the garden with easy care, raised beds and borders, and then divide the rest of the space into a gravel garden and paved patio area. Place sculptural, decorative features or a pond at the far end of the garden to lead the eye across it, and site dining areas close to the house. Use evergreen hedging as a screen.

▲ Ornamental focus
In an easy care garden, a wide range of decorative elements can be used to make an interesting focal point. The simple sculptural shapes of individual pieces, such as an avant-garde recliner, a large simple container, or a boulder, demand attention. Here a large amphora is the garden's central focus and is given extra prominence with a setting of pebbles and terra-cotta tiles.

◄ Gravel garden
Covering the soil with landscape plastic virtually eliminates the need to weed. After planting through the membrane, disguise the covering with a range of decorative aggregates from gravels and pebbles to crushed brick. Over larger areas, it's important to introduce other shapes and textures. Here, a line of wooden crossties directs the eye to the container, which is set on a mosaic of slate shards ringed with stones. Select plants of differing heights, colors, and textures to complement the gravel surface.

Integrated seating

Gravel garden

Decorative sculptural features

Evergreen hedging

Easy-to-clean hard landscaping

Raised beds

Easy care garden

WHAT IS ACHIEVABLE?

Keep an open mind. It's easy to be seduced by an attractive garden design, but it's important to be practical about what you can realistically achieve and how well the design will suit you and your lifestyle.

▼ SET YOUR PRIORITIES

When deciding on a design for your garden, think about how you live and the resources you have available. In addition to how much the garden will cost to build, also take into account how much maintenance it will need, and what skills and time that will require. For example, a border of varied shrubs planted through a weed-suppressing membrane with an attractive mulch will need much less care over time than a bed of annuals. It's also vital to choose a design that suits your site. Soil type and pH largely determine the plants you can grow, and exposure will influence where you position features such as seating areas. Slopes, drainage, and access for machinery and materials are important factors, too.

To look their best, these extensive plantings of clipped hedges and pleached lime trees require time-consuming care.

POINTS TO CONSIDER

Time available
Estimate the time needed to build the design, as well as that needed to maintain the plan. Looking after this topiary bed, for example, would be a time-consuming labor of love.

The budget
Shop around to get the best prices for materials, and compare quotes for labor and tool rental. Building a raised bed like this from lumber is cheaper than using bricks.

DIY or hire someone?
Do you have the skills to complete the design yourself, or will you need professional help? Laying a brick path like this yourself is fairly easy; pouring a concrete one is less so.

SITE CONSTRAINTS

The success of any design is greatly improved by understanding the plot, particularly soil type, growing conditions, and microclimate. In unfamiliar locations, look at what is thriving in nearby gardens, and seek local advice on seasonal variations. Making even small improvements, like creating shelter, can increase the range of plants you can grow, but get to know the plot before making major changes.

▲ Soil and exposure

Many plants require specific soil conditions, such as acid, alkaline, moist, or well-drained, which will influence what you can grow. Exposure also affects plants, which often have a preference for sun or shade, but is equally important when siting features: seating areas, for instance, are best in warm, sunny spots. Watch the garden during the day to see where sun and shade fall, and adjust your plans and planting accordingly.

Planting large shrubs will create areas of shade in your garden for those plants that will benefit from it.

▲ Open space and shelter

Unlike sheltered spots, open gardens can be prone to gusting winds, which may damage plants and will test the durability of garden buildings. Even urban gardens can be exposed, suffering damage caused by wind racing between neighboring buildings. Sheltered sites are often warmer and allow a wider range of plants to be grown. Garden structures can be more lightweight, and more open designs are possible.

A sheltered location provides the ideal site for large-leaf plants that would be damaged by wind.

◄ Access and obstacles

Whatever you're planning for your garden, don't forget that you need to be able to bring materials in and take debris out. In a ground-floor unit that could even mean carrying everything across the living room carpet. Find the best location for deliveries and decide where to store them. It may be advisable to seek access from neighbors.

Don't assume you can change everything in your garden to suit your design. Existing trees and other features may be protected, so check with the local extension office.

A wheelbarrow, is ideal for moving large or heavy materials on or off site, providing you have access for one.

WHERE TO START

For most people, moving to a new home involves taking on a garden shaped by at least one previous owner. If you are a new gardener, adopting a richly planted garden can be exciting as well as daunting. To avoid mistakes, learn as much as you can before taking action.

▲ Assess the site

An established garden may contain mature trees and shrubs, some hard landscaping, and a variety of structures and buildings. Carrying out a thorough site review will highlight problem areas as well as plants and features to retain or enhance. Do a soil analysis to find any deficiencies. Look for shrubs and trees in need of pruning, regeneration, or removal, or that are mismatched.

Take photographs throughout the year to document the seasonal changes of plants and flowers.

▼ WAIT AND SEE

If possible, leave the major reconstruction of a mature, well-stocked garden for up to a year. There may be plants that aren't visible at the time you move in, and it's easy to dismiss a dull shrub in the fall only to find it completely transformed with blossoms and taking center stage in early spring. Delaying not only allows you to experience the seasons, but also to view color schemes, to see where the light falls, and to assess the amount of privacy the planting creates. It also allows you to review the productivity and health of mature plants and decide whether any need restoration or removal. Mark the position of bulbs or herbaceous plants that you want to keep before they die back. It is a good idea to make a planting plan of existing material in advance of digging and restructuring borders. Local horticultural colleges, social media, garden centers, and nurseries can help identify mystery specimens as well as problems with pests and diseases.

Spring is the season when plants begin to emerge.

Check for unsightly gaps in your summer borders.

Leave plants to develop their fall features.

Structural plants and seed heads create winter interest.

QUICK FIXES

While you're working out the details of a major overhaul, consider giving your garden an interim mini-makeover; this will refresh tired-looking hard landscaping and rejuvenate beds and borders. There are plenty of improvements that can be made with immediate benefits, which won't cost a great deal. Tackle eyesores such as dilapidated sheds or badly pruned trees first, and if summer is approaching, make upgrading terraces and patios a priority.

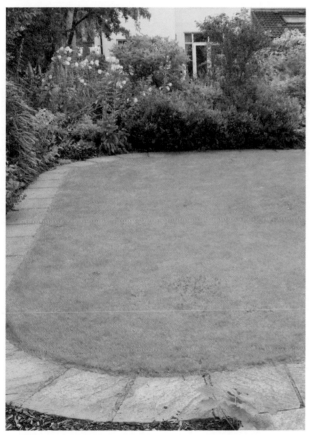

▲ Reshape beds and lawns

You can turn a lawn into a feature simply by giving it a crisp, well-defined shape. For a modern touch, go for geometric shapes, such as intersecting rectangles, squares, or circles. Replace meandering border edges with strong, sweeping curves that lead the eye to a focal point. Adding a brick or paver mowing edge makes upkeep easier and gives the lawn some designer flair.

Reshaping this established lawn and adding edging has given the whole garden a new, fresh look, improving the appearance of flower borders, too.

► Freshen up

Apply a fresh coat of paint or stain to existing features. On old walls, clean off loose flakes, and scrub away any algae before repainting. Wobbly fences can sometimes be rescued rather than replaced; hide mismatched or missing panels with willow screens or trellis. Replace torn roofing on sheds and garden buildings, restore broken panes, and replace any cracked paving slabs.

Revitalize old fences with fresh paint.

► Clean up

Pulling unwanted plants, removing debris, and generally decluttering provides an instant uplift. Weed paths and patios, and rent a pressure washer to restore grimy paving. Remove unused plant supports, cut back dead stems, and weed beds. Mow and edge lawn, and repair worn patches. Finish by sweeping and washing surfaces.

Power wash patios to remove stains.

► Cut back

Left untouched for a few years, some shrubs can outgrow their allotted space. Fast-growing types can also become clogged with unproductive wood, spoiling their shape and flowering ability. Cutting back sprawling plants can restore balance in a border and will free up space for new plantings. Neglected climbers might also need some attention.

Prune unruly shrubs back to size.

OLD GARDEN, NEW GARDEN

Starting with a bare site is the easiest way to design and build the garden you want. New-construction sites are a blank canvas, but if you have taken over an existing plot, you may need to clear it first. Keep the best plants and features, and don't be afraid to remove the rest.

► CLEAR AWAY DEBRIS

When clearing a site, you are likely to come across a wide range of materials for disposal. Some plant waste can be composted, sent as green waste to local composting, or you can hire a shredder to chip larger, woody branches, which makes excellent mulch. As a last resort, you can also burn dry organic waste and untreated wood on still, dry days.

For bulky materials that can't be composted, shredded, or burned, like trash or debris, rent a dumpster or check what your local waste management company will pick up.

Wear gloves when clearing a site in case of sharp or hidden debris.

◄ REMOVE PLANTS

Established gardens may contain plants that you don't want to keep. Perennials, bulbs, and small shrubs can be dug up and given away or possibly replanted

elsewhere. Most trees and shrubs can't realistically be moved, so are best cut down and dug out. To remove large specimens, contact a tree surgeon for advice, and where necessary, remove stumps too large to dig out using a "stump grinder," which can be rented. Some localities may require permits for tree removal. Check with the appropriate authorities. When clearing plants, remove all obvious weeds, then lay down a weed-suppressing fabric, securely pegged down, to help keep the area weed-free in future. As a last resort, if the plot is overrun with tough perennial weeds, use a chemical weed killer.

Removing trees may require a permit.

In some cases, weed killer may be the best solution.

▶ NEW CONSTRUCTION

If you buy a house in a new development, you may start out with just a stretch of bare ground in place of a garden. Although unsightly, this fresh start gives you the ideal opportunity to design your dream garden from scratch. Other than the barest bones, such as a sidewalk, new-build gardens are devoid of existing features that might otherwise restrict your choices. Such a blank canvas also allows you to start designing and building as soon as the weather allows, and access for machinery and deliveries is often easier.

The downside of construction sites is that with a lack of established trees and shrubs, it can take several years before the garden develops a sense of maturity or privacy. Depending on how the site was used before it was developed, there may also be issues with soil quality (see below). You may also find there are planning restrictions and bylaws, often specific to that development, limiting what you can plant and build, especially in front yards.

New gardens often lack plants and features but offer a wealth of design opportunities.

▼ Assess the soil

New build soils are often very poor. In a new garden, don't assume that rubble was removed from the site; it may have been buried under a thin layer of topsoil. Dig test holes across the site to check, and also look out for other soil problems, such as compaction (see right). Mark out any problem areas so you can resolve them later or plan around them. Also check how deep the topsoil goes, measure its pH, send soil to be tested at a laboratory, and assess whether it is mostly clay, sand, or loam (see pp.20–21).

▼ Soil compaction

It's not unusual to find a cosmetic topsoil dressing used to disguise an impenetrable base of compacted soil, caused by heavy machinery. Compacted soil contains little air and drains poorly, which restricts plant growth. Scrape back the topsoil to look for patches of soil that are hard to dig, and fork through the soil as much as possible, incorporating bulky organic matter, such as composted bark. Compaction is most common on heavy clay soils and can take several years to alleviate.

▼ Other considerations

Look at deeds and covenants to find out whether your development has requirements for plantings. Often only plantings visible from the street are regulated. Check the routing of gas and water pipes, drains, and electricity cables before work begins to prevent them being disturbed or damaged.

Dig test holes to assess the quality of your soil.

Puddles may indicate areas of compacted ground.

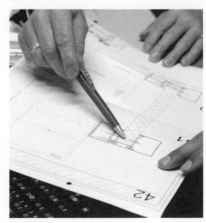

Check your site plan when designing your garden.

SURVEYING THE SITE

Analyzing the key characteristics of your lot will help you create a garden that works. If you know your challenges, such as a border that floods in the winter or an area that's always in shade, you can find planting or landscaping solutions.

▶ CONSIDER THE SOIL

Understanding the type and structure of your soil is of utmost importance. Plants require differing conditions, and knowing what you have allows you to make better planting choices. Although certain soil types can be improved, it's best not to try too drastic a change: a thin, alkaline soil formed over limestone bedrock will have a high pH—ideal for lavender, but lethal for pieris, rhododendrons, and other ericaceous plants that require deep, acidic, humus-rich soil. Adding peat or chemicals to increase the soil's acidity may solve the issue in the short term, but water rising from the bedrock will return the ground to its original state, and it's usually better to work with the existing pH. The consistency and drainage of soil can also adversely affect construction projects, such as ponds or building foundations, so plan carefully to avoid disappointment.

Soil pH
Use a pH test to analyze your soil. Most plants prefer conditions around pH 6.5. But be aware: some, such as pieris, prefer acidic conditions, around pH 5.5. Alkaline soils suppress clubroot disease of cabbage family plants.

Heavy soil
Clay-rich or "heavy" soils can be tough to dig. If they dry out, they can become solid or cracked. Since they drain poorly, they can become very sticky when wet. Add organic matter to improve the soil structure.

Sandy soil
Sandy, stony, or gravelly soils drain quickly and therefore tend to lack water-soluble nutrients, which are easily washed away. Rake in fertilizer, and apply a 2–3 in (5–8 cm) mulch of well-rotted manure or compost.

▼ EXPOSURE AND SHELTER

Factors such as the direction in which your garden faces, how much sun it receives, where the prevailing wind blows from, and how sheltered the lot is should strongly influence your garden design and planting decisions. By observing the sun as it moves across the garden, you can identify which areas will make the best locations for eating and relaxing—you could have one patio for breakfast or morning coffee

and another for evening dining. These observations will also help you position a herb or vegetable plot or a gravel garden, which all need as much sunshine as possible. As the sun moves from east to west, the house, neighboring trees, buildings, and hedges can cast shadows over different areas. The amount of shade will also vary according to the time of year: in the summer the sun is higher, which results in more of the garden receiving warmth and light.

South-facing garden (midday)

West-facing garden (midday)

North-facing garden (midday)

East-facing garden (midday)

▲ Frost pockets

Hot air rises, and in sloping gardens the cold air will sink to the bottom of the grade. If prevented from escaping by a dense hedge or wall, it accumulates, forming a frost pocket. Select plants carefully because tender and newly planted ones, especially evergreens, may not be able to survive the cold in winter months.

Observe your garden to identify frost pockets. They can be very localized: the plants surrounding the *Sambucus*, *Acanthus*, and grasses above are unaffected.

▼ Exposed seaside sites

Strong winds can strip moisture from foliage and damage weak stems, so the more sheltered your garden, the better your plants will cope. Use tall wind-, salt-, and cold-tolerant plants to create a "shelter belt," to shield the plot from prevailing winds. This barrier of plants will allow you to grow more delicate types in sheltered spots.

Use tough plants such as large, spiky phormiums and tall, feathery pampas grass on exposed, sea-facing exposures. Their height and foliage make them an asset, but even plants such as these benefit from a shelterbelt to reduce exposure.

DEALING WITH SLOPES

Gradients add interest to a garden, allowing you to create different levels, but they can pose a challenge. Achieving level surfaces and easy access may require substantial digging, soil retention, and drainage.

▼ CREATING LEVELS

Gently sloping sites provide a wealth of opportunities to create interesting paths, steps, and spaces. Individual areas can be easily leveled, either by cutting in and building retaining walls or by building upward to form decks and terraces. On larger plots, or on those that slope in more than one direction, different levels can be interconnected to create a multi-level space. Where gradients are gentle, this is something you can probably achieve yourself, or at least with minimal help and advice.

Major earth-moving is very expensive and difficult, however, and on steeply sloping sites it may be better to design with the gradient rather than try to level it. Instead, try to work with the natural contours. Seek expert advice to see what is achievable and what it may cost.

A multi-level terrace like this provides a variety of linked spaces.

▼ RETAINING THE SOIL

When cutting into a slope to make a level area, you may need to retain surrounding soil to hold it in place. On gentle slopes, a low wall or a row of railroad ties may be adequate, which you could install yourself. Steeper sites, with more soil to hold back, require substantial retaining structures, capable of supporting the weight of soil as well as the water it contains. Speak to a professional landscaper, or for walls over 3 ft (1 m) high, contact an engineer.

Use railroad ties to level shallow slopes.

Substantial walls are needed to retain steeper sites.

▶ CHANGING LEVELS

An essential aspect of any sloping site is being able to move between levels safely and easily. Ramps and steps are the obvious solution, and whichever you choose, plan them carefully. They should be wide and deep enough to climb safely, but shallow enough so you don't struggle to reach the top. The materials used should not become slippery in wet weather, and you may need to plan in surface drainage and handrails. You may be able to achieve this yourself on simple slopes, but seek advice on steep, challenging sites.

Simple steps are easy to build with basic DIY skills and provide space for decorative pots.
Shallow ramps are the safest way to ascend a slope. One like this could be made using decking planks.

Steep steps are useful where space is limited but can be dangerous or difficult to climb without a secure handrail.

Retaining wall

Shallow steps are safer and easier to climb but take up more space. Ideal for larger plots, wider steps can be decorated with planters.

Continuous ramps are ideal for wheelchairs and bikes but must be long enough to be sufficiently shallow. This takes up a lot of space.

Stepped ramps take less space than full ramps and are easier than steps for wheelbarrows and wheelchairs. The surface must not be slippery.

▶ PROVIDING DRAINAGE

Drainage is important on sloping sites to control the direction in which ground- and rainwater travels. Unchecked, water flows downhill, either below or over the surface, and can collect anywhere, even indoors. Drainage is especially important in areas with heavy soils and in urban locations, where there is run-off from roofs, paths, and roads. Angle your hard surfaces to direct water away from buildings, and dig gravel-filled sumps, or interceptor drains, to control water movement. Building raised beds can lift plants out of wet conditions. Again, seek professional advice if unsure.

Groundwater

Surface water

Gravel-filled sump

Interceptor drains capture groundwater as it travels through the soil. Gravel-filled sumps drain water running over the surface.

Interceptor drain

CREATING BOUNDARIES

The role of a boundary is to define a space, whether that's the whole plot or an area within it. Boundaries have many functions, from providing privacy and intimacy to forming the backbone of the entire garden design.

▼ SETTING LIMITS

Garden boundaries have the fundamental task of containing the site and providing a physical barrier to intruders, prying eyes, and the weather. In most gardens, they are highly visible and form the backdrop to everything else. When designing with boundaries, there are two approaches: either try to blend them in, or make a feature of them. Once in place, the materials and style you choose are hard to change, so design your boundaries carefully.

Lush planting softens this wall, blurring its lines.

Stark modern fencing sets the tone here.

▲ DEFINING SPACES

Dividing spaces often makes them seem larger, especially when the different areas are then given a specific use, such as for formal dining or as a play area for children. You don't need tall barriers to create the divisions— you can achieve the same effect with low walls, woven screens, and see-through planting. The idea is merely to suggest a space and purpose. Using screens also means that the divisions are temporary and can change as your need for different spaces evolves.

Bright paint and a low wall mark out this seating area.

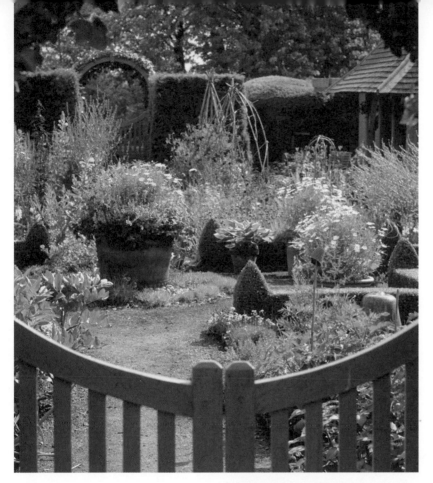

◄ BEYOND THE BOUNDARIES

Garden boundaries don't have to block views or be continuous and unbroken, and can be used to lead the eye to specific features. Niches clipped into hedges provide a prime spot for a statue, while trellis panels inserted into fences can reveal a neighboring focal point. Alter the height along the length of your boundaries to give a varying sense of enclosure and openness. Gates don't just provide access, they can also be used to frame views in or out of the garden and can be made features in their own right.

Within the garden, leave gaps in divides and screens to give a taste of what lies beyond. This will also allow you to take full advantage of garden features by enabling them to be enjoyed from different angles. Be creative with the design of your garden, and consider how and from where you will view its features.

A moon gate like this defines the entrance and frames the view.

► MATERIALS TO CONSIDER

When deciding on what materials to use for garden boundaries, it is important to consider the overall design first. Aesthetically, natural materials suit traditional designs better but can look out of place in contemporary plans, and vice versa. On a practical level, think about durability and what the boundary is for. If it's intended to keep people out or to act as a windbreak, you'll need something sturdy. Likewise, if your garden is exposed to the elements, even temporary internal dividers will need to be fairly robust. Maintenance is also a factor. Hedges need trimming regularly in the summer, and fences last longer if they are treated every year. Even walls need looking after.

Brick walls offer a traditional look.

Fences and screens are quick to erect.

Traditional hedges take several years to establish.

Trellis fencing is useful for internal garden divides.

SURFACES

Surfaces are one of the main elements of a garden, literally underpinning almost everything else. They can be expensive and time-consuming to install, but get it right, and they will last a lifetime.

▼ CHOOSING MATERIALS

There are many factors to consider when deciding on surface materials. Cost and appearance are obvious, but don't overlook practicality: think about the site and how it will be used. For example, choose tough, hard-wearing materials for heavily used areas such as paths. Consider porous materials, like gravel, at the foot of sloping sites where drainage is an issue. If access is difficult, think about using lightweight materials that can be easily carried to the site.

Another important consideration is that, although the surface is the most visible element, it is often the easiest to complete; it is the foundation that can be challenging. Decking, for example, needs minimal footings which you can do yourself, but stone tiles require a solid base, best left to professionals. The payback, however, is that while a deck lasts 10–15 years, tiled surfaces can last indefinitely.

Hard surfaces are best for seating areas; lawn is ideal for play spaces.

DRAINAGE

Hard surfaces must drain in a controlled way to prevent puddles from forming and to stop rainwater from entering buildings. Slope surfaces and incorporate drainage channels to direct flow. Ensuring good drainage also helps keep smooth surfaces, like slabs and tiles, from becoming slippery when wet.

Plants between paving slabs can help absorb excess water from the nonporous surface. Trim as needed if they spread.

► HARD SURFACES

Hard surface materials include bricks, blocks, slabs, and tiles, whether natural or man-made. Their advantage is that they provide a firm, level surface that is very hard-wearing. They are also available in a wide range of materials, suitable for most designs. Smaller units, like bricks, are best for sloping or angular sites, where corners are required, or where materials must be carried on site. Slabs are ideal for paving areas quickly and are simple to lay. The drawbacks, depending on the material, are the need for foundations and drainage, and often the price.

◄ GRAVEL

Gravel is very versatile and comes in a range of colors and textures. It can be laid almost anywhere, regardless of slopes and corners, and requires only a weed-proof membrane for a foundation. It can be carried in bags to the site, and if bought in bulk can be very economical. It can be used as a temporary solution. Laying it requires no special tools or skills, so is easy to do yourself. The downsides are that it does not form a solid surface and can make walking—and pushing wheelbarrows and strollers—harder. Weeds may eventually grow through it.

► DECKING

Decking is usually made of weather-resistant, pressure-treated wood, which must be treated regularly to protect against rot. Decks are adaptable, ideal for sunny areas, and can be built to suit most sites, whether on different levels or awkwardly shaped. Their advantage is that they are easy to build, using basic tools and DIY skills, and the materials are cheap. You can also adapt or expand them over time. The drawbacks are that decks can be slimy when wet, and that wood decays and needs replacing. Composite decking is made from recycled plastic and wood and lasts longer.

◄ LAWNS

Lawns are the most traditional garden surface. Like gravel, they are ideal for sloping and awkwardly shaped sites, and the materials can be easily brought on site, assuming the soil beneath is suitable. They are also ideal for families, providing a safe surface for children and one that will grow back if damaged. A big drawback is maintenance, since they require regular mowing in summer and treatment and care in fall and spring. They are not suitable for shady sites and can turn to straw in hot summers, although they usually recover.

GARDEN BUILDINGS

Even the humble tool shed can become an attractive feature when positioned and finished with care, so it's worth integrating your garden buildings into your design. With sheds, greenhouses, and other work buildings, pay particular attention to access and location.

▶ SITING STORAGE

Sheds offer convenient storage for items, such as tools, potting mix, toys, and bicycles. In a small plot, consider bench storage or a locker. Fit sheds with a sturdy padlock, and check homeowner's insurance to see whether they are covered. Consider location carefully. It might be better to put a shed out of sight—down a side passage or behind shrubs and trees—rather than in full view.

When selecting a shed, examine the quality of the joints, frames, and fittings of doors and windows, and reject any where you see chinks of light through the framework. The base should feel solid, and the roof should have a decent overhang and be good and sturdy.

Wooden sheds look attractive but need paint, stain, or preservative treatments to prevent rot. Rustproof metal or fiberglass types may be easier to maintain.

◀ Access

If you will be maneuvering large equipment, such as a lawn mower or wheelbarrow, in and out of your shed, select a model with large entrances and doors that open fully. Wide access paths are ideal, and you may want to replace steps with a ramp, or gravel paths with paving, for easy access. For leisure buildings, garden offices, and studios—where you will not regularly need to move bulky items—use steps and stairways to enhance the architectural impact of the structure; surround it with plants to integrate it into the garden. For any garden building, ensure that the base is level and that surrounding surfaces and paths slope away slightly to divert rainwater.

Make a grand entrance by using a striking spiral staircase for access to an exterior office or studio.

▶ GREENHOUSES

Commonly constructed from metal, such as lightweight aluminum, or from naturally rot-resistant woods like cedar, greenhouses are available to suit any garden design. A sheltered location is best, avoiding nearby walls, hedges, and trees that cast unwanted shade. Locate your greenhouse away from property lines to lessen the risk of vandalism.

Consider what you are likely to grow: a lean-to on the north side of a wall would be perfect for a cool, shady fernery, but much more light will be needed for ripening grapes. An east–west orientation for a freestanding greenhouse is ideal for raising spring seedlings and overwintering plants. Choose a model with roof vents and exterior shading blinds to keep plants cool in summer; if you need heat and light, lay power lines to supply electricity.

A large, traditional greenhouse makes an attractive feature in a rural garden. Surround it with plants to soften its appearance.

Get planning permission when siting a garden room.

Customize a shed with a stained-glass window.

Install a playhouse and walkway.

Fit a garden office with an insulating sedum roof.

◀ TYPES OF BUILDINGS

There is a wide range of garden buildings available, but if you can't find the design you want, some companies will create unique pieces or can convert an existing building. You might need a building permit depending on the size, height, and proximity to property lines, so check before starting.

Customize a wooden building using paint, stains, or even a stained-glass window, or leave structures a natural shade to blend in with their surroundings. For a green roof, try pre-planted sedum matting; you may need to strengthen the structure to take the extra weight. Fit insulation in sheds, garden offices, and workshops, especially if you plan to heat them. Consult an electrician when installing heating and lighting.

LIGHTING

Outdoor lighting can serve a variety of purposes, from providing safety and security to creating a relaxing atmosphere. It can transform the look of your garden at night, so decide which plants or focal points you want to illuminate, and then choose lights to fit your design.

▼ SECURITY

Lighting up entrances to the house can be decorative and welcoming but can also help deter burglars; if possible, keep a clear line of sight to the road. LED wall lights can be set to turn on at dusk and off in the morning, but this can result in light pollution that disturbs wildlife. A more eco-friendly option is to install security lights fitted with infrared movement sensors that illuminate your home as people approach it. Adjust sensitivity so that lights aren't triggered by passing cats and rabbits. Also keep nearby plants pruned to prevent them from activating the lights on a windy night. Be sensitive in the placement and power of lights to avoid upsetting your neighbors.

A clear line of sight along well-lit paths leaves no hiding places for unwelcome visitors.

▲ SAFETY

If you plan to use the garden at night, you'll need to light paths and steps for safety. Concentrate on potential hazards, such as ponds, or where ground levels change or fall off sharply from a pathway. Use post lights or low-level mini spotlights angled to cast light over the edges of paving or decking, or install recessed paving lights; choose a style that complements the design of your house and garden. Recessed deck lights are relatively easy to install and will highlight the edge of the deck as well as changes in level. Safety lights don't have to be on continuously: sensors are available that will turn lights on as you approach and off again after a set time. You can also control garden lights using a remote or cell phone.

Outdoor LED post lights are plugged into a power box. Solar-powered lights are also available.

◀ DECORATION AND MOOD

With strategic lighting it's possible to transform the look of a garden at night. Individual mini spotlights, uplights, and downlights can be used to illuminate sculptures, decorative wall panels, garden buildings, and structures, such as pergolas. Used sparingly, colored lights will add drama to plain walls, and recessed lights can make a feature of steps and retaining walls. Fountain lights make water features sparkle at night, while submersible lights add drama to contemporary pools.

Uplighting a tree picks out the texture of the bark and leafy canopy. With diaphanous subjects like grasses, shining low-level lighting through the stems and flowers works well. Tiny string lights woven through overhead climbers and wall shrubs creates a romantic atmosphere.

Use recessed lighting to illuminate a seating area and to highlight focal plants and screening.

▶ LIGHTING OPTIONS

There is a range of lighting types, so pick those that fit your design. Any lights powered by a main circuit must be installed by an electrician.

LED lights make striking features. They can be plugged into a transformer in a waterproof unit in the garden or attached to the house. Submersible LEDs can be used to illuminate ponds and water features.

You can also buy wireless, battery-powered lights that are recharged by plugging them into a USB socket. Solar-powered lights are eco-friendly and many will work even in winter; position them so they can absorb enough sunlight to recharge.

Candles and lanterns are inexpensive and create a wonderful atmosphere. Make sure to position them well away from flammable materials and plants.

Lantern-style lights provide an atmospheric touch to a garden.

Solar-powered lights are safe and easy to install.

Ensure that candles are safely positioned.

LED lighting should be installed by a professional.

DESIGN PRINCIPLES

Decide on a look for your garden—sleek contemporary, relaxed informal, or strongly structured traditional—and base your layout on this. Consider different ways of navigating the garden, where to place various features, and in what direction main sight lines will run.

◄ SHAPES AND SPACES

Designs work best if there is a good balance between flat, open spaces, such as lawns, decking, and patios, and upright elements, such as trees, borders, and buildings. The vertical features provide contrast with the horizontal, and help divide up the plot. Overlap bold geometric shapes for a simple but unusual design.

Mark out the key zones on a rough plan, designating approximate areas of use, such as seating or planting. Decide whether you've given sufficient space to different areas, and try different ideas. If the lawn or terrace is too big relative to the borders, the garden could feel stark and uncomfortably open. On the other hand, lack of open space could feel claustrophobic.

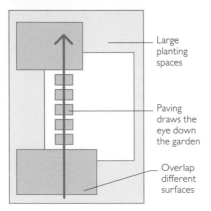

Large planting spaces

Paving draws the eye down the garden

Overlap different surfaces

Right angles Use straight-sided shapes to make the garden seem bigger—position down the center for length, or side to side for width.

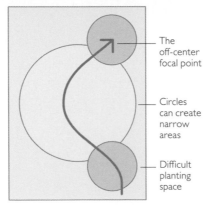

The off-center focal point

Circles can create narrow areas

Difficult planting space

Circles Use the circular areas to create an organic, natural-looking design. Here, the eye is led through the center to the rear right corner.

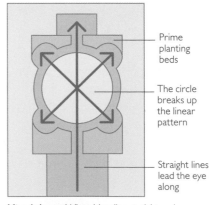

Prime planting beds

The circle breaks up the linear pattern

Straight lines lead the eye along

Mixed shapes When blending straight and rounded shapes, keep the design simple, or it can create odd-shaped planting areas.

▼ ROUTES AND NAVIGATION

Deciding the garden's access points and figuring out how to move around it results in a pattern of pathways that will influence the overall design. A straight path forming the primary route down the center creates a formal look. Strengthen the axis further by placing a focal point at the far end. A route that meanders creates a more relaxed ambience, with the promise of partly hidden spaces to explore. A circular route can provide access to all parts of the garden, linking to different areas, such as a dining terrace or utility area.

Use sharp topiary to accentuate formal symmetry.

Create a winding, riverlike walkway lined with slate.

A circular path makes the whole plot accessible.

▼ FOCAL POINTS

In a small plot, use one strong focal feature, such as this large slate vase, to draw the eye; for a traditional feel, place it at the end of a straight walkway. Positioned in a corner, it can pull focus along a diagonal axis to make a short plot feel longer. Choose features in interesting shapes, textures, and colors to contrast with their surroundings.

▼ EXPERIMENT WITH PLANS

The plans below illustrate just how different the same-sized plot could look, simply by rearranging the position and shape of various key garden features. Each design contains lawns, borders, a pond, and a patio, but the left-hand plan is formal and very orderly while the plan on the right-hand side is fluid, relaxed, and dynamic.

Place a grid over your plan—by keeping the lines adjacent to the paper's edges you will find it easier to plot the straight-lined grid formation of the first design. Alternatively, rotate this grid by 45 degrees to plot your features on the diagonal, as in the second design. Link features together by plotting them on a curved, swooping line.

Choose plants that act as a foil for your feature.

Hide an unsightly shed

Use tall trees to mask a garden shed

Fill deep borders with plants

Surround the house with paving

Use a grid-like layout and parallel screens of trees and hedging to encourage the development of secluded, intimate areas.

Use decking as a focal point

Create deep swathes of plants

Frame the garden with tall trees

Extend the curve with brickwork

Use organic shapes and a small number of materials to create a space that is relaxing and will be easy to maintain as plants develop.

DRAWING SIMPLE PLANS

Once you've examined your garden's soil and exposure and chosen which features you want to include, you can begin designing. You'll need an accurate site plan, so be sure that you measure carefully.

▶ REGULAR SHAPES

On a piece of letter- or legal-sized paper, sketch out a rough outline of the garden, drawing it approximately to scale. If the site is attached to—or flows around—a building, make this your main point of reference.

Using a long tape measure, note the exact shape and dimensions of the building, including the position of doors and windows, and also the distances between the building and the property lines. This will show the full extent of the garden area. Next, measure the length and angles of the garden boundaries and also the distances from corner to corner to help you figure out the true shape of the plot, relative to the house.

Finally, note any remaining elements, including any existing features or buildings that you intend to keep, and mark their positions in relation to the property lines and house.

Add in features once the boundaries are set

Measure the length of each property line

Measure the distance between the house and property line

▶ Property lines
Measure all four sides of your garden, then the house and its distance from each of the property lines.

House

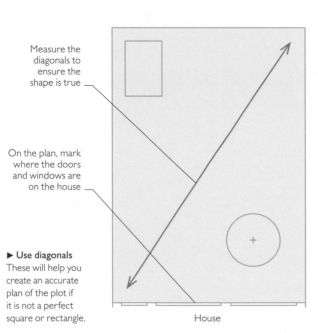

Measure the diagonals to ensure the shape is true

On the plan, mark where the doors and windows are on the house

▶ Use diagonals
These will help you create an accurate plan of the plot if it is not a perfect square or rectangle.

House

Locate retained features as accurately as possible

Plot key plants relative to the house and property lines

▶ Features
Plot the positions of features that you plan to keep, taking measurements from the house.

House

▼ MEASURING TO SCALE

Once you've gathered your measurements, transfer them to a scale drawing on graph paper. Choose a scale that relates to the size of your plot and the amount of detail you require. For a small garden, a scale of 1:25 (½in/1 cm on paper measures 10in/25 cm on the ground) or 1:50 is ideal. When transferring measurements to the plan, a ruler and a pair of compasses will be useful for plotting features. Draw it using a fine-line pen, and make photocopies so you can experiment with ideas.

▼ IRREGULAR SHAPES

To measure out an irregularly shaped garden accurately, you will need to use offsets. These are worked out by first laying a tape measure along the length of the garden at a 90-degree angle to the house. Holding a second tape measure at 90 degrees to the first, measure the distance to the boundary on each side at regular intervals, also recording the measurement to any feature you plan to keep. Scale down the measurements, and draw out the plot, linking the boundary offsets to draw the perimeter.

1 Begin by drawing the facade of the house along one edge. Use a pen and a ruler to mark the size and position of windows and doors.

2 Draw in the property lines and then the diagonal measurements. If the lines don't match up, adjust the boundary lines accordingly.

3 Draw in the position of trees and their canopies using measurements taken in relation to the house and boundaries.

4 Finish by plotting the position of sheds, ponds, patios, and other hard elements. Don't waste time filling the plan with features you don't intend to keep.

Features such as trees can be added later

Use crosses to denote door and windows

House

◀ **Base line** Measure the house and property lines as a starting point to the plan, and add more detailed measurements as you calculate them.

At frequent intervals, measure from the tape to the boundary

Measure all relevant features to be retained

House

◀ **Measure out** Lay a tape measure down the length of the space at a 90-degree angle to the house, then take offsets from it.

CREATING A DESIGN

There are a number of useful ways to solidify your ideas and help you visualize the various stages of development in your garden plans. Start off with a basic sketch or photo and roughly superimpose your design. It's also handy to have several copies of a scale plan to experiment with.

1 BUBBLE PLANS

This is one of the easiest ways to visually display your ideas and will help you establish the best positions for functional areas and decorative features. Bubble plans help show the relationship between, and relative scale of, component elements, such as lawns, borders, seating areas, and play equipment. Link and overlap the bubbles, and change their size and orientation as you experiment. You may find it useful to color code the bubbles according to their different uses.

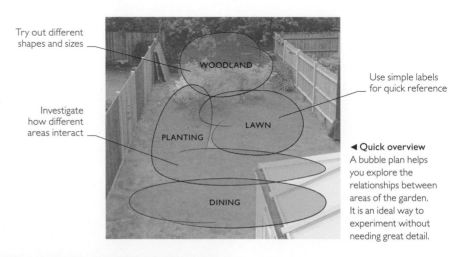

Try out different shapes and sizes

Investigate how different areas interact

WOODLAND

LAWN

PLANTING

DINING

Use simple labels for quick reference

◀ Quick overview
A bubble plan helps you explore the relationships between areas of the garden. It is an ideal way to experiment without needing great detail.

Explore perspective by adding in trees

Consider replacing existing elements

Experiment with vertical features

▶ Get perspective
Drawing over a photo provides a three-dimensional view that you may find difficult to draw freehand.

2 SKETCH OVER PHOTO

Take photographs of your space from as many different angles as possible. These will act as a handy reminder for drawing plans, especially for checking the position of trees and buildings outside the perimeter. Try to get a view from above to help you better visualize the garden. When experimenting, place sheets of tracing paper over one of your photographs, and sketch out a range of three-dimensional ideas. The photograph's boundaries and trees will help keep the drawn elements to scale, but try not to let existing features, such as patios or borders, influence your design. Sketches like these are invaluable for showing others what you have in mind, because many people find bird's-eye plans difficult to visualize.

3 OVERHEAD PLAN

Create a scale plan showing the exact size and location of all the garden's features—you may want to employ a qualified garden designer to do this for you. Draw in vertical elements, such as fences, hedges, and trees. Map out horizontal surfaces, and if possible, draw in individual paving units or decking planks. Going into detail will help you predict the costs accurately. If your garden slopes and there are dramatic changes in level, annotate these clearly, or produce a cross-sectional plan. More complex drawings for steeply sloping gardens may need to be produced by a surveyor for ease of planning.

Distinguish between different materials

Mark the exact number of units required

◄ **View from above** Try to make your plan as accurate and detailed as possible. Draw furniture and features to scale.

4 PLANTING PLAN

If your planting plan is for a landscaper or nursery, be precise so they know how many plants to supply and what spacing to use. Indicate lines, drifts, or blocks of the same plant using symbols, a numbered key, or a color code (see pp.116–117). Show where shrubs, trees, or topiary will overlap ground-level planting.

Label areas that you want to be sodded

Show plants to be grown under trees

LAWN

◄ **Be precise** Indicate on your plan how far large plants are likely to spread and develop. This will help with accurate planning and prevent later problems.

5 THE FINAL STAGES

When a design is drawn to scale and shows accurate locations and dimensions of all its elements and features, as well as the layout of electric cables, lighting, and drainage, it is ready for use. Whether you do all the work yourself or pass it on to a contractor, the plan will be invaluable when measuring and laying out. Laminate it, or make several copies, since it will probably end up muddy and torn.

6 THE FINISHED GARDEN

By following a detailed plan, you maximize the chances of a smooth, organized project. Once construction and planting are completed, add finishing touches that will enhance your design. Here, the furniture (right) echoes the clean lines and square shapes of the stonework.

PUTTING UP FENCE POSTS

The strength of a fence lies in its supporting posts. Choose 3×3 in (75×75 mm) pressure-treated wooden posts, and set them in quick-drying concrete or alternatively support in concrete spurs. Your chosen fencing panels can then be nailed in place.

▶ **A new fence** makes an attractive backdrop to planting, and will last for years if put up correctly.

FENCING BASICS

Installing a new fence post involves digging a deep hole and partially filling it with gravel to provide a firm foundation. The post is then set vertically using "post-mix" concrete that dries in under an hour. Ask your neighbors' permission if you need access, and hang the finished side of the panel facing their lot.

YOU WILL NEED

Claw hammer or screwdriver
Tape measure, bubble level, rope
Bricks, lumber, gravel
Spade
Fence posts and finials
Metal spike or pole
Lumber battening
"Post-mix" concrete

Fence post

Post-mix concrete

Gravel

Soil

1 If replacing an existing fence, dig out any weak or damaged posts first. If these are set in concrete, use improvised levers to pry them out of the ground.

2 Mark where the new post holes need to be. Dig them 12 in (30 cm) square, and roughly a third as deep as the fence will be tall—deeper in exposed sites.

3 Place pieces of rock in the bottom of the hole, and stand the post on top. Holding the post vertical, pack gravel around the sides until the hole is half filled.

4 Use a heavy metal pole or a length of wood to ram the gravel in place and help settle the material. Top off as required so the hole remains about half full.

5 To test that the post is vertical, hold a bubble level against each of its four sides. Adjust as needed. Check the post is at the right height for the panel.

6 To keep the post upright, tack on a temporary wood brace, affixed to a peg driven into the soil. Affix it to the side that won't have fencing panels attached.

7 Fill the hole with water, and let it drain to settle the gravel. This will also improve the adhesion of the concrete. Check that the post is completely vertical.

8 Add quick-drying "post-mix" concrete to the hole, and leave to set fully before hanging the panels. To protect the tops, nail on wooden finials to deflect rain.

FENCING OPTIONS

The style of the fencing you choose has a major impact on the overall effect of your garden; the right choice can act as a foil for planting or make a bold design statement. Select the highest-quality materials that you can afford for the most attractive and durable results. A concrete or wooden gravel board at the fence base prolongs the life of the panels.

Natural screen
A framed and oiled willow screen provides a neat yet natural backdrop for planting.

Hurdle
These surprisingly robust, hand-woven panels are perfect for English-style gardens.

Trellis panel
With an inset of trellis down the center, these panels are ideal for training climbers.

Shiplap
One of the cheapest and most popular fencing options, but not the most durable.

METAL SPIKE SUPPORTS

If you have firm, rock-free soil, metal spike supports are an option. Position the spike in place, and insert a "dolly," a post-driver, into the square cup. Hit the dolly with a mallet to drive the spike into the ground. Check the angle to ensure that it is straight; they are difficult to remove once inserted. When the spike is in the ground, remove the dolly and insert the post, tapping it into place.

Featheredge
These sturdy panels of vertical softwood lumber are a good choice for boundaries.

Picket fence
This simple wood fence has rustic charm, yet also works well for a modern property.

LAYING A PATH

Paths can be laid using a wide range of materials. Bricks, blocks, and other small units are hard-wearing and adaptable for slopes and angles. Creating a simple block path requires only basic tools and is easy to do yourself.

▶ **Taller edging** blocks can be used to hold back soil from paths that run alongside raised garden borders. They prevent soil from washing onto the path when it rains, keeping it neater.

PAVING BASICS

Block paths are laid onto a very simple foundation, consisting of a compacted layer of soil, gravel, and sand set into the ground. The blocks are then laid on top and held in place with sand and gravel.

Edging blocks (optional)
Blocks
Soil
Fine gravel
Sand
Coarse gravel

YOU WILL NEED

Tape measure, bubble level
Pegs and string
Hammer and nails
Spade, trowel
Shuttering boards
Coarse gravel
Sharp sand, fine gravel
Hand rammer or plate compactor
Paving blocks or bricks
Rubber mallet
Garden brush

1 Measure the path, and mark with string and long wood pegs, spaced every 5 ft (1.5 m). Allow enough room for shuttering boards and decorative edging.

2 Dig out enough soil between the string to accommodate layers of gravel and sand as well as the blocks. Check levels along the path using a bubble level.

3 To prevent puddles, the path must slope gently to one side to drain. Angle it away from house or garden walls to avoid water problems. Check levels again.

4 Nail the shuttering boards to the pegs to enclose the area of the path. Check levels once more; any adjustments can be made by easing the pegs up and down.

5 Spread a 3–4 in (8–10 cm) layer of coarse gravel along the length of the path. Use a hand rammer or rented plate compactor to tamp it down thoroughly.

6 Spread a layer of sharp sand over the gravel. Level the surface by pulling a length of wood across the path toward you. Fill in any hollows with extra sand.

7 Here, shallow blocks that sit on the sand's surface are used. Full-sized paving bricks should be tamped into the sand and left above the surface by ¾ in (2 cm).

8 Paving bricks are butted up close together, but other paving types require regular spaces. When you have finished laying and tamping, brush finer sand into the gaps.

9 Once the path is laid, consider removing one or two small pavers to provide planting holes. Plant with low alpines; these will soften the appearance of the path.

10 Finish off block paths by brushing decorative gravel into the gaps between them. This isn't necessary for brick paths since the blocks are butted up together.

MATERIALS

There is a broad range of materials available for laying block paving using this method, with natural and man-made products in a wide variety of sizes and finishes. Price and appearance are obvious factors when choosing, but also consider how durable the material will be, whether you can get it on site easily, and how simple it is to lay.

Granite stones
Tough, natural, and nonslip, these work for uneven surfaces and areas of heavy use.

Paving bricks
These are cheap to buy, easy to lay, and come in a wide variety of colors and styles.

Mixed materials
In informal plans, use a mixture of tiles, slabs, and stones for an eclectic look.

Concrete blocks
These are a cheaper alternative to granite but give a similar effect when laid.

Other materials
Paths don't have to be stone. Consider other materials, such as wooden crossties.

Crazy paving
Embed stone or slab pieces into gravel and sand, or into mortar for a more solid finish.

LAYING A PATIO

Slabs and pavers are available in a wide range of shapes, sizes, and materials and make a neat, practical surface. Laying large, regular pavers is relatively easy; preparing the foundation is the hardest part of the job.

▶ **The patio surface** forms the backbone of the design with subtle colors and smooth surfaces that blend into the background. Finely mortared joints complete the look.

PATIO BASICS

Patio slabs and pavers are laid onto a simple foundation consisting of compacted soil, fine gravel, and sand set at a slight gradient for drainage. Each slab or paver is then sat onto five "dabs" of mortar and tapped level. To finish, wet or dry mortar is worked into the joints to create a solid, weathertight surface.

Pavers
Leveling sand (optional)
Lawn
Compacted gravel
Soil

YOU WILL NEED

Pegs and string
Builder's square
Spade or sod cutter
Rake
Builder's trowel and brick jointer
Hand rammer or plate compactor
Bubble level
Pavers or slabs
Fine gravel, sharp sand
Ready-mix mortar
Rubber mallet or club hammer
Spacers
Stiff brush

1 Mark off the area to be paved with pegs set at the height of the finished surface, and join with string. Use a builder's square to check corner angles are 90 degrees.

2 Remove any turf with a spade, or rent a turf cutter for large areas. (Reuse turf or compost it.) Dig out the soil to 6 in (15 cm) deep, plus the thickness of the paving.

3 Use a hand rammer or powered compactor to tamp down the foundation area. Adjust the marker pegs to ensure the finished surface has a slight gradient for drainage.

4 Spread a 4in- (10cm-) deep layer of fine gravel over the area, rake level (ensuring you retain the slope), then tamp firm with a hand rammer or plate compactor (*above*).

5 Level out the gravel, where required, with sand. Lay the first pavers along the perimeter string, placing each on five trowelfuls of wet mortar.

6 Tamp down the pavers using a rubber mallet or the handle of a club hammer. Insert spacers to ensure evenly-sized joints, and support the outer slabs.

7 Remove spacers after two days, once the pavers are firm, and brush dry ready-mix mortar into the joints between them. The mortar will harden over a few days.

8 For a neater finish, use a builder's trowel to push wet mortar into the gaps, then smooth the surface with a brick jointer (*above*). Avoid staining the surface of the pavers.

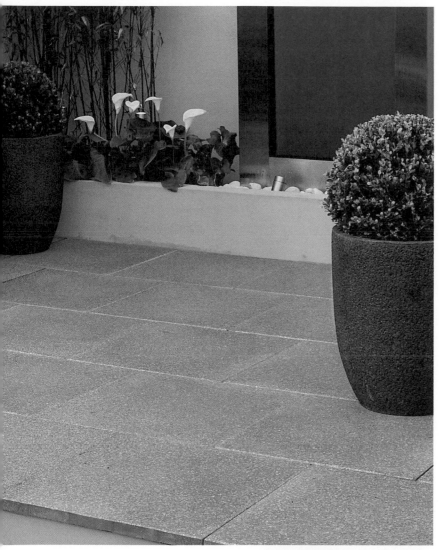

MATERIALS

The range of materials to use for patios is vast, with choices to suit all designs and budgets. Laying a patio is time-consuming and costly, so consider your choice of materials carefully. Some materials are more durable than others, while others, including some natural stones, need routine care. Also remember, styles change through the years.

Concrete slabs
There is a huge variety to pick from, some natural or modern, others more basic.

Natural stone
Attractive but costly; some types need annual treatment to make them weatherproof.

Tiles
Tiles can't be laid with the "dab" method (*left*) but must be laid on a solid concrete bed.

Molded slabs
These add texture and interest to a finished patio. Use sparingly to create a feature.

MAKING CUTS

To finish the patio you may need to cut some pavers to size or shape, using a stone saw (*see right*). First, measure and mark out the cut you need to make, and lay the paver on a deep layer of sand. Holding the stone saw firmly, draw the blade along the desired cut until complete. For your own safety, wear goggles, gloves, ear protection, and a dust mask when cutting.

Patio kits
Centerpiece designs, such as this stylized sun, come as a kit and fit together like a puzzle.

Reclaimed stone
Using reclaimed stone will give your patio a "period" look, but can be very expensive.

HOW TO INSTALL A DECK

Decking is very adaptable and can be built to fit most sites, blending with modern and traditional garden styles. It is usually built from hardwood or pressure-treated softwood and often comes in kit form.

▶ **Decks can offer** the ideal solution to awkward lots that feature slopes or poor access. They can be raised to level a site, and the materials are fairly lightweight.

DECKING BASICS

Decks consist of a wooden frame supported by evenly spaced posts. The posts are set upright into holes filled with gravel and concrete, then trimmed to provide a level base. The deck is constructed on top to create an even, raised platform.

Spacers between decking boards

Internal joist attached to support post

Edging lumber attached to support post

Wood spacer attached to internal joist

YOU WILL NEED

Pegs and string, tape measure

Builder's square, bubble level

Weed-proof membrane

Spade

Gravel

3 x 3 in (75 x 75 mm) support posts

Post-mix concrete

4 x 2 in (100 x 50 mm) lumber joists

Drill

Galvanized nuts, bolts, washers, screws, nails, brackets

Saw and hammer

Decking boards

Spacers

1 Mark out a rectangular or square deck with pegs and string. Check the corners are at a 90-degree angle using a builder's square. Mow any grass very short.

2 Lay a weed-proof membrane over the area, overlapping joints by 18 in (45 cm). Roll it back when setting the outer posts, but cut through it for internal supports.

3 You will need a post in each corner and the rest spaced in a grid pattern, one every 4 ft (1.2 m). Dig the holes 15 in (38 cm) deep, and fill 3 in (8 cm) deep with gravel.

4 Fill the hole with water to dampen the gravel, and allow to drain. Insert the post, and pour in post-mix concrete (see p.84), using a level to check if it is vertical. Leave it to set.

5 Cut edging boards to length, and drill bolt holes through them and also the posts. Attach one end of the first edging board to a post using nuts and bolts.

6 Level the first board, and affix in place with nuts and bolts. Trim the post ends flush. Repeat these steps until all three sides are affixed, then tighten the bolts firmly.

7 Predrill holes, and use nails to affix internal joists between the edging boards across the shortest span, spacing them 16 in (40 cm) apart. Make sure they are all level.

8 To hold the joists rigid, cut short lengths of lumber, and insert them between the joists at 4 ft (1.2 m) intervals. Secure them using long nails or metal brackets.

MATERIALS

Decks are predominantly made of lumber and often come in kit form. Being made of wood, they are easy to adapt and personalize with your own ideas, although ready-made deck accessories are available. The advantage of decks is that they are easier to change than traditional patios, allowing you to be more creative with materials.

Wooden decking
The most common material for decking is wood that has been treated against rot.

Plastic decking
Rot- and weatherproof, plastic surfaces are ideal in low-care garden designs.

Decking tiles
Made from light softwood, these tiles are easy to replace when they start to wear.

Wood stain
Pretreated lumber can either be left natural or transformed with a colored stain.

Railings
Some decks must have safety railings, which can be a feature in their own right.

Finials
Personalize your deck posts with attractive finials, which come in many designs.

9 Cut a decking board to length. Predrill holes in the board, then attach it to each joist using two corrosion-resistant decking nails or countersunk screws.

10 Cut remaining boards to size, and attach them to the deck, making any joints above the joists. Space the boards ¼in (5 mm) apart, using spacers, to allow for expansion.

LAYING A LAWN

The quickest way to achieve a beautiful lawn is to lay sod in early fall or spring to give the grass plenty of time to establish. Watering is critical to prevent drying out. To cover a large area, sowing seed is a cheaper option.

▶ **A well-maintained lawn** creates a sense of space in the garden, as well as providing the perfect foil for border flowers.

LAWN BASICS

Buy your sod from a reputable supplier, and if possible, inspect it before purchasing to ensure that it is weed- and disease-free. Prepare the site carefully before laying the sod, and ensure that you lay the pieces very closely together to create tight seams. Once the strips are in place, you can cut a curved edge using a garden hose or rope as a guide.

Sod

Subsoil

Topsoil

Granular fertilizer

YOU WILL NEED

Spade or fork

Rake

Hoe

All-purpose granular fertilizer

Sieved topsoil mixed with horticultural sand

Wooden plank

Broom

Garden hose

Edging iron

1 Two months before the sod arrives, weed the site thoroughly and dig a little organic matter into the soil.

2 Level the area with a rake and apply an all-purpose fertilizer. Keeping your weight on your heels, tread over the length of your plot, and repeat at a right angle across the width.

3 Rake the ground level to remove any depressions. Leave for five weeks for the soil to settle, then hoe to remove weeds.

4 Carefully unroll the sod, laying whole pieces and working out from an edge. Stand on a plank to distribute your weight, and tamp down with a rake.

5 Continue to lay the sod in rows, and stagger the joints like a wall of bricks; this produces a much stronger structure. Use an old knife for cutting if necessary.

6 Create a tight seam between pieces by butting them together so they almost overlap and then pressing the crease down firmly with your thumbs..

7 Don't use small pieces of sod at the edge of the lawn; they will dry out and shrink— instead lay them in the middle of the site. Firm in well with a rake.

8 To shape lawn edges, use a garden hose or rope to mark out the curves, and then cut around your template with an edger or sharp spade.

SEEDING A LAWN

For large areas of lawn, seeding is the cheapest option and, although it will be about a year before the grass can take heavy use, it should start to green up and look good in under a month. The best time to sow is in late spring or early fall when the soil is warm and moist.

1 Prepare the site as for sod. Before sowing, remove weeds, and add a layer of fertilizer. Weigh out seed for a square yard (meter), and pour into a paper cup; mark where seed reaches.

2 Rake soil level. Remove any stones and other debris. Mark out a square yard (meter) using canes or string, then measure out the right amount of grass seed using the marked paper cup.

3 Scatter half the seed in the cup over the marked area in one direction, and then the other half at a right angle. Set out the next square, and repeat the sowing process.

4 Rake the seed into the soil to just cover it. Water with a can fitted with a rose, or spray lightly with a hose. Cover the area with bird-proof fleece. The seedlings should appear within 14 days. Water regularly.

9 To help adjacent pieces of sod grow together and root firmly, brush in a blend of sieved topsoil and horticultural sand, using a stiff broom.

10 Keep the lawn well-watered during dry spells (particularly in summer) to avoid shrinkage. Take care not to overwater in winter, as this may kill the grass. If cracks do appear, brush in some soil.

MAKING A PERGOLA

A pergola is a series of cross-beams linked together to form
a covered walkway, providing the perfect support for climbing
plants. A wood frame kit, demonstrated here, makes it easy
to put the structure together.

▶ Create a shady retreat
by training climbing plants up and
over your pergola using wires
attached to the upright posts.

PERGOLA BASICS

Each pergola arch consists
of a crosspiece supported by
two upright posts. Most have
extra crosspieces along the
length of the roof timbers
to strengthen the roof and
support the areas between
the upright posts—these
additional crosspieces do
not sit on uprights, so
are unsupported.

Extra crosspiece

Crosspiece
attached to
two upright
posts forms
an arch

Roof timber

Side timbers

Upright posts

YOU WILL NEED

Pergola kit
Pegs and string, tape measure
Builder's square, bubble level
Vice
Drill and screwdriver
Galvanized screws or bolts
Hammer
Temporary wooden battens (optional)
Spray paint
Spade
Gravel
Metal spike
Ready-mix fast-set concrete

1 Unpack and identify all the
pieces. Mark out the layout of the
pergola on the ground with pegs
and string, using a builder's square
to check right angles.

2 To make an arch, attach each
end of a crosspiece to the top of
an upright post. Nail wooden
battening between the upright
posts to keep them from splaying.

3 Mark the two post positions for
the first arch using spray paint. Dig
out holes about 2 ft (60 cm) deep
and 12 in (30 cm) across. Fill with
4 in (10 cm) of gravel.

4 Ram the gravel firmly in place with
a metal spike. Place the posts in the
holes, and check that each one is
vertical by holding a bubble level
against each of its sides.

5 Holding the posts steady and
upright (or using wooden battens
if necessary), concrete the first
arch into place (see p.84).

6 Position the second arch,
allowing for a slight overlap.
Dig post holes, and check their
position by placing side timbers
on their respective uprights.

7 Using a bubble level, check that
the side timbers are horizontal and
the uprights are vertical before
concreting the posts in position.
Repeat steps 3–7 for all the arches.

8 Once the concrete has set,
screw or bolt all the side timbers
in place, butting the joints together.
It's best to predrill the holes to
prevent splitting.

OBELISKS

Wooden obelisks suit almost any garden design, be it formal or a relaxed English-country style. Use them draped with clematis or other flowering climbers to add height to a border, as a feature to flank an entrance, or to create a focal point at the end of a walkway.

Although you can make an obelisk from scratch (if you have good DIY skills) or from a kit, ready-made structures are available in a range of materials and sizes and can be inexpensive. Choose a contemporary metal structure for a mixture of climbing roses and clematis, or a more short-lived woven wicker frame to support a profusion of colorful sweet peas (*Lathyrus*).

Woven
For a rustic look, choose a woven obelisk for beans in a productive garden.

Metal
Delicate climbing flowers provide a contrast to a modern metal obelisk.

9 Screw or bolt the extra crosspieces in place midway between the uprights. Check that all the fixtures on the frame are tight.

10 Predrill holes, and screw the roof timbers on top of the crosspieces. Leave the wooden battens in place until the concrete has completely set.

MAKING A POND

Designing a pond with a flexible synthetic rubber or PVC liner allows you to create a feature of any size and shape. Mask the edges of the liner with overhanging stones on a bed of waterproof mortar.

▶ **Plant up your pond** with water lilies and marginal plants once the waterproof mortar is completely dry.

POND BASICS

A pond crater usually has a deeper section in the center; the depth must be at least 18 in (45 cm) to prevent the pond freezing solid in winter. The pit is covered with underlay to cushion the liner. For the amount of liner to buy, add twice the depth of the pond to its maximum length plus width.

Rolled-up surplus liner

Decorative stone slabs

Planting shelf

Waterproof mortar

Pond liner

Soil

Pond or carpet underlay

YOU WILL NEED

Garden hose

Spade

Pickax

Bubble level/plank

Sand

Pond or carpet underlay

Flexible pond liner

Waterproof mortar, bucket, trowel

Sharp knife

Decorative stone

1 Use a hose to mark the outline of the pond; the relative inflexibility of the hose will create a smooth, curving shape.

2 Before you start digging, skim off turf for reuse elsewhere. Keep the fertile topsoil separate from the subsoil, and loosen compacted subsoil with a pickax.

3 Dig out the pond to a depth of 18 in (45 cm). Leave a shelf 12–18 in (30–45 cm) wide around the edge, then dig out the center to a further depth of 18 in (45 cm).

4 Use a bubble level placed on a straight piece of wood to check that the ground around the top of the pond is level. Remove loose soil and large or sharp stones.

5 Line the sides and base of the pond with pond or carpet underlay. On stony soils, spread a 2 in (5 cm) layer of sand over the base first.

6 Center the liner over the hole, letting it slide down in its own weight. Leaving plenty of surplus, pleat the liner to fit it to the shape of the pond. Fill with water.

7 When the pond is full, trim the liner leaving 18 in (45 cm). Pleat the excess so it lies flat, and bury the edges in the soil. Lay a bed of mortar; don't let it fall into the water.

8 Bed the edging stones into the mortar, overhanging them by 2 in (5 cm) to hide the liner. Stand vertical stones on a piece of rolled-up surplus liner.

BUILD A BUBBLE POOL

Suitable for even the smallest gardens, a bubble pool makes an interesting water feature. Adjust the flow so that the water bubbles up over the top of the pot and down the sides. Seek advice from a qualified electrician to install an outdoor electricity supply, and ensure that all electrical connections are fitted with a ground-fault circuit-breaker.

1 Dig a hole bigger than the size of the water reservoir that will be positioned below the bubble pool. Install a waterproof electricity supply with assistance.

2 Edge the hole with damp sand, and position the reservoir, packing the area around it with sand. When in place and level, place the pump inside, and add the lid.

3 Place the pot over the reservoir with the pump pipe protruding through the hole in the base. Seal the pipe in place with silicone sealant, and leave to dry.

4 Attach the delivery pipe to the water flow adjuster, then attach them to the pump tube inside the pot. The delivery pipe should sit just under the rim of the pot. Fill the reservoir and pot with a hose.

9 Wait a week for the mortar to set, then add aquatic plants and marginals. Top baskets with a layer of well-washed pea gravel.

10 If adding fish, float their bag on the water, and open the top to allow more air inside. Release the fish into the pond after 20 minutes.

BUILDING A RAISED BED

Creating a wood-framed raised bed is easy, especially if the pieces are pre-cut to length. Untreated wood is best for growing edibles, to avoid any risk of chemicals leeching into the soil. If the bed is to sit next to a lawn, add a brick mowing edge.

▶ **A neat mowing edge** makes the perfect finish for your raised bed and creates a clean edge as well as a decorative feature.

RAISED BED BASICS

To create a raised bed, stack wood, overlapping the joints at the corners. Partially fill with a layer of debris, including stones and broken crocks for drainage, to fill deep beds before adding at least 6 in (15 cm) of topsoil or compost, and topping with a layer of mulch.

Pre-sawn lumber for a neat finish

Deep layer of topsoil

Top planks rest on the base

Brick mowing strip

Mix of soil and debris for good drainage

YOU WILL NEED

Spade

Pre-cut wooden planks

Bubble level

Tape measure

Rubber mallet

Drill

Screwdriver

Heavy-duty exterior grade screws

Debris and topsoil (ideally mixed with well-rotted garden compost or manure)

Bark

1 Dig out strips of turf wide enough to accommodate the wood. Pressure-treated wood or reclaimed hardwood are economical options.

2 Lay out the boards in place, and check that they are level with a bubble level; use a plank of wood to support a shorter bubble level. Check levels diagonally, too.

3 Make sure that the base is square by checking that the diagonals are equal in length. For a perfect square or rectangular bed, it's a good idea to use pre-cut wood.

4 Using a rubber mallet, gently tap the wood so that it butts up against the adjacent piece, remaining level and upright. Remove soil as needed.

5 Drill holes through the end planks into the adjacent pieces at the top and bottom. Secure with long, heavy-duty exterior grade screws.

6 Attach the next layer on top of the base, joining them together and making sure the joints overlap those below. Check levels before screwing together.

7 For extra drainage, partially fill the base with debris—this may not be necessary in shallower beds. Add at least 6 in (15 cm) of quality topsoil, free from perennial weeds.

8 Fill up to about 3 in (8 cm) from the top, then mulch with a layer of bark or gravel. Plant your bed with ornamentals or productive plants, and water in well.

MATERIALS

Consider size carefully when selecting a material for a raised bed: railroad ties will allow you to create a large bed, but unless you are very tall, you should build your beds no more than 4 ft (1.2 m) across so you can reach to the center. Beds can be narrower if you choose, and taller beds are ideal if you want your plants within easy reach.

Ties
Unused railroad ties can be built up layer by layer to suit your needs.

Stone
Perfect for a country-style border of rambling ornamentals. Doesn't require mortar.

Wicker
Choose a lined, woven wicker bed for a short-term, rustic, English-garden appearance.

Brick
Create beds of any size using bricks, making sure that you include drainage channels.

Ready-made kits
The simplest option, ready-made raised bed kits are available in various sizes.

Slate
Use reclaimed slate tiles set upright to edge and support temporary raised beds.

MAKING A MOWING EDGE

Dig out a strip of soil deep enough to accommodate the bricks plus 1 in (2.5 cm) of mortar. Lay a level of mortar mix in the bottom of the trench as a foundation, and set the bricks on top with a small gap between each. Check that the bricks are level, and tap them into position with a rubber mallet. When fully set, brush dry mortar between the bricks, working it in with a trowel.

PLANT YOUR GARDEN

From rambling climbers to majestic bamboos, the gorgeous plants offered in this chapter suit every garden, regardless of soil conditions, exposure, or size. Follow the planting recipes to create year-round interest—from naturalized spring bulbs and wildflower summer meadows to fall berries and colorful winter stems.

PLANT FAMILIES

Plants in each of the major groups have different characteristics and behave in different ways, so it is useful to have a basic understanding of how they look and perform before creating a planting design for your garden.

TREES

These large, woody evergreen or deciduous plants usually produce a canopy of leafy stems above a single clear trunk, although many conifers have branches from top to bottom. Trees lend height to designs and provide shade in sunny sites, but position them carefully as they are difficult to move once established.

SHRUBS

Together with trees, shrubs form the backbone of a garden design. They can be evergreen or deciduous and come in many different shapes and sizes, but all are characterized by a permanent framework of woody stems. Grown for their attractive foliage, flowers, and stems, shrubs provide color and interest all year.

PERENNIALS

Living for three years or more, a few perennials are evergreen, but the majority are deciduous, their top growth dying down in winter and reappearing in spring. Their stems are generally nonwoody, and many multiply to form large clumps. They are mainly grown for their flowers; some also provide foliage interest.

GRASSES AND BAMBOOS

Grasses grow from the stem and leaf bases and produce strap-like foliage. They encompass annuals and evergreen and deciduous perennials, and their flowers are wind-pollinated. Sedges are very similar to grasses, but tend to be evergreen, while bamboos are simply grasses with woody stems.

BULBS

A bulb is a plant with a food-storage organ that sustains its growth when the optimal conditions prevail. The group includes true bulbs, such as daffodils; corms, such as crocuses; tubers, including dahlias; and rhizomes, like irises (see p.160). They are valued for their colorful flowers; some also have decorative foliage.

ANNUALS AND BIENNIALS

Plants that grow, flower, and die within one year are known as annuals; those that produce stems and leaves in their first year, then bloom and die in the second year are biennials. The flowers of hardy types are often used to brighten up borders, while tender plants that flower all summer are ideal for pots.

CLIMBERS

These plants climb host plants or structures to search out sufficient light. The group includes evergreen and deciduous forms; some have soft stems while others are woody. Most need a framework of trellis or wires, or a host tree or shrub to climb, and cling via a number of different methods (see p.144).

WATER PLANTS

Plants that live in and around water comprise four main categories: oxygenators help keep the water clear by starving out weeds; aquatics, such as water lilies, root at the bottom of a pond; marginals live at the water's edge; and bog plants typically grow in the moist soil that surrounds a natural pond.

PLANTING FOR A LIFESTYLE

The plants you choose and the way that they are used have an impact on the time you will need to spend caring for them. If you want an easy-care garden, opt for robust, hardy plants that perform year after year and require little maintenance.

High maintenance

If you enjoy being outside and tending your garden, you can choose from a wide range of planting designs and garden styles. Include a lawn if you don't mind mowing, and try tender plants that require tending in a warm greenhouse or room indoors over the winter. Ambitious gardeners can also sow annuals each year in beds and containers, and plant tender summer bulbs, such as dahlias and gladioli, which need lifting and bringing indoors in the fall. Trees with flowers that require frost protection, such as magnolias, are also options if you are happy to cover them with fabric when temperatures dip.

Moderate care

Those who enjoy gardening but only have limited time can still maintain a lawn and perhaps a few large container displays, as well as trees, shrubs, and perennials in beds and borders. Any plant in a pot needs more nurturing than one in the ground, where it has access to greater reserves of nutrients and water, but large containers require watering less frequently because they hold greater volumes of soil. You could also plant climbers like clematis that only need to be pruned annually, and some hardy bulbs, which are left in place in the winter.

Low maintenance

Small trees and hardy shrubs make life easy for gardeners. Most require very little maintenance if planted in the right conditions. Shrubs may need trimming back every couple of years, while trees shouldn't require much pruning, except to remove dead or diseased stems. Hardy perennials are also easy; just cut back the dead growth in the fall or early spring.

High-maintenance gardens filled with annuals, tender summer bulbs, and lawns require constant care in the growing season.

Low-maintenance gardens include easy-care perennials, such as grasses, shrubs, and *Hylotelephium* (sedum). Gravel is a low-maintenance surface option.

DESIGNING WITH PLANTS

To create an exciting design, combine a range of plants with contrasting structures, textures, and forms. You can also produce a specific look, such as a contemporary or English style, simply by using specific plants or grouping them in a particular way.

PLANT FUNCTIONS

Before planning a planting design, take time to compile a list of your favorite plants. Visit gardens and jot down the names of any that inspire you, and look through books, magazines, and plant catalogs for additional ideas. Make sure that the plants on your list will thrive in your garden, and then map out a simple plan (see pp.116–117).

Start by planning trees and shrubs to add height and structure to your design. Then fill in around these plants with perennials and ground cover plants, and include plenty of seasonal interest with a range that perform at different times of the year. Finally, inject drama with focal plants set in key positions within your design.

Beautifully blended shapes, colors, and textures create a dynamic visual feast in this garden.

Structural plants
Woody plants, like trees and shrubs, can be used to create a structure, such as a hedge or flowering screen, a tree-lined walkway, or a mixed group to form a backdrop to a flower bed.

Mid-range plants
Most perennials fall into this group, together with small shrubs. Use them between structural plants, or combine them with grasses to produce rippling seas of color and texture.

Focal plants
Plants with bold colors and shapes catch the eye, directing the line of vision to a planting design, punctuating the end of a pathway, or sharpening the focus on a patio.

Ground cover
Ground-hugging plants can be shrubs, grasses, or perennials. Smothering weeds with their leafy stems, they help fill difficult areas beneath trees and next to sun-baked patios.

Seasonal plants
All the main plant groups include seasonal interest. Both trees and shrubs offer flowers and fall leaf color, while bulbs, annuals, and perennials provide seasonal blooms.

GROUPING PLANTS

Your choice of plants and their grouping and arrangement should reflect the garden style you are trying to create. A traditional approach for a border design is to line plants up in order of size, with the largest at the back and smallest at the front; beds work in a similar way with plants of ever-decreasing sizes fanning out from the tallest in the middle.

Modernists have adopted a different approach, and use blocks of a single species to mirror Cubist paintings. English-garden designs interlink oval-shaped swathes of perennials to create a natural effect, while modern perennial designs are also inspired by nature, weaving together wide ribbons of tough hardy perennials and grasses to create an undulating landscape of flowers and foliage.

Traditional designs

To create a traditional border, either plant a hedge, or use shrubs and tall grasses to form a backdrop, and add perennials with contrasting leaf shapes and flowers in front. Pom-pom-headed alliums work well with floating grasses, while flat-headed achillea make a good match for flower spikes. Edge the front of your design with ground cover plants, compact grasses, and annuals to form a line of flowers.

Contemporary blocks

Inspired by the modernist art movement, planting in blocks produces a clean, minimalist design. You can use a single type of grass, such as a *Miscanthus* species, which will have a dynamic effect when the leaves rustle in the wind; clumps of bulbs or perennials, such as irises; or heavier blocks of closely clipped box or yew. Set them out on an asymmetrical grid, and use lawns and pools to break up the planting.

Woodland planting

Even small gardens can play host to a woodland design. Underplant a small collection of trees with shade-tolerant shrubs, grasses, ferns, and other perennials that would naturally occur in similar sites in the wild, but don't be tempted to cram in lots of different species, since this will look too styled. Add some meadow flowers in open areas around the trees and in brighter areas within your woodland to mimic a glade.

Natural-looking designs

Contemporary designs combine a limited palette of hardy perennials and grasses in bold swathes to resemble a prairie or steppe landscape. These designs work best on medium-sized to large sites, but you can shrink them down to fit smaller spaces by reducing the number and diversity of plants. Perennials such as *Rudbeckia*, *Eupatorium* and *Hylotelephium* are ideal, combined with grasses like *Stipa*, *Miscanthus*, and *Calamagrostis*.

WHAT PLANT WHERE

When selecting plants for your garden, it's important to test your soil and assess your site carefully before you start (*see pp.66–67*). Failure to do so may end in disappointment, with sun-loving plants in shady sites growing tall and gangly as they strain to find the light, or shade-loving plants scorching in full sun.

Test your soil's acidity, too, because mistakes can be costly if plants are given the wrong conditions. For example, azaleas, rhododendrons, camellias, and pieris only thrive in acidic soil and will suffer in chalky, alkaline conditions. Remember, too, that the soil close to a house wall or permanent structure will be significantly drier than other areas of the garden—these areas are called "rain shadows."

Roses will not flower well, if at all, in a shady site, and their stems may grow tall and leggy. Plant them in open, sunny areas in nutrient-rich, moist but well-drained soil.

All ferns thrive in shade as their fronds will scorch in full sun. Most also require moist soil, although a few, including *Dryopteris filix-mas*, cope with drier conditions.

CREATING A PLANTING STYLE

Plants enhance and define a garden style or theme. Geometric beds set out in a symmetrical pattern instill a sense of formality; contemporary plans are defined by minimalist planting, while curving borders filled with billowing grasses and native flowers convey a wilder look.

► FORMAL STYLE

Chic and orderly, formal styles are all about control. To achieve the look, lay out your beds in a symmetrical pattern, and use clipped hedges to define them. Take your lead from the formal gardens of Versailles in France, and plant low hedges of box filled with colorful gravel, roses, or lavender to create a theatrical effect. Lollipop-shaped trees or topiary will lend height and structure. Enclose flowering perennials or annuals with looser shapes in square or rectangular beds. Formal styles are easy to care for; simply clip the hedges and topiary twice a year

Formality is created using balanced design, mini-fountains, and a mirror.

◄ COTTAGE STYLE

Evoking an English country cottage, the English style has long captured the imagination of gardeners with a passion for plants. It is essentially a romanticized version of 19th-century cottage gardens, where most of the planting was productive with a few flowers thrown in to create a colorful mix.

Today, flowers tend to dominate these designs; perennials and annuals are woven together in swathes, and beds are punctuated by structural shrubs, such as bay. Rose- and clematis-covered arches and arbors are also typical of these gardens, adding height and structure to designs, while scented roses and lavender are included for their fragrance. This is a high-maintenance style, ideal for energetic plant lovers.

Classic combinations of delphiniums, lupines, and scabiosa are edged with frothy *Alchemilla mollis and Persicaria* spilling over onto gravel or brick pathways.

▶ URBAN STYLE

City gardens tend to be small and need to look good all year because the whole space is permanently on view. They may also be overlooked by neighboring properties and require tall planting to increase privacy. Inject color with painted walls, which make great foils for evergreen foliage specimens, such as bamboos and phormiums, or use plants including heucheras, daylilies (*Hemerocallis*), and sedums to add color. Also use plants that perform well without taking up valuable ground space. Ideas include pleached trees (*see pp.118–119*) along the boundaries to enhance privacy, and climbers that provide walls of flowers and foliage. In a roof garden lightweight pots of windproof hardy grasses, geraniums, and lavender are ideal.

Colors and shapes of bamboos and grasses, box topiary, and purple heucheras stand out against painted surfaces.

◀ MEDITERRANEAN STYLE

Use the sun-baked landscapes of the Mediterranean region to inspire you with plants that evoke a rural setting or a café-style courtyard. In a medium-sized or large garden, try mass plantings of lavender with the odd scarlet poppy dotted here and there to mirror the fields of southern France. Alternatively, use large terra-cotta pots filled with this quintessential Mediterranean herb on a patio. Established olive trees offer much-needed shade in both country and city gardens and are hardy enough to survive winters outside in a sheltered spot and free-draining soil. Patios edged with rockroses (*Cistus*) and self-seeded annuals create a sense of relaxed informality.

A gravel scree, laid on a weed-proof membrane, makes an easy-care foil for sun-loving lavenders and poppies.

▲ WILDLIFE GARDENS

Ever popular, wildlife gardens offer an attractive natural setting for people, plants, insects, birds, and animals.

A pond or pool is a vital ingredient, unless you have small children where open water can pose a danger, and can be planted with a whole range of beautiful aquatic and moisture-loving plants *(see pp.176–177)*. Include an area of long grass and nectar-rich flowers to lure bees and insects. Star attractions for beneficial insects include the butterfly bush *(Buddleia)*, *Mahonia*, thyme, lavender, asters, and foxgloves. A mixed hedge and a fruit tree will provide nesting sites and winter food for birds.

Wooden walkways, fringed with naturalistic plantings of iris and ornamental thistle, allow easy access for close study of water life.

▶ CONTEMPORARY STYLES

Sharp and sophisticated, contemporary designs are based on the principle "less is more." Map out your garden on an asymmetrical grid with planting limited to key areas, and a restricted palette of different species. Architectural plants will help define the style. Set out topiary box balls in rows or blocks, or try spiky bearded irises in a regimental line. Many contemporary designers also employ tightly trimmed hedges to carve up the space and divide different areas of the garden. In a courtyard, a tree with an eye-catching shape, such as an *Acer palmatum*, would make an effective focal point against a brightly painted screen.

Glossy bamboo stems are underplanted with white peonies in chunky marble chips in this green and white minimalist garden.

◄ FAMILY GARDENS

Gardens for grown-ups and children have to be multi-functional, offering both a relaxing and stimulating environment. If your garden is large enough, break it up into "rooms," with areas for entertaining and spaces to play. Throughout the garden, the planting has to be resilient and bounce back if walked on or hit by flying balls. Decorative grasses are ideal since many are perennials—snapped flower heads will, in most cases, simply stimulate the plant to produce more blooms.

Use tough plants, such as *Aucuba*, *Elaeagnus*, and *Euonymus*, around swings and sandboxes. They are practically indestructible.

DESIGNING CONTAINER DISPLAYS

As well as using plants in beds and borders, add a selection of containers to embellish your garden style. Choose pots that suit your theme, and fill them with foliage and flowers to decorate patios or provide focal points in the garden.

Pots made from metals like zinc and man-made materials tend to suit contemporary designs, especially when molded into smooth, geometric shapes. Use a set of three large, identical containers planted with leafy phormiums, astelias, or topiary for a modern look, or try squat pots filled with houseleeks (*Sempervivum*) or aeoniums.

Classic and period garden styles can be enhanced with pots made from terra-cotta or natural stone, or composites that resemble these. Patio roses make superb feature plants for large urns in a traditional setting, or try an old trough filled with herbs, perennials, or alpines in an English-garden plan. If you have a natural-style garden, complete the look with a rustic container made from recycled wood.

Rustic
Use recycled fruit boxes, old kitchen pans, or wooden planters for an English or natural style.

Tropical
Colorful glazed containers suit tropical foliage and leafy shrubs or topiary specimens.

Contemporary
Metallic containers lend a modern note to a patio or garden. Team them with architectural foliage.

Traditional
Terra-cotta containers are ideal for traditional gardens, and their earthy tones suit cottage plants.

INTRODUCING COLOR AND TEXTURE

Awakening our senses, color can excite and energize us or create a calm, tranquil atmosphere. Combine hot pinks, reds, and oranges in areas where you want borders to sparkle, and cool blues, greens, purples, and white close to relaxing seating and dining areas.

THE COLOR WHEEL

Many artists and designers use a device called a "color wheel" to help them create pleasing color combinations. The wheel is made up of the primary colors (blue, red, and yellow) and secondary colors (green, orange, and purple). The secondary colors are directly derived from the adjacent primaries, for example when blue and red paints are mixed they make purple, and red and yellow combine to produce orange. The same principle applies to the tertiary colors, which result when adjacent secondary and primary colors are mixed.

You can use the wheel to create a color palette in the garden. Combine colors directly opposite each other, such as yellow and purple, to create dramatic contrasts that will help to enliven a planting design, or try adjacent colors to produce more subtle blends.

Shades and tones of purples and greens create an elegant planting combination.

CHOOSING COLORS

As well as using the wheel for ideas, also consider the effects that colors have on the senses. Hot hues, including red, yellow, and orange, are bright, arresting colors that catch the eye: use them as focal points in borders or in pots on a patio. These sizzling shades will also seem to shorten a space and can make a garden look smaller if set at the back.

Cool colors, such as blue, green, and mauve, have the opposite effect and help lengthen a view, just as colors pale toward the horizon. Blues and mauves are easy on the eye, but a plan with only these colors may look flat, so inject warmer colors to liven it up.

USING COLORS

Use the color wheel as a guide when mixing and matching colors in your garden, and try the following ideas to create successful designs. You can also incorporate shades and tints of the main hues: shades are colors with additional black, making darker hues, while tints are colors mixed with white and are paler.

Single color and duotone designs allow you to create a sophisticated look. The famous white garden at Sissinghurst in the UK has inspired many to adopt a monochrome palette, using a combination of white flowers and silver and variegated foliage. Or try planting a border with just two colors, such as purple and yellow, or pink and mauve.

Opposite colors on the color wheel will produce a successful design when used in combination with each other. These contrasting colors are known as complementary shades and are used by many top garden designers. Try pairing purple salvias with bright yellow *Doronicum* (left), or opt for maroon alliums with lime green euphorbias.

Triadic colors are those that are evenly spaced around the color wheel. Like opposite colors, they often create a sense of excitement since they are contrasting hues. Triadic color combinations are useful if you have cool hues, such as purple and blue, which need a matching hot shade to enhance the design.

Adjoining colors create harmonious combinations—when you select soft purples and blues, the effect is soothing. Paler tints that reflect light will help inject highlights into your plan. If you are more adventurous, try a fiery mix of the hot shades, such as red and orange, with a foil of darker shades, and watch your borders blaze under the sun.

USING PLANT TEXTURES

Successful planting designs combine leaf, stem, and flower textures as well as colors. Select shiny leaves, berries, and fruits to reflect light into gloomy areas, and use soft, downy foliage close to the front of a bed or border where its tactile texture can be fully appreciated. Also, plant trees with rough or peeling bark to create focal points in winter gardens.

When creating your planting designs, pair up plants with contrasting textures. Try matching grasses with plants that produce felted or ferny leaves. Think, too, about the texture of flowers, combining the satin petals of roses, for example, with the spiky bracts and rough, prickly flower heads of sea holly (*Eryngium*) or the brushlike blooms of red hot pokers (*Kniphofia*).

Prickly
The prickly stems of roses and spiky sea holly flowers (*above*) contrast well with silky petals.

Silky
The petals of large flowers, such as tea roses (*above*), camellias, and hibiscus have a satin-like texture.

Shiny
The leaves of *Fatsia*, camellias, and other plants add a shiny texture, as do berries and fruits.

Matt
Plants with matte leaves include *Gunnera*, *Cercis*, hydrangeas (*above*), and many others.

Soft
Stachys byzantina (*above*) and *Verbascum bombyciferum* are prized for their downy foliage.

Hard
The rigid trunks of trees, like *Acer pensylvanicum* (*above*), contrast well with their soft canopies.

SEASONAL EFFECTS

Creating a spectacular design with year-round appeal requires careful planning. Find inspiration and ideas by visiting open gardens at different times of the year, note the plants that are looking their best, and add these to your displays.

▶ WINTER

Many herbaceous perennials are beneath the soil at this time of year, but those with sturdy stems and enduring seed heads make decorative displays when married with grasses and evergreens. Colorful dogwoods (*Cornus*) also come into their own in the winter with their scarlet or bright yellow trunks, while white birches (*Betula*), golden bamboos, and the red trunks of *Prunus serrula* are picked out by the sloping rays of the winter sun. A few shrubs dare to bloom, including *Mahonia japonica*, witch hazels (*Hamamelis*), and scented winter box (*Sarcococca*). Conifers add evergreen interest with blue-, and gold-leaf types injecting extra color.

Flash frosts transform the garden, adding sparkle to conifers, plumed grasses, and the leaves of shrubs such as purple *Cotinus*.

◀ SPRING

Heralding the start of the growing season, spring arrives with a burst of color as the sun warms the soil and buds unfurl. Delicate blossoms adorn tree branches like bolts of lace, while a few shrubs beneath their canopies also put on an early show. Magnolias are the queens of the spring garden, their beautiful flowers striking a pose against the graceful stems. Perennials are also starting to show their faces in the spring with a range of beautiful hellebores and also dainty bleeding hearts (*Lamprocapnos*) leading the way.

Cherry blossoms are the star in this spring garden, complemented by mass planting of tulips in harmonizing colors.

▶ SUMMER

Long, sun-drenched days epitomize early summer when the garden is in full swing with plants vying for attention at every turn. The choice is vast, but remember that too many contrasting plants can look messy. Include a few attractive foliage subjects to offset perennials and flowering shrubs. Trees perform a similar function and also help regulate temperature fluctuations in the garden. As summer draws on, beds and borders may look past their prime, so include Michaelmas daisies (*Symphyotrichum*), rudbeckias, crocosmias and decorative grasses that flower as the season comes to a close.

Summer color continues with dahlias, salvias, Lavatera, and repeat-flowering begonias and French marigolds.

◀ FALL

It's easy to forget about fall when you're planting a border in the spring, but this can be a dramatic season with flaming red and orange foliage firing up the proceedings and branches laden with shimmering fruits. Trees and shrubs valued for their fall tints and berries include maples, cherries, crab apples, *Sorbus*, *Cotoneaster*, *Cotinus*, and *Viburnum opulus*. The violet beadlike berries of *Callicarpa bodinieri* are also well worth including. Some flowers, such as *Verbena bonariensis*, Michaelmas daisies, and *Abelia*, continue to bloom as temperatures plunge, while hydrangeas, *Hylotelephium* (sedums), and the grasses that bloomed earlier have ornamental seed heads, many of which will persist into the winter. Include some fall-flowering bulbs, such as nerines and crocuses, at the front of a sheltered sunny border.

The fiery leaves of *Acer palmatum* and dense red berries of a towering *Cotoneaster* set the garden on fire in the fall.

MAXIMIZING PLANT POWER

Think of your garden as an outdoor room, with leafy walls and a protective canopy of trees and structures. You can either fill the room with plants to confer a sense of enclosure, or restrict the planting to key areas to create an airy open space.

▶ CREATING A ROOM

To create an intimate area for dining or relaxing, use trellis covered with climbers or a hedge or bamboo screen to enclose the space. In a small garden, you could wrap a seating area with tall, airy perennials and annuals, but this will only give shelter during the summer months.

Low plants allow more light to penetrate and can extend the views through a garden, but they may also expose the boundaries, which will make the area look smaller. To create the illusion of a larger space, plant tall shrubs and trees to disguise fences and walls, and site a low hedge toward the end of the garden with a doorway cut into it or a path weaving around it so that the garden appears to continue beyond it.

A backdrop of dense yew provides privacy for a decked seating area, and clipped low hedging adds to the sense of discovery as you approach.

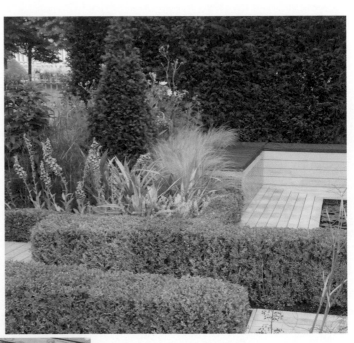

◀ WALLS OF FLOWERS AND FOLIAGE

The walls around a garden may provide useful vertical spaces for flowers and foliage and help create a three-dimensional design. Think of the surfaces as you would those in the house, and paper them with climbers, including ivy, roses, clematis, and jasmine. Introduce screens within the garden to create different areas, such as a kitchen and lounge. The screens can be decorated and will create microclimates, providing conditions for a greater range of plants. Use a mixed hedge to make a wall of decorative flowers, foliage, and berries.

Integrate a seating area into a garden wall, and clothe it with attractive climbers or wall shrubs.

▼ MAKING AN ENTRANCE

Make dramatic entrances to your garden rooms with decorative doorways. Train a pair of trees, such as hornbeams—which have flexible stems and tolerate clipping—to form an archway over a gate. Period and formal gardens suit a simple doorway, such as an arch, cut into a closely clipped yew hedge.

Contemporary designs require something a little different. One idea is to flank the entrance with lines of grasslike *Libertia* set against rusty steel panels, or try a metal arch with an evergreen *Trachelospermum* with its scented white summer flowers, trained over it.

A rustic arch or pergola at the entrance to a English garden is adorned with scented roses and honeysuckle to set the scene as visitors pass through.

PLANTING IN RESTRICTED SPACES

Pack your courtyard, balcony, or roof terrace with plants in pots affixed to walls or suspended in baskets. Green roofs will also increase your planting space and make great wildlife habitats, as will a few well-chosen climbers used to clothe bare walls, or even a full living "green wall" vertical planting system, now widely available.

Space savers

Planting in tiny spaces requires a little ingenuity. As well as using climbers to cover the walls, dress them up with pots and window boxes filled with seasonal flowers and foliage, or train an espaliered tree to a wall or fence and use the space in front for some well-behaved flowering perennials or small shrubs. Pencil-thin conifers and fan-trained trees also take up very little ground space and make great accent plants in pots or borders.

Light ideas

The weight of plants and pots can pose problems on balconies and roof terraces, so select light metal containers or polycarbonate and recycled plastic types. Faux terra-cotta, lead, and stone pots are very realistic and, once planted, it is difficult to distinguish them from the real thing. Trees grown on dwarf rootstocks (*see p.125*) will add height to a tiny garden, while grasses, bulbs, and perennials offer year-round interest. You can even plant a dwarf shrubby evergreen, such as *Lonicera nitida*, in a long, deep container to create a slim green screen.

Green roofs

There is a variety of green roof systems to choose from, but check the load-bearing capacity of your roof before investing in one. You can choose between easy-care succulents or more sophisticated grass and flower plans if your roof will take the weight of the deeper soil required. As well as looking fantastic, green roofs also provide excellent habitats for birds and insects, help insulate your property, reduce flash flooding by absorbing rainwater, and minimize noise pollution in homes near airports and highways.

CREATING A SIMPLE PLANTING PLAN

Planting plans are really easy to draw up, and they will help you organize your ideas and plot the position of the plants. You can also use a plan to visualize how much space you have and the number of plants needed for your design.

MEASURING AND VISUALIZING YOUR BORDER

Before making a plan, first carry out a survey of the site, checking how much sun it receives and the soil type (see pp.66–67). Then measure your planting area accurately, and draw the outline to scale on graph paper (see pp.80–81). Look through your chosen list of plants, and double check that each will suit the specific conditions of the bed or border, and note their heights and spreads to calculate the space they require.

Many people find it difficult to look at a two-dimensional plan and visualize how their three-dimensional planting design will look, so try using props to create an impression. Set out tripods, buckets, and pots that are approximately the same heights and spreads as your plants in the area you have allocated for them. Even top designers use this trick to check that their planting ideas will work on the ground.

◀ **Visualization technique**
Mocking up your planting plan using garden equipment is a good way to find out what works.

MAKING A PLAN

You can either plot your plants to scale within your outline plan using professional symbols (see below), or simply use a bubble diagram to show roughly where you are proposing to site different species (see p.82). The benefit of a scale drawing is that you can estimate the number of plants you will need more accurately. Large plants, such as trees and shrubs, are relatively easy to plot using a compass to draw circles to scale. Remember that young trees and shrubs will be smaller than your plan suggests, so fill in the spaces with annuals or perennials that can be lifted and moved easily as your woody plants grow. Plot smaller plants, such as perennials and bulbs, in groups rather than as individual plants.

CALCULATING PLANT QUANTITIES

The quantity of trees and large shrubs you require will be obvious from your plan, but perennial numbers may be more difficult to calculate. To help you make an accurate estimate, mark out a square yard on the ground, then buy one or two mature plants, and place them in the square. Allowing some space for spread, you can then calculate the number needed to fill a square yard and therefore the quantities required for your border. Bulbs can be packed very closely together, and if you are planning on large-scale plantings, check out specialty suppliers that offer discounts for bulk purchases.

Plant symbols
These are the most widely understood and commonly used planting plan symbols, which are part of a visual design language.

Wall shrub

Conifer Climber

Perennials

Existing tree

New tree

Shrubs

Bulbs

Hedge

THE FINAL PLAN

This garden design, by top British designer Chris Parsons of Hallam Garden Design, is for a small woodland area, featuring three silver birches (*Betula utilis* var. *jacquemontii*). To produce a similar plan for your own garden design, first mark out the trees using circles, and calculate the areas beneath the canopies that will sustain shade-loving plants, such as the epimediums used here. Tall grasses are accent plants that need sun, so should be set where the trees cast little or no shade. Note that the more dramatic plants, such as *Helleborus foetidus* and the purple *Actaea simplex*, have been used as single specimens, while a mass of the yellow-flowered *Alchemilla mollis* fills the areas in between and spills onto the gravel patio.

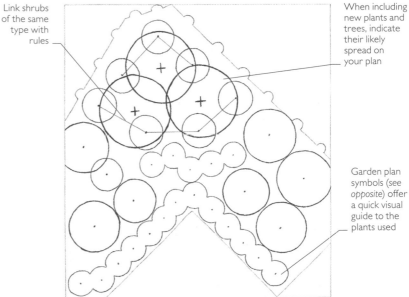

Link shrubs of the same type with rules

When including new plants and trees, indicate their likely spread on your plan

Garden plan symbols (see *opposite*) offer a quick visual guide to the plants used

YOU WILL NEED

1 *Betula utilis* var. *jacquemontii*
2 *Actaea simplex* 'Brunette'
3 *Alchemilla mollis*
4 *Helleborus foetidus* Wester Flisk Group
5 *Epimedium* x *versicolor* 'Sulphureum'
6 *Calamagrostis* x *acutiflora* 'Karl Foerster'

INTRODUCING TREES

Offering color and structure throughout the year, trees are an essential ingredient for any garden design. As well as lending height and beauty, they cast cooling shade, absorb greenhouse gases, and provide homes and food for wildlife.

▶ CREATING A WOODLAND SETTING

You can create a woodland effect with just a few well-chosen specimen trees in a small garden or with a more varied selection on a larger lot. Look for varieties with unusual stems for a striking effect even after the leaves have fallen in the winter. The dappled shade cast by your chosen trees will offer sufficient light for a collection of shade-loving plants. When choosing underplanting for your plan, look for a selection of plants that will provide year-round interest.

A mix of textured trunks, underplanted with rhododendrons, hostas, ferns, and ivies, frame the steps to a woodland pond. The corky bark of *Cordyline australis* contrasts with the papery surfaces of silver birches, and a lantern tree brings a splash of color to the canopy.

▲ ADDING HEIGHT AND PRIVACY

Any tree will add height to a garden, but to give a more contoured effect, underplant it with shade-tolerant shrubs. Trees' imposing stature can be deployed to great effect in a city garden overlooked by many windows. Use species with airy canopies to shield a seating area; plant them close to the space that needs extra privacy, rather than on the boundary where taller trees will be needed to mask upstairs windows. Alternatively, plant a wall of pleached trees, which form a line of clear, stilt-like stems topped by a screen of leafy branches just above head height.

A row of pleached hornbeams creates a suspended boundary—perfect for adding privacy without resorting to dense hedgerow planting.

▼ USING TREES AS FOCAL POINTS

When selecting a tree for a focal point, opt for a year-round star performer. Choose a cherry or crab apple that will be covered with delicate blossoms in the spring, provide a leafy canopy in the summer, and put on a finale of blazing colors and shining fruits in the fall. Alternatively, in a modern or formal garden, you could opt for a shapely evergreen or an elegant topiary specimen. Site your tree in the center of a lawn, at the end of a pathway, or in a border to punctuate a corner or curve in the design, and use small trees in pots to make an impact on a patio or in a courtyard garden.

The glow of this Japanese maple's beautiful summer foliage stands out in an otherwise verdant scheme.

◄ FRAMING FEATURES

A long, tree-lined lane makes an impressive entrance, and a similar effect is possible in a small garden with fewer trees and a little pruning and training. Plant six to ten trees on either side of a pathway, and train their stems on frames to form arches of foliage. Use the same technique with a pair of matching trees to create a decorative arbor over a seat.

Highlight a focal point, such as this sculpture, by positioning it center stage at the end of a leafy walkway.

◄ PROVIDING COLOR AND TEXTURE

Before buying trees for color effects, look for those that offer more than one decorative feature. Spring blooms have instant appeal but last just a few weeks, while the deep red bark of a *Prunus serrula* or stunning white birch trunks provide color all year. If flowers are your passion, include a few different species, such as a cherry and the early summer blooms of *Cornus kousa*, to extend the display.

Plenty of good tree choices are available for fall color, prolonging the season of interest into early winter when the fallen leaves carpet the ground. Textures also add an extra dimension to planting designs; consider the pleated foliage of hornbeams or the spiky needles of pines and other conifers.

Match an ornamental cherry (see pp.124–125) with contrasting deep-red foliage specimens and evergreen conifers for theatrical impact in the garden.

SELECTING AND PLANTING ORNAMENTAL TREES

Every space has room for a tree, whether it's a majestic oak in a large plot or a compact conifer on a patio. Choose a healthy specimen, plant it with care, and water well for a beautiful feature that will last for many years to come.

When buying trees, you will find that most are sold as container-grown plants. Look for those in white or black woven fabric bags (known as Air-Pots), which are designed to promote healthy roots and encourage trees to establish well once planted. Trees are a long-term investment, so buy from specialty nurseries, where stock will be grown in ideal conditions and a quality guarantee or replacement is offered if plants fail.

Hedging and fruit trees are also available in bare root form from late fall to late winter. These are young, dormant plants removed from fields and supplied without a pot. They are cheaper than container-grown trees but must be planted as soon as you purchase them.

A greater choice of trees is usually available if you buy them container grown; most large, mature specimens are only available in this form.

SELECTING SIZES AND SHAPE

Check the plant label carefully, and seek advice before buying a tree to ensure that its size and shape suit the style of your garden, and that it will fit your space when it matures. Also site your tree carefully when you get it home; if planted in the wrong place, it will be very difficult to move once established.

Spreading These may be small or large, but all spreading trees produce horizontal branches and are often wider than they are tall. They are ideal as focal points in a lawn or gravel garden but may take up too much space in a small plot.

Weeping Trees with this graceful look include the weeping willow as well as many smaller trees, such as flowering ornamental cherries (*Prunus spp*). Use the elegant silhouette of a weeping tree as a focal point in the garden for maximum impact, or add trees with light canopies to a mixed border.

Fastigiate With erect branches, held close together, fastigiate trees have a slim shape that makes them perfect for small gardens or tight spaces. Conical trees produce horizontal branches from the top to the bottom of the trunk; the shape is similar but broadens out more.

Round-headed Many trees, such as this hornbeam (*Carpinus betulus* 'Variegata') produce a rounded canopy on a single clear stem; those with this shape usually allow light beneath them for underplanting. You can prune the stems to accentuate the lollipop shape and use the tree as a focal point.

WHEN AND WHERE TO PLANT

The best time to plant trees is in the late fall, although container-grown types can be planted at any time as long as the ground is not frozen, waterlogged, or bone dry. Bare root trees must be planted in the winter at the same depth as they were grown in the nursery field—indicated by a brown soil mark on the stems. Check your soil and exposure (see pp.66–67), and match your tree choices with your garden conditions since planting a tree in the wrong place may cause it to grow lopsided or fail to thrive. Remember that trees cast shade and draw large quantities of moisture and nutrients from the soil, affecting other plants growing nearby. They can also undermine foundations with their roots, so be careful to site your tree at a distance from buildings. Where there is space, consider a tree with a strong structure to act as a stand-alone focal point.

A row of slender silver birches planted directly into a lawn can act as an informal division between areas, as well as adding height and shade in the summer.

Create a focal point with a flowering tree, such as this decorative dogwood (*Cornus kousa* var. *chinensis*), in the center of a lawn, or use one at the end of a vista to draw the eye.

GARDEN WISDOM

Don't plant too deeply
Trees that are planted too deeply may fail to establish well or even die because their trunks become too wet and rot. Ensure your tree is planted so the point where the roots start to flare out from the trunk is at soil level—you may need to scape away some soil from container-grown trees to see this point.

Use a cane as a guide.

PLANTING A CONTAINER-GROWN TREE

Get your new tree off to a flying start by preparing the ground well before planting. Loosen the soil with a fork to improve drainage, remove weeds, and incorporate some organic matter and all-purpose fertilizer at the specified rate over 6–10 ft (2–3 m) of ground surrounding the planting area to ensure that your tree is well nourished. Stake large trees after planting (see p.122) to prevent damage from wind-rock.

1 Soak the tree roots thoroughly. Dig a planting hole the same depth as the root ball and up to three times as wide. Break up any compacted soil around the sides with a garden fork.

2 Place the tree in the hole, and check the planting depth by laying a stick or bamboo cane across the top (see *Garden Wisdom box, below*). This may be easier if you remove the container first.

3 When the container has been removed, scrape away excess soil from the base of the trunk, and tease out any roots that have grown around the edge of the root ball.

4 Put the tree back in the hole, and spread the roots out evenly. Water in well, thoroughly soaking the roots. Ask someone to help you hold the tree upright while you replace the excavated soil.

5 Replace the excavated soil in and around the roots, and firm in well with your foot to eliminate any air pockets, but be careful not to compact the soil. Water the tree well. Apply a mulch, leaving a gap around the trunk.

AFTERCARE AND MAINTENANCE

Most newly planted trees will need extra irrigation for up to two years until they are fully established. Drought stress can cause permanent damage, so it is vital that you water frequently and sufficiently so that moisture reaches the roots.

After planting, winter-planted deciduous trees will not need further watering until early spring when they come into bud; evergreens may require extra irrigation during a dry winter. Water deeply once or twice a week from spring to fall. Use a hose, but turn the tap only halfway on to restrict the water flow, and soak a wide area up to 6 ft (2 m) around the trunk to encourage the roots to follow the moisture. Keep the same area around the tree free of weeds to give it the best chance of thriving.

Apply a thick mulch, such as composted bark chips, after planting and watering in to suppress competing weeds and seal in moisture; keep the mulch clear of the tree's trunk to prevent rot.

Staking trees

Large trees will require staking to guard against wind rocking the plant and tearing new roots. After three years, they will have sufficient anchoring roots to hold them steady, and the stake can be removed.

An angled stake is commonly used, although an upright one can be used for bare root trees. Drive in a wooden stake at a 45-degree angle, leaning it into the prevailing wind. Use a flexible tree tie to secure it about a third of the way up the trunk. On windy sites, use two upright stakes on either side of the root ball, attached to the trunk with long ties. Check ties every few months, loosening if necessary to prevent damage to the tree as it grows.

Watering bags slowly release moisture, wetting the roots more efficiently than surface watering.

When staking, use adjustable tree ties that can be loosened as the tree grows.

TREES FOR WILDLIFE

One of the major benefits of owning a tree is the huge variety of wildlife it attracts to the garden. Birds nest among the branches and feed on the flower buds and berries; insects are also drawn to all parts of these majestic plants.

Berries are an attractive feature in a garden, as well as providing a valuable source of food for birds and other animals in the winter months when food is scarce. If you have space, plant several fruiting trees that ripen at different times to ensure a long-lasting supply. Good choices for an abundance of berries are hawthorn (*Crataegus*), *Cotoneaster* x *watereri* 'John Waterer', mountain ash (*Sorbus*), mulberry (*Morus nigra*), elderberry (*Sambucus*), and cherry (*Prunus*). Most windfalls are readily eaten by birds, small mammals, and insects.

Other excellent trees for wildlife include thorny types that provide cover from predators, such as hawthorn and holly (*Ilex*), and those with nectar-rich flowers for bees and other insects, including crab apples (*Malus*). Hazels (*Corylus*) are also useful, producing an abundance of nuts for overwintering creatures.

Sambucus nigra

Corylus avellana

Crataegus persimilis

Ilex aquifolium 'Madame Briot'

TREE GROUPINGS

PARADISE ISLAND

Tree ferns (*Dicksonia*) lend a tropical flavor to any planting design and mix well with the purple foliage of a Japanese maple (*Acer*) and lush ferns (*Dryopteris*). Add a dash of color with some moisture-loving bright red astilbes set around a pond. Although reasonably hardy, tree ferns will need some winter protection (see *p.130*).

1 In fall, turn over the planting area, and add some well-rotted manure a few weeks before planting. Plant the Acer using the technique outlined on page 121, and water in well.

2 You can also plant the astilbes and ferns at the same time, using the method for planting perennials on page 137. Plant the ferns between the trees, and the astilbes in sun.

3 In mid-spring, plant the tree ferns at the back of the bed in the same way as you planted the Acer. Water the crowns, not the roots of the ferns, and cover the bed with an organic mulch.

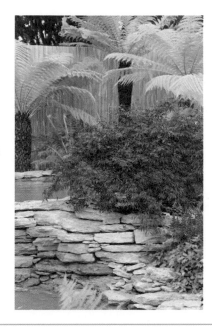

YOU WILL NEED

1 *Dicksonia antarctica*

2 *Acer palmatum* var. *dissectum* Dissectum Atropurpureum Group

3 *Astilbe* 'Köln'

4 *Dryopteris affinis*

VIBRANT WINTER BORDER

Willows (*Salix*) have a graceful look, and some are also valued for their colorful winter stems. Young stems produce the best effects, so pollard them in late winter by removing all stems above a clear trunk every couple of years. Dogwoods (*Cornus*) also have bright winter trunks; cut them back to the ground every year in late winter.

YOU WILL NEED

1 *Salix alba* var. *vitellina* 'Britzensis'

2 *Cornus sericea* 'Flaviramea'

3 *Cornus alba* 'Sibirica'

4 Dwarf conifers

5 *Erica carnea*

6 Variegated ivies

1 Plant your trees and shrubs in fall after turning over your border and incorporating plenty of well-rotted organic matter. Set out your plants in their pots.

2 Plant the *Salix* at the back with a frill of ivies in front, but not too close to the tree. The *Cornus* are about hip-height; site them in the middle of the border.

3 Plant the conifers in the gaps and the low-growing *Erica* at the front. Apply an organic mulch. Water the plants for two growing seasons.

ORNAMENTAL CHERRIES

Celebrated for their dazzling spring flowers, many ornamental cherries have a range of other eye-catching features, including decorative bark, fall leaf color, beautiful structure, and glistening fruits that provide food for birds and other wildlife. They are also available in a range of sizes to suit gardens large and small.

Prunus padus 'Colorata'

Choose from a huge range of flowering cherries for a spectacular display of delicate blooms in your garden each spring. Some types also have coppery-red young foliage, and many display excellent fall color, so when making your selection, look for a cherry that offers more than one season of interest. There is a wide variety of species and types available (*see below*); be sure to ask suppliers for a compact or dwarf type if you need a tree for a small garden.

▶ **Create a sensational spring border** with an abundance of floral underplanting such as viola, tulips, and tiarella paired with the beautiful blossom of *Prunus* 'Kanzan' and *P. triloba*.

CHERRIES TO CHOOSE FROM

Prunus avium The wild cherry is a tall tree best suited to large gardens. As well as masses of white flowers in the spring, it has good fall color along with red fruit.

Prunus padus The bird cherry is ideal for urban gardens. Its long flower panicles are accompanied by green leaves that turn yellow and bronze in the fall.

Prunus rufa The Himalayan cherry is grown for its wonderful reddish-brown and amber bark. This small tree also bears small clusters of pale pink flowers.

Prunus serrula The Tibetan cherry has willowlike leaves and small flowers. It is prized for its mahogany-red bark that peels as it ages, adding color and texture.

Prunus sargentii This Sargent's cherry has single pink spring flowers and chestnut-brown bark, while fall tints are often fiery. It casts a light shade.

Whatever type of garden you have, an ornamental cherry is guaranteed to boost its spring appeal. Choose from single or double flowers in shades of white or pink. Check the final height and spread of your chosen tree before buying to make sure that it will fit the space you have. Some have a weeping look, such as *Prunus* 'Cheal's Weeping', which has arching branches laden with double pink flowers, while others, including *Prunus* 'Spire', are more upright, providing a vertical accent.

There are many compact forms that are suitable for small gardens, such as the pink-flowered Prunus 'Accolade', 'Kanzan', and 'Pandora', or the dainty *Prunus* 'Shimidsu-zakura' with white blooms.

Ideal as focal points in the center of a yard or paved patio garden, cherries also make eye-catching features in mixed borders. Alternatively, plant a cluster of trees to mirror Japanese gardens during the cherry blossom festivals. Try underplanting with spring bulbs that flower at the same time, such as grape hyacinths and snake's head fritillaries, and include some late flowers like Japanese anemones to complement the fall leaf color.

Plant your tree in a sunny site, although some tolerate part shade, and free-draining soil. To plant a tree in the ground, see page 121, or plant in a large pot (see *right*). Many cherries have a beautiful natural style and need little pruning, but if you do cut back your tree, do so in the summer to reduce the risk of silver leaf disease (see *p.267*).

POTTING A CHERRY

If you're short of space, you can still enjoy an ornamental cherry's gorgeous spring blooms by planting a tree in a container, which will restrict its size and keep it from outgrowing its container. Make sure that you choose a large, weatherproof pot with drainage holes in the base.

1 Place broken crocks in the bottom of the pot. Wearing gloves, add a layer of commercial potting mix, and mix in controlled-release fertilizer, following the product guidelines.

2 Soak the tree roots in a bucket before planting. Coax out any roots that are circling around the root ball, and stand the tree on the potting mix, ensuring it is upright.

3 Plant the tree at the same level it was growing at in its original pot. Fill in with potting mix and firm down, leaving a 2 in (5 cm) gap between the rim of the pot and the mix for watering.

4 Give the planted tree a good soak. Water regularly—every couple of days in the summer—and feed annually in the spring with a slow-release fertilizer. Underplanting will add floral interest through the summer.

Prunus x *subhirtella* **'Autumnalis'** This popular cherry produces delicate blooms sporadically through the fall and winter and is ideal for small gardens.

Prunus **'Taihaku'** The great white cherry is a popular and celebrated Japanese variety. Its winning features include large white flowers, coppery young foliage, and fall color.

Prunus x *yedoensis* **'Somei Yoshino'** The Japanese Yoshino cherry bears almond-scented, white blooms on arching branches in mid-spring, followed in the fall by dark red fruits.

STYLES WITH SHRUBS

Spanning a vast range of woody plants from sprawling ground huggers to statuesque specimens, shrubs are a diverse group that also includes stylish evergreens, colorful foliage plants, and spectacular flowering types.

▶ FILLING DIFFICULT SITES

When looking for a plant to fill a difficult site, you will always find a shrub to suit. There are those that thrive in deep shade, such as skimmias and daphnes, while sun-loving bottlebrush will sail through dry periods. In poor soils, buddleias are almost guaranteed to succeed, and sprawling specimens like *Cotoneaster horizontalis* will cover a slope or bank. There are even shrubs that are happiest in the salt-laden air near the beach, such as sea buckthorn (*Hippophae*) and *Tamarix*.

Squeezing into a gap, the bright red flower spikes of this crimson bottlebrush add color and texture.

▲ INJECTING FOLIAGE INTEREST

Shrubs are indispensable foliage plants with the evergreens providing permanent color and deciduous types offering bright new spring leaves and fall fire. Those with colorful foliage inject highlights into dull green displays, while variegated evergreens perform a similar function, illuminating gloomy areas with splashes of light. Choose shrubs with dramatic leaf shapes to provide points of interest: the bold, glossy, fingerlike forms of *Fatsia japonica* and the pointed spikes of a yucca are sure to catch the eye.

Mix the spiky, dark red foliage of a *Berberis* with grasses and perennials in a border for contrast and long-lasting interest.

◄ CREATING CONTAINER FEATURES

Many shrubs make excellent container specimens, and when planted in large pots, most are easy to care for. Compact evergreens offer sculptural year-round displays, either planted on their own or with seasonal companions. Alternatively, choose a small conifer with textural foliage and architectural shapes, such as a pencil-thin juniper or the round *Pinus mugo* 'Mops'. To create a flowering container display, look no further than the vast range of patio roses, available in almost every color except blue. Shrubs that flower for many months, such as the new hydrangea hybrids, also make elegant container plants and will make a superb focal point on a patio.

The long-lasting blue flowers of this *Hydrangea serrata* 'Blue Deckle' make a beautiful and enduring shrubby container feature.

▲ PROVIDING STRUCTURE AND SCREENING

Use a selection of shrubs to create walls and structures in your garden; box and others with dense foliage make excellent hedges for edging, boundaries, and low screens. Shrubs with elegant forms, like hebes and *Nandina*, offer sculptural interest in borders and gravel gardens. Try plants with arching stems, like *Buddleia alternifolia*, in an open site. Large foliage shrubs are also useful, providing beautiful backdrops to planting designs.

Perfectly trimmed evergreen hedges provide sturdy, structural contrast with the soft, romantic planting in this early summer garden.

◄ ADDING SEASONAL FLOWERS

The choice of flowering shrubs is vast and varied, ranging from inconspicuous winter flowers to big, bright blooms. Most shrubs flower for only a brief time, but since there are options for every month, you can enjoy color all year. The fragrant flowers of witch hazels get the ball rolling in the winter, followed by a huge selection of spring blooms and early summer gems, including the scented *Philadelphus*. The colorful flowers of summer, such as fuchsias, roses, and hydrangeas, are followed by fall blooms like heathers (*Erica*), which maintain interest as the seasons turn.

***Rhododendron mucronulatum's* vibrant pink blooms** bring a splash of much-needed color into the winter garden, especially when paired with a witch hazel's yellow flowers.

SELECTING AND PLANTING SHRUBS

Most hardy shrubs need very little care once established, making them ideal for those with little time to spare. Tender types require more attention, but when grown in pots they can be easily moved indoors for the winter.

Their sheer diversity makes shrubs a highly appealing group of plants, but before you buy, check the labels carefully for final heights and spreads because different species can have widely differing habits. Azaleas are a case in point, with the deciduous *Rhododendron luteum*, for example, growing to a lofty 12 ft (4 m) in height, while the compact evergreen

Rhododendron 'Rosebud' reaches no more than 3 ft (90 cm).

Look for healthy plants that show no signs of disease on the leaves and stems, and slip them out of their pots to check that the roots are not congested, since this will hinder their development once planted. Also reject any that have poor or underdeveloped root systems.

Always check your chosen shrubs are healthy and undamaged before purchasing.

SHRUBS FOR DIFFERENT CONDITIONS

To guarantee the best performance, choose shrubs that suit your site and soil; in the wrong conditions their foliage and flowers are likely to suffer.

As well as checking plant labels, also consider shrubs' native habitats. Those from warm climates like the Mediterranean need a sunny location in free-draining soil and often have small leaves that deflect the heat and light. Forest or woodland natives are shade lovers and can be identified by their larger, dark green foliage, which is perfectly adapted to absorb the low light beneath tree canopies.

Check that shrubs do not require specifically acid or alkaline soils before buying to prevent an expensive mistake. Most shrubs will tolerate both, but there are some exceptions.

Sun Shrubs with small, silver or gray-green leaves, such as rockroses (*Cistus, above*), lavender, and Russian sage, need a sunny site. Plants with colorful leaves, such as *Berberis thunbergii* and the purple forms of smoke bush also thrive in sun

Shade Many large-leaf and some pretty flowering shrubs, such as hydrangeas (*above*), prefer a shady site. A few variegated shrubs, such as *Elaeagnus*, also cope with shade but need a little sun to bring out their colors.

Acidic soils Some shrubs, such as camellias (*above*), rhododendrons, and *Pieris*, are only happy if grown in acid soil. Others that prefer acidic conditions include witch hazel, heathers, *Enkianthus, Leucothoe,* and *Arctostaphylos*.

Alkaline soils A greater number of plants will tolerate alkaline conditions, including sun lovers, such as *Ceanothus (above), Cytisus,* and *Hebe,* and plants for shade, such as *Deutzia, Sarcococca,* and *Viburnum tinus*.

PLANNING A SHRUB BORDER

Many shrubs produce a dense thicket of branches and form a block of solid color, so arrange them in height order, with the smallest at the front. Also select plants with different heights and structures, and think of them as living sculptures to create a visually exciting display. For example, you could use a *Cornus controversa* 'Variegata', with its horizontal flowering stems, behind compact shrubs with contrasting strap-like or rounded foliage (*see below*).

You can also enhance the interest of some small-leaf shrubs, such as box or shrubby honeysuckle (*Lonicera nitida*), by clipping them into topiary shapes. Try planting a prized specimen in a large pot, and set it at the front of, or within, your border. Also consider shrubs with decorative or unusual foliage to inject textural and color contrasts, and add grasses, sedges, and perennials, such as rudbeckias or asters, to bring flowers and color to your border in the late summer and fall when few shrubs are in bloom.

Pair the delicate white flowers of a *Cornus controversa* 'Variegata' with a silvery *Pittosporum* and red annual *Atriplex hortensis* var. *rubra*.

GARDEN WISDOM

Heavy loads

Architectural shrubs, such as clipped bay, palms, and fatsias, make excellent container plants. However, large shrubs or those in weighty containers can be very heavy, so it is wise to plant them in situ or set them on plant trolleys, which can be wheeled around your plot with ease. You can buy decorative cast iron trolleys that make attractive additions to a patio display.

Plant heavy pots *in situ*.

PLANTING A SHRUB

If your soil is very heavy or light and sandy, improve it before planting, and select suitable shrubs (*see p.66*). A few weeks before planting, till the area to reduce soil compaction, and incorporate some organic matter. Plan your layout carefully, and site shrubs with sufficient space for them to grow to their full size. While they are maturing, fill in any gaps with annuals and perennials, which can be lifted and moved when necessary.

1 Measure the distance from neighboring plants to ensure your shrub has space to mature. Dig a hole about twice the width of the container and the same depth as the root ball.

2 Place the shrub, in its container, into the hole, and use a cane as a guide to ensure that the shrub will be at the same level when planted as it is in its pot. Water it thoroughly.

3 Enrich the excavated soil with controlled-release fertilizer. Remove the shrub from its pot, and place it in the hole. Fill in around the roots with the enriched soil.

4 Firm the soil down around the roots with your fingertips to expel any air pockets. Water in well, and apply a mulch of well-rotted organic matter, leaving a gap around the stems.

CARING FOR SHRUBS

Many shrubs require very little aftercare, but they will need regular watering until their roots are fully established. Water during the growing season from spring to fall; evergreens may also need watering during prolonged dry spells in winter. Once established, most shrubs will only require extra water during a severe drought. Mature shrubs should not need feeding, either—just lay a mulch of well-rotted organic matter, such as manure or compost, around them each spring. If your plants are looking unhealthy or if your soil is poor, apply an all-purpose granular fertilizer before mulching.

Supplement poor soil with all-purpose fertilizer.

Overwintering tender shrubs

Many tender shrubs, such as *Cordyline australis*, will not survive a harsh winter unprotected, but this should not deter you from growing them. The easiest solution is to grow compact types in small pots and bring them under cover during the winter. If your plants are too large or your pots too heavy to move, cover them with a double layer of horticultural fabric. Make sure you also wrap up the container to insulate the roots, especially if your plants are in terra-cotta pots, which may crack in cold conditions. Alternatively, make a cage

Frost-proof delicate roots by insulating pots with burlap, fabric, or bubble wrap.

around shrubs planted in the ground, using chicken wire attached to canes. Pack the cage with dry straw for insulation, and cover it with plastic to keep out the rain. This method should keep the plant dry. Remember to remove the plastic on warm days to prevent the plant from "sweating" and rot from setting in.

SMALL SHRUBS FOR EDGING

Diminutive shrubs make excellent edging plants, either clipped to form a low hedge, or planted in a line at the front of a bed or border.

Thymes are useful edging for sunny, formal, or wildlife gardens, where their flowers will attract many beneficial insects. They are available in a variety of colors and look attractive when used to cover slopes and banks, especially when planted in colorful blocks (*top left*). Consider combining them with other herbs, such as lavender.

Excellent choices for low, formal hedges or as edging for a potager include box, *Buxus sempervirens* (*top right*), and forms of *Euonymus fortunei*; their linear structure lends them to traditional garden designs.

On acid soils, include heathers and heaths to form a dense carpet of evergreen, needlelike foliage. They naturally form domed shapes (*bottom left*) and can be clipped to accentuate this trait. Line up plants, use them in clusters, or plant in swathes for a natural effect (*bottom right*). Different types flower in fall, winter, spring, and summer, and by mixing and matching a range you can create an edge with flowers all year.

Scented strips of thyme.

Crisp corners on box hedging.

Compact spheres of heather.

Soft swathes of heather.

SHRUB GROUPINGS

COOL CONTEMPORARY ROSE BED

Disease-resistant roses, such as Winchester Cathedral, make beautiful focal features in a bed of perennials. The monochromatic plan is perfect for a contemporary or formal garden, where the elegant flowers create an air of cool sophistication. The rose is best in full sun, but the surrounding plants will cope with some shade.

YOU WILL NEED

1 *Actaea simplex* 'Brunette'
2 *Veronica spicata* 'Alba'
3 White violas
4 *Rosa* Winchester Cathedral
5 Hardy white geraniums
6 *Alchemilla mollis*

1 To plant the rose, follow the steps on page 133, setting it in a place of pride in the middle of the border. Water the other plants.

2 Plant the low-growing violas, *Alchemilla*, and geraniums in the front and the taller *Actaea* and *Veronica* behind or to one side.

3 Water well, and add an organic mulch, leaving gaps around the stems. Keep the border watered while the plants are establishing.

RICH MIX

The sumptuous dark purple foliage and structural look of the *Cotinus* dominates this design and is set off by layers of foliage color and form, with a golden hop (*Humulus*) growing over a rail in front of a *Cotoneaster* hedge. The box (*Buxus*) balls provide a formal note, while the perennials pick up the color of the *Cotinus*. The plants will thrive in full sun or partial shade and moist but free-draining soil.

YOU WILL NEED

1 *Cotinus* 'Grace'
2 *Cotoneaster* hedge
3 *Humulus lupulus* 'Aureus'
4 *Lysimachia ciliata* 'Firecracker'
5 *Buxus* topiary

1 This plan will get off to a good start if planted in the fall. Prepare the bed by digging and incorporating well-rotted organic matter.

2 Plant the shrubs as described on p.129. The hop is a twining climber and will need a support to scramble over (see p.145).

3 Either clip the box balls *in situ*, or buy ready-made topiary specimens. Apply an organic mulch, keeping it clear of the stems. Water well.

CLASSIC ROSES

Reigning supreme as queen of the flower garden for hundreds of years, the rose's exquisite beauty, elegance, and fragrance remains unrivaled. Today, modern disease-resistant hybrids that combine the best of the species' charms have caught the eye of contemporary designers and made roses more fashionable than ever.

Rosa 'Sunblest'

With around 150 species of roses and thousands of hybrids and cultivars to choose from, you cannot fail to find a rose that appeals to your sense of style and taste. Choose from elegant hybrid teas, the classic flowers of traditional rose gardens; thorny species with their large, beautiful blooms and glossy rose hips; or compact patio roses to dress up a summer container. In confined areas, use the vertical space, and train a climber to decorate your walls and fences with foliage and sumptuous blooms.

TYPES OF ROSE

Shrubs This diverse group includes species roses that usually bear single flowers over a relatively short period, as well as modern shrub roses that flower for longer and include a wider range of flower forms.

Hybrid tea Sometimes called large-flowered roses, these have blooms of a classic shape, with long, pointed buds opening to petals that surround a central cone. The flowers are borne singly; many are fragrant.

Floribunda Also known as cluster-flowered roses, floribundas are similar to hybrid teas but with a more informal style, bearing flowers in great quantities from the summer to fall. Many are scented.

Old Bearing one flush of flowers in the summer, often followed by large hips, old roses include groups such as Alba, Bourbon, Damask, Moss, and China roses. Most are very thorny, and many have a rich scent.

Patio and dwarf polyantha Patio roses are dwarf floribundas, growing to just 18–24 in (45–60 cm) in height. Polyanthas are rarely scented but are tough bushes of a similar size with lots of small flowers.

Miniature These repeat-flowering, dwarf shrubs have very compact growth and rarely spread. Flowers are tiny and rarely scented, and appear in flushes of 3–11 from summer to fall. Ideal for containers.

Ramblers With long, flexible stems, rambling roses produce one flush of clustered, small to medium flowers in early summer. They grow vigorously and are ideal for training over fences and pergolas, and into trees.

Climbers With a more rigid framework than rambling roses, climbing roses are a diverse group, including some types of hybrid tea and floribundas; most flower from summer to fall.

PLANTING ROSES

Roses thrive in a sunny location in fertile, moisture-retentive soil. If your soil is free-draining, dig in plenty of well-rotted farmyard manure a few weeks before planting to increase water retention. Whatever your soil type, apply a 2 in (5 cm) mulch of manure after planting, leaving a space around the stems.

1 Dig a bucketful of organic matter into your proposed planting area. Then dig a hole a little deeper and twice the diameter of the container in which your rose is growing.

2 Place the rose, in its pot, into the hole. Using a cane, ensure the graft union (swelling at base of the stems) will be below the surface, or slightly above in heavy soil. Add fertilizer to the excavated soil.

3 Water the rose and leave to drain before removing from its pot. Apply mycorrhizal fungi to the base of the hole according to the directions—this will aid root growth.

4 Wearing gloves, place the rose in the hole. Backfill around the root ball with the excavated soil, and firm in gently around the stems with your hands. Water in well.

With such variation in flower form and structure, roses are among the most versatile of all garden plants. Traditionalists may like them confined to their own beds, but if you choose this style, opt for disease resistant roses that will not succumb to black spot and lose their leaves. Alternatively, mix and match roses with other shrubs and perennials, which not only extends the season of interest but also helps disguise leggy or leafless plants.

Standard roses make striking features in parterres and formal gardens and look stunning when underplanted with lavender. Or use one as the centerpiece in a large container display on a patio surrounded by summer bedding.

Species shrubs, such as *Rosa alba* and *R. rugosa*, and modern hybrids are excellent choices for hedges, their thorny stems providing cover for wildlife and acting as a deterrent against human intruders. Climbers

▲ **Make the most** of the vertical space in your garden by training vigorous rambling roses up bare walls and boundary fences.

and ramblers are also effective in wildlife gardens but really come into their own in English-style designs. The tried-and-tested pairing of roses and clematis epitomizes a romantic idyll when plants are left to scramble over an arch or around a doorway.

Plant container-grown roses at any time of year and bare root roses in the winter, after soaking their roots in water just before planting. Many roses fall prey to the fungal disease black spot, which, although not fatal, produces ugly black spots on the leaves and stems and causes foliage to fall. Reduce the risk by selecting disease-resistant hybrids. Aphids (see *p.360*) do not kill established plants, but may damage new flower buds and stems.

PLANTING WITH PERENNIALS

Celebrated for their infinite variety, perennials (see p.12) never lose their charm and remain as popular as ever. With flowers of every color, texture, shape, and form, this group includes plants for both sun and shade, and varieties suitable for all types of soil.

▶ FILLING THE GAPS

Perennials are ideal for filling gaps and adding ground-cover interest between shrubs and beneath trees in mixed borders and woodland gardens. Shade lovers, such as hellebores, suit situations where their planting partners block the sun, putting on an early show of flowers beneath a deciduous tree, or use ferns to carpet the ground with a leafy design. In sunnier spots, your options are wider, but choose tough perennials, like achilleas, that can cope with competition for moisture from their neighbors.

In this neutral-colored scheme, *Alchemilla molli*s and a purple *Actaea simplex* add color and texture.

▲ INJECTING TROPICAL FLAVOR

In warm, sunny, sheltered areas, re-create the gardens of tropical places close to home with a combination of tender perennials and hardy types with eye-catching looks. Set the scene with large-leaf plants, and add to the effect with colorful leaves and vibrant flowers. Tender plants are best grown in pots and brought inside before frost comes to avoid damage. Match these with hardy perennials that can remain outside all year.

Pair the hardy banana (*Musa basjoo*) with fiery cannas and annual purple *Ricinus* to inject an exotic flavor to a border.

◄ PROVIDING SUMMER ABUNDANCE

No plant group can compete with perennials for sheer flower power. The queens of the summer border, they include traditional favorites, such as delphiniums and peonies. These prima donnas dazzle and glow, but others, like pastel-hued *Astrantia major,* are more delicate and reserved, forming a chorus to the bright stars and tempering the flower display.

From early to midsummer, perennial borders are heavy with flowers, but the choice diminishes as fall approaches. To keep your garden in full bloom at this time, seek out late starters like red hot pokers (*Kniphofia*) to carry you through the late season.

Create a cottage garden brimming with summer blooms such as tall spikes of *Delphinium*, purple salvias, and classic roses.

▲ DECORATING DRY LANDSCAPES

Drought-tolerant perennials are perfect for gravel gardens and desertlike landscapes. These styles are ideal if you garden on dry, sandy soil, and if you choose your plants carefully, you should not have to water them once they're established. Small succulents, together with *Rhodanthemum* and *Stachys,* will form a dense carpet of color on a gravel or scree surface; mix them with taller plants like salvias and valerian (*Centranthus*) to add height.

To create this look, mix grasses with flowering perennials, such as yarrow (*Achillea*) in a range of yellows and oranges.

◄ CREATING NATURAL-LOOKING EFFECTS

Prairie designs are best suited to larger gardens where plants can be amassed in bold swathes. Choose a limited selection of perennials that enjoy the conditions you can provide, and plant them in large groups. A number of perennials also suit meadow plantings. To create this style, imagine the plants have self-seeded between the grasses. Create small groups here and there, dotting a few of the same species close to these clusters.

Combine swathes of catnip (*Nepeta racemosa* 'Walker's Low') with *Betonica officinalis* 'Hummelo' and *Salvia nemorosa* 'Amethyst'.

SELECTING AND PLANTING PERENNIALS

Perennials provide spectacular flowering displays for many months of the year. Although some tall types require staking, most will look after themselves, reappearing year after year following their winter rest.

STAGGERING VARIETY

From the towering *Eupatorium purpureum* to the low, sprawling *Campanula poscharskyana,* there is a perennial for any area or planting design. They are available in a huge range of colors and shades, making it difficult to decide which to plant. Begin by assessing your site and soil and selecting those that do best in these conditions (*see p.66*). Next, map out your border or planting area, and assign plants according to their size and stature. Generally, lofty plants provide a backdrop to medium-sized and ground-hugging perennials, but remember that a few, such as the ever-popular *Verbena bonariensis* and elegant *Dierama pulcherrimum,* can be planted toward the front of a design because they have slender stems and an airy, see-through structure. Finally, take your pick from the wide range of flower colors and foliage varieties to complete your design.

Spectacular blooms

For borders bursting with color, include a few flamboyant blooms. Try peonies, which boast large flowers prized for their ruffles of delicate petals in pink, red, or white. Lupines join the peonies in early summer and produce eye-catching cones of small flowers in many hues, while in midsummer, the towering spires

Plant perennials in groups of three or more. Buy mature plants or young "plugs," which are more cost effective for bulk purchases.

of delphiniums are hard to beat, with their spikes of open flowers in shades of blue, purple, pink, and white. Also add a selection of oriental poppies. Although their sumptuous blooms are relatively short-lived, the decorative seed heads that follow extend their interest.

▶ **A pink rhododendron bush**, surrounded by foxgloves, red valerian, and *Centaurea montana* (perennial cornflower), brings a splash of color to a border in spring and early summer.

PLANNING A LONG SEASON OF INTEREST

There are perennials for all seasons, starting with hellebores (*top left*), which flower between late winter and mid-spring. Next are the dainty forget-me-not–like blooms of *Brunnera,* and dancing flowers of *Epimedium* and *Lamprocapnos spectabilis,* all of which prefer some shade, followed later in spring by aquilegias in a variety of shapes and colors. A host of geraniums and vibrant geums (*top right*) then appear in the early summer.

For dramatic color from late summer to fall, opt for blue or red asters (*bottom left*) and golden rudbeckias, toned down with the white daisies of *Leucanthemum.* In the fall, try the knee-high, sun-loving *Ajania pacifica* (*bottom right*), which bears yellow button-like flowers surrounded by beautiful silver-edged lobed foliage. The evergreens then come into their own in the winter, with round-leaf bergenias, grassy *Libertia,* and colorful heucheras leading the show.

Helleborus × *hybridus* 'Pluto'

Geum coccineum

Aster amellus 'Rosa Erfüllung'

Ajania pacifica

GARDEN WISDOM

Planting depths explained

Most perennials should be planted at the same depth as they were when in their original pots, but exceptions include those that dislike damp soil around their stems, such as *Verbascum, Sisyrinchium,* and *Hylotelephium.* Plant these 1–1½in (2–3 cm) above the surface, and pull up the soil around the root ball to encourage water to drain off. Moisture-loving plants, including hostas, prefer to be planted more deeply so that their roots are never exposed to the dry conditions nearer the surface.

PLANTING A PERENNIAL

To prepare the ground for planting, dig up the soil to aerate it, reduce compaction, and remove any weeds. Then dig in some organic matter, such as well-rotted manure or compost. Most perennials are planted in the early fall or spring; more tender types or those that dislike cold, wet conditions, such as *Verbena bonariensis,* are best planted in the spring, allowing them a full growing season to establish before winter.

1 Dig a hole twice as wide as the plant pot and a little deeper. Set the plant in the hole, and check that it will be at about the same depth when planted as it was in its original pot.

2 Fork the bottom of the hole to loosen any compacted soil, and rake in a little general fertilizer to the hole. Water the plant well, then carefully slip it out of its pot.

3 Gently tease out any circling roots from the root ball. Place the plant back into the hole. Fill in around the root ball with soil, firming it down with your fingers.

4 Water the plant well, and apply an organic mulch of compost or well-rotted manure. Lay gravel around plants that like their stems kept dry, such as achilleas, stachys, and sedums.

AFTERCARE

If you plant perennials in their optimal conditions, they should only need watering for one season after planting. Some may require extra irrigation during extended periods of drought, but don't be tempted to water plants whose leaves droop at midday, because this is simply their mechanism for conserving moisture—they should bounce back again in the evening.

Once they are established, hungry perennials, such as *Symphotricum novae-angliae*, will need an application of all-purpose granular fertilizer once a year in spring. Also mulch around perennials with organic matter, such as well-rotted manure, compost, or bark chips, at the same time.

Tall plants, such as delphiniums and some asters, will need staking, especially in exposed sites. Insert stakes in spring when new growth appears, and tie in the stems as they grow. Stake single stems with bamboo canes; insert hazel twigs or pea sticks, or use link or ring support

Stake clump-forming plants, such as peonies, early in the season, raising as the plant grows.

frames around clump-forming plants. These may not look very attractive at first, but the plants will soon grow large enough to disguise them.

Cutting back perennials

Perennials require very little other maintenance, and most will be happy doing their own thing for the rest of the growing season. Some plants, such as hardy geraniums, will form fresh foliage if you cut them back after they have bloomed. Others, including

Dianthus, will produce a fresh flush of blooms if deadheaded. In the late fall, cut old plant stems down to ground level unless their foliage or seed heads are attractive over the winter, in which case wait until spring. Remove the old foliage of evergreens, including bergenias, in the spring to allow space for new leaves to form.

PERENNIALS FOR DIFFICULT SITES

Versatile and beautiful, perennials can be relied upon to fill even the most challenging sites. Plan carefully, and you will be able to create year-round interest in any garden.

Alpines are perfect for squeezing between paving or the gaps in a dry stone wall. *Aubrieta (top left), Alyssum,* and *Arabis* will fill these areas with exhilarating spring color, while *Frankenia* and *Cerastium* offer later seasonal interest.

The grayish, blue-leaf evergreen *Euphorbia rigida (top right)* is ideal for sunny slopes and produces frothy yellow flowers in spring, or choose the fernlike, silver-leaf *Artemisia* 'Powis Castle' for sun-baked gravel gardens.

In dry shade, use the pretty *Vinca minor (bottom left)*, with its waxy stems of evergreen foliage and beautiful blue spring flowers, or *Lamium*, with variegated foliage.

Most ferns are at home in deep shade, while other good choices for shady borders include low-growing *Pachysandra*, *Alchemilla mollis*, and *Brunnera*, or *Bergenia* and some *Lysimachia* where taller plants are required. For damp shade, try hostas *(bottom right)*, which produce attractive foliage (but most need protection against slug and snail attacks).

Crimson *Aubretia*

Euphorbia rigida

Vinca minor

Hosta 'Francee'

PERENNIAL GROUPINGS

HIGH-SUMMER COLOR

Nothing compares to a midsummer border brimming with colorful perennials. This mix of contrasting yellows, blues, and purples with red highlights also combines interesting shapes and styles which lead the eye around the design. Plant this group in a sunny area, and apply an organic mulch over the border each spring.

YOU WILL NEED

1 *Lupinus* 'The Governor'
2 *Pittosporum tenuifolium* 'Silver Queen'
3 *Anchusa azurea* 'Loddon Royalist'
4 *Achillea* 'Moonshine'
5 *Rosa* Rose of Picardy
6 *Verbascum* 'Gainsborough'

1 In spring, turn over the border, add some organic matter, and set out your plants. Plant flower spikes next to flat-headed achilleas.

2 Plant the tall lupines and verbascums in groups of three or more toward the back of the border, but ensure they are still in sun.

3 Water the border well after planting and regularly for the first year. In late winter, cut back the old perennial stems.

PRAIRIE DRIFTS

This beautiful border comprises large drifts of stout perennials that, together with groups of grasses, provide stunning late summer color. The plants also offer interest in fall when the blooms fade and seed heads form, followed in winter by straw-colored stems that look fabulous when iced with frost. Plant in a sunny site.

YOU WILL NEED

1 *Deschampsia cespitosa*
2 *Hylotelephium spectabile*
3 *Echinacea purpurea* 'Rubinstern'
4 *Lythrum virgatum*
5 *Eupatorium*

1 Before planting in early fall or spring, dig plenty of organic matter into the border to enrich the soil.

2 Buy ten or more plants of each type, and plant them in teardrop-shaped, interlinking swathes. Vary heights and textures to create the effect.

3 Keep plants well watered for the first growing season until they are established. Leave the dried stems over winter, and then cut them down in spring.

PERENNIALS FOR FOLIAGE

Swathes of flowers look wonderful in beds and borders, but many perennials bloom for a relatively short period. For a longer-lasting design, select plants for foliage effects as well as for blooms, and combine different shapes and colors for a long season of interest.

Perennials follow the general pattern of most plants, with larger-leaf species tending to prefer shade, and those with small, silver, or downy foliage enjoying sunny sites. Most colorful foliage perennials need some sun to bring out their hues, but a range of variegated plants, such as arums and pulmonarias, do well in the shade. Contrast plants with different features (*see right*), and use each type in bold groups or swathes for the greatest impact.

FOLIAGE OPTIONS

Large leaves One of the best perennials for large leaves is *Bergenia* (*above*), with its oval, leathery leaves and clusters of pink flowers in early spring.

Colorful foliage For the widest variety, opt for heucheras (*above*), which thrive in most soil types. Hostas include a good choice for shady sites.

Swordlike leaves Sun-loving phormiums (*above*) are hardy and make exceptional focal plants. Shade-tolerant astelias produce a similar effect.

Patterns *Brunnera* cultivars (*above*), and *Pulmonaria* species, many of which are variegated, will brighten up shady areas with their patterned foliage.

Grassy leaves *Ophiopogon* species (*above*) are compact plants with variegated leaves or black grasslike foliage. *Libertia* is a taller option for beds and borders.

Dryopteris affinis

Fingerlike foliage Not all euphorbias are perennials, but the striking reddish-purple foliage of *Euphorbia amygdaloides* 'Purpurea' makes it one of the best.

Ferny leaves Choose an *Achillea* (*above*) for a mix of fernlike foliage and flowers. Ferns themselves make beautiful specimens for shade.

Soft, downy foliage For tactile effects, try downy leaf lambs' ears, *Stachys byzantina* (*above*), and the velvety foliage of *Verbascum bombyciferum*.

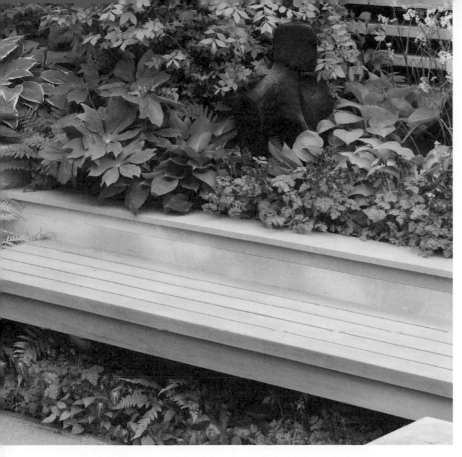

◄ **Nestle shade-loving perennials,** such as *Hosta* and *Dicentra* 'King of Hearts', under a bench to add an extra layer of planting to a secluded corner of the garden.

PLANTING FERNS IN A POT

Even if you don't have much space, you can create a lush green display by planting a mix of contrasting ferns in a container on a patio. These are ideal in a shady spot.

1 Choose a pot with holes in the base to allow for adequate drainage. Apply a layer of potting mix. Add some slow-release fertilizer granules.

2 Soak the ferns in a bucket of water for 15 minutes. Place them, still in their original containers, in the pot to ensure that you are happy with the arrangement.

3 Tip the ferns out of their containers, and place on the layer of potting mix. Fill in around the root balls, firming the mix gently with your fingers.

4 Plant the ferns at the same depth as in their original containers, leaving a gap of 2 in (5 cm) between the pot rim and top of the soil to allow space for watering. Water in well.

Leafy perennials are versatile plants, suitable for gardens of all sizes, with diminutive types squeezing comfortably into tiny spaces and dramatic crowd-pleasers, like phormiums, providing excellent container plants for patios. Add to these the mid-sized perennials, which create bold, textured effects when used *en masse* in larger spaces. There are even tough little plants, including the prettily patterned deadnettle, *Lamium maculatum,* that will survive the dry shade beneath trees.

Make the most of perennials in a small urban garden by tucking shade lovers, such as hostas, pulmonarias, and ferns, beneath a bench, or use them to produce a frill of foliage alongside a pathway. In boggy areas close to a pond or pool, inject drama into a larger garden with the massive leaves of a *Gunnera manicata,* or use the well-shaped *Ligularia* and *Rodgersia* species where space is more restricted. Areas that bask in full sun will provide the perfect home for an edging of furry lambs' ears (*Stachys*), swathes of colorful succulents, including purple forms of *Hylotelephium telephium,* and focal plants such as *Melianthus major.*

Plants grown for foliage effects come from a wide range of habitats, so check the labels for specific site and soil requirements before you buy. Many, like ferns (*see right*), make excellent container specimens, but remember to keep perennials in pots well watered and feed them annually in the spring with an all-purpose granular fertilizer to keep the foliage looking lush.

INTRODUCING CLIMBERS AND WALL SHRUBS

Climbers and wall shrubs are versatile plants, perfect for decorating small gardens where space is tight or for covering large structures and screens. Prized for their lush foliage, they also offer a variety of decorative fruits and flowers.

▶ PROVIDING WALLS OF SCENT

The beauty of a scented climber is that the blooms are perfectly placed at nose height. The choice is vast, with climbing and rambling roses producing a range of heady scents. Deciduous honeysuckles (*Lonicera periclymenum*) and jasmines (*Jasminum*) are also hard to beat for fragrance, while scented evergreens include the star jasmine (*Trachelospermum jasminoides*). Wisteria's purple or white lanterns of flowers reign supreme in the spring, blessing gardens with a rich scent. Best grown on a sturdy pergola or frame, this towering beauty needs plenty of support.

Star jasmine (*Trachelospermum jasminoides*) is a highly scented evergreen that is easily trained onto wires or trellis. Although the summer flowers are small, they emit a delicious fragrance.

▲ CREATING LEAFY SCREENS

When grown up a wooden or chain link fence or a trellis, climbers offer a fast-growing alternative to a hedge. These hybrid fence-covering hedges are known as "fedges," and ideal plants include ivy (*Hedera helix*) and the deciduous Virginia creeper (*Parthenocissus*). For a shady wall or fence, try the climbing hydrangea, which produces a leafy screen with flat, white flowers. The stunning pink, white, and green *Actinidia kolomikta* is a great choice for a sunny site.

The dramatic foliage of *Parthenocissus tricuspidata* creates a dense, leafy wall with beautiful fall tints.

▲ DECORATING STRUCTURES

Soften the hard lines of a pergola, arch, fence, or shed with a veil of braided stems, textured foliage, and flowers and fruits for all seasons. Wire up vertical supports for twiners, and ensure your structure will take the weight of heavy-limbed specimens. Try combining two varieties, but check plant labels for vigor to ensure one half of a climbing pair will not swamp the other. Also consider wall shrubs, such as *Pyracantha*, which makes screens of spiny stems, evergreen foliage, and masses of fall and winter berries.

The classic combination of roses and clematis makes a romantic, English-garden style feature of these iron railings.

◄ ADDING HEIGHT TO CONTAINER DISPLAYS

Climbers are not just for beds and borders. In a courtyard or on a patio, create focal points with large pots of annuals. Traditional flowering climbers, such as sweet peas, are ideal for an English-garden design, supported by a tripod of rustic canes. For a contemporary effect, choose an unusual flower shape such as Rhodochiton. Patio clematis are also worth considering, their compact growth festooned with summer flowers.

An eye-catching container wigwam of scrambling sweet peas (*Lathyrus odoratus*) provides a floral focal point in a border.

◄ CLIMBING THROUGH TREES AND SHRUBS

Deciduous trees provide the perfect hosts for large scrambling climbers like roses and early-flowering clematis. These vigorous plants will need a little support from bamboo canes at first, but once latched onto the tree branches, they will soon find their way up through the canopy. Choose pairings of trees and climbers carefully to give a long season of interest with flowering seasons in quick succession. For summer and fall color, add a late-flowering species, such as the flame creeper (*Tropaeolum speciosum*). Adorn shrubs with more compact climbers; try a scrambling annual like the cup and saucer vine (*Cobaea scandens*), or in a tropical-style garden, choose sizzling orange *Eccremocarpus* flowers.

Pair a pale pink climbing rose with a deciduous tree to support an abundance of beautiful flowers, creating atmosphere and a fragrant seating area in a secluded corner of the garden.

SELECTING AND PLANTING CLIMBERS AND WALL SHRUBS

There are many beautiful climbers and wall shrubs available and plants for both sun and shade, but whatever you choose, make sure you know how yours climb, and provide them with appropriate supports.

Climbers have developed a range of methods by which they scramble up vertical surfaces, and understanding the one your chosen plant uses will help you provide the right support for it. Twining climbers, such as clematis and honeysuckle, need trellis, wires, or a large shrub or tree to cling to, while some vigorous climbers, including wisteria, become very heavy over time, so make sure the supporting structure will hold their eventual weight.

A self-clinging plant, such as ivy or Virginia creeper (*Parthenocissus*), will climb over a house wall without your help, but once established, these plants need to be cut back regularly and may damage gutters and downspouts.

Look for plants with lots of healthy stems, and remember to remove plastic or metal ties fixing them to their canes before planting.

CLIMBING TYPES

Climbers have a variety of methods to cling to their hosts, from sticky pads to twining stems and tendrils. Read the labels on plants when you buy, or examine stems and shoots to decide what support they need. Even the self-clinging types will require some canes at first to guide the stems to their supports.

Aerial roots Self-clinging climbers, such as ivy and climbing hydrangea, use aerial roots to attach to surfaces. Ivies will scramble over anything in their path, from trees and shrubs to walls, fences, and posts.

Adhesive pads Some self-clinging climbers, including Virginia creeper and Boston ivy, produce adhesive pads that stick the plants to their supports. They will need no other help from you after they have attached themselves.

Hooks and thorns Plants such as roses use hooks and thorns to latch onto taller plants. They will grow well through a host plant but will need to be tied to trellis or wires against a wall or on a structure like a pergola.

Twining stems or tendrils Popular climbers, such as passion flowers and honeysuckle, thread their way through a host plant using twining stems or tendrils. Cover a structure, such as a fence or arch, with mesh or wires for them to cling to.

COVERING WALLS AND SCREENS

To cover walls and fences, roses and twining climbers like clematis will usually need additional wire or trellis supports. If using trellis, attach two wooden slats to the vertical surface, and screw the trellis onto them. This creates an air space behind the trellis, which allows climbers to get a better grip.

When attaching horizontal wires, drill parallel sets of holes at 18 in (45 cm) intervals up the wall or fence posts, and insert anchors into the holes (these are not required in wooden posts). Screw in vine eyes, and attach durable garden wire. Tighten the vine eyes to pull the wires taut. To encourage your climber to cover the surface evenly, spread the stems out, and attach them to the wires or trellis with soft twine. Rose stems flower more profusely when trained horizontally, so train as many as you can along the wires.

Decorate a rustic wall with clematis, supported by wires and vine eyes that will be hidden from view.

GARDEN WISDOM

Wiring up posts

The posts of a pergola or arch are easy to wire up. Simply twist in four screw eyes on each side of the post at the top, and repeat at the bottom. Affix plastic-covered wires between them, and twist the eyes until the wires are taut. Alternatively, give climbers more support by wrapping wire or plastic netting around the posts and securing it with metal pins.

Quick and easy supports.

PLANTING A CLIMBER

Affix wire supports or trellis panels in place before you plant your climber against a wall or fence. Then dig up and enrich the soil with organic matter, such as well-rotted compost or manure. Avoid planting your climber too close to the wall or fence because the soil there is likely to be very dry. Most hardy climbers are best planted in the fall; plant more tender types, such as potato vines (*Solanum*), in the spring.

1 Dig a planting hole about 18 in (45 cm) from a fence (or a little closer to a post), making it twice as wide and slightly deeper than the plant pot. Place the pot in the hole to check the planting depth.

2 Place bamboo canes in the hole, and arrange them in a fan shape. Attach the canes to the horizontal wires on the fence to provide a temporary support for the climber until it reaches the wires.

3 Water the plant, then remove it from its pot. Place it in the hole, and lean it toward the fence; ensure the root ball is not above the soil surface. Add fertilizer to the excavated soil.

4 Fill in around the roots with soil, firming it down with your fingers. Make a saucer-shaped depression with the surrounding soil around the base of the climber to create a water reservoir.

5 Tie the stems loosely to the canes with twine. Water the plant—the reservoir will guide moisture to the roots. Apply a mulch of organic matter or bark chips, leaving a space around the stems.

AFTERCARE

Climbers take a couple of seasons to fully establish and may need extra water during this time. Water every week during dry spells from early spring to fall; evergreens may need watering during the winter, too. Turn the tap halfway on, and aim your hose at the base of the plant to thoroughly soak the root area. Alternatively, attach a rose to a watering can, and empty the whole can around the plant.

Each spring, apply a mulch of organic matter, such as well-rotted manure or garden compost, leaving a gap around the climber's stems. If your soil is reasonably fertile, most plants will not require additional feeding once established. If growth is slow or your climber is lacking vigor, apply an all-purpose granular fertilizer in spring. Tie in young stems throughout the growing season to ensure supports are covered evenly. For pruning advice, see pages 316–317.

BEAUTIFUL BERRIES

The flowers of climbing plants are eye-catching, but those with berries should not be underestimated for late-season ornamental value and a long season of interest. Good choices include the glossy violet, red, pink, or white berries of *Billardiera longiflora,* which make an unusual garden feature, or the red, beadlike rose hips that stud the stems of rambling roses, such as

Billardiera longiflora Dainty greenish-yellow flowers are followed by the colorful fruits that adorn this pretty evergreen in fall. It requires a sheltered, sunny location to survive the winter; cover it with fabric during cold spells.

Rosa 'Seagull' and *R.* 'Albertine', adding to their appeal after the flowers have faded.

Alternatively, choose *Ampelopsis brevipedunculata,* whose white berries shine like pearls before maturing to a rich purple-blue, or the bright orange, red, or golden berries of wall shrubs such as *Pyracantha*, which will bring a splash of color to a gloomy corner.

Rose hips Many roses produce pretty hips, but if you deadhead the flowers you'll remove the fruits, too. Leave a few stems of ramblers unpruned after flowering, and don't deadhead repeat-flowering climbers after midsummer.

WALL SHRUBS FOR YEAR-ROUND INTEREST

Woody plants that can be trained on a wall or fence but have no ability to climb are known as wall shrubs. There are beauties for all seasons, with the blue-flowered *Ceanothus*, such as *C.* 'Concha' (*top left*), which bears abundant clusters of blooms, and the flowering quince, *Chaenomeles*, leading the way in spring.

In the summer the golden-yellow blooms of *Fremontodendron* 'California Glory' (flannel bush, top right) will brighten up a sunny wall. Alternatively, try the dainty bell-like, pendent flowers of the evergreen *Abutilon megapotamicum* (*bottom left*), or tender *Carpenteria californica* (tree anemone), with its fragrant, cup-shaped flowers.

Fall color comes in spades from the profuse berries of pyracanthas and cotoneasters, while winter is the time when the silky tassels of *Garrya elliptica* (*bottom right*) appear. The variegated evergreen foliage of *Euonymus fortunei* cultivars, such as *E. f.* 'Emerald 'n' Gold' and 'Silver Queen' are also useful in the winter, adding interest to a shady wall.

Ceanothus 'Concha'

Fremontodendron 'California Glory'

Abutilon megapotamicum

Garrya elliptica

CLIMBER GROUPINGS

QUICK-COVER SCREEN

Annual climbers, such as morning glory (*Ipomoea*) and black-eyed Susan (*Thunbergia*), quickly climb over a wire trellis to create a temporary screen or backdrop to a raised bed or container. Both need free-draining soil and a sunny site to encourage the flowers to bloom.

1 Plant *Ipomoea* and *Thunbergia* seeds in pots indoors in early spring. When the frost has passed, fill a raised bed or large container with commercial potting mix. Affix a trellis to the back of the display.

2 After the frost, plant two seedlings of each plant at the base of the trellis, and daylilies that match the colors of the climbers on either side. Firm in the soil with your fingers.

3 Water in the plants, and keep the bed or container well watered throughout the summer. The climbers will not need to be tied to the trellis, but ensure the stems cover it by spreading them out evenly.

YOU WILL NEED

1 *Ipomoea* 'Heavenly Blue'
2 *Thunbergia alata*
3 *Hemerocallis* (daylily)

CLASSIC COMBINATION

The dainty, small-flowered rambling rose hybrid *R.* 'Minnehaha' makes an ideal partner for *Clematis* 'Comtesse de Bouchaud'. Just as the scented rose begins to fade, the clematis bursts into bloom and keeps the show going until early fall with its pastel pink flowers. Both the rose and clematis will need a sturdy trellis, wired wall or fence, or a tree for support. Underplant them with contrasting blue perennials, such as the hip-high *Campanula lactiflora*; its bell-like blooms persist throughout summer and will cover any leggy stems at the base of the climbers. All plants will be happy in full sun or partial shade and moist but well-drained soil.

1 These climbers like fertile soil, so dig plenty of organic matter into the bed before you start planting, and add some fertilizer.

2 Plant the clematis and rose as shown on page 145, about 24 in (60 cm) apart. Firm in the soil well around the stems, and water in the plants.

3 Plant the campanulas about 18 in (45 cm) in front of the climbers. Keep the bed well watered for the first two growing seasons.

YOU WILL NEED

1 *Clematis* 'Comtesse de Bouchaud'
2 *Campanula lactiflora*
3 *Rosa* 'Minnehaha'

Clematis × durandii

CLIMBING CLEMATIS

The flexible, flowering stems of clematis provide many ways to create exciting effects in the garden, and with a vast range of colors, shapes, and forms to choose from, it's no wonder they're so popular. From tree huggers to container varieties, there's a clematis for every garden size and flowers for almost every month of the year.

Clematis comprise a large group of climbers and include a range of different flower types and growth habits. The larger species, such as *Clematis montana* and *C. tangutica*, need little support when allowed to scramble through host trees and shrubs. The large- and late-flowering hybrids are not as vigorous and, like all clematis, need wires or trellis to climb vertical structures. Late-flowering viticella types are similar in habit to the large species and ideal for weaving through host plants.

Clematis offer a rich source of exciting features for year-round displays, with patio hybrids; large-flowered early summer performers; the subtle, bell-like blooms of late-flowering species; and the sweet aroma of winter- and

TYPES OF CLEMATIS

Early-flowering species These include the tall, often scented, open-flowered montanas, ideal for growing through trees, and the smaller, early-flowering alpina and macropetala species.

Large-flowered hybrids The large, showy blooms of the early-summer-flowering hybrids make up a large and varied group with a broad color palette. Many hybrids also sport stripes and color blends.

Late-flowering hybrids These include *C. jackmanii* and its many relatives, and the flowers tend to be smaller than the earlier-flowering hybrids. The color ranges mirror those of the large-flowered types.

Double-flowered hybrids Much sought after, double-flowered clematis are prized for the ruffles of petals that surround the central anthers, giving the flowers a fuller, more rounded appearance.

early spring-flowering forms. And for the brief moment in midwinter when clematis are not in bloom, *C. tangutica* brightens gloomy days with its lantern-shaped seed heads.

Some clematis types, , such as *C. montana* and its cultivars, can reach up to 30 ft (10 m), and when planted with a host tree that flowers just before its late spring blooms appear, the pair provide many weeks of color. The late-flowering

viticella types also make good partners for trees and shrubs, or allow them to scramble through herbaceous plants in a border.

To cover a wall, fence, or screen, train a large clematis along wires. A good choice for late-season color is *C.* 'Bill McKenzie', which forms a tangle of leafy stems and bright yellow nodding flowers followed by decorative seed heads. The myriad clematis hybrids afford eye-catching displays for pergolas, arches, and posts, and all combine well with climbing roses, jasmine, and annual morning glory (*Ipomoea*).

Plant clematis in moist but well-drained, fertile soil; they thrive in full sun or partial shade. Keep the roots cool by shading them with other plants or placing a layer of pebbles or flat stones at the base. To prevent the fungal disease clematis wilt, plant in deep, fertile soil, and ensure the plant's roots don't dry out.

◄ **Send a clematis** such as *C.* 'Perle d'Azur' scrambling over a wall for an informal mass of colorful blooms in the late summer.

PRUNING CLEMATIS

There are three methods of pruning clematis: most plant labels will tell you which group your plant belongs to, and when it is best to prune.

Group 1
Shear over vigorous winter- and spring-flowering clematis after flowering to keep them tidy. Renovate old, congested plants by cutting them back almost to ground level after flowering.

Group 2
Early summer-flowering clematis, including the large-flowered hybrids, require light pruning. Remove dead and diseased growth, and cut back remaining stems to a pair of healthy buds.

Group 3
Clematis that flower after midsummer should be cut back hard in winter or early spring. Prune the stems to a pair of strong buds 6–12 in (15–30 cm) above the ground. New stems will soon appear.

Patio clematis As well as some compact hybrids, such as *C.* 'Bees' Jubilee' (*above*), the clematis in Raymond Evison's Boulevard collection have been bred specifically for containers.

Evergreen species *C. armandii* (*above*) and *C. cirrhosa* are popular for their evergreen foliage and their profusion of late winter and early spring flowers. Those of *C. armandii* are sweetly scented.

Small-flowered species This group includes the late-flowering viticella clematis, the yellow-red *C. koreana* (*above*), yellow *C. tangutica*, and *C. flammula* with its clouds of tiny star-shaped blooms.

BAMBOO AND GRASS EFFECTS

From wispy fountains of rustling leaves to stands of colorful poles topped with feathery foliage, grasses and bamboos lend stature and drama to any planting design.

▶ INJECTING COLOR AND FORM

Planting flowers isn't the only way to ensure a broad spectrum of color in your garden: bamboo varieties are available with beautiful purple, ice-blue, gold, or black stems. Some, like the blue-stemmed *Borinda papyrifera* and *Phyllostachys*, measure up to 15 ft (5 m) in height and provide a fantastic way to add color and drama to your outdoor space if you have the room to make the most of them.

Grasses can also add a splash of color, and unusual cultivars make great focus plants. Look for varieties with striking yellow stripes or spectacular scarlet tips, such as *Miscanthus sinensis* 'Zebrinus' or the scarlet-tipped *Imperata cylindrica* 'Rubra'.

In this gravel garden, clumps of black and yellow-stemmed bamboos (*Phyllostachys nigra* and *P. aureosulcata* f. *aureocaulis*) lend height and color to a foliage design.

▲ PROVIDING TEXTURAL CONTAINER DISPLAYS

Grasses make exceptional container specimens, either planted on their own or together with annuals and perennials in mixed displays. Add structure and interest to patio designs with a mix of tall, leafy fountains; golden flowing types; and those with long, soft flower heads, and bronze or blue-gray foliage. Bamboos also look great in containers but are very demanding, requiring plenty of water all year.

Combine evergreen *Stipa tenuissima* and *Carex comans* with deciduous *Eragrostis* for a multicolored display.

▼ CREATING SCREENS AND HEDGES

Densely planted bamboos make unusual hedges and are outstanding windbreaks. Use noninvasive types such as *Fargesia* and *Phyllostachys*, planted in the ground or grown in containers. Seek expert advice, because invasive types can be very difficult to eradicate.

Some deciduous grasses, including *Miscanthus sinensis*, can also be used for screening. Their dried stems and flowers will still provide cover in the winter but need to be cut down in the spring, when the plants offer no shelter for a few weeks before the new growth takes over.

Plant tall bamboos in large terra-cotta containers to create a flexible screen for a sheltered seating area.

◄ MAKING MEADOWS

Soft grass species provide the perfect foil for bright annual meadow flowers. Alternatively, use them on their own to produce a summer hay meadow with feathery flowers and decorative seed heads. As well as looking beautiful and needing to be mowed just one or two times a year, depending on the type you choose, meadow grasses also provide the perfect habitat for insects and invertebrates. The grasses are usually available in seed form and should be planted as for a meadow (see p.340).

Sow meadow grasses beneath deciduous trees to soften their silhouettes with a sea of airy foliage.

◄ ADDING INTEREST TO MIXED DISPLAYS

Both deciduous and evergreen grasses provide a textural contrast to perennials and offer an airy foil to blocks of shrubs. Tall grasses make excellent backdrops to herbaceous plantings in sunny areas, while well-behaved bamboos that do not spread too rapidly perform a similar function—but do keep an eye on their growth. There are many beautiful grasses and sedges for the middle of beds, including those with see-through stems; low-growing *Carex* and fescues are perfect for the front of a display.

A wonderful choice for height, *Stipa gigantea* does not dominate thanks to its see-through flower heads. Add contrast at the front with the golden sedge, *Carex elata* 'Aurea'.

SELECTING AND PLANTING BAMBOOS AND GRASSES

Tough and versatile, there are grasses and bamboos for sunny or shady locations and dry or damp soils. Select them carefully to produce a year-round display of foliage, flowers, stems, and seed heads.

Grasses are a varied group and can be found on every continent on the planet; those selected for garden use have graceful styles and decorative flowers and seed heads. They range from tiny types, such as the squat fescues, to towering giants like *Arundo donax*, which reaches up to 12 ft (4 m) in height. Most grasses prefer full sun and free-draining soil, although *Holcus, Milium,* and the prairie cordgrass *Spartina* thrive in moist conditions and some shade. Most bamboos and the evergreen *Carex* family and other sedges, which closely resemble grasses, are also perfect for shady sites and damp soils.

Planting an invasive species can be a costly, irreversible mistake. A good nursery can offer invaluable advice on invasiveness before buying.

SELECTING WELL-BEHAVED BAMBOOS

Bamboos are simply grasses that form woody stems, and they tend to be more tolerant of shady conditions than their close relatives; a few, including forms of *Pleioblastus*, are even happy in deep shade. They thrive in moist but well-drained soil.

Despite their elegant appearance, some bamboos have a dark side—their invasive, spreading roots can take over a garden, transforming beautiful planting designs into dense jungles. Bamboos that fall into this group include *Indocalamus*, *Pleioblastus*, *Pseudosasa*, *Sasa*, and *Sasaella*. If you want to grow these, restrain their roots by planting them surrounded by bamboo control sheets.

Clump-forming species, such as *Fargesia, Chusquea, Thamnocalamus, Himalayacalamus, Phyllostachys,* and *Semiarundinaria* are better behaved, but will still benefit from a root barrier to keep them in check.

Phyllostachys One of the most popular tall, clump-forming bamboos. Choose from golden-, black-, or green-stemmed types; all are ideal for use as screening or as focal points.

Thamnocalamus A tall, graceful bamboo that is a beautiful garden specimen. It has small leaves and either blue, fading to deep red, or pinkish-brown stems.

Fargesia All members of the *Fargesia* family are well behaved, hardy, and tolerate dry soils. They make excellent hedges and look stunning when grown in large patio containers.

Borinda This noninvasive bamboo is closely related to *Fargesia* and *Thamnocalamus*. Its vivid blue stems and strong upright growth are a colorful focal point or screen.

WHEN AND WHERE TO PLANT

Most grasses, sedges, and bamboos are available in pots and can be planted like perennials (see *p.137*) at any time of the year, unless the soil is frozen, very dry, or waterlogged. However, it is best to plant them in the spring, allowing a full growing season for them to establish before winter. Some bamboos, especially those used for hedging, are also available as bare root plants in the winter; plant them as soon as you receive them.

Grasses suit most sunny mixed borders and gravel gardens, and they also make effective container plants. Bamboos will be happy in both sunny and partially shaded areas and are best used as focal points or backdrops to mixed planting designs or to create a screen or hedge. Most grasses and bamboos dislike waterlogged soils, so add sand to heavy clays to improve drainage, and incorporate plenty of well-rotted manure or garden compost into all types of soil a few weeks before planting.

Grasses can be planted alongside herbaceous perennials to create contrast and variety in beds.

PLANTING A BARE-ROOT BAMBOO

Available from specialty nurseries, bare root bamboos tend to be cheaper than those grown in containers, and most are available via mail order. The drawback is that you will need to plant them as soon as possible to prevent them from drying out and failing to thrive once planted. When you receive them, stand the plants in a bucket or large pot filled with soil or moss, keeping them damp until you are ready to plant. Then prepare your bed by digging it up to loosen any compacted soil, and apply some well-rotted manure or compost.

1 Dig a hole deep enough to fit the whole root ball, and use a fork to loosen the soil at the bottom. Add a layer of well-rotted manure or compost to the base.

2 Unwrap the bamboo, and place it in the hole. Check that the soil marks on the stems (culms) will be at ground level when the bamboo is planted.

3 Keep the plant upright with one hand, and carefully work the excavated soil in between the roots. Fill in the hole gradually, and water to remove any air pockets around the roots.

4 Firm the soil with your fingers, pushing it between each of the stems. Water in well, and apply a mulch of rotted manure or composted bark, keeping it clear of the stems.

AFTERCARE AND MAINTENANCE

Grasses rarely need extra irrigation once established because they have adapted to survive periods of drought. Bamboos may need watering for longer and will need a constant supply of water if grown in containers, so you may want to invest in an automatic system, such as a drip hose or drip nozzles attached to a garden hose. An automatic timer will also allow you to regulate watering times.

Apart from watering, bamboos and grasses require very little extra maintenance. In spring, comb out the dead growth from evergreen grasses and sedges with a leaf rake or kitchen fork. The dead stems of deciduous grasses have decorative value in the winter, but should be cut back in the spring.

Cut out dead bamboo stems when you see them, and mulch plants every year in the spring with rotted manure or composted bark. Leave a carpet of dead foliage beneath the plants. This contains silica, which bamboos need in order to form wood.

Automate watering to ensure that plants receive enough water to establish successfully.

Use a root barrier to prevent vigorous bamboo plants from overtaking the garden.

Controlling bamboos

Bamboos spread via underground root systems or rhizomes that travel horizontally just beneath the soil surface, throwing up new stems as they do so; some can be invasive. To prevent them from taking over, dig a narrow trench around your clump, and insert a commercial root barrier of nonperishable material, such as strong plastic, or a wall of slate slabs. Alternatively, use a sharp spade to slice through the roots around your bamboo, and dig out and remove the severed roots.

GARDEN WISDOM

Two for one
Grasses are very easy to divide, and if you buy a large clump in a pot, you can instantly make two smaller plants. Since grasses bulk up pretty quickly, this can be an economical way of filling a border. To divide your grass, dump it out of its container, and then either pull the root ball apart with your hands, or cut it with a sharp pruning saw. Plant the divided sections immediately in moist growing mix in a container or in the ground.

BEAUTIFUL SEED HEADS

Among the most alluring features of decorative grasses are their seed heads, which can grace a garden from midsummer to winter if you mix and match varieties, and are especially valuable during the winter months when there is little else to see. Choose a variety of different types, such as feathery plumes and caterpillar-like brushes.

The best grass choices for winter-interest seed heads include forms of Stipa, Pennisetum, and the reed grasses, Calamagrostis, as well the larger grasses, such as pampas grass (Cortaderia) and the many forms of Miscanthus.

Stipa calamagrostis
The feather grass is so named because in late summer it forms beautiful plumes of greenish-white flowers, shaped like giant feathers. These then dry to produce tawny seed heads that last through the winter.

Pennisetum alopecuroides
In late summer the fountain or foxtail grass bears long stems of pinkish-brown, foxtail-like flowers that dry to form decorative seed heads. It needs a sunny, sheltered site to survive the winter.

Briza Both the annual *Briza minor* and perennial quaking grass, *B. maxima*, produce spear-shaped seed heads that dance in the breeze during summer and fall. Plant in full sun and any soil—even in wet conditions.

BAMBOO AND GRASS GROUPINGS

POOL OF COLOR

Add depth and drama to a garden with differing textures and colors of grasses. The eye lingers on the bands of 'Pink Feather' pampas grass, *Calamagrostis*, *Miscanthus*, and *Pennisetum* in this display. Taller, structural background plants such as *Arundo donax* (a giant reed) and *Stipa gigantea* bring depth to the arrangement.

1 In fall, dig over the site, removing weeds and compaction. For each 3 sq ft (1 sq m), work in a bucket of rotted organic matter.

2 Buy the plants in spring, and set them out, with ripples of grasses leading the eye across to the taller background plants.

3 Add a mulch of gravel around the grasses to reflect light and suppress weeds. Water during dry spells for the first two summers.

YOU WILL NEED

1 *Stipa gigantea*
2 *Miscanthus* 'Adagio'
3 *Miscanthus* 'Ferner Osten'
4 *Cortaderia* 'Pink Feather'
5 *Calamagrostis* 'Karl Foerster'
6 *Pennisetum macrourum*
7 *Calamagrostis brachytricha*
8 *Pennisetum villosum*
9 *Pennisetum* 'Fairy Tails'

JAPANESE-STYLE DISPLAY

Graceful bamboos planted in glazed containers lend an Asian note to a patio design. Most require large pots, but you can use smaller ones if you're prepared to repot regularly. In this context you can also use more invasive types like *Pleioblastus*, since the pots contain the roots' spread. The bamboos will be happy in a partially shaded area.

1 Choose a selection of pots with drainage holes, then add a layer of good quality growing mix to each pot. Add some slow-release fertilizer granules.

2 Water the plants, and then tip them out of their containers. Plant the bamboo in the pots at the same level they were at in their original containers. Firm in the growing mix around the stems.

3 Water the pots regularly during the growing season. Each spring, remove the top layer of growing mix, and add fresh, mixed with some slow-release fertilizer granules. Repot the plants as necessary.

YOU WILL NEED

1 *Phyllostachys bambusoides* 'Holochrysa'
2 *Pleioblastus variegatus*
3 *Indocalamus tessellatus*
4 *Pleioblastus variegatus* 'Tsuboii'
5 *Fargesia murielae*

FOCUS ON GRASSES

Knit together a range of different grasses to form a spectacular textured border, or mix and match with complementary perennials for a colorful display of flower and foliage forms. The graceful leaves and delicate flowers shimmer and glow when backlit by morning or evening sun, so try to place your border to capture this effect.

Grasses range from lofty giants that stretch up over 6 ft (2 m) or more to tiny tufts that barely reach ankle height with a whole variety of sizes in between. Weave a selection of tall types in swathes through a large border using prairie-style planting, or use them to form a backdrop in a smaller space. Also integrate evergreen and deciduous grasses for year-round appeal. In the summer, the wisps of delicate flowers will appear in a range of colors and contrast with the bold shapes of the leaves. In the winter, many deciduous types lose their summer colors but retain their structure, creating interest at a time of year when there is little else on display.

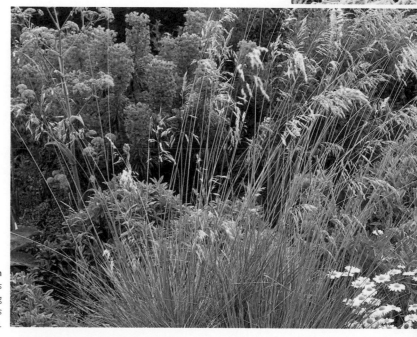

▶ **Mix blue-green** *Helictotrichon sempervirens* with plants of contrasting shapes and colors, such as *Euphorbia* and *Leucanthemum*.

Chasmanthium latifolium 'River Mist'

CHOICE OF GRASSES

Miscanthus Eulalia grasses are deciduous, upright, and drought tolerant; most are fairly large. The flower plumes are borne in the late summer.

Pennisetum Deciduous fountain or foxtail grasses have arching foliage and long, soft flowers. Most do not exceed 3 ft (1 m).

Deschampsia 'Goldtau' is a popular border cultivar with deciduous dark green leaves and cloudlike sprays of tiny, golden summer flowers.

◄ **In winter**, displays of *Phlomis russeliana*, *Hakonechloa macra* 'Aureola', and *Pennisetum* look beautiful when dusted with frost.

Panicum species with contrasting perennials, such as *Eupatorium*, Michaelmas daisies (*Symphyotrichum*), and *Verbena bonariensis*.

In smaller gardens or at the front of large borders, try a mix of *Calamagrostis brachytricha*, with its beautiful late summer, feather-like plumes, the wispy *Stipa tenuissima*, and silvery-blue *Helictotrichon*. Match these with rusty-orange achilleas, cream *Astrantia major*, and dark red *Hylotelephium* 'Herbstfreude'. Also use the flowing form of *Anemanthele lessoniana* at the edge of a border to add a sense of movement as it spills over a path or patio.

All the border grasses suit gravel gardens, which also make good seedbeds for annuals. Sprinkle the seeds of *Briza minor*, with its dainty, dangling, summer flowers, through a gravel border for a natural effect; it will self-seed thereafter, repeating the effect year after year. Other annuals to try include *Lagurus ovatus*, or bunny tails, which features furry little pom-pom blooms, and *Setaria macrostachya*, with its caterpillar-like flower heads.

Most grasses need a sunny site to thrive, so choose the brightest spot in your garden for the best display. Most species also like free-draining conditions and will withstand periods of drought once established. Ideally, plant them in the spring to allow the root systems a full season to develop before winter. Although most grasses prefer sun, *Deschampsia* will tolerate some shade and thrives in a range of soil types.

In large borders, weave together a selection of medium-sized and large grasses, such as *Miscanthus*, *Calamagrostis*, *Deschampsia*, and

PLANTING GRASSES

1 Dig a hole as deep as and a little wider than the container. Place the plant in the hole to check that the top of the root ball will be level with the soil when you plant it out.

2 Water the plant well. Remove it from its container and gently tease out the outermost roots. This encourages them to spread and develop well after planting.

3 Place the plant in the hole, and fill in around the root ball with the excavated soil, firming it with your fingers. Water it well using a can with a fine rose. Water regularly until it is established.

4 The dead growth of deciduous grasses can be left over the winter; use a leaf rake or kitchen fork to remove dead growth from evergreens in the early spring.

Anemanthele This knee-high evergreen has gauzy flowers and arching clumps of foliage with yellow and red tints from fall to spring.

Stipa Choose popular, wispy-leaved *Stipa tenuissima* or *S. gigantea* with evergreen leaves and tall stems of golden, oat-like flowers.

Calamagrostis Most feather reed grasses are good in borders. They bear deciduous upright foliage and feather-like flower heads.

Helictotrichon Evergreen blue oat grass is steely-blue and a good foil for flowering plants. Its flowers appear from late spring to summer.

Panicum Prairie-type switch grass has clusters of tiny flowers that float above clumps of wide leaves. Some types have blue-gray foliage.

USING BULBS EFFECTIVELY

From diminutive winter-flowering snowdrops to the soaring stems of vibrant dahlias in the fall, bulbs, tubers, corms, and rhizomes offer a huge choice of flowers for all seasons, while their diversity of color and style will enrich any garden.

▶ INFUSING GARDENS WITH SCENT

Many bulbs boast colorful blooms, but a number are also celebrated for their delicious fragrance. Position them at the front of borders, or grow them in pots near the house. To create a perfumed paradise, seek out beautiful scents for all seasons, starting in spring with forms of *Narcissus jonquilla*, *N. tazetta*, and *N. poeticus*, as well as hyacinths and bluebells. In the summer, select the powerfully scented oriental and longiflorum lilies, or try the Turk's cap *Lilium martagon* in shady sites. End the year with the fall-flowering *Crinum* x *powellii*.

Vibrant in scent and color, the blooms of *Lilium* Golden Splendor Group make beautiful edging for a walkway.

▲ DECORATING LAWNS

Create carpets of color and texture by planting spring bulbs beneath the grass in the fall. Plant bulbs, such as snake's head fritillaries, in a random pattern to mimic a wildflower meadow, or in a more formal garden, try planting in narrow lines to create stripes of delicate flowers. Experiment with color combinations: choose a limited range of pastel shades, or plan for an explosion of color. Leave the bulbs to die down naturally before mowing in late spring, and the plants will then multiply to give even greater displays in future years.

Soften a formal, structured design by planting lines of delicate *Anemone blanda* 'White Splendour' and 'Blue Mist'.

◄ MAKING SEASONAL DISPLAYS

Inject color into your patio displays throughout the year with a range of bulbs for different seasons. Some, such as snowdrops, will flower year after year if planted in a cool spot; team them with other woodlanders, such as small ferns and hellebores. Other diminutive, early-flowering bulbs, such as irises and species tulips, are perfect for a sink or trough as part of an alpine collection. Grow dwarf narcissi and *Muscari* in window boxes and wall pots, and combine these with heucheras, violas, and evergreen grasses for color from winter to late spring. In the summer, surround a central planting of tall dahlias or cannas, and edge with trailing plants.

For a late summer display, plant striking dahlias with the feathery fronds of *Pennisetum orientale* and arching stems of *Gaura lindheimeri*.

▲ CREATING TROPICAL EFFECTS

Tender bulbs grown for their sparkling blooms, such as dahlias, cannas, and gladioli, fit perfectly into planting designs that mirror the landscapes of the Far East or Caribbean. Plant them in late spring in free-draining soil or in containers, and combine their vibrant flowers with a foil of lush foliage. Some hardy bulbs work particularly well as part of this kind of themed display.

Create a tropical paradise using cannas with their flame-like flowers and colorful leaves. Intersperse with heleniums and rudbeckias.

◄ WELCOMING IN SPRING

Gracing beds and borders with sunny yellows, hot pinks, sizzling reds, and cool blues, spring bulbs are a great way to kick off the growing season. Some, such as snowdrops, will appear once winter comes to a close and will be followed in quick succession throughout the season by dwarf irises, crocuses, and daffodils. By the middle of spring, the garden will be ablaze with hyacinths, fritillaries, and the queens of the show, tulips. Underplant taller types with spring bedding in complementary shades.

For an eye-catching display of color, plant pots of bright pink, red, and yellow tulips, and mix and match them with violas, saxifrage, and grasses.

SELECTING AND PLANTING BULBS

Bulbs are very easy to grow; simply plant them a few months before they are due to bloom. Most prefer full sun and free-draining soil, but some will thrive in shady sites beneath deciduous trees.

This diverse group of plants offers interest almost all year, from snowdrops at the end of the winter to colchicums and nerines in the fall, with a vast array of bulbs in bloom in between. For a year-round display, start with colorful spring bulbs, such as tulips and daffodils, and mix in some alliums, which will flower on the cusp of the new season, their pom-pom blooms providing dramatic accents in beds and borders. Lilies are the stars of summer, with their large, fragrant blooms in shades from cool white to deep maroon stealing the show. From midsummer, spice up your garden with tender dahlias, gladioli, cannas, and long-flowering Peruvian lilies (*Alstroemeria*), and end the year with a display of delicate nerines, if you have a sunny, sheltered garden to suit them, or cyclamen and colchicums in colder spots.

Label bulbs planted in pots so that you can identify them before they burst into flower.

WHAT IS A BULB?

It can be confusing when you discover that the word "bulb" is often used as a blanket term for any plant that has an underground food-storage organ. As well as true bulbs, there are three other forms: corms, rhizomes, and tubers.

Each type of bulb has evolved to cope with a variety of growing conditions and allows the plants to survive when dormant and during adverse conditions, such as during prolonged periods of drought.

◄ True bulbs
Daffodils, tulips, and *Eucomis* (see left) are all true bulbs. The bulbs are made of leaves layered like an onion, covered with a protective papery skin or tunic. Lily bulbs are looser in form and lack a skin—plant them on their sides to prevent water from seeping in and rotting them.

◄ Corms
Gladiolus and crocus (see left) are typical corms. These are formed by the swollen bases of the plants' stems and are more rounded in shape than true bulbs. They produce one or two buds at the top, and tiny cormlets grow around the base.

◄ Rhizomes
The most common rhizomatous plants are bearded irises (see left), although Dutch and reticulata irises are bulbs. Rhizomes have a swollen root that grows horizontally near the soil surface and produces several buds along it, which then develop into leaves and flower stems.

◄ Tubers
Tubers fall into two categories: root tubers, such as dahlias, which are basically enlarged roots, and stem tubers, like begonias, which are swollen underground stems similar to rhizomes (see left). Tubers produce buds or eyes along their length, and each can form a new plant.

WHEN TO PLANT

Spring flowers

Plant spring-flowering bulbs, such as daffodils, tulips, grape hyacinths (*Muscari*), crocuses, and other hardy types in the fall to overwinter and then flower the following year. Most can be planted early in the season, but leave tulips until late fall to minimize the risk of the plants developing the disease tulip fire.

Summer flowers

Alliums, which flower in early summer, are best planted in the fall, but the majority of other summer bulbs should be started off in the spring. Plant tender types, such as dahlia tubers and gladioli corms, in pots indoors to be moved out later, or plant outside when the soil has warmed up and the worst frost has passed.

Fall and winter flowers

Plant nerine bulbs in a warm, sheltered, free-draining site or in a container in the fall to flower the following year. Cyclamen and colchicums are also planted in the fall. Snowdrops are an exception: plant them after they have flowered when still in leaf, known as "in the green."

PLANTING DEPTHS AND LAYERING

For bulbs to flower successfully, you need to plant them at the optimum depth. Most, including daffodils, grape hyacinths, and alliums, should be planted at about three times their own depth (*see below*).

However, there are exceptions. Tulips prefer deeper planting, at four times their own depth, while cyclamen species should be planted with the top of the tuber at or just below the soil surface.

Bulbs make beautiful container plants, and by layering two or three different types in one large pot you can either produce a sequential display or, with careful planning, one that will flower simultaneously for a big burst of color.

To create a long-lasting display, place a layer of potting mix at the bottom of a pot. Lay some tulip bulbs on it, then add more potting mix on top and set small crocus bulbs on this. Finish off by adding the final layer of potting mix. Store the pot in a sheltered spot and move into the sun in spring.

▶ **Planting depths**
Tulip bulbs should be planted at a depth of about four times their height; daffodils should be planted at three times theirs.

Daffodil   Tulip

▶ **Layering early**
and late bulbs together, such as crocus and tulips, will create a longer display.

PLANTING IN A BORDER

Choose healthy, disease-free, firm bulbs, and select a site with free-draining soil. If you have heavy clay, either dig in plenty of sand and well-rotted manure a month or so before you start, or plant your bulbs in pots. Bulbs can be planted *en masse* in a large trench or hole or naturalized in grass (*see p.162*). Mark the area where you have planted your bulbs to prevent digging them up later by mistake.

1 Dig a hole to a depth of about 3–4 times the height of your bulbs and large enough to accommodate them at the correct planting distances. Lightly fork over the bottom.

2 Apply some granular fertilizer to soil in the hole. Then set out the bulbs with the pointed growing tips facing upward. Discard any that are soft or show signs of disease.

3 Fill in the hole with soil, being careful not to damage the growing tips. Firm it down with your hands to push out any air pockets around the bulbs.

4 Cover the area with chicken wire held down with pins or rocks to prevent animals from digging the bulbs up. Remove the wire when the first shoots appear in the early spring.

AFTER FLOWERING

After spring bulbs have bloomed, remove the flower heads to prevent them from setting seed, and apply a bulb fertilizer. Allow the foliage to die down naturally before cutting it off. Many bulbs will bulk up year after year to produce large clumps, but tulips may stop flowering if they are not lifted every year after the leaves have died down. Dig them up carefully with a fork, and remove any diseased bulbs. Clean the soil from the healthy bulbs, and store them in paper bags or boxes in a cool dry place. Replant them in late fall. If large swathes of snowdrops have developed, you can lift and divide them in spring after they have flowered. For further dividing advice see pages 332–333. Lift tender bulbs, such as dahlias, begonias, and gladioli before it frosts (see p.165).

NATURALIZING BULBS

Decorate your lawn with a sprinkling of colorful bulbs. Arrange them in random groups or swathes, or opt for ordered stripes across the lawn (see p.158). You could also plant them in rings around the base of large trees or shrubs. Choose robust types, such as snowdrops, daffodils, or crocuses, which can compete successfully with the grass and spread over time, creating a colorful carpet of blooms.

Before planting in fall, remove perennial weeds, such as dandelions, and mow the grass. If you are planting bulbs over a wide area, scatter them across the lawn and plant each individually—a bulb planter will make this job easier.

Plant smaller areas by lifting a section of sod. Use a sharp spade to cut an "H" shape into the grass. Holding the

Gently push bulbs into the soil, ensuring that you plant them at the correct depth, and provide them with enough space to spread.

spade horizontally, slice under the sod, and carefully roll it back to reveal the soil. Add a small amount of fertilizer, and space the bulbs out on the soil; you may need to dig deeper to accommodate larger bulbs like daffodils. Gently replace the flaps of sod, firm down gently, and water well.

UNUSUAL VARIETIES

Create a talking point by growing a range of unusual bulbs in borders or containers for a striking mix of foliage and flower forms. Seek out specialty suppliers for the widest choice, and ensure that your site and soil are suitable; growing bulbs in containers will allow you to control the growing conditions more easily.

In spring, try the elegant maroon or cream bells of the stately bulb *Fritillaria persica* (bottom left). Unlike its diminutive cousin the snake's head fritillary (*F. meleagris*), this large plant grows up to 5 ft (1.5 m) in height, creating a dramatic statement in a border. *Triteleia hyacinthina* (top left) is smaller but equally impressive, producing umbels of starry white flowers on slim stems.

For summer color, try *Dichelostemma* (top right) with its tubular bell-like blooms in reds, pinks, and purples, and the elegant corn lily, *Ixia viridiflora* (bottom right), which produces dainty star-shaped blooms. Also add a few brightly colored *Sparaxis* hybrids, which come in an assortment of fiery shades, and in pots, beds, or borders are guaranteed to turn heads throughout the summer months.

Triteleia hyacinthina

Dichelostemma ida-maia

Fritillaria persica

Ixia viridiflora

BULB GROUPINGS

SPRING HOT SPOT

Fire up your late spring garden with a range of hot-hued tulips, including orange-red 'Ballerina' and pinkish-red 'Jimmy', mixed with sizzling euphorbias. Add a cooling note with the dainty white bell-shaped flowers of a Solomon's seal (*Polygonatum*), held on graceful, arched stems. Plant in an area that receives some sun.

1 Prepare the border in early fall by digging in well-rotted organic matter. Then plant the *Polygonatum* at the back of the border.

2 Plant the *Euphorbia* about 18–24 in (45–60 cm) in front, leaving a space for the tulips. Wait until late fall to plant the tulips.

3 Plant groups of *Tulipa* 'Ballerina' between the perennials and *T.* 'Jimmy' in front. The bulbs will then appear in mid-spring.

YOU WILL NEED

1 *Tulipa* 'Ballerina'
2 *Polygonatum* x *hybridum*
3 *Tulipa* 'Jimmy'
4 *Euphorbia griffithii* 'Fireglow'

CONTRASTING COLORS

Mixing and matching spring bulbs in a riot of bright colors makes a dazzling display beneath a blooming cherry or crab apple tree. Use flowering perennials, such as primulas and saxifrages, to complement your designs, and interplant with perennials that bloom later so that their foliage disguises the dying leaves of the bulbs. Lift the tulips after flowering, and store the bulbs in a dry area.

1 Prepare a bed in a sunny area, as for the plan above. In early fall, plant the saxifrages and primulas at the front of the border.

2 Plant the *Muscari* and hyacinth bulbs at the same time as the perennials, but leave gaps for the tulips, and mark the planting areas.

3 In late fall, plant the tulips between the markers for the hyacinths and *Muscari*. The border will be in full bloom from mid-spring.

YOU WILL NEED

1 *Tulipa* 'Ballade'
2 *Tulipa* 'Golden Apeldoorn'
3 *Hyacinthus*
4 *Muscari*
5 *Saxifraga*
6 Purple primulas

DAZZLING DAHLIAS

Prized for their bright, bold, and extraordinarily diverse blooms, dahlias are impossible to ignore. Choose from fiery oranges and reds, cool whites, and pretty pinks to boost your beds, borders, and container displays from midsummer to late fall.

Dahlia 'Hillcrest Royal'

Comprising so many different forms, dahlias offer something for everyone. Those with a penchant for large, dramatic focal plants will be drawn to the giant-flowered types that exceed 10 in (25 cm) in diameter. For more relaxed or informal designs, opt for the small or medium-sized blooms, and if you are planting pots, try the miniatures, which measure just 4 in (10 cm). In addition dahlias are divided into ten main groups that reflect the size, shape, and structure of their flower heads (*see below*).

Most dahlias bloom from midsummer to the first frost, providing a long season of color and texture. There are tall types in each of the flower categories that make excellent back-of-the-border plants, with some reaching up to 5 ft (1.5 m) in height. By

TYPES OF DAHLIAS

Single The flowers are usually open with a single set of petals surrounding a central disk. They are usually less than 4 in (10 cm) across.

Anemone The fully double anemone flowers have two sets of petals surrounding a dense group of shorter tubular petals in the center.

Ball These fully double flowers are ball-shaped or slightly flattened at the top and produce densely packed, almost tubular petals.

Water lily With broad, overlapping petals that resemble those of a water lily, these fully double flowers have no central disk.

Decorative These flowers are fully double with no central disk and have a domed look. The petals are often tear-shaped or oval.

positioning them among other late-flowering grasses and perennials you can also disguise the stakes that are needed to support their stems.

For pots or the front of a border, choose the compact forms. Look for the label "dwarf bedder," which describes plants that do not exceed 2 ft (60 cm) in height. The gallery dahlias, with flowers named after famous artists and art movements, such as D. 'Art Deco' and D. 'Gallery Cézanne', fall into this group. Remember, too, that many small or miniature flowers are held on tall plants, so check labels carefully before buying.

Choose a range of flower types to add interest to your planting design—try pairing tiny pom-poms with large cactus blooms for an exciting contrast. As well as their compelling flowers, many dahlias also offer colorful foliage. The dark bronze leaves of the 'Bishop' range, for example, are well worth including in borders and container displays.

Plant dahlias in a sunny spot with sufficient space to allow them to grow to their full potential. Plant the tubers in the ground a few weeks before the final frost in the late spring, or grow plants in pots indoors; harden them off by placing them outside during the day for a couple of weeks, and plant them out when the frosts have passed.

◀ **Let your prima-donnas** take center stage by setting them against a foil of cool green foliage. Dahlias' vivid blooms perform their star turn just when most summer flowers are fading.

OVERWINTERING TUBERS

By lifting your dahlia tubers, storing them carefully indoors over the winter, and planting them out again in the spring, you can enjoy their beautiful flowers in your garden year after year. Check the stored tubers regularly during the winter; if any mildew or rot has developed, cut it out with a clean, sharp knife.

1 After the first fall frosts have blackened the foliage, trim stems back to 6 in (15 cm) with pruners. Use a fork to lift the tubers, label them, and store upside down for two weeks.

2 Once the tubers have dried out, place them right side up in boxes of dry vermiculite, and keep them in a cool, dry, frost-free place over the winter.

3 In the spring, plant the tubers in pots of fresh potting mix, and grow them inside. Plant outside when the frosts are over. For tall dahlias, add a stake when planting.

Pom-pom A smaller version of the ball dahlias but with a more spherical shape, pom-poms are never more than 2 in (5 cm) in diameter.

Collarette Similar to single dahlias with broad outer petals, but distinguishable by the inner "collar" of smaller petals around a central disk.

Cactus The narrow, pointed petals of the fully double flowers are straight or curled inward, giving a spiky, spherical appearance.

Semi-cactus The spiky, pointed petals of the semi-cactus dahlia have broader bases than cactus types and curve at the tips.

Miscellaneous This broad category includes dahlias that do not fit into any of the other groups, including peony, lilliput, and orchid types.

EASYGOING ANNUALS AND BIENNIALS

They may be short-lived, but annuals and biennials make up for their brief spell in the limelight with a wealth of dazzling flowers. Some also sport colorful foliage, and most are easy to grow from seed, sown direct or indoors.

▶ CREATING FLEETING COMBINATIONS

Shrubs and perennials can leave gardens looking underplanted until they become more established, but with a sprinkling of annuals and biennials you can fill your borders with blooms without cramping the permanent plants. Hardy annuals can be sown where required for almost instant effect—although they may not grow if sown too close to shrubs—while biennials have a two-year life cycle and give color early the following year. Many annuals and biennials, including love-in-a-mist (*Nigella*) and forget-me-nots (*Myosotis*), self-seed freely; you may only need to sow once to enjoy them in your garden for many years to come.

Summer annuals, such as these chrysanthemums (*Chrysanthemum carinatum*) and pot marigolds (*Calendula officinalis*), grow fast and bulk out beautifully to fill bare ground.

▲ MAKING FOILS OF FOLIAGE

Although the flowering annuals draw the eye, foliage plants provide equally compelling displays. Multicolored coleus, with patterned leaves in rich purples, reds, yellows, and greens, are a match for any bloom, while tall *Perilla frutescens* provides the perfect backdrop to colorful flowers. Silver-leaf and trailing annuals are useful foils for container displays, or for something a little more dramatic, consider *Euphorbia marginata* with its tall stems of green and white leaves and the exotic hand-shaped foliage of *Ricinus communis*.

The leaves of coleus (*Solenostemon*) come in a huge variety of shades and patterns—try planting several together to create a riot of color in a border.

▲ GOING WILD

Meadow planting is increasingly popular, not just because it has a natural beauty, but once established they are low-maintenance—simply cut back once or twice a year (*see p.341*). The brightest and most beautiful annual flowers thrive in very poor soils, so some may require you to strip off the topsoil before sowing your seed mixes. You can also sow annual mixes to add sparkle to perennial meadow flower displays, creating a backdrop of subtle color topped off with bright poppies and corn marigolds.

This small orchard is underplanted with meadow-style annuals including poppies (*Papaver species*) and love-in-a-mist (*Nigella damascena*).

◄ PLANTING CLASSIC CONTAINERS

The long flowering season and colorful blooms of annuals make them the perfect plants for pots and baskets. In the spring, garden centers are brimming with traditional favorites, including petunias, impatiens, and geraniums in every shade under the sun. However, most of these are tender, so keep your plants under cover until early summer to avoid losses. Although it's tempting to cram your containers with lots of different flowers, their effect will be lost if they're all competing for attention. To prevent this, select one feature plant, such as a white-flowered marguerite, and team it with matching flowers and foliage plants.

Cascading lobelia with its mass of tiny blue flowers and cool white impatiens create a beautiful pastel container design with a pink fuchsia.

◄ BRIGHTENING THE GLOOM

Most annuals and biennials will not burst into bloom unless flooded with sunlight, but a select few thrive in some shade. Natural woodlanders such as foxgloves (*Digitalis*) grow best in the dappled light beneath deciduous trees, while annuals that flourish in partial shade include sweetly scented tobacco plants (*Nicotiana*), colorful impatiens, and violas with fall-, winter-, spring-, and summer-flowering forms, so you're sure to find one that will suit your conditions.

Nestling beneath a cluster of silver birches, foxgloves (*Digitalis species*) inject a splash of eye-catching color into this small woodland garden.

SELECTING AND PLANTING ANNUALS AND BIENNIALS

Most annuals and biennials are easy to grow from seed, providing an inexpensive way to fill your garden with a sea of color. If you don't have the space or time to sow seeds, choose from the wide selection of young plants.

Buying young annual plants is the quickest way to fill containers and borders with color.

You will find a huge choice of annual and biennial seeds online or via mail order from specialty suppliers. Hardy annuals, such as love-in-a-mist (*Nigella*) and pot marigolds (*Calendula*), can be sown directly outside in mid-spring; sow them where you want them to flower. Sow tender and half-hardy types in the early spring in a heated greenhouse or on a windowsill indoors. For these you will need seed trays or pots, seed starting mix, and some patience, because they must be nurtured until they are ready to go outside after the last frost (*see pp.328–329*). If you sow with care, you can be rewarded with 20–50 plants or more per packet.

Plug plants offer another economical way of purchasing annuals and biennials. These are seedlings that need to be potted into larger containers or trays when you receive them, but they cost much less than mature plants. Specialty suppliers offer a good range, although not as extensive as the choice of seeds. Finally, you can buy mature plants, which provide instant effects and are ideal if you want just a few plants to fill a summer container or to add color to a border.

Shade Plant a partially shady site with the blue flowers of *Myosotis sylvatica* 'Music'.

Sun A colorful mix of *Papaver rhoeas* will brighten up a sunny border or meadow.

PROVIDING IDEAL CONDITIONS

There is a range of annuals and biennials for almost any location, so select those that suit your site.

To encourage the best performance from your plants, you will need to provide them with sufficient light—browse through a seed catalog, and you will find that the majority of annuals listed prefer to grow in a sunny location. Colorful types, including marigolds, lobelia, petunias, and asters, will light up a sunny spot with their striking blooms. However, there are a few annuals, including busy lizzie (*Impatiens*), nasturtiums, and fibrous-rooting begonias, that are happy in partial shade, while foxgloves (*Digitalis*) and forget-me-nots (*Myosotis, see left*) are among the biennials that will thrive in partially shaded sites.

The majority of sun lovers prefer average to free-draining soil and can tolerate periods of drought. For example, cornflowers and annual poppies (*see left*) are ideal for a meadow on a large expanse of dry, sandy soil. True annual wild flowers perform best on infertile soil. If you want to grow wild flowers and if yours is too rich, you will find that grasses and weeds dominate and the flowers will not be able to compete. To remedy this, strip off the top layer of soil before sowing, since this usually contains the highest levels of nutrients.

Plants from tropical areas that are grown as annuals for bedding, such as coleus (*Solenostemon*) and heliotrope, as well as woodlanders such as foxgloves, prefer moist soil conditions. Also, annual bedding plants that are used for summer container displays, such as petunias, asters, and marigolds, will perform best when they are grown in moist potting mix.

EASY SEEDS

Growing annuals and biennials from seed is not difficult as long as you can provide the right conditions at the crucial stages of their growth—check individual seed packets for site and soil advice. However, if you are new to sowing seeds and want to guarantee success, put the following at the top of your list: hardy nasturtiums, pot marigolds, love-in-a-mist, California poppies, English marigolds, *Iberis*, and *Cerinthe major*. These are among the most dependable hardy plants. Sow outdoors where they can flower in free-draining soil and a sunny site to promote a good display of blooms.

Sow the following tender seeds indoors in the early spring for a sparkling collection of summer flowers: annual dahlias, cosmos, petunias (select the upright plants as the trailing forms are less reliable), *Bidens, Tagetes*, and zinnias.

SELF-SEEDING PLANTS

Annuals and biennials that self-seed either true to type or with minor variations:

Agrostemma (Corn cockle)
Calendula officinalis (Pot marigold)
Centaurea cyanus (Cornflower)
Clarkia amoena (Satin flower)
Collinsia bicolor (Chinese houses)
Digitalis purpurea (Foxglove)
Eschscholzia californica
  (California poppy)
Hesperis matronalis
  (Dame's violet, sweet rocket)
Lunaria annua (Honesty)
Malcolmia
Myosotis (Forget-me-not)
Oenothera biennis (Evening primrose)
Papaver (Poppy)
Silene armeria (Campion)
Tropaeolum majus (Nasturtium)
Verbascum (Mullein)

SOWING BIENNIALS

Spring-flowering hardy biennials, such as wallflowers (*Erysimum cheiri*), should be sown between spring and early summer in the year before they bloom. They grow best in a sunny site and free-draining soil, so dig plenty of organic matter, such as well-rotted manure or compost, into heavy clay soils in the fall before sowing.

1 Remove any weeds and stones from the soil before sowing, and rake it to ensure an even surface. Sow seed thinly and evenly, and then water using a watering can with a fine rose.

2 When seedlings reach 2 in (5 cm) tall and have a few leaves, lift them carefully with a fork. Retain plenty of soil around the roots. Water the soil around the plants thoroughly an hour before lifting.

3 Replant 6–8 in (15–20 cm) apart, firming them in with your fingers. Keep them well watered in summer. If they are not in their final position, you can lift and replant them again in the fall.

4 Plant them in sunny borders with tulips and other spring bulbs or in a container. Many biennials do not like excessive winter rain, so protect them with a cloche during wet periods.

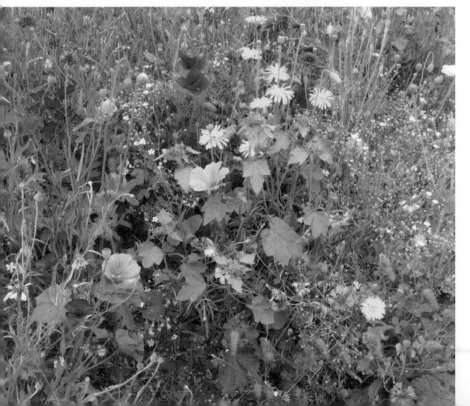

Sow meadow mixes in poor soils and in full sun for a dazzling flower display.

PLANT CARE

Watering young seedlings is vital if you want them to grow into mature, healthy plants, but once they are established, many require little extra irrigation except during long periods of drought. The exceptions are those grown in containers, which will need watering daily during hot spells and every few days at other times.

Feed container-grown annuals with slow-release fertilizer granules when you plant them. This one application should provide them with sufficient nutrients for most of the season, but if displays start to flag at the end of summer, top them off with a dose of liquid fertilizer.

Remove faded blooms regularly since this encourages the plants to form flowers rather than putting their energies into making seeds. Don't deadhead the flowers if you want to collect seeds to sow next year.

Zinnia 'Carousel' is attractive to beneficial insects.

FLOWERS FOR BEES AND BUTTERFLIES

Many annuals and biennials are rich in nectar and attract pollinating insects, such as bees, butterflies, hoverflies, and moths. These beneficial insects are especially useful in productive gardens, where pollinators are needed to set fruits, such as cucumbers and strawberries, and seeds like fava and runner beans.

Another good reason to stock your garden with insect-friendly plants is to maximize bee food supplies since worldwide populations of these vital insects are in serious decline as a result of the loss of their preferred flower-rich habit, and any extra help you can give them will benefit your garden, too. The best nectar-rich plants to include in your displays are spring-flowering *Iberis*, sweet alyssum (*Lobularia maritima*), and sweet williams (*Dianthus barbatus*). Cornflowers (*Centaurea cyanus*), corn cockles (*Agrostemma githago*), and other meadow flowers, the yellow and white poached-egg plant (*Limnathes douglasii*), pot and French marigolds (*Calendula* and *Tagetes*), California poppies (*Eschscholzia*), *Cerinthe major*, and *Phacelia tanacetifolia* produce blooms for insects throughout the summer.

CUT FLOWERS

Some annuals make stunning cut flowers for the home. Combine *Moluccella laevis*, with its tall spikes of unusual green flowers, with larkspur (*Consolida ajacis*), and try the annual aster *Callistephus chinensis* in late summer and fall arrangements, or *Bracteantha*, which can be used fresh or dried.

Moluccella laevis (*top left*) The bells of Ireland make the perfect foil for colorful flowers. Grow in full sun in moist, free-draining soil. Chill the seed for five days in the refrigerator, and soak before sowing.
Consolida ajacis (larkspur, *top right*) This pretty annual looks like a dwarf delphinium with spikes of blue, pink, or white flowers. Sow seed in spring, and enjoy vases of blooms all summer.
Callistephus chinensis (*bottom left*) Sow seeds of the annual or China aster indoors in early spring. Plant out after last frost in a sunny site with moist, free-draining soil. Buy long-stemmed varieties for indoor displays.
Xerochrysum bracteatum (*bottom right*) The everlasting flower is so called because it will literally last for years when dried. Sow the seed indoors in early spring, and plant out after the last frost in a sunny site and free-draining soil.

Moluccella laevis

Consolida ajacis

Callistephus chinensis

Xerochrysum bracteatum

ANNUAL GROUPINGS

CREATIVE MIX

Annuals can be used as excellent fillers for the gaps in borders between groups of perennials that have yet to become established. Here, orange French marigolds (*Tagetes*); leafy, lime-green *Ipomoea batatas;* and white cosmos brighten up a sunny border of Shasta daisies (*Leucanthemum*), penstemons, and dahlias.

YOU WILL NEED

1 White *Cosmos bipinnatus*
2 *Penstemon*
3 *Tagetes*
4 *Leucanthemum*
5 *Ipomoea batatas* 'Sweet Caroline Light Green'
6 Yellow dahlias

1 In early spring, sow cosmos, *Ipomoea*, and marigold seeds indoors in pots or trays. Keep the seedlings in a warm place, and water frequently.

2 When all danger of frost has passed, plant out the seedlings in a sunny border, and protect them against slug and snail attacks.

3 Water well while plants are establishing; they will cope with some drought later in summer. Apply a liquid fertilizer if the annuals start to flag.

SUMMER BRIGHTS

Sun-loving annuals and tender perennials that are grown as annuals, such as *Pelargonium* and *Osteospermum*, will thrive in the shelter of a south-facing brick wall. The wall will also absorb heat from the sun during the day and radiate it back out during the evening, emitting even more of the heat these plants enjoy. Combine bright reds with yellows for a fiery display, together with blue nemesias and the leafy *Helichrysum* to provide a contrasting foil to the hot shades.

YOU WILL NEED

1 *Begonia* 'Waterfall Encanto Orange'
2 *Nemesia* 'Golden Eye'
3 *Pelargonium* 'Horizon Deep Scarlet'
4 *Helichrysum petiolare*
5 *Osteospermum* 'Banana Symphony'

1 In late spring, buy young plants or "plugs," and grow them indoors. After the last frost, fill large pots with potting mix.

2 Leave a gap of about 4 in (10 cm) between the mix and pot rim, and add some slow-release fertilizer granules.

3 Plant pots, setting the smallest plants and cascading foliage at the front of the pots. Water the plants every other day in summer.

STRIKING SUNFLOWERS

For many, a love affair with sunflowers begins at an early age when, as children, we watch them grow from tiny seeds into towering giants. Many artists have been inspired by their graphic blooms, while the sturdy stems and cheerful, open flowers are great for cutting. In addition, the seeds offer a rich source of food for birds.

Helianthus annuus

Sunflowers have been bred to be tall plants, measuring 8–15 ft (2.4–4.6 m) in height with heavy heads held on sturdy stems punctuated with rough, heart-shaped leaves. However, smaller cultivars are also available, with many dwarf varieties growing to just 12 in (30 cm). The classic golden petals and chocolate-brown centers are not the only colors available. For a more sophisticated palette, choose from pale cream, dusky pink, or dark, smoldering maroon blooms.

To picture the conditions sunflowers enjoy, just think of sun-drenched fields of golden flowers in the south of France. Use this image as inspiration, and plant

TYPES OF SUNFLOWERS

Multi-stemmed varieties Ranging in size from towering giants to more compact types, these have a branching style and produce an abundance of slightly smaller blooms than the single-stemmed plants.

Double-flowered The cushion-style flowers are more rounded in appearance than those with single blooms. Good choices include yellow 'Teddy Bear', orange 'Golden Cheer', and red 'Double Dandy'.

Dwarf varieties Ideal for the front of a sunny border or in pots, the dwarf varieties come in an assortment of colors, like shades of yellow, cream, orange, and red. They measure up to 24 in (60 cm) in height.

Tall single stem Grow incredibly tall varieties, such as 'Giant Russian' and 'Titan', which rise up to 10 ft (3 m) and 12 ft (3.6 m) respectively. These types produce a single large flower at the top of each pole-like stem.

Bi-colored Among the most popular are those that resemble pinwheels, with rings of color radiating from the center. 'Pastiche' is a pale-colored form, while 'Florenza' sports dark red and cream blooms.

Cream-flowered For an elegant border, select a pale cream type. 'Vanilla Ice' and 'Italian White' are both tall varieties, while 'Buttercream' has yellow-tinted flowers and will only reach about 3 ft (1 m) in height.

Dark-flowered Strikingly different, these are popular for their rich red, maroon, or brown flowers. Choose 'Earthwalker' for its terra-cotta and brown blooms, russet-colored 'Ruby Sunset', or dark maroon 'Black Magic'.

bold swathes of blooms. Group them with other late-flowering sun lovers, such as *Echinops, Kniphofia, Veronicastrum virginicum*, hardy salvias, and ornamental grasses, including species of *Stipa, Miscanthus*, and *Panicum*.

In smaller gardens, opt for the dwarf or medium-sized varieties. Sunflowers with small blooms look best in borders, where giant-flowered types can look overbearing. Use yard-high sunflowers in colors to match your palette at the back of a sunny informal or wildlife design, or line up compact types to edge formal beds or fill a parterre. Sunflowers make good container specimens, too. Dwarf types are the obvious choice, but taller plants can be equally effective in large pots. Try them with an edging of annual millet (*Pennisetum glaucum* 'Purple Baron') and ferny *Lotus maculatus* for a contrast in form and texture.

Sunflowers are best sown from seed in pots in the early spring (*see right*), but they can also be sown directly in the ground in mid-spring in a sunny, sheltered spot. Guard against slugs, and bird-proof your seedbed with netting until plants are about 4 in (10 cm) tall. Stake sunflowers in windy sites, tying them in regularly as they grow.

PLANTING SUNFLOWERS

1 Fill small pots with seed starting mix, and make a hole in the center with your finger. Place one seed in each hole, and then cover. Ensure pots have drainage holes, or use biodegradable types.

2 Water with a can fitted with a fine rose to protect the delicate seedlings from damage. Keep the seed pots in a warm, frost-free place during germination.

3 Plant out seedlings once they reach about 6 in (15 cm) tall, when the danger of frost has passed. Support taller varieties with canes, especially in exposed sites.

4 Dwarf sunflowers are ideal for patio containers; taller varieties are best planted direct in sunny borders. Keep plants well watered until they are fully established. Mature plants will cope with some drought.

◄ **Brighten up your border** with a bold-colored mix of medium-sized sunflowers, *Salvia*, lilies, and *Tropaeolum*. Use whites and complementary blues as a foil to the bright flowers.

WATER GARDENING

Water enhances a garden with graphic reflections, sparkles of light, and a whole range of diverse plants that thrive in and around ponds and pools. Combine colorful deciduous plants with a few evergreens for year-round interest.

▶ DRESSING UP FORMAL FEATURES

Formal water features require restraint. Choose just one or two plants to add interest to a raised pool, rather than cramming in a whole range of different types. Match the flat pads and elegant flowers of water lilies with the dramatic vertical leaves of horsetails or miniature reeds to create a sophisticated design. Alternatively, use a basket of beautiful spear-shaped foliage, such as *Pontederia cordata* to create a focal point in an otherwise clear pool.

To keep the water in your formal feature clean and free of algae, try adding a black dye, which that will inhibit the growth of weeds and accentuate plant reflections; some shade from the leaves of water lilies will help, too (see *pp.180–181*).

The sleek, geometric lines of this raised pond provide the perfect backdrop for the architectural reed foliage. Lily pads decorate the water's surface with elegant patterns.

▲ MAKING A HOME FOR FISH

Fish help bring a pond to life, but many feed on aquatic plants, so choose tough greenery that will regenerate after being nibbled. Good choices include grassy, clump-forming *Acorus calamus*, marsh marigolds (*Caltha*), and pickerel weed (*Pontederia*), which will also provide cover from herons and other predators. Position plants carefully in aquatic baskets topped with well-washed pea gravel.

The floating foliage of water lilies (*Nymphaea*) provides fish with much-needed shade and protection.

▲ PLANTING BEAUTIFUL BOGS

Bog and moisture-loving plants include a compelling range with brightly colored flowers and dramatic foliage. A natural pond will be edged with the damp soil these plants require, but if your conditions are too dry, make a bog garden by digging out an area and lining it with perforated plastic to help retain moisture (*see p.342*). In the spring, edge your pond with a range of flowering plants, such as primulas teamed with a carpet of low-growing bugle (*Ajuga reptans* 'Multicolor'). If space allows, spectacular displays can be created by mixing the massive leaves of a *Gunnera* with vivid red or pink *Astilbe* and purple-leaf *Filipendula rubra*.

Create a kaleidoscope of color around a pond with the bright red flower spikes of *Astilbe*, variegated hostas, and spiky irises.

◄ INTRODUCING SMALL DESIGNS

You don't have to deny yourself a water feature if you have just a small patio or balcony garden. A watertight glazed container filled with a dwarf water lily or an arum lily (*Zantedeschia aethiopica*) will add a touch of class to a modern garden design, or opt for a more informal barrel pool, easily constructed from an old barrel lined with plastic. Plant it with a selection of compact aquatics, such as ragged robin (*Lychnis flos-cuculi*) and marsh marigolds (*Caltha palustris*), opting for a good mix of foliage and flowers, being careful not to overwhelm the feature.

Add a new dimension to a small garden with a pool planted with iris (*Iris laevigata*) and water forget-me-nots (*Myosotis scorpioides*).

◄ CREATING A WILDLIFE HAVEN

Any amount of water will attract wildlife, including insects, frogs and toads, birds, and small mammals. To create the most attractive and safe environment, ensure that one side of your pool slopes down into the water so that creatures can get in and out easily, or use containers in and around a raised feature to act as stepping stones. Protect aquatic creatures from predators with marginals for cover, and create a refuge for land animals by edging at least half the pond with bog plants. Although native aquatics will give your pond a natural look, some, like *Iris pseudacorus* and the cattail *Typha latifolia*, are very invasive. Instead, look out for better-behaved compact varieties, and add oxygenating plants to keep the water clear.

Plant a wide variety of marginals and bog plants, such as these irises, to provide shelter and nesting places for creatures living in and around your pond.

SELECTING AND PLANTING WATER PLANTS

Caring for aquatic plants is not difficult, and after planting many take care of themselves, although in small ponds, vigorous types may need dividing occasionally, and you will have to remove pond weeds.

Before planting a pond, check that your favorite plants suit its size and location. Site ponds and water features away from overhanging trees since these may cast too much shade for your plants to thrive. The fallen leaves in the fall also produce harmful toxins as they decompose in the water. Ideal plants for small ponds include marsh marigolds (*Caltha palustris*), *Sagittaria*, Butomus, the corkscrew rush *Juncus effusus* f. *spiralis*, and dwarf water lilies, as well as the oxygenating plant hornwort. Larger, deeper ponds provide the conditions needed to support a greater range of plants, including many water lilies.

Choose plants for boggy, marginal areas, as well as aquatics, to create a smooth transition from pond to land.

WHAT PLANT WHERE

There are four main types of water-dwelling plants. To enjoy the benefits of all of them, make shallow ledges in the pond for marginals, which live at the water's edge, and create an area of moist ground around the sides to accommodate bog plants. Ensure a depth of about 20 in (50 cm) or more for aquatic plants, whose leaves float on the water's surface, and include oxygenating plants, which either behave like aquatics or float in the water.

Bog plants These thrive in a moist or wet soil. There is a wide range available, which includes some of the most colorful waterside plants, such as several irises, primulas, *Lythrum*, and *Lysimachia*.

Marginal plants Growing in a few inches of water, these plants soften the line between water and land. Some have colorful flowers (*Mimulus*), and many have dramatic foliage (*Sagittaria*).

Aquatic plants These deep-water plants root on the bottom of ponds. There are relatively few plants in this group, but it includes water lilies, which require a minimum water depth of 20 in (50 cm).

GARDEN WISDOM

Pond depths explained
Plant labels state a preferred water depth, indicating where the plant needs to be set in your pond. The figure refers to the distance between the top of the root ball and the water surface. Place marginal plants that need to be at water level with the top of the plant basket level with the pond surface.

Oxygenators Essential plants in a pond, oxygenators provide oxygen and absorb nutrients otherwise used by algae. Some, like *Ranunculus aquatilis*, flower above the water surface.

marginal plant depth

aquatic plant depth

KEEPING WATER CLEAR

Weeds can ruin the appearance of a pond and compete with valuable ornamentals for light and nutrients. Help keep them in check by including oxygenating plants in your plan; these starve weeds of the nutrients they need to thrive. Check before buying to avoid introducing invasive oxygenators, since these can cause environmental problems by clogging up natural waterways if they escape from domestic ponds (*see list, right*). Avoid algae problems by not stocking too many fish and by proper maintenance.

If you have a contemporary pool with just a few plants and an expanse of clear water, you may want to use a commercial black dye designed for water features. The dye blocks the light, minimizing the growth of submerged pond weed and algae.

OXYGENATORS

Plants to include
Ceratophyllum demersum (Hornwort)
Potamogeton crispus (Curly pondweed)
Orontium aquaticum
Cabomba caroliniana
Ranunculus aquatilis
Aponogeton distachyos

Plants to avoid
Azolla filiculoides (Fairy fern)
Crassula helmsii (New Zealand pygmy weed)
Eichhornia crassipes (Water hyacinth)
Elodea nuttallii (Nuttall's waterweed)
Hydrocotyle ranunculoides (Floating pennywort)
Lagarosiphon major (Curly waterweed)
Ludwigia spp. (Water primrose)
Myriophyllum aquaticum (Parrot's feather)

PLANTING CONTAINERS

Large containers and half barrels can make attractive diminutive pools for patios and small gardens. Plant them with aquatics and marginals in fine-meshed plastic pond baskets, which are available in an assortment of shapes and sizes. Alternatively, if your container has an uneven base or curved sides, buy a flexible aquatic bag, which will fit snugly into it.

1 Choose aquatic baskets or bags that will fit the size of your plants when they are mature. Place a layer of aquatic potting soil in the bottom of each bag or basket.

2 Insert plants, and fill around the root balls with soil, gently firming it down. If you are planting oxygenators, use a pencil to make holes in the compost, insert the stems, and firm down.

3 To prevent soil from floating out of the bag or basket and muddying the water, cover the surface with a layer of pea gravel.

4 Place your plants in the container, and stand them on bricks if they are not at the correct level when sitting on the bottom. Slowly fill the container with water.

Water lilies limit algal growth by reducing light availability, making it difficult for algae to survive.

AFTERCARE AND MAINTENANCE

Remove any dead or diseased foliage as soon as you see it to prevent it from polluting the water. In small ponds, you can deadhead water lilies and marginals to keep your displays looking neat, but this is not strictly necessary. Although you can minimize weeds, some will inevitably find their way into your pond. Remove excess duckweed with a fishing net, and wind algae around a stick to pull it out. Leave the weeds on the edge of the pond for a day or two to allow trapped animals to return to the water. Dispose of aquatic weeds on a compost heap; never down a drain or in a ditch.

Top off the water levels of ponds and small water features regularly during hot summers. Check that any submerged planting baskets have not fallen off their supporting bricks—you may also need to remove bricks from beneath baskets of water lilies as they mature and the stems grow up to the surface.

If pests, such as aphids, slugs and snails, become a problem, lure natural predators, including frogs, toads, and newts, to your pond by creating damp habitats for them under stones or logs close by, and avoid pesticides. If plants become unruly or outgrow their planting baskets, lift and divide them in the spring. See pages 344–345 for further information.

Cut away any diseased or yellowing foliage, to maintain the appearance of your pond and prevent the spread of disease.

Remove algae from the water since it can hamper the growth of other plants. Vigilant removal will eliminate the problem over time.

EYE-CATCHING BLOOMS

Some pond plants are demure and unassuming, offering a simple foliage backdrop, but specimens such as these are the beauty queens, prized for their eye-catching flowers. Water irises offer a fleeting splash of color in early summer, elegant arums add a sophisticated note to midsummer displays, while the dramatic scarlet flares of *Lobelia cardinalis* and fiery *Mimulus* appear later in the year.

Iris laevigata (top left) Japanese water irises come in shades of blue, purple, and white, and dress up ponds and water features with their elegant blooms, bulking out quickly to form large clumps, which you can divide easily to make more plants.
Mimulus (top right) The monkey flower bears an abundance of small, red flowers (*M. cardinalis*) or yellow blooms with red throats (*M. guttatus*) among a mass of light green foliage.
Zantedeschia aethiopica (bottom left) Arum lilies are among the most beautiful of all aquatic plants. The white types are the hardiest, while many rich pinks and purples are tender and need a frost-free home in the winter.
Lobelia cardinalis (bottom right) This showy marginal is hardy in USDA Zones 3 to 9. The rewards for growing it are 3 ft (1 m) spikes of brilliant red flowers from late summer to fall.

Iris laevigata

Mimulus

Zantedeschia aethiopica

Lobelia cardinalis

WATER PLANT GROUPINGS

LILY POND

An elegant formal pool makes the perfect stage setting for a water lily (*Nymphaea*) or two. Ensure your pool is deep enough for your chosen lilies, and if you want to include marginals, such as irises, raise them up to their optimal level on ledges around the sides or on bricks.

1 Plant the water lilies as shown on page 181 in fine-meshed aquatic baskets, and place them on the bottom of the pool. Then plant the irises and arum lilies.

2 Use the planting method outlined on page 177. Set the irises at a depth of 4–6 in (10–15 cm) and the root balls of arum lilies 6 in (15 cm) below the water surface.

3 Include a few oxygenating plants to keep the water clear. Plant the edges with bergenias, *Lysimachia*, and other perennials, using the method on page 137.

YOU WILL NEED

1 *Zantedeschia aethiopica*
2 *Bergenia*
3 *Nymphaea* 'Pygmaea Rubra'
4 *Nymphaea alba*
5 *Iris laevigata* 'Variegata'
6 *Iris laevigata* var. *alba*
7 *Lysimachia nummularia* 'Aurea'

STREAMSIDE PLANTING

Take advantage of the permanently moist soil beside a stream to grow some beautiful bog and moisture-loving plants, such as primulas, *Persicaria*, and ferns.

Horsetails (*Equisetum*), which can be invasive in the soil, are best restricted to planting baskets and set in the water. Disguise the baskets with rocks and pebbles.

1 If your stream is artificial and the edges are dry, create boggy conditions by digging out a trench on either side of the water.

2 Line the trench with pond liner, and use a fork to puncture it at regular intervals. Replace the soil on top, incorporating some well-rotted manure, too.

3 Plant the primulas, ferns (*Dryopteris*), and Persicaria into the moist soil. Plant the horsetails in fine meshed baskets (see p.177).

YOU WILL NEED

1 *Canna indica*
2 *Carex comans*
3 *Primula pulverulenta* Bartley hybrids
4 *Equisetum hyemale*
5 *Persicaria microcephala* 'Red Dragon'
6 *Dryopteris filix-mas*

PERFECT WATER LILIES

Few can resist the magical quality of these starry summer flowers floating on a pool of sparkling water. Whether your chosen design plan requires formal elegance or has a wild, natural look, whether you have a large lake or small barrel pool to plant, you can be sure to find a water lily to suit your purpose.

When selecting a water lily (*Nymphaea* species), first assess the size and depth of your pond or water feature. Large species lilies, such as *N. alba*, spread up to 6 ft (1.8 m) across the surface and require a minimum water depth of 3 ft (1 m), while tiny types, including *N. tetragona*, are happy in tubs or small pools.

As well as producing exquisite flowers, the majority of water lilies are tough, functional plants. Their exotic-looking blooms belie their hardy nature—most will survive the harshest winter unscathed—while the platelike leaves inhibit the growth of algae. The exceptions are the exotic blue- and purple-flowered water lilies, which are not hardy and must be given winter protection.

For the best effects in large or medium-sized pools, ensure your water lilies are not crowded by too many other plants, or they will lose their impact. Plant a single lily in a raised pool for a sophisticated look in a formal garden. In an informal or wildlife garden design, build a pond with a pebble beach effect, and plant your water lilies in the deeper water at the other end.

Create stunning containers with beautiful white water lily blooms as a focal point.

Water lilies combine well with other aquatics, including irises, *Pontederia cordata*, and the arrow-shaped foliage of *Sagittaria sagittifolia*. For a patio display, plant a dwarf water lily in a glazed container or watertight tub, and pair it with one or two well-behaved marginal plants, such

Nymphaea 'Conqueror'

TYPES OF WATER LILIES

Vigorous types Only suitable for large, deep, natural ponds, these impressive water lilies include the wild, white-flowered *N. alba*, the popular red hybrid *N.* 'Escarboucle' (*above*), and the white *N.* 'Gladstoniana' with its dinner plate–sized blooms.

Small and dwarf These diminutive water lilies, including *N.* 'Pygmaea Helvola' (*above*), are the perfect choice for small ponds and large containers. They need 18 in (45 cm) of water (less for the dwarfs), and spread up to 1–3 ft (30–90 cm).

Medium-sized This large group includes hybrids in white, yellow, pink, and red. They need a pond depth of 1–2 ft (30–60 cm), and spread about 4 ft (1.2 m) over the surface. Popular cultivars include the fragrant *N.* 'Marliacea Albida' (*above*).

◀ **Floating on the surface,** the water lily's leaves shade the water, restricting the growth of algae.

PLANTING A WATER LILY

When choosing water lilies, look for healthy plants free from algae and other weeds. Make sure you position them in a sunny site, and don't overfeed the plants.

1 Choose an aquatic plant basket with fine-meshed sides. Add a layer of aquatic potting soil. Carefully remove the water lily from its original container, and position it in the center of the basket.

2 Fill the basket with more potting soil; gently firm in. Wipe the leaves gently with a cloth to remove any duckweed or algae, and spray with water to prevent drying out.

3 You can stabilize the surface of the soil in the basket by covering it with a layer of pea gravel. First rinse the gravel in water several times to remove dust and impurities.

4 Place the basket in the pond, raising it up on bricks if the water lily's leaves do not reach the surface of your pond or container. The bricks can be removed as the stems grow.

as the miniature cattail, *Typha minima*, and the magenta blooms of *Iris versicolor* 'Kermesina'.

Water lilies object to fast-moving water, so are not suitable for streams or areas close to waterfalls or fountains. They also prefer a sunny location to flower well and may not bloom in the shade. Plant them in aquatic baskets (*see right*); when they outgrow their allotted space, divide them and repot the smaller plants. In frost-prone areas, grow tender varieties in a sunroom.

Scented Fragrant water lily blooms are available in all plant sizes, including the medium-sized rose-pink *N.* 'Rosennymphe' (*above*), the vigorous vanilla-scented *N.* 'Marliacea Carnea', and the dwarf *N. odorata* var. *minor*.

Colorful foliage Many water lilies have variegated foliage, providing interest and a decorative look when the flowers are not in bloom. The maroon-flecked, purplish-green leaves of *N.* 'James Brydon' (*above*) are a good choice.

Tender types These include exotic blue and purple varieties, as well as flowers in the usual water lily color range. Some will survive outside in the summer, but for the rest of the year they will need a minimum temperature of 50°F (10°C).

GROW YOUR OWN

Whether you have an plot in a community garden or just a small patch of growing space in your own garden, this chapter will equip you with all you need to produce delicious homegrown fruit and vegetables. You can also use vegetables like ruby chard and globe artichokes as ornamental plants in your flower beds and borders.

WHAT TO GROW

Pick up a seed catalog, and the choices are inspiring.
There are practical considerations, such as the space and
time available, but beyond that, select for taste and variety,
and enjoy growing the fruits and veggies you love to eat.

▶ QUALITY AND TASTE

Homegrown vegetables always
seem to taste better than store
bought, especially crops, such as
sweet corn, lettuce, and peas,
which deteriorate within hours of
picking. Consider heritage varieties
not sold in stores, which offer more
interesting tastes and qualities.
Grow vegetables you enjoy,
organically if you prefer, and focus
on those that are expensive to buy,
such as baby varieties, asparagus,
new potatoes, and shallots. Also
consider varieties resistant to pests
and diseases, which improves yield
and makes them easier to grow.

▶ ORGANIC CROPS

If you are concerned about using
synthetic pesticides, you may wish to
grow them organically. Some can simply
be planted early or late to avoid the
worst problems, while others are
available in varieties that have natural
pest and disease resistance. Sowing or
planting the crops in different beds each
season also helps prevent the buildup of
soil diseases. In addition, you can also
help keep your vegetable beds healthy
by growing plants that encourage their
predators (see p.356). Some have the
bonus of being ornamental, too.

◀ TIME AVAILABLE

The amount of time you have to dedicate to your garden is a crucial factor in deciding what to grow. If you only have a few hours a week, and your growing space is a distance away from home, choose crops that are largely self-sufficient once established and do not need constant feeding, watering, staking, and tying in. Equally, if you can't get there to harvest regularly, don't grow vegetables that need constant picking. If your plot is closer to home, and you have some time every day to give to tending your fruit and vegetables, you can grow more demanding crops.

▲ CONTINUOUS HARVEST

For a continuous supply all year, choose crops and varieties that mature at different rates, and sow them every three weeks or so. You can also choose varieties for storing, such as late-season apples. Maximize your space by intercropping slow-growing vegetables, such as rutabaga, with quick-maturing lettuces, for example.

▲ ROOM TO GROW

The size of your plot will determine the amount and type of crops you can grow. If space is short, don't grow something that will only produce enough for one meal. Make the most of your space with fast-growing or high-yielding varieties, choose dwarf forms for containers, and plant trailing crops, trained vertically.

WHERE TO GROW

How and where you grow your vegetables depends on your soil, site, and exposure. Large gardens and community plots can offer ideal conditions, especially with a greenhouse, but there are raised-bed options for smaller gardens, and crops that can be grown in sunny beds and borders.

TRADITIONAL BEDS

If you have enough space and good, well-drained soil, consider growing vegetables in traditional narrow beds, sited to take best advantage of your exposure. The best width is 4 ft (1.2 m), which allows you to work without stepping on and compacting the soil. For this reason, it is a good idea to build a path between the beds to walk along, ideally wide enough for a wheelbarrow. In plots without beds, lay boards to work. To make the beds more attractive, which may be important on smaller plots, add elements such as brick paving, or surround beds with herbs or step-over fruit trees.

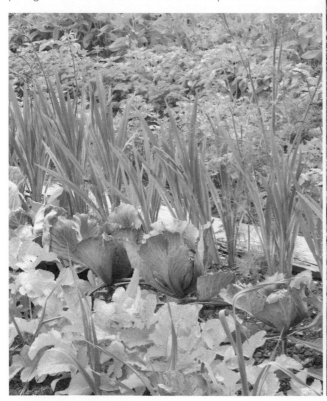

▶ RAISED BEDS

If your soil is poor, growing crops in raised beds may be the simplest solution. They are easy to build, (see *pp.98–99*), and if filled with high-quality topsoil, they can provide ideal growing conditions for a wide variety of crops and herbs. The good drainage in a raised bed helps the soil warm up more quickly in spring, giving your crops a head start, although you will need to water and feed more often. Raised beds also add interest to your garden and bring your crops up to a more comfortable working height.

◀ UNDER COVER

In cooler areas, crops like tomatoes and eggplants grow best under cover in a greenhouse or polytunnel. If you can fit one of these in, you will find it invaluable. The warmth and protection provided means a growing season from early spring until temperatures and light levels drop in late fall. You can sow early crops under cover, give seedlings a head start, and protect tender plants.

Greenhouses and tunnels should be located in full sun, away from trees and overhanging branches, but also in a position that is not too exposed. Installing power will allow you to run heaters, lights, and propagators, and having a water supply nearby is also useful.

CONTAINERS

Containers are suitable for growing a wide range of fruit and vegetables and are a useful solution in smaller plots where border space is limited or if the soil is poor or unsuitable. They also allow you to grow crops in ideal positions or close to the house for easy picking. You can use any container, provided it has drainage holes in its base: from traditional terra-cotta and glazed earthenware to all sorts of recycled materials, such as metal washtubs.

Plants grown in containers require feeding and regular watering, particularly in hot, dry weather. Where space allows, use larger pots since these retain moisture better and provide more growing space. Smaller containers are portable, allowing you to move plants as needed (to avoid full sun or shade, for instance). Most vegetables can be grown in containers, but also consider dwarf fruit trees, fruit bushes, and strawberries.

Repurposed containers make excellent plant pots, as long as they have holes in the bottom to allow excess water to drain out.

Window boxes

For those with minimal growing space, window boxes are a useful option and bring produce within easy reach. Dwarf or cascading varieties are the best to grow, including lettuce and tomatoes. Herbs are also good, especially for your kitchen windowsills. Always ensure boxes are firmly secured to prevent them from falling, especially from upper windows.

Window boxes suit colorful crops.

Growing bags

These provide a flexible way to grow vegetables and are sold prefilled with growing mix and ready to plant, or empty to fill yourself. They can be used inside or out, and for a wide range of annual crops, such as tomatoes and zucchini. Deep bags can also be used for root crops, such as potatoes. Discard or refill with fresh soil or growing mix each year.

Growing bags make patio crops easy.

Hanging baskets

Hanging baskets offer similar benefits to small containers and allow you to use walls or fences as growing spaces. Cascading and low-growing crops are the most suitable, but for the best crop, don't over-plant. Position the baskets in sunny, sheltered spots away from wind, attaching the brackets securely. In summer, water daily, and feed every week.

Hanging baskets crop at eye level.

◀ WALLS AND FENCES

To help maximize your yield, make use of walls, fences, and other upright structures in the garden, including pergolas, to grow climbing vegetables and to train fruit, such as red currants. As long as they are sited in a sheltered spot, these provide useful places to grow plants vertically without taking up valuable ground space. Walls are especially good for tender plants, like peaches.

Before planting, attach trellis or wires to walls and fences to provide support and to make it easier to train stems. Improve the soil at the base of the structure with well-rotted organic matter, especially near walls. Regularly water any plants growing under overhangs.

▲ CONVENIENT COVER

If you don't have space for a greenhouse, a cold frame or mini-greenhouse is the next best thing. These are ideal for raising seedlings and protecting plants in cold snaps. By opening them up on warm days, you can harden off plants ready for planting. Mini-greenhouses are perfect for growing tomatoes and peppers and can be folded away at the end of the season when crops are finished, or used to protect tender fruit.

▲ MIXED PLANTING

Exclusive vegetable-only beds are not necessary because you can grow many crops in flower beds and borders. Some plants, such as globe artichokes, winter kale, and Swiss chard, are ornamental in their own right. Mixed planting is an excellent way to make a small garden productive and provides interest when flowers have faded. The mix of plants also helps "hide" crops from pests and attracts beneficial and pollinating insects.

TOOLS AND EQUIPMENT

Having the right tools on hand makes growing your own produce much easier. Most are things you will use elsewhere in the garden, so are a worthwhile investment. Start with the essentials, and build up your toolbox over time.

Choosing tools

The tools you need to grow fruit and vegetables are fairly basic; even if you're new to gardening, you probably own several of them already. When buying tools, choose the best quality you can afford, and keep them in good shape so they will last for years to come. Gather them together after use, wipe them clean, and store them in a dry place.

Spades and forks These are vital for preparing the soil, digging holes, and hilling up. Spades are more use on light soils. Forks are best for heavier soils and for lifting plants.

Hand fork and trowel Both are useful for planting, harvesting, and for tending small areas of soil or containers. Use a small fork for weeding. Long-handled types are available.

Rake Use a rake to create a fine tilth when sowing and covering seed. Rakes are also handy for clearing plant debris when crops are finished. They have many general uses in the garden.

Pruners These are used to prune fruit trees and bushes and should be kept sharp. They are also used to harvest larger fruit and vegetables, such as cucumbers, without damaging stems.

Hoes These tools are invaluable for weeding between plants, tending the soil before planting, and making seed drills. Of the various types, Dutch hoes are the most versatile.

Pruning saw If you have fruit trees or shrubs, a sharp pruning saw is the best tool for pruning larger branches without causing damage. It can also be used for ornamental trees and shrubs.

Garden fabric This lightweight fabric is ideal for protecting young plants against frost or for draping over spring-flowering fruit trees. Keep it handy for when late frosts are predicted.

Netting Protect fruit and vegetable crops from insects and birds using fine- and medium-grade netting. Very fine, insect-proof mesh protects crops such as carrots and cabbages.

Cloches Use these to warm the soil in spring before planting, to protect newly planted crops, and to encourage an early harvest. There are types to suit large or small plots.

Canes and pea sticks These are needed in the fruit and vegetable garden to provide support for tall or weaker plants. Keep a range of sizes to suit different crops.

Seed and module trays These are useful when raising your own vegetable plants from seed. They tend to be fragile and short-lived but are cheap to replace.

String and raffia Use raffia to tie tender stems to supports; use string for more robust jobs. Choose natural fibers since, unlike plastic twine, these will rot down in the compost heap.

Garden totes Modern totes are made of rubber or plastic and are useful for carrying small items, such as crops, seedlings, or tools, as well as compost and garden debris.

Dibble These are useful for sowing large seeds individually, such as beans, or for transplanting young seedlings. They can also be used to plant bulbs.

Hand sprayers Keep these handy for spraying pesticides, to spray water on tomato flowers to improve pollination, or to increase humidity around indoor crops.

PREPARE A SITE

Before sowing or planting vegetables, you first need to prepare the site. When starting from scratch, this involves creating new beds or preparing new containers. Existing plots may just need a good clear up: weeding, feeding, and preparing the soil in time for spring.

STARTING FROM SCRATCH

To create a new fruit and vegetable plot, choose a sunny, sheltered spot away from frost pockets, ideally where the soil is fertile and well-drained. Mark the shape of the beds, making them no wider than 4ft (1.2m) so you can reach plants in the middle, and leaving room between them for a wheelbarrow. If building raised beds, break up the soil surface before building the sides, then fill with improved topsoil. Conventional beds also need turning over and preparing before being planted.

Make raised beds no wider than 4ft (1.2m) so that the crops can be easily tended.

PREPARING THE SOIL

Digging the soil is essential to keep it healthy. It's best done in the fall or winter to give it time to settle before planting in the spring, but don't dig the soil when it is wet or frozen. Working in rows, dig to a spade's depth, lifting and flipping the soil back on itself; at the same time, dig in well-rotted organic matter. On new beds, weed the area first, remove any large stones and debris, and fork it over to break up large clods.

Dig the soil to at least one spade's depth. Work across the bed and from one end to the other to avoid standing where you have already dug.

Improve the soil with well-rotted organic matter, such as manure or garden compost. On heavy clay soils, dig in composted bark.

Apply balanced fertilizer before planting, or use organic pelleted chicken manure. Water well if it doesn't rain within a day or so.

GETTING A HEAD START

In colder areas, the soil can be slow to warm up in the spring, which delays seed germination, slows plant growth, and can reduce harvests. To make up time or even get ahead, use covers in late winter and early spring to warm the soil and to dry the surface a little, making it easier to work. Do not cover clay soils; they don't drain and so need to dry by surface evaporation.

First dig the soil (*see below left*), and rake the surface fine and flat. Cover the bed with plastic sheeting to keep out the rain and trap heat; secure the edges by digging them into the soil. Black plastic is best for new beds; it will help kill weeds, although clear plastic traps more heat. You can use garden fabric, but since it is permeable, it is less effective than plastic.

Remove the covers after a few weeks, just prior to sowing or planting, or make cuts and plant through, leaving the cover in place to suppress summer weeds.

▶ **Cloches**
warm and dry soils (even clay soils), protect young plants, and provide invaluable extra warmth for tender crops such as melons and cucumbers.

RAISED BEDS, POTS, AND GROWING BAGS

In the fall, remove any weeds and plant debris, fork over the soil surface of existing raised beds, and incorporate well-rotted manure or compost. Unless your soil is clay, cover the bed with plastic sheeting during winter to keep down weeds and to warm the soil before planting.

In the spring, remove the covers and any lurking weeds, and lightly fork over the soil. Apply a balanced fertilizer before planting to give new crops a boost. Newly built raised beds are ready to plant as soon they are filled with soil. If you are growing crops in existing containers, use fresh growing mix, which also helps discourage pests and diseases from building up. When planting new containers, plant smaller ones under cover, harden off, and move them outside later, when the risk of frost has passed. Place large containers in sunny, sheltered spots, ensure they have plenty of drainage holes, and fill with growing mix. To prepare growing bags, fluff up the growing mix by shaking it before opening the bag, then put them in their final position, make drainage holes, and cut holes in the top for planting. Water well and allow to drain before planting.

Growing bags make ready-to-go planting places for crops such as tomatoes, greens, and peppers.

SOW YOUR OWN

Raising crops from seed is usually the only way to grow sufficient plants for a worthwhile harvest. Always check the seed packet for specific instructions, but otherwise a few golden rules apply: provide the correct temperature and soil conditions; prepare seeds if necessary (see p.329); and sow indoors or outside at the recommended time of year.

SOWING INDOORS

Although some seed can be sown directly in the ground, some crops, such as tomatoes, eggplants, and peppers, need to be sown under cover in early spring and then planted out later. Sow seed in trays, modules, or biodegradable pots, which can be planted straight into the ground once the seedling has developed. Use heated propagators, or cover pots with clear plastic bags to provide extra warmth to encourage germination.

1 Prepare the seed trays or modules by filling them with seed growing mix, leaving a gap below the rim. Break up any large lumps, and firm it down gently to remove any air pockets.

2 Water the mix lightly before sowing. If seeds are very fine or are mixed with sand, pour a small amount into the palm of your hand so that you can easily control them as you sow. Larger seeds can be sown individually.

3 Sow seed thinly on the surface of the growing mix or, if sowing in module trays, place one or two seeds in each module. Lightly cover the seeds with a thin layer of growing mix, depending on their size, and water lightly.

4 Put the tray in a warm place, and check daily to make sure the soil is moist and to see if any seeds have germinated. Move the growing seedlings into new trays when the second pair of leaves appear.

5 As they grow, seedlings will develop a stronger root system and will be easier to handle. Push them out of their seed trays or pots from below, and replant them into larger pots filled with potting mix.

6 Keep seedlings well watered. Transfer them to a greenhouse or cold frame when they are ready to harden off (see right): they should have 4–6 true leaves. Water them well before planting out, and try to retain as much potting mix as possible.

PLUG PLANTS

If you don't have the time or space to grow plants from seed, or you only want a few, buying plug plants is the solution, although it is more expensive than raising plants from seed. Plugs are available by mail order or from garden centers, but the choice of varieties can be limited. In mid-spring, select plugs with undamaged leaves and healthy root systems. If you buy via mail order, they will be sent to you at the optimal planting time. Water well, and repot or plant out immediately.

HARDENING OFF

Plants grown indoors or overwintered in heated greenhouses should be gradually acclimated to lower temperatures before they are planted outside. This process is known as "hardening off" and starts after the last frosts. Move plants into a cool greenhouse or cold frame for a month, or cover with cloches, removing the lid during the day, and increasing their exposure to outdoor temperatures.

SOWING OUTDOORS

In the spring, many vegetables, such as beets, carrots, spinach, and turnips, can be sown directly into the ground. To prepare a seed bed, turn over the bed at least two weeks before sowing, removing any weeds, and incorporate well-rotted manure or garden compost. If time permits, allow weeds to germinate, then remove them by hoeing.

1 In spring, warm the soil if necessary using cloches or plastic sheeting (see p.193). Rake the soil to a fine tilth, and use string to mark lines. If possible, water the day before sowing. Make a drill by pulling the edge of a draw hoe along the length of the string.

2 Sow seeds along the drill as thinly as possible, or for larger seeds, singly, spacing them according to the instructions on the packet. For some crops this will be their final position, but sow generously since they can be thinned later.

3 Gently cover the seeds with soil, and firm the seedbed with the back of the rake to ensure the seeds are in good contact with the soil, then very lightly and carefully rake over the surface. Water the soil carefully to avoid disturbing the seeds. Mark the position of the row with a label.

A YEAR IN THE VEGETABLE GARDEN

The vegetable garden is a busy place for many months of the year, starting with ground preparation and sowing seeds in spring, followed by crop care and harvesting through summer and into fall. Use the winter months for clearing up, digging beds, and planning for the year ahead.

SPRING

Preparation

• **In early spring**, give your greenhouse a really good cleaning. Remove any bubble plastic if the frost is over, and clean all the window panes—inside and out. Replace any cracked panes, and check that automatic vents are working. Paint any wood panels, and wash down the greenhouse floor and shelves with water and disinfectant.
• **Turn over the soil** to ensure that it has not become compacted—try to avoid stepping on it if possible.
• **Put supports in place** for climbing plants; construct wigwams from bamboo canes to support climbing beans.
• **In late spring**, prepare beds for early summer sowings.

Sowing seeds

• **Sow vegetable seed** in a greenhouse to give both hardy and tender varieties a head start. Begin with eggplants, beets, cucumbers, peppers, and tomatoes.
• **Sow hardy vegetable seed** such as fava beans, Brussels sprouts, cabbages, carrots, kale, leeks, lettuce, peas, and parsnips under cloches outdoors in early spring.
• **In mid-spring**, sow seeds such as green and runner beans, sweet corn, beets, broccoli, cabbages, carrots, cauliflower, spinach, and Swiss chard directly in the ground, and cover with cloches if frost threatens.
• **In late spring**, sow summer and winter squash seeds under cover in a greenhouse.

Planting out

• **In early spring**, plant out early seed potatoes, garlic, and onion and shallot sets.
• **In mid-spring**, plant out mid-season potatoes and globe and Jerusalem artichokes.
• **Lift and pot on seedlings** of leeks, eggplants, and early summer cabbages, and harden off those that will be planted outside. Use cloches or cold frames to protect vulnerable seedlings from frost or pests.
• **In late spring**, harden off, and plant out seedlings, such as peppers, tomatoes, celery, and Brussels sprouts.
• **Begin to transplant well-developed seedlings** of cauliflower, zucchini, and Florence fennel, and provide them with protection from cloches as necessary.
• Plant out store-bought, pre-grown herbs in late spring.

Routine care

• **Remove and dispose of weeds** as they appear.
• **Hill up potatoes** to protect them from frost.
• **Put fabric on young plants** on chilly nights.
• **Water plants regularly**, especially those in containers.
• **Top-dress plants** in containers if necessary.

Harvesting

• **Harvest cabbage**, cauliflower, kale, purple sprouting broccoli, Swiss chard, asparagus, and green onions.

Other tasks

• **Prune perennial herbs**, such as rosemary, thyme, and sage. Divide clump-forming herbs and replant if necessary.
• **Shade the greenhouse** by applying whitewash to the glass.

Sow seed under cover for a head start.

SUMMER

Sowing seeds
• **In early summer**, sow beets, carrots, zucchini, outdoor cucumbers, beans, herbs, peas, radishes, squash, rutabagas, Swiss chard, and turnips. Continue to sow successionally over the summer months, and make late-summer sowings for fall and winter harvests.

Planting out
• **Transplant all indoor-sown seedlings** to their final outside positions in early summer.

Routine care
• **Feed and water plants regularly**, particularly as the weather warms up and the plants begin to bear a crop.
• **Keep plants well weeded**, and clear beds of debris.
• **Tie in climbing plants**, and nip off their topmost shoots to encourage bushy growth.
• **Remove side shoots** from indeterminate tomatoes.
• **Hill up** potatoes and leeks.

Harvesting
• **Harvest crops** such as beets, fava beans, cabbages, cauliflower, zucchini, cucumbers, artichokes, lettuce, peas, garlic, onions, tomatoes, eggplants, sweet corn, peppers, potatoes, carrots, and Swiss chard. Harvest fruits as they appear, as this will encourage crops, such as zucchini and peppers, to produce a greater yield.

Other tasks
• **Feed, weed, and water greenhouse plants** regularly, and ventilate on hot days to prevent temperatures from rising too high. As summer goes on, shade the greenhouse by applying whitewash to the glass, and on very hot days damp down the floor by splashing water on it. Remove pests and diseases on sight, or buy biological controls.

FALL AND WINTER

Sowing seeds
• **In early fall**, sow spinach and Swiss chard under cover, and transplant spring cabbages outside. Sow hardy lettuce varieties for winter and early spring picking.
• **Plant out fall garlic,** shallots, and hardy onion sets, and sow fava beans, carrots, and peas to overwinter.
• **From midwinter onward**, sow hardy crops under cover ready for planting out in early spring, such as fava beans, early carrots and cauliflower, leeks, lettuce, onions, shallots, spring cabbages, and peas.

Harvesting
• **Harvest the last crops** of many vegetables, including beets, carrots, chiles, cucumbers, cabbages, green and runner beans, peppers, potatoes, sweet corn, tomatoes, squash, and turnips. Kale, leeks, and parsnips should also be ready for harvesting as required, but can be left to stand in the ground longer.
• **Over the winter**, continue to harvest Brussels sprouts, cabbages, kale, parsnips, and leeks.

Other tasks
• **In fall**, remove any spent plants, and give the greenhouse a good cleaning after the busy summer months before bringing in the plants that will overwinter there.
• **Tidy the garden**, removing all dead plants—if the debris is disease-free, transfer it to the compost heap.
• **Gather up any fallen leaves** to use to make leaf mold.
• **Dig well-rotted manure** into beds and borders.
• **Plan your crop rotation**, and order seeds, onion sets, seed potatoes, and bare root plants. Chit your seed potatoes.
• **If the greenhouse is not heated**, line the windows with bubble plastic to slow heat loss and take the edge off short frosts. Check plants for pests and diseases, and ensure their potting mix is slightly moist but not wet.

Hand weed vegetable beds to avoid damaging crops.

Collect fallen leaves for leaf mold.

Harvest sprouts ready for Christmas.

HEALTHY CROPS

No crops are immune to pests and diseases, and you will inevitably come across a few problems in the course of growing your own fruit and vegetables. Prevention is better than cure, and many setbacks can be avoided by good garden management and giving your plants the best care and attention.

Although almost any crop you grow will be under threat from some type of pest or disease, certain groups of crops, such as brassicas, are especially prone to specific diseases, like clubroot. Fortunately, there are alternatives to simply reaching for a bottle of pesticide: basic plant care is the place to start. Regular feeding and watering will encourage plants to become as strong and naturally robust as possible. You can also start them off under cover to give them an advantage or grow resistant varieties. Weeds can provide breeding grounds for pests and diseases as well as competition for crops, so remove them on sight. In some cases, appropriate chemical controls may be the best option; ensure that you use them safely (see p.359).

CROP ROTATION

This technique provides optimal growing conditions for your plants. The basic premise is to avoid planting the same groups of vegetables in the same place more than once every four years. This discourages the buildup of diseases that affect specific plant groups and also allows plants to benefit from the nutrients left behind in the soil by its previous occupants. Think of your crops as belonging to three distinct groups for rotation:
• potatoes and tomatoes
• brassicas, such as cabbages and broccoli
• legumes, such as peas and beans, with onions and roots, such as carrots and parsnips.

Bed one

Year one: Potato family and tomatoes

Year two: Legumes—peas, fava beans, green beans, runner beans—and also onions, carrots, beets, parsnips, and celeriac

Year three: Brassicas—Brussels sprouts, cabbage, cauliflower, kale—radishes, and turnips

Bed two

Year one: Legumes—peas, fava beans, green beans, runner beans—and also onions, carrots, beets, parsnips, and celeriac

Year two: Brassicas—Brussels sprouts, cabbage, cauliflower, kale—radishes, and turnips

Year three: Potato family and tomatoes

Bed three

Year one: Brassicas—Brussels sprouts, cabbage, cauliflower, kale—radishes, and turnips

Year two: Potato family and tomatoes

Year three: Legumes—peas, fava beans, green beans, runner beans—and also onions, carrots, beets, parsnips, and celeriac

▶ GENERAL HYGIENE

Good gardening practice is key to producing healthy plants and a high yield of good-quality produce. Plant out healthy seedlings, plants, or trees into well-prepared, disease-free soil, and tend them using clean tools. It is important to keep the growing area clear of dead or decaying plants—remove any diseased plant material as soon as you see it, and destroy it; do not place it on the compost heap since you will risk further infection. Keep plants well fed and watered so that they are better able to fight diseases.

◀ BARRIERS, TRAPS, AND CONTROLS

Attacks from various pests can be prevented if you protect fruit and vegetables. Covering plants in tents of fine, insect-proof netting or horticultural fabric provides a barrier against pests, such as carrot fly, cabbage root fly, flea beetle, aphids, butterflies, and birds. Grease bands wrapped around tree trunks stop winter moths from climbing up to lay their eggs. Traps, such as sticky wasp traps, can be used to catch and kill specific pests. Organic slug pellets help control slugs, and nematodes applied regularly in the growing season are a biological control for slugs.

▶ RESISTANT VARIETIES

Your chance of success with certain crops is greatly increased if you grow resistant varieties, bred to withstand specific problematic pests, for example, carrots bred to resist carrot fly. Another option is to choose varieties that have been awarded the All America Selection designation. These crops have good general resistance to pests and diseases, are reliable, not prone to reversion, do not require special care, and are widely available. The list is regularly reviewed and updated as new varieties become available.

◀ ORGANIC GROWING

Choosing to grow fruit and vegetables organically is a personal decision, but some gardeners find that it improves the health and vigor of their plants. They also feel better eating unsprayed crops and knowing exactly what has gone into producing them. Your plant health need not suffer if you refuse to use chemicals: allow nature to assist by reducing pests and diseases with the help of natural predators and biological controls (see pp.356–358). Using natural fertilizers, such as compost and manure, is also a part of this philosophy.

CONTINUOUS HARVEST

The key to achieving a succession of fruit and vegetables is careful planning. The aim is to produce enough food to consistently supply you throughout the seasons without being overwhelmed by excess or having nothing on hand.

INTERCROPPING

This technique maximizes your space and yield by allowing you to grow more than one crop simultaneously, using small crops in the gaps between larger crops. Plants such as sweet corn are ideal: with tall stems that cast little shade, they can be underplanted with lettuce, radishes, or onions, or grown with squashes beneath and beans climbing the stems—a planting trio dubbed the "Three Sisters" by indigenous groups across the Americas. You can also intercrop with ornamentals that attract pollinators, like the poached-egg plant, or those that divert pests, such as nasturtiums.

CATCH CROPPING

The catch cropping technique is similar to intercropping but specifically involves sowing fast-maturing crops—usually those that take about 30 days or so to mature from seed, such as radishes or salad leaves—before or after slower-growing ones, such as parsnips or leeks. This allows the quick-growing crops to take advantage of ground that will not be required until the long-term plants are further developed. Fast-growing seed can also be sown successionally in small batches every few weeks. This will provide a manageable supply so you do not end up with a glut.

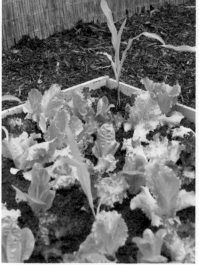

SUCCESSIONAL SOWING

Prevent gluts by sowing seed in batches, every few weeks, rather than all at once so that cropping is spread over a long period. These crops do not store well so are best used fresh.

Fast-growing crops:
Baby beets • baby carrots • baby spinach • calabrese • cauliflower • green beans • kohlrabi • lettuce • bok choy • peas • radishes • salad leaves • green onions • summer cabbages

◄ **Fast-growing crops** such as lettuce can either be grown successionally or as catch crops that precede the emergence of slower plants.

STORING VEGETABLES

If you find yourself with a larger yield than you can consume, or poor weather threatens and you need to harvest large amounts at once, there are plenty of ways to minimize waste.

Use airtight jars to store chutneys and pickled vegetables.

Surplus vegetables can be reliably stored in various different ways to keep for the leaner winter months. Many can be cooked and used to make chutneys, pickles, and preserves, which will allow you to enjoy them long after harvesting. Store some vegetables chopped or whole, either pickled in vinegar or brine, or blanched and frozen. If you have the equipment, many crops can be used to make delicious homemade wines in a matter of months, such as parsnips and rhubarb.

Alternatively, use vegetables, such as broccoli, peppers, and tomatoes, to make soups, freezing them if you don't want to eat them right away. If you lack inside storage space, large harvests of root vegetables can be easily stored outside if protected from frost.

FREEZING

This is an excellent way to store a variety of crops for up to six months, and one of the best ways to preserve their fresh flavors, if you freeze them promptly. Blanch all vegetables in boiling water before freezing to preserve color, texture, and flavor.

Herbs are particularly good for freezing—chop them finely and freeze in an ice cube tray.

Freeze extra green beans, fava beans, runner beans, and sprouting broccoli.

Sweet corn should be frozen quickly since it rapidly loses sweetness after harvesting.

PRESERVING

A traditional technique for storing vegetables is to pickle them raw in cold vinegar or cook them and use in chutneys or preserves. These techniques conserve the flavor of the vegetables, which will often improve over a couple of months.

Pickle vegetables, such as cucumbers, peppers, beets, cabbages, garlic, and shallots cold in vinegar, leaving for a month to mature.

Use a range of crops, such as beets, zucchini, and beans to make chutneys or preserves, or mixed vegetables to make relish.

CLAMPING

Choose a sheltered patch of well-drained soil that won't be needed over the winter, and cover it with an 8 in (20 cm) layer of sand. Dig up the vegetables, trim away any top growth, and make a pyramid with them on the sand. Cover with an 8 in (20 cm) layer of straw, then a 6 in (15 cm) layer of soil, leaving one section of straw exposed.

Root vegetables such as carrots, celeriac, parsnips, rutabagas, turnips, and potatoes, can be stored throughout the fall and winter.

Green beans are best if trimmed before freezing.

Beet chutney will keep well until needed.

Potatoes can be stored in clamps for months.

VEGETABLE CROP PLANNER

Use this table to check when to sow, plant, and harvest your crops.
The planting times are approximations. For local information, please
check the USDA Zone Map and your extension office.

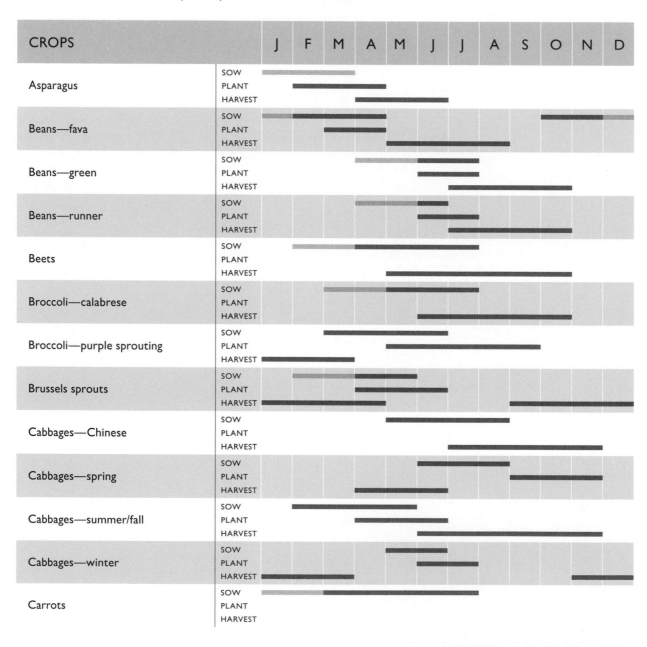

CROPS		J	F	M	A	M	J	J	A	S	O	N	D
Asparagus	SOW												
	PLANT												
	HARVEST												
Beans—fava	SOW												
	PLANT												
	HARVEST												
Beans—green	SOW												
	PLANT												
	HARVEST												
Beans—runner	SOW												
	PLANT												
	HARVEST												
Beets	SOW												
	PLANT												
	HARVEST												
Broccoli—calabrese	SOW												
	PLANT												
	HARVEST												
Broccoli—purple sprouting	SOW												
	PLANT												
	HARVEST												
Brussels sprouts	SOW												
	PLANT												
	HARVEST												
Cabbages—Chinese	SOW												
	PLANT												
	HARVEST												
Cabbages—spring	SOW												
	PLANT												
	HARVEST												
Cabbages—summer/fall	SOW												
	PLANT												
	HARVEST												
Cabbages—winter	SOW												
	PLANT												
	HARVEST												
Carrots	SOW												
	PLANT												
	HARVEST												

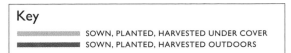

Key

	SOWN, PLANTED, HARVESTED UNDER COVER
	SOWN, PLANTED, HARVESTED OUTDOORS

CROPS		J	F	M	A	M	J	J	A	S	O	N	D
Cauliflower—summer	SOW												
	PLANT												
	HARVEST												
Cauliflower—winter	SOW												
	PLANT												
	HARVEST												
Celeriac	SOW												
	PLANT												
	HARVEST												
Celery—self-blanching	SOW												
	PLANT												
	HARVEST												
Celery—trench	SOW												
	PLANT												
	HARVEST												
Cucumbers	SOW												
	PLANT												
	HARVEST												
Cut-and-come-again greens	SOW												
	PLANT												
	HARVEST												
Eggplants	SOW												
	PLANT												
	HARVEST												
Endive	SOW												
	PLANT												
	HARVEST												
Florence fennel	SOW												
	PLANT												
	HARVEST												
Garlic	SOW												
	PLANT												
	HARVEST												
Globe artichokes	SOW												
	PLANT												
	HARVEST												
Green onions	SOW												
	PLANT												
	HARVEST												

CROPS		J	F	M	A	M	J	J	A	S	O	N	D
Jerusalem artichokes	SOW												
	PLANT	██										██
	HARVEST	██								██			
Kale	SOW				██							
	PLANT						██					
	HARVEST	██							██			
Kohlrabi	SOW		░░	██								
	PLANT					██						
	HARVEST						██					
Leeks	SOW	░░		██								
	PLANT						██					
	HARVEST	██							██			
Lettuces	SOW	░░		██								
	PLANT											
	HARVEST			██							░░	
Onions—overwintering	SOW								██			
	PLANT									██		
	HARVEST						██					
Onions—summer	SOW	░░						██				
	PLANT			██								
	HARVEST							██				
Parsnips	SOW	░░	██									
	PLANT											
	HARVEST	██								██		
Peas	SOW	░░		██						░░		
	PLANT			██								
	HARVEST					██						
Peppers—chile	SOW		░░									
	PLANT				░░							
	HARVEST						░░	██				
Peppers—sweet	SOW			░░								
	PLANT	░░				██						
	HARVEST						░░	██	░░			
Potatoes—early	SOW											
	PLANT			██								
	HARVEST					██						
Potatoes—late	SOW											
	PLANT			██								
	HARVEST									██		
Potatoes—mid-season	SOW											
	PLANT			██								
	HARVEST								██			

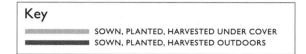

Key
- ▨ SOWN, PLANTED, HARVESTED UNDER COVER
- █ SOWN, PLANTED, HARVESTED OUTDOORS

Legend: ▨ = under cover, █ = outdoors

CROPS		J	F	M	A	M	J	J	A	S	O	N	D
Pumpkins	SOW				▨	▨	█						
	PLANT					▨	█						
	HARVEST									█	█		
Radishes—summer	SOW	▨	▨	▨	█	█	█	█					
	PLANT												
	HARVEST				█	█	█	█	█	█	█	█	
Radishes—winter	SOW							█	█				
	PLANT												
	HARVEST	█	█	█							█	█	█
Rhubarb	SOW	▨	▨	▨									
	PLANT	█	█	█							█	█	█
	HARVEST				█	█	█	█					
Rutabaga	SOW					█	█						
	PLANT												
	HARVEST	█	█	█							█	█	█
Scallions	SOW			█	█	█	█	█	█	█			
	PLANT												
	HARVEST	█	█	█	█	█	█	█	█	█	█	█	█
Shallots	SOW	▨	▨	▨	█								
	PLANT		█	█	█								
	HARVEST							█	█	█			
Spinach	SOW	▨	▨	▨	█	█	█	█	█	█			
	PLANT												
	HARVEST			█	█	█	█	█	█	█			
Squashes—summer	SOW				▨	▨	█						
	PLANT					▨	█	█					
	HARVEST							█	█	█	█		
Squashes—winter	SOW				▨	▨	█						
	PLANT					█	█						
	HARVEST									█	█		
Sweet corn	SOW				▨	▨	█						
	PLANT												
	HARVEST								█	█	█		
Swiss chard	SOW				█	█	█	█	█	█			
	PLANT				█	█	█	█					
	HARVEST	█	█	█	█	█	█	█	█	█	█	█	█
Tomatoes	SOW		▨	▨	▨								
	PLANT				▨	▨	█						
	HARVEST								█	█	█		
Turnips	SOW		▨	▨	█	█	█	█					
	PLANT												
	HARVEST						█	█	█	█	█	█	█

LETTUCE

Probably the easiest and most rewarding of crops, fast-growing lettuce can be grown in the smallest of spaces, including containers, and will provide you with fresh salads all summer and even into the winter months.

	SPRING	SUMMER	FALL	WINTER
SOW/PLANT				
HARVEST				

Crisp, fresh lettuce is a summer staple.

HOW TO GROW

Lettuce needs a bright spot, shaded from midday sun, and grows best at temperatures of 50–68°F (10–20°C). It also prefers moist, free-draining soil, improved with well-rotted organic matter. For an early-summer harvest, sow hardy types outdoors in the late winter. Tender varieties can also be sown under cover in the winter and early spring, ½ in (1 cm) deep in modules to be planted outside when the frost has passed. For summer crops, sow outdoors once temperatures rise to above 41°F (5°C). Lettuce should be thinned or planted 6–12 in (15–30 cm) apart, but this depends on the variety, so always check the packet.

Keep plants well watered, especially during dry spells to help prevent bolting, and weed them often to reduce competition. Loose-leaf varieties can be harvested leaf by leaf as soon as they are large enough; harvest traditional hearting varieties as soon as a small heart develops, cutting them cleanly through their stems with a sharp knife. To prevent disease, clear away all plant debris after picking.

TYPES AVAILABLE

Loose-leaf lettuces don't form a heart and can give a continuous supply of leaves if grown as a cut-and-come-again crop (see facing page).

Butter lettuces are some of the most popular varieties and have soft, round heads with either flat or frilly leaves.

Romaine and semi-Romaine lettuces (sometimes called cos lettuces) are upright and more oval in shape with longer, crisper leaves.

Head lettuces have round, dense heads and very crunchy leaves—this group includes iceberg lettuces.

VARIETIES TO TRY

Loose-leaf
'Catalogna' • 'Cocarde' • 'Green Salad Bowl' • 'Laurenzio' • 'Lollo Bionda' • 'Lollo Rossa' • 'New Red Fire' • 'Red Salad Bowl' • 'Rossa a Foglia Riccia da Tavolo' • 'Verde a Foglia Riccia'

Butter
'All The Year Round' • 'Buttercrunch' 'Cassandra' • 'Clarion' • 'Marvel of Four Seasons' • 'Mottistone' • 'Tom Thumb'

Romaine
'Chartwell' • 'Dazzle' • 'Freckles' • 'Frisco' 'Little Gem' • 'Little Gem Pearl' • 'Lobjoits Green Cos' • 'Nymans' • 'Pandero' • 'Parris Island' • 'Pinokkio' • 'Tintin' • 'Winter Gem'

Head
'Challenge' • 'Great Lakes' • 'Iceberg' • 'Red Iceberg' • 'Saladin' • 'Sioux' • 'Webbs Wonderful' • 'Winter Density'

CUT-AND-COME-AGAIN

Quick-maturing leaf crops are perfect for growing as a cut-and-come-again salad. Just one sowing will provide you with tasty leaves for several weeks. It's the ideal way to grow salad if you have limited space.

	SPRING	SUMMER	FALL	WINTER
SOW/PLANT				
HARVEST				

Grow fresh, handy salad in patio containers.

HOW TO GROW

As the name suggests, cut-and-come-again crops are sown, harvested young, left to grow back, then cropped again. Leafy crops are best suited to this approach, and you can buy seed mixes for different tastes and uses. Sow seeds as you would lettuces (*see facing page*) indoors in early spring in pots, or outside in pots or into well-drained,

fertile soil, once the temperature has risen above 41°F (5°C). After 2–3 weeks leaves should be ready to pick. To harvest, either pick the larger leaves individually, leaving the smaller ones to grow, or cut back the whole plant with scissors. The latter approach is quicker, although the plants are slower to recover. Once they have regrown, however, plants

can be harvested again in the same way. Plants will regrow a number of times, but for the strongest crop, resow a fresh batch every three weeks for a succession.

Keep the plants well watered at all times, and feed crops in containers every two weeks. Clear plant debris after picking to avoid diseases, and keep plants well weeded.

TYPES AVAILABLE TYPES AVAILABLE

Corn salad, also known as lamb's lettuce, produces a steady supply of small leaves when picked individually and continues into winter.

Mibuna is similar to mizuna (*below*), and is grown for its slender summer leaves. It can be harvested whole or as single leaves.

Land cress has a peppery taste and can be used instead of watercress. Harvest as seedlings, or leave to grow for about six weeks.

White mustard has a mild mustard flavor, and can be harvested at seedling stage (*above*) or when more mature as young plants.

Bok choy is commonly grown as a mature crop (see *p.209*), but the seedlings are just as tasty and provide instant salad. It has a mild flavor.

Mizuna has a mild mustard flavor and a crisp texture. It can be harvested as seedlings or allowed to grow for a few weeks.

LOOSE LEAF CROPS

There's a surprising range of leafy crops that take little space and are easy and attractive plants to grow. They give a delicious crop of crisp, tasty leaves and stems and most are ideal for smaller gardens and containers.

	SPRING	SUMMER	FALL	WINTER
SOW/PLANT				
HARVEST				

Swiss chard 'Lucullus'

HOW TO GROW

Leaf crops are generally quick-growing and prefer a sunny spot with well-drained, fertile soil that has been improved with plenty of well-rotted organic matter, such as garden compost or manure. Where space is limited, small crops can be grown in containers (see below).

For an early start, sow under cover into modules in spring, and plant them outdoors when the risk of frost is over. Sow main-season crops directly outside in the soil into drills, thinning them to their final spacing, according to the crop and variety. Cover young plants with fabric if cold weather is predicted.

Keep the plants well-watered throughout the growing season, and weed often to reduce competition and encourage quick growth. Some leaf crops can be harvested as whole, mature plants, but most are picked as individual leaves (see right).

▶ **Pick leaf crops** when young or fully grown, depending on space available.

WATCH OUT FOR …

Downy mildew causes yellow patches with fluffy mold beneath them on leaves, which may die, weakening plants. Remove infected leaves, and improve airflow.

Fungal leaf spot causes dead patches on the leaves, which may merge, killing larger areas. Remove infected leaves and fall debris.

Slugs and snails are major pests, spoiling leaves or eating whole plants. Apply slug pellets, use beer traps, or lay gritty trap barriers.
(For more pests and diseases advice, see pp.356–369.)

GROWING IN CONTAINERS

1 Ensure the container has drainage holes before filling with compost, leaving a gap below the rim to allow for easy watering. Make shallow drills, sow seeds, and cover. For an early start, sow indoors.

2 Seeds germinate after about two weeks, depending on the crop. Move indoor-raised crops outside when the risk of frost has passed. Water the plants well, and feed every other week with a balanced liquid fertilizer.

3 Container-grown crops are best harvested regularly as individual leaves, picked when young and tender. Leave the plants to grow, but sow more seed to give a prolonged crop. Replace older plants every few weeks.

▶ SPINACH

Packed with vitamins, spinach is grown for its delicious leaves; smooth-leaf varieties can be eaten raw in salads, crinkled varieties are best cooked. Grow it in moist, rich soil, shaded from full sun, and keep it well watered at all times to prevent bolting. Sow seed direct outside, ¾in (2 cm) deep, spaced 1in (2.5 cm) apart in rows 12in (30 cm) apart. Thin to 3–6 in (7–15 cm).

Varieties to choose:
'Bordeaux' F1 • 'Crocodile' F1 • 'Emelia' • 'Ottawa'
'Polar Bear' F1 • 'Triathlon'

◀ SWISS CHARD AND SPINACH BEET

The large, crisp leaves can be harvested young for salads or grown larger for cooking. Grow in rich, moist soil; the plants are not as temperature sensitive as lettuce and less prone to bolting. Sow seeds outside in the spring for a summer crop; mid- to late summer for a winter crop. Sow 1in (2.5 cm) deep, 6 in (15 cm) apart.

Varieties to choose:
'Bright Lights' • 'Lucullus' • 'Perpetual Spinach'
'Rainbow Chard' • 'Rhubarb Chard'

▶ ENDIVE

Sugarloaf endive and radicchio (red-leaf endive) produce dense leafy heads in the late summer, which are similar to lettuce but have a bitter taste. Sow outside in early to midsummer, ½in (1 cm) deep in rows 12in (30 cm) apart. Thin the seedlings to 9–12 in (23–30 cm) apart. Weed and water regularly, and cut leaves from midsummer once the hearts have formed.

Varieties to choose:
Radicchio: 'Palla Rossa Bell' • 'Rossa di Verona'
Sugarloaf: 'Borca' • 'Pan di Zucchero'

◀ CHINESE CABBAGE

Also known as Chinese leaves, this quick-growing crop is ready to harvest after 6–7 weeks. The cylindrical heads of densely packed leaves are good raw or stir-fried. Sow directly outside in succession from late spring onward, ½in (1 cm) deep, thinning to 12 in (30 cm) apart for large heads, 6 in (15 cm) apart for smaller ones.

Varieties to choose:
'Kasumi' F1 • 'One Kilo SB' • 'Richi' F1 • 'Wa Wa Sai' F1
'Wong Bok' • 'Pak Choy'

TOMATOES

Tomatoes are a popular crop, producing summer crops in a wide variety of colors, shapes, and sizes. Depending on the type, they can be trained as cordons, left as bushes, or allowed to cascade from hanging baskets.

	SPRING	SUMMER	FALL	WINTER
SOW/PLANT				
HARVEST				

Harvest fruits when fully ripe and evenly colored.

HOW TO GROW

In cool areas tomatoes crop better in a greenhouse, but grow outside in much of the US. Sow seeds in modules or small pots indoors at a temperature of 64–70°F (18–21°C) in the early spring. Pot into individual pots, 3 in (8 cm) in diameter when large enough to handle, and harden off outdoor varieties once all threat of frost has passed. Plant outside into pots or growing bags or into fertile, well-drained soil 30 in (75 cm) apart. If planting into greenhouse borders, space plants 2 ft (60 cm) apart. Provide support, water regularly, and feed weekly once the first flowers appear in the summer. Remove yellowing leaves as they appear, and pinch off cordon varieties as needed.

TYPES AVAILABLE

Beefsteak tomatoes produce the largest fruit but can be slow to ripen and give fewer fruit per plant than other types.

Cherry tomatoes are very free-fruiting, producing long chains of berry-sized fruit. Some varieties are suitable for patio containers.

Plum tomatoes have larger, fleshier fruit than cherry types and a rich flavor. There are varieties suitable to grow inside or outdoors.

Heirloom varieties produce tasty fruit in a variety of shapes and colors, including striped.

VARIETIES TO TRY

Tomatoes have either a bush (B), trailing (T), or tumbling (see facing page).

Cherry tomatoes:
'Balconi Red' (tumbling) • 'Chocolate Cherry' (T) • 'Gardener's Delight' (B or T) • 'Gold Nugget' (T) • 'Romello' (B) • 'Sungold' (T) • 'Tumbling Tom' (tumbling)

Plum tomatoes:
'Black Plum' (T) • 'Crimson Crush' (T) • 'Moneymaker' (B) • 'Roma' (B) • 'Summer Sweet' (T)

Beefsteak tomatoes:
'Big Red F1' (T) • 'Beefeater' (T) • 'Marmande' (T) • 'Mountain Magic' (T) • 'Pink Wonder' (T)

Heirloom tomatoes:
'Green Sausage' (B) • 'Purple Russian' (T) • 'Antique Roman' (T) • 'Tigerella' (T)

Use tall garden canes or flexible strings for indoor cordon tomatoes.

TRAINING AND SUPPORT

Bush tomatoes, which are usually grown outdoors, are the simplest to support and train; insert canes around the plants, and tie in the branches to help take the weight of the developing fruit. The bigger the crop, the more canes needed.

Trailing tomatoes are trained as single stems and are usually grown under cover. To provide support, insert tall canes next to each plant, avoiding the roots, and tie in the stems at intervals as they grow. If using growing bags, attach the canes to the greenhouse frame to give extra support. Check and tie in plants every week, and pinch off the main growing tips when they reach the top of the supports. Stop outdoor cordons once they have produced 4–5 fruit trusses.

To encourage tomatoes to fruit and to limit their size, pinch off the side shoots that develop in the joints between the leaves or flower trusses and the main stems. If these grow, they waste plant energy on unwanted growth and also shade the fruit, preventing it from ripening. Bush and tumbling varieties do not need to be pinched off. As the plants grow, remove the leaves below the lowest truss of ripening fruit to promote airflow and reduce disease.

GROWING IN CONTAINERS

Tomatoes grow best in containers filled with new potting mix or in growing bags, since this reduces the risk of soil-borne disease. It also allows you to place plants in a warm and sheltered location.

If growing in pots, place rocks in the base of a 15 in (38 cm) diameter pot, fill it with good-quality peat-based growing mix, and plant one plant in each. If planting into a standard growing bag, make drainage holes in the bottom first, then plant 2–3 tomatoes in each. To grow tumbling tomatoes in hanging baskets, line the basket with pierced plastic to help retain moisture, and fill with growing mix. Position the plants near the edge so the stems can tumble over the sides. Hang the basket in a sheltered spot out of the wind, and water every day.

▶ **Tumbling tomatoes** are ideal for small spaces. Baskets can be planted decoratively with flowers.

WATCH OUT FOR ...

Tomato blight causes the leaves to discolor, dead tissue to develop on the stems, and the fruit to rot. Grow resistant cultivars. Do not replant in the same compost if growing in a greenhouse bed.

Blossom end rot causes the base of the fruit to turn brown, then drop off. It is commonly caused by erratic watering; destroy infected fruit, and water regularly. (*For more pests and diseases advice, see pp.356–369.*)

FEEDING AND WATERING

Feeding and watering are the most important things to get right. Water regularly and evenly; allowing the plants to dry out then occasionally soaking them causes fruit to split, as well as blossom end rot (*see left*). Tomatoes are hungry plants and need weekly feeding with a high-potash liquid fertilizer as soon as the plants flower, and twice weekly once the first fruits appear. Follow the instructions on the packet. Liquid organic feeds are also available.

Irregular watering can cause cultural problems, such as split fruit and blossom end rot.

PEPPERS AND CHILES

These plants are closely related, but choose carefully because they have very different tastes. Sweet peppers have a mild flavor and often a succulent texture, while chile peppers are their fiery siblings with a spicy kick.

	SPRING	SUMMER	FALL	WINTER
SOW/PLANT				
HARVEST				

HOW TO GROW

Pepper and chiles are best grown outside in a hot, sunny, sheltered spot. Buy pot-grown seedlings in spring, or sow seed under cover, kept at 70–75°F (21–24°C). Pot into individual pots when seedlings are large enough to handle. Repot when the roots fill the pot, and either grow under cover, or harden off to plant outside. Grow them in containers or in sunny beds, spacing them 12 in (30 cm) apart, with 2 ft (60 cm) between rows. Water regularly as the weather warms, and feed once a week with a high-potash tomato fertilizer. Pinch off and support tall plants with canes if necessary. Peppers change color and flavor as they ripen; harvest when green for a milder flavor, or when red or orange for a richer taste (hotter in the case of chiles). Although ripe crops have the best flavor, leaving them to fully ripen will result in a smaller harvest.

TYPES AVAILABLE

Sweet peppers are mild-tasting and produce large, fleshy fruits that ripen from green to red. They can be grown inside or out.

Scotch bonnets are notoriously hot and are widely used in Jamaican cooking. They need a long, hot summer to grow well.

Jalapeño chiles are plump with thick flesh, and vary in spiciness according to variety. They crop best in warm, sunny conditions.

Cayenne chiles are long, slender, thin-skinned, and packed with seeds. They can be very fiery and are good for drying.

VARIETIES TO TRY

Sweet peppers differ mainly in color and shape, while there is a far greater variety of chiles to choose from. Scoville unit ratings will indicate how hot a given variety will be.

Sweet peppers
'Bell Boy' • 'Big Banana' • 'Corno di Toro Giallo' • 'Gourmet' • 'Purple Beauty' • 'Redskin'

Chile peppers
Mild:
'Ancho' • 'Hungarian Hot Wax'

Medium:
'Apache' • 'Padron' • 'Inferno'

Hot:
'Cherry Bomb' • 'Etna' • 'Long Thin Cayenne' • 'Summer Heat'

EGGPLANTS

Also known as aubergines, eggplants are a mainstay ingredient in many cuisines. In cooler climates they are best grown under cover, but otherwise require little effort to give a rewarding crop.

	SPRING	SUMMER	FALL	WINTER
SOW/PLANT				
HARVEST				

HOW TO GROW

Eggplants need warmth to fruit well and do best in a greenhouse or sunroom, but will crop outside in milder areas. Sow seed in early spring into pots or modules kept at 70–75°F (21–24°C). Pot the seedlings, and grow them under cover at 61–64°F (16–18°C) until late spring. To encourage bushiness and more flowers, pinch off the growing tips when the plants reach 12 in (30 cm) high. Harden off if growing outside, and plant 24 in (60 cm) apart in a warm, sheltered, sunny spot in fertile, well-drained soil after the last frost. Outdoor plants can also be grown in large containers left standing in the sun. Plants under cover can be grown in large containers or growing bags, or planted into greenhouse borders.

Water plants more regularly as the temperatures rise and fruits appear, and feed every week with a high-potash tomato fertilizer. To encourage fewer, larger fruit, pinch off the first flower as it appears, and thin fruits to three or four per plant. As the plants grow, support the main stems by tying them into canes or trellis. Harvest the fruits when full-sized and ripe. They are at their best when their full color has developed and the skin is shiny. If the skin begins to dull, the plants have matured too much and will taste dry and bitter. After fruiting, discard all plant debris, including used growing mix from pots.

Eggplants grow well in containers indoors, or outdoors if given a sheltered spot. Keep them well watered and fed.

WATCH OUT FOR …

Glasshouse whitefly feed on plants, sucking their sap, spreading viruses, and reducing harvests. Leaves may start to yellow and feel sticky to touch. Hang sticky traps or use biological control.

Gray mold is most common in poor, wet summers and causes fluffy mold on leaves and flowers, reducing the crop. Remove infected growth, and improve airflow.
(*For more pests and diseases advice, see pp.356–369.*)

Harvest early, rather than late. Older eggplants taste bitter and slow the growth of developing fruit.

CUCUMBERS

You have not experienced the true fresh, juicy flavor and crispy texture of cucumbers until you have grown your own. With varieties that can be grown easily inside or out, there's no reason not to give them a try.

	SPRING	SUMMER	FALL	WINTER
SOW/PLANT				
HARVEST				

Harvest cucumbers by cutting them off using a knife or pruners. Pick regularly to encourage new fruits.

HOW TO GROW

Cucumbers need a sunny location with moist, fertile soil or compost and are ideal for growing in containers or the soil. Sow seed under cover at 70°F (21°C) in small pots in early spring for indoor crops, mid-spring for outdoor varieties. Harden off cucumbers for planting outside when four weeks old, and plant out after the last frost, putting supports in place first. Space the plants 18 in (45 cm) apart. Sow seeds direct in summer. Keep plants well watered, especially when in fruit, watering indoor plants daily in the summer. Feed with a general liquid fertilizer every two weeks after the first flowers appear.

TYPES AVAILABLE

Ridge cucumbers are grown outside on the ground or trained up supports. They have tougher skins, which may have small spines.

Heritage cucumbers are grown outdoors and generally produce smaller, rounded yellow or white fruit that are ideal for salads.

Greenhouse varieties produce long, smooth, thin-skinned fruit that need to be grown under cover to set reliably.

VARIETIES TO TRY

All-female varieties (F) are more expensive to buy than standard types, but produce better-tasting cucumbers (see right).

Greenhouse varieties
'Addison' • 'Bodega' • 'Bologna' • 'Camaro' • 'Carmen' • 'Cucino' FI (F) • 'Flamingo' • 'Louisa' • 'Passandra' FI (F) • 'Socrates' • 'Picolino' FI (F) • 'Telegraph Improved'

Outdoor varieties
'Burpless Tasty Green' • 'Bush Champion' • 'Long Green Ridge' • 'Lungo Verde Degli Ortolani' • 'Marketmore' • 'Masterpiece'

Heritage varieties
'Boothby's Blonde' • 'Crystal Apple' • 'Double Yield' • 'Miniature White' • 'White Wonder'

Providing support

Cucumbers can be left to trail along the ground, but they crop better and take up less space if trained up a support. For outdoor plants, make a simple wigwam using 5–6 tall canes, tied at the top. In a greenhouse, insert one cane per plant, holding it upright by attaching it to the frame. To use all the space available, train plants along the inside of the greenhouse roof on long, sturdy wires, and tie them in.

► **Cucumber plants** grow quickly so should be tied in regularly; the swelling fruit can become heavy.

▲ **Cane frames** provide an easy-to-make, robust support for outdoor crops.

Containers

Cucumbers thrive in containers and growing bags, inside or out. When planting containers, place crock pieces over the holes, use peat-based growing mix, and leave a large gap between the surface and the rim for easy watering. If you use growing bags, make several drainage holes in the bottom first, and insert the supports before planting.

► **Growing bags** are ideal for cucumbers and reduce the risk of soil-borne diseases affecting your plants.

"All-female" varieties

If modern indoor cucumbers are pollinated, the fruit that develops can be misshapen and bitter-tasting. Avoid this by growing "all-female" varieties or by removing any male flowers before they open.

◄ **Female** flowers are easy to spot since they have an immature fruit behind the petals.

WATCH OUT FOR ...

Squash, cucumbers, zucchini, and pumpkins are related and are affected by the same pests and diseases (see pp.221–223).

Cucumber mosaic virus causes mottled leaves, weak growth, and poor harvests. Destroy infected plants, and grow resistant varieties.

Powdery mildew coats leaves in white fungal growth. Keep plants well-watered, and improve airflow. (For more pests and diseases advice, see pp.356–369.)

GROWING GHERKINS

Gherkins are immature cucumbers that are grown the same way as outdoor varieties. Sow seed under cover in pots, harden off, and plant out when the risk of frost has passed. Water and feed regularly, and harvest the fruits when 1–3 in (2.5–7.5 cm) long. Harvest often, and pickle fruits right away. Although cucumbers can be picked small as gherkins, specially bred varieties are more successful.

Varieties to try:
'Diamant' • 'Piccolo di Parigi' • 'Venlo Pickling'

SWEET CORN

The minute a cob is picked, the sugar in the kernels starts turning to starch, reducing its tenderness and sweetness. When you grow your own and eat them fresh, you won't believe the difference in taste.

	SPRING	SUMMER	FALL	WINTER
SOW/PLANT				
HARVEST				

Fresh sweet corn is much sweeter than store bought.

HOW TO GROW

Sweet corn requires a hot season to produce a good crop, so plant in a sheltered, sunny site with well-drained soil. In colder areas, sow seed in the spring under cover in a heated propagator, set to a minimum temperature of 61–70°F (16–21°C). Grow the seedlings at room temperature, and harden them off once the risk of frost has passed. To produce full-sized cobs, the flowers must be fully pollinated, which is done by the wind. Help ensure this by growing the plants together in blocks (*see below*). It is best to sow seed under cover, even in mild areas, to deter mice.

For a succession of crops, sow at two-week intervals into the summer. Water well, and cover plants with fabric if cold nights persist. Plants do not need support, but if the stems are rocked by wind, support by mounding soil around them. Water regularly once the plants start to bear crops.

As the cobs ripen in late summer, the silks darken and turn brown. Test to see if the cobs are ready (*see right*) before removing. Leave late-season cobs to ripen as long as possible before the first frost. The flowers of baby sweet corn don't need to be pollinated; pick the fruits before the silks darken.

Check to see if cobs are ready by exposing the cob and pressing a fingernail into a kernel. If it exudes milky sap, it is ready to harvest.

PLANTING OUTDOORS

1 To encourage good pollination, plant sweet corn in blocks, 18 in (45 cm) apart, so the pollen can be blown by the wind from plant to plant. Baby corn can be planted more closely, 6 in (15 cm) apart.

2 Sweet corn is slow to develop, and young plants cast only light shade. Take advantage of the space below them as they develop, and underplant with a quick-growing catch crop, such as beets, radishes, or kohlrabi.

VARIETIES TO TRY

"Super sweet" (S) hybrids produce sweeter kernels than traditional varieties; "Tender sweet" (T) are sweeter and more tender. They must not be pollinated by other varieties or their special qualities are lost.

'Incredible' (S) • 'Lark' (T) • 'Marshall's Honeydew' (T) • 'Mirai White M421' (S) • 'Prelude' (S) • 'Seville' (S) • 'Sundance' • 'Swift' (TS) • 'Minipop' (baby corn)

FLORENCE FENNEL

Attractive to look at as well as to eat, this lacy-leaf vegetable is grown for its aniseed-flavored, slightly tender stem bases. It is prone to bolting and develops best in mild, warm conditions.

	SPRING		SUMMER		FALL		WINTER	
SOW/PLANT								
HARVEST								

HOW TO GROW

This choice vegetable prefers a sunny, sheltered location and moist, rich soil, improved with lots of well-rotted organic matter—less than optimal conditions will cause the plants to bolt. Sow indoors into small pots to avoid disturbing the roots when transplanting, or sow outside when all risk of frost has passed. Harden off indoor-grown seedlings, and plant them out in late spring, spacing plants 12 in (30 cm) apart. Water well and regularly, especially during dry spells, keeping the soil permanently moist. Grow the plants early in summer, and keep well watered to help prevent bolting. Weed often, and cover the stems with soil as they grow, to blanch and make them sweeter. If nights turn cold, cover with fabric or cloches.

Florence fennel is ready to harvest about 12 weeks from sowing, when the stems are about the size of tennis balls. Don't allow them to grow larger, or they will become tough. Unless you want the plants to resprout (*see below*), harvest by pulling the plants up whole.

▶ **Florence fennel** is attractive enough to grow as an ornamental and is a good crop planted in containers. Resow regularly throughout the summer for a steady supply.

RESPROUTING FENNEL

1 Cut the swollen stems off just above ground level with a sharp knife. Unless you need the space for other crops, leave the roots in the ground to regrow and produce a second crop of leaves.

2 Keep the stumps well watered, and within two weeks the plant will produce new shoots. Although these won't grow into full-sized bulbs before fall, the tasty, feathery leaves can be used fresh as an herb in soups and salads.

WATCH OUT FOR ...

Rhizoctonia is a fungal disease that causes seedlings and mature plants to rot off at the base. There are no chemical controls. Rotate crops, and don't grow lettuce or radishes in the same soil afterward.

Bolting, where plants quickly run to seed, is a common problem when growing Florence fennel. It is caused by stress. Transplant seedlings carefully, and keep them well watered, weeded, and fed. Once bolted, plants cannot be saved.

RHUBARB

Cooked like fruit and eaten in desserts, rhubarb is technically a vegetable because, like celery, it is the leaf stems that are eaten. It is very easy to grow, and mature plants crop from spring to summer.

		SPRING	SUMMER	FALL	WINTER
PLANT					
HARVEST					

HOW TO GROW

Rhubarb is best planted in a sunny spot, although it does tolerate some shade with well-drained, moisture-retentive soil that has been enriched with well-rotted organic matter. Plant bare root plants while dormant, late fall to early spring; container-grown plants can be planted any time if well watered. When planting container-grown plants, make sure the bud is at the same depth in the soil as it was in the pot, and position plants 3 ft (90 cm) apart. Water plants well during dry spells in the first year, and mulch with well-rotted organic matter in the spring, avoiding the crown itself. Cut the flowering stems that appear in the summer, remove dead leaves in the fall, and mulch.

Stems are tender and ready to harvest when reddish and just before the leaves unfurl, unless they are forced (*see below*). Pick as needed until early summer, then let the plant recover. Twist the stems so they come away cleanly, rather than cutting them. Do not harvest any stems from new plants in their first year, then harvest only lightly in their second.

▶ **Rhubarb leaves** are toxic—remove them from the stems before cooking. They are safe to add to the compost heap.

FORCING EARLY STEMS

1 For early, tender stems, cover the plant before it emerges with a large container to block out the light, such as a forcer (*above*) or a bucket weighed down with bricks. Check for slugs and snails first.

2 Remove the long stems as needed until mid-spring, then uncover the plant, and allow it to grow naturally. To let the plant recover, do not force it the following year. For best results, apply this technique to early or forcing varieties.

WATCH OUT FOR ...

Slugs and snails attack young or forced stems, eating or damaging growth. Apply pellets sparingly, or use beer traps, or biological control.

Crown rot causes the center of the plant to decay, especially where the leaves join. It is caused by various diseases, most often in wet weather. There are no chemical controls. Cut out the infection before it spreads. (*For more pests and diseases advice, see pp.356–369.*)

CELERY

Versatile in cooking, celery is a fairly tricky vegetable to grow well and requires some effort. Novice gardeners should look for modern self-blanching varieties, which are easier to grow than trench types.

	SPRING		SUMMER		FALL		WINTER	
SOW/PLANT								
HARVEST								

HOW TO GROW

Celery prefers an open site with moist, rich, well-drained, slightly acid soil that has been improved with plenty of well-rotted organic matter, such as garden compost. Dig this into the soil in the season before you plan to grow.

Sow seeds (which can be slow germinating) under cover in early spring into modules or small pots. The seeds need light to germinate, so cover very lightly with growing mix, if at all. Keep the sown seeds at 60°F (15°C), then transfer seedlings into larger pots once they are large enough to handle. Grow them

under cover at a temperature of 50°F (10°C) until all risk of frost has passed, then harden off and plant outside in the early summer.

Plant self-blanching varieties 9 in (23 cm) apart in blocks and trench celery 12–18 in (30–45 cm) apart in a prepared trench (*see right*). Water in well, keep the area free of weeds, and feed once every two weeks with a balanced liquid fertilizer throughout the growing season. Harvest celery after 4–8 months when the heads are big enough to use. Trench celery is the hardiest and can be left in the ground for winter; self-blanching must be pulled before the first frost.

Blanching celery

Traditional trench celery needs to be covered to produce crisp, tender blanched stems. Dig a trench 12 in (30 cm) deep by 18 in (45 cm) wide, and spread well-rotted organic matter in the bottom, topped with soil. Space plants 6 in (15 cm) apart in the trench. When they reach 12 in (30 cm) high, wrap the stems with cardboard to keep the soil out, and earth up against the sides. Do this two or three more times in summer, so only the leaves remain visible at harvest time. Alternatively, plant new self-blanching varieties, which, when planted in blocks, create enough shade to blanch the stems.

▶ **Blanching celery stems** makes them more tender to eat, but green stalks are more nutritious.

VARIETIES TO TRY

Traditional celery is grown in trenches; self-blanching types are easier to grow.

Trench celery
'Blush' • 'Ideal' • 'Giant Pink' • 'Giant Red' 'Martine' • 'Pascal'

Self-blanching/naturally pale celery
'Crystal' • 'Green Utah' • 'Ivory Tower' • 'Loretta' • 'Tango' • 'Victoria'

ZUCCHINI AND MARROWS

The only difference between zucchini and marrows is their size. When harvested small, zucchini has a delicate flavor and tender skin; marrows develop a thicker skin over time. The edible flowers are a delicacy.

	SPRING	SUMMER	FALL	WINTER
SOW/PLANT				
HARVEST				

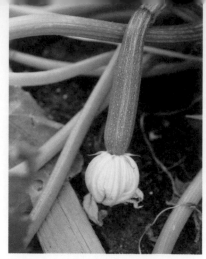

Zucchini forms behind the female flowers.

HOW TO GROW

Zucchini and marrows can be grown in beds or large containers and need a warm, sunny spot with fertile soil. Sow seed under cover in early spring (*see below*), or outdoors under a cloche, 1 in (2.5 cm) deep when the risk of frost has passed. Plant bushy varieties 24 in (60 cm) apart and trailing types, which can be trained up canes, 3–4 ft (90 cm–1.2 m) apart. Water well, and feed with a liquid fertilizer every week. Break the stems to harvest zucchini at 4 in (10 cm) long, or for marrows, thin the fruit to two or three per plant, and allow them to grow to 8–12 in (20–30 cm).

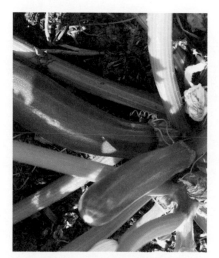

Pick zucchini young and tender, but leave marrows to develop a thick outer skin.

VARIETIES TO TRY

Zucchini
Most zucchini are green, but some are yellow (Y), which makes them easier to see when harvesting:
'Clarion' F1 • 'Defender' F1 • 'Gold Rush' F1 (Y) • 'Jemmer' F1 (Y) • 'Romanesco' • 'Supremo' F1 • 'Venus' F1

Marrows
Marrows are large zucchini but there are also varieties available that are particularly suited to growing as marrows:
'Badger Cross' F1 • 'Bush Baby' • 'Tiger Cross' F1

SOWING AND PLANTING

1 Sow seeds indoors, 1 in (2.5 cm) deep into small pots to avoid disturbing the roots when planting them out later on.

2 Grow them indoors in a greenhouse or on a bright windowsill. They will be large enough to plant out after 4–6 weeks, so don't sow too early.

3 Harden off, and plant out once the risk of frost has passed. To avoid root damage, water the plants first so they slide more easily from their pots.

4 Plant into containers or beds, and keep them well watered throughout the growing season. Larger containers retain moisture more effectively.

SUMMER SQUASH

Summer squash are a lot like zucchini in terms of growing, cooking, and eating, but they come in a much wider variety of shapes and textures. They are attractive plants and fun to grow.

		SPRING		SUMMER		FALL		WINTER	
SOW/PLANT									
HARVEST									

Summer squash can be grown among nasturtiums in the garden.

HOW TO GROW

Summer squash prefer moist, rich soil and crop better in hot summers. Sow seed under cover in early spring into small pots, harden off, and plant outside into large containers or beds when all risk of frost has passed. Plant bushy varieties 18 in (45 cm) apart and trailing types 3–4 ft (90 cm–1.2 m) apart. Seed can also be sown outside under cloches at this time, 1 in (2.5 cm) deep. Water well, and when squash appear, feed with a high-potash fertilizer every week. Tie trailing varieties to supports, and pinch the tips when they are 24 in (60 cm) tall. Harvest squash while small for best flavor, cutting their stems at the base with a sharp knife. Wear gloves—older stems may have needle-sharp bristles.

◄ **Train squash up** supports or netting to save space and keep them clean.

WATCH OUT FOR ...

Squash, cucumbers, zucchini, and pumpkins are related and are affected by the same pests and diseases (*see p.215 and pp.222–223*).

Cucumber mosaic virus affects squash as well as cucumbers, causing the foliage to become yellow and mottled, weakening the plants and reducing the crop. There is no cure for this disease, so plants must be destroyed.
(*For more pests and diseases advice, see pp.356–369.*)

TYPES AVAILABLE

Patty pan squash have a flattened shape with a bumpy ring. The plants double as garden ornamentals when trained against fences.

Round squash are often highly decorative, producing fruits with colorful patterned skins that can be smooth or knobby in texture.

VARIETIES TO TRY

The patty pans (P) are more decorative than plain round (R) varieties, although they taste similar when cooked.

'Custard White' (P) • 'Moonbeam' F1 (P) • 'Peter Pan' (P) • 'Scallop Yellow Bird' (P) • 'Summer Ball' (R) • 'Sunburst' F1 (P) • 'Tromboncino'

PUMPKINS

Pumpkins are a familiar sight at Halloween, carved into jack-o'-lanterns, and are more popular for decoration than as edible crops. However, they are easy to grow, fun for all, and spectacularly announce the onset of fall.

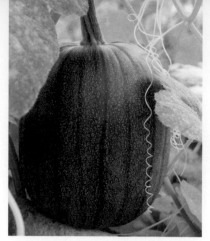

Pumpkins need time to develop and space to grow to a good size, in full sun.

	SPRING	SUMMER	FALL	WINTER
SOW/PLANT				
HARVEST				

HOW TO GROW

Pumpkins are a type of winter squash (see *facing page*) and require plenty of time to develop their bold coloring, as well as a lot of space. Sow seed indoors in mid-spring into small pots to help minimize root disturbance when planting outside. Harden off the seedlings once the risk of frost has passed, and plant 3–5 ft (1–1.5 m) apart in a sunny, sheltered spot in well-drained, fertile soil that has been prepared with plenty of well-rotted organic matter, such as garden compost or manure. (If you're short on space, plant pumpkins directly into a well-rotted compost heap.) Water in, and mulch well, covering with cloches or fabric during cold spells. Water regularly, particularly in hot, dry weather, and feed with a liquid fertilizer every other week. Lift trailing varieties off the ground with netting. If you want large pumpkins, thin the baby fruits, limiting each plant to bearing just two or three. For pumpkins to eat fresh, pick when they reach a good size. For large, decorative fruit, let them grow on and color up, but pick them before the first frost.

DRYING AND STORING

Pumpkins can be stored to eat later in the year but must be prepared properly. Leave the fruits on the plant to develop a thick skin, then cut them off, leaving a long stalk (this delays rotting, which starts at the stalk end). "Cure" the pumpkins by leaving them outside in the sun for around ten days to dry. If rain is forecast, move them indoors or cover them. Turn them occasionally so that the whole surface dries. Once "cured," store the pumpkins in a dry, well-ventilated, frost-free space that is consistently cooler than 59°F (15°C). Check occasionally for signs of damage or decay.

▶ **Keep developing fruit clean** by raising them up with a thick mulch of chipped bark or straw or with a brick.

VARIETIES TO TRY

'Atlantic Giant' • 'Baby Bear' • 'Becky' • 'Jack Be Little' • 'Jack of All Trades' • 'Mammoth' • 'Mars' F1 • 'Rouge Vif d'Etampes' • 'Sunshine'

WATCH OUT FOR ...

Pumpkin, cucumbers, zucchini, and squash are related and are affected by the same pests and diseases (see *p.215, p.221, and p.223*).

Slugs will attack all parts of young plants and may hide beneath the large leaves. Spread slug pellets, or use beer traps or biological control to keep slugs away from vulnerable plants.
(For more pests and diseases advice, see *pp.356–369.*)

WINTER SQUASH

Closely related to pumpkins, their plump cousins, winter squash produce smaller, tastier crops, grown for their sweet, nutty flavor. They are also more decorative, developing interesting colors and shapes, and longer storing.

	SPRING	SUMMER	FALL	WINTER
SOW/PLANT				
HARVEST				

HOW TO GROW

Winter squash requires long, hot summers to ripen fully and prefers a sunny, sheltered spot. They grow best in moist, fertile soil, improved with lots of rich, well-rotted organic matter, such as garden compost. Sow seed indoors during mid-spring into small pots to prevent disturbing the roots when planting out. Harden off seedlings once the risk of frost has passed, and plant out 3–5 ft (1–1.5 m) apart. Water in and mulch well, and cover with cloches or fabric if the weather is still chilly. Water plants regularly, particularly in hot, dry weather, and feed with a liquid fertilizer every couple of weeks. Squash are trailing plants that take up a lot of space but can be trained over supports, such as cane wigwams or trellis. Tie in trained stems regularly to help support the heavy fruit.

Squash are ready to harvest in late summer when the fruit develops a hard skin and the stem starts to crack. If you want larger fruit, thin them out, leaving two or three per plant. Like pumpkins, winter squash can be stored for many weeks after harvesting if they have been "cured" first (see *facing page*). Leave them on the plants as long as possible but harvest before the first frost.

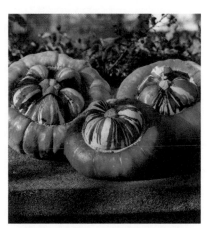

'Turk's Turban' squashes are among the most distinctive and attractive. They can be enjoyed as decoration until used for cooking.

PLANTING OUT

1 Plant squash seedlings outside when the risk of frost has passed but before they become pot-bound or grow too large to handle easily. Squash germinate and grow quickly, so don't sow them too early.

2 Water the seedlings before removing the pots so they slip out easily, and plant the seedlings at their original depth. Water well, and add a mulch of organic matter to feed them and to retain moisture. Sprinkle slug pellets lightly as a precaution.

WATCH OUT FOR …

Squash, cucumbers, zucchini, and pumpkins are related and are affected by the same pests and diseases (see p.215 and pp.221–222).

Glasshouse red spider mite can attack plants during hot summers, sucking sap, discoloring leaves, and seriously weakening plants. Spray plants with an appropriate insecticide when symptoms first appear.
(*For more pests and diseases advice, see pp.356–369.*)

RADISHES

Crisp and peppery red-skinned radishes are a familiar summer snack and salad ingredient that are quick and easy to grow. However, there are also unusual Asian radishes to try as well as varieties to harvest in winter.

	SPRING	SUMMER	FALL	WINTER
SOW/PLANT				
HARVEST				

HOW TO GROW

All types of radishes grow best in a sunny spot with moist, free-draining soil. Avoid growing them in stony or recently manured soil, since this causes the roots to split or fork. Summer radishes are very quick growing, ready to pick in just 2–6 weeks from sowing. For an early start, sow them indoors in modules in early spring, ½ in (1 cm) deep, and plant them out in late spring. Sow outdoors from late spring to late summer in rows 6 in (15 cm) apart, and thin seedlings to 1 in (2.5 cm) apart. They can also be grown successfully in containers. Best pulled young, they become tough and tasteless if left too long.

Winter radishes are slower growing than summer types, taking 8–10 weeks; harvest in the fall when the size of turnips. Sow seed in midsummer in rows 12 in (30 cm) apart, and thin to 6 in (15 cm) apart. Keep the soil moist to encourage rapid growth and succulent roots. Unless needed, leave mature roots in the ground until midwinter, then lift and store them under cover: somewhere dry, well-ventilated, and frost-free. Check the roots regularly for signs of damage or decay.

Daikon radishes are grown in the same way as winter types. Sow seed directly in drills from mid- to late summer, and harvest in the fall. The roots can be left in the ground until needed. Unlike summer radishes, neither these or winter types are suitable for containers.

WATCH OUT FOR ...

Flea beetles eat small holes in the leaves, which cause seedlings to die off, and weakens growing crops. Sow or plant out young plants with garden fabric.

Cabbage root fly maggots burrow into the radishes, stunting their growth and causing decay. Cover plants with insect-proof netting.
(For more pests and diseases advice, see pp.356–369.)

TYPES AVAILABLE

Summer radishes are quick-growing and are eaten raw. They are the easiest to grow in small gardens, and there are lots to choose from.

Winter radishes can be eaten raw, grated in salads, but their tougher flesh is best enjoyed cooked. They have a mild flavor, not peppery.

Daikon is an Asian vegetable, widely sold in supermarkets. It can be eaten raw if finely chopped and is commonly cooked in stir fries.

BEETS

Beets have recently been having a well-deserved comeback. Packed with antioxidants, these colorful roots, available in shades of orange, yellow, and white as well as red, are gracing plates and plots once more.

Beet 'Boltardy'

	SPRING	SUMMER	FALL	WINTER
SOW/PLANT				
HARVEST				

HOW TO GROW

Beets prefer a sunny location with well-drained, fertile soil that has been improved with well-rotted garden compost or manure. If you have heavy soil, warm it in the winter with cloches several weeks before sowing. Sow outdoors in early spring, 1 in (2.5 cm) deep, 4 in (10 cm) apart, in rows 12 in (30 cm) apart. Beet "seeds" are actually cases that contain a cluster of seeds, so thin out surplus seedlings as they appear, leaving only the strongest one. If you live in a colder area, protect germinating seeds with cloches or fabric.

Beets need regular watering throughout the growing season, particularly in dry spells, to prevent the roots from becoming woody. Weed around them carefully by hand—a nick on the roots with a trowel or hoe will damage them and cause them to bleed. For the best flavor, pull roots when they are golf-ball sized, first loosening the soil with a hand fork. As an extra crop, you can also harvest the young leaves, but pick sparingly to avoid checking growth.

WATCH OUT FOR ...

Aphids suck sap, weakening the plants and slowing growth. Crops can be delayed or reduced. Spray heavy infestations with a suitable insecticide (see p.359).

Leaf-mining fly larvae feed within the foliage, causing brown blotches. Remove infested leaves since there are no chemical controls available. (For more pests and diseases advice, see pp.356 369.)

GROWING PATIO CROPS

1 Sow pre-soaked seeds sparingly into patio planters, cover them with 1 in (2.5 cm) of growing mix, and water them in well.

2 Beet seeds germinate about a week after sowing. Keep the growing mix moist, and site the container in a sunny location. Protect against slugs.

3 Depending on variety, harvest after 6–8 weeks, and resow a second or third crop. Water regularly during the summer to prevent them from bolting (running to seed).

VARIETIES TO TRY

Traditional red beet varieties bleed easily, staining clothes and surfaces, so you may prefer other colored types that don't leave unwanted marks.

Red varieties
'Alto' F1 • 'Boltardy' • 'Boro' F1 • 'Cylindra' • 'Detroit 6 Rubidus' • 'Red Ace' F1

Other colors
'Albina Vereduna' (white) • 'Burpee's Golden' (orange) • 'Chioggia Pink' (pink)

CARROTS

In a large plot you can grow enough carrots to last for months, but even in small spaces you can produce a good crop, especially of the smaller varieties. Alternatively, try growing some with unusual shapes and colors.

	SPRING		SUMMER	FALL	WINTER
SOW/PLANT					
HARVEST					

Young roots are deliciously sweet.

HOW TO GROW

Sowing early and main crop varieties will provide you with carrots from summer until winter if you have the space. Carrots prefer a dry site with light, fertile soil that has not been manured in the last 12 months. Make sure there are no stones or clods of soil because this will produce forked or misshapen roots.

Sow early varieties in early spring under cloches, insect-proof mesh (see p.191), or fleece, and main crops in the open or under mesh in mid-spring; sow seed in succession throughout the growing season. For a late crop, sow an early variety in midsummer. Sow at a depth of ½–¾ in (1–2 cm) about 1 in (2.5 cm) apart, and thin plants to 4 in (10 cm) apart as they grow. Allow 12 in (30 cm) between rows. Thinning releases scent from the foliage, which attracts carrot fly (see right). Thin in the evening to reduce the effect. Weed around the seedlings by hand. Full-sized carrots are ready for harvesting after 12–16 weeks, depending on the variety. Baby carrots are ready in 8–10 weeks.

WATCH OUT FOR ...

Aphids attack the leaves, sucking sap and carrying viruses. Apply approved insecticides, or grow under very fine insect-proof mesh.

Carrot flies lay eggs near young plants, which hatch into maggots that burrow into the roots. Protect plants with fabric or fine netting. Avoid disturbing the plants during the day since this can attract the flies.
(For more pests and diseases advice, see pp.356–369.)

◄ **Fine netting** prevents the female carrot flies from laying eggs near your crop. The netting only has to be 2 ft (60 cm) high since the flies stay close to the ground. Leave it in place all season.

TYPES AVAILABLE

Rounded carrots produce short roots and are ideal for growing in containers or in gardens where the soil is thin and stony.

Finger carrots require deeper, finer soil to produce long, unforked roots, although they can be grown as baby carrots where soil is shallow.

VARIETIES TO TRY

Round varieties
'Atlas' • 'Early French Frame' • 'Parmex' • 'Rondo'

Finger varieties
'Adelaide' F1 • 'Fall King 2' • 'Flyaway' F1 'Maestro' • 'Mignon' • 'Nantes 3' • 'Purple Haze' • 'Resistafly'

KOHLRABI

Kohlrabi produce striking stems and leaves and would make an attractive addition to an ornamental display. Their swollen stems have a delicious nutty flavor, like a cross between celery and cabbage.

	SPRING	SUMMER	FALL	WINTER
SOW/PLANT				
HARVEST				

HOW TO GROW

Kohlrabi are tolerant plants and will grow well in most garden soils, sandy or heavy, but will crop best in rich soil, improved with plenty of organic matter. When planting, avoid beds where traditional brassicas have been grown in the last three years to avoid clubroot (see *top right*); kohlrabi is a member of the brassica family.

For early crops, sow seeds under cover in modules, and plant outside in the late spring after all frost has passed. Sow outdoors in the late spring to early summer when the soil has warmed up. Cold soil may cause plants to bolt (run to seed and spoil). Sow in rows 12 in (30 cm) apart, ¾ in (2 cm) deep and 9 in (23 cm) apart. Kohlrabi is fast

growing, ready to pick when the stems reach golf-ball size, around 7–8 weeks after sowing. Crops left to grow larger become tough and tasteless. For a constant supply throughout the season, sow in repeated batches every two weeks throughout the spring and summer. Water plants regularly to prevent roots from becoming woody; they won't require additional feeding.

Kohlrabi can be grown successfully in containers, and repeated crops can be planted in the same potting mix all season; it may need refreshing after each harvest and should be discarded in the fall. Position in a sunny spot, and keep plants well watered. Feed container-grown plants every other week using a balanced liquid feed.

As a bonus crop, when harvesting the mature stems also pick the young, tender leaves and use them as summer greens.

TYPES AVAILABLE

Purple varieties can be slower to mature and hardier. Sow them later than white-skinned varieties for late summer and fall crops.

White varieties are a good choice for quick harvests and can be sown as "catch crops" while other vegetables become established.

VARIETIES TO TRY

Purple-skinned varieties
'Azure Star' • 'Blusta' • 'Kolibri' F1 • 'Purple Danube' F1

White-skinned varieties
'Korfu' • 'Lanro' • 'Logo' • 'Olivia' F1 • 'Rapidstar' • 'Superschmelze'

POTATOES

The humble spud comes in myriad shapes and colors and has many uses in the kitchen, from summer salads to all-season fries. Potatoes are easy to grow, even in small spaces and containers.

Potato 'Yukon Gold'

	SPRING	SUMMER	FALL	WINTER
SOW/PLANT				
HARVEST				

HOW TO GROW

Potatoes need an open, sunny site with moist, well-drained, fertile soil, improved with plenty of well-rotted organic matter, such as garden compost. Sold as "seed" potatoes (small tubers), they are labeled as "early," "mid-season," or "late," depending on when they are ready to harvest.

To suppress weeds, cover the planting area with sheet plastic and plant the tubers through it. Once "chitted" (see below), plant earliest potatoes in early spring; protect against frost by covering with fleece or drawing soil over tender shoots when frosty nights are forecast.

Plant mid-season varieties in mid-spring; and late varieties from mid- to late spring. Plant tubers 4–6 in (10–15 cm) deep, and cover the chits with 1 in (2.5 cm) of soil. Space them 12 in (30 cm) apart with 24 in (60 cm) between rows for earliest, 30 in (75 cm) for late types. Keep plants well watered, weed regularly, and "hill up" (see facing page) as needed.

Harvest earliest types in early summer, scraping away some soil first to see if they are large enough. Mid-season will be ready in midsummer, and latest from late summer to fall. Unearth them with a fork, taking care not to spear them. Clear all plant debris from the soil.

VARIETIES TO TRY

Early
'Accent' • 'Concorde' • 'Epicure' • 'Foremost' • 'Pentland Javelin' • 'Red Duke of York' • 'Swift' • 'Vivaldi' • 'Winston'

Mid-season
'Belle de Fontenay' • 'Charlotte' • 'Estima' • 'Kestrel' • 'Kondor' • 'Lady Christl' • 'Picasso' • 'Ratte'

Late
'Desiree' • 'Golden Wonder' • 'King Edward' • 'Maris Piper' • 'Navan' • 'Nicola' • 'Picasso' • 'Pink Fir Apple' • 'Salad Blue' • 'Sarpo Mira'

GARDEN SPEAK

Chitting potatoes
Potatoes can be "chitted" before planting, which involves giving them an early start indoors. To do this, place the seed potatoes with their "eyes" facing upward in trays or egg cartons in a warm, light place so that short green shoots, or "chits," appear. Once the chits are ¼–½ in (5–10 mm) long, the tubers are ready to be planted out. Chitting advances maturity so the potatoes can be harvested earlier, giving them some protection from slugs and blight.

PLANTING POTATOES

1 Chit early potatoes inside; mid-season and late crops can be planted unchitted. Only plant undamaged tubers.

2 Tubers can be planted into individual holes if only growing a few or in long trenches for larger crops. Plant the chits facing upward.

3 Fill the holes or trench, covering the tubers with 1 in (2.5 cm) of soil. When planting chitted tubers, be careful not to knock off the developing shoots.

Hilling up

When the developing stems reach 6 in (15 cm) tall, start "hilling up" by mounding up the surrounding soil to cover the shoots, burying them by half their height. Repeat every few weeks as the shoots grow. This prevents tubers being exposed to sunlight, which turns them green and makes them poisonous. It also helps stifle weeds and deters blight (*see bottom right*). and can protect early varieties from frost. Potatoes grown through black plastic sheeting don't require hilling up.

▶ **Hill up potatoes** carefully to avoid damaging the stems, which are brittle at the base and can snap. Hilling up also helps control weeds.

Harvesting

If you're not sure when to harvest potatoes, look for telltale signs above ground. Earliest varieties are ready when their flowers begin to open or the buds drop. Late types are ready when their foliage yellows, although they can be left in the soil until mid-fall to bulk up. Cut back stems 10 days before lifting.

◀ **Open flowers** mean that the early crops are ready to lift, but late crops still need time to grow.

Growing in containers

If you don't have much space, you can grow a decent crop of potatoes in a container or strong bag. Ensure that it is at least 12 in (30 cm) deep with drainage holes, and half-fill it with growing mix. Place one or two potatoes on top and cover with 4 in (10 cm) of growing mix. Add growing mix to half-cover the shoots as they grow, and water regularly. Harvest the potatoes as soon as they are ready. This method is suitable for all crops.

New potatoes are ideal for growing in strong plastic bags. Harvest the crop by tipping the potatoes out once they have matured.

Potatoes can be grown in any container that drains well and is deep enough for the tubers to develop fully, like a trash can.

Storing late potatoes

Lift potatoes on a dry day, and leave them to dry on the soil surface. Discard any that are diseased or damaged, and use smaller tubers fresh since they deteriorate sooner. Once the skins are dry, remove excess soil, but don't clean them further to avoid damaging the skins. Store the tubers in paper bags or in trays, somewhere dry, well ventilated, and frost-free. Check them often for damage or decay.

WATCH OUT FOR ...

Potato cyst nematodes cause leaves to yellow and plants to die off early, reducing the crop. There is no control. Rotate crops, and use resistant varieties.

Potato blight causes dead patches on the leaves and stems and on the tubers, which then rot. It is prevalent in damp summers. Use resistant cultivars, or grow early varieties since blight occurs later in the season. Destroy infected plants. (*For more pests and diseases advice, see pp.356–369.*)

ROOT AND STEM CROPS

Roots are mainly long-term crops, best suited to larger plots where you can plant a worthwhile number and can leave them to grow undisturbed. Reliable, they offer a welcome feast when few fresh crops are available.

		SPRING		SUMMER		FALL		WINTER	
SOW/PLANT									
HARVEST									

Turnips can be harvested young.

HOW TO GROW

This group of vegetables needs an open, sunny site with deep, light soil, free from large stones. They will crop in heavy soil as long as it drains well; in shallow soils, choose varieties with shorter roots. Sow seed in spring, under cover for celeriac, directly outside in drills for the others, planting out or thinning to their preferred final spacings. Keep plants well weeded to reduce competition, and water as required; avoid allowing the crops to become dry because the developing roots may then split when watered.

In smaller plots, interplant slower-growing parsnips and rutabagas (see p.200) with quicker crops, like radishes and bok choy, sown directly to make better use of the space. In milder areas, leave the roots in the ground in fall and winter until needed. In colder, wetter areas, lift and store them.

▶ **Protect crops** stored in the soil over the winter with a layer of straw or fabric.

SOWING AND GROWING

1 When sowing directly in the soil, sow seeds in small clusters spaced at the correct planting distance. After germinating, thin each cluster of seedlings, leaving the strongest. Water plants well as they grow.

2 Keep the seedlings weed-free, taking care not to damage the developing roots with the hoe; hand weed if possible. If intercropping, harvest and resow as soon as the catch crops are ready, but avoid disturbing the main crop.

3 Harvest some roots as soon as they reach a usable size, but leave others in the ground to grow longer; avoid disturbing adjacent plants. Remove all plant debris after harvesting to prevent the buildup of diseases.

▶ TURNIPS

Turnips are quick growing and can be harvested as baby roots after 6–7 weeks or left 11 weeks to grow larger. They prefer cool, moist conditions and need a fertile soil, improved with well-rotted organic matter. For an early crop, sow seed under cover in spring in modules and plant outside when the seedlings have one or two leaves. Instead of thinning, they can also be grown as clusters.

Varieties to try:
'Armand' • 'Atlantic' • 'Golden Ball' • 'Manchester Market' • 'Purple Top Milan' • 'Primera' • 'Snowball'

◀ RUTABAGAS

Rutabagas are slow-growing, ready to harvest in winter after 20–26 weeks. They need a sunny site with light soil that drains freely but doesn't dry out. Sow outside in late spring, in drills ¾ in (2 cm) deep. Cover with fleece or mesh to exclude cabbage root fly. Thin seedlings to 9 in (23 cm) apart, and water and weed regularly. Harvest the roots when 4–6 in (10–15 cm) across, and protect roots left in the soil in winter with a layer of straw.

Varieties to try:
'Brora' • 'Helenor' • 'Magres' • 'Marian' • 'Virtue'

▶ PARSNIPS

Parsnips need an open, sunny site with light soil that has been deeply dug to allow the roots to grow long and straight. Sow seeds direct in mid- to late spring once the soil starts to warm; germination can be erratic. Thin seedlings to 4–8 in (10–20 cm) apart, depending whether you want smaller or larger roots. Water sparingly to encourage deep-rooting, and harvest in late summer.

Varieties to try:
'Albion' • 'Countess' • 'Gladiator' • 'Panache' • 'Pinnacle' • 'The Student' • 'White Gem'

◀ CELERIAC

Although celeriac is commonly thought of as a root crop, it is the swollen stems that are eaten. It grows in sun or shade but prefers moist, rich soil improved with organic matter. Sow seed in spring in modules at 50°F (10°C); grow under cover, harden off, and plant out in late spring or early summer, 12 in (30 cm) apart with the crowns showing above the surface. Water regularly in summer, and harvest from early fall to late winter.

Varieties to try:
'Brilliant' • 'Giant Prague' • 'Monarch' • 'Prinz'

ONIONS AND SHALLOTS

Easy to grow and indispensable in the kitchen, onions are a good crop for beginners. Try your hand at raising sweet-tasting shallots and red-skinned onions, as well as the more traditional garden varieties.

	SPRING	SUMMER	FALL	WINTER
SOW/PLANT				
HARVEST				

French shallots: easy to hold and slice.

HOW TO GROW

Onions are undemanding to grow but prefer a sunny, sheltered spot and well-drained soil, enriched with organic matter. They can be raised from seed sown in the spring, or you can give yourself a head start and buy "sets," which are small bulbs to plant outside. Sow seed under cover into modules, and harden off the seedlings before planting them out in late spring. They can also be sown directly outside in drills in late spring, once the soil has warmed up, giving a useful late summer harvest.

Plant onion sets directly outside from early to mid-spring, 2–4 in (5–10 cm) apart in rows 12 in (30 cm) apart, pushing them into the soil with the tips uppermost until just protruding. Many shallots grow too slowly from seed, so plant sets from late winter to early spring, 6 in (15 cm) apart in rows 12 in (30 cm) apart.

Onions and shallots need little attention except regular watering and weeding. Once the leaves start to turn brown, bend over the tops to help ripen the bulbs. When ready in summer, lift the bulbs with a fork, then dry and store (see *facing page*).

TYPES AVAILABLE

Red onions are generally smaller and sweeter than traditional brown-skinned onions and can be finely sliced and eaten raw.

Brown onions have the strongest, most pungent flavor, and there are many to choose from. Some can be harvested small for pickling.

Round shallots need a long season and grow as small clumps, not individual bulbs. They are richer and sweeter tasting than onions.

French shallots are similar in flavor and growth pattern to the round ones, but are easier to chop because of their elongated shape.

VARIETIES TO TRY

Brown onions
'Ailsa Craig' • 'Bedfordshire' • 'Golden Bear' • 'Setton' F1 • 'Sturon'

Red onions
'Hyred' F1 • 'Kamal' • 'Red Baron' • 'Red Brunswick'

Overwintering onions
'Radar' • 'Senshyu Semi-globe Yellow' • 'Shakespeare'

Round shallots
'Delvad' • 'Golden Gourmet' • 'Pikant' • 'Prisma' F1 (raise from seed) • 'Red Gourmet'

French shallots
'Jermor' • 'Longor' • 'Mikor' • 'Pesandor' • 'Vigarmor' • 'Zebrune'

GROWING ONION SETS

1 Plant onion sets pointed-end up, pushing them lightly into the base of shallow drills. They can also be planted in containers for a small crop.

2 Onions need little routine care during the growing season. Keep them well weeded, but water only when established. Check them for signs of disease.

3 When the crop is ready to store, leave the bulbs on the soil surface to dry. Cover large crops if rain is predicted; small crops can be brought under cover.

4 Check stored onions for signs of disease or decay. Don't compost discarded bulbs since some diseases spread easily and are tricky to control.

Overwintering onions

Sometimes called Japanese or "overwintering" onions, these are hardy varieties that grow through the winter to harvest in midsummer. Sow seed in late summer directly into a bed outside, or plant sets mid- to late fall into well-drained soil. Plant more closely than summer varieties since some will be lost during the winter. Feed the plants twice in winter with a nitrogen-rich granular fertilizer, and thin them out in the spring. This technique can only be used with hardy onions—others bolt in cold weather.

Braiding onion bulbs together using their leaves is the traditional way to dry them and makes an interesting fall decoration.

Storing

Harvest onions and shallots when their leaves turn yellow and fall over; in midsummer for shallots, early to late summer for onions. Once lifted, lay the bulbs on the soil in the sun to dry out, ideally on wire mesh to allow air to circulate around them. If the weather is wet, dry the bulbs in a sunny, warm spot indoors. When the skins have turned papery, remove the leaves and any soil, and store them somewhere light and well ventilated. Lay them out in rows, braid them into ropes using their leaves, or store them in nets.

WATCH OUT FOR ...

Onion fly larvae eat the roots and bulbs, causing plants to yellow, wilt, and even die. Rake soil to expose pupae to birds, and cover young plants with garden fabric.

Onion white rot causes foliage to yellow and wilt, and white mold appears on the base of bulbs, which rot. Destroy infected plants, and rotate crops. (*For more pests and diseases advice, see pp.356–369.*)

GROWING GREEN ONIONS

Fast-growing green onions are a staple of summer salads and Asian cooking and are ready to harvest 4–6 weeks after sowing. They prefer fertile, well-drained soil and a sunny site. Sow successionally all summer from early spring, every month, into pots or shallow drills, ¾in (2cm) deep, 12in (30cm) apart, allowing ½in (1cm) between them. Weed regularly, and water in dry conditions. Harvest when 6in (15cm) high and of your preferred thickness.

Green onion 'Guardsman'

GARLIC

A member of the onion family, this versatile ingredient, highly valued for its culinary qualities, is extremely easy to grow. Although it takes time to mature, it grows through winter, takes up little space, and is good in pots.

		SPRING	SUMMER	FALL	WINTER
SOW/PLANT					
HARVEST					

Garlic can be purple- or white-skinned.

HOW TO GROW

Garlic needs warmth to ripen and grows best in a sunny site with rich, moist, well-drained soil. Ideally, plant in fall or early winter; spring-planted garlic will produce smaller bulbs because they have less time to mature. Separate the bulb into cloves, and push the largest ones (discarding any tiny ones) into the soil with the points upward; the tips should be just below the surface. Allow 4 in (10 cm) between cloves, and space rows 8 in (20 cm) apart. Keep the area around the plants free of weeds and the soil moist, particularly in dry conditions. Check regularly to make sure birds have not pulled out the cloves; if so, push them back into the soil.

Garlic is ready to lift when the leaves turn yellow and wilt. Using a hand fork, lift the bulbs, and lay them out to dry in the sun, ideally on wire mesh to allow good airflow. If the weather is wet, dry them indoors on trays, or hang them up in braids. Once dried, garlic can then be stored in braids or nets somewhere cool and well ventilated. If you prefer, harvest garlic while the stems are still green. This "wet" garlic has a milder flavor and should be used quickly because it will not store.

WATCH OUT FOR ...

Onion white rot (see p.233) causes foliage to wilt and bulbs to become moldy and rotten. It affects all members of the onion family, including garlic.

Rust causes orange patches on leaves, which wither and die, weakening the crop. Avoid planting in damp, shaded areas. There is no chemical control; remove infected material, and improve airflow.
(For more pests and diseases advice, see pp.356–369.)

PLANTING AND GROWING

1 Garlic needs a cold period to grow well and is best planted in the fall or winter. Plant it in beds or in larger containers.

2 Control weeds during the spring and summer, and keep plants well watered. Even if plants bolt (run to seed), they still give a good harvest.

3 After harvesting garlic, don't grow other members of the onion family, including leeks and shallots, in the same soil to prevent the buildup of diseases.

VARIETIES TO TRY

Supermarket garlic can be unreliable. Bulbs supplied by nurseries are virus-free and are bred to suit local conditions. Culinary bulbs are grown in warmer regions and won't tolerate cool growing conditions.

'Arno' • 'Californian Late' • 'Cristo' • 'Early Wight' • 'Germidour' • 'Early Purple Wight' • 'Solent Wight'

LEEKS

Although often thought of as a winter vegetable, leeks can be harvested from late summer to late spring and can be grown with little effort. They store well outside to prolong the harvest.

		SPRING		SUMMER		FALL		WINTER	
SOW/PLANT									
HARVEST									

HOW TO GROW

Leeks need a sheltered, sunny site and fertile, well-drained, ideally slightly acid soil; preferably heavy and moisture-retentive. Turn over the bed the fall before planting, and incorporate plenty of well-rotted compost or manure. For an early start, sow seed under cover in late winter in trays or modules, to a depth of 1 in (2.5 cm). When risk of frost has passed, harden off seedlings when pencil-thick, and transplant them into deep holes, 6 in (15 cm) in depth, 6 in (15 cm) apart with 12 in (30 cm) between rows. Water around the stems, and allow the water to settle the soil around them rather than backfilling and firming by hand. Seed can also be sown directly outside in drills from early to mid-spring. For a continuous crop, sow at regular intervals, and transplant when seedlings are 8 in (20 cm) tall.

Once established, weed often, but water only in dry spells, and apply a high-nitrogen granular fertilizer in midsummer to late winter for early to late crops. As the leeks grow, pile earth around the stems to exclude light ("hilling up"); this blanches the stems, making them white and sweet-tasting— deep planting is a good start to this process. Harvest as needed, late summer to late spring.

Storing leeks

To keep harvested leeks at their best, especially at the end of season when you need to clear the beds, bury the stems in shallow trenches. This keeps them fresh and frees up space for new-season crops.

◄ **Heeled in** leeks stay fresh for a few weeks until needed as long as the stems are covered with soil.

PLANTING OUT

1 Transplant from a seedbed or plant out leek seedlings in spring. Use a dibble to make deep individual planting holes, 6 in (15 cm) in depth.

2 Trim the roots with a knife or scissors so seedlings are easier to drop into their planting holes. This may slow growth, but the roots soon grow back.

3 Water well so the water washes the soil back into the deep planting holes without leaving large air pockets. This also prevents damage to the leek stems.

PEAS

Sweet, tender peas are well worth growing yourself for a taste that surpasses anything you can buy in the store. If you don't like shelling peas, try a sugar snap type, which can be eaten pod and all.

VARIETIES TO TRY

Podding peas
'Ambassador' • 'Early Onward' • 'Feltham First' • 'Hurst Greenshaft'

Sugar snap peas
'Cascadia' 'Lusaka' • 'Nairobi' • 'Sugar Ann'

Snow peas
'Delikata' • 'Oregon Sugar Pod' • 'Sweet Sahara' • 'Sweet Sensation'

	SPRING	SUMMER	FALL	WINTER
SOW/PLANT				
HARVEST				

HOW TO GROW

Peas grow best in rich, moist soil, improved with well-rotted organic matter, and a sunny spot that does not get too hot. Sow seed outside according to when you want your harvest, from early spring to early summer. Make a trench 2 in (5 cm) deep and 10 in (25 cm) wide, water well, then sow seeds at least 2 in (5 cm) apart, backfilling with soil. If you have space, plant another row 18–36 in (45–90 cm) away, depending on how tall the variety is, to allow space for picking and weeding. To gain a more continuous crop, sow at intervals when the preceding sowing is 2 in (5 cm) tall. For a head start, sow podded varieties indoors in late winter into long troughs or plastic guttering (*see right*), and plant out

in spring. Cover early sowings with fabric to protect plants against frost, and sow quick-growing snow peas and sugar snap peas in the late spring and early summer.

Once sown, position supports along the row for the plants to climb. All peas need supports; twiggy sticks are ideal for dwarf or shorter varieties; taller varieties benefit from a trellis, rows of bamboo canes, or netting. Keep plants well watered in warm weather; if planted into fertile soil, they won't require extra feeding. When the first pods are ready, pinch off the growing tips (which you can eat in salads). Peas are generally ready to pick about three months after sowing and are best harvested small and tender.

Sow indoors into plastic guttering for an extra early crop. Plant outside by sliding the pea seedlings out into a prepared trench.

TYPES AVAILABLE

Snow peas are eaten whole and should be picked just as the peas inside start to swell. Best eaten lightly steamed.

Sugar snap peas are allowed to develop longer than snow peas; pick when the pods fill out but the peas are tiny.

Podding peas are traditional garden peas that are shelled before eating. Pick them young for the best flavor and texture.

FAVA BEANS

Not for nothing are these plants, also called broad beans, traditional favorites of the garden; they are at their best when freshly picked. They are also easy to grow, producing good yields of tender crops in early summer.

		SPRING	SUMMER	FALL	WINTER
SOW/PLANT					
HARVEST					

HOW TO GROW

In the fall, choose a sunny, sheltered spot with well-drained, fertile soil, and dig in plenty of well-rotted organic matter, such as garden compost or manure. For early crops, sow seed under cover in pots in late fall, transplanting the seedlings outside in early to mid-spring. Sow seed outside in the fall in a sheltered site. Space seed 8 in (20 cm) apart in rows 18 in (45 cm) apart. For crops during the summer, sow successionally in early and mid-spring, when the previous sowing is 4 in (10 cm) tall. Support growing plants with twigs or bamboo canes, using smaller sticks for dwarf varieties. Mulch around the plants with compost, keep plants well weeded, and water regularly, especially when plants are in flower. Once the first pods have appeared at the base of each plant, pinch off the growing tips. This encourages the beans to mature more quickly and promotes a larger crop.

Harvest when the pods start to swell and the beans inside are thumbnail-size; they become tough and starchy if they grow too large. Pick regularly, cutting the pods off rather than pulling them to prevent damage to the plants. Eat as fresh as possible.

▶ **Fava beans** mature from the bottom of the stem upward. Each plant will crop over a few weeks as the pods develop.

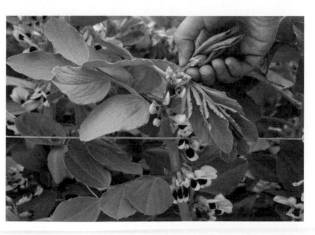

▶ **Removing the tips** once the first pod sets encourages quicker ripening and also deters blackfly, which target the soft growth. The tips can be eaten.

GREEN BEANS

Whether you grow bush varieties or climbers, green beans are the perfect crop for a small garden because just a few plants will keep you well stocked all summer. They're also a good choice for containers.

		SPRING	SUMMER	FALL	WINTER
SOW/PLANT					
HARVEST					

Green beans can be dried as haricots.

HOW TO GROW

Green beans need a warm site, sheltered from the wind, and prefer well-drained soil with organic matter dug in the fall before planting (*see below*). Sow seeds in spring indoors in modules or deep pots, 2 in (5 cm) deep. When plants are about 3 in (8 cm) tall, harden them off, and plant outdoors once all frost has passed. For a later crop, sow seeds outside when the soil is warmer.

Support climbing varieties with tall canes 6–8 in (15–20 cm) apart, one per plant. Plant bush varieties 6 in (15 cm) apart; they grow without support. Water frequently when in flower or cropping. Pick pods often while they are big enough to use but are still tender.

◄ **Encourage the plants** to twine around the supports, and pinch off the tips as they reach the top of the canes.

WATCH OUT FOR...

Green beans suffer many of the same pests and diseases as runner beans (*see facing page*).

Anthracnose causes red-brown spots on the pods, followed by pink slime in wet weather. No chemical controls; remove infected plants, or grow resistant varieties.

Bean halo blight causes small spots with bright surrounding rings on leaves, which die, reducing yield. Remove and destroy infected leaves.
(*For more pests and diseases advice, see pp.356–369.*)

VARIETIES TO TRY

Climbing varieties have a good crop in a small space; bush beans do well in pots.

Climbing varieties
'Borlotto Lingua di Fuoco 2' • 'Cobra' • 'Hunter' • 'Pantheon' • 'Sultana'

Bush varieties
'Annabel' • 'Delinel' • 'Ferrari' • 'Purple Teepee' • 'Sonesta'

Digging a bean trench

To encourage the best crop, a traditional method is to dig a trench 2 ft (60 cm) deep and as long as your planned rows of beans the fall before sowing. Loosen the soil at the base with a fork, then pile up vegetable and plant waste (the sort normally destined for the compost heap). Backfill with soil, and leave it to settle. By spring the soil will be rich and moisture retentive, ideal for green and runner beans (*see right*).

RUNNER BEANS

Worthy of a place in the border as well as the vegetable patch, these climbing beans race up their supports in a flurry of lush growth, creating leafy columns of brightly colored flowers. The beans are delicious and plentiful.

	SPRING	SUMMER	FALL	WINTER
SOW/PLANT				
HARVEST				

Runner beans mature in stages, so pick often.

HOW TO GROW

Runner beans need a sunny, sheltered location with deep, fertile soil, improved with organic matter the fall before planting. They grow best in bean trenches (*see below left*). Sow seeds under cover in mid-spring in deep pots, harden them off, and plant outdoors once the risk of frost has passed. Provide support (*see below*), planting one plant per cane. Runner beans can also be sown outside in late spring. Sow two beans per cane, thinning to the strongest plant. Water the plants well, especially when in bloom, or the flowers may drop off and won't mature into beans.

If planted into well-prepared soil, the developing beans won't need additional feeding.

Tie plants into their supports, pinching off the tips when they reach the top to prevent beans from forming out of reach. Harvest the beans while they are young and tender, about 4 in (10 cm) long, and before the seeds start to swell. Surplus fresh beans can be frozen.

If you have found a variety you like, allow some pods to develop fully in late summer. Collect the beans, and dry them on a sunny windowsill. Store them somewhere dry, cool, and frost free, and sow them again the following year.

WATCH OUT FOR ...

Runner beans suffer many of the same pests and diseases as green beans (*see facing page*).

Blackfly can form large colonies quickly, sucking sap and weakening plants. Spray heavy infestations with a suitable insecticide.

Rust can occur in wet conditions. Leaves and stems develop orange or brown pustules, then wither and die. Dispose of infected growth, and improve air flow around plants.
(For more pests and diseases advice, see pp.356–369.)

VARIETIES TO TRY

Most runner beans have either white or red flowers and are an attractive feature in the garden before the beans form.

Red-flowered beans
'Achievement' • 'Celebration' • 'Enorma' • 'Hestia' (bicolor) • 'Lady Di' • 'Painted Lady' (bicolor) • 'Polestar' • 'Stardust'

White-flowered beans
'Desiree' • 'Moonlight' • 'White Apollo' • 'White Emergo' • 'White Lady'

Providing support

Runner beans are tall climbers and reliably produce heavy crops, so they need strong support. Put these in place before sowing directly or planting out. The supports should be about 6 ft (1.8 m) tall and are most easily made from bamboo canes or bean poles. In smaller gardens, make individual frames using 5–6 uprights, or make a line of them (*see right*). Where space allows, or if you are growing a large crop, make a linear support with two rows of uprights, linked together with a cane along the top for added strength.

CABBAGES

One of the most popular of the brassica group of vegetables, cabbage has varieties to plant and harvest nearly all year. The selection includes textured savoys, sweet spring greens, and vibrant red-leaf varieties.

	SPRING	SUMMER	FALL	WINTER
SOW/PLANT				
HARVEST				

Savoy is a distinctive choice.

HOW TO GROW

Cabbages grow in sun or partial shade and prefer moist, fertile, slightly alkaline soil that has been improved with plenty of well-rotted organic matter, such as garden compost. The soil should also be firm to help support the large heads, especially in the winter. Depending on the type (see right), you can sow cabbage successively all year. Sow in early spring for summer cabbage; sow in late spring for fall and winter crops, and sow mid- to late summer for cabbage the following spring. Sow seed ¾ in (2 cm) deep under cover in modules or outside in a seedbed, and plant out or transplant the seedlings when they have 3–4 leaves. Keep plants well-watered until established, weed regularly, and remove any dead leaves. Harvest the cabbage when ready using a sharp knife, and clear away any plant debris.

WATCH OUT FOR ...

All brassicas suffer similar pests and diseases (see pp.242–245).

Clubroot attacks brassica roots, stunting growth and killing plants. It can last in the soil for 20 years, and there is no cure. Destroy infected plants, rotate crops, and lime the soil. Strong seedlings are less vulnerable. Some varieties show resistance, labeled (C) opposite.

Mealy cabbage aphids suck sap and weaken plants. They hide under the leaves. Spray with insecticide. (For more pests and diseases advice, see pp.356–369.)

◄ **Use collars** to protect young plants from cabbage root fly (see. p.244).

SOWING AND GROWING

1 Cabbages are hardy plants, but for an early start, sow in spring under cover into trays or modules. This will help produce stronger plants with greater resistance to clubroot..

2 When planting out, hold the cabbage by the leaves to avoid damaging the roots. Use a dibble to make planting holes about 6 in (15 cm) deep, water the hole before inserting the plant, then firm it in gently.

3 To harvest, use a sharp knife to cut the whole plant off at the base. Remove all debris to prevent the buildup of diseases, but don't disturb neighboring plants. Stumps may resprout if left in the ground, especially if a cross is cut in the top.

► SPRING CABBAGE

For spring crops, sow seed in late summer, and plant out in early to mid-fall. Space plants 10 in (25 cm) apart. Water well until established, then again only in dry spells. In winter, hill up the stems to help support the plants, and remove any dead or yellowing leaves. In spring, harvest by cutting the cabbages whole.

Varieties to try:
'Advantage' • 'Excel' F1 • 'Durham Early' • 'Frostie' F1 • 'Greyhound' • 'Spring Hero'

◄ SUMMER AND FALL CABBAGE

Sow seed in succession, early spring to early summer, to give a harvest through summer and fall. Make early-spring sowings under cover into modules, and harden plants off once they have 3–4 true leaves. Plant out 15–18 in (38–45 cm) apart once hard frosts have passed; cover plants with fabric on colder nights. Apply a granular feed when adjacent plants start to touch across rows.

Varieties to try:
'Deadon' • 'Derby Day' • 'Golden Acre' • 'Hispi' F1 • 'Kilaton' F1 (C) • 'Kilazol' F1 (C)

► WINTER CABBAGE

For crops through winter, sow seed in batches from late spring to early summer. Plant out or transplant when seedlings have 3–4 leaves, spacing them 18 in (45 cm) apart. Apply a granular fertilizer when adjacent plants start to touch. Hardier varieties can be left in the soil in winter until needed, others should be cut and stored in nets; they will last 6–8 weeks if kept cool.

Varieties to try:
'Celtic' • 'Cordesa' (C) • 'Ormskirk 1' F1 • 'Rigoletto' • 'Savoy King' • 'Tarvoy' • 'Tundra'

◄ RED CABBAGE

Harvested in summer to fall, sow seed for red cabbage from early to late spring; plant out or transplant the seedlings 18 in (45 cm) apart, once they have 3–4 leaves. Cover early crops with fabric to protect against frost. Water well until established, weed regularly, and apply granular fertilizer when neighboring plants start to touch. Harvest when the heads feel uniformly solid.

Varieties to try:
'Kalibos' • 'Lodero' (C) • 'Marner Large Red' • 'Red Flare' • 'Rookie' • 'Ruby Ball' • 'Ruby Perfection'

KALE

This vitamin-packed vegetable fell out of favor for a while but is now hugely popular. It is a hardy and easy-to-grow plant, as architectural as it is flavorful, and brings interest and sustenance to the winter garden.

	SPRING	SUMMER	FALL	WINTER
SOW/PLANT				
HARVEST				

HOW TO GROW

Kale is a hardy crop and will survive outside in the worst winter weather. It tolerates most soil types but prefers well-drained soil that has been improved with well-rotted organic matter, such as garden compost. It also benefits from firm, compacted soil, which helps support its tall stems. Sow seeds in mid-spring in pots or modules under cover, and plant out in the late spring and early summer. Plant 18 in (45 cm) apart, being careful not to damage the roots. Firm the plants in, and water thoroughly. Continue to water only sparingly, except in dry conditions, to encourage tougher leaves to overwinter.

Keep plants well weeded, and remove yellowing leaves as they appear. If lots of the leaves start to turn yellow in the early fall, apply a high-nitrogen granular or liquid fertilizer to restore color. If you are growing taller varieties, especially in exposed gardens, stake the plants before they are damaged by strong winds

Harvest kale from fall to spring, picking the tender leaves from the center of the crown to encourage regrowth. Remove any flowers that appear, but leave the older leaves in place to help protect the center. Harvest until the plants flower; the leaves then turn bitter.

Kale can also be grown as a cut-and-come-again salad (see p.207). Harvest when 2–3 in (5–8 cm) high, or later at 6 in (15 cm).

Colorful kale varieties make an attractive winter feature in the garden. They are ideal for smaller plots, allowing you to incorporate vegetables into mixed planting designs.

TYPES AVAILABLE

Curly kale varieties are sweeter-tasting and more tender than traditional smooth-leaf kale. They look attractive in the garden during winter.

Smooth-leaf kale is only grown for the tender leaves at the center of the plant. Some varieties make handsome border plants.

BRUSSELS SPROUTS

Few vegetables provoke as strong a reaction as Brussels sprouts—people either love or hate them. Easy to grow, sprouts taste sweetest after a few hard frosts and can be roasted and stir-fried as well as boiled.

	SPRING	SUMMER	FALL	WINTER
SOW/PLANT				
HARVEST				

HOW TO GROW

Brussels sprouts prefer a sunny site and neutral, moist, well-drained soil, improved with well-rotted organic matter. However, avoid very rich soils, which produce loose, open sprouts. They also benefit from a sheltered site and firm soil to prevent the laden stems being blown over in the winter. Sow seeds in trays or modules under cover in early spring, or outdoors into a seedbed in mid-spring. Thin direct-sown seedlings to 3 in (7.5 cm); plant out indoor-sown plants in mid-spring, when 4–6 in (10–15 cm) high, spacing them 31 in (75 cm) apart. Plant deeply, with the first true leaves level with the soil surface to ensure the plants won't blow over when their crop develops. Water well during dry spells, and cover with netting as the first sprouts form. Hill up around the stems to provide extra support, or stake plants growing on exposed or windy sites.

Start harvesting in the fall when the sprouts are firm, working from the bottom of the stem up, removing a few from each plant at a time. Alternatively, dig up the whole plant when it is covered in sprouts, and hang the stem in a cold, frost-free place (or stand it in a bucket of water), and pick as required.

GROWING SPROUTS

1 Firm the soil around new plants to help support the tall stems as they grow. Attach plant collars to protect against cabbage root fly.

2 Support the plants as they grow by hilling up with soil. In more exposed areas, insert canes or stakes to prevent plants from being rocked by the wind.

3 Use a sharp knife to harvest the sprouts, or twist them off with your fingers. Cut sprouts soon spoil, so only harvest when needed. Cut stems last several days.

BROCCOLI

Packed with vitamins and highly ornamental, broccoli is an asset to any garden. Choose from white or purple winter sprouting types, which bear an abundance of tender stems, or the large domed heads of summer calabrese.

		SPRING	SUMMER	FALL	WINTER
SOW/PLANT		███████	███████		
HARVEST		███████	███████	███	██

Broccoli 'Early White Sprouting'

HOW TO GROW

Broccoli grows best in a sunny site in rich soil that has been improved with plenty of well-rotted organic matter, such as garden compost or manure. The two types, sprouting and calabrese, are sown in different ways. Sow sprouting broccoli under cover into small pots or modules in early spring for early varieties, midsummer for late crops. From mid-spring it can also be sown directly outside in seedbeds and covered with cloches or fabric. Plant out or transplant seedlings into their final positions in late spring, once the frost has passed, leaving 24 in (60 cm) between plants and rows.

Summer calabrese dislikes root disturbance and should be sown outside where it will grow in soil that has been raked to a fine tilth. Sow in drills ½ in (2 cm) deep, 12 in (30 cm) apart, with 18 in (45 cm) between rows.

Keep both types well watered in the summer, and cover with netting so the heads are protected against birds. The heads can become heavy, so support plants using canes, or hill up the base of the stems. Harvest summer or winter heads before the tiny flowers within the florets open. Pick sprouting broccoli often to encourage an extended crop; the more you pick, the more it crops. Cut calabrese heads in the summer when less than 4 in (10 cm) across to encourage more flowering shoots; use a sharp knife to cut the florets, starting with the central head.

WATCH OUT FOR ...

All brassicas suffer from similar pests and diseases (see pp.240–245).

Cabbage root fly lay eggs near brassica plants, hatching into maggots that eat the roots. Plants are weakened and may die. There are no chemical controls; fit brassica collars around young plants.

Pigeons may attack plants during winter and spring, eating the foliage and flowers. Cover plants with netting, or build a scarecrow.
(For general advice, see pp.356–369.)

TYPES AVAILABLE

Calabrese is a quick-growing crop and is harvested the summer after sowing. Pick the heads while they are small for the largest harvest.

Sprouting broccoli is a winter staple and will crop for several weeks; harvesting the stems encourages growth.

VARIETIES TO TRY

Calabrese
Clubroot resistant varieties (C) are available.
'Apollo Brokali' F1 • 'Belstar' F1 • 'Fiesta' F1 • 'Monclano' F1 (C)

Sprouting
Different varieties of sprouting broccoli produce purple heads (P) or white (W).
'Claret' F1 (P) • 'Early White Sprouting' (W) • 'Rudolph' (P) • 'White Star' (W)

CAULIFLOWER

Cauliflower can be harvested most of the year, but it is sometimes challenging to grow. The extra effort is well rewarded, however, with delicious homegrown florets and colored types rarely seen in supermarkets.

	SPRING	SUMMER	FALL	WINTER
SOW/PLANT				
HARVEST				

HOW TO GROW

Cauliflower can be grown year-round, but sowing times differ for summer or winter varieties. All types of cauliflower need fertile, well-drained soil that is firm enough to support the heads and has been improved with well-rotted organic matter. For early summer crops, sow seed under cover in the fall in small pots, or sow in midwinter for a slightly later crop. If you don't have much space, try growing miniature summer varieties, which can be grown 6 in (15 cm) apart.

For a fall crop, sow under cover or outside under fabric in early spring.

Harden off seedlings before they reach 2 in (5 cm) tall, then transplant outside, 24 in (60 cm) apart. For winter varieties, sow in late spring outdoors where they can grow on, 30 in (75 cm) apart.

Keep the plants well watered as they grow, and feed them with liquid fertilizer in midsummer. If growing white varieties, shield the curds from the sun (*see below*). Harvest the heads while firm, cutting the stem with a sharp knife.

▶ **Cauliflower 'Romanesco'** is an unusual lime green variety with distinctive, pointed curds. It is sometimes described as a calabrese but is really a fall cauliflower.

BLANCHING THE HEADS

1 Cauliflower curds can discolor in bright sun. Prevent this by folding or tying 4–5 outer leaves over the center. Make sure the curds are dry to prevent them from rotting. Keep the leaves in place until harvest.

2 The curds are ready to pick when large enough to crop but still firm to touch. Do not harvest cauliflowers until you plan to use them; they soon deteriorate. When harvesting, cut the curd with some surrounding leaves to keep it fresh for longer.

GLOBE ARTICHOKES

The most elegant and statuesque of kitchen garden plants, globe artichokes wouldn't look out of place in an ornamental border. The huge flower buds are a delicious treat.

		SPRING	SUMMER	FALL	WINTER
SOW/PLANT					
HARVEST					

Globe artichokes can also be grown as ornamentals.

HOW TO GROW

Globe artichokes prefer a sheltered, sunny location in well-drained, moisture-retentive soil that has been enriched with well-rotted organic matter, such as garden compost. They are most commonly planted as young plants, bare root from fall to spring or as container-grown plants at any time if well watered afterward. If you want several plants, sow seed under cover into pots in late winter or early spring. Harden the seedlings off, and plant them out in early summer, 3 ft (90 cm) apart with 3–4 ft (90 cm–1.2 m) between rows. Water well and regularly during dry spells, and feed using a balanced general fertilizer in the spring.

To help new plants establish, remove any flowers produced the first year. In later years, the buds can be thinned to produce larger heads. When harvesting, timing is crucial; using pruners, cut the flower buds when they reach golf-ball size but before the scales start to open. Cut heads last a few days but are best used quickly. Harvest too late, and the heads are inedible.

Remove dead material when the plants die back in the fall, and if you live in a frost-prone area, protect the crown with a layer of straw over the winter. Plants should be replaced every three years. Take offsets (young shoots) in the spring from your existing plants and grow those.

Globe artichokes are large perennials and grow best in rich soil. Mulch plants in the fall or spring with well-rotted organic matter.

WATCH OUT FOR ...

Black bean aphids attack the stems and leaves, sucking sap, distorting growth, and weakening the plants. If severe, treat with a suitable insecticide (see p.359).

Petal blight is common in wet seasons and causes flower heads to turn brown, then shrivel and develop fluffy mold. There are no chemical controls. Remove infected heads, avoid planting in shady sites, and keep plants healthy.
(For more pests and diseases advice, see pp.356–369.)

JERUSALEM ARTICHOKES

Despite both being called "artichokes," globe and Jerusalem artichokes are not related. Globe artichokes are grown for their flower heads, while the Jerusalem type is a root crop, producing fleshy tubers in the fall that are eaten like potatoes and have a nutty flavor.

Related to the sunflower, Jerusalem artichokes are hardy perennials and grow well even in poor sites. They grow to over 6 ft (2 m) tall and can be used as a windbreak, although they will cast shade. The plants spread quickly and can be invasive if not harvested in fall. Lift the tubers when the foliage dies back. Replant some tubers to grow on, and harvest the rest. Use them fresh.

VARIETIES TO TRY

If growing globe artichokes in smaller gardens, choose varieties with colored heads (C), and plant in mixed borders. Watch for:

'Green Globe Improved' • 'Gros Vert de Laon' • 'Purple Globe' (C) • 'Romanesco' (C) • 'Violetta di Chioggia' (C)

ASPARAGUS

These succulent spears appear only briefly in the late spring, but once established, they crop for many years with very little maintenance. Tender spears appear in the late spring and can be harvested for several weeks.

	SPRING	SUMMER	FALL	WINTER
SOW/PLANT				
HARVEST				

The spears are delicious steamed.

HOW TO GROW

This perennial plant grows in the same spot for up to 20 years, so choose the site carefully. It prefers a sunny, sheltered location with well-drained soil, improved before planting with plenty of well-rotted organic matter. It is usually grown from young bare root crowns, planted in the spring (see below), or can be planted as container-grown specimens at any time of year if well watered. For the most productive plants, choose all-male varieties. If you want a lot of plants and are willing to wait for them to grow, asparagus can also be grown from seed. Sow the seed under cover

in late winter into modules, then plant out the seedlings in the spring once they have been hardened off.

New crowns should be allowed to establish themselves for at least two years before harvesting (see below). Keep the plants well watered all summer, mulch with well-rotted organic matter in the fall, and apply a balanced granular fertilizer in the spring, before and after harvesting. During summer, support the tall, ferny growth with canes, and keep plants well-weeded. At the end of summer, cut down the yellowing growth to 1 in (2.5 cm) above the soil, and clear away all plant debris.

VARIETIES TO TRY

All-male asparagus hybrids (M) are the best choice because they don't waste energy producing seed, giving stronger crops. Most named varieties are sold as plants or as bare root crowns.

'Ariane' • 'Backlim' F1 (M) • 'Connover's Colossal' • 'Gijnlim' (M) • 'Jersey Knight' • 'Pacific Purple' • 'Theilim' F1 (M)

PLANTING AND HARVESTING

1 Dig a trench, 8 in (20 cm) deep, add rich organic matter, and mound up the base. Position the bare root crowns, spacing them 12 in (30 cm) apart, and spread out the roots. Cover them with soil, and water well.

2 Mature plants, planted at least two years earlier, should be picked as the new shoots appear in spring. Cut off the spears 1 in (2.5 cm) below soil level when they are about 8 in (20 cm) tall. Remove every spear to encourage more to grow.

WATCH OUT FOR ...

Slugs and snails eat the emerging spears in the spring and can be particularly damaging. Apply slug pellets, use beer traps, or use anti-slug nematodes as biological control.

Asparagus beetle larvae and adults feed on the spears and foliage, weakening the plants. Destroy them on sight. Spray badly affected plants with a suitable insecticide.
(For more pests and diseases advice, see pp.356–369.)

ANNUAL HERBS

Fast-growing annual herbs are a must in the garden, even if you only have space for a few pots. They thrive in beds or containers, so plant them close to your kitchen door or backyard grill to pick fresh whenever needed.

		SPRING	SUMMER	FALL	WINTER
SOW/PLANT					
HARVEST					

Thai basil has a subtly different flavor, making it an interesting variety to grow.

HOW TO GROW

Annual herbs are quick and easy to grow from seed sown in batches from late spring to summer to give a constant supply into fall, or sown under cover in winter if given enough light and warmth. When they are large enough to plant out, they can be grown outside in beds and containers in a sheltered, sunny site in moist, well-drained soil or compost. When planting in beds, avoid very fertile sites; this promotes leafy growth that is poorly flavored. Similarly, feed herbs planted in containers only sparingly. Watering is more important however, since cilantro and dill are prone to suddenly bolting (running to seed) if plants become dry. Harvest the leaves and stems as needed, picking regularly to encourage new growth. Keep some for drying, freezing, or for making into pesto.

◄ **Once in flower**, annual herbs are past their best, but continue growing to collect seed.

WATCH OUT FOR ...

Aphids are attracted by the leafy growth, sucking sap and weakening plants. Avoid using insecticides; encourage natural predators, such as ladybugs, blast the pests off with water, or use organic control.

Slugs and snails are major pests, s poiling leaves or eating whole plants. Apply slug pellets, or use nematodes as biological control.
(*For more pests and diseases advice, see pp.356–369.*)

SOWING UNDER COVER

1 To avoid disturbing roots when planting out, sow basil and parsley into large-module trays that provide space for the seedlings to develop. Use a growing mix for starting seeds.

2 Make hollows in the growing mix at the correct depths, and sow seed into them. Cover with compost, water, and cover the trays with clear plastic to keep moist. Keep the trays at the required temperature.

3 Seeds germinate at different rates, so check often. As soon as seedlings appear, remove any covers, and keep them warm. Thin them as they grow to leave the single strongest plant per module. Harden off and plant out.

▶ BASIL

This is a tender annual with aromatic leaves and stems. Sow seed under cover into module trays in spring, harden off, and plant out in a sheltered, sunny border or container, or grow on under cover. Pinch off regularly to encourage bushier growth. Container plants can be brought in and grown over the winter in a bright spot. There are many types to consider, some quite decorative.

Varieties to try:
'Aristotle' • 'Genovese' • 'Lime' • 'Neapolitan' • 'Purple Ruffles' • 'Sweet Green' • 'Siam Queen' • 'Thai Sita'

◀ PARSLEY

This is a biennial herb, commonly grown as an annual for its tasty flat or crinkled leaves. Sow seed under cover in spring into modules to prevent root disturbance, which can trigger bolting; germination can be slow. Harden off and plant out into moist, well-drained soil in sun or partial shade. Seed can also be sown outside in summer in drills. Keep plants well-watered during spring and summer, and remove any flowers that appear.

Varieties to try:
'Envy' • 'Moss Curled 2' • 'Paravert' • 'Plain Leaved 2'

▶ DILL

This tall herb is grown for its mild-tasting leaves and seed and makes a decorative addition to borders. Sow directly in spring in its final growing position into moist, fertile soil. If transplanted, disturbed, or allowed to become dry, dill will bolt. Sow successively in batches until midsummer. Harvest the leaves before the plant flowers, and use them fresh or dried. Collect the seeds as they turn brown and dry, then store them.

Varieties to try:
'Diana' • 'Dukat' • 'Tetra'

◀ CILANTRO

Cilantro is a tall annual, grown for its tasty leaves and seed (known as coriander). Sow seed in regular batches, directly outside in their final growing positions from early spring to late summer. It prefers a moist, well-drained soil; grow in full sun for seed, partial shade for leaves. Keep plants well watered to prevent bolting. Harvest and use the leaves fresh, and freeze any surplus. Allow the seed to turn brown and dry before collecting it.

Varieties to try:
'Calypso' • 'Confetti' • 'Slow Bolt'

HARDY BORDER HERBS

Once established, hardy perennial and shrubby herbs provide a wealth of different flavors and scents year after year. Many form large clumps or bushes, so you won't need many plants to supply all your culinary needs.

		SPRING	SUMMER	FALL	WINTER
SOW/PLANT		████	██		
HARVEST			████	████	██

Sage and thyme like a sunny spot.

HOW TO GROW

Most perennial and woody herbs originate from the Mediterranean and prefer a hot, sunny location with poor, dry soil. Good drainage is essential, and if planting on heavy soil, first dig in some coarse sand and bulky organic matter, such as composted bark. Perennial herbs are normally sold container-grown, and are planted in spring and summer when in active growth. Some, like tarragon and mint, spread quickly and can be invasive, so should be planted into containers placed into the soil to restrict their growth.

Hardy herbs are easy to grow and often develop stronger scents and flavors when neglected. In addition to watering in dry spells, support taller herbaceous herbs, like mint, in summer but cut all growth to the ground in fall. They also benefit from being divided every couple of years (see *pp.332–333*). Once established, shrubby herbs like sage and bay require only a light trim in spring to keep them in shape.

Many hardy herbs can also be grown in containers, provided they have good drainage. Plant into cactus growing mix, and site the pots in sunny, sheltered locations. Water regularly; feed herbaceous herbs monthly, shrubby ones annually.

WATCH OUT FOR ...

Slugs and snails eat the softer leaves and stems, especially in spring. Herbaceous herbs are most affected. Apply slug pellets, use beer traps, or lay gritty traps.

Cats can be a particular problem on herb beds, which they often use as litter areas. Use cat repellent sprays or powders, or insert twigs or stems and netting to act as a barrier. (*For further advice, see pp.356–369.*)

PLANTING AN HERB BED

1 Choose a sunny spot, and prepare the soil by adding sand to heavy soils or organic matter to lighter soil. Weed the area thoroughly.

2 Lay plastic membrane before planting the herbs to suppress weeds. This will help warm the soil earlier in spring and retain moisture in summer.

3 Use a sharp knife to cut holes in the membrane, and plant through it. For a formal design, consider edging the bed with a low hedge.

4 Choose a variety of herbs that prefer the same growing conditions. Arrange them before deciding their final positions, allowing space for them to grow.

► **Mint** is a spreading perennial that can be invasive, so contain its roots. It needs moist, well-drained soil and will tolerate some shade.

◄ **Rosemary** is an evergreen shrubby herb, best planted in poor, well-drained soil in a sunny site. Harvest the stems regularly.

► **Thyme** is a low-growing evergreen perennial that will form a dense carpet. It is ideal for patio containers and window boxes.

◄ **Sage** is an evergreen shrubby herb, best grown in a sunny location in well-drained soil. It can be short-lived in cooler areas.

► **Bay** is a reliable evergreen shrub. It can be grown in large patio containers if clipped regularly. Does not tolerate frost.

◄ **Oregano** is a low-growing perennial herb, ideal for containers. It needs a sunny spot and well-drained soil. There are many varieties.

► **Chives** This grasslike perennial will tolerate some shade and forms a spreading clump. Its leaves and flowers can be eaten.

◄ **Tarragon** is a spreading perennial herb. There are two main types, Russian and French; French is more highly regarded for flavor.

FRUIT IN THE GARDEN

Growing your own fruit may conjure up images of space-hungry orchards and strawberry fields, but with a bit of careful planning, fruit trees, bushes, and vines can be included in even the smallest garden designs.

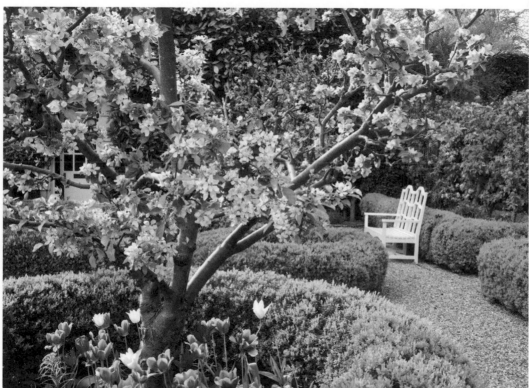

▲ DUAL-PURPOSE FRUIT

Although grown for their crops, many fruit trees and bushes are highly decorative. Spring-flowering apples and cherries are as attractive as many ornamental types, with the bonus of fruit in summer and fall. Fruit bushes, such as blueberries, give a good show even in containers, easily rivaling conventional flowering shrubs.

▶ MIXED PLANTING

Rather than creating a fruit garden, plant fruit in mixed beds and borders. Most fruit trees can be underplanted with ornamentals, and some make attractive focal points, while many bushes are good companions to border and patio ornamentals. You can even add delicious summer strawberries to your hanging baskets.

◄ PATIO CONTAINER

Containers offer a useful way to grow fruit in gardens where the soil is poor, the site is cold and exposed, or you don't have space in the borders. Some fruit, such as blueberries, need an acid soil and are usually grown in containers, as are tender crops like peaches, which can be moved to a sheltered spot when flowering. Most fruit can be grown in pots and will need regular feeding and watering during summer; some may need support.

▲ DWARF VARIETIES

If you don't have space for larger trees or want to grow several on a smaller plot, choose dwarf or grafted varieties. The yield will be smaller than full-sized trees, but the quality and flavor are identical. Choose trees on rootstocks to suit your needs, whether growing them in pots or borders. Also consider family trees, with two or more varieties on one stem.

▲ WALL-TRAINED FRUIT

If you have a sunny wall, this is a spectacular and space-saving way to grow fruit. You can buy some plants already partially trained, or you can do the training yourself. Fruits, such as peaches and nectarines, thrive when grown this way, particularly on warm brick walls, and are easier to cover with fabric or netting to protect the blossom and fruit. A wide range of trees from cherries to pears are suitable for wall-training. Grapes are an obvious candidate. Wall-training requires some skill, which can be learned over a few seasons.

BUYING AND PLANTING FRUIT

When you have decided what crops you'd like to grow, you then need to decide how, where, and when to buy your plants; whether you need more than one; and the best way to plant them.

BUYING NEW FRUIT PLANTS

Fruit plants are widely available in large garden centers, which offer a reasonable choice all year. Trees and plants are usually supplied in containers and can be planted immediately. Specialty nurseries generally offer a wider selection of fruit, often supplied bare root in winter, and often by mail.

Container-grown plants

The advantage of container-grown plants is that they can be planted at any time of year, if well watered afterward. You can also inspect plants for health and vigor before you buy them. When buying container-grown fruit, avoid those with weeds in the soil or bulging pots. Ease the plants from their pots, and reject any that are pot-bound, which will root poorly. Plant as soon as possible; keep them watered if this isn't possible.

Bare root plants

Lifted and sold when dormant, bare root plants are available only from late fall until spring. They are supplied without soil surrounding their roots so should be planted right away, or temporarily planted, "heeled in," to prevent them from drying out. Bare root plants are often cheaper than container-grown specimens, and the range available is larger.

Container-grown plants can be planted at any time of year. Inspect them carefully before deciding which trees to buy.

They are usually supplied by specialty nurseries, although garden centers may also sell some bare root plants, such as raspberry canes.

FLOWER POLLINATION

The blossoms of fruit trees and bushes are pollinated by insects, and many varieties must be cross-pollinated by another plant of the same species in order to fruit. If you have limited space, buy self-pollinating varieties; you will only need one plant, although trees fruit better if cross-pollinated. Alternatively, find out what type of pollinator your tree needs before buying, and check nearby gardens to see if there are suitable varieties.

For successful cross-pollination, compatible trees must flower together (be in the same "pollination group"). Some apples and pears are "triploids," meaning their pollen is sterile and they require two pollinators to fruit.

PLANTING BARE ROOT FRUIT

Plant bare root fruit trees and bushes as soon as possible to prevent the roots from drying out. The planting technique differs from planting container-grown plants (see p.121), because roots are exposed and can be easily damaged. Bare root plants often establish more quickly than container-grown, rooting directly into the new soil.

1 Dig a suitably large hole, and lower the plant in place, using a cane to ensure the mark on the stem is level with the soil surface. Tease out the roots gently, and spread them out evenly inside the planting hole.

2 Mix organic matter into the soil, and backfill, working it gently in between the roots. Make sure the plant is planted upright, then water the soil every few spadefuls to ensure there are no air pockets trapped between the roots.

3 If planting trees or larger shrubs, support the main stems using stakes and adjustable ties that can be loosened as the plant grows. Support smaller shrubs using canes. Remember to check ties regularly for adjustment.

4 Once the tree or shrub is planted, and supported if necessary, water it thoroughly to help settle soil around the roots. Mulch around the plant to retain moisture, and water regularly during dry spells until established.

PLANTING WALL-TRAINED FRUIT

Training fruit against walls and fences is a useful way to use empty vertical surfaces for crops, but they must be planted correctly. The important thing is to provide basic support first, such as horizontal wires or trellis, so the plants can be tied in as they are planted. Additional supports can then be added as the plants grow.

1 Horizontal wires, spaced 2 ft (60 cm) apart, are ideal for training fruit against walls and fences and are easy to affix using vine eyes or screw eyes (above). Use strong, galvanized wire, which is very long lasting.

2 If planting a row of wall-trained fruit, mark the planting distances first so they are evenly spaced. Cordon trees and soft fruits can be planted more closely than free-standing plants, as little as 12 in (30 cm) apart.

3 Once planted, train the stems and branches as required, whether vertical, angled, or fan-trained, and tie them onto the wires with soft string. Use canes to hold young stems straight, and remove them once mature.

4 Rain may have difficulty reaching the roots of wall-trained fruit, so plants should be watered frequently until well established. Mulch plants to help retain moisture, and water mature fruiting plants well during dry spells.

A YEAR IN THE FRUIT GARDEN

Most fruiting trees and plants are perennials, so there is no need to sow or plant them every year. Because they are in the ground for many years, routine care is vital if good crops are to be produced. Fruit left to its own devices often produces poor yields and can be prone to problems.

SPRING

Preparation
- **Early spring** is your last chance to spray trees with a winter wash to deter pests, such as aphids.
- **Mulch around the base** of all fruit trees and bushes using well-rotted manure or compost.
- **Top-dress container-grown plants,** and feed fruit trees and bushes with an appropriate fertilizer.
- **Water and feed plants regularly** as temperatures rise and the plants come into vigorous growth.

Sowing seed
- **Sow melon seeds** under cover in mid- to late spring in a heated greenhouse; sow in midsummer if your greenhouse is unheated.

Planting out
- **Plant strawberry runners** when the soil has warmed up, and cover with cloches or fabric until after the last frost. To help build up the plants, don't let them fruit in their first year. Pick the flowers off in mid-spring.
- **Plant bare root trees** and bushes in early and mid-spring, as long as the soil is not frozen. This will be your last opportunity. (Container-grown types can be planted at any time of year.)
- **Finish planting raspberry canes** in mid-spring.

Routine care
- **Keep trees and plants well weeded**, being careful not to damage their roots.
- **Prune fan-trained peaches** and nectarines.
- **If frost protection is not already in place**, cover any tender plants with horticultural fabric to protect the blooms. Plum and cherry trees may also need protection.
- **Hand-pollinate** vines or trees that are growing under glass, which may not be accessible to insect pollinators.
- **In mid-spring**, prune and tie in fig trees.

- **In late spring**, train your grapevines, pinching off the vine shoots to leave two laterals (see *p.275*).
- **Prune out dead and damaged growth** from plum trees, and remove any unwanted shoots on trained trees.
- **Tie blackberries**, loganberries, and tayberries into their supports if necessary.
- **Once flowers appear**, cover soft fruits with netting to protect the developing fruits from birds.
- **Apply a mulch of straw** around the base of strawberry plants to suppress weeds and keep the fruit clean.
- **Check regularly for signs of pests and diseases**, especially sawfly caterpillars, which may target gooseberry and currant bushes. Deal with them as they appear (see *individual fruit guides or pp.356–369 for further general information*).

Harvesting
- **Harvest any early gooseberries** that have been grown under cover.

Keep strawberries clean on a bed of straw.

SUMMER

Routine care

• **In early summer**, peg down or remove the runners from fruiting strawberry plants.
• **Thin out fruits** of apple, pear, plum, peach, apricot, and nectarine trees, and grapevines.
• **Net cherry trees** to deter birds.
• **Make sure plants are well watered**—especially those in containers—and mulch to conserve moisture and suppress weeds.
• **Feed plants** with high-potash fertilizer as the fruits develop.
• **Remove any dead and diseased shoots** and plants, and destroy them rather than composting.
• **Check for signs of pests and diseases**, and take immediate action should any appear.
• **Continue to tie in trained plants**, such as blackberries and other hybrid berries.
• **Prune currant bushes** and gooseberries.
• **In late summer**, prune fruited stems of apples and pears. Prune damsons and plums after fruiting.
• **Deadhead herbs** after flowering.

Harvesting

• **Harvest tree fruits as they appear**, and prune nectarines, apricots, and peaches once they have fruited.
• **Pick ripe currants** and gooseberries as they appear.
• **Blueberries, strawberries, summer-fruiting raspberries, and currants** should be ready for picking by midsummer.

Other tasks

• **Once strawberries have fruited**, remove old straw and leaves. Cut out fruited raspberry canes.

FALL AND WINTER

Routine care

• **In fall**, weed thoroughly around all plants, and cut off and remove any damaged or diseased shoots.
• **Finish any summer pruning** of tree fruits, and tie in any wayward shoots on trained plants.
• **Make sure stakes are secure** and firmly in the ground, and check the tree ties are in place.
• **Move any tender plants indoors,** such as citrus.
• **Cut out old canes of blackberries** and hybrid berries after they have fruited.
• **In winter,** remove any netting from plants to prevent damage if snow falls.
• **Apply winter washes to trees and bushes** as needed. Apply a top-dressing of sulfate of potash to all plants.
• **Cover peaches, apricots, and nectarines** to protect their blooms from peach leaf curl and early spring frost, and wrap up containers to protect against frost damage.
• **Prune apples and pears** if frost is not forecast.
• **Prune fall raspberries**, gooseberries, and currants.
• **Cover strawberries** with cloches or fabric.
• **Move container-grown plants under cover** to encourage an earlier crop.
• **Take precautions** against pests and diseases.

Harvesting

• **Pick fall raspberries** until the first frost, and harvest any remaining everbearing strawberries.
• **Harvest the last ripening fruits,** and store any excess.

Other tasks

• **In fall**, order any new bare root trees or bushes, and prepare the soil for them.
• **In winter**, plant bare root plants as soon as they arrive if the soil isn't frozen.

Thin plum fruitlets to encourage full-sized fruit.

Prune pear and apple trees in winter for the best crop.

Use fabric to protect plants from frost.

MANAGING A GLUT

For many fruit crops, even more so than vegetables, the harvest is fast and furious in summer and fall, often presenting you with a glut. Fortunately, there are ways to even out the harvest, and by using simple preserving techniques, you need not waste a single berry.

▼ EVEN OUT THE HARVEST

All types of fruit have their own cropping periods, but with careful planning you can aim for a selection that gives a steady, mixed harvest, from gooseberries and strawberries in early summer to late apples and grapes in fall. Most fruit is also available in early-, mid-, and late-season varieties, which extends their season by several weeks.

You can also extend the growing season of certain container-grown fruit, such as everbearing strawberries, by moving them under cover in the spring or fall.
Blueberries have a long harvest period, with early varieties ready in July and late ones cropping into September.

▼ STORE APPLES AND PEARS

Established apple and pear trees tend to be bountiful and most likely to give you a surplus crop. Early-fruiting varieties should be eaten fresh, but late croppers will last for weeks or months if stored correctly.

Harvest apples when they pull away in your hand; pick the pears when still underripe. To store, select only unblemished fruit and place them in single layers in shallow containers or on shelves. Store the fruit in a cool, frost-free, well-ventilated spot under cover, and check them regularly for signs of decay.
Apples and pears can be wrapped in tissue or newspaper. Store them in a container that allows air to circulate.

▼ FREEZING FRUIT

Freezing freshly picked fruit is the best way to preserve the flavors, colors, and textures while at their peak. All sorts of fruit can be stored this way, whether frozen whole like gooseberries, pitted like cherries, or first cut into usable slices, like apples and peaches.

Some soft fruits have a tendency to clump together when frozen, especially small berries, and are best frozen individually on trays. When frozen, they can then be placed into bags and containers. You can also use this method to prevent sliced fruit from sticking together when frozen. Date all frozen fruit, and use within 3–6 months to enjoy it at its best.

Freeze small berries in a single layer on a baking tray before moving into labeled freezer bags or containers.

▶ PRESERVING

Canning is a traditional method of preserving fruit (either whole or in large pieces) and can be used for a wide range of tree and bush fruit. There are various ways to can fruit, but all involve putting the fruit in bottles or jars with hot or cold sugar syrup, heating, then sealing them with air-tight lids. The jars should be stored in a cool, dark place, and used throughout fall and winter.

Fruit can also be bottled in alcohol to produce flavored alcohol, such as raspberry vodka, or steeped in wine or cider vinegar to make fruit-flavored vinegars. Only preserve clean, undamaged fruit.

Sterilize all containers by washing thoroughly in hot, soapy water before drying completely in a warm oven.

▼ JAMS, SAUCES, AND CORDIALS

The traditional approach to preserving fruit is to boil it in sugar and water to make thick-set jams or syrupy cordials. This is a simple way of preserving many types of fruit, including currants, strawberries, gooseberries, blackberries, raspberries, apples, and plums, either as single or mixed flavors.

Jams will last for up to six months. Fruit sauces often contain spices, and are cooked until thickened but still runny. They keep for a few weeks. Cordials are strained to a thin syrup, which is then diluted with water to drink right away. The syrup will last a few days or can be frozen in ice cube trays as individual portions.

Some soft fruits require additional pectin, which can be purchased, to produce a thick-set jam.

FRUIT CROP PLANNER

Use this table to check when to sow, plant, and harvest your fruit. The planting times are approximations. For local information, please check the USDA Zone Map and your extension office.

CROPS		J	F	M	A	M	J	J	A	S	O	N	D
Apples	SOW												
	PLANT	■	■									■	■
	HARVEST								■	■	■		
	PRUNE	■	■					■	■			■	■
Apricots	SOW												
	PLANT	■	■									■	■
	HARVEST								■				
	PRUNE			■	■			■	■				
Blackberries and hybrids	SOW												
	PLANT	■	■									■	■
	HARVEST							■	■	■			
	PRUNE												
Blueberries	SOW												
	PLANT	■	■									■	■
	HARVEST								■	■			
	PRUNE	■	■									■	■
Cherries	SOW												
	PLANT	■	■										
	HARVEST						■	■	■				
	PRUNE			■	■		■						
Currants—black	SOW												
	PLANT	■	■									■	■
	HARVEST						■	■	■				
	PRUNE	■	■									■	■
Currants—red and white	SOW												
	PLANT	■	■									■	■
	HARVEST						■	■	■				
	PRUNE	■					■	■				■	■
Figs	SOW												
	PLANT	■	■									■	■
	HARVEST								■	■			
	PRUNE		■	■			■	■	■				
Gooseberries	SOW												
	PLANT	■	■									■	■
	HARVEST					■	■	■					
	PRUNE	■					■					■	■

Key
- SOWN, PLANTED, HARVESTED UNDER COVER
- SOWN, PLANTED, HARVESTED OUTDOORS

CROPS		J	F	M	A	M	J	J	A	S	O	N	D
Grapes—outdoor	SOW												
	PLANT	■	■									■	■
	HARVEST									■	■		
	PRUNE			■	■	■	■	■	■			■	■
Peaches and nectarines	SOW												
	PLANT	■	■									■	■
	HARVEST								■	■			
	PRUNE					■	■	■	■				
Pears	SOW												
	PLANT	■	■									■	■
	HARVEST									■	■	■	
	PRUNE							■	■	■			
Plums, damsons, and gages	SOW												
	PLANT	■	■									■	■
	HARVEST							■	■	■	■		
	PRUNE				■	■	■	■	■	■			
Quinces	SOW												
	PLANT	■	■									■	■
	HARVEST										■	■	
	PRUNE	■	■									■	■
Raspberries—summer	SOW												
	PLANT	■	■									■	■
	HARVEST						■	■	■				
	PRUNE								■	■	■		
Raspberries—fall	SOW												
	PLANT	■	■								■	■	■
	HARVEST							■	■	■	■		
	PRUNE	■	■										
Strawberries—summer	SOW												
	PLANT		■	■	■			■	■	■			
	HARVEST				■	■	■						
	PRUNE												
Strawberries—everbearing	SOW												
	PLANT			■	■	■	■	■	■	■			
	HARVEST						■	■	■	■	■		
	PRUNE												

APPLES

Apple trees can be grown in the smallest of spaces and can be trained into different forms, such as fans or cordons, to suit any site. As well as producing delicious fruit, they also provide spectacular displays of blooms in the spring.

		SPRING	SUMMER	FALL	WINTER
PLANT					
HARVEST					

Worcester Pearmain is a dessert variety.

HOW TO GROW

Plant apple trees in a warm, sunny location—although cooking varieties are more tolerant and can be trained on north-facing walls. All prefer free-draining, fertile soil but will tolerate all but very wet or dry conditions. Bare root trees can be planted in late fall to early spring; container-grown apples can be planted at any time as long as you incorporate plenty of compost or manure. Freestanding trees require staking; trained varieties, such as fans and cordons need a system of posts and wires or can be trained onto a fence or wall. Remove any fruit for the first two years to encourage the tree to establish fully and develop a branching structure.

Apple varieties, such as 'Golden Noble', can be bought on rootstocks of different vigor to suit your particular needs.

Pollination

Apple flowers must be pollinated to bear fruit, and unless apple trees are growing nearby, you'll need to plant at least two varieties from the same pollination group (trees are listed A to D: early to late), according to when they flower. Some are termed "self-pollinating" but will crop better if cross-pollinated. Some, like 'Bramley's Seedling', are triploid. These need two pollinator varieties to bear fruit but cannot be used as pollinators themselves. Seek expert advice.

If you only have room for one tree and no pollinator, consider a "family tree," with two or more varieties grafted onto one plant.

Rootstocks

Apple trees are sold grafted onto rootstocks to control their size and vigor. Choose one that best suits your garden and your own needs.
M27 Most dwarfing, ideal for trees planted in containers. Trees grow to 5–6 ft (1.5–2 m).
M9 Dwarfing, needs good soil, but suitable for large containers. Trees grow to 6 ft (2 m).
M26 Semi-dwarfing, ideal for large containers, cordons, and fans. Trees grow to 8 ft (2.5 m).
MM106 Semi-vigorous, ideal for fans. Trees grow to 12–17 ft (4.5–5 m).
MM111 Vigorous, requires space. Trees grow to 17–21 ft (5.5–6.5 m).
M25 Very vigorous, suitable for large gardens. Trees grow to 25 ft (8 m).

VARIETIES TO TRY

Cooking varieties
'Bramley's Seedling' (triploid) • 'Golden Noble' (C) • 'Howgate Wonder' (C) • 'Lane's Prince Albert' (D)

Dessert varieties
'Court Pendu Plat' (D) • 'Discovery' (B) • 'Egremont Russet' (A) • 'Fiesta' (B) • 'James Grieve' (B) • 'Golden Delicious' (C) • 'Lord Lambourne' (A) • 'Pixie' (C) • 'Sunset' (B)

Fruiting types

Most apple trees are "spur-bearing," which means their fruit is produced on short, stubby spurs that form on stems at least two years old. Over time more spurs form, giving more fruit, until they eventually become overcrowded and need thinning out in winter (*see right*).

Other varieties are referred to as "tip-bearing" and carry much of their fruit at the ends of stems produced the previous summer. When pruning these trees, the aim is to remove stems and branches that have fruited, and to encourage new shoots that will fruit in following years. Before pruning your trees, make sure you know what type they are first.

Pruning and training

All apples should be trained into shape when first planted. Established, freestanding trees need only basic pruning in winter. Trained trees are additionally pruned in summer.

Pruned growth

After planting, prune one- or two-year-old trees to 24–30 in (60–75 cm) high, leaving 3–4 lateral stems. Cut these back by two-thirds.

Prune spur-bearing trees to maintain an open center. Prune strong new side shoots back to 4–6 buds; reduce weaker growth by half. Thin out crowded fruiting spurs and remove dead wood.

Prune tip-bearing apples, cutting side shoots over 12 in (30 cm) long back to a bud. Tip-prune the main branches. Maintain an open center and prune dead or diseased stems.

Fruit thinning

In midsummer, after the "June drop," when the tree drops excess fruitlets, those that remain should be thinned to allow them to grow to full size. When trees are left to overcrop, the apples are smaller and may not ripen fully, and the overladen branches can snap. Thin fruit clusters to one or two fruitlets per 4–5 in (10–12 cm) of stem on dessert apples, and single fruitlets every 6–8 in (15–20 cm) on cooking apples. Remove undersized, diseased, or damaged fruitlets first.

Established cordons need little winter pruning, other than thinning congested spurs. In mid- to late summer, cut new shoots from the main trunk back to three leaves and side shoots from existing spurs to one leaf.

Established fans should be pruned as if each arm were a cordon. In summer, cut new shoots from the main arms back to three leaves and prune all side shoots to one leaf each. Remove any shoots that appear from the main trunk.

Thinning Removing excess fruitlets in the summer is essential to achieving a healthy crop of decent-sized fruit.

Store surplus apples during the winter on shelves in a cool, dry, frost-free place, such as a garage. Check them regularly for signs of decay.

WATCH OUT FOR ...

Apple sawfly lay eggs that hatch into tiny maggots that burrow into the developing fruit. Some fruit will fall as a result, others are left with unsightly scars across the skin. Dispose of fallen fruit; any that continue to ripen are safe to eat.

Codling moth caterpillars are another cause of maggoty apples. Control the larvae by spraying with an insecticide (*see p.359*) in June and again three weeks later.
(*For further advice, see pp.356–369.*)

PEARS

The buttery texture and delicious taste of pears make this fruit a must for any garden. They have a reputation for being tricky to grow but are as easy as apples, their only weakness being susceptibility to early frosts.

	SPRING	SUMMER	FALL	WINTER
PLANT	�no		▪	▪▪
HARVEST		▪▪	▪	

'Concorde' is a tasty variety to eat fresh from the tree.

HOW TO GROW

Pears require a warm, sunny spot and should be planted away from frost pockets, where their early spring flowers could be destroyed by hard frosts, resulting in little or no fruit at harvest time. The site should also be sheltered from strong winds that could damage blooms and cause fruit to fall early.

Pears prefer a rich, well-drained soil with lots of organic matter dug in, such as compost or manure. Bare root trees should be planted while dormant, from late fall to late winter, but container-grown pears can be planted at any time if kept well watered until established.

In smaller gardens, pears can be grown in containers or trained as space-saving espaliers, cordons, and fans against walls and fences, although they are too vigorous to grow as stepovers. Remove all fruit for the first couple of years after planting to allow the tree to establish a strong root system and a healthy framework of branches.

Pollination

Pear flowers must be pollinated to fruit, so unless there are pear trees in neighboring gardens, you must plant at least two varieties from the same pollination group. Trees are termed A to C (early to late), according to when they flower. Triploid pears need two pollinators and certain varieties do not have compatible pollen, so seek advice when buying them.

WATCH OUT FOR ...

Scab causes corky patches on apples and pears, which may shrivel and fall. Remove infected fruit (see p.359).

Pear midge lays eggs on the flower buds in spring. Maggots feed inside the fruitlets, causing them to blacken and drop. Destroy infested fruitlets.

Birds and wasps attack mature fruit, especially if the skin is damaged. Net small trees, and hang wasp traps in the branches. (For more advice on pests and diseases, see pp.356–369.)

VARIETIES TO TRY

Dessert varieties
'Aurora' (C) • 'Bosc' (B) • 'Conference' (B) • 'Flemish Beauty' (C) • 'Gorham' (C) • 'Golden Spice' (B) • 'Gourmet' (A) • 'Parker' (B) • 'Pattern' (B)

Cooking varieties
'Clapps Favorite' (C) • 'Luscious' (C) • 'Nova' (C) • 'Spartlett' (C)

Pear blooms are vulnerable to frost damage, so avoid planting in cold sites and frost pockets. At night, protect young trees with garden fabric.

Rootstocks

Pear trees are always grafted onto quince rootstocks to restrict their size. Trees left growing on their own root system would become too large for most gardens.

Quince C—Semi dwarfing, suitable for trained specimens. Needs fertile soil. Trees grow to 10 ft (3 m).

Quince A—Vigorous and less fussy about soil conditions. Can be used for fans, cordons, and freestanding trees. Trees grow to 20 ft (6 m).

Fruit thinning

Fruitlets that have managed to avoid the spring frost and "June drop" (*see far right*) will need thinning in midsummer to ensure they grow to their full potential. If allowed to overcrop, the fruit will be undersized and may fail to ripen fully; overladen branches may snap.

   Thin out pear clusters to one or two fruitlets every 4–5 in (10–12 cm) on freestanding trees and to single fruitlets at the same spacing on cordons, fans, and espaliers.

When thinning fruitlets, take the opportunity to remove any that are especially small and those that show signs of disease or damage.

"June drop" is a natural process in which trees shed overcrowded or damaged fruit in early summer, usually July. Wait until it has passed before thinning out the remaining fruitlets.

Pruning and training

Freestanding trees are pruned in the winter the same way as apples (*see pp.262–263*). As they are vulnerable to frost, they are often trained against walls as espaliers or fans.

Attach horizontal wires to a wall or fence, 12 in (30 cm) apart. Plant a branched, one- or two-year-old tree against them, pruning it to leave two branches 18 in (45 cm) above the soil. Train the branches laterally using canes.

The first summer after planting, use canes to train new side shoots that develop from the two main branches into a basic fan. Remove any that grow toward the center of the tree or outward from the wall. Tie young stems with soft string.

The first full winter after planting, prune the tips of all lateral branches back by one-quarter to one-third in length. Check all branches are securely tied in place. Remove any unwanted stems growing directly out from the main trunk.

During the second summer, attach more canes and tie in additional side shoots to form the ribs of the fan, creating a balanced shape. If required, remove congested growth by pruning long side shoots on the main ribs back to three leaves.

Picking and storing

Judging when pears are ready to pick can be tricky since culinary varieties only soften when cooked, and eating varieties should be picked when slightly underripe—the final ripening is done in the fruit bowl. To test if an early- or mid-season pear is ready, taste for sweetness—it should still be firm. Once picked, late pears need storing to ripen in a dry, dark, well-ventilated place, such as a garage. Check them often because pears can quickly go from being under- to overripe in a matter of days. Be careful when picking pears; the skin damages easily, and the fruit will then spoil.

PLUM FAMILY

Plums are one of the easiest fruits to grow as they require little pruning and often crop heavily. Self-pollinating varieties mean only one tree is needed, and there is a range of cooking and eating types to suit all tastes.

		SPRING	SUMMER	FALL	WINTER
PLANT					
HARVEST					

Mouth-watering plums are a sure taste of summer.

HOW TO GROW

To give a good crop, plum trees need plenty of moisture and require a moist soil that drains freely. They also prefer a sheltered site to protect their early spring flowers from damaging frost. Bare root trees should be planted in the winter; those grown in containers can be planted at any time if kept well watered. Plum trees are too vigorous to train as cordons or espaliers but can be grown freestanding, as fans, or in containers if you choose trees grafted onto dwarfing rootstocks. Plums are prone to a number of diseases (see *facing page*) that can kill trees if infected growth isn't pruned out quickly. Check trees regularly.

Rootstocks

Plum trees are supplied grafted on rootstocks that restrict their size and encourage regular harvests. Two rootstocks are commonly used:
Pixy Semi-dwarfing, suitable for trees in containers. Trees grow up to 7 ft (2.2 m).
St. Julien A Semi-vigorous. Trees grow up to 9 ft (2.7 m).

TYPES AVAILABLE

Plums are popular, with varieties suitable for cooking or eating fresh from the tree. A few are more versatile and can be used for both.

Gages have possibly the most delicious fruit within this group. They are usually sweeter and have a rounder shape than plums.

Damsons are smaller than plums and gages and tend to have a darker skin and sharper flavor, making them excellent for cooking.

Bullaces bear the smallest, most abundant fruit of all and are very hardy. They are only suitable for cooking due to their tart flavor.

VARIETIES TO TRY

Most plums are self-pollinating (SP); some need separate pollinators (see *facing page*).

Plums
'Avalon' (dessert; pollination group A) • 'Blue Tit' (cooking/dessert; SP) • 'Early Laxton' (cooking/dessert; B) • 'Marjorie's Seedling' (cooking/dessert; SP) • 'Opal' (cooking; SP) • 'Victoria' (cooking/dessert; SP).

Gages
'Cambridge Gage' (partly SP) • 'Denniston's Superb' (SP) • 'Golden Transparent' (SP) • 'Old Green Gage' (C).

Damsons
'Farleigh Damson' (C) • 'Merryweather Damson' (SP) • 'Prune Damson' (SP).

Bullaces
'Black Bullace' (SP) • 'Langley Bullace' (SP) • 'White Bullace' (SP).

Pollination

Self-fertile plums pollinate their own flowers, so you only need to grow one tree. Others need separate pollinators that flower at the same time. When buying plums, choose those from the same pollination group, labeled A to C (early to late) according to flowering time.

Plums flower in early spring and are at risk of frost damage. Cover young and container-grown trees with garden fleece when frosts are predicted. Remove during the day to allow insects to pollinate. Young fruitlets are also vulnerable to frost.

Picking

Plums are ready to pick when slightly soft. They often ripen at different times on the same tree, so several pickings may be required. Plums and gages are ready mid- to late summer, damsons and bullaces toward fall. Pick fruit with the stalk still intact.

Ripe plums don't keep long, so eat them soon after picking. Firm and slightly underripe plums will ripen in the fruit bowl over a couple of weeks.

WATCH OUT FOR ...

Plum leaf-curling aphid suck sap from the leaves, causing them to curl and become misshapen. Treat with pesticides in midwinter and again at bud burst (see p.359).

Silver leaf enters wounds, causing a gray sheen on the leaves that may turn brown and fall. As the disease spreads, branches die back, until the whole tree dies. Prune infected material but sterilize tools between plants; silver leaf is easily spread. (For further advice, see pp.356–369.)

Pruning and training

Plum trees should be pruned as little as possible to avoid silver leaf (see below) infecting the wounds. Only prune plums when in active growth in spring and summer.

Pruned growth

Prune new freestanding trees by removing the main stem above the uppermost side shoots, and shorten 3–4 healthy branches by half or two-thirds to promote bushiness.

To prune established trees, thin congested stems to improve airflow between branches, take out weak or damaged growth, and remove overly vigorous upright new shoots.

Prune new fan-trained trees by removing the main stem and leave only two branches 16in (40cm) long either side of the main stem, 10in (25cm) above the soil. Train the two fan arms using canes affixed to wires.

The first summer, select new side shoots to train against the wires and tie in new growth. Cut back surplus shoots to one leaf, and any growing the wrong way or from below the fan arms. Repeat in following years.

CHERRIES

Modern cherry trees are ideal for smaller gardens since many are self-pollinating, so you only need to grow one tree. Compact types are available and give a fine display of spring flowers, as well as delicious summer fruit.

		SPRING	SUMMER	FALL	WINTER
PLANT					
HARVEST					

Picked one by one, fresh cherries are a summer treat.

HOW TO GROW

There are two types of cherries: sweet and tart. They are grown in different ways, so be sure you know which you want. Sweet kinds are sensitive and need a sunny, sheltered site. In cooler areas, they are best grown trained against warm walls. Tart cherries are less demanding and crop well even in cool, shaded locations. Bare root cherries should be planted in winter; those grown in containers can be planted at any time. All prefer rich, free-draining soil, so add plenty of well-rotted compost when planting. They can tolerate slightly alkaline or acidic conditions, but avoid heavy soils, or the shallow roots may rot. Cherries are prone to silver leaf disease (see p.267), so prune well.

Pollination

Many modern cherry varieties are self-pollinating and will pollinate their own flowers, which means you only need to plant one tree. Others require cross-pollination in order to fruit, so unless there are compatible varieties growing nearby, you'll need to plant two or more cherries from the same pollination group. These are listed A to D (early to late), according to flowering time.

Cherry blossoms can be pink or white and are generally borne in spring.

Rootstocks

Cherries are naturally very large trees, too big for most gardens, and traditionally required long ladders to harvest the fruit. Modern trees are now supplied grafted onto rootstocks that restrict their size and make them more suited to domestic gardens. The most common rootstocks are:

Gisela 5 Dwarfing, suitable for trees in containers and wall-trained specimens. Requires good soil. Trees grow up to 6–10 ft (2–3 m).

Colt Semi-dwarfing, suitable for trees in large containers or fan-trained specimens. Any soil. Trees reach 12–15 ft (4–5 m).

TYPES AVAILABLE

Tart cherries are too sour to eat directly from the tree but make great jam, sauces, or fillings for pies. They are the easiest to grow.

Sweet cherries are delicious eaten fresh from the tree but can also be cooked. They require a warm, sheltered site to ripen fully.

VARIETIES TO TRY

Most cherries are self-pollinating (SP) but some must be grown with other varieties from the same pollination group. Self-pollinating cherries will crop better if cross-pollinated.

Tart cherries
'Montmorency' (SP) • 'North Star' (SP) • 'Sand' (SP)

Sweet cherries
'Bigareau Napoleon' • 'Black Tartarian' (SP) • 'Bing' • 'Kansas Sweet' • 'Lapins' (SF) • 'Mona' • 'Ranier' • 'Stella' (SP)

Pruning and training

To avoid silver leaf, a disease that can be fatal to some fruit trees, cherries are pruned only when in active growth. Prune young cherries in the same way as plums (see p.267); prune mature freestanding trees to create an open, balanced shape.

Pruned growth

Established tart cherry trees crop on wood produced the previous year. After picking, prune out fruited stems, and thin congested growth (above). Sweet cherries need pruning in the spring to remove dead or diseased growth.

To prune established tart cherry fans (not shown), remove old growth in the spring to promote new stems, and remove any wayward shoots. After fruiting, cut back fruited stems, which will be replaced by the new growth.

Established sweet cherry fans are pruned by cutting side shoots back (above) to 5–6 leaves in the summer. New growth and uprights should be tied in horizontally. After fruiting, pruned side shoots should be cut to three leaves.

Protection

Cherries flower in the early spring, which means the blooms can be damaged by hard frosts. Unless planted in a sheltered site, protect young trees with garden fabric. Trees should also be protected against birds, which will quickly strip a tree of fruit. Net trees before the fruit starts to ripen, making sure birds can't sneak underneath.

WATCH OUT FOR …

Cherry slug worms are slimy sawfly larvae that leave skeletal patches on leaves. Spray with insecticide (see p.359).

Cherry blackfly sucks sap and causes leaf curling in early summer. Use an insecticide (see p.359) in spring when aphids first appear on the foliage.

Spotted wing drosophila lays eggs in developing cherries, spoiling the fruit with its larvae and the rot that follows. Use an insecticide (see p.359).
(For more pest and disease advice, see pp.356–369.)

Net your cherries before they ripen since birds won't wait. Secure netting to the ground to prevent birds from becoming trapped inside.

Picking and storing

Harvest cherries as soon as they are soft to the touch, picking them by the stalk to avoid damaging the skin. Use pruners or scissors to remove them from the tree. Sweet cherries last a week after picking and can be frozen. Tart cherries require cooking to make them palatable.

Use scissors and snip fruit stems to avoid damaging the skins. This will make harvesting a slow process but fresh cherries are worth it.

PEACHES AND NECTARINES

Fuzzy peaches and their smoother cousins, nectarines, are delicious but can be a challenge to grow in cooler climates. Success comes with a bit of effort and the right conditions— few summer fruit crops are as rewarding.

Freestanding trees need a very sheltered position.

	SPRING	SUMMER	FALL	WINTER
PLANT				
HARVEST				

HOW TO GROW

Peaches and nectarines are fully hardy, but their early spring flowers are easily damaged by frost, which prevents fruiting; the young fruitlets are vulnerable, too. To provide adequate protection, train them as fans, and grow them against warm, sunny, south- or southwest-facing walls or

fences. Dwarf trees can also be grown freestanding in containers filled with commercial growing mix. Bare root trees are planted in the winter; container-raised trees can be planted any time if kept well watered afterward. All varieties prefer rich, well-drained, slightly acidic soil with a pH of 6.5–7.0. Prepare the ground before planting by digging in plenty of organic matter, such as garden compost. To prevent silver leaf infecting wounds (see p.267), prune only when the trees are in active growth during spring and summer.

◄ **Juicy peaches** may be tricky to grow, but they are deliciously rich and tasty. A fruiting tree also provides a point of discussion in the garden.

Protection and pollination

During late winter, the trees need protection from rainfall to help prevent peach leaf curl, and in the spring, protection from frost. Container-grown trees can be brought under cover. Outdoor, fan-trained trees should be covered with bubble insulation or plastic sheeting and garden fabric. When the flowers start to open, remove the covers on bright, dry days to allow insects to pollinate them, which is needed for fruiting. If the weather remains wet, you'll need to pollinate the flowers by hand, using a soft brush.

Good airflow is important for preventing diseases, so don't wrap trees completely, and remove covers when the weather allows.

VARIETIES TO TRY

Some peach varieties show good disease resistance (DR) to peach leaf curl (see right for more information). Nectarines are a more reliable crop.

Peaches
'Avalon Pride' (DR) • 'Garden Lady' (dwarf) • 'Peregrine' • 'Rochester' • 'Red Haven'

Nectarines
'Early Rivers' • 'Fantasia' • 'Lord Napier' • 'Nectarella' • 'Pineapple'

WATCH OUT FOR ...

Peach leaf curl causes red blisters on the leaves, which drop, weakening the tree. Spores enter the buds in late winter, carried by rainfall. Cover the tree with plastic sheeting in the winter, remove infected leaves, and pick up all fallen leaves in the fall.

Glasshouse red spider mite causes fine mottling on the foliage and early leaf fall, especially on trees in sheltered spots. Introduce a predatory mite, *Phytoseiulus*, to control the pest.
(For further advice, see pp.356–369.)

Pruning and training

To provide a sheltered spot, peaches and nectarines are usually trained against walls on lateral wires. They are pruned twice a year in the spring and summer.

Pruned growth

The first spring after planting a one- or two-year-old tree, cut the main stem, leaving one branch each side, 10 in (25 cm) above the soil. Cut the branches to 14 in (35 cm) and tie them horizontally on canes.

The first summer, as side shoots grow, select three each side, one below the branches, two above, and train them on canes. Cut other shoots to one leaf. In the spring, cut back the ribs by a quarter.

Prune established fans in the spring to remove dead or damaged growth and wayward stems. On each rib, choose two side shoots to grow on, and remove the others. After harvesting, cut back fruited stems to make way for those left to grow on.

Prune established, freestanding trees by removing one-quarter of the stems that fruited last year, cutting back to healthy, pointed buds. Remove any dead or damaged wood, and thin out old branches that have stopped bearing fruit.

Thinning

Developing peach and nectarine fruitlets need thinning in the early summer to allow the remaining fruits to ripen fully and reach their optimum size. This process also helps prevent laden branches from snapping and damaging the tree. Thin to one per cluster, at a spacing of 4 in (10 cm) apart, when the fruit is the size of hazelnuts, then to 8 in (20 cm) when they are walnut-sized.

◄ **Harvest fruit** when they are slightly soft near the stalk, cupping and twisting them off. Fresh fruit won't keep long, so eat them soon.

GROWING APRICOTS

Apricots are closely related to peaches and are grown in the same way, most commonly as fans on south-facing walls. Dwarf varieties can also be grown in containers. They are less susceptible to peach leaf curl than peaches and nectarines, and modern varieties, like 'Flavorcot' and 'Tomcot', flower later so are less prone to frost damage. Protect the developing fruit from birds. Apricots are ready for picking when they start to soften in the summer and pull easily from the tree.

Apricots to try include: 'Alfred' • 'Flavorcot' • 'Goldcot' • 'Moorpark' • 'New Large Early' • 'Petite Muscat' • 'Tomcot'

◄ **Apricots fruit** on stems produced the previous year. Trees are pruned in spring and summer to promote new growth and replace fruited stems.

QUINCES

These trees are an asset in any garden with their fragrant, pale pink spring blossoms; gnarled bark; and large, attractive, unusual fall fruit. Slow ripening, the fruit is best eaten cooked in jams and pies.

	SPRING	SUMMER	FALL	WINTER
PLANT				
HARVEST				

Ripening fruit make a colorful feature.

HOW TO GROW

These trees are easy to grow and need little care once established. They require a warm, sheltered site and prefer deep, fertile, free-draining, acidic soil (pH of 6.5). Bare root trees should be planted in the winter; container-grown trees can be planted at any time if kept well watered afterward. Dig in plenty of organic matter when planting, such as well-rotted garden compost, and mulch annually in the spring with more of the same material.

Fall fruits should be left to ripen as long as possible, but watch out for frost.

WATCH OUT FOR ...

Quince leaf blight is a fungal disease, most prevalent in wet summers. It causes small red-brown spots on the leaves, which turn yellow and drop, weakening the tree. Destroy fallen leaves. Prune to form an open canopy with good airflow. Quinces are usually pest free. (*See pp.356–369.*)

Splitting fruit is commonly caused when trees in fruit have been allowed to become dry. Avoid this by watering well during dry spells.

Picking and storing

Quinces rarely ripen fully in cool climates and should be left as long as possible before picking. Even so, they are still likely to be too hard and sour to eat fresh from the tree. To promote ripening indoors, store unblemished fruit over the winter in a frost-free, ventilated place. Check regularly for damage or decay.

Spring color
Quince flowers are highly attractive and are showy in the spring.

Rootstocks

Quinces are often grown on their own root system but may be grafted to restrict their size, making them more suitable for a small garden. Two rootstocks are commonly used.
Quince C Suitable for small gardens. Trees grow to 10ft (3m).
Quince A Suitable for larger plots. Trees grow to over 12ft (4m).

VARIETIES TO TRY

When choosing varieties, you'll often find quinces listed under their botanical name, *Cydonia oblonga*. This is not to be confused with Japanese quince (*Chaenomeles*).

'Champion' • 'Lusitanica' • 'Meech's Prolific' • 'Vranja'

Pruning and training

Quinces are normally grown as freestanding trees and are pruned in the winter. They are too vigorous to train or to grow against walls.

Pruned growth

To prune established trees, cut back strong side shoots to 12in (30cm), and tip-prune the main branches in winter. Keep an open center.

FIGS

Native to the Mediterranean, figs are easy to grow and ideal for planting in containers. Unlike most fruit trees, they are not too particular about soil conditions and will fruit in poor, shallow soil as long as it drains well.

	SPRING	SUMMER	FALL	WINTER
PLANT				
HARVEST				

In cold areas, pack trees with straw for winter.

HOW TO GROW

Figs need a warm, sunny site and do best trained on a south- or southwest-facing wall, where they can be easily protected from pests and frost with nets and fabric. Figs fruit best with restricted roots, so plant in a "fig pit." Plant bare root trees in the winter, and container-grown trees at any time if well watered. Figs set fruit in late summer; they will overwinter and ripen the following summer. Remove any figs bigger than peas in late fall, leaving only tiny embryo fruits at the tips to overwinter.

Make a fig pit using 12 in (30 cm) concrete slabs sunk into the soil to form a box. Line the bottom with a few inches of crushed stone or pottery.

Picking and storing

It's time to pick the figs once they are fully colored, slightly soft, and the stalks start to bend. Look for drops of nectar appearing at the base of the fruit, but don't pick too early. They won't ripen further. Gather them when ripe and consume immediately.

VARIETIES TO TRY

'Brown Turkey' • 'Brunswick' • 'Rouge de Bordeaux' • 'White Marseilles'

Pruning and training

Whether trained against a wall or grown freestanding, figs should be pruned in the spring to remove old growth, and again in the summer to encourage the formation of fruitlets. Fig sap can irritate skin, so wear gloves when pruning trees.

To prune freestanding trees, in spring, select long, old stems that only fruit at the tips and cut them back to within 2–3 in (5–8 cm) of the trunk or branch (*above*). Remove congested growth from the center and any dead or diseased wood. Also cut back frost-damaged shoots to healthy growth. In summer, pinch off growing tips once they have 5–6 leaves, to stimulate new fruit production. This will also let in the sun to ripen last year's fruit.

To prune established, wall-trained trees, in late spring, cut back old, unproductive main branches to one bud (*above*). Prune half of all side shoots growing from the trunk and branches back to one bud. Remove any dead or diseased growth, any crossing branches, and any wayward shoots. Tie in new growth. In the summer, pinch off side shoots once they have 5–6 leaves to encourage fruit formation. Tie in new growth to the wires.

GRAPES

Wine grapes can successfully be grown outdoors in most cool climates, and many modern varieties are also sweet enough to eat, at least when cooked. True dessert grapes grow best under cover, but you will need space.

	SPRING	SUMMER	FALL	WINTER
PLANT				
HARVEST				

Ripening grapes should be watered well.

HOW TO GROW

Grapevines are fully hardy but prefer a sheltered site away from strong winds and frost pockets. They need full sun to ripen the fruit and are best planted against south-facing walls or fences. Grape vines will grow in a wide range of soils, including chalk, sand, and clay, and will tolerate poor, shallow conditions. Bare root vines should be planted in the winter; container-grown vines can be planted at any time. They need little additional feeding once established, since their long roots dig deep. Being climbing plants, grape vines need support and can grow to be very large. The simplest way is to grow them as cordons (see *facing page*). They can be allowed to climb over pergolas, but will fruit poorly.

Container-grown grapes are widely available in garden centers, but contact specialty nurseries for the best selection.

Indoor grapes

Certain dessert grapes require long, warm seasons to ripen fully and can only be grown successfully in large greenhouses or sunrooms. Growing grapes indoors requires year-round care, so consider carefully before planting.

Growing under cover allows you to grow a wider range of dessert grapes as long as you have plenty of space available.

TYPES AVAILABLE

Wine grapes are commonly grown outside, although the fruit is often too sour to eat fresh. Use them for cooking or wine making instead.

Dessert grapes are delicious fresh from the vine and can be grown outside if you choose the right varieties. Others must be grown indoors.

VARIETIES TO TRY

Grapes ripen green, referred to as white (W), or red (R), depending on variety.

Outdoor wine grapes
'Barbera' (R) • 'Chardonnay' (W) • 'Chenin Blanc' (W) • 'Primitivo' (R) • 'Trabbiano' (W)

Outdoor dessert grapes
'Catawba' (R) • 'Delaware' (R)

Training techniques

Grapes are vigorous climbers and must be trained on a system of horizontal wires in order to have a good crop. There are two different techniques commonly used:

Pruned growth

The single cordon system, often used indoors, involves a single, 6 ft (2 m) tall stem that is permanently trained upright and pruned to develop a system of fruiting spurs.

In the summer one new shoot is allowed to develop per spur. New growth is trained on wires and bears fruit. Fruited stems are pruned out in the winter.

The double guyot system, most commonly used for outdoor grapes, involves keeping only three stems and removing the rest in the winter. The center stem is pruned to 3–4 buds, the outer two should be carefully bent out horizontally and tied to the wires to grow in the summer (*above*).

In the summer, new stems develop from the horizontal limbs and bear fruit. At the same time, three new shoots are allowed to develop from the central stem but are not allowed to flower. In the winter when all fruited growth is removed, these three stems are left to start the cycle again.

Thinning and harvesting

As fruit clusters develop in the summer, they should be thinned to promote healthier, full-sized fruit. Left unthinned, the grapes will be undersized and will not ripen fully. They will also be prone to disease, which could spread to other clusters. To give time to establish, vines should not be allowed to bear fruit for their first two years.

In the summer, use a pair of pruners or round-tipped scissors to carefully thin individual berries. Avoid damaging remaining fruit.

Continue thinning until the bunch is reduced in size by a third. Take the opportunity to remove weak or damaged fruit.

Grapes are ready when they are soft, taste sweet, and their skin has taken on a translucent quality. Remove them by cutting through the stem with pruners.

WATCH OUT FOR …

Birds and wasps may target outdoor vines while the fruits are ripening. Use wire or plastic netting to deter birds, and hang wasp traps nearby.

Gray mold, also known as botrytis, causes fungal growth on stems, leaves, and fruit. Fruit often decays before ripening. Destroy all infected material, and prune congested growth to improve air circulation. (*For more advice on pests and diseases, see pp.356–369.*)

STRAWBERRIES

Every garden has room for strawberry plants, which give sweet, succulent fruit when planted in pots, baskets, and growing bags, as well as in traditional beds. Choose the right varieties, and enjoy them from spring to fall.

Snap the stems to pick fruit.

		SPRING	SUMMER	FALL	WINTER
PLANT					
HARVEST					

HOW TO GROW

Strawberries need full sun to ripen completely, and prefer free-draining, fertile, acid (pH 6.0–6.5) soil. They also grow well in raised beds and especially in containers and baskets, which suit their trailing style. Plant in the spring or summer, depending on type, 18 in (45 cm) apart in rows spaced at 30 in (75 cm). To avoid soil-borne diseases, don't plant in beds recently used for tomatoes, potatoes, or chrysanthemums. After cropping, cut back old leaves to expose the crown to sunlight. This will encourage better fruiting the following year. Replace plants grown in the soil every four years and those in containers every two years.

Strawberries are self-fertile but need insects or wind to transfer the pollen to the stigma.

TYPES OF STRAWBERRIES

Traditional strawberries are either "summer-fruiting," which are the tastiest, or "everbearing," which crop over a longer period.

Alpine strawberries are perennial plants and crop for many years. Although their fruits are small, they are sweet and flavorful.

VARIETIES TO TRY

Summer-fruiting strawberries crop from early to midsummer. Everbearing types fruit in early then late summer and into mid-fall. Replace plants annually. Alpine varieties fruit freely throughout summer.

Summer-fruiting
'Alice' (early) • 'Cambridge Favourite' (mid) • 'Elsanta' (mid) • 'Honeoye' (early) • 'Pegasus' (mid) • 'Symphony' (late)

Everbearing types
'Albion' • 'Buddy' • 'Flamenco' • 'Mara des Bois' • 'Muricata'

Alpine strawberries
'Alexandria' • 'Baron Solemacher' • 'Mignonette' • 'Rugen'

Containers

Strawberries can be grown in almost any type of container with adequate drainage holes, including hanging baskets, stackable towers, traditional strawberry planters, and growing bags. All will need watering at least once a day during the growing season and should be fed weekly with a high-potash tomato fertilizer. Turn containers often to avoid leaving some fruit in the shade.

Keep the fruit clean

Strawberries grow on the ground and, to keep them clean, they are best lifted off the soil. Straw mulch is commonly used; barley straw is considered the best since it is softer. Fiber mats wrapped around each plant are also popular and easy to use. You can also plant through black plastic stretched over a slightly raised bed. As well as keeping fruit clean, this warms the soil, retains moisture, and suppresses weeds.

▲ **Cover fruit** with netting to protect them from birds. Always replace it after harvesting.

PROPAGATING

To maintain a good crop, strawberry plants should be replaced at least every two years. It's well worth propagating your own so you have a constant supply of replacement plants. This is easy to do because strawberries naturally produce "runners," which are little plantlets that you can continue growing. Propagate only healthy runners and remove the rest to encourage plants to concentrate their energy on producing fruit.

1 When runners start to develop in the summer and the young plantlets have strong leaves, lift them from the soil, but leave them attached to the parent plant.

2 Sink small pots filled with potting mix into the soil. Plant one plantlet per pot, keeping them in place with bent wire staples. Keep them well watered.

3 After 4–6 weeks, the plantlets will develop roots of their own and can be separated from the parent. Grow them on their own, potting and planting outside as necessary.

Forcing strawberries

Strawberries can be encouraged to crop at least one or two weeks early by placing a cloche over them in spring. Container-grown plants can also be moved into an unheated greenhouse in spring to fruit earlier. In fall, move everbearing varieties under cover to prolong their fruiting season. Make sure plants are placed in the sun to help ripen the fruit.

▶ **Check the fruit** every day. Strawberries ripen quickly in summer and soon spoil.

WATCH OUT FOR ...

Gray mold, or botrytis, enters through the flowers and remains dormant until the fruit matures. Destroy all infected plant debris.

Vine weevil grubs destroy the roots, particularly on container-grown plants. Adults chew notches from the leaf margins, but the white grubs cause more serious damage. Control with nematodes in late summer. (*For more pests and diseases advice, see pp.356–369.*)

RASPBERRIES

The rich scent and taste of raspberries is the very essence of summer, and they are very easy to grow. Plant summer- and fall-fruiting types, and enjoy a plentiful harvest from high summer until the first frost.

		SPRING	SUMMER	FALL	WINTER
PLANT					
HARVEST					

Ripe berries leave the core when picked.

HOW TO GROW

Raspberries prefer a moist, slightly acid soil with a pH of about 6.0. They need a sunny site for the fruit to ripen, although they will tolerate some shade. Raspberries are leggy plants, so put a support structure of posts and wires in place before planting. Plant bare root canes (see right) from late fall to late winter; container-grown plants can be planted at any time if kept well watered afterward. Canes should be planted 16 in (40 cm) apart in rows spaced at 6 ft (2 m) intervals. Plant them shallowly to prevent the roots from rotting, and cut the tops of the canes back to 8 in (20 cm) immediately after planting. When the canes start to send out new shoots, the original cane can then be cut down to ground level. Raspberries need watering regularly during dry periods. Feed them in the early spring with a rose fertilizer containing iron and magnesium, or apply a mulch of well-rotted organic matter, such as garden compost, spread around the base of the canes.

◄ **Water canes** at cool times of day, using a can or hose to direct water at the base.

Bare root canes

Bare root raspberries are usually sold during the fall and winter in bundles of 10–20 canes. This is a cheap way to buy a lot of plants, but they should be planted as soon as possible. To prevent damaging the roots and reduce planting stress, stand the bundle in water for an hour before unwrapping it.

TYPES AVAILABLE

Summer-fruiting raspberries come into fruit mid-season and usually crop for about three weeks, depending on the variety grown.

Fall-fruiting raspberries crop from late summer to the first frost. Like summer varieties, their berries can be red or yellow.

VARIETIES TO TRY

Summer-fruiting
'Canby' • 'Encore' • 'Lauren' • 'Reveille' • 'Tulameen'

Fall-fruiting
'Autumn Bliss' • 'Double Delight' • 'Durham' • 'Joan J' • 'Polka'

Support

Raspberries are tall, rambling plants and need support throughout the growing season. For a single row of canes, tightly stretch three wires horizontally, spaced 30 in (75 cm), 3 ft (1 m), and 5 ft (1.5 m) above the ground, between two 8 ft (2.5 m) posts. For a double row (*see below*), use two parallel wires, supported by cross-members, spaced 3 ft (1 m) and 5 ft (1.5 m) above the ground, and pulled taut between upright posts.

Summer-fruiting raspberries are tall plants and must be given adequate support.

WATCH OUT FOR ...

Raspberry beetle grubs cause the ripening fruit to dry up at the stalk end. Maggots may be found inside the fruits. Control by spraying with a suitable insecticide (*see p.359*) as the fruits begin to ripen.

Cane blight is a fungal disease that causes stems to brown and become brittle, and they may then snap off at the base. Destroy infected canes. (*For more pests and diseases advice, see pp.356–369.*)

Pruning and training

It's important to know what sort of raspberries you have before pruning them. Summer-fruiting varieties crop on canes produced the previous year; fall types fruit on canes produced during the current year. Mix them up, and you might remove fruiting stems by mistake.

Prune summer-fruiting raspberries in late summer, cutting all fruited canes to the ground. This allows light and air into the remaining canes produced during the current year, helping prevent disease.

Tie in new-season, summer-fruiting canes to their wire support after pruning out old fruited growth in late summer. Space canes 4 in (10 cm) apart, and loop taller stems over the top wire. In spring, prune to 6 in (15 cm) above the top wire.

Prune fall-fruiting raspberries in the spring by removing all the canes to ground level. Step carefully to avoid damaging any new shoots that may be appearing from the soil. Rake up fallen leaves to keep the site clean.

New fall-fruiting raspberry canes can be grown without supports but bear a better crop that is easier to pick if gathered up with string. Support may be needed in exposed sites. Remove any weak, diseased, or damaged stems.

BLACKBERRIES AND HYBRIDS

Blackberries can be picked from hedgerows, but garden varieties generally have bigger, juicier fruit. You can also choose from several hybrid forms, which are just as easy to grow but offer something slightly different.

VARIETIES TO TRY

Some blackberry varieties are thornless (TL), making them easier to harvest.
'Fantasia' • 'Helen' (TL) • 'Loch Ness' (TL) • 'Oregon Thornless' (TL) • 'Silvan'

	SPRING	SUMMER	FALL	WINTER
PLANT				
HARVEST				

HOW TO GROW

Blackberries and their hybrids are vigorous climbing plants and prefer a sheltered site. Blackberries will tolerate light shade and poorer soil, while the hybrids need full sun and richer growing conditions. Bare root canes should be planted in winter, when all stems should be cut back to healthy buds 8 in (20 cm) above the soil. Container-grown plants can be planted all year if kept well watered. Enrich the soil prior to planting by digging in well-rotted organic matter. Feed annually with rose fertilizer, or apply more organic matter in the spring, and water plants well, especially when in fruit.

▲ **Successful pollination** is essential for the fruit to develop fully and reach full size.

▶ **Harvest regularly** since blackberries and the hybrids ripen over several weeks, and it will take several sessions to pick the whole crop.

HOW TO PROPAGATE

1 Blackberries and hybrids can be easily propagated in late summer by bending a new stem to the ground and burying the tip to a depth of 4 in (10 cm). Firm it down, water well, and leave it attached to the main plant.

2 The stem will have rooted by the following spring, when it can be lifted from the ground and either potted or transplanted. Keep the young plant well watered until it establishes fully, and don't allow it to fruit for the first two years.

WATCH OUT FOR ...

Blackberry cane spot causes gray or purple spotting on the canes, which die back. Infected canes should be destroyed immediately.

Raspberry beetle may also affect crops (see p.279).

Raspberry spur blight causes purple-gray areas around buds on the canes. The following year, canes produce weak growth and may wither and die. Cut out and destroy any infected canes.
(For further advice, see pp.356–369.)

Pruning and training

Blackberries and the hybrids are grown against wires and can be trained in several ways (*below*). Fruit is produced on canes formed the previous summer, so the aim is to separate these canes from new growth that will fruit next year. Wear gloves because blackberries can be very thorny.

The trailing fan method differs from the upright fan method. Here, fruited stems are also removed in the fall, and one-year-old growth is tied in to form a fan. The difference is that the new growth is trained across the ground, then trained up to the wires in the fall to replace the fruited growth. This method suits bigger gardens with ground to spare.

The alternate bay method involves training the new season's growth on the opposite side to where the fruiting stems, produced last year are trained. In effect the fruiting side of the plant alternates left or right from one year to the next. Fruited stems are removed in the fall. This method is a good choice for smaller gardens.

The alternate bay method involves training the new season's growth on the opposite side to where the fruiting stems, produced last year, are trained. In effect, the fruiting side of the plant alternates left or right from one year to the next. Fruited stems are removed in fall. This method is a good choice for smaller gardens.

HYBRID BLACKBERRIES

These hybrid berries are mostly the result of cross-breeding between raspberries and blackberries and have similarities to both parents. Each hybrid has its own eating qualities. All are vigorous climbers.

Boysenberry

This is a cross between a loganberry (*below*) and a blackberry. It crops for 3–4 weeks in midsummer and produces a large crop of succulent, dark-purple fruit. They look much like blackberries but are larger, and their flavor is considered superior. Naturally thornless forms are available from specialty suppliers.

Loganberry

A cross between blackberries and raspberries, the sharp-tasting fruit most resemble the latter and are best eaten cooked. The loganberry is naturally spiny, but thornless forms are also available from specialty suppliers. Allow the fruit to ripen fully and turn dark red before picking from mid- to late summer.

Tayberry

Resulting from a cross between blackberries and raspberries, the rich red berries are larger and sweeter than loganberries and appear in midsummer. Allow the fruit to turn dark red before picking. They are sweet enough to eat fresh from the plant but are best when cooked for jams and pies.

Japanese wineberry

While this is a separate species rather than a hybrid, it is very similar, producing bright red, raspberrylike berries in mid- to late summer. Its stems are covered with attractive red bristles, and it is often grown partly as an ornamental. This dual purpose makes it a good choice for smaller gardens.

BLACK CURRANTS

One of the easiest fruit bushes to grow, black currants even do well in containers, producing healthy berries, packed with vitamins. They can be eaten fresh but taste far better in jams, pies, and summer drinks.

		SPRING	SUMMER	FALL	WINTER
PLANT					
HARVEST					

Fruits are a magnet for birds; net them (*see right*).

HOW TO GROW

Black currants require moist, fertile soil and prefer full sun but will also ripen, albeit later, in some shade. Plant bare root shrubs in the winter; container-grown plants can be planted at any time if well watered. Dig in well-rotted organic matter, and plant deeply (*see below*). Black currants grow well in containers filled with commercial growing mix. Before the fruit is ready to harvest, from mid- to late summer, cover plants with netting to deter birds. Water well during dry periods, and feed in the spring with granular fertilizer or well-rotted organic matter, such as garden compost.

Support fruiting plants with string and canes to prevent branches laden with fruit from drooping and snapping off.

PRUNING AND TRAINING

Black currants fruit on one-year-old wood. They should be pruned in the winter (*below*) to encourage new fruit-bearing shoots. Plants can also be pruned in the summer to allow light in to ripen the fruit and improve air circulation between branches, which helps deter disease.

| Pruned growth

In the winter, prune established shrubs by cutting a third of the oldest branches off at ground level and removing dead, damaged, or diseased wood. Horizontal branches that are lying close to the ground should also be removed. Don't prune healthy young stems.

HOW TO PLANT

1 Dig a hole deeper than the root ball is tall, and shovel some well-rotted garden compost into the base.

2 Check the level, and ensure that the crown of the plant is positioned in the hole slightly below the soil surface.

3 Backfill the hole with soil, and water the plant in well. New stems will develop from below soil level.

VARIETIES TO TRY

Modern varieties have been bred for improved disease resistance. These are often denoted by 'Ben' in their names.

'Baldwin' • 'Ben Connan' • 'Ben Gairn' • 'Ben Hope' • 'Ben Lomond' • 'Ben Sarek' • 'Big Ben' • 'Ebony' • 'Titania'

RED AND WHITE CURRANTS

With a slightly tart taste, these colorful berries are the basis of many sauces and desserts. They are very easy to grow and can be trained or grown in pots, depending on how much space you have available.

	SPRING	SUMMER	FALL	WINTER
PLANT				
HARVEST				

VARIETIES TO TRY

Red currants
'Jonkheer van Tets' • 'Junifer' • 'Laxton's No.1' • 'Red Lake' • 'Rovada'

White currants
'Blanka' • 'Versailles Blanche' • 'White Grape'

HOW TO GROW

Red and white currants prefer fertile, well-drained, acid soil with a pH of 6.5–7.0. They need a warm, sunny location but will tolerate some shade. Bare root shrubs should be planted in the winter; container-grown shrubs may be planted at any time if well watered. The shrubs are usually grown as bushes on a short stem or "leg" 6 in (15 cm) tall. Alternatively, they can be trained as fans, cordons, standards, or stepovers. Like most soft fruits, they require protection from birds as the fruit starts to develop. Feed plants in the spring with a granular fertilizer or well-rotted organic matter. Plant shrubs in containers into a good quality commercial potting mix.

Red currants fruit on buds at the base of last year's wood and also on old spurs. They should be pruned hard in winter to encourage new spurs, similar to gooseberries (see p.284).

Net all currants before they ripen to prevent birds from stripping the plants bare.

Pick fruit as "strings" when all the berries have turned red and look slightly opaque. Replace netting after each harvest.

◄ **White currants are sweeter** than red currants but don't have such an attractive, jewel-like appearance.

WATCH OUT FOR ...

Gooseberry sawfly larvae eat the leaves, except the stalks, and can defoliate red currant or gooseberry bushes. Pick off the caterpillars or spray with insecticide (see p.359).

Leaf spot disease causes brown spots to appear on leaves. Remove and destroy any that are infected.

Currant blister aphid causes leaves to crinkle at the tips and red, blister-like blemishes. It can be tolerated as little damage is done.
(For further advice, see pp.356–369.)

GOOSEBERRIES

These very hardy fruit bushes are a good choice for cold, exposed gardens. Firm, tart, and juicy, gooseberries are especially good cooked; their old-fashioned appeal is becoming more widely appreciated.

	SPRING	SUMMER	FALL	WINTER
PLANT				
HARVEST				

Some varieties ripen green, others, dark red.

HOW TO GROW

Gooseberries require a moist, fertile soil and will tolerate some shade. Commonly grown as freestanding bushes, they are usually planted on a short 6 in (15 cm) stem, called a "leg." Where required, they can also be trained as stepovers, cordons, and standards, or as fans on north-facing walls. Bare root shrubs should be planted in the winter; container-grown can be planted at any time of year if well watered. Dig well-rotted organic matter into the planting hole. Space bushes 4 ft (1.2 m) apart and cordons 14 in (35 cm) apart.

Thin the fruit from the early summer, removing alternate berries, which can be used in cooking. This encourages full-sized fruit, which can be harvested once ripe from midsummer onward. Net young fruit to protect it from birds. Be careful when harvesting since the bushes have long, sharp thorns.

Water plants well during dry spells, and feed in the spring with a granular fertilizer or well-rotted organic matter. Freestanding shrubs may need support with canes in the summer to prevent laden branches from collapsing or snapping.

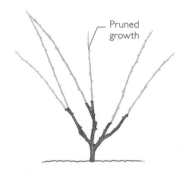

◄ Ripe fruit is best eaten fresh but can also be stored in the fridge or frozen.

VARIETIES TO TRY

Dessert varieties (D) can be eaten raw; culinary fruit (C) are best for cooking; dual types are suitable for both uses (C/D).

'Captivator' (C) • 'Careless' (C/D) • 'Greenfinch' (C) • 'Invicta' (C/D) • 'Leveller' (D) • 'Whinham's Industry' (C/D)

Pruning

Established gooseberry bushes are pruned in the winter and summer. The main aim is to create an open, airy center and keep older fruiting wood productive.

Pruned growth

In the first winter after planting, choose 4–5 healthy stems, and cut them back by half to three-quarters. Remove all other stems and shoots coming from the "leg" at the bottom.

To winter-prune established shrubs, tip-prune main stems, and cut back side shoots to 1–4 buds. The center of overgrown shrubs should be thinned by a quarter. In the summer, prune side shoots to five leaves.

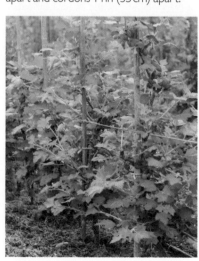

Cordon-trained plants can be grown much closer together than freestanding shrubs, which is ideal for smaller gardens.

BLUEBERRIES

Native to the US, these delicious berries need minimal pruning or training and grow well in patio containers. The sweet, summer fruit is packed with goodness and tastes even better when cooked.

	SPRING	SUMMER	FALL	WINTER
PLANT				
HARVEST				

Fruit ripens over a span of time, so harvest regularly.

HOW TO GROW

Blueberries need moist, acid soil with a pH of 4.0–5.5. They prefer full sun but will tolerate some shade. Plant bare root shrubs in the winter; plant container-grown shrubs at any time if well watered. Add leaf mold of composted pine needles to the planting hole to maintain acidity, and mulch in the spring with more of the same. Space blueberries 4 ft (1.2 m) apart, water well during dry spells, and net developing fruit against birds. Blueberries are partially self-pollinating and can pollinate their own flowers, but they crop better if other varieties are planted nearby. Don't allow pot-grown plants to dry out, and feed regularly, especially when in fruit.

Unless your soil is acidic, grow blueberries in large containers filled with potting mix for acid lovers, available from garden centers.

◄ **Pollination** is essential for fruit formation and is ensured by planting two or three varieties that flower at the same time.

VARIETIES TO TRY

'Berkley' • 'Bluecrop' • 'Bluetta' • 'Duke' • 'Coville' • 'Earliblue' • 'Herbert' • 'Patriot' • 'Spartan' • 'Top Hat'

WATCH OUT FOR ...

Birds can strip plants of berries in a matter of hours. Net bushes before the fruit starts to ripen, and secure it at ground level so birds can't sneak underneath.

Blueberry stem blight is a fungal disease that enters the plants through wounds and pruning cuts. It causes the leaves to brown and die, weakening the plant and reducing the crop. Remove and destroy all infected growth.
(*For further advice, see pp.356–369.*)

Pruning and training

Blueberries are pruned from late winter to early spring, when the swelling buds show which parts of the plant are alive. Avoid pruning stems with lots of healthy, fat buds; these will bear fruit in the summer.

▶ **To prune established shrubs**, prune out a few of the oldest stems, leaving 4–6 main shoots. Tip-prune stems that fruited last year, cutting back to strong buds. Remove lateral branches growing too close to the base, and thin the center of overgrown shrubs. Never remove more than a quarter of the shrub at once.

CARE FOR YOUR GARDEN

The essence of good gardening is care and maintenance, and a little bit of know-how and some expert tips can go a long way. This chapter equips you with key techniques, such as propagation and pruning, as well as advice on tools, timing, feeding, and watering to help you make a success of everything you do in the garden.

EARLY TO MID-SPRING

After the long winter, the first hint of spring in the air means that it's time to start tidying and preparing the garden for the warmer months to come. You'll still need to watch out for frost, but look ahead, and start planning your spring and summer borders.

► PROTECT AGAINST FROST

March and April can still be frosty, especially at night, so keep an eye on the weather forecast, and protect tender plants if a frost threatens. Cloches, horticultural fabric, or even cut-down plastic bottles will give frost protection. You can also use cloches on areas of bare soil to warm it up for sowing.

▼ TRANSPLANT SEEDLINGS

If you come across any self-sown annual or biennial seedlings in your beds and borders, pot them up or transplant them to a more permanent growing location if necessary. You can begin to harden off seedlings raised in pots under cover, but do not plant them outside until the threat of frost has completely passed.

▲ FEED FISH

March is the time to start feeding fish in your ponds. Take stock of your plants: marginals may need trimming, and aquatics may need moving or dividing. Pond pumps can now be taken out of storage, checked, and replaced in the pond.

▶ NEAT LAWNS AND BORDERS

Spruce up your lawns and borders for spring. Start by mowing the lawn after its winter break, then trim and tidy any ragged edges by hand. Inspect the lawn, checking for perennial weeds (see pp.352–353), and reseed any bare patches (see p.93). In borders, keep an eye out for germinating weed seedlings, and remove them with a hoe when you spot them. Once your beds and borders are tidy, mulch them with a thick layer of organic matter to suppress weeds.

◀ GUARD AGAINST SLUGS AND SNAILS

Young growth is particularly vulnerable to attack from slugs and snails, so protect it using nematodes as a biological control, or scatter organic slug pellets.

▲ PROTECT FRUIT BLOSSOMS

Late frost can still happen in early spring, so be careful to protect fruit blossoms and young fruitlets until there is no further threat. The buds and flowers of peaches, nectarines, and cherries open early and are prone to frost damage. Protect wall-trained and free-standing trees with fabric.

▲ PLANT TREES

Use your last chance to plant bare root trees in March, while they are still in a near-dormant state. If you have missed out on bare root stock, container-grown trees can be planted throughout spring and will be available from garden centers. If you plant young fruit trees and bushes, pinch off any flowers this year to encourage a good root system.

LATE SPRING TO EARLY SUMMER

June is the month when the garden is at its peak—borders look perfect, and summer vegetables and soft fruit are flourishing. Keep an eye out for pests over the summer months, and water plants regularly but wisely during drier spells.

▶ PROTECT PLANTS FROM SLUGS

Slugs and snails are especially fond of young growth, particularly that of delphiniums and hostas, and can attack young buds before they have even emerged from the soil. General controls, such as organically approved slug pellets, can be very effective, but other organic methods such as beer traps are also worth trying. Microscopic nematodes can be purchased and watered in and will infect slugs, helping control them in spring and summer. Another way to try and stop these pests in their tracks is to use a physical barrier such as eggshells or a layer of coarse sand.

▲ PLANT OUT VEGETABLES

Vegetables sown earlier in the year, such as globe artichokes, leeks, and celery, can be planted out in May once they are robust enough. Tender marrows and zucchini can also be planted out once the threat of frost has passed.

▶ MOVE POTS OUTSIDE

Any tender or exotic plants, such as citrus trees, that you have brought indoors over winter can now be moved back into the garden after a gradual acclimatization to outdoor temperatures (the shock of a sudden change can cause leaves to drop).

◄ KEEP WATERING

As temperatures start to rise, it's important to keep plants well watered, especially those that have just been planted out. As plants become established and develop bigger and more effective root systems, they will need watering less frequently. Established plants only need a good soaking in dry conditions if they show signs of wilting.

▲ HARVEST FRUIT

Remove cloches from strawberries now to let the fruit ripen in the summer sun, ready for imminent picking. Tuck straw under the developing fruits to keep them dry and away from the soil. Keep all fruit well watered in dry spells to ensure a good crop of quality fruits throughout the summer.

▲ PLANT SUMMER BEDDING

Beds and borders planted with spring bedding can be cleared now as summer approaches, ready for tender summer bedding plants, such as *Bacopa*. A wide selection will be on display at nurseries and garden centers and can be safely planted out from May into June.

▲ TRIM HEDGES

Formal evergreen hedging that is free of nesting birds should be lightly trimmed by hand now. Hand shears will give a better result than a mechanical hedge trimmer, which can bruise leaves instead of cutting them cleanly, resulting in brown and unsightly foliage. It's much better to trim it regularly to keep it in shape. Use a length of taut twine or a cane as a guide to help you keep the line straight as you work.

MIDSUMMER

Now's the time to relax and enjoy your garden, as all the hard work you invested in sowing and planting earlier in the year starts to pay off with borders and beds looking their best for the long summer evenings. Devote your energies to keeping the garden well watered in hot weather.

▶ SUPPORT YOUNG PEAS

Sweet peas and peas have rather straggly growth and like to be supported. Small twigs are a good way to do this, and strong, straight prunings from other shrubs in the garden will also work well. The tendrils of the peas will cling to the sticks.

▼ HARVEST EDIBLE FLOWERS

Nasturtiums and other edible flowers, such as violas and roses, make delicious and eye-catching additions to summer salads. Gather the flowers as required, choosing flawless, pest-free blooms wherever possible.

▶ PICK RASPBERRIES

Summer-fruiting raspberries should ripen this month. The "plug" or core will remain behind on the bush, and the berries should come away easily when ripe. If they don't, they're not ready to be picked. Pick ripe fruits regularly so they are not allowed to rot on the bush.

◀ DEADHEAD FLOWERS

Removing faded blooms will prevent plants from setting seed and keep roses coming for the rest of the summer. An easy way to deadhead straggly plants, such as pansies and petunias, which have smaller flowers and are more difficult to trim, is to cut them back with pruners or shears.

▼ CARE FOR BASKETS

Colorful summer hanging baskets will be at their best now with their profusion of plants but will need daily watering and regular feeding in the hot weather. If they start to flag and droop, unhook the baskets, and plunge them into a bucket of water to revive the plants.

◀ WATER FOR BIRDS

During hot, dry summer spells, water for birds will be scarce, so provide pools, ponds, and baths for them wherever possible. As well as a continuous supply of drinking water, water for bathing is also important and helps keep birds' feathers in good condition.

◀ PLANT OUT LATE BEDDING PLANTS

To ensure that any late summer bedding plants, such as *Petunia, Alyssum,* and *Nemesia,* have enough time to settle in and flower for the rest of the summer, plant them out as soon as possible in baskets, containers, and borders. Replace any tired-looking plants in your borders with healthy new specimens, and fill gaps to keep your garden looking lush throughout the season.

LATE SUMMER TO MID-FALL

Flower borders may be starting to fade, but late summer is a time of "mellow fruitfulness" in the garden. Most summer crops can be gathered, with tomatoes, peppers, sweet corn, and squash reaching their peak. Use the warm days for cleaning and organizing tasks, too.

▶ HARVEST APPLES AND PEARS

The first apples and pears in the garden should be ready to pick from August onward. When you see one or more apples on the ground, this is a sure sign that the fruit is ready to harvest. If you cup an apple in your hand and gently twist it, a ripe fruit should detach effortlessly from the tree, stalk intact. If it does not come away easily, leave it on the tree for a few more days before testing again. Pears should be harvested while slightly underripe and ripened indoors (see p.265).

▲ FEED TOMATOES

Continue to feed tomato plants with a high-potash feed applied weekly. Water plants every evening if possible. If you have green tomatoes toward the end of the season, bring them indoors to ripen on a sunny windowsill or in the fruit bowl. Remove any yellowing leaves, and thin any foliage clustered around the trusses of fruit. As well as allowing more light to reach the fruits and ripen them, this will improve air circulation around the plants and reduce the possibility of botrytis, also known as gray mold.

▲ FIX TREE BAND TRAPS

Female winter moths are unable to fly, so will climb apple and pear tree trunks to lay their eggs during winter. To catch them, fix sticky tree band traps around the trunks. Use the bands on stakes, too, to prevent moths from reaching the trees via tree ties.

▼ LIFT ONIONS

When the foliage collapses, onions are ready to harvest. On a dry day, gently ease the onions out of the soil, and leave them out to dry. To ensure that they store well and do not rot, they must be completely dry—if the weather turns wet, cover them with a sheet of plastic, or move them indoors.

▲ NET PONDS

Leaves will start to drop as fall approaches, so ensure that you cover your pond with special netting to prevent dead leaves from falling in and affecting the water quality. Nets will also protect your fish from herons and other predators.

◄ RAKE LEAVES

Fallen leaves will collect on your lawn in the fall and can kill off the grass if left in a thick layer, as well as encouraging slugs and snails if left lying over and around plants. Rake leaves up regularly, and use them to make leaf mold (see pp.22–23).

▲ PRUNE LAVENDER

Once your lavender plants have flowered and started to fade, go over the plants with a pair of pruners, cutting them back. This will encourage side shoots to grow and give plants a bushier, more compact look. Rambling roses should also be pruned after flowering (see pp.318–319).

LATE FALL TO WINTER

Although flowers can be scarce in the garden over the winter months, berries, evergreen foliage, and trees with decorative bark will cheer up the garden and add interest. Take stock of the gardening year as it ends, and use the time to begin planning your spring displays.

▶ BRING HERBS INDOORS

Most container herb plants are too delicate to survive the winter outdoors, so bring them under cover in their pots for the colder months before temperatures begin to drop. This will ensure a steady supply to liven up your winter dishes when other produce is less plentiful. Position pots on a windowsill to catch as much winter sunshine as possible, and pinch off growing tips when necessary to promote a bushy look.

▲ LEAVE SEED HEADS

Many grasses, such as the huge range of *Miscanthus* varieties available, have attractive seed heads that can be left on the plants over fall and winter. Their dry plumes look attractive, especially when dusted with winter frost.

▶ PLANT FRUIT TREES

Now's the time to order and plant bare root trees. Prepare the ground first by digging in plenty of well-rotted organic matter to improve the soil structure. A feed of general fertilizer will also help get your trees off to a good start.

◄ WINTER-PRUNE SHRUBS

February is the month to prune many woody plants, including winter-flowering shrubs, such as *Hamamelis*, once their flowers have faded. Summer-flowering shrubs, such as the butterfly bush (*Buddleja davidii*), that flower on new wood later in the summer can be cut back, using loppers if necessary. The twiggy prunings can be used as plant supports elsewhere in the garden, or shredded to be added to the compost heap or to make a mulch that can be applied in spring when the ground is a little warmer.

◄ FEED THE BIRDS

Food for birds is in short supply over the colder months, so put food out for them on a regular basis; different mixes are available for feeders and for bird tables and ground feeding. Clean out bird boxes of old nesting material to encourage birds to nest in them again next year. Birds will be looking for winter roosts, so do this as soon as possible. If they are already familiar with a box by spring, they are more likely to select it as a nesting site.

▲ STORE WINTER SQUASHES

Pumpkins and winter squashes can be left on the vine during the fall to reach their maximum size and develop brightly colored skins. Do not leave on the plant over winter as they may rot or be eaten by pests. Once "cured" in the sun for ten days, they can be stored. Keep them in a dry, well-ventilated, frost-free place, checking regularly for damage or decay.

▲ CLEAN TOOLS AND EQUIPMENT

Take advantage of the quieter winter months in the garden to check over and clean all your garden equipment before storing it. Clean or discard any old pots and trays that you're not intending to reuse, as well as checking tools and getting the lawn mower serviced and sharpened. You won't need to mow the lawn itself over the winter—just avoid walking on it in frosty weather to try to prevent damage.

Water individual pots regularly in dry conditions and when growing under cover. Use a rose to prevent displacing soil in small pots.

REVIVE A WILTED BASKET

If a summer hanging basket begins to flag, plunge it into a sink, bowl, or bucket of water. Once the potting mix is moist, remove it, and let excess water drain away. Replace dead plants, and trim damaged growth.

Restore baskets by immersing them in water and leaving them there for a little while. They will draw the moisture they need through their roots.

HOW TO WATER

To ensure your plants thrive rather than wilt or struggle to survive, it's important to water them efficiently. If you understand the needs of different plants, you can use techniques that deliver water where it is needed most.

EFFICIENT WATERING

Adequate water and sound watering methods are essential for healthy plant growth. Poor watering does more harm than good: drenching plants with abandon can leave roots exposed if potting mix is washed away or soil is eroded by the fast flow of water. If there is puddling on the soil surface and the ground becomes waterlogged, roots may rot.

Water is a valuable resource, both in environmental terms and for your wallet if you are on a water meter. The aim of effective watering techniques is to reduce the need for watering and use water effectively and economically when you do water.

To reduce moisture loss through evaporation, water plants in the cool of the evening or early in the morning. This ensures water reaches roots with minimum waste. Timing is critical. Although it may occasionally be necessary to water in the heat of day, avoid it if you can.

If beds, borders, or vegetable patches need watering, avoid the temptation to freshen them up by sprinkling water lightly over a wide area. Light watering won't penetrate the soil and may encourage roots to develop closer to the surface. This makes plants more susceptible to drought and in need of repeated watering. Instead, give individual plants a thorough soaking by watering directly above the root area. Let the water soak in before applying more.

Needy plants

Start with newly planted seedlings, then established plants. Close attention needs to be paid to newly sown grass or recently planted beds and borders, plants in pots, and most fruit and vegetables. Elsewhere, keep an eye on plants growing under trees and

To reduce water waste, water directly at the base of individual plants so that moisture gets straight to the roots.

Thoroughly water young plants individually as you transplant them. Continue to water regularly while they become established.

Get up early and water plants at the very beginning of the day when the sun is not at its hottest—this way you'll lose less to evaporation.

hedges along with those planted under an overhang or trained against a wall or fence. Generally, established plants growing in soil do not require watering, but their growth is usually improved by watering in drought conditions.

Watering baskets and containers

Summer rainfall seldom keeps hanging baskets and containers moist; the foliage will often act like an umbrella, keeping the potting mix beneath dry. To ensure plants in pots thrive, water regularly and thoroughly, especially in the summer. When planting containers, leave a 2 in (5 cm) gap between the top of the potting mix and the lip of the container to act as a well for water to gather and then filter down to the roots of the plants.

To water baskets, remove the rose from a watering can, and pour water slowly beneath the foliage, directly onto the potting mix. Place trays under patio containers to act as a reservoir in summer. Although plants in pots are most demanding while in active growth, they also need occasional watering in dry spells over the winter.

EASY WATERING

Watering cans are probably the only watering equipment you'll need for a small garden, but a hose is a better option for a large plot and will make life easier. Instead of attaching a hose to a tap indoors, install an outdoor tap (building codes vary; consult a professional before altering your plumbing). There are many devices available to improve the efficiency of watering and make life easier; a long-handled wand can be fitted to a hose to reach individual plants, or a timer can be fitted to a tap to deliver water via a drip hose or an automatic irrigation system.

Sprinklers release a huge amount of water. They are best used only on newly laid lawns in dry conditions. Always check for watering restrictions in case of drought.

Drip feeders along a length of hose can be used to water at intervals along a bed or in pots.

Low-level watering systems attached to buried hoses will deliver water close to the roots.

Garden hoses will avoid a lot of time spent carrying watering cans around the garden.

Timer systems enable you to water at optimal times of day, even when you are not around.

Drip hoses on the soil surface or buried around perennials put water where plants need it.

Extended watering heads mean you can water plants directly from a distance.

An old barrel is an attractive feature as well as serving a practical purpose. Make sure it is watertight, and position it under a downspout.

USING GRAY WATER

Waste water from the sink, bath, and washing machine can be recycled in the garden. Avoid polluting it with detergents by using environmentally friendly products, and dilute this "gray water" before using it.

Don't pour waste water down the sink—water your ornamentals with it instead. Avoiding using gray water on edible crops.

SAVING WATER

Conserving water is essential if you have a meter, but there are other incentives. Climate change, urban spread, and the expense of processing tap water make it increasingly important to use water wisely.

WISE WATERING

Most rainwater washes down the drains; reduce waste by ensuring as much as possible reaches plants. When planning a garden, ensure that the direction of the slope over a path, patio, or drive directs water to lawns or beds. Lawns are particularly resilient, and in temperate climates rarely need special watering once established. Build in ways to collect and store rainwater, and add moisture-retaining mulches to soil.

Collecting rainwater

Although underground rainwater harvesting systems can be installed, it is far cheaper and easier to use water barrels. These can be sited to collect rainwater from any roof with gutters and down-spouts, and come in all shapes and sizes from huge tanks to slimline models ideal for small gardens. To plumb in a water barrel, remove a lower section of downspout so it empties into a barrel placed beneath it, then add an overflow pipe to take away excess water. Or you can stand the barrel next to the downspout and link them with a divertor kit.

Mulching

Covering the soil surface with mulches, such as gravel, leaf mold, garden compost, composted bark, or well-rotted manure, helps reduce water evaporation and also stifles weeds that compete for moisture. Mulches are best applied from mid- to late

Attach barrels to downspouts by the house, a shed, or greenhouse to catch rainwater. Keep a lid on to prevent evaporation and mosquitoes.

Drainage pipes from a raised patio can provide an additional water source for flower beds situated below them at a lower level.

spring and in the fall, when the soil is moist and warm. Avoid mulching in winter and early spring; the soil is cold and the mulch may slow it from warming up. Mulching retains moisture most effectively if applied to damp soil, so unless it has rained recently, water the area well first, and allow the surface to

drain. Spread the mulch 2–3 in (5–7.5 cm) thick over the soil, being careful not to pile it up against stems or smother low-growing plants. On new beds and borders, consider laying a permeable membrane before mulching to protect against weeds (see p.350). Plant through slits, and cover the membrane with mulch.

Camouflage unattractive sheets of permeable membrane with gravel or fine bark chips. This will give the area a neat, weed-free finish.

Gravel laid around the base of individual plants is enough to keep in moisture around the roots. Water the plants well first to be most effective.

DROUGHT LOVERS

Acanthus spinosus
  (Bear's breeches)
Cistus x *lenis* 'Grayswood Pink'
  (Rock rose)
Elaeagnus angustifolia
Eryngium x *oliverianum*
Euphorbia myrsinites
Foeniculum vulgare 'Purpureum'
  (Bronze fennel)
Iris unguicularis
Lavandula (Lavender)
Salvia officinalis (Common sage)
Salvia rosmarinus
  (Rosemary)
Sempervivum arachnoideum
  (Hen-and-chickens)
Stachys byzantina (Lambs' ears)
Stipa tenuissima (Feather grass)

HOW TO WATER POTS LESS

Plants in containers dry out faster than those in the ground. To keep watering to a minimum, don't overplant, ensure plants are not pot-bound, and use large pots, which hold more potting mix and retain moisture better. Choose a potting mix intended for the type of plants you plan to grow.

Choose your material carefully. Plastic pots hold moisture more effectively than porous terra-cotta. If you grow plants in metal pots, avoid placing them in full sun to keep the potting mix and roots cool.

Group plants in containers together so they shade each other, and stand them on saucers that will act as a reservoir for excess water. Cover the potting mix surface with bark chips, gravel, garden compost, or a decorative material to reduce evaporation.

A mulch of bark chips or other biodegradable material will hold in moisture.

Add water-retaining crystals to potting mix before planting. These release water as needed.

Terra-cotta pots look beautiful but do not retain water as well as plastic containers.

Group pots together and the plants will shade each other, keeping their roots cool.

Fit pots with individual drip attachments from a garden hose, operated by a timer.

Larger plastic containers retain moisture well and are suitable for thirsty plants and crops.

HOW TO FEED

Ensure your garden is full of flourishing plants by providing them with the correct nutrients as and when they need them. Get the feeding right, and they will respond with healthy leaf, fruit, and flower growth.

Soluble fertilizer is easy to apply to plants and can be mixed and applied with a watering can. Check the package for dilution rates first.

FEEDING FACTS

It's important to get feeding just right. Too little results in weak growth, while too much promotes soft, sappy shoots that attract the attention of aphids, become vulnerable to frost damage, and may need support.

A careful look at a plant should tell you if it is lacking an essential nutrient. Leaves that yellow at the edges and between the veins show signs of iron deficiency.

FEEDING TECHNIQUES

There is a wide range of plant foods available, from manure and compost to liquid, granular, and powdered feeds. Some are inorganic—man-made; others are organic—derived from plant and animal waste.

Some feeds have equal proportions of the three major plant nutrients (nitrogen, phosphorus, and potassium, represented by the symbols N, P, and K), which promote all-around healthy growth. Others have a higher percentage of a particular nutrient; these are designed to encourage root, foliage, or fruit development. Specialty granular and liquid feeds are also available for specific plants or purposes, like orchid, tomato, citrus, and bonsai fertilizer, and ericaceous and sequestered iron fertilizers.

Granular fertilizer can be scattered on the soil around the base of the plant and will deliver nutrients straight to roots as it is washed in.

Dry fertilizers

Granular or powdered fertilizers are mainly used to feed established plants in beds or borders or to boost soil fertility before planting. Apply in early spring, scattering it around established trees, shrubs, and perennials, or working it in to broad patches of soil. If you need to treat a large area, divide it into square yards (meters) with canes for more even distribution. Always wear gloves when handling dry fertilizer.

Slow-release fertilizers

Added to the soil or mixed into compost in powder or granular form, these fertilizers feed plants gradually over time. They are particularly useful if you are short on time, as only one application is needed. Follow the

Bulky organic fertilizers are invaluable, feeding plants by boosting the soil's nutrients while also improving its structure.

package instructions for application, and wear suitable gloves when handling it.

Liquid fertilizers

Fast-acting liquid fertilizers can be applied to soil or potting mix, once diluted, or added to a sprayer and used as a foliar feed. Liquid feeds that are high in potash are ideal for improving yields of plants such as tomatoes, peppers, and strawberries,

or to extend the display of flowering annuals. Kelp is a good organic fertilizer for garden plants. Dilute concentrated feeds according to the package instructions, or use the more expensive ready-mixed feeds. Yellowing leaves (chlorosis) can be a sign of nutrient deficiency. Liquid feeds can offer a quick fix, but first be sure that the symptom does not have another cause, such as poor drainage or disease.

Manure

Simply adding bulky farmyard manure into the soil improves its structure and water-retaining ability, encourages beneficial organisms, and adds nutrients. Ideally, apply well-rotted manure in the fall, either as a 2–3 in (5–7.5 cm) deep mulch to established beds, or dug into large areas being prepared for planting in the spring.

Liquid fertilizers act quickly once diluted in water, and when applied to the soil or leaves, will soon revitalize flagging plants.

Plants in pots need more feeding than those in the ground. Top-dressing large containers with a balanced fertilizer helps them thrive.

Well-rotted manure is best applied in the late winter, so it can gradually rot into the soil, nourishing it ready for spring growth.

Making garden compost

Making your own compost is easy and makes sense economically and environmentally, too. Fill your bins with a mixture of green and brown waste. Green waste includes lawn clippings, annual weeds, plant trimmings, and other soft material that rots down quickly, bringing nitrogen and moisture to the mix. Shredded cardboard and dead leaves

are good brown-waste materials—they are dry, rich in carbon, and give compost structure. Green materials rot to a smelly sludge, but brown materials balance out the compost to produce a rich, crumbly texture. Do not add animal waste, meat, cooked food, diseased plants, or fresh perennial weeds.

1 Choose a compost bin to suit your needs, and position it in the garden where it can be easily accessed and tended.

2 Add uncooked kitchen waste as well as healthy plant materials and grass clippings to your heap. Pick out any perennial weeds or diseased plants.

3 Build up your heap in layers of green and brown material to blend the materials and give the finished compost a good structure and texture.

4 Turn the heap periodically with a garden fork to mix up all the rotting materials and aerate the heap; this also helps the mixture compost more thoroughly.

CONTAINER GROWING

There are thousands of plants that will thrive in containers—in fact you can grow just about anything in them, from trees to miniature bulbs, fruit and vegetables, and aquatic plants such as water lilies.

Containers make the perfect home for many plants and are an ideal solution if you have limited space or want herbs or plants on hand.

PLANTING POTS

Whether you want to create a vibrant display of summer color or just a focal point, the key to success with containers is to make sure all the plants' needs are met.

Pick containers that suit your plants and style of garden. Good-quality terra-cotta suits a formal, classic space, while galvanized steel cubes, cylinders, or conical pots look good in a more contemporary garden. Black or white terrazzo (faux marble) oozes sophistication and suits many garden styles. If

you have a balcony or roof garden, use lightweight pots.

The size of the pot you need depends on the plant. Make sure it is large enough for the root ball, with space around the sides and base for the roots to grow. Use large pots for trees, shrubs, or groups of plants, while smaller containers can house herbs, bulbs, or perennials.

Using the correct potting mix is vital. Shrubs, trees, and other perennials growing permanently in pots grow best in a potting mix that retains moisture well and is fairly

Planting a patio pot

Patio containers are easy to plant, but it's worth spending a few minutes preparing pots before you start. Choose a pot with a drainage hole that will accommodate the plants easily with room for growth. Fill potting mix to within 2 in (5 cm) of the rim. Once you have planted, keep this gap between the surface of the potting mix and lip of the container to keep

water from spilling over the edges when watering. Stand containers on pot feet to allow excess moisture to drain away. This prevents moisture building up at the base of pots, leading to waterlogging and root damage. Pools of water may stain the ground and the container, and encourage roots to grow out of the base of the pot, which can look untidy.

1 If you are using terra-cotta pots, prepare them for planting by first giving the insides a good soaking using a watering can or hose.

2 If the pot is large, cover the base with styrofoam or rubble to avoid using more potting mix than you need. This also prevents the mix washing out of the drainage hole.

3 Fill the pot, leaving a gap at the top to allow for watering. Mix a granular fertilizer into the soil according to the instructions on the package.

4 Position plants in the pot, leaving enough space between them to allow for growth. Gently firm down the soil around the roots, and water in well.

heavy, preventing pots from toppling over. Peat-based mix is ideal for temporary displays of annual plants or vegetables. Once planted, add a decorative mulch over the surface of the potting mix. It looks good, stifles weeds, and locks in moisture.

Group pots together to create an interesting display. Use a few different styles of pots, but keep it simple for a unified look.

A simple pot supporting a well-shaped plant can create a focal point in a garden or can be used to draw the eye to what lies beyond it.

TOP-DRESSING

Plants that are permanently grown in pots can run out of steam and should be given a boost in spring. Top-dressing is simply removing the top layer of potting mix and replacing it with fresh material mixed with an appropriate fertilizer.

Top-dress containers with fresh potting mix, then cover with a mulch of bark chips or decorative pebbles to keep the moisture in and prevent weeds from germinating.

Planting a hanging basket

Hanging baskets can be planted for year-round interest or to provide a blast of color in specific seasons. Baskets are available in a wide range of sizes and styles and have either solid or open sides. Those with open sides require liners to retain the potting mix; choose one the right size, made of cardboard, plastic-backed jute, coconut fiber, or artificial moss. To make planting easier, sit your basket in a large pot or bucket to prevent it from moving around. Fill it using specially formulated hanging basket potting mix, or make your own blend using potting mix mixed with controlled-release fertilizer granules and water-retaining crystals.

1 If your hanging basket is not already lined, cut your preferred lining material to size, and press it into place. Cut planting holes in the sides.

2 Half-fill the basket with a mixture of potting mix, fertilizer, and water-retaining granules. Insert the plants into the compost through the side holes.

3 Add more potting mix to the basket once all the side plantings are in place, then position the plants to grow on the top of the basket or to trail down.

4 Firm down plants, then give the hanging basket a good watering using a fine rose. Leave the basket to drain in the pot or bucket before hanging in position.

Encourage a good display from your plants by removing spent flowers, which may promote new flowering stems.

STAKING PLANTS

Weak-stemmed or top-heavy perennials need supports in summer, which should be put in place in early spring. Use link stakes to surround large clumps, and wire-mesh rings on legs for multi-stemmed perennials.

Help plants hold their heads high for all to see in summer by putting supports in place before they get too big.

A GOOD DISPLAY

Every gardener wants a great display of color in the garden, and it's not hard to achieve with good plant care. There are a few simple tricks that will help you keep ornamental plants flowering better, and for longer.

PROLONGING FLOWERING

Deadheading spent flowers, pinching off growth, and dividing crowded bulbs and perennials are effective techniques used to encourage plants to perform at their best. They are carried out at different times of year, and all are simple to do.

Deadheading

Most plants divert their energy into producing seeds when their flowers start to fade, but you can encourage them to continue flowering longer by regularly removing spent heads. Dying flowers on soft-stemmed plants can be snapped off with your thumb and forefinger; use pruners for thicker stems or where accuracy is needed, such as on roses. This technique can be used on many shrubs, perennials, and annuals.

A small number of plants are sterile and don't set seeds, which means they will continue to flower even if you don't remove the deadheads. You may still wish to remove dying flowers, however, to improve the plant's overall appearance and to reduce the risk of disease or rotting in damp weather. In contrast some plants are prolific self-seeders, such as annual poppies, and can become a nuisance in the garden. In this situation, deadheading before seeds are produced will prevent unwanted seedlings from appearing all over.

Pinching off

Left to their own devices, some perennials, bedding plants, and flowering pot plants produce thin, spindly shoots, leading to a disappointing display of color.

Removing spent flowers not only makes the plant look better but also encourages the plant to direct its energy into making new blooms.

Pinching off the growing tips stops vertical growth and encourages the growth of stems lower down, creating a bushier plant.

However, by pinching these shoots back early in the season you can encourage plants to produce bushier growth from lower down, which will give the plant a more balanced shape. It also creates more robust plants that are less likely to collapse, while also encouraging the production of more flowers. Some plants, like annual sweet peas, only need pinching off once, but others, such as fuchsias and petunias, need regular attention during summer.

Generally, plants need pinching off when they are about a third of their ultimate height; aim to remove around 1–2 in (2.5–5 cm) of growth.

Thinning overcrowded bulbs

Over a number of years, most bulb species form clumps that gradually become so overcrowded that the plants stop flowering—described as becoming "blind." To rejuvenate them, carefully lift the clumps with a fork as the leaves die down in fall, and divide them into separate bulbs. Remove any dead, diseased, or unhealthy bulbs, and replant the rest into well-prepared soil. Most bulbs will need thinning every three to four years, but let flowering performance guide your decision; lift and divide bulbs when the flowering season deteriorates.

Established bulb colonies can be difficult to lift from the soil in one piece, so work from all sides and lift smaller, individual clumps.

PLANT LIST

Perennials that benefit from occasional division
Achillea (Yarrow)
Astilbe
Coreopsis (Tickseed)
Helenium (Helen's flower)
Hylotelephium spectabile (Ice plant)
Iris
Monarda (Bergamot)
Rudbeckia (Coneflower)
Stachys byzantina (Lambs' ears)

Perennials that dislike disturbance
Anemone x hybrida
Aquilegia (Columbine)
Crocosmia (Montbretia)
Dierama (Angel's fishing rod)
Helleborus
Lamprocapnos spectabilis (Bleeding heart)
Paeonia (Peony)

Lifting and dividing perennials

Many perennials outgrow their allotted space or lose vigor with age, forming unproductive mounds of foliage that do not flower well. Others form unsightly rings of plants around a bare center. Revive plants by dividing them when dormant, either in late fall or early spring—plants split early in the year establish better because the soil is damp but quickly warms up. Most perennials need dividing every two or three years, but some grow more vigorously than others, requiring frequent division, while others flower better when congested, are slower growing, or resent disturbance. Dividing perennials is a useful way to propagate them (see p.332).

1 Carefully lift the plant, using a fork. Take care not to damage the roots as you do so. Gently shake off excess soil as you remove the clump.

2 Separate plants by inserting two spades back-to-back in the center of the clump and pushing them away from each other to split the mound.

3 Divide the larger clumps into smaller, more manageable pieces using your hands. Discard any unhealthy-looking sections, and pull out any weeds.

4 Replant the newly divided sections into their new positions at the same depth as before. Firm the soil around the roots well.

TENDER PLANTS

During colder months, plants are vulnerable to frost, low temperatures, biting winds, and excessive rain. Losing a few plants is inevitable in a very hard winter, but you can reduce the risk with protective measures.

Mature tender plants may be too large to bring under cover during the winter, so you will need to protect them where they grow.

MOVING UNDER COVER

If you are overwintering crops, extending the growing season, or making early or late sowings in the ground, use plastic tunnels, cloches, or fabric to protect plants from hard frosts and excessively wet conditions.

A simple cloche provides enough protection for young plants in mid-spring when there is still risk of frost.

WINTER PROTECTION

A sudden cold snap will take its toll on tender plants, so don't be caught unaware. Wrap up plants well in advance, and prepare them for the worst weather to help them get through the winter unscathed.

While tender bulbs and tubers are best lifted from the ground, vulnerable shrubs, climbers, and other plants can be protected from the elements *in situ* with burlap, horticultural fabric, and straw. Wrap plants in late fall or before the first frost. Protect branches of shrubs, such as *Cestrum,* fuchsia, and *Clerodendrum,* with a sheet of horticultural fabric held in place with twine. Encase the lower stems of tender climbers with dry straw wrapped with burlap.

Sensitive architectural plants need extra care. Place straw in the crown of tree ferns and palms, then gather up the fronds, and wrap in fabric. To protect bananas, cut off the leaves, and encircle the trunks with chicken wire. Stuff this with straw, and cover it all with plastic sheeting to keep out the rain—loosen the covers during milder weather to allow air to circulate.

Plants in containers

Plants in pots are particularly vulnerable to cold weather, and a sudden cold snap or a prolonged period of icy weather can cause damage to roots or tender shoots. Move plants to a cool sunroom, porch, or frost-free greenhouse if possible; dormant plants that don't

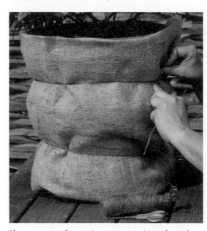

Keep roots of container-grown plants frost-free outside in winter by wrapping the pots with bubble wrap or burlap, secured with twine.

Tender blossoms on wall-trained fruit trees can be protected *in situ* from frost damage over the winter by covering with horticultural fabric.

need light, such as fuchsias, can also be moved into garages and sheds. If you don't have space or the pots are too heavy to move, take other precautions.

Keep the roots protected from frost by wrapping the container with bubble wrap, burlap, or fabric, and tie it securely in place with garden twine. Alternatively, push pots up against the wall of the house, where it is slightly warmer, and pack them together tightly so they help insulate each other. Protective material can then be wrapped around the whole group. Sheets of fabric can also be wrapped around the tops of plants to protect foliage, buds, or early flowers, particularly on fruit trees.

Excessive moisture caused by winter rain can also cause problems for container-grown plants. Wet potting mix or puddles at the base of pots can starve roots of oxygen and they may then rot, causing the plant to die. Reduce problems by moving pots into a sheltered spot or under an overhang, and raise containers off the ground on pot feet to allow excess moisture to drain and air to circulate around the roots.

Tropical plants, such as bananas (*above*) and palms, are vulnerable to frost. If you can't move them under cover, mulch them well with straw.

TENDER PLANTS
Bougainvillea
Brugmansia
Callistemon (Bottlebrush)
Canna (Indian shot plant)
Clerodendrum bungei (Glory flower)
Cordyline australis (New Zealand cabbage palm)
Dahlia
Dicksonia antarctica (Tree fern)
Eucomis (Pineapple lily)
Fuchsia
Galtonia
Gladiolus
Hedychium (Ginger lily)
Leonotis leonurus (Lion's tail)
Melianthus major (Honey bush)
Musa basjoo (Japanese banana)
Pelargonium
Punica granatum (Pomegranate)
Tigridia (Tiger flower)

Lifting and storing tender bulbs and tubers

Unless you have a mild winter climate and well-drained soil, lift your tender bulbs and tubers and store them under cover during winter to prevent them from rotting in damp soil or being damaged or killed by penetrating ground frost. Dahlias, *Eucomis*, cannas, gladioli, *Tigridia*, *Galtonia*, and other summer-flowering species should be lifted during the fall once the foliage starts to die back. Lift the bulbs and dry off completely to prevent them from rotting, then store under cover in a garage, shed, or any dry, frost-free place. Label them before storing for easy identification when they are planted outdoors again in the spring. Check bulbs occasionally for signs of decay.

1 Lift bulbs out of the soil in fall using a fork, being careful to avoid damaging them with the prongs. Discard any damaged bulbs.

2 Remove soil, trim off dying top growth, and lay the bulbs out on a wire rack. Once they are dry, store the bulbs in boxes or trays of sand in a frost-free place.

1 Lift tubers out of the ground during fall using a fork, digging around the edge of the clump to prevent damage to the roots.

2 Shake off excess soil, trim away any dying foliage and stems, and let the tubers dry out completely. Once dry, dust off the remaining soil, and store the tubers.

Many trees benefit from regular pruning to control their size and produce an attractive shape. It also promotes strong new growth.

PINCH PRUNING

You will need pruning tools to make a clean cut to woody or thick branches, but soft and sappy growth can be pruned by hand. Pinch off this growth with your thumb and forefinger to encourage a bushy plant.

Young, fresh growth can be pinched off neatly between thumb and forefinger without causing damage.

PRUNING

You can influence the way plants grow through pruning, which will also increase their production and ensure they look their best. Knowing when and where to prune, and which technique to use, will help your plants flourish.

WHY PRUNE?

Pruning plants worries some gardeners, but armed with the right tools and a little knowledge, you can improve the look and vigor of your plants without harming them.

Hard pruning results in more vigorous growth further down the plant. At the end of each shoot is a terminal bud that is stronger than those along the sides, which grow to form side shoots. Cutting off the terminal bud directs the plant's energy to the side buds, resulting in a bushier, fuller plant.

There are many reasons why you might need to prune plants in this way. Left to their own devices, some plants become a messy tangle of overgrown branches, promoting conditions ripe for pests and diseases. Overgrown plants also tend to be less vigorous, resulting in a poorer display of flowers or the production of fewer fruit.

Pruning helps maintain an attractive shape and prevents plants from suffocating compact neighbors, especially in small gardens where space is at a premium. Many beautiful effects can be achieved by careful pruning. Cutting some plants back hard will result in foliage that is larger and brighter than mature leaves, while cutting back the shoots of plants grown for winter stem color encourages a flush of bright new

Make an angled cut downward on stems that bear alternate buds along their length. Select a healthy bud and prune just above it.

On plants with opposite buds on their stems, prune just above a pair of healthy buds, making a clean, straight cut.

Choosing and using the right tools for the job is essential to prevent damaging plants, which in turn can lead to infections.

PRUNING TOOLS

To prune properly you need a small selection of good-quality tools. It is important that they are maintained well so they make clean cuts that do not damage plant growth.

Different tools are needed for different jobs. Choose hand pruners for the accurate pruning of stems up to ½ in (1.5 cm) in diameter and keep them sharp and clean. Handheld pruning saws are ideal for thicker branches. Telescopic loppers are used for cutting stems up to 1 in (2.5 cm) thick, growing above head height. Handheld shears are best for topiary, while electric and gas-powered trimmers are useful for cutting most hedges.

Long-arm loppers make trimming stems above head height easier and safer and do away with the need for ladders.

shoots. Regular pruning to remove diseased or damaged material also keeps plants in good health. Pruning needs depend on the type of plant, and for some, a light trim is all that is necessary to maintain a good display.

WHEN TO PRUNE

The timing of pruning is important: if you prune at the wrong time, you might remove flower buds or leave plants vulnerable to damage by frost. A good rule of thumb for any shrub or climber is to prune lightly shortly after flowering as the blooms start to fade—an exception is forsythia, which can be pruned hard to control its size. If the plant flowers after the summer solstice, you can usually prune back hard in spring. Of course, there are exceptions to this rule (such as mophead and lacecap hydrangeas, which have their flower heads left in place through winter and are then pruned lightly in spring), so research specific plants. Evergreen shrubs are usually pruned between late spring and fall. Soft growth is vulnerable to frost, so prune to allow plenty of time for regrowth to toughen up before cold weather arrives.

To prune back stems and branches, you only need a pair of sharp pruners.

Remove thicker stems of large shrubs and trees with a sharp-toothed pruning saw.

A bow saw is ideal for removing branches of 6 in (15 cm) or more and cutting them into logs.

Loppers make it easier to cut woody stems of ½ in (1 cm) thick, especially where access is tricky.

Electric hedge trimmers make light work of cutting and shaping long or tall hedges.

Shears are invaluable for trimming smaller hedges, but also for cutting long grass.

PRUNING SHRUBS

To keep shrubs looking their best, prune them regularly to keep them within bounds and maintain a well-balanced structure. Pruning at the right time will keep them healthy and encourage masses of flowers.

Prune little by little if you are unsure how much of the stems' length to remove. You can always prune a little more if necessary.

WHY PRUNE SHRUBS?

Most shrubs will grow happily without intervention, but unless you prefer a natural look, unpruned plants look out of place in traditional gardens. Annual pruning will keep shrubs at a size suitable for your garden, prevent them muscling out other plants, and stop them spreading onto pathways.

Pruning also improves the flowering or fruiting performance of shrubs. Older wood is less vigorous than younger shoots, and removing this material encourages plants to be more productive. Timing is key, to avoid mistakenly removing developing flower buds.

Although some shrubs respond to hard pruning with a flush of new growth, others are slower growing and only require minimal pruning to keep a balanced shape.

Routine tasks

To ensure healthy plants, remove dead, diseased, or dying growth as you notice it. If left, diseased portions can spread into other parts of the plant. Either cut out the damaged branch, or cut back to healthy wood.

Pruning early-flowering shrubs

Shrubs that flower in spring and early summer on wood formed the year before, such as *Philadelphus*, *Weigela*, *Kerria*, *Forsythia*, *Buddleja alternifolia*, *Kolkwitzia*, and *Deutzia* should be trimmed when blooms fade. This will encourage a flush of new branches and the production of flowers closer to the ground, where they are easier to enjoy. If left, plants will become lanky and the flowers will be held higher up the plant. To improve their appearance and keep them under control, remove thin and wispy growth, then cut back branches that held flowers to strong side branches, aiming to maintain an open, balanced framework.

1 As soon as *Philadelphus* has finished flowering, cut back about a quarter of the oldest flowering stems to 6 in (15 cm) above the ground.

2 First remove any dead, damaged, or diseased stems, cutting them back to the base of the plant using sharp, clean pruners.

3 Prune out stems of the previous year's growth, cutting them back to about 2 or 4 buds from the old wood. This will encourage a new flush of growth.

4 Finally, trim the tips of any strong young stems that are already present in the plant. This encourages them to branch further down, resulting in more flowers.

Some shrubs grow unevenly, spoiling the symmetry of the plant; if a plant has developed more growth on just one side, lightly prune the stronger shoots on the bushy side, and hard prune the weaker ones to restore balance.

Congested branches reduce airflow and light to the center of the plant, which can result in disease. Thinning out growth and removing crossing or unwanted branches will improve the resilience of the plant.

A shrub that looks out of shape and unbalanced should be pruned to give it more structure and create a healthier framework.

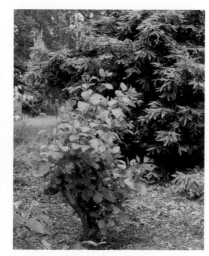

Once pruned, the plant puts on a whole new flush of vigorous growth and begins to take on a more attractive shape.

ALSO RECOMMENDED

Shrubs pruned in summer after flowering:
Buddleja alternifolia
Deutzia
Exochorda
Kolkwitzia
Philadelphus
Photinia villosa
Ribes sanguineum
Syringa
Weigela

Shrubs pruned in spring:
Buddleja davidii
Caryopteris x clandonensis
Cotinus
Forsythia
Fuchsia
Hibiscus syriacus
Hydrangea
Lavatera
Perovskia

Pruning late-flowering shrubs

Shrubs that flower on the current season's growth (wood), such as lavender, roses, *Spiraea japonica*, fuchsias, *Caryopteris*, and buddleja should be pruned in early spring. This gives them plenty of time to form vigorous new branches to carry blooms in summer. There are a number of ways to prune these plants: *Leycesteria, Perovskia,* and those that do not produce a woody framework can be pruned to almost ground level, while others can be allowed to develop a permanent framework with the branches cut back each year to maintain their shape. After pruning, give plants a boost by scattering a general granular fertilizer over the soil.

1 Prune late-flowering shrubs, such as *Hydrangea paniculata,* in the dormant season well after flowering.

2 Using a sharp pair of pruners, begin by removing dead, diseased, and damaged wood, cutting back to healthy growth and stem joints.

3 Cut out up to one-fifth of the oldest wood all over the plant, reducing stems to within 2–3 in (5–8 cm) of the ground. It is easiest to do this with a pruning saw.

4 Remove any weak or twiggy growth, too, and cut out any crossing or straggling stems to create a well-balanced shrub with an open center.

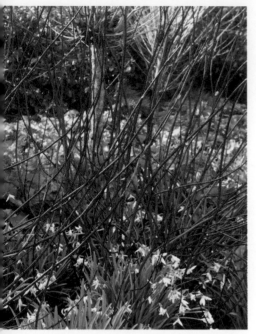

The flame-red stems of dogwood provide a much-needed splash of color in winter. This annual spectacle is maintained by hard pruning.

PRUNING FOR A PURPOSE

Some shrubs are grown for their foliage or for their colorful stems, which are at their best after leaf fall. By pruning these plants hard early in the year, you can create magical effects in the dark, cold winter months.

SPECIAL EFFECTS

It might look brutal at first, but many shrubs respond positively to hard winter pruning by rewarding you with a mass of fresh, new, colorful stems, or by developing leaves that are much bigger, are a better shape, or are more colorful than those produced by unpruned plants.

A number of shrubs will become quite large if left to their own devices, but by cutting them back hard annually in spring, or at least once every few years, you can contain their size and also encourage healthy, decorative leaves.

Avoid pruning plants in the fall, because decay fungi might enter the pruning cuts and cause damage or even death.

Before you start, check that specific plants will respond well to hard pruning. Remember that although cutting back will improve foliage or stems, it might also mean a loss of flowers for that season. Not all plants will tolerate hard pruning, and some may not survive such treatment.

Coppicing and pollarding

Shrubs grown for their winter stems tend to merge into the background for

Pruning for colorful winter stems

Dogwoods, willows, and ornamental brambles are prized for their colorful winter stems, which emerge as their leaves drop in the fall. To ensure a great display each year, these plants need pruning annually, once established, in early spring to encourage a flush of new stems. Known as coppicing, this pruning technique aims to create a permanent low, stubby

framework close to the ground. After they have been cut back, new, vibrant shoots will grow vigorously in time for winter. If you are worried about the vigor of your plants, for example for some variegated shrubs, prune more lightly, to encourage new growth. This will also keep the shrub at a larger size.

1 Just before growth begins in early to mid-spring, cut out old, stray stems using pruners to give the plant some shape.

2 Cut away last year's shoots and all nonwoody growth to within 3 in (7.5 cm) of the main stems to get better access to the center of the plant.

3 Once you have clear access to the main stems, cut back hard all shoots to 2–3 in (5–8 cm) from the base of the plant, cutting just above the join with the main stems.

4 Once you have finished pruning, feed plants with fertilizer, and give the area around their roots a good mulch with compost or well-rotted manure.

SPECIAL PRUNING

Plants that respond well to pruning

Acer negundo 'Winter Lightning'

Catalpa bignonioides
(Indian bean tree)

Cercis siliquastrum
(Judas tree)

Cornus species
(Dogwood)

Cotinus species
(Smoke bush)

Davidia involucrata
(Handkerchief tree)

Eucalyptus gunnii
(Cider gum)

Rubus species
(Ornamental bramble)

Salix species
(Willow)

Sambucus nigra 'Aurea'
(Elder)

PRUNING FOR FOLIAGE

Some shrubs are pruned hard to produce winter stems, and others can be given similar treatment to encourage more eye-catching foliage. The Indian bean tree (*Catalpa bignonioides*), Judas tree (*Cercis siliquastrum*), foxglove tree (*Paulownia tomentosa*), and others respond by producing larger leaves than those on unpruned plants. Cider gum (*Eucalyptus gunnii*) has curved, oval leaves when mature. If cut back hard, it responds by producing attractive juvenile leaves.

▲ **Prune back hard** in the spring for a more impressive display. Certain plants produce their most attractive foliage with juvenile leaves.

◄ **Pollarding** trees and shrubs encourages them to bear their most eye-catching young growth, raised above ground level.

much of the year, only coming into their own in the fall after the leaves drop. If left, their stems appear dull and lose their vibrancy of color, but cutting them back annually, or at least every other year, will promote a flush of new colorful shoots.

Willows and dogwoods can be pruned using a technique known as coppicing, which encourages a mass of colorful winter stems. Begin training plants just after planting by pruning back all shoots hard, close to their base. The following spring and in subsequent years, prune the tree in the same way to produce a stumpy framework.

Pollarding (see p.321) is another method used for pruning dogwoods and willows to produce spectacular winter stems. Instead of being pruned back close to the ground, plants are pruned above a clear trunk. The branches are cut back to previous cuts on the top of the trunk to leave a lollipop shape. After cutting back plants hard, feed around the roots and mulch.

The foliage of many deciduous variegated shrubs is far more vibrant if pruned annually. The usual techniques for these plants are pollarding and stooling, which should be carried out between late winter and early spring, before leaves appear. To stool plants, cut back stems to within 2–3 in (5–7.5 cm) of the ground. To grow as a pollard, cut back shoots to within 2–3 in (5–7.5 cm) of the trunk. Apply a balanced granular fertilizer at 2 oz per sq yd (70 g per sq m) to assist new growth after pruning.

Variegated plants can quickly become overrun by non-variegated shoots, so prune them out on sight to maintain interesting foliage.

PRUNING CLIMBERS

Climbing plants and wall shrubs provide vertical color and interest, but if neglected they will soon grow out of bounds, becoming shy to flower or casting unwanted shade. Pruning once a year will keep them at their best.

A little judicious pruning will give you walls of color throughout the seasons, and even a seemingly informal garden requires a little work.

BASIC CLIMBER PRUNING

Without a helping hand some plants will run away, outgrowing their designated space and becoming an ugly tangle of shoots. Others will lose vigor and produce few flowers, berries, or fruit.

Annual pruning helps keep climbers attractive, productive, and in check, but you can make life easier by selecting plants that suit your garden, along with their allotted space or support. This reduces the need to prune too often, making it easy to keep your climbing plants under control.

Whether you're growing self-clinging climbers (see p.144) or those with lax stems that need training against supports to flourish, your aim is to create a well-balanced framework that covers the area. Remove any weak or damaged shoots, and prune wayward growth to encourage branching. As the climbing plant matures, older, woodier stems will need pruning to promote more vigorous shoots.

Types of cut

Plants that have a network of woody stems are easily pruned using pruners

Pruning honeysuckle

Honeysuckles are prized for their highly scented flowers and will happily climb over supports. However, they can break ranks and invade the space of other plants or cause damage to overburdened supports or structures. Pruning and training in spring will help keep them in check as well as productive and healthy.

1 To encourage even coverage, cut out old woody stems at the base or just above a point where strong growth is emerging.

2 Remove unwanted new shoots as they grow to keep plants within bounds. Cut away these wayward stems close to the main framework, and tie them into their supports.

Pruning ivy

Ivy's vigorous and dense growth means it must be pruned regularly to stop it from becoming a nuisance. Plants can be pruned in late spring or early summer to reduce the height, width, and density of growth; they can also be sheared or cut back hard. Check plants before pruning to avoid disturbing nesting birds.

1 Ivy can be an irritant, so wear gloves to prune it. Peel away and cut off all unwanted ivy. Check for dead, damaged, or diseased growth and then prune that, too.

2 Ivy will attach itself to most surfaces and cling on. If it has strayed into territory where it is unwanted or might cause damage, peel it away from the wall by hand.

to ensure accurate cuts and a tidy finish. If growth is needed to fill a certain area, pruning cuts can be made above outward-facing buds pointing in the direction needed. Pruning like this would be a chore on those plants that form a dense

If your climber needs drastic pruning, cut away all the unproductive material beneath the foliage using a pair of hand shears.

mass of spindly growth, so prune these stems en masse with shears or pruners. Wall shrubs, and climbing plants with evergreen foliage, can be clipped tightly with shears to keep them neat and bushy.

When to prune

The timing of pruning is generally the same for climbers as it is for other shrubs. Evergreen climbers grown for their foliage can be pruned in spring, while those grown for their flowers need pruning at specific times to avoid removing flower buds. Early-flowering plants that flower on the previous season's wood should be pruned after flowering, while those that flower in mid- to late summer on the current season's growth can be pruned in winter or early spring. Clematis fall into three pruning groups and are categorized according to when they flower (see p.149)

PRUNING WALL SHRUBS

Unlike true climbers, which are largely self-clinging, wall shrubs have no natural means of supporting themselves vertically, so branches are usually tied into a network of wires, trellis, or other supports. Like all shrubs, these need pruning annually to keep them within bounds; to prevent them from becoming too heavy and pulling away from supports; and, if grown for their flowers, to encourage a good display.

Start by pruning horizontal branches to reduce the width, then cut taller vertical stems to reduce the height. Foliage plants can be pruned in spring, but for others their pruning depends on their flowering times (see pp.312–313).

Prune back wall shrubs, such as this *Euonymus fortunei*, in late spring to shape them and keep them contained. Pruning by hand with pruners creates a neater finish.

WISTERIA

Wisteria will grow rampantly if left to its own devices, producing masses of leafy growth at the expense of flowers. Pruning diverts the plant's energy from making leaves to producing flower buds, while

reducing the mass of whiplike shoots helps light reach the network of branches inside. Although wisterias can cover a large area, don't trim them back quickly with a pair of shears; precise pruning twice a year with pruners yields better results.

In summer, prune back vigorous shoots and long, whiplike stems to about four or six leaves from the main stem, creating shoots that are 6 in (15 cm) long.

In winter, cut back all the stems you shortened in summer to about two or three buds, or so they are approximately 3–4 in (8–10 cm) in length.

Cut away horizontal stems first on large-growing shrubs, such as *Garrya elliptica*, in spring, then reduce the height to the required level by cutting off vertical stems.

PRUNING ROSES

Roses are among our best-loved plants, valued for their scent, variety, color, and multiple uses in the flower garden. They are relatively easy to train and prune to ensure a great display each year.

New buds are a useful clue to the direction in which a new shoot will grow. Prune back to an outward-facing bud to avoid congestion.

HOW TO PRUNE ROSES

Roses need pruning for a variety of reasons. Left to grow as they please, they will flower for a few years but then begin to produce weak stems that carry fewer blooms. The plant is likely to develop a mass of congested stems, which reduces the amount of light and air reaching its center. These unhealthy conditions weaken new growth and provide the kind of conditions that encourage pests and diseases to prosper. Choose a pruning technique that suits the type of rose you are growing. For most pruning work, hand pruners are fine, but thicker branches should be removed with a pruning saw.

Climbing and rambling roses (see facing page) need trimming to keep them within the bounds of pergolas, arches, and fences. Bush roses, which include hybrid tea and floribunda varieties, are usually grown in beds and borders. After removing dead, diseased, and dying growth, hybrid teas should be pruned back in early spring, reducing healthy main stems by a quarter to encourage plenty of well-placed flowering shoots. Aim

Pruning shrub roses

Early spring is the best time to prune shrub roses, starting with any dead, diseased, or dying material. Your aim is to create a strong, open framework with a good airflow to prevent fungal diseases. Cut a few of the oldest stems back to the ground, then reduce healthy main stems by a quarter. Use a slanting cut, directly above an outward-facing bud, and snip sloping away from the bud. As well as pruning these roses annually, keep the floral show going longer by deadheading flowers as they start to fade. Despite their slow-growing nature, patio roses are pruned in the same way to keep them compact and flowering freely.

1 Prune roses between late fall and early spring, before leaves appear. First remove any dead or damaged stems from the plant.

2 Prune any over-vigorous shoots by shortening them to about half their original length using pruners. You may want to wear gloves to do this.

3 Cut back any other stems by about half if they look as though they will affect the balance of the shape of the plant when growth begins again in spring.

4 Once you have finished pruning, apply fertilizer around the roots of the plant, and add a layer of mulch, keeping it clear of the main stem.

for a strong, open structure that is uncluttered in the center.

Less vigorous floribundas are not pruned so hard. Cut back shoots to within 6–8 in (15–20 cm) of the base of the plant, leaving a framework of 6–8 of the strongest stems.

Crossing and rubbing branches will cause damage to the plant, which can lead to disease. These stems should be removed as they appear.

Lightly prune miniature roses in spring, cutting wayward branches back by a third and pruning to shape. Patio roses also need pruning to boost flowering, and the shoots of ground-cover roses need to be cut back to keep them within bounds; remove thicker branches on old plants to stimulate new growth.

Aftercare

After pruning, water roses well, and apply a granular rose fertilizer over the root area. Finish by mulching plants, leaving a gap between the mulch and the stems. During summer you can extend flowering by deadheading flowers that are within reach all over the plant to encourage more to develop. Use your fingers to snap off fading blooms at the slightly swollen section of the stem just below the flower, or use pruners.

REMOVE ROSE SUCKERS

Grafted roses often produce unwanted, vigorous, and less ornamental growth from their roots. Remove these by twisting them off at the base. Avoid cutting them at ground level as this stimulates regrowth.

Rose suckers are easy to spot at the base of plants. They detract from the plant's appearance and sap its resources.

Pruning rambling roses

Rambling roses generally need less pruning than climbers, but if their allocated area or supports have been covered, you may want to prune back the stems to regain control and improve their flowering. Ramblers should be pruned in late summer once they have finished flowering.

1 Remove one in three of the oldest stems entirely using loppers, cutting the stems back to just above the soil surface.

2 Cut back any stems that have flowered or are making the plant look unruly, then shorten side shoots by about two-thirds of their length using pruners.

Pruning climbing roses

Climbing roses are not self-clinging and need their shoots to be tied to supports. They are best pruned in late fall after the flowers have faded, or in winter. Remove dead, diseased, or dying branches, and cut out old branches if the plant is heavily congested, to promote fresh new growth.

1 Spur-prune last season's flowering stems back to two or three healthy buds to encourage them to produce more flowering stems.

2 Train any straggling new and old stems to fill gaps in the allocated framework for a neat finish. Tie them into their supports using garden twine.

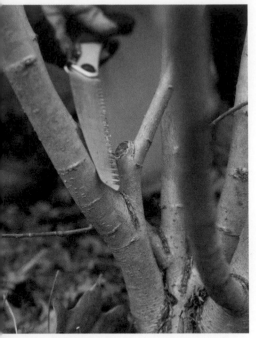

Neglected shrubs, or those that have seen better days, should be cut back hard as an alternative to digging them up.

PRUNING TO RENOVATE

Many woody plants become a tangled mass of congested branches if irregularly pruned, but few are beyond salvation. Most plants can be restored using some drastic but essential pruning techniques.

SHAPING UP

Regularly pruning helps maintain the appearance and health of shrubs, but if plants have been neglected or have grown too large, or you have inherited a garden with out of control plants, more drastic action may be required.

Overgrown plants are unlikely to flower well, and new growth tends to be weak and less vigorous than in well-tended plants. Apart from becoming an eyesore and losing their attractive shape, neglected plants can also cast unwanted shade in a garden, restricting the growth of other plants and preventing you from planting perennials, bulbs, or other plants to make the most of your space. Pests and diseases are also more prevalent among unpruned plants due to their weaker growth, a buildup of dead stems and plant debris, and the reduced light levels and air circulation passing through the crown.

The key to dealing with overgrown shrubs is to cut them back hard,

Using the three-cut pruning method

Sometimes trees require more radical pruning than just trimming a few unwanted branches or shoots. If a branch has become diseased, damaged, or unsafe, it is often better to remove it altogether. Or it may be that you want to improve the tree's overall shape and appearance. If you are removing a whole branch, it needs to be done in stages rather than with one cut near the trunk. This will prevent any damage to the tree should the heavy branch break mid-cut, taking with it the bark on the trunk. Such damage can expose the trunk and the whole plant to serious infections, such as silver leaf (see p.368), which may prove fatal.

1 Using a pruning saw or pruners (depending on the width of the branches), first remove side shoots and the end of the branch.

2 Using a pruning saw in one hand and holding the branch close to the trunk, make a cut under the branch further along, then cut through from above.

3 Holding the stump steady, make the final cut to remove the branch just outside its "collar," cutting through from above with a pruning saw.

4 Make sure the final cut leaves a clean wound; if there is any damage, neaten up the cut. You do not need to apply any wound paint to the stub.

usually to bare stumps, and this should be done in late spring or summer, after the plants have finished flowering. Feed well to promote regrowth. Many plants respond well to this treatment, throwing out a flush of new growth, and soon start to earn their place again. Regard this as a last-ditch attempt to save the plants however, because although this technique works well with many plants, some may not recover and so may need to be dug up and replaced

Hard-pruning evergreens

Many evergreen shrubs can be hard-pruned. Bushy plants with lots of branches at ground level, such as mahonia (*see below*), can be pruned to leave just a cluster of stumps. Plants that grow from single trunks, such as camellia, should be reduced to around 24 in (60 cm) high with side stems cut close to the main

branch. Despite looking severe, a flush of young stems will appear from this stump, although it may take several years for the plant to reach flowering size again. *Aucuba japonica* (spotted laurel), escallonia, *Prunus laurocerasus* (cherry laurel), and *Viburnum tinus* can all be pruned this way.

Stems and side shoots of some deciduous shrubs can be pruned back hard in spring to improve their overall appearance.

POLLARDING

Dogwoods and some willows, along with eucalyptus and other trees and shrubs, are valued for their juvenile, colorful winter stems. The best displays come from plants that have been heavily pruned or pollarded.

To produce colorful winter stems, all previous stems need cutting back hard in spring to encourage vibrant new shoots.

Pruning mahonia

Mahonia is a statuesque shrub grown for its attractive evergreen foliage and its winter and spring flowers, many of which are highly scented. You can keep mahonias short and bushy by pruning plants immediately after flowering, cutting them back to healthy new shoots. Over time however, plants can become very large with dense

growth that will cast unwanted shade and muscle out any less robust plants growing nearby. To restore the shape of plants or to keep them within bounds, prune them hard from midwinter to early spring when flowers have faded. Only overgrown mahonias need this treatment.

1 First remove all the stems from the tops and sides of the plant using a pruning saw. Cut them back close to the main stems.

2 Once you have cut back the tall growths, remove any damaged, diseased, or crossing stems and old growth to leave five or six strong stems.

3 Once the upper stems have been removed, cut back all the stems to about 3–4 ft (90–120 cm) high, or to 2 ft (60 cm) if you want a smaller plant. Feed the plant well.

4 By summer, the plant will have recovered and produced many fresh new stems and leaves from the stumps. It will not require such drastic pruning again for years.

HOW TO CUT A HEDGE

Hedges are invaluable for dividing a garden, for use as a windbreak or boundary, or to provide background to a border, but unlike fences, they need regular care to keep them healthy, neat, and looking their best.

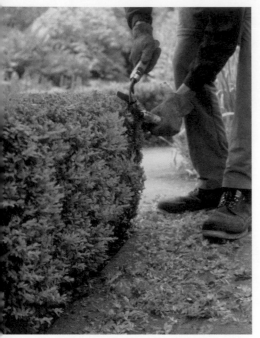

Formal hedges and topiaries rely on a neat, well-maintained shape for impact. Trim them as necessary to keep them looking good.

SHAPING UP

An attractive hedge can become an unshapely mess if neglected, so make sure it is trimmed regularly—whether this is just once a year or several times during the growing season, as is necessary with certain fast-growing conifers. Sections of hedge may die if not cared for, and the hedge overall can begin to lose its usefulness. Low-growing hedges or short runs can be kept in shape easily with a pair of sharp hand shears; an electric, cordless, or gas-powered trimmer will make light work of larger hedges. Use hand pruners to trim hedges planted with large-leaf evergreens, such as laurel, to prevent leaving tattered leaves.

Formal and informal hedges

Hedges generally fall into two categories—formal and informal—both of which can make excellent windbreaks, barriers, or partitions. Formal hedges are clipped tightly to maintain a geometric shape. Hornbeam, beech, privet, holly,

Cutting an evergreen hedge

Evergreens, such as yew (*Taxus baccata, shown below*), make excellent dense hedges and are often planted as a boundary to divide a garden or as a dark backdrop to herbaceous perennials. Unlike most conifers, they respond well to hard pruning and can be trained to any height or shape. Aim to maintain a fairly narrow hedge. You may wish to trim so that the base is slightly wider than the top; then in winter snow will fall down the sides rather than accumulate. Plants can put on around 12 in (30 cm) of growth each year, so keep them in shape by pruning in late summer. Although neglected hedges can be restored, they tend to spread outward over time.

1 Decide how much you want to remove when trimming. If you want straight edges, stretch a string along the top to act as a guide.

2 Using a powered hedge trimmer and safety equipment, trim the sides in sweeping movements, keeping the blade parallel to the hedge.

3 Standing on a well-supported platform, use the hedge trimmer to cut along the top of the hedge, keeping the blade flat to create a straight edge.

4 Brush away all hedge trimmings from the top and sides of the hedge once you have finished trimming. Remove them, along with any at the base.

laurel, yew, and Leyland cypress are often used for this style. Formal hedges will need trimming every 4–6 weeks in summer to keep a neat shape with slightly tapered sides.

Informal hedges are left to grow more naturally and suit a relaxed style of garden. Because they are not clipped hard, the plants flower or fruit and are usually pruned back into shape once the display is over. Forsythia, escallonia, berberis, hawthorn, and spindle are suitable for this kind of hedge. These hedges often attract wildlife, such as birds, so trimming should be avoided at nesting time, which can last well into the summer.

DISEASE CONTROL

Reduce disease problems by removing any hedge trimmings immediately after cutting. Rake up material left at the base, and flick hedges with a rake to dislodge loose clippings. Make the job easier by placing sheets below the hedge before trimming to catch clippings.

Compost any disease-free hedge trimmings, but destroy any that show signs of pests or disease.

Formal hedges make beautiful features, either as a focal point or a backdrop to other plants. They need regular attention to look their best.

Informal hedges are well suited to more relaxed garden designs with a natural feel. They also require less precise pruning.

Renovating a hedge

If you've inherited a hedge that is too wide or overgrown, you can restore its shape with some hard pruning, carried out in stages over a two-year period. In the first year, trim the hedge as normal, then cut one side back hard. The following year, if growth has been vigorous on the side that's been hard pruned, trim this side as normal, and cut back the other side hard. If there is poor growth on the side that was hard pruned, feed and mulch well and wait another year. Although drastic, many plants respond well to this technique, including beech, hornbeam, yew, holly, cotoneaster, and pyracantha. Always seek advice, since some plants, including most conifers, won't tolerate this.

1 Carry out major renovation work on deciduous hedges in winter and evergreens in late winter, while they are dormant.

2 After trimming, cut the branches of the hedge back to the main stems. Set sticks along the length to guide you and help create an even surface.

3 Continue to cut along the length of one side of the hedge to the end. Cut back along the top to create a straight line as you work along.

4 In the winter of the following year, if the hedge has responded to trimming, do the same work to the other side of the hedge to create an even and balanced shape.

Neatly clipped pieces of topiary are an elegant feature on patios, on either side of a doorway, or as focal points in the garden.

STERILIZING TOOLS

Be vigilant when trimming plants, especially if they are showing signs of pest or disease damage. Clean all tools with disinfectant and water, and collect all trimmings to reduce the risk of infection.

Clean tools as you move between plants by spraying them with a disinfectant solution and wiping the blades clean.

BASIC TOPIARY

If you believe topiary is just for skilled experts or, at best, an expensive purchase, think again. Many simple shapes are easy to establish from scratch and with regular care are attractive features that last for years.

SHAPING UP

Manicured topiary balls, cones, cubes, lollipops, spirals, or cloud-pruned trees provide sculptural shapes, structure, and a dash of elegance, in pots or in beds and borders.

Boxwood, holly, yew, Portuguese laurel, *Phillyrea*, bay, and many other evergreen and deciduous plants respond well to being closely clipped. Boxwood is prone to the disease boxwood blight (see *p.365*); be vigilant if choosing this shrub. Partially and completely trained specimens are available, but a cheaper alternative is to create topiary shapes from scratch using untrained plants.

Before clipping, gather together the right tools. You need a pair of good-quality shears for cutting large plants and handheld clippers for detailed work or cutting smaller pieces of topiary. Use pruners to snip off thicker branches or remove any that spoil the shape. While working, regularly dip cutting tools into a bucket of water to prevent sap from building up on the blades.

Making a standard tree

A traditional lollipop-shaped standard, where a rounded head of foliage perches above a clear, straight stem, makes an elegant, vertical feature. Bay, Portuguese laurel, holly, myrtle, and hornbeam are easily manipulated in this way.

Pick a plant with a single, strong central leader that will act as your main stem, and tie it to a cane or stake. Gradually clear the lower stem of shoots, then snip back the leader to encourage bushy growth to develop, and clip to a rounded shape.

If you want to create a lollipop shape, prune back the topmost stems to create a loose ball. Clip to define the shape as the plant grows.

To create a strong supporting stem, tie the main stem into a cane with twine, and clear it of all side shoots and foliage.

Maintaining a shape

To ensure the crisp silhouette isn't lost under shaggy new growth, clip plants regularly. It's easy to restore them by visually following the contours of the shape, or make a template or use a cane as a cutting guide. Step back often to check your work. Clean up in early summer and again in late summer for a crisp winter outline. Yew only needs pruning once, in summer, while fast-growing shrubs, such as boxwood, may need trimming more regularly, but avoid trimming evergreens late in the season, otherwise the new growth that is stimulated will not have time to harden off before the first frost.

If you don't feel confident about pruning topiary by eye, the best way to get the shape right is to use a template.

Once you have trimmed an approximate ball, judge future prunings by eye, stepping back from time to time to check your progress.

PLANT LIST

Topiary-friendly plants:

Buxus microphylla
(Small-leaf boxwood)

Carpinus betulus
(Common hornbeam)

Cryptomeria japonica

Fuchsia varieties

Ilex crenata (Box-leaf holly)

Juniperus chinensis
(Chinese juniper)

Myrtus communis subsp.
tarentina (Tarentum myrtle)

Phillyrea latifolia

Pittosporum tenuifolium

Prunus lusitanica
(Portuguese laurel)

Quercus ilex (Holm oak)

Salvia rosmarinus 'Miss
Jessopp's Upright' (Rosemary)

Santolina chamaecyparissus
(Cotton lavender)

Viburnum tinus

Creating a topiary cone

Cone shapes are among the easiest to create and maintain. Yew, bay, box-leaf holly, and many other plants with dense foliage are ideal, and shapes are best started on bushy, untrained plants. If you want a tall cone, choose a substantial plant with a strong central leader. You can use very young plants, but remember these will take several years to reach a good size. Cone shapes can be created by pruning by eye, or you can use guides. Rest three canes on the sides of the cone, pushing them into the ground. Secure them at the top, and bind the sides together with garden wire to make an evenly shaped wigwam, then prune around it.

1 To create a topiary cone, take a healthy, bushy, previously untrained plant. Remove some of the messy straggler stems first.

2 Stand above the plant, looking down on it, and prune in an outward direction using shears, working your way around the sides of the plant.

3 Still using large shears, go back around the plant, neatening the sides. Stand back and look at the shape a few times as you work to make sure it is balanced.

4 To keep your topiary cone at its best, trim whenever it begins to lose shape. Stop pruning in early fall to reduce the risk of frost damage to new growth.

Raising your own plants from seed or cuttings is very rewarding and is an economical way to fill your beds, borders, and containers.

PROPAGATING PLANTS

New plants can be raised easily using simple techniques that include growing from seed, taking cuttings, or dividing existing plants. This is a rewarding and inexpensive way to increase your plant stocks.

Most plants can be propagated in several ways, but some methods are more successful for certain plants. Raising plants from seed may be the only option if you want to grow a rare or unusual variety that is not readily available at nurseries; it can be more economical, too. Taking cuttings is an ideal way to increase your stock of plants, such as shrubs, perennials, or succulents, and there are several methods for doing this, associated with different times of the year. Clump-forming perennials, including alpines and many herbs, can be propagated by dividing their crowns in spring and fall.

Propagating outdoors

Plants can be propagated both indoors and out. In the garden, seeds of hardy vegetables or annuals can be sown directly into the soil where they are to grow. Apart from some exceptions, most are best sown in spring after all

danger of frost has passed. Hardwood cuttings of trees and shrubs, taken during the dormant season, can be inserted in the ground in a warm, sheltered part of the garden, then carefully dug up and planted out into their final positions when roots have formed.

Propagating under cover

Plants can be propagated throughout the year if you have a greenhouse, since the staging allows plenty of room for plants to develop. The warmth and shelter they offer means you can sow flowering or edible plants earlier than usual— later sowings or cuttings often catch up in here, too, because of the improved growing conditions. You will need good ventilation and some form of shading to shelter plants from the scorching sun in summer. An unheated structure or simple cold frame provides some warmth

COLLECTING SEED

An inexpensive way to get new plants is to collect seed. Many annuals can be easily grown this way; seed from shrubs and perennials may need special care to germinate.

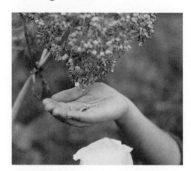

Collect seeds in late summer and fall as the seed heads become brown and dry. Shake the heads into a paper bag.

Hardy seeds can be sown outdoors in spring as the soil warms up without being started under cover. Others must wait until after the last frost.

Taking cuttings from plants will give you identical versions of your favorite plants with minimal effort.

Cold frames allow for earlier sowing and can be used to acclimatize plants grown indoors to outside temperatures in late spring.

Cloches are perfect for protecting young plants or those that are borderline hardy until the last frost has passed.

PROPAGATION MATERIALS

To make propagation easy, put together a simple kit of needed tools and materials to keep near your potting area. A selection of different-sized pots, seed trays, and cell trays with clear plastic lids, along with compost, are useful for all types of propagation. Use a sharp knife or pruners for taking cuttings. A dibble allows you to insert them into pots smoothly and without damage; it can also be used to pull out seedlings. Cover seeds with vermiculite, perlite, or a fine layer of compost sifted through a metal sieve. Use a small watering can with a rose fitted to water seedlings without damaging them. Keep plant labels and a pencil or waterproof pen handy.

and extra protection. In many cases heat is only needed in the early stages of propagation, whether it is to germinate seeds or root cuttings. Additional heat is usually not necessary once plants start to grow.

You can also raise seeds or take cuttings early in the year in a sunroom or on a windowsill, as long as there is plenty of light. You don't even need a propagator. Small pots can be covered with a clear plastic bag held in place with an elastic band. The bags can then be removed as soon as seeds have germinated or cuttings have formed roots and started to grow.

Many plants can be raised successfully in a light place indoors. A bright kitchen windowsill is ideal, or place them on a table or close to a window in a sunroom. Avoid placing them in shady corners, though, as plants will not grow.

It's always useful to have propagating equipment on hand for when you need it. Label plants as you prepare them to save confusion later.

A windowsill in a sunny, draft-free location is a good alternative if you do not have room for a greenhouse in your garden.

Mini-greenhouses are useful for protecting plants and seedlings at key times of the year and can be dismantled when not needed.

A propagator tray with a lid can be really useful. The warmth generated gets seeds off to a great start. Make sure the lid has an adjustable vent to allow air to circulate.

GROWING FROM SEED

Watching plants grow from seeds you have sown yourself is a magical experience. You can raise just about any plant from seed: annuals, perennials, and vegetables—and even trees.

Watching seedlings germinate and develop can be very satisfying. Keep them well watered.

WHAT SEEDS NEED

Most seeds are easy to germinate if they are given the right combination of water, air, dark, and warmth. Some seeds require light to germinate and are sown on the surface of potting mix without covering.

For best results, use good-quality seeds and clean equipment to avoid diseases. Seeds sown indoors require a fine potting mix that is capable of easily drawing up moisture—it should be firmed, rather than compacted, which inhibits the take-up of water. If you are sowing seeds in the ground, weed first, remove stones, and create a soil texture that almost resembles fine bread crumbs.

F1 and F2 hybrids

Many annuals, perennials, and vegetables are classed "F1 hybrids." These have been bred for uniformity, health, vigor, and, in the case of vegetables, high yields. They are more expensive due to the breeding work that has gone into their development, but offer more consistent results. They won't breed true from their own seeds, so don't bother collecting their seeds to use the following year. F2 hybrids are the progeny of self- or

Sowing seed indoors

Prior to sowing, make sure your container is large enough for your chosen seeds and that it is immaculately clean to avoid spreading soil-borne diseases. Fill it with commercial seed starting mix. If you are using seed trays, firm down the potting mix gently with a piece of flat wood; use the base of another pot if sowing in traditional round containers. After sowing, place pots in a place where the seed can germinate.

Some will benefit from a heated propagator, or a simple cover of glass, a clear plastic bag, or plastic wrap. After germination, water carefully with a watering can fitted with a fine rose. To avoid displacing plants or potting mix while watering, start by pouring the water away from the container, then move the spout methodically over the plants.

1 Take a clean seed tray that has holes in the bottom for drainage, and fill it with potting mix. Gently firm down the potting mix.

2 Carefully scatter the seeds over the surface of the potting mix, following the instructions on the packet for sowing depth and distances.

3 If necessary, cover the seeds with a thin layer of potting mix, sifting it to gently cover but not smother seeds. Alternatively, cover with a thin layer of vermiculite.

4 Water the soil and seeds gently, being careful not to displace the soil or seeds. Use a fine rose on a watering can to help you do this carefully.

Sow seeds outside in drills at the depth and spacings specified on the seed packet. Use a cane in the drill to keep them in straight lines.

Thin out seedlings grown in pots or trays to prevent overcrowding; this will also inhibit the spread of any diseases, such as damping off.

To prevent patchy germination of seedlings, rather than even distribution across the container, always firm and level growing mix carefully prior to sowing, and be careful to sow the seed evenly across the surface of the growing mix.

Seedlings can sometimes become leggy, but to avoid this, remove them from heated propagators as soon as they have germinated, and place pots in a well-lit place. This should ensure growth remains even. If seedlings appear to become lopsided, rotate the pot daily so they are evenly exposed to light.

Overwatering is one of the most common causes of seeds not growing well, while underwatering can cause them to wither; try to get the balance right.

cross-pollinated F1 plants. F2 seeds are seldom sold, but many occasionally be superior to open-pollinated seeds, while cheaper than F1 hybrid seeds.

Hardening off

Plants that are raised indoors but are destined for the garden will need to be hardened off to help them cope with lower temperatures and air movement. Acclimate them to life outdoors two to three weeks before

Move plants outside into sheltered spots on warmer days, and bring them in at night to start getting them used to outside temperatures.

they are due to be planted out by placing them in a cold frame. Keep vents open during the day, but close them at night. If you don't have a cold frame, take trays outside during the day and bring them in at night.

Inducing germination

Some seeds have hard shells or a chemical inhibitor in their seed that air and moisture cannot easily penetrate, making them difficult to germinate. Among them are beets, cotoneaster, euonymus, morning glory, and laburnum. You can help the process along by softening seed coats by soaking them in warm water, scratching them with sandpaper, or nicking them with a knife—this process is known as scarification.

Most sowings are successful, but problems can arise if you use old seeds or those that have been stored incorrectly, which may fail to germinate. Follow the sowing dates on seed packets and keep your seeds in a cool, dry, dark place until you are ready to sow them.

DAMPING OFF

Seedlings are vulnerable to damping off, a disease that can run riot and cause stems to collapse at soil level. To prevent this, start with clean pots, sow thinly, and always use fresh starting mix and tap water, rather than rainwater.

Once it sets in, damping off will tear through trays of seedlings, leaving no option but to start from scratch with new seeds, fresh starting mix, and a clean tray.

Taking cuttings is an excellent way to get new stock from favorite plants that need replacing, or as an insurance for tender ones over winter.

TAKING CUTTINGS

Cuttings can easily be taken from many plants and will readily form roots if grown in the right conditions. For best results, select strong, healthy shoots, and use sharp pruners or a knife when preparing them.

TYPES OF CUTTINGS

Taking cuttings is one of the most widely used forms of propagation because it ensures the new plants created have the exact physical characteristics of the parent. Many popular trees, shrubs, fruit bushes, climbers, conifers, perennials, herbs, and tender house plants can be propagated in this way.

Cuttings can be taken at different times of the year at different stages of the plants' growth. Softwood cuttings are taken from spring to early summer using very new growth and have the

highest potential of taking root. However their young leaves are at risk from dehydration, which means they need care and attention.

Semi-ripe cuttings are taken in late summer using growth that has started to harden. These cuttings root more slowly than softwood cuttings but are easier to care for and less likely to dry out.

Hardwood cuttings are taken in winter from deciduous shrubs and trees and are very straightforward, requiring low levels of aftercare.

Softwood and semi-ripe cuttings

HARDWOOD CUTTINGS

Some woody plants can be propagated in winter, when dormant. Cut pencil-thick stems into 6 in (15 cm) lengths, and insert them into pots or in the ground, leaving 1 in (2.5 cm) of stem showing.

Take hardwood cuttings by trimming off lengths, cutting one end at an angle so that you can identify the top and the bottom.

Taking semi-ripe cuttings

Semi-ripe cuttings are taken in late summer, when stems start to harden and growth slows. At this stage, stems have food reserves that will help them survive. Cuttings do not need heat to form roots, but do prefer high humidity. Once potted, put them in an unheated propagator or cover with a clear plastic bag. Place on a windowsill or in an unheated greenhouse or cold frame.

1 Select from the parent plant (such as Boxwood, shown) a healthy, young stem that is beginning to harden and is not floppy.

2 Cut off a piece of stem about 4 in (10 cm) long using clean pruners. Keep the cuttings in a plastic bag while you gather the rest.

3 Remove the leaves from the lower two-thirds of the stem. Pinch off the sappy tips. Once planted, it will start to grow within a few weeks.

are inserted into pots filled with moist, well-drained potting mix to root, while hardwood cuttings can be placed in pots or directly into soil in a warm, sheltered site outdoors. The latter can take many months to form roots, so choose a planting spot where the cuttings can be left undisturbed. The cuttings should have formed roots by the following fall, when they can be transplanted to their final location.

Although not usually needed, some cuttings can be encouraged to form roots more quickly by dipping the bottom end in a specialized rooting hormone liquid. Shake off the excess before planting as normal in soil.

Rooting hormones can help cuttings grow roots, particularly semi-ripe or hardwood ones. Gently dip the rooting end in before planting.

Stem cuttings can be left to root in potting mix in individual pots, seed trays, or positioned around the edges of one pot.

PLANT LIST

Hardwood cuttings
Buddleja (Butterfly bush)
Chaenomeles (Japanese quince)
Cornus alba (Dogwood)
Sambucus (Elder)
Ribes (Flowering currant)
Salix (Willow)

Softwood cuttings
Fuchsia
Hydrangea
Pelargonium
Salvia (Sage)
Solenostemon (Coleus)

Semi-ripe cuttings
Buxus (Boxwood)
Lavandula (Lavender)
Lavatera
Philadelphus
Pyracantha
Viburnum

Taking softwood cuttings

Softwood cuttings are usually taken between mid-spring and early summer on young growth that has been produced in the current year. Many house plants, perennials, and shrubs can be propagated using this technique. Cuttings readily form roots if placed in a heated propagator, which will keep their bases at a temperature of between 70–75°F (21–24°C). However, their immature leaves dry out quickly, so it's important to keep material damp when collecting cuttings (place them in a moist bag) and to keep the humidity high inside the propagator until they have rooted. Open vents daily to reduce condensation, and keep light levels high.

1 Select healthy, very young growth at the end of stems *(from plants such as Cotton lavender, shown)*. Cut lengths 2–3 in (5–8 cm) long.

2 Using a clean penknife or sharp blade, cut the stem just beneath a leaf joint. Do this carefully and cleanly—torn stems attract disease.

3 Any leaves left below the surface of the soil are likely to rot, so trim the cutting carefully to remove them, leaving just a few leaves at the top.

4 Place the cuttings carefully into a seed tray of potting mix or into pots. Make sure the leaves are clear of the surface by not planting cuttings too deeply.

LAYERING AND DIVIDING

Propagating plants by layering and division are simple techniques that enable you to make more of your favorite plants while controlling their spread and keeping them healthy and vigorous.

Dividing plants by pulling them apart or cutting them into pieces is a very simple way of creating lots of new plants from a single specimen.

CREATING NEW PLANTS

While some propagation methods require careful attention or the use of shelter or heat to induce plants to root, others require minimum effort and are almost foolproof.

Division is probably the easiest of all propagation techniques: plants are simply split into smaller pieces and replanted outdoors. Layering is useful for shrubs and climbers that are not easily propagated by cuttings—rather than remove a portion of growth, as in taking cuttings, shoots form roots while still attached to the parent plant.

Dividing perennials

Herbaceous perennials that spread to form clumps are easily propagated by division in spring or fall. To do this, lift plants from the ground with a fork, taking care not to damage the roots. Lightly rooted plants can simply be divided by pulling them apart by hand, while those with sturdier root systems,

LAZY CUTTINGS

Some plants are easy to propagate by hand and require no tools or special equipment. Gently tease apart sections or individual shoots, keeping plenty of root attached, then plant into pots or in the ground.

Plants such as Sedum, Saxifraga, Sempervivum, and other creeping plants, are ideal candidates for this type of easy division technique.

Root cuttings

A number of perennials and shrubs can be propagated from pieces of root lifted from the ground between November and late February, such as tree poppy (*Romneya*), *Catalpa, Paulownia,* oriental poppies, Japanese anemones, and *Verbascum*. For best results, plant roots of pencil thickness, but if using finer roots, lay them on the soil surface, and cover with a thin layer of compost.

1 Lift plants from the ground using a fork, avoiding damaging the roots. Gently tease apart the clump with your hands.

2 Shake off excess soil carefully, and select a few healthy roots that are of pencil thickness from the clump.

3 Cut lengths 2 in (5 cm) long and insert them into pots filled with growing mix. Place in an unheated greenhouse or cold frame.

such as *Hemerocallis*, will need splitting with a spade or a knife. Those with fibrous roots, such as *Achillea*, are best divided using two garden forks—place them back-to-back in the center of the plant, and separate the clump by pushing the forks away from each other. Whichever method you use, discard any dead material, and replant portions as soon as possible in well-dug soil to prevent the roots from drying out. Division helps rejuvenate congested plants.

Dividing bulbs

Many bulbs increase readily during the growing season, forming new bulbs from the parent plants. To propagate your favorites and to keep clumps floriferous, divide them every few years.

Divide bulbs before growth begins in spring, prizing clumps from the ground with a fork. Replant larger bulbs in the ground, and grow smaller bulbs in pots for several years until they are large enough to plant out.

Runners and suckers

Although you have to actively propagate some plants, many are self-propagating, naturally producing runners or suckers. *Tetrapanax, Rhus,*

Divide small clumps as you would larger ones, by inserting two forks into the middle of the clump and pushing them away from each other.

Kerria, Ajuga, Aralia, Euonymus fortunei, and strawberries can all be propagated this way. These growths can be carefully removed from the parent plant, along with a portion of roots, and planted elsewhere. Removing runners and suckers also helps you control the spread of plants.

You can grow new strawberry plants from old by rooting their self-propagating runners. Simply pin them to the soil, and let them root.

Layering shrubs and climbers

This simple technique can be used to propagate many shrubs and climbers, some of which, such as rhododendrons, may be difficult to propagate by other methods. A shoot is encouraged to form roots while still attached to the parent plant by bending it down and burying it in the soil. After the layer has rooted (usually after about a year), it can be detached from the parent and planted on where it is to grow.

1 Select a flexible, healthy stem, and make a slanting cut on the underside of it at the point where the stem will reach the ground.

2 Make a shallow trench in the soil about 4–6 in (10–15 cm) away from the parent plant, and bend down the shoot, positioning the cut on the soil surface.

3 Peg the layer in place with a loop of wire, then tie the tip of the shoot to a cane in the ground to encourage it to grow upward.

PLANT LIST

Plants for division
Achillea
Aster
Festuca
Hemerocallis (Daylily)
Hosta
Hylotelephium (Ice plant)
Ophiopogon
Paeonia (Peony)
Pulmonaria
Thalictrum

Plants for layering
Camellia
Clematis
Jasminum (Jasmine)
Lonicera (Honeysuckle)
Magnolia
Rhododendron
Wisteria

Lawns are the ultimate outdoor carpet, providing a multi-purpose surface suitable for relaxation or play in any space.

CHOOSING SOD

Sod can vary in quality, so buy from a reputable supplier, and check it for weeds. Meadow sod is cheap, but often of poor quality, while domestic sod is hard-wearing and best for family lawns. Fine sod is ideal for a showpiece lawn.

Always check sod before you buy. Reject any with weeds, bare patches, or yellowing edges; these suggest that they are long overdue for planting.

LAWNS

Nothing sets off a landscape design like a verdant blanket of grass. Whether you're looking for a hard-wearing family lawn or a manicured showpiece to complement your plants, lawns are easy to begin from scratch.

NEW LAWNS

Technically, you can create a new lawn at any time, but it is more likely to succeed if started at the right time of the year. Lawns sown in fall tend to establish quickly as the soil is still warm, and the wet weather prevents it from drying out. The next best time is in spring, although seedlings will have to cope with frost, cooler soil temperatures, and competition from weeds.

Sod is generally laid between early fall and late winter, and although it is possible to create both sod and seed-sown lawns during summer, they will require copious watering to help them establish.

After laying or sowing a lawn (see pp.92–93), you will need to give it close attention until it has established and is ready for use. Grass seed will germinate within 7–21 days, and you should ensure that the soil does not dry out during this time. If the weather is dry, use a sprinkler to keep the ground moist. Hungry birds can disturb seeds, so cover the newly sown area with straw. When the grass is about 2½ in (6 cm) high, give the lawn its first cut. Use a rotary mower with the blades set high to avoid dragging the delicate seedlings out of the ground. Repeat several times during the growing season, but avoid any other traffic on the lawn for at least ten weeks after sowing to allow the grass to develop a strong root system.

Sod is easier to establish. After laying, keep it well-watered, especially during dry weather. When the grass shows signs of new growth, cut it with a mower set on a high setting. Wait at least six weeks before using the lawn, and then avoid anything but light traffic. When the pieces have connected without any gaps, your

Starting from scratch is sometimes the only option, but you may have to wait a little time before your lawn is ready to be used.

Wildflower meadows give a natural look and need less routine care. They should be mowed in a particular way and at certain times of year.

new lawn is ready to be used. (Fill any gaps that do appear with soil).

Low maintenance

Although newly created lawns need careful attention, you don't need to toil endlessly over an established lawn. Allowing the grass to grow longer and raising the height of the blade means you will mow less often, and the lawn should be able to cope better in drought situations.

An alternative to a traditional lawn is a wildflower lawn. Lay special sod containing native flowers, such as yarrow, ragged robin, and cowslip, and a mixture of ornamental and native grasses that can be left to grow long.

Old, tired lawns

If you inherit a neglected lawn, you may be able to restore it with a program of renovation starting in spring. Mow on a high setting, then feed with a general-purpose spring feed. Ten days later, apply a lawn weed killer. Level out bumps and hollows, and reseed any bare patches. Keep the lawn well watered during dry periods. If the lawn has more weeds than grass, it may be better to start again from scratch.

LAWN-CARE TOOLS

You only need a few tools to keep your lawn in good shape: a mower, rake, edger, and shears are sufficient, although other equipment may be necessary, depending on the size or state of your lawn. By far the most important lawn-care tool is a mower. Choose carefully: push mowers or compact cordless mowers suit small lawns, while a cylinder mower fitted with a rear roller is the best option for creating perfect stripes on a larger lawn. Mulching mowers reduce maintenance because clippings are shredded and returned to the lawn. Riding mowers are ideal for those with more than half an acre.

A mower is an indispensable piece of lawn machinery. Choose one that is right for your size of lawn and will fit into the storage that you have when not in use.

A leaf rake is useful for removing any moss and debris clogging up your lawn.

If your lawn suffers from compacted soil, literally breathe life into it using an aerator.

Neat edges define a lawn, and handheld edging tools will give your yard a crisp edge.

If there are more weeds than grass, it may be time to start again, or treat lawns with weed killer, and reseed bare patches.

Edging shears trim grass at the edges without damaging plants in borders.

String trimmers are ideal for the areas mowers can't reach, or for small areas..

Manual seed spreaders can also be used to spread seeds or lawn fertilizers. Rent one if necessary.

CARING FOR YOUR LAWN

If you are aiming for an immaculate lawn, you need to do a little more than mow it every few weeks. Regular feeding, watering, weeding, and trimming are necessary to give you a lawn to be proud of.

The perfect lawn demands tender loving care and a few tricks to get the lush, verdant look just right. You will also need the right tools.

MOWING SAFETY

To prevent accidents, always ensure mowers are turned off when you are cleaning or otherwise maintaining them. Do not put hands or feet near blades when the mower is in use.

HOW OFTEN TO MOW

There are no hard-and-fast rules about how often you should mow, so be guided by the rate of growth of your lawn and the type of finish you want. Unless the weather is extremely mild, your lawn is unlikely to need cutting in winter, but it will need regular trimming from early spring until the fall.

Hard-wearing family lawns will need cutting once a week, while those maintained for their ornamental looks may need trimming up to three times a week at the height of their growing season. Start with the blades on their highest setting, then reduce the height of the cut as the season progresses; an eventual height of 1 in (2.5 cm) is ideal for domestic lawns, while ¾ in (2 cm) is suitable in spaces where a more manicured look is required.

Stripes and edges

Alternating dark and light green stripes gives a sharp finish to a formal lawn. To achieve this, you need a mower with a rear roller. Mow in parallel rows, with each row in the opposite direction to the next. The stripes are most obvious from a distance, especially from above.

After mowing, put the finishing touches to your lawn by trimming the edges. Use a pair of long-handled edging shears to remove any overhanging grass. Edges can become uneven over time, so redefine them with a half-moon edging tool. Use a piece of wood as a straight-edged cutting guide. Remove all cuttings and trimmed sod.

Watering and feeding

Recently created lawns will require regular watering in order to thrive, but once established, lawns are remarkably tolerant of drought.

Electric mowers should always be turned off at the main switch before you inspect or replace cutting blades.

Apply special lawn fertilizers in liquid or granular form during spring and fall to give lawns the nutrient boost they require.

Collect grass cuttings after mowing, and add them to your compost heap, preferably in layers with brown material (see p.303).

Although grass may turn brown in extended dry periods, the damage is largely superficial, and the grass will bounce back when the rain returns. Longer grass deals better with drought, so raise the blades of your mower to their highest setting. This encourages plants to become deeper rooted and avoids the risk of scalping the surface, which will pull out dry grass by its roots, leaving ugly bald patches in the lawn.

Most lawns will do well if fed twice a year. Give them a quick boost in spring with a liquid or granular formulation high in nitrogen, then strengthen up the roots for winter with a fall feed. Avoid using spring feeds later in the year since this can result in soft sappy grass, vulnerable to frosts.

Rolling a lawn

A heavy roller, which can be rented if necessary, is traditionally used in spring to resettle the surface of the lawn after winter, especially if fall-laid sod was damaged by frost. However, rolling is not essential and can cause problems. The heavy weight may compact the soil, impeding drainage and leading to the conditions favored by moss.

Keep lawn edges defined and crisp-looking by trimming them with edging shears. Trim the wispy grass, and avoid cutting into the lawn.

If the edge of the lawn or a path begins to look uneven or has lost its definition, carefully go around it with a half-moon edger.

Bare patches of lawn can be easily restored by raking the soil and sowing new seed. Apply fertilizer, and water well for quicker growth.

Get ready for winter

Fall is a good time to carry out maintenance on your lawn to get it in shape to cope with winter. A layer of dead grass and other material, known as thatch, can build up on the surface of the soil, impeding drainage, encouraging moss, harboring fungal diseases, and preventing the strong growth of grass. This can be removed by scarifying it—vigorously raking it with a leaf or using an electric scarifier. Wet weather can make lawns boggy, so relieve compaction caused by heavy foot traffic by aerating with a fork or aerator. This helps improve drainage and prevents the conditions favored by moss.

1 Clear any leaves or other debris from the lawn in fall. Rake the lawn surface firmly to remove any embedded debris or moss.

2 Using a garden fork or a special aerator (as shown here), spike holes into the lawn all over the surface to aerate it and improve drainage.

3 Brush dry, fine sand into the holes to prevent them from closing up, allowing air and water to pass freely into the root zone. Only use horticultural grade sand.

4 Spread dry top-dressing over the surface to help improve drainage and to level out hollows. Use a brush or the back of a rake to work it into the grass evenly.

Most lawns suffer from minor problems, especially if they are used as a family play space. The majority are easy to fix with a little care.

WET LAWN DAMAGE

Rain can cause problems on compacted or poorly drained lawns. Waterlogging starves roots of oxygen, and moss and damp-loving weeds will prosper in these conditions.

LAWN PROBLEMS

Almost every lawn shows problems from time to time, often after a long period of drought or a wet winter when moss takes hold. Most can be remedied, and there are useful quick fixes for uneven edges and bare patches.

UNEVEN SURFACE

Lumps and bumps often become noticeable in spring after a winter of little attention, or in summer when anthills cause bare patches in the grass. Bumps make mowing the lawn difficult because they tend to be scalped by the mower. You can deal with them by raising the height of cut, but the better solution is to make a quick repair.

Very small bumps can be leveled by removing cores of soil with a hollow tine aerator. To repair larger bumps, you need to cut a cross over the lump using a half-moon edger, then peel back the four corners of sod. Remove some of the soil, smooth the soil surface, then fold back the sod into place carefully.

Making repairs

Like lumps, hollows in the ground look ugly and are likely to contain longer grass that the mower cannot reach. Small depressions can be repaired gradually by filling them with a sandy top dressing, adding ½ in (1 cm) at a time. (*See facing page for advice on larger depressions.*)

Edges may crumble or break because of wear and tear and also as a result of mowing. To repair these, carefully cut out a rectangle of sod including the broken edge. Cut precisely, with sharp vertical edges and right-angled corners. Turn the piece of sod around so that the good edge is on the outside. Keep the broken part within the lawn, fill it with topsoil, and then resow it with some grass seed. The combination of new seed and regular mowing will encourage the lawn to spread and fill the patch.

Damaged patches within a lawn are equally easy to repair. Remove a rectangular piece of sod by

Leaves and other debris make lawn sod slippery underfoot, causing sliding and damage to the grass.

Adjust the height of your mower's blade to avoid damaging bumpy surfaces; raising it in dry conditions helps grass survive drought.

Mossy hollows can develop in lawns where the soil has been compacted by frequent walking. Consider installing stepping stones.

cutting around the damage with a half-moon edger—use a straight-edged piece of wood as a cutting guide. Put the blade of a spade under the sod, keeping it parallel with the surface and digging down to as shallow a depth as possible. Remove the damaged piece, rake over the exposed soil, then cut an identically shaped piece of sod, and plug the gap. Alternatively, prepare the soil, resow with seeds, and cover it with

netting to protect it from birds. Avoid walking on resown patches until they are established.

Stepping stones

If your lawn suffers in wet weather or needs protection from heavy traffic, try laying stepping stones through it to reduce wear on the grass. Space slabs, stones, or circles of wood on the grass, making sure they are evenly spaced and checking the

distance between them to make sure they are a comfortable step apart. When happy with the pattern, cut around them with a half-moon tool and remove the sod beneath.

Remove soil to the depth of the stepping stone, along with an extra 2 in (5 cm). Level the base and add a 2 in (5 cm) layer of compacted sand. Place the stepping stones on top, keeping them level with the lawn so you can mow across them.

Stubborn perennial weeds or those with deep tap roots can be treated with weed killer or dug out by hand with a fork or kitchen knife.

Repair worn edges by removing sod and turning it around so the good edge is on the outside. The inner bare patch will grow over.

Rake out thatch and other debris that clogs up the lawn. Moss, combined with other materials, competes with the grass and hinders its growth.

Filling a large depression in a lawn

Over time, lawns can develop lumps and bumps as parts sink or endure heavy traffic. If larger hollows are causing problems with the mower, it makes sense to try to fill them, which means lifting the grass and adding more soil to level it. To repair these bumps, cut a cross through the hump with a half-moon edger,

then carefully fold the four flaps back, being careful not to break the sod. Add some soil, then replace the sod. If the hollow is still visible, repeat until it appears level. When you are satisfied with the appearance of the lawn, replace the corners, and firm the grass back into place with the back of a rake.

1 Cut through the surface, making a cross shape on the grass. Using a spade laid parallel to the soil, slide it under one corner of sod.

2 Repeat, lifting the four corners of the sod and gently folding them back onto the soil surface, taking care not to break any of them as you do so.

3 Add some soil to the hollow, using your hand to fill the dip, and level off the surface of the soil. Add more topsoil as necessary until it is level.

4 Replace the sod, and firm back into place with the back of the rake. Brush some more topsoil in between the cracks to help the sod knit together.

MINI MEADOWS

Wildflower meadows are an attractive alternative to a traditional lawn and will attract wildlife and provide vibrant color for many weeks. They can be time-consuming to establish but are simple to maintain.

Long, waving grasses are reminiscent of summer meadows and work well as a natural lawn or when used to edge a formal one.

MEADOW OPTIONS

A meadow will add a natural touch to a garden, and there are many exciting seed mixes available, along with plants that will add a bold splash of color from spring to summer. To make a meadow that will return year after year, use perennial seeds or plants. For a one-time spectacle or to fill a bare patch with a splash of color, sow a mixture of annual varieties.

An existing lawn or patch of grass can be turned into a meadow, but you will have better results if you start with a bare piece of ground.

Wildflower sod is available for those who are pressed for time and want to create a meadow quickly.

Let it grow

The simple way to create a meadow look is to allow your lawn to grow long and let the grass flower. To add extra color, plant wildflower plugs in groups within the grass, along with small bulbs. Plant in the fall after cutting the grass short. To keep fertility low, which will encourage wildflowers, do not use lawn fertilizers and always remove clippings so nutrients cannot reenter the

Sowing a wildflower meadow

The best way to establish a wildflower meadow is to sow seeds onto bare soil in spring or fall at a rate of ¼oz per 10 sq ft (5 g per square meter). Spring-sown seeds will germinate easily, but those sown in fall can rot over the winter if your soil is heavy and wet. Start preparing the site about six weeks before sowing. Strip away all vegetation and weeds, then remove all of the topsoil from the area to be sown, replacing it with less-fertile subsoil. Finally, prepare the bare soil as you would for sowing a new lawn (see p.93). Replacing the soil is not feasible over a very large area, so reduce fertility by sowing nutrient-hungry crops for a season.

1 Wildflower seed mixes are sown in small quantities; to make it easier to see where you have sown, mix the seeds first with silver sand.

2 Prepare the soil to be sown by turning it over and removing any large stones or debris. Then firm it down, and rake the surface to give a fine, even texture.

3 Mark out evenly sized squares over the area to be sown using bamboo canes. This makes it easier to sow the right amount of seed evenly.

4 Rake the seed into the soil very lightly using a leaf rake. Water the seed in well using a fine spray. Cover the area with straw to ward off birds.

Paths mown through long grasses make a lovely natural feature as well as a practical solution to navigating your mini-meadow.

Annual flowers add a glorious splash of color through long grass. You can choose your favorite flowers or sow mixed packets of seed.

HERB LAWNS

Chamomile and thyme lawns are attractive alternatives to a traditional lawn, although they also need considerable upkeep. They suit areas that receive only light foot traffic.

To establish an herb lawn, prepare the site as you would for sowing a new lawn in spring (see page 93). Choose a ground-hugging variety of thyme or a nonflowering chamomile, such as *Chamaemelum* nobile 'Treneague', and plant plugs or plants at 4–10 in (10–25 cm) intervals, depending on the size of plant. Water the plants in well, and keep the site weed-free until established. Do not walk on the lawn for 12 weeks after planting, and allow only light traffic over it for its first year.

soil. It can take several years to establish a balance between grass and wildflowers.

Wildflower meadow mixes

There are many types of seed mixes available that contain different varieties, color blends, or suit a specific soil type or location. Perennial meadow mixes tend to prosper in low-fertile soil. Where soil fertility is too high, for example in an existing border, sow a cornfield annual mix that includes plants such as cornflower, corn poppy, corn marigold, and corn cockle. Barley and wheat seed add an authentic touch. Perennial wildflowers tend not to flower in their first season, so to ensure interest in the first year, choose a mix that contains some faster-growing annuals.

Cutting your meadow

Although meadows do not require as frequent cutting as traditional lawns, they do need mowing occasionally. Meadows that flower in summer are generally cut from early fall to early spring, while those designed for spring color should be cut from midsummer. If you have a mixture of flowers that appear at different times, cut once a year in early fall. The height of cut should be no lower than 3 in (8 cm). Remove all clippings to keep soil nutrient levels low.

MEADOW PLANT LIST

Centaurea nigra
(Common knapweed)

Daucus carota (Queen Anne's lace)

Galium verum
(Lady's bedstraw)

Leucanthemum vulgare
(Ox-eye daisy)

Malva moschata
(Musk mallow)

Plantago lanceolata
(Ribwort plantain)

Prunella vulgaris
(Self-heal)

Rumex acetosa
(Common sorrel)

Salvia pratensis
(Meadow clary)

Sanguisorba minor
(Salad burnet)

Silene dioica (Red campion)

Thyme plants make a lush, aromatic lawn, spreading to create a pretty, edible carpet studded with pink flowers in summer. Use several varieties for a patchwork effect.

Chamomile is a classic alternative lawn. It is a harder plant to establish than thyme, but in light, moist soils it will become a pretty, fragrant carpet of low-growing plants.

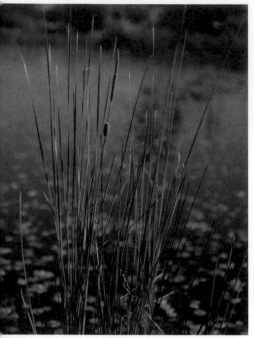

There is a water feature to suit any garden. If you have the space, a large wildlife pond makes an attractive garden asset.

CLEAN POND PUMP

Streams, fountains, waterfalls, and other features rely on pumps to keep water moving. To ensure they continue to work properly, remove pumps from ponds in early winter to check and clean them.

To prepare ponds for winter lift pumps out of the water and give them a good clean, removing weed and debris, then dry carefully before storing until spring.

PONDS AND WATER

Whether you have a large pond or a simple bubble fountain, water in any form will add interest to your garden, creating sound and movement, attracting wildlife, and enabling you to grow aquatic plants.

ROUTINE CARE

The aim of most water gardeners should be to have a healthy pond or water feature, where plants and creatures thrive in a body of clear water. However, this cannot be achieved by leaving the pond to its own devices. Without intervention, a pond can become engulfed by plants, while a buildup of algae or pond weed can lead to unsightly, murky water. To keep ponds and water features in good shape, you have to maintain them year round.

A key task is to remove plant debris as it appears. Deadhead marginal or aquatic flowers, and remove dying foliage to prevent it from rotting in the water.

To keep the surface of ponds clean, remove excess amounts of floating weeds. Use a net to scoop out mats of tiny-leaf duckweed, and twirl hairlike blanketweed from the surface with a stick or garden cane. Before putting weeds on the compost heap, place them at the edge of the pond overnight so any creatures you have unwittingly removed can return to the water. Check around the edge of the pond and among marginal plants for any traditional garden weeds, too, and pull them out.

Over a hot summer, the level of ponds can drop as water evaporates, leading to a reduced surface area and less oxygen available for fish. Keep ponds at the right level by topping them off once a week with rainwater from a barrel, if possible. If you don't have a water barrel, use water from a hose, topping off

Marginal and aquatic plants in baskets need repotting when roots burst through baskets. Check them in spring and pot on if necessary.

Plant marginal plants at the edge of ponds in baskets or mesh pots to prevent them taking over and crowding out other plants.

frequently to prevent the shock of the colder water disturbing the fish.

Leaves can drop for many weeks in fall; rather than fishing them out on a daily basis, stretch wire over the surface to catch them until nearby trees and shrubs are bare, or rake leaves from overhung ponds regularly.

Pond equipment is expensive to install and needs maintenance, so remove and clean lights, filters, and pumps annually.

Maintaining water quality

The importance of water quality can vary depending on the style of pool or pond. Crystal-clear water is usually required for formal features, while slightly cloudy water can be overlooked if you have a wildlife pond. However, your aim should be to keep your water as clean as possible with good habits.

There are hundreds of different types of algae that can cause problems in ponds, from those that cause a "pea soup" effect in the water to others that form a dense mat of growth on the surface.

Use rainwater to top up ponds if possible as it is very low in nutrients, so does not encourage algae. Consider adding a UVC filter, which binds any algae particles together in the water and then filters them out.

Filters help keep the water clean; a mechanical filter will sit on the pond floor, while a biological filter must be placed at the highest point. These types contain beneficial bacteria that convert organic waste into useful nutrients.

Another option is to use natural filtration to keep ponds clean. For example, in swimming ponds about fifty percent of the total area is taken up by aquatic plants, which remove nutrients from the water to prevent algae from forming. Instead, consider using barley straw, which releases hydrogen peroxide as it rots, suppressing algae (see below left).

Basic pond-care equipment

To maintain your pond, you will need a hand net, a cane or pole for removing blanketweed, netting to cover the pond in the fall, and a selection of mesh baskets for plants.

To operate ponds with moving water, you will need a pump. A submersible pump is sufficient for gently moving features, but a more powerful surface version will be needed for fast-flowing streams, waterfalls, or fountains.

WATER FEATURES

While ponds, pools, and streams are generally better suited to a larger garden, even a smaller plot can accommodate a water feature. If you have an outdoor electrical supply, a wall-mounted fountain, where water trickles from a spout into a pool below, is a great way to use vertical space, while a bubble fountain or pebble pool can transform an unused corner. For a simple pond, fill a low barrel with tiny aquatic plants (see p.97), or use a shallow container that can double as a bird bath.

A pretty terra-cotta pot with a bubbling fountain is an attractive and soothing focal point in a small garden if you don't have space for a larger pond.

Barley straw can be used to suppress algae. Add it in spring, and remove it once it turns black, usually within about six months.

Keep pond surfaces clear of blanketweed, which can quickly overrun a pond. Twirl the weed around a stick for easy removal.

Create a miniature water garden by standing marginal plants, such as marsh marigolds, *Sagittaria*, and *Butomus*, on stacked bricks within a barrel pond.

MAINTAINING POND PLANTS

Aquatic plants need less maintenance than many plants growing in beds and borders, but to keep them looking good, they need attention during the growing season so the pond continues to be attractive.

The best displays in ponds and water rely on a balance between well-maintained aquatics and oxygenating plants, kept in careful check.

ROUTINE CARE

Most pond plants are fairly vigorous, and after a few years of growth, begin to outgrow their designated space and need to be divided and thinned out. Submerged oxygenating plants, such as hornwort, whorled milfoil, and water crowfoot, can quickly become a dense mass of growth that gets entangled with other plants. These plants should be thinned out in spring or fall by lifting baskets out of the pond and trimming back growth.

Do not remove too much growth because you will expose the surface of the pond to sunlight, creating the right conditions for algae to grow.

Some aquatics, especially marginals, form dense clumps that need to be divided to provide a good floral display and to prevent them from crowding out neighboring plants. Irises, Japanese rush, dwarf reed, flowering rush, water mint, marsh marigold, and many others should be lifted in spring, split into smaller sections, and replanted.

Dividing and planting irises

Irises growing in containers will eventually become a mass of congested shoots and pot-bound roots. At this stage they will rarely flower, and plants will lose vigor. Check whether plants need dividing in late spring or early fall, lifting containers out of the pool to see whether there is a mass of roots poking through the mesh at the sides and bottom. Most irises can be divided by hand by tugging them apart gently, but if roots are held tightly together, they should be divided with a knife. Repot divisions individually, and return them to the pond. This basic technique can be used to propagate and rejuvenate many clump-forming aquatics.

1 Dig the clump out of the pond using a spade or fork, being careful not to damage the roots or disturb the pond too much.

2 Place the clump on the ground, and divide it using a spade. Separate out these smaller clumps into individual plants for replanting.

3 Choose the healthiest-looking divisions, discarding any past their prime, and, taking one plant at a time, lower them into an empty aquatic planting basket.

4 Once the plant is in position in the middle of the new basket, start to fill around it with garden soil or specialty aquatic soil. Firm down, and put gravel on the surface.

Most pond plants do not need feeding, but water lilies need plenty of nutrients to thrive. Feed plants when just coming into new growth in spring. Place sachets of aquatic fertilizers next to the crown of the plant, and cover with pea gravel.

Remove all flowers on aquatic plants as they start to fade, to prevent them from rotting and discoloring the water. This also prevents them forming seed heads and colonizing neighboring baskets. At the same time, trim off any dead, dying, or diseased growth, including lily pads.

Planting aquatic plants

Aquatics are usually grown in mesh containers, which are available in many sizes to suit different plants. These pots allow water to flow freely in and out, enabling the plant to take up nutrients from the water while preventing the roots from spreading out. Growing in baskets also makes it easy to move plants around to change the look or to remove them if they need dividing.

First, line your basket with a piece of burlap or plastic mesh. This prevents the soil from escaping through the sides and clouding the water. If planting very tall marginals, place a brick or stone in the base to keep it stable and prevent it from blowing over in high winds. Fill the basket with garden soil or a specialty aquatic soil, leaving a 1 in (2.5 cm) gap between the soil surface and the rim of the pot. Soak the soil with water, then make a hole large enough for the roots of the plant. Place the plant in the hole, cover the roots with more soil, and firm into place. Cover the surface with a ½ in (1 cm) layer of pea gravel to stop the surface from being washed away. Water again to remove any air pockets. In shallow ponds, baskets can easily be lowered in by hand, but if the water is deep, you may need to thread heavy duty string through the sides of the basket and lower it.

Oxygenating plants are often sold in bunches and do not need any preparation before planting. Simply push them into a basket of soil, making sure they are firmed in well to prevent them from floating free. If you have a pool with a soil bottom, they can be planted into the base instead. Floating aquatics can simply be placed on the surface of the water.

The rounded leaves of duckweed are a common sight on ponds and need to be skimmed off the surface to keep them in check.

Cover the soil surface with gravel before submerging aquatic plants in baskets. It prevents the soil from escaping.

AQUATIC PLANTS

Aponogeton distachyos (Water hawthorn)

Ceratophyllum demersum (Hornwort)

Hottonia palustris (Water violet)

Iris pseudacorus (Yellow flag)

Iris versicolor (Blue flag)

Myriophyllum verticillatum (Whorled milfoil)

Nymphaea 'Aurora' (Water lily)

Nymphaea 'James Brydon'

Orontium aquaticum (Golden club)

Pontederia cordata (Pickerel weed)

Ranunculus aquatilis (Water crowfoot)

Sagittaria sagittifolia (Arrowhead)

Stratiotes aloides (Water soldier)

Trapa natans (Water chestnut)

Typha minima (Dwarf reed)

AQUATIC INVADERS

Some fast-growing plants should be avoided—they escape from ponds and colonize waterways. Culprits include water lettuce (*Pistia stratiotes*) and Canadian pondweed (*Elodea canadensis*).

Parrot's feather (*Myriophyllum aquaticum*, *above*) is a pernicious, invasive weed that will quickly overrun your pond or pool unless it is removed.

FISH AND WILDLIFE

A pond stocked with fish or one that provides a natural habit for a community of native creatures adds interest and beauty to your garden. Ensure your pond teems with life by creating ideal conditions for its occupants.

Dragonfly nymphs, along with newts and frogs, will soon colonize a natural pond and are fascinating for children and adults to observe.

CARING FOR FISH

Fish are very easy to take care of, but if you want a thriving population, you will need to do some work. Choose fish varieties that are suitable for the size of your pool; use a maximum of 20 in (50 cm) of fish body length, when fully grown, per square yard of water surface as a guide. Rather than stocking a pond at one time, introduce fish in two groups, about ten weeks apart; if too many are added at once, there will be a buildup of excrement that will pollute the water and will be detrimental to the fish's health.

Fish are best introduced during the warmer months of the year to prevent them from becoming almost dormant in cooler water. Do not pour fish in bags straight into the pond, but add them gradually so they can acclimate (*see below*).

Although fish will feed on insects and plants in the pond, they still need extra food pellets or flakes. Ensure that you add the correct amount based on the size of your pond and the number of fish in it, following the instructions on the package. The amount fish eat largely depends on

DETERRENTS

Given the opportunity, herons will try to hunt your fish. Stretch heron netting over the water, or create a low fence around the perimeter using wire to keep them at bay.

Installing a decoy heron close to a pond is believed to discourage the real birds from visiting to steal fish. Herons will revisit ponds repeatedly, taking every fish.

Introducing new fish

If you are stocking a new pond or adding new fish to an existing community, do this during the warmer months to avoid stressing the fish with a drop in temperature. At first, keep your fish in their transfer bags of water, floating the bag unopened on the surface of the pond. When the temperature of the water inside and outside the bag is more or less the same, release the fish into the pond.

1 Fish are usually sold in bags with their own water. Add a little of the pond water to that in the bag and reseal the bag.

2 Float the unopened bag on the surface of the pond until the temperature of the water in the bag matches that of the pond.

3 When the water in the bag has cooled sufficiently, open the bag, and allow the fish to swim free into the pond.

If you want to encourage specific wildlife into your pond, find out what sort of habitat is preferred, and include the right elements.

Frogs feast on all sorts of pests, especially slugs. You can watch their life cycle from spawn to tadpole to frog played out in your pond.

PREPARING FOR WINTER

Ponds are vulnerable during winter weather. Expanding ice can cause concrete liners to crack and water to seep out. Fish also suffer because the water's surface can freeze over in severe weather due to the narrow gap of air between the surface of the water and ice being replaced by gases produced by decaying vegetation. In ponds with concrete liners, floating a small ball on the surface of the pond in winter is most effective; not only will this keep a patch free of ice, but it will absorb the pressure and prevent fractures. To create a ventilation hole for fish, either add a floating electric pool heater or melt an 18-in- (45-cm-) wide patch with boiling water.

Hold a saucepan of boiling water against the pond's surface to melt a breathing hole if a thin layer of ice has formed.

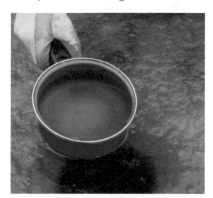

Float a tennis ball on the surface of the water as temperatures drop. If the surface ices over, it can be removed to leave a hole.

the temperature of the water; in winter they eat less, but get hungrier as the water warms up in summer. Generally, give them high-protein food in summer and a low-protein formulation in winter.

Keep an eye out for diseases so you can nip problems in the bud and prevent them from spreading to other fish. Fungal growth, cuts, ulcers, missing scales, lumps, and infected eyes are all possible signs of problems, as is a change in behavior, such as refusing to eat. If you are concerned, consult a fish care book to see if you can diagnose the disease and find a suitable cure.

Herons are the greatest predator of pond fish, and suitable deterrents should be put in place (see facing page). To protect fish from cats, fill the marginal shelf with plants so they cannot get close to the water.

Caring for wildlife

The success of a pond in attracting wildlife largely depends on its design. If you are creating a pond from scratch, aim to design it with a simple shape, along with a ramp, peninsula, or inlet to encourage wildlife to enter. A good

way to do this is to build a pebbly beach on a sloping side using large and small pebbles. Use larger stones around the edge of the pond, and grade their size as you work up the slope. Continue building beneath the surface of the pond to create a ramp down to the floor of the pond. Native aquatic plants are loved by indigenous wildlife, so include some of these along with more vibrant exotics. Surround the pond with plenty of plants to provide cover, enabling visiting creatures to feel protected. Avoid adding fish to a wildlife pond. They are voracious predators of some smaller creatures.

Observe wildlife in the pond, but try not to disturb surroundings and water habitats, which may frighten away shy animals. Wildlife ponds do not need cleaning as often as formal features, but whenever thinning out oxygenators or removing other plants from a pond, place them on the side for a day or so to allow any creatures that have been accidentally removed to find their way back in. Do this in spring rather than in the fall, when pond creatures may be going into hibernation.

HELP AND ADVICE

Even the most careful gardener will occasionally find plants that are fading or a crop overrun with a troublesome pest. No garden is immune from pests and diseases, and recognizing the symptoms and finding appropriate controls is your best defense. This section will help you identify and tackle the main culprits.

CONTROLLING WEEDS

Weeds can colonize any garden quickly, and while weeding can be time-consuming, it is a necessary job. However, there are ways to prevent weeds taking hold.

DESIGNING OUT WEEDS

Weeds need space to grow, so try to keep bare soil to a minimum when designing and planting your garden. Choose vigorous perennials and shrubs that can compete against weeds, and plant them closely so new weeds can't get a foothold. Before planting, weed the area thoroughly, being sure to remove perennial weed roots, and water new plants well to ensure they establish quickly.

Regularly weeding new plantings from the outset will give your plants an advantage over emerging weeds when new growth appears the following spring.

An alternative approach is to learn to live with the more attractive annual weeds and only control problem perennials. Use the chart on page 352 to help identify them. Alternatively, keep planting to a minimum and grass over large areas.

Mulch around ground-cover plants to provide extra protection against weeds.

WEED-PROOF MEMBRANES

Laying permeable, weed-proof membrane around your plants is the most effective way to deter weeds and is most easily installed on new beds and borders. Water still penetrates to plant roots, but weed shoots and seedlings are unable to break through and eventually die. The membrane also retains moisture in the soil, further benefiting your plants, and can be disguised with attractive gravel or bark chips.

1 To prepare a weed-free border, cultivate the soil first, digging in organic matter, removing any weeds, and laying down weed-proof membrane. Anchor the membrane's edges, or dig it into the soil, and lay out your plants on top.

2 When you have decided where to place your plants, use a sharp knife to cut crosses in the membrane, then fold the flaps open to create planting windows. Dig planting holes in the soil, and sink your plants in.

3 Firm the plants in, water well, and fold the membrane flaps around the plant. Lay gravel or bark over the membrane to a depth of about 4 in (10 cm). Keep plants well watered and top off the mulch every year or so.

GROUND-COVER PLANTING

When planted together, vigorous, low-growing plants can be used as a living mulch, suppressing weeds by absorbing water and nutrients, blocking out light, and forming a physical barrier. Evergreen shrubs and perennials are the most effective and give year-round protection. Deciduous plants can also be used, although you may need to weed between them in spring and fall until new growth appears. If you only need temporary cover, plant bushy annuals such as *Tagetes* (French marigold) closely together, or choose a trailing type such as *Tropaeolum majus* (nasturtium). For extra protection, mulch between ground-cover plants, especially while they establish.

Evergreen climbers will also blanket the soil.

Trailing conifers make excellent ground cover.

Flowering herbs provide color and deter weeds.

WEEDING MANUALLY

Pulling weeds by hand or using a hand fork is the best way to remove them from small beds or confined areas, where you risk damaging adjacent plants. Pulling them out by hand allows you to work between plants without disturbing them; loosen the soil with a fork to release deep-rooted weeds. You may have to gently untangle plants from creeping or climbing weeds such as bindweed.

Cutting weeds off at the base with a hoe is the best way to tend larger, more accessible areas. It is most effective when done in dry weather, so the weed seedlings wilt and die quickly without a chance to recover. Annual weeds are easily hoed out; perennial weeds are best dug out or, if necessary, treated with a systemic weed killer.

USING WEED KILLERS

For large areas infested with perennial weeds, weed killers may be necessary as a last resort. Choose a "systemic" type, which is absorbed by the plant, killing it completely—although several applications may be needed for tough weeds such as ground elder. "Contact" weed killers kill the leafy growth quickly and are best reserved for annual weeds only.

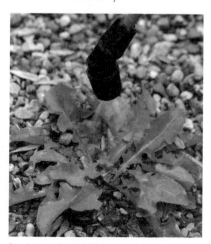

Ready mixed weed killer sprays can be used on their narrowest "jet" setting to spot treat weeds.

TROUBLESOME WEEDS

Weeds can develop unnoticed in the garden, giving them time to establish and spread. This can spoil the appearance of your borders and give your plants unwelcome competition. Use this guide to identify weeds and nip them in the bud.

ANNUAL AND PERENNIAL WEEDS

Some annual weeds set seed within weeks, and there can be several generations in a single year. Remove them before they flower; more seed means more weeds. Perennial weeds are easy to remove when young but the longer they are left, the harder it becomes. To control them effectively, be persistent and thorough.

Annual meadow grass This annual grass forms small tufts, often in the gaps between paving stones where it can be difficult to remove. It is also common in borders and containers.

Bindweed This perennial weed is a vigorous climber and can quickly smother border plants. Use canes to train it away from your plants, and spray it with a suitable weed killer.

Brambles Spreading by roots, suckers, and seed, these woody climbers can form an impenetrable barrier. Regular digging will help keep them under control, or use an appropriate weed killer.

Chickweed This annual appears quickly whenever the soil is cultivated, and forms a spreading mat. Late plants overwinter until spring if left; it sets seed in just six weeks.

Couch grass This perennial grass grows in beds and lawns, where its tough roots spread among neighboring plants and make it hard to control. It spreads easily by root fragments.

Dandelion Most commonly seen in lawns, this perennial weed spreads via wind-borne seeds. Although deep-rooted, they are easy to dig out. Mowing lawns regularly helps control them.

Fat hen This is a slower-growing annual weed, producing one generation per year. It flowers from midsummer onward and produces masses of seed that last for years in the soil.

Ground elder This is a low-growing, perennial weed that often spreads among border plants, making it difficult to dig up or spray. It will quickly resprout from tiny root pieces.

Groundsel With its fluffy seed heads, this annual weed spreads quickly and in large numbers. It will grow anywhere and can easily smother young seedlings. Weed it out by hand.

Hairy bitter cress This annual weed grows very quickly and is often brought into gardens with container-grown plants from nurseries and garden centers. Weed by hand before it flowers.

Japanese knotweed A very vigorous perennial that is hard to control once established. It resprouts from small root pieces. It is vital to control it so it is not a nuisance elsewhere.

Oxalis Several species of this bulb-forming perennial are garden weeds and spread by tiny bulbils that are buried deeply and are difficult to remove completely. Treat with weed killer.

Shepherd's purse This upright, wiry weed is more common in the vegetable bed than in borders but will grow anywhere. It flowers from midsummer, producing masses of seeds.

Stinging nettles More common on new or neglected sites, this perennial weed forms large clumps with thick mats of roots. It can be controlled by digging and cultivating the soil.

Willow herb Forming tall, upright spikes, this perennial spreads by creeping underground roots as well by as seeds that are freely spread by the wind. Remove plants before they flower.

Rhododendrons are an example of a plant that requires specific growing conditions. Without them, plants will soon deteriorate.

DIAGNOSING PROBLEMS

Understanding why plants are unhealthy can be tricky because different problems can cause similar symptoms. The trick is to pinpoint the likely cause by a process of elimination, although there can often be more than one.

All plants need some care, even established trees and shrubs, and it doesn't take long for neglected plants to suffer. Plants that aren't looked after are likely to have weak or congested growth that is prone to pests, diseases, and physical damage. Although they may flower, the display will be disappointing. As a first step, research what care your plants require, and see where you might be going wrong.

Wilting leaves can indicate various problems.

SOIL, SITE, AND EXPOSURE

All plants have preferred growing conditions, but some may tolerate a wide variation. It helps to know what these are, so check when you buy new plants. Those on lighter soils often succumb to nutrient deficiencies and wilting, while plants on heavier soils risk rotting in prolonged wet weather, especially in winter. Some plants thrive in full sun, while others can be scorched, needing cooler corners. Sun lovers perform poorly in shade, leading to spindly growth and few flowers.

Growing conditions also change through the year, which can affect plant health. Frost and sun-scorch are seasonal risks, but changing wind patterns, lengthening shadows, lower light levels, and cooler soils are also factors to consider.

Unexpected frost can kill tender plants.

Bright sun can scorch plant leaves.

Waterlogging causes plant roots to rot.

Shade weakens plants that prefer full sun.

Common nutrient deficiencies

Plants need nutrients for healthy growth, but they must be in balance. Even well-tended soils can lack specific nutrients, causing poor displays or yields and leaving plants prone to pests and diseases. Changes in leaf color can help diagnose which nutrients are in short supply.

Nitrogen Foliage turns pale green, and yellowing young leaves are seen in spring. Overall growth is weak, and plants spindly. Apply a high-nitrogen fertilizer. Mulch helps stabilize nitrogen levels.

Iron Plants develop yellow leaf edges on young leaves, spreading between the veins. Growth is weak. Most common on alkaline soils. Apply a product containing chelated iron around the roots.

Magnesium Older leaves turn yellow, with red or brown coloration spreading between veins. Most common on light, sandy soils; apply a fertilizer containing magnesium.

Calcium Present in the soil, calcium is not taken up by plants that are too dry; keep them moist. It causes distorted leaves, cracks, and spots on fruit, and bitter pit and blossom end rot (*shown*).

Other deficiencies

Boron Affects many crops and ornamentals; growing tips die, growth is stunted, fruit and leaves distort. Apply "Borax" (sodium borate) to the soil, although be sure to use the correct dose; excess boron also causes problems.

Manganese Similar symptoms to iron deficiency; young leaves turn yellow or pale green, but veins remain green. Affects many plants, often acid lovers that are grown in alkaline soil. Spray plants with manganese sulfate, or apply to the soil.

Molybdenum Occurs in acid soil and affects brassicas, causing the leaves to turn yellow and become stringy. Apply fertilizer containing sodium molybdate or lime the soil to raise pH.

Potassium Leaves turn blue or yellow, with brown blotches or leaf edges. Leaves may roll inward, and flowering and fruiting is weak. This affects many plants; apply a high-potassium feed.

OTHER FACTORS

There are lots of factors that affect how well your plants grow, some more obvious than others. If you have ruled out issues with soil, site, care, and pests and diseases, consider what else has changed that could affect plants. Are they more shaded than before due to neighboring plants, or could they be suffering from competition? Has there been any new construction nearby that may have changed exposure or soil drainage? Another thing to consider is the plant itself. All plants have a lifespan, and yours may be declining due to old age. Some shrubs live less than ten years; some trees less than 40.

Poor plant health can be difficult to diagnose and can be the result of many different causes. Consider the plant's overall growing conditions, and seek advice from your local nursery.

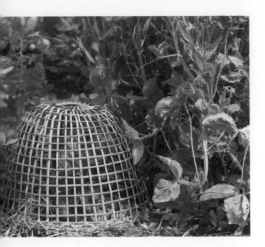

CONTROLLING PESTS AND DISEASES

Plants are naturally attacked by pests and diseases, and while the vast majority will thrive, there are some that will succumb. There are several practical steps you can take before reaching for a chemical solution.

Plants are not helpless and have their own natural defenses to help them fend off and recover from pests and diseases. The trick is to help your plants help themselves. Keeping them growing strongly is the best defense: give them sufficient moisture and plant food to encourage healthy growth. Avoid high-nitrogen feeds or feeding in late summer, however, because this encourages soft, sappy growth that attracts pests and diseases and is prone to frost damage.

Prune plants regularly to promote strong growth, and remove weak or diseased material each year.

For long-term health, give your plants the best possible growing conditions, choosing the right plants to suit the site. Make sure they establish fully and don't compete with each other for moisture and nutrients. For an added advantage, seek out resistant varieties, especially of edible crops.

Water well; stressed plants are easy targets.

PEST-PROOF PLANTING

Invertebrates are adept at locating specific plants to feed on; many do this by identifying volatile chemicals (odors) given off by plants. These are undetectable to humans, but easily sensed by insects from some distance away. Once the insects are nearby, they also use sight and taste to determine if a plant is suitable. However, insect-damaged plants give off different odors than undamaged plants, and natural enemies use these odors as a way to locate their prey.

To combat and make use of these natural processes, try mixed growing, such as adding fruit trees and bushes in borders and vegetables among summer bedding. This can lead to

less pest damage than growing crops in large groups and conventional rows. A variety of plants often has a greater diversity of predators and prey, leading to a better balance and reduced damage.

Nasturtiums climb or trail on the ground and can easily be accommodated in mixed beds.

French marigolds can help protect plants from whitefly and carrot fly and are attractive in beds.

TAKING SIDES

Gardens are mini ecosystems with an ongoing battle being fought unseen between predator and prey. Take advantage of the fact that the pests that feed on your plants are all prey to other organisms, and encourage predators in your garden. These allies need somewhere to live, so provide basic habitats for them. Create a pond for slug-eating amphibians; provide nest boxes for birds and supply winter shelter for beneficial insects, such as ladybugs. Beneficial predators also need food, so don't rush for the pesticides when pests first appear. Leave them to build up, and wait for your allies to find them.

This approach will not eradicate pests, but will help balance their numbers. It best suits the relaxed gardener, who is happy for nature to take its course.

Food and water tempts beneficial insects, birds, and animals to your garden, helping reduce the number of unwanted pests.

Hoverflies Many of these wasp and bee mimics feed on aphids as larvae and are valuable garden pollinators. Encourage them by planting lots of colorful, nectar-rich flowers.

Ladybugs These insects feed eagerly on aphids as larvae and adults. They are among the earliest predators to appear, often emerging in spring as the temperature rises.

Birds Many species play an important role in eating pests throughout the year, picking off aphids or larger pests, like slugs and caterpillars. Provide nest sites and drinking water.

Amphibians Frogs and toads scour the garden at night, looking for slugs, insects, and other prey. If you don't have room for a pond, provide cool, damp areas where they can shelter.

Ground beetles Several species of beetles feed on garden slugs and often live in the cool, shaded spots slugs prefer. Place large stones on the soil for them to hide under undisturbed.

Hedgehogs Although not often seen, hedgehogs are an ally, eating slugs, snails, and other invertebrates from spring to fall. Provide habitats and summer drinking water as well as a winter nest area.

CHECK FOR PROBLEMS

It isn't possible to prevent pests or diseases from attacking your plants, but you can reduce the damage caused. Your best defense is to check plants regularly, and act quickly. Symptoms of plant diseases are often easy to spot, so look out for weak growth or discolored or distorted leaves, flowers, and fruit.

Pests may be less obvious because they are mobile and can hide on or around the affected plant. Some leave tell-tale signs, such as slug trails, but others are harder to identify. Check plants at night, when many pests are active, and look under leaves or around the base of plants for likely culprits.

Check plants carefully and regularly. Pests may be nocturnal or very small, and can hide in nooks and crannies between leaves or in the soil.

USE BARRIERS AND TRAPS

Consider using physical barriers to protect your plants from damage. Tree and shrub guards will protect against animal pests, such as deer and rabbits, and nets keep birds away from crops. To guard against insects, cover young plants with cloches or fine netting, or use plant collars to prevent them from gaining access to your plants. Slugs and snails are voracious pests, so protect vulnerable specimens with a scattering of slug pellets, use copper tape to protect container-grown plants, or use coarse sand or crushed eggshells as a barrier.

Not all pests can be kept out with barriers, so use traps instead. Sticky yellow traps are ideal for controlling whitefly under cover. Outside, use beer traps for slugs, pheromone traps to lure codling moths, and bottle traps to catch wasps feeding on summer fruit.

BIOLOGICAL CONTROL

Instead of chemicals, biological control is an environmentally friendly way to tackle certain pests and can be bought via mail order. It is most commonly used to protect indoor crops, although it can also be used outside. The technique involves introducing a beneficial predator, such as a nematode, to feed on the pest. To be effective, there must be sufficient prey, and the conditions must be suitable.

Bottle cloches are impenetrable to slugs and crawling insect pests and promote growth.

Suspended traps filled with sugary water are irresistible to wasps, which meet a sticky end.

Encarsia formosa is a parasitic wasp, often used to control whitefly in greenhouse crops.

CHEMICAL CONTROLS

Synthetic insecticides and fungicides can be effective at treating plant problems, but many gardeners use them only as a last resort. Many pests move on in time or are eaten by predators, and many diseases can be avoided by keeping plants strong and healthy. When plants are clearly suffering, however, chemical control may be the best option, although it is important to use an appropriate treatment and to apply it correctly. Always check product packaging, and seek advice if necessary.

Fungal diseases, such as rose black spot, can be difficult to control once established.

Insecticides

There are two basic types of insecticide used to kill insect pests. "Contact" insecticides are sprayed directly onto pests, or kill pests that touch treated surfaces. They must be applied thoroughly, soaking the plant's leaves, and reapplied at set intervals. "Systemic" insecticides travel through plant tissues and kill insects that feed upon them. This type protects plants over time.

Be aware that insecticides are indiscriminate and also kill beneficial insects; apply them sparingly in the evening when pollinating insects are not active.

Fungicides

Used to treat fungal diseases (not bacterial or viral), fungicides are most effective when used to prevent infection rather than cure it. Once plants are infected, the best strategy is to remove all affected growth and to treat new shoots as they appear. Depending on the product used, the fungicide should be reapplied at recommended intervals and may be required throughout the season.

If plant disease is a recurrent problem, try to improve plant health as a long-term solution, or consider growing different plants. Fungicides are a short-term treatment.

Using chemicals safely

Follow the instructions on the package carefully when you apply garden chemicals. Don't be tempted to increase the dose—you risk harming yourself and your plants. Avoid spraying on windy days to prevent drift, or in full sun, which could scorch plant foliage. Aquatic life is very sensitive, so never spray near ponds or streams.

To store chemicals, keep them in their original packaging and keep them in a frost-free place away from children and pets. Dispose of surplus treatments carefully, and never use out-of-date chemicals.

Ready mixed insecticide sprays are convenient to buy and use. They also reduce the risk of overdosing your plants. Always wear protective gloves when spraying pesticide.

Fungicides only treat fungal diseases, such as mildew (*above*). Growth affected by bacterial or viral diseases must be pruned out and should be burned to destroy the infection.

Store chemicals in a safe place, clearly labeled and away from children. Safely dispose of old chemicals that are no longer recommended or licensed for use; it is illegal to keep or use them.

A–Z OF COMMON PESTS

APHIDS

Plants affected: *various.*
Also known as green- or blackfly (but can be other colors), these insects feed in large colonies on plants, often on softer new growth. Severe infestations weaken plants, distort growth, and may reduce yields. They also spread viruses, and their sticky excretion, "honeydew," allows the growth of black sooty mold. Spray severe attacks with insecticide.

ASPARAGUS BEETLE

Plants affected: *asparagus.*
Adults and larvae attack plants, eating the leaves and outer surface of the stems, defoliating plants. Stems may die, weakening plants and reducing future yields. There are two generations a year, in late spring and summer. Pick off the black, red, and yellow adults and cream-colored larvae, or spray with organic insecticide.

BIRDS

Plants affected: *various.*
Many species attack plants, pecking the leaves, flowers, and fruit. The damage is usually annoying rather than harmful, although birds will strip fruiting cherry, raspberry, and strawberry plants. Erect a scarecrow or net plants when fruiting.

CABBAGE ROOT FLY

Plants affected: *all brassicas.*
The maggots eat the roots, stunting growth and causing plants to wilt in dry spells. Young plants can be killed; adult plants may produce smaller harvests. Protect young plants with collars around their bases to prevent adult flies from laying their eggs, plant out stronger seedlings that will fend off attack, or cover plants with insect-proof netting.

CAPSID BUG

Plants affected: *various.*
These small, green, sap-sucking insects attack tender plant shoots and flower buds, secreting a toxin that kills plant cells. As the shoots develop, the emerging leaves are peppered with holes; affected flowers may abort or open deformed. Most common in late spring to late summer; spray with insecticide.

CARROT FLY

Plants affected: *carrot, celery, parsnip, parsley.*
Carrot fly maggots tunnel into the taproots, forming holes just under the skin that collapse, leaving the roots prone to secondary infections. Stored roots are also prone to decay. There are two or three generations a year from late spring to fall. Sow during midsummer to avoid the first generation, grow resistant varieties, grow under insect-proof mesh, or cover plants with fabric.

CHERRY AND PEAR SLUG WORM

Plants affected: *Chaenomeles, cherries,* Crataegus, *pears, plums, and* Sorbus.
These caterpillar-like larvae, which have a slimy, sluglike appearance, graze on the upper surface of leaves from late spring to mid-fall, causing the remaining tissue to dry up and turn brown. There are two or three generations a year.

CODLING MOTH

Plants affected: *apples and pears.*
Small caterpillars tunnel into the fruit, feed in the core, then tunnel out,

Aphids attack many plants, usually the new growth.

Carrot fly maggots can spoil the crop.

Codling moth caterpillars can ruin mature fruit.

leaving the mature fruit unpalatable. Use pheromone traps to capture adults and to indicate when spraying is needed. Use a suitable insecticide in midsummer to kill the caterpillars as they hatch.

CURRANT BLISTER APHID

Plants affected: *currants.*
This sap-sucking pest feeds on the leaves at the shoot tips in spring, distorting growth and causing a blistered appearance that is unsightly but not damaging. Spray heavy infestations with pesticide.

CUTWORMS

Plants affected: *various.*
These are the soil-dwelling caterpillars of various moths that eat roots, causing plants to wilt and die and damaging tubers. At night they feed above ground, eating plant leaves. Check the soil around plants for caterpillars, control weeds, and cultivate the soil regularly. There are no chemical controls.

FLEA BEETLES

Plants affected: *brassicas, potatoes, and many ornamentals.*
These tiny beetles eat holes in the leaves, which may turn brown and die. Seedlings can be killed by severe attacks, and mature plants can be checked. There are many species, which attack a wide range of plants from mid-spring to late summer. Sow under fleece or plant out seedlings under fleece in good weather to encourage rapid growth.

GLASSHOUSE RED SPIDER MITE

Plants affected: *various.*
These tiny mites form huge colonies, sucking sap and causing the foliage to become dull and mottled, often with a silvery sheen. Fine webs may also appear between leaves and stems. Most common on indoor plants, these mites occur outside in warm summers and can seriously weaken plants. Use biological control, or spray plants using a suitable pesticide.

GLASSHOUSE WHITEFLY

Plants affected: *various.*
These sap-sucking, white-winged insects are most common on indoor plants but also occur outside in warmer summers. They quickly breed and infest plants, weakening them, and encourage sooty mold with their sugary secretions. Hang sticky yellow traps near plants to monitor numbers of whitefly. For indoor crops, use *Encarsia formosa*, a parasitic wasp, as a biological control. Alternatively, or for outdoor plants, treat using a suitable insecticide.

GOOSEBERRY SAWFLY

Plants affected: *gooseberries, red and white currants.*
Plants are rapidly and severely defoliated by caterpillar-like insects in late spring and summer and are often reduced to bare stems by the time crops are ready in early summer. Check plants from mid-spring and remove by hand.

LARGE AND SMALL WHITE BUTTERFLIES

Plants affected: *mainly brassicas.*
The caterpillars of large and small white butterflies eat holes in the outer leaves and crowns, causing considerable damage to crops and reducing yields. There are two generations a year from spring to fall. Cover plants with fine insect netting or 1/8 in (4 mm) mesh butterfly netting to deter adults, check plants often and pick off, or spray with insecticide.

LEAF MINERS

Plants affected: *various.*
These are the larvae of various flies, moths, sawflies, and beetles that burrow into the leaf tissue, forming obvious tunnels. The damage looks bad but is usually harmless. Protected inside the leaf, the insects are difficult to control. On smaller plants, pick off badly affected leaves.

Flea beetles disfigure leaves and weaken plants.

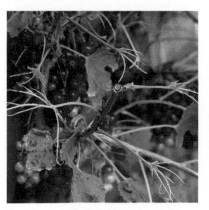

Gooseberry sawflies will also attack currants.

Large white butterfly caterpillars feed on leaves.

LEATHERJACKETS

Plants affected: *various.*
Crane fly (daddy long legs) larvae; these pests live in the soil, eating plant roots. They can cause brown patches on lawns and kill seedlings and young plants, including vegetables, from late winter to midsummer. Use nematodes as biological control.

LILY BEETLE

Plants affected: *lilies and fritillaries.*
Both the bright red adults and excrement-covered, maggot-like larvae eat leaves and flowers and can ruin plants quickly. Active from spring to fall. Check plants and pick them off by hand, or spray with insecticide.

MEALYBUGS

Plants affected: *various, mainly indoor plants.*
Covered with white, waxy fluff, these sap-sucking pests are more common on house plants. Forming colonies in leaf joints and other inaccessible places (root mealybugs attack roots), they are hard to control. Spray with insecticide, or use biological control.

MEALY CABBAGE APHID

Plants affected: *all brassicas.*
Forming large colonies on the undersides of leaves from mid-spring to mid-fall, these gray-white aphids suck sap, causing yellowing leaves and distorted growth. Heavy attacks can kill shoots, causing multi-headed plants. Mealy cabbage aphid damage is usually superficial but heavily infested plants can be treated with a suitable insecticide.

MOTHS

Plants affected: *various.*
Moth larvae can occasionally be a significant pest to crops. Look out for the tomato hornworm on tomatoes in late summer. Most moth species are host-specific. Pick off any larger larvae that you spot by hand. Look under leaves for eggs, or spray with a suitable insecticide.

ONION THRIP

Plants affected: *onions, leeks, shallots, and garlic.*
White maggots eat the roots in early summer, causing plants to collapse. In late summer maggots may also tunnel into bulbs, causing rot to set in. Destroy infested plants; there are no pesticide controls. Plant onion sets, which are not as vulnerable as seedlings, and cover plants with fine, insect-proof netting.

PEAR PSYLLA

Plants affected: *pears.*
These aphid-like insects suck the sap from leaves and produce large, sticky drops of honeydew that can coat the tree and fruit. They are highly resistant to most available insecticides. Oil sprays, combined with insecticide, can be effective when applied during dormant season.

PLUM LEAF CURLING APHID

Plants affected: *plum trees.*
This aphid forms large colonies on the undersides of plum leaves, sucking sap and causing the leaves to curl inward in spring and early summer. Young trees may be weakened, but the damage is mainly superficial; new leaves will develop. Spray young trees with insecticide.

POTATO CYST NEMATODES

Plants affected: *potato, tomato.*
Leaves yellow and die from soil level upward in mid- to late summer, killing the plants. Small white or brown cysts can be seen on the roots. Nematodes build up and persist in the soil for many years, preventing a worthwhile crop. No chemical controls; rotate crops, or plant resistant varieties.

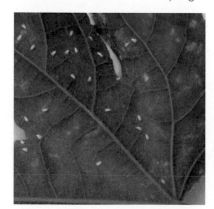

Glasshouse whitefly are found on indoor plants.

Glasshouse red spider mite is hard to control.

Lily beetle adults are easy to spot on plants.

RASPBERRY HORNTAIL

Plants affected: *raspberries, blackberries, and hybrids.*
Females insert their eggs just under the epidermis of blackberry and raspberry canes. A few days later eggs hatch into small larvae that spirally girdle the tips of the canes and cause wilting. Removing and destroying infested canes when they wilt removes the larvae and helps reduce the total population.

ROOT APHIDS

Plants affected: *beans, carrots, lettuce, parsnips, roses, and pinks.*
These sap-sucking pests feed on the roots, weakening plants and causing them to wilt in sunny weather; crops are reduced. They are difficult to control because they are protected by the soil; keep plants well watered in dry spells and rotate crops.

SAWFLIES

Plants affected: *various.*
There are many types of sawfly, mostly plant-specific. The caterpillar-like larvae feed on young fruit, or tunnel into the leaves, sometimes causing distorted growth. Depending on the type, damage can be rapid and extensive. Control with insecticide, or pick off and destroy infested fruit and leaves.

SCALE INSECTS

Plants affected: *various.*
These sap-sucking insects resemble small shields stuck to the leaves and stems and attack indoor and outdoor plants. There are many species with varying life cycles, and they feed on a range of host plants. They weaken plants and can reduce harvests and also attract sooty mold with their sticky excretions. Spray when nymphs are present with insecticide.

SLUGS AND SNAILS

Plants affected: *various.*
Not all slugs and snails damage plants, but those that do attack a wide range of plants, eating leaves, stems, and fruit. They are most active in cool, wet weather and feed throughout the year, especially at night, as long as the temperature is above 40°F (5°C). They can never be eliminated from a garden, so focus on protecting vulnerable plants. Apply slug pellets sparingly, or use beer traps or biological control.

VINE WEEVIL

Plants affected: *various.*
The slow-moving, black adult beetles eat leaf margins, making distinctive notches, but the white larvae cause most damage. These eat roots, causing plants to wilt and often killing them.

They also tunnel into tubers, leaving them prone to other infections. Container-grown plants are most at risk, especially those with fleshy roots, although even woody shrubs can be attacked. Pick off adult beetles, drench potting mix with pesticide, or apply a biological control.

WIREWORMS

Plants affected: *various.*
These are the larval stage of click beetles and live in the soil, eating the roots of seedlings and tunneling into root crops. They are most common where new beds have been cut into lawns and fall in line after a few years of cultivation. There is no pesticide control. Dig root crops early to reduce damage.

Plum leaf curling aphid affects all forms of plum.

Apple sawfly larvae spoil the appearance of fruit.

Vine weevil larvae eat roots, killing plants.

A–Z OF DISEASES AND DISORDERS

APPLE SCAB AND PEAR SCAB

Plants affected: *apples, pears.*
Caused by closely related fungi, these diseases are most prevalent in damp conditions. Fruit are affected by dark, scabby marks; these often just affect the skin, but severely affected fruit may crack. Leaves develop dark blotches and may fall, and blisters may form on twigs. Remove affected growth and fruit, and dispose of fallen leaves. Prune in winter to improve air flow. Olive, pyracantha, willow, and some other trees and shrubs can also be affected by scab diseases.

BACTERIAL CANKER

Plants affected: Prunus *species.*
Most common in wet seasons, this disease causes sunken areas of bark to develop on branches and stems, which ooze yellow sticky resin as they develop. Buds may fail to open, and leaves die back; eventually whole branches die, and plants may be killed. Prune and destroy infected growth as soon as it appears, and grow resistant types.

BEAN CHOCOLATE SPOT

Plants affected: *fava beans.*
Brown spots develop on upper leaf surfaces with dark streaks on the stems, flowers, and pods, which may spread and connect. Yield is reduced, and severely affected plants may die. This is a fungal disease, most common in damp conditions, and can be seed-borne. Grow on well-drained soil, avoid high-nitrogen fertilizers, and space plants widely.

BEAN HALO BLIGHT

Plants affected: *Green and runner beans.*
This is a bacterial disease, causing water-soaked dead areas with a yellow rim to develop on leaves. The leaves then yellow and may die, weakening plants and reducing yield. Stems and pods can also be affected. It is spread by overhead watering. Destroy infected plants in the fall, and grow resistant varieties.

BITTER PIT

Plants affected: *apples.*
Apple fruits develop small, sunken, brown spots, spoiling their appearance, and the flesh may taste bitter. Large fruits and heavy cropping trees are most susceptible. Bitter pit is caused by calcium deficiency, brought on by the tree being too dry. Water well and spray with calcium nitrate.

BLACK CURRANT REVERSION DISEASE

Plants affected: *black currants.*
Plants affected by this virus problem have smaller leaves with a change of leaf shape and number of veins. They flower weakly, and produce small crops. They may show swollen buds ("big buds"), which is not a symptom of the virus, but of the mite that transmits it. There is no cure. Destroy infected plants and only buy certified disease-free plants.

BLOSSOM END ROT

Plants affected: *tomatoes, peppers.*
This condition causes dark sunken patches on the base of fruit, making them inedible. It is caused by dry soil conditions, leading to calcium deficiency. Water plants regularly, and remove affected fruit.

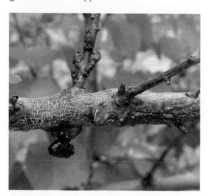

Bacterial canker can kill infected plants.

Bean chocolate spot causes brown leaf marks.

Bitter pit can be avoided by watering apples well.

BLUEBERRY STEM BLIGHT

Plants affected: *blueberries.*
This fungal disease infects wounds, cuts, and damaged areas, causing clusters of leaves to turn brown and die, staying attached to the plant at first and falling off later. Infection spreads quickly, and whole stems die back. Prune out affected growth.

BLACKBERRY CANE SPOT

Plants affected: *blackberries, hybrids.*
This is a fungal disease that causes silver-gray spots with purple margins on stems and leaves in early summer. In severe cases individual canes die back, reducing yield. Remove and destroy infected canes.

BLOSSOM WILT

Plants affected: *apples, pears, cherries, plums, apricots, and peaches.*
Fruit tree flowers wilt and turn brown but stay attached to the plants; the disease may also spread to leaves and fruiting spurs, killing them. It is most common in damp weather. Prune out affected shoots and dispose of any rotten fruit.

BOXWOOD BLIGHT

Plants affected: *boxwood; related species.*
Fungal disease that defoliates plants, particularly during wet weather and in sheltered spots. Leaves turn brown and fall causing bare patches, stems are streaked with black and young stems die back. In wet weather, white fungal material is visible beneath infected leaves. Control is difficult, so avoid buying any plants with signs of blight. Cut back mildly affected plants and dispose of potentially diseased fallen leaves and adjacent topsoil. Protect recovering foliage with fungicides. In severe cases remove affected plants, replanting with another species.

BRASSICA RING SPOT

Plants affected: *brassicas.*
This fungal disease causes dark angular spots, often with yellow edges, on the leaves and stems. Leaves may yellow and fall, weakening plants. It is most common in cool, wet conditions. Remove infected leaves, clear plant debris, and grow resistant varieties.

CANKER

Plants affected: *apples, pears, mulberry, and many ornamentals.*
Caused by fungi, cankers can affect a wide range of woody plants. Common symptoms are raised or sunken areas of dead bark, which spread and cut off the sap, causing buds, leaves, and branches to die back. Cut out any infected growth.

CLEMATIS WILT

Plants affected: *clematis.*
This is a fungal disease affecting certain large-flowered hybrid clematis varieties. It causes leaves and stems to suddenly wilt and collapse, dying back to the base. Established plants will resprout, but younger specimens can be seriously weakened. Remove all infected growth. Note that wilting in clematis often has other causes, such as pest, weather, or physical damage.

CLUBROOT

Plants affected: *all brassicas.*
This is a serious disease that distorts roots, causing the foliage to become pale and pink-tinted, with the stems and leaves wilting even when plants are well watered. Yield can be seriously reduced and plants may even die. Destroy all infected material, increase soil drainage, and raise pH using lime. Plant out large healthy seedlings, and grow resistant varieties.

CORAL SPOT

Plants affected: *various broadleaf trees and shrubs.*
This fungal disease causes woody stems to die back and bright orange pustules to develop on the dead bark. It is carried by water splashes and pruning tools and enters plants via open wounds. It is most damaging to plants that are already under stress from other problems. Destroy infected material, cut back to healthy growth, and clean pruning tools.

Canker can kill branches and whole trees in time.

Clubroot affects brassicas, stunting their growth.

Damping off can decimate young seedlings.

CROWN ROT

Plants affected: *various, mainly bulbs and perennials.*
Caused by fungal or bacterial infections, leaves and stems wilt and die, and the base of the plant rots away and may smell unpleasant. Remove infected material, which often means the whole plant. Avoid wounding stems, planting too deeply, or mulching close to stems.

CUCUMBER MOSAIC VIRUS

Plants affected: *many vegetable crops and ornamentals.*
Plants are stunted, and the foliage may be distorted with yellow mottling. Flowering may be reduced and flowers discolored, and the fruit of any affected cucurbits can be distorted, discolored, and inedible. The virus is easily spread between plants, often by aphids, and there is no cure. Control aphids, avoid handling plants, grow resistant varieties, and destroy infected specimens quickly.

DAMPING OFF

Plants affected: *various.*
This disease kills seed and seedlings, causing stems to collapse and roots to rot. Prevent it by using sterile growing mix and trays, sowing thinly, and watering using tap water.

DOWNY MILDEW

Plants affected: *various.*
This disease, most common on plants in damp conditions, causes yellow patches on the upper leaf surfaces, with fuzzy white, gray, or purplish mold below. These spread, killing leaves and weakening plants. Remove infected material, improve air flow, and avoid overhead watering.

FIRE BLIGHT

Plants affected: *some members of the Rosaceae family, including apples, pears, and* Pyracantha.
Flowers, leaves, and stems wilt, and branches may die back rapidly. Bark sinks inward and sticky ooze may be secreted. This bacterial disease is most common in warm, wet weather; prune and destroy infected material, and sterilize pruning tools.

FUSARIUM WILT

Plants affected: *various.*
This fungal disease causes plants to wilt and die, and older leaves appear scorched. Cutting into stems may reveal reddish-purple streaks. There is no cure. Destroy infected plants, clear plant debris, and avoid planting the same species in an affected patch of soil for several years.

GRAY MOLD

Plants affected: *various.*
This fungal disease is prevalent in cool, damp conditions, especially on plants overwintered under cover. Fluffy mold appears on leaves, flowers, and fruits, and whole stems may wilt and die. Remove infected growth and all debris, and improve air flow around plants under cover.

HONEY FUNGUS

Plants affected: *various trees, shrubs, and perennials.*
Affected plants can die suddenly or may die back over a number of seasons; the leaves discoloring and wilting or failing to emerge in spring. Infected plants develop white, mushroom-smelling, fungal mycelium under the bark of the stem base and roots. Black, shoelace-like strands may also be found in the surrounding soil. Dig up and destroy infected plants, removing as much root as possible. Plant less susceptible species.

LEAF SPOTS

Plants affected: *various.*
Round or irregular spots, sometimes surrounded by a yellow halo, can be caused by various bacterial or fungal infections. Spots may connect, and some leaves may die, but the damage is usually minor; it can be a sign of poor plant health. Remove

Downy mildew causes discolored patches.

Gray mold thrives in cool, damp conditions.

Onion white rot can destroy a crop in summer.

infected leaves, rake up any that fall, and improve plant health.

LEEK RUST

Plants affected: *various members of the onion family.*
Outer leaves develop small, bright orange pustules, and may die off, weakening the plants. Inner leaves are rarely affected, and crops are still edible if affected leaves are removed. Most common in damp conditions. Clear plant debris after harvest, space plants widely, and grow resistant cultivars.

ONION WHITE ROT

Plants affected: *onions, shallots, garlic, and leeks.*
This serious disease causes leaves to yellow and wilt, and white, fluffy mold appears around the base of developing bulbs. There is no cure, and the soil where affected plants have been grown will be contaminated for many years. Remove and dispose of affected plants, and avoid moving contaminated soil around.

PARSNIP CANKER

Plants affected: *parsnips.*
This fungal disease causes dark, cankered areas on the roots. It is caused by a number of different fungi, some of which can also cause

leaf spotting. Points of root damage are frequently colonized by the canker, including feeding damage from carrot fly larvae. There are no chemical controls of parsnip canker. Grow resistant varieties, and sow closely in late spring to produce smaller roots, which are less susceptible.

PEACH LEAF CURL

Plants affected: *peaches, nectarines.*
New leaves in spring are puckered and blistered, turning red before dropping off. A second flush of leaves may develop; these are unaffected, but trees can be weakened if attacked over several years. Remove infected leaves quickly, and feed and water plants well. Cover with clear plastic in late winter and spring to protect leaves from rain, which spreads the fungal spores. Spray with fungicide in spring and fall.

PHYTOPHTHORA ROOT ROT

Plants affected: *various.*
This damaging disease causes the roots and stem base of affected plants to rot, and overall growth is weak. Foliage is sparse and may become discolored, stems die back, and the whole plant may be killed. If the bark is removed at the base of the main stem, the tissues below are stained reddish-brown. It is most

common on poorly drained soil. There is no cure; destroy infected plants, and remove the soil.

POTATO BLIGHT

Plants affected: *potatoes, tomatoes.*
This disease is most common in warm, wet seasons. It causes brown patches on leaves that wither and die. Stems develop dark patches and collapse, and infected tubers have sunken patches and discolored flesh and usually rot. Destroy infected growth, hill up to protect tubers, and grow resistant varieties.

POTATO COMMON SCAB

Plants affected: *potatoes, beets, radishes, rutabagas, and turnips.*
This is a bacterial disease that causes rough, corky patches on the skin of tubers. Yield isn't reduced, and the unsightly scabs can be removed when peeling the tubers. It is most common in hot, dry summers. Improve the soil with organic matter, water well, and grow resistant varieties.

POWDERY MILDEW

Plants affected: *various.*
This common disease causes white fungal growth on leaves, stems and fruit. Growth can become yellow and distorted; affected fruit (such as grapes) can split. Affected plants are unsightly

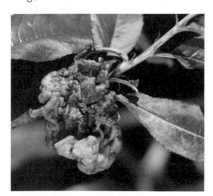
Peach leaf curl weakens plants and reduces yields.

Potato blight is most common in wet seasons.

Powdery mildew affects a very wide range of plants.

and may be weakened, but are rarely killed. Remove infected growth, water plants well, and improve air flow around each plant.

QUINCE LEAF BLIGHT

Plants affected: *quince trees.*
Numerous small, dark spots appear on the leaves and commonly merge together. Leaves yellow and fall, fruit may be spotted and misshapen, and shoot tips may die back. This fungal disease is most common in wet weather. Remove and destroy infected growth, and clear plant debris in the fall.

RASPBERRY SPUR BLIGHT

Plants affected: *raspberries, hybrids.*
Dark patches appear on the leaves in summer, and purple areas form on the stems around the buds. The affected areas turn a gray or silver color during fall and winter. The following spring, the new shoots wither and die, and crops are heavily reduced. It is most common in wet seasons. Remove and destroy all infected stems, and thin out canes.

RED CORE

Plants affected: *strawberries.*
This uncommon disease causes stunted growth in late spring and early summer, when leaves turn orange or brown.

Berries are small and ripen early. The disease is worse on heavy, wet soils and persists for years. Destroy infected plants, and replant elsewhere.

ROSE BLACK SPOT

Plants affected: *roses.*
This fungal disease causes purple-black spots on leaves that usually yellow and drop. The spots disfigure plants, which are weakened by the repeated leaf fall. Remove infected leaves and growth, and clear away all fall debris. Resistant varieties are available but resistance may not last the lifetime of the plant. Fungicides can also be applied as a preventive measure.

REPLANT DISEASE

Plants affected: *roses and fruit trees.*
Newly planted roses and fruit trees fail to thrive and may die back, but there are no obvious problems, such as over- or underwatering. Replant disease commonly occurs where the same species has been grown before; the full cause is not known, but is thought to be various soil-borne pests and pathogens attacking the roots. Plant something else instead, or remove as much soil as possible before replanting.

RUST

Plants affected: *various.*
Most common in wet conditions, this disease is caused by various fungal species, many of them host-specific. It commonly causes orange or brown pustules on the leaves and stems, which may yellow, wither, and die. Severe attacks can weaken and kill plants. Remove infected material, improve air flow around plants, and grow resistant varieties. If necessary, treat ornamental plants with fungicide.

SILVER LEAF

Plants affected: *plums, cherries, apples, and some other woody plants.*
Leaves develop a silver sheen, and if affected branches over 1 in (2.5 cm) in diameter are cut across, brown staining can be seen inside. Stems and branches die back, and established trees may be killed. It is caused by a fungal infection that enters plants through wounds and pruning cuts. There is no cure. Prune and destroy infected growth, cutting stems to 6 in (15 cm) beyond where staining is visible. Prune trees in summer when infection is less likely, and plant resistant varieties and rootstocks.

SCLEROTINIA ROT

Plants affected: *various.*
This disease causes the basal leaves of plants to wilt and yellow, and a

Rose black spot ruins the appearance of plants.

Rust affects many crops and ornamental plants.

Silver leaf is damaging and easily spread by pruning.

rapidly spreading brown rot appears on the stems. Large amounts of fluffy white fungal growth often develops, and black, seedlike structures appear. It is most common in cool, damp conditions. There is no cure. Destroy all infected material as soon as possible.

SOOTY MOLD

Plants affected: *various.*
This is black or gray mold that forms on the surface of leaves, growing on the sugary excretions ("honeydew") produced by sap-sucking insects, such as aphids. Although it doesn't attack the plant, it prevents light from reaching the leaves and can reduce vigor. It also looks bad. In some cases it may be possible to control the pest producing the honeydew. The mold growth can be wiped or washed off.

TOMATO BLIGHT

Plants affected: *tomatoes, potatoes.*
Caused by the same pathogen as potato blight, this disease causes dark patches on the leaves, which die back, and lesions on the stems, which usually collapse. Infected fruit turns brown and eventually decays. It is most common on outdoor-grown plants, especially in wet summers. Destroy infected material as soon as symptoms appear. If indoor crops are affected, wash out the greenhouse thoroughly

after the plants are removed. Effective resistant varieties are now available.

TURF RED THREAD

Plants affected: *lawn grasses.*
Patches of turf turn reddish or become bleached, then characteristic, small, pinkish-red, threadlike growth develops. Grass is rarely killed but becomes unsightly. It is most common on poorly fed and aerated lawns. Scarify the grass, feed with a nitrogenous fertilizer, and aerate the lawn.

VERTICILLIUM WILT

Plants affected: *various.*
Symptoms of this fungal disease are most prominent during hot, dry conditions. Leaves on affected branches discolor, turning brown or yellow between the veins, wilt, and die, although not all branches will be infected at the same time. Branches may die back, and if cut open, there will be brown or purple-brown streaks inside. There is no chemical control. Destroy infected plants, including the roots, and remove the surrounding soil. Conifers and grasses are immune to the disease.

VIOLET ROOT ROT

Plants affected: *various.*
Plants are stunted with yellowing leaves, and when lifted, the roots

are covered with a dense network of purple fungal strands. It is most common on wet, acid soils and persists for several years. Remove infected plants before they disintegrate, and improve drainage.

VIRUSES

Plants affected: *various.*
There are many viruses that affect plants, although most cause yellowing leaves, often in a mottled or mosaic pattern. The method of spread varies according to the virus. Insect transmission (such as by aphids) is common; handling or propagating from infected plants is another cause. Viruses weaken plants and commonly reduce flowering and lower yield. There is no cure, and infected plants should be destroyed to prevent the virus from spreading.

WHITE BLISTER

Plants affected: *vegetable brassicas, honesty, and some other ornamentals.*
Shiny white fungal pustules develop on the undersides of leaves, singly or in rings. The affected leaves become puckered and distorted, and the upper surface forms sunken yellow pits. This disease is most common in damp conditions and may persist in the soil. Remove infected leaves and heavily affected plants, and grow resistant varieties.

Tomato blight is most common on outside crops.

Verticillium wilt attacks a wide range of plants.

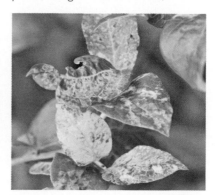
Viruses cause a wide range of debilitating symptoms.

PLANT CHOOSER

This gorgeous catalog of plants is designed to help you find the perfect plant for every corner of your garden. Search by type, whether you're looking for a fall shrub, a summer climber, or a spring perennial, or browse through the problem-solver pages to find something to cover shady ground or thrive in a sun-baked border.

ANNUALS, BIENNIALS, AND BEDDING

***Antirrhinum majus* 'Liberty Yellow'
(Liberty Classic Series)**
Bearing distinctive, rich gold, freesia-like
blooms all summer, these snapdragons are
perfect for summer bedding and for cutting.
‡ 18 in (45 cm) ↔ 12 in (30 cm) ☀ ◊ ❀

Calendula officinalis
The bright orange-yellow, daisylike flowers
of the pot marigold are produced from
summer through to fall. Deadhead to
keep the show going.
‡ 30 in (75 cm) ↔ 18 in (45 cm) ☀ ◊ ❀❀❀

***Cosmos bipinnatus* Sensation Series**
This popular annual cosmos produces
large pink and white flowers on elegant
thin stems above the fine, feathery leaves
throughout summer.
‡ 36 in (90 cm) ↔ 24 in (60 cm) ☀ ◊ ◖ ❀❀❀

***Digitalis purpurea* Camelot Series**
This is one wonderful foxglove among many.
Tall spires of freckled, bell-like flowers are
produced in shades of white, pink, lavender,
or cream.
‡ 4 ft (1.2 m) ↔ 24 in (60 cm) ☀ ☀ ◖ ❀❀❀

Eschscholzia californica
The California poppy is a low-growing annual
for the front of a sunny border. The bright
orange and yellow flowers are very attractive
against the ferny foliage.
‡ 12 in (30 cm) ↔ 6 in (15 cm) ☀ ◊ ❀❀❀

***Felicia amelloides* 'Santa Anita'**
This delicate subshrub has bright green
foliage. Large, daisylike flowers with blue
petals and bright yellow centers open
from late spring to fall.
‡↔ 24 in (60 cm) ☀ ◊ ❀

Hibiscus trionum
Flower-of-the-hour produces a succession
of stunning cream flowers with burgundy
centers from summer to early fall. Each
flower lasts only for a single day.
‡ 24 in (60 cm) ↔ 12 in (30 cm) ☀ ◖ ❀

***Lantana* 'Radiation'**
Vibrant yellow and red flower heads
are produced throughout summer above
the wrinkled, dark green leaves of this
tender subshrub.
‡ 18 in (45 cm) ↔ 10 in (25 cm) ☀ ◖ ☗

Limnanthes douglasii
This low-growing annual, known as
the poached egg plant, bears masses of
cup-shaped, white flowers with yellow
centers throughout summer.
‡ 6 in (15 cm) ↔ 4 in (10 cm) ☀ ◊ ❀❀❀

❀❀❀ FULLY HARDY	❀❀ HARDY IN MILD REGIONS/SHELTERED SITES	❀ PROTECT FROM FROST OVER THE WINTER	❀ NO TOLERANCE TO FROST
☼ FULL SUN	☼ PARTIAL SUN	❀ FULL SHADE	◊ WELL-DRAINED SOIL	◖ MOIST SOIL	◗ WET SOIL

Nemesia strumosa 'KLM'
Named for the Royal Dutch Airlines, this bushy annual with toothed and slightly hairy leaves is covered in masses of tiny blue and white flowers in summer.
‡ 12in (30cm) ↔ 6in (15cm) ☼ ◊ ◗ ❀

Nicotiana 'Domino Salmon-pink'
During mid- to late summer this tobacco plant is clothed with star-shaped, salmon-pink flowers, which open up in the early evening and emit a delicate scent.
‡ 18in (45cm) ↔ 16in (40cm) ☼ ☼ ◊ ◖ ❀

Nigella damascena Persian Jewels Group
Mixed shades of blue, pink, and white add charm to this English garden favorite, love-in-a-mist. Both flowers and seed heads are good for cutting.
‡ 16in (40cm) ↔ 9in (23cm) ☼ ◊ ❀❀❀

Osteospermum 'Buttermilk'
Sun-loving Cape daisies are mainly grown for their bright and cheerful flowers; these are borne from spring to fall, but close in shady conditions.
‡ 24in (60cm) ↔ 12in (30cm) ☼ ◊ ❀❀

Papaver rhoeas
Field poppies are ideal for creating a splash of color in a sunny area of the garden. Various flower colors are available, from white to red and mauve.
‡ 24in (60cm) ↔ 6in (15cm) ☼ ◊ ❀❀❀

Viola 'Bowles's Black'
A pretty annual viola with dainty, midnight blue-black flowers. Perfect for rock gardens, containers, or for growing between the cracks in paving stones.
‡ 6in (15cm) ↔ 3in (8cm) ☼ ◊ ❀❀❀

Zinnia marylandica Zahara Coral Rose (Zahara Series)
Zinnias produce an abundance of bright summer flowers. This variety bears frilly pink pompom blooms.
‡ 12–18in (30–45cm) ↔ 12in (30cm) ☼ ◊ ❀

ALSO RECOMMENDED

Ageratum houstonianum 'Blue Danube'

Campanula medium 'Bells of Holland' (Canterbury bells)

Cerinthe major 'Purpurascens'

Clarkia amoena (Satin flower)

Convolvulus tricolor 'Blue Flash'

Eustoma grandiflorum

Gaillardia pulchella Lollipop Series

Helianthus annuus 'Music Box' (Sunflower)

Iberis umbellata Fairyland mixture (Common candytuft)

Lathyrus annuus (Sweet pea)

Lobularia maritima 'Snow Crystals'

Lunaria annua (Honesty)

Nemophila menziesii (Baby blue eyes)

Omphalodes linifolia (Venus's navelwort)

Sanvitalia procumbens (Creeping zinnia)

Sutera cordata Snowstorm Series Giant Snowflake ('Danova906')

Tagetes patula 'Naughty Marietta'

Tropaeolum majus Alaska Series

PLANTS FOR SUMMER CONTAINERS

Agapanthus praecox subsp. _orientalis_
The sky-blue, tubular flowers of this tall
perennial are borne in clusters at the top of
strong stems that rise from clumps of broad,
dark green leaves.
↕ 3 ft (1 m) ↔ 2 ft (60 cm) ☀ ◐ ❋

Ageratum 'Adriatic'
From summer until the first frost, this plant
produces small mid-blue flowers in dense
clusters above downy, green, oval leaves.
Water well in containers.
↕ 8 in (20 cm) ↔ 12 in (30 cm) ☀ ◌ ◐ ❋

Argyranthemum 'Jamaica Primrose'
The soft yellow daisy flowers of
this easygoing plant are beautifully
complemented by the ferny, deeply
divided mid-green leaves.
↕↔ 3 ft (1 m) ☀ ◌ ◐ ❋

Brachyscome iberidifolia
The blue, violet, or white daisylike flowers
of this bushy annual appear from mid- to
late summer, held above deeply divided
gray-green foliage.
↕↔ 18 in (45 cm) ☀ ◌ ◐ ❋

Calibrachoa Cabaret Series
From summer to fall, this mound-forming,
trailing plant bears bright pink, trumpet-
shaped flowers in profusion. They are set
against dark green leaves.
↕ 5 in (13 cm) ↔ 18 in (45 cm) ☀ ☀ ◐ ❋

Dianthus 'Becky Robinson'
The pretty, semi-double flowers of this
compact perennial are clear pink, bordered
with deep red. Cut or deadhead them to
prompt repeat flowering.
↕ 18 in (45 cm) ↔ 16 in (40 cm) ☀ ◐ ❋❋❋

Fuchsia 'Celia Smedley'
An upright fuchsia bearing deep red flowers
and pink sepals from midsummer, 'Celia
Smedley' will give its best display if given
well-fertilized, loamy potting mix.
↕ 5 ft (1.5 m) ↔ 3 ft (1 m) ☀ ☀ ◌ ◐ ❋

Gazania Talent Series
Providing a vivid splash of yellow in a container
display, the open, daisylike flowers appear
over a long period. The leaves are felted and
grayish-green.
↕↔ 10 in (25 cm) ☀ ◌ ❋

**_Impatiens walleriana_
'Tempo Lavender Butterfly'**
The strong lavender-pink flowers of this
variety are long lasting and provide a bright
display from summer to fall.
↕↔ 10 in (25 cm) ☀ ◌ ◐ ❋❋

❀❀❀ FULLY HARDY ❀❀ HARDY IN MILD REGIONS/SHELTERED SITES ❀ PROTECT FROM FROST OVER THE WINTER ❀ TOLERANCE TO FROST

☼ FULL SUN ☼ PARTIAL SUN ❊ FULL SHADE ◊ WELL-DRAINED SOIL �ొ MOIST SOIL ◔ WET SOIL

Ipomoea tricolor 'Heavenly Blue'
A fast-growing climber with twining stems, this variety of morning glory bears sky-blue, funnel-shaped flowers with white centers throughout the summer.
↕ 10ft (3m) ☼ ◊ ❀❀

Lobelia erinus Cascade Series
This trailing lobelia bears masses of tiny dark blue flowers from summer through to mid-fall; they last better if given a position in partial shade.
↕↔ 6in (15cm) ☼ ☼ ◊ ❀

Pelargonium 'Caligula'
This miniature zonal pelargonium has dark green leaves and bright scarlet double blooms. Deadhead regularly to prolong their season until the first frost.
↕ 5in (12cm) ↔ 4in (10cm) ☼ ◊ ❀

Petunia Surfinia Pink Vein
With large pink flowers with deeper hued veins and centers, this trailing petunia grows vigorously and makes a strong display in a container. Deadhead regularly.
↕ 16in (40cm) ↔ 36in (90cm) ☼ ◊ ❀

Ricinus communis 'Impala'
Suitable for a large container, this tall, fast-growing shrub has deeply divided bronze leaves up to 12in (30cm) across. The small red flowers are followed by red seed heads.
↕ 5ft (1.5m) ↔ 3ft (1m) ☼ ◊ ❀

Tropaeolum majus
Nasturtiums are popular for their bright yellow, orange, or red flowers. Both the flowers and pale green leaves are edible, adding color and flavor to salads.
↕ 12in (30cm) ☼ ◊ ◔ ❀

Verbena 'Sissinghurst'
Large round clusters of bright magenta flowers are borne from summer to fall, providing bold color against the dark green leaves of this easy-to-grow plant.
↕ 8in (20cm) ↔ 3ft (1m) ☼ ◊ ◔ ❀❀

ALSO RECOMMENDED

Aloysia triphylla
  (Lemon verbena)

Argyranthemum 'Vancouver'

Begonia Nonstop Series

Bidens ferulifolia

Brugmansia x *candida*
  'Grand Marnier'

Campanula isophylla
  (Falling stars)

Canna 'Assaut'

Chrysanthemum 'Mary Stoker'

Cosmos bipinnatus
  Sensation Series

Fuchsia 'Thalia'

Gazania Mini-Star Series

Limnanthes douglasii
  (Poached egg plant)

Matthiola incana Cinderella
  Series (Gillyflower)

Narcissus 'Tête-à-Tête'

Nemesia strumosa 'KLM'

Nerium oleander (Oleander)

Pelargonium 'Happy Thought'

Petunia 'Purple Wave'

Prostanthera rotundifolia
  (Round-leaved mint bush)

Rosa 'The Fairy'

SPRING-FLOWERING BULBS

Anemone blanda 'White Splendour'
The white daisylike flowers of this anemone are held on upright stems above the deeply toothed leaves, making a prolific display in spring.
‡ 4 in (10 cm) ↔ 6 in (15 cm) ☼ ◊ ✿✿✿

Camassia leichtlinii
The leafless stems of this striking plant bear dense spikes of star-shaped white or blue-violet flowers with six petals. Long, slim leaves grow at the base of the stems.
‡ 5 ft (1.5 m) ↔ 12 in (30 cm) ☼ ☼ ◊ ◊ ✿✿

Convallaria majalis 'Albostriata'
Short spikes of white, sweetly scented flowers are borne on arching stems in late spring, surrounded by handsome gold-striped, broad green leaves.
‡ 8 in (20 cm) ↔ 12 in (30 cm) ☼ ☼ ◊ ◊ ✿✿✿

Crocus chrysanthus 'E.A. Bowles'
The rich yellow of the goblet-shaped flowers of this crocus is emphasized by the purple feathering on the outer petals and the dark green, white-striped leaves.
‡ 3 in (8 cm) ↔ 2 in (5 cm) ☼ ◊ ✿✿✿

Cyclamen coum subsp. coum f. coum Pewter Group This cyclamen has dark green leaves with a pewter sheen. The flowers appear from late winter to early spring and range from white to crimson.
‡↔ 4–5 in (10–12 cm) ◊ ◊ ✿✿✿

Erythronium dens-canis
With heavily marked green leaves and dainty, nodding flowers in colors from white to pink, this dog's-tooth violet makes a pretty display in early spring.
‡ 6–10 in (15–25 cm) ↔ 4 in (10 cm) ☼ ◊ ✿✿✿

Fritillaria meleagris
A native of English grasslands, this fritillaria looks stunning planted en masse in grass. The pink-purple or white flowers have a distinctive checkered pattern.
‡ 12 in (30 cm) ↔ 3 in (8 cm) ☼ ☼ ◊ ◊ ✿✿✿

Galanthus nivalis
The fragrant white flowers of the common snowdrop are a classic sight in early spring. Given the right conditions, it will self-seed easily to make spreading colonies.
‡ 6 in (15 cm) ↔ 3 in (8 cm) ☼ ◊ ◊ ✿✿✿

Hyacinthus orientalis 'City of Haarlem'
In late spring this hyacinth produces a dense spike of intensely fragrant, primrose-yellow flowers. The leaves are bright green and lance-shaped.
‡ 10 in (25 cm) ↔ 3 in (8 cm) ☼ ◊ ✿✿✿

❋❋❋ FULLY HARDY	❋❋ HARDY IN MILD REGIONS/SHELTERED SITES	❋ PROTECT FROM FROST OVER THE WINTER	❋ NO TOLERANCE TO FROST
☼ FULL SUN	☼ PARTIAL SUN	❋ FULL SHADE	◊ WELL-DRAINED SOIL ◊ MOIST SOIL ◊ WET SOIL

Iris 'George'
This vigorous dwarf iris flowers in early spring, producing fragrant, deep violet-purple flowers up to 3 in (8 cm) across, with bright yellow markings on the falls.
‡ 4 in (10 cm) ↔ 3 ft (1 m) ☼ ❋ ◊ ◊ ❋❋❋

Leucojum aestivum 'Gravetye Giant'
Resembling a giant snowdrop, the summer snowflake bears nodding white flowers with green tips in spring. Narrow green leaves provide a subtle backdrop.
‡ 36 in (90 cm) ↔ 3 in (8 cm) ❋ ◊ ❋❋❋

Muscari armeniacum
Dense spikes of fragrant, bell-shaped, deep blue flowers with a pale blue or white rim are produced on upright stems surrounded by narrow mid-green leaves.
‡ 8 in (20 cm) ↔ 4 in (10 cm) ☼ ◊ ◊ ❋❋❋

Narcissus 'Ceylon'
This large, very vigorous daffodil has showy, long-lasting flowers with deep yellow petals and orange-rimmed cups. The strap-shaped leaves are dark green.
‡ 16 in (40 cm) ↔ 5 in (12 cm) ☼ ◊ ❋❋❋

Puschkinia scilloides
Slender, bell-shaped flowers in pale blue with a fine deeper blue line down the center of each petal make a pretty display on compact stems in early spring.
‡ 6 in (15 cm) ↔ 2 in (5 cm) ☼ ❋ ◊ ❋❋❋

ALSO RECOMMENDED

Allium acuminatum
Allium aflatunense
Anemone tschernjaewii
Calochortus luteus (Yellow mariposa)
Chionodoxa 'Pink Giant'
Colchicum luteum
Crocus 'Blue Pearl'
Ferraria crispa
Fritillaria imperialis 'Lutea' (Crown imperial)
Fritillaria verticillata
Hyacinthoides non-scripta (English bluebell)
Hyacinthus orientalis 'White Pearl'
Iris 'Natascha'
Ixia viridiflora
Leucojum vernum (Spring snowflake)
Muscari botryoides 'Album'
Narcissus 'Silver Chimes'
Ornithogalum magnum
Ornithogalum oligophyllum
Scilla siberica 'Alba' (Siberian squill)
Sparaxis tricolor
Tulipa 'Giuseppe Verdi'

Scilla bifolia
Particularly attractive naturalized in grass or beneath deciduous trees, this early-blooming plant bears blue-violet star-shaped flowers on one side of the stems.
‡↔ 6 in (15 cm) ☼ ◊ ❋❋❋

Tulipa 'Spring Green'
With a feathery green flash on each ivory petal, this Viridiflora Group tulip is a cool and elegant presence in a mixed or color-themed border. It flowers in late spring.
‡ 16 in (40 cm) ☼ ◊ ❋❋❋

SUMMER AND FALL BULBS

Allium hollandicum 'Purple Sensation'
The deep purple, spherical flower heads of
this early summer-flowering, stately allium
look stunning when planted with silver-
leaved, shorter plants.
‡ 32 in (80 cm) ↔ 3 in (7 cm) ☼ ◊ ❀❀❀

Allium sphaerocephalon
Known as the round-headed leek, this plant
sends up golf ball–sized flower heads in
midsummer. They are a rich, bright purple
and are a magnet to bees.
‡ 36 in (90 cm) ↔ 2 in (5 cm) ☼ ◊ ◊ ❀❀❀

Alstroemeria ligtu hybrids
These midsummer-flowering perennials
bear sprays of delicate flowers in a wide
variety of colors, from white to shades
of pink, yellow, and orange.
‡ 20 in (50 cm) ↔ 30 in (75 cm) ☼ ☀ ◊ ◊ ❀❀❀

Canna 'Striata'
A statement plant with rich, yellow-
striped green leaves and bright orange
flowers carried on dark red-purple stems
in midsummer.
‡ 5 ft (1.5 m) ↔ 20 in (50 cm) ☼ ◊ ❀

Colchicum fallale
Fall crocuses flower when least expected,
their large pale lilac blooms suddenly
appearing in the fall before the leaves
emerge in the spring.
‡ 4–6 in (10–15 cm) ↔ 3 in (8 cm) ☼ ◊ ◊ ❀❀❀

Crinum x powellii
A very decorative plant, this lily produces
flared trumpet blooms, up to ten at a time,
at the top of tall, rigid stems from late
summer to mid-fall.
‡ 3 ft (1 m) ↔ 24 in (60 cm) ☼ ◊ ◊ ❀❀

Crocosmia masoniorum 'Firebird'
This dazzling, bright red crocosmia makes a
fabulous mid- to late-summer display when its
spikes of vivid flowers arch over the fans of
bright green leaves.
‡ 32 in (80 cm) ↔ 18 in (45 cm) ☼ ◊ ◊ ❀❀❀

Cyclamen hederifolium
Fluted pink flowers are carried above
the soil surface in fall before the foliage
appears. The heart-shaped leaves are dark
green with silver patterning.
‡ 4 in (10 cm) ↔ 6 in (15 cm) ☼ ☀ ◊ ❀❀❀

Dahlia 'Bishop of Llandaff'
The vivid red flowers of this dahlia
look dramatic against the black-red
foliage, making it a striking addition
to a late summer border.
‡ 3 ft (1 m) ↔ 18 in (45 cm) ☼ ◊ ◊ ❀❀

❀❀❀ FULLY HARDY   ❀❀ HARDY IN MILD REGIONS/SHELTERED SITES   ❀ PROTECT FROM FROST OVER THE WINTER   ❅ NO TOLERANCE TO FROST

☼ FULL SUN   ◉ PARTIAL SUN   ◉ FULL SHADE   ◊ WELL-DRAINED SOIL   ◐ MOIST SOIL   ● WET SOIL

Dierama pulcherrimum
The delightful name of angel's fishing rod perfectly suits this elegant perennial, whose pink bell flowers move gracefully on long stems in the slightest breeze.
↕ 5 ft (1.5 m) ↔ 24 in (60 cm) ☼ ◊ ◐ ❀❀

Fritillaria imperialis
Stately and strong-growing, the crown imperial stands regally within a border. Clusters of orange flowers radiate from the top of tall stems in early summer.
↕ 5 ft (1.5 m) ↔ 12 in (30 cm) ☼ ◊ ❀❀❀

Gladiolus murielae
Fragrant, pure white flowers with deep burgundy centers are carried on the tall, arching stems of this exotic gladiolus during late summer and into fall.
↕ 3 ft (1 m) ↔ 2 in (5 cm) ☼ ◊ ❀❀

Iris pallida 'Variegata'
The long, tapering, yellow-striped leaves of this elegant iris surround a succession of showy, scented blue flowers in early summer. A perfect plant for a hot border.
↕ 4 ft (1.2 m) ↔ indefinite ☼ ◊ ❀❀❀

Lilium regale
The large, white, trumpet-shaped flowers of the regal lily are purple on the outside and held in clusters on tall stems, creating an eye-catching display in midsummer.
↕↔ 6 ft (2 m) ☼ ◊ ❀❀❀

Nectaroscordum siculum subsp. bulgaricum
The flowers on this onion relative are green, white, and burgundy. Grouped in sprays on top of tall stems, they are a pretty sight in early summer.
↕ 4 ft (1.2 m) ↔ 18 in (45 cm) ☼ ◉ ◊ ❀❀❀

Nerine bowdenii
South Africa has given gardeners many spectacular plants, and this is no exception. Stems of vivid pink, spidery flowers appear from bare soil in fall.
↕ 24 in (60 cm) ↔ 6 in (15 cm) ☼ ◊ ❀❀

ALSO RECOMMENDED

Summer-flowering
Allium 'Gladiator'
Alstroemeria 'Moulin Rouge'
Cardiocrinum giganteum (Giant lily)
Dahlia 'Hillcrest Royal'
Dichelostemma congestum
Ismene x spofforthiae 'Sulphur Queen'
Lilium 'Starfighter'
Polianthes tuberosa 'The Pearl'
Ranunculus asiaticus var. flavus (Persian buttercup)
Watsonia meriana
Zantedeschia elliottiana (Golden arum lily)

Fall-flowering
Acis autumnalis (Autumn snowflake)
Amaryllis belladonna 'Hathor'
Colchicum bivonae
Cyclamen mirabile
Scilla scilloides
Nerine bowdenii 'Alba'
Nerine 'Orion'
Zephyranthes grandiflora

SPRING AND EARLY SUMMER PERENNIALS

Anemone ranunculoides
With small, bright yellow, five- or
six-petaled flowers, this spring-flowering
plant resembles a buttercup. It is ideal for
naturalizing in a woodland garden.
‡↔ 8 in (20 cm) ☼ ◊ ◊ ✿✿✿

Aquilegia vulgaris 'Nivea'
Clusters of white flowers borne on upright
stems with grayish-green, divided leaves make
this plant a pretty addition to a border,
especially in a shady spot.
‡ 36 in (90 cm) ↔ 18 in (45 cm) ☼ ☼ ◊ ✿✿✿

Bergenia ciliata
In the spring this evergreen perennial has small
white flowers that become pink. Its large, round,
hairy leaves make it attractive after the flowering
season, too.
‡ 12 in (30 cm) ↔ 18 in (45 cm) ☼ ☼ ◊ ◊ ✿✿✿

Brunnera macrophylla
A clump-forming perennial excellent for
ground cover, this plant produces slender
sprays of star-shaped flowers resembling
forget-me-nots in early spring.
‡ 18 in (45 cm) ↔ 24 in (60 cm) ☼ ◊ ◊ ✿✿✿

Digitalis grandiflora
This species of foxglove produces its pale
yellow flowers in early summer. It is a
short-lived, clump-forming perennial
ideal for an informal border.
‡ 3 ft (1 m) ↔ 18 in (45 cm) ☼ ◊ ◊ ✿✿✿

Eranthis hyemalis
In early spring bright yellow, cup-shaped
flowers grow from green bracts resembling
deeply divided leaves; naturalized in grass,
they make a pretty carpet.
‡ 4 in (10 cm) ↔ 4 in (10 cm) ☼ ◊ ◊ ✿✿✿

Euphorbia polychroma
The yellow flowers of this bushy,
rounded perennial provide bright color
over several weeks in spring, set against
mid-green leaves.
‡↔ 20 in (50 cm) ☼ ◊ ◊ ✿✿✿

Geranium cinereum 'Ballerina'
One of the earliest hardy geraniums
to bloom, this variety has cup-shaped,
purplish-pink flowers with purple veins and
dark centers, carried in profusion.
‡ 4 in (10 cm) ↔ 12 in (30 cm) ☼ ◊ ✿✿✿

Geum rivale
A native of waterside locations, water avens
is ideal for a bog garden or a site beside a
pool. In late spring it produces nodding,
bell-shaped, deep pink flowers.
‡↔ 24 in (60 cm) ☼ ◊ ◊ ✿✿✿

❀❀❀ FULLY HARDY ❀❀ HARDY IN MILD REGIONS/SHELTERED SITES ❀ PROTECT FROM FROST IN THE WINTER ❀ NO TOLERANCE TO FROST

☼ FULL SUN ☼ PARTIAL SUN ❀ FULL SHADE ◊ WELL-DRAINED SOIL ◊ MOIST SOIL ◊ WET SOIL

Helleborus argutifolius
Given the right conditions, this hellebore puts on a profuse display of pale green flowers with bold stamens held above its sometimes prettily marbled leaves.
↕ 24 in (60 cm) ↔ 18 in (45 cm) ☼ ❀ ◊ ❀❀❀

Iris sibirica 'Butter and Sugar'
In early summer this Siberian iris produces abundant large flowers with creamy white standards and butter-yellow falls veined with green.
↕ 3 ft (1 m) ↔ indefinite ☼ ◊ ❀❀❀

Lamprocapnos spectabilis
The main charm of this plant is in the pretty pink heart-shaped flowers held on arching stems in spring, but the deeply divided leaves are also very attractive.
↕ 30 in (75 cm) ↔ 20 in (50 cm) ❀ ◊ ◊ ❀❀❀

Lupinus 'Chandelier'
From early to midsummer, 'Chandelier' bears spires of bright yellow pea flowers. If deadheaded it may sometimes bloom again in the early fall.
↕ 36 in (90 cm) ↔ 30 in (75 cm) ☼ ❀ ◊ ❀❀❀

Maianthemum racemosum
From late spring to midsummer this plant bears conical spires of small, slightly scented white flowers on tall stems, followed by red berries.
↕ 36 in (90 cm) ↔ 18 in (45 cm) ❀ ❀ ◊ ❀❀❀

Paeonia cambessedesii
Single, deep rose-pink flowers are borne in mid-spring above notably attractive foliage, dark green above with purplish-red veins, stalks, and undersurfaces.
↕↔ 22 in (55 cm) ☼ ◊ ❀❀

Polygonatum x hybridum
Small white tubular flowers hang from elegantly arching stems with glossy green oval leaves, making it a super plant for borders and woodland gardens.
↕ 4 ft (1.2 m) ↔ 3 ft (1 m) ❀ ◊ ❀❀❀

Primula x bulleesiana
A lovely hybrid candelabra primula, this plant produces flowers that are mainly terra-cotta in color but may range from grayish-yellow to maroon.
↕↔ 24 in (60 cm) ❀ ◊ ❀❀❀

Pulmonaria 'Diana Clare'
A vigorous, densely clump-forming hybrid, 'Diana Clare' has beautiful silver-flushed, lance-shaped foliage and bright purple-blue flowers.
↕ 12 in (30 cm) ↔ 18 in (45 cm) ❀ ❀ ◊ ❀❀❀

SPRING AND EARLY SUMMER PERENNIALS _CONTINUED_

Pulsatilla vulgaris
In spring nodding, cup-shaped flowers in purple, pink, or white with bright yellow centers are borne on upright stems above feathery light green leaves.
↕↔ 9 in (23 cm) ☼ ◊ ❀❀❀

Rhodanthemum hosmariense
The yellow-centered white daisy flowers of this subshrub make a great show from spring through to fall, growing from mounds of ferny silver-gray leaves.
↕ 4–12 in (10–30 cm) ↔ 12 in (30 cm) ☼ ◊ ❀❀

Saxifraga Southside Seedling Group
This mat-forming, evergreen plant produces arching spires of white blooms with strong red markings in late spring and early summer.
↕ 12 in (30 cm) ↔ 8 in (20 cm) ☼ ◊ ❀❀❀

Symphytum x _uplandicum_ 'Variegatum'
A clump-forming perennial good for ground cover in wild gardens, this has large, hairy leaves with cream margins and blue or purple-blue tubular flowers.
↕ 3 ft (1 m) ↔ 24 in (60 cm) ☼ ☀ ◖ ❀❀❀

Tanacetum parthenium 'Aureum'
This fast-growing, short-lived, bushy perennial has white flowers with dark yellow centers, borne in summer on upright stems above aromatic foliage.
↕↔ 18 in (45 cm) ☼ ◊ ❀❀❀

Thalictrum aquilegifolium 'Thundercloud'
From rounded leaflets of ferny foliage rise tall stems with clusters of tiny mauve-pink flowers in summer. The seed heads are also attractive.
↕ 3 ft (1 m) ↔ 12 in (30 cm) ☀ ◖ ❀❀❀

Trollius x _cultorum_ 'Alabaster'
The globe-shaped, rich cream flowers of this plant are borne on slender, upright stems in spring above attractive, deeply divided, mid-green foliage.
↕ 24 in (60 cm) ↔ 18 in (45 cm) ☼ ☀ ◖ ◗ ❀❀❀

ALSO RECOMMENDED

Achillea 'Fanal'

Anchusa azurea 'Loddon Royalist'

Asphodeline lutea (Yellow asphodel)

Convallaria majalis (Lily of the valley)

Diascia personata

Epimedium 'Amber Queen'

Erysimum cheiri 'Blood Red'

Geranium macrorrhizum 'Ingwersen's Variety'

Geum 'Bell Bank'

Heuchera species

Leucanthemum x _superbum_ 'Aglaia'

Lupinus 'The Chatelaine'

Meconopsis grandis (Himalayan blue poppy)

Papaver orientale (Oriental poppy)

Primula veris (Cowslip)

Ranunculus aconitifolius

Salvia x _sylvestris_ 'Mainacht'

Trillium grandiflorum (Wake-robin)

Viola x _wittrockiana_ Ultima Series

SUMMER AND FALL PERENNIALS

Acanthus spinosus
This handsome, clump-forming perennial is a striking architectural presence in a border with tall spikes of purple-hooded, white, tubular flowers.
↕ 4 ft (1.2 m) ↔ 24 in (60 cm) ☼ ◊ ❊❊❊

Achillea 'Paprika'
A vigorous, tough variety of yarrow, this plant produces flat clusters of striking red flowers with yellow centers held above the feathery, mid-green leaves.
↕↔ 24 in (60 cm) ☼ ◊ ◊ ❊❊❊

Agapanthus 'Blue Giant'
With exceptionally large flower heads, 'Blue Giant' makes a strong statement with its deep blue, bell-shaped blooms held on tall, stiff stems in late summer.
↕ 4 ft (1.2 m) ↔ 24 in (60 cm) ☼ ◊ ❊❊

Anemone x *hybrida*
This group of Japanese anemones encompasses single, semi-double, and double types in white or pink; 'Honorine Jobert' is a popular single white.
↕ 4–5 ft (1.2–1.5 m) ↔ indefinite ☼ ❊ ◊ ❊❊❊

Aster amellus 'King George'
From late summer to late fall this bushy perennial bears a profusion of large, daisylike, violet-blue flowers with yellow centers held in loose clusters.
↕↔ 20 in (50 cm) ❊ ◊ ❊❊❊

Astrantia major
Small, greenish-white or pink-tinged flowers, produced over a long season, are a pretty display above massed divided, mid-green leaves.
↕ 24 in (60 cm) ↔ 18 in (45 cm) ☼ ◊ ❊❊❊

Delphinium Blue Fountains Group
These dwarf delphiniums form clumps of dark green, divided foliage, from which rise dense spires of white-eyed flowers in shades of blue from pale to dark.
↕ 3 ft (1 m) ↔ 24 in (60 cm) ☼ ◊ ❊❊❊

Dianthus 'Bovey Belle'
The bright purple, double flowers of this modern pink are good for cutting as well as for color in the border, offering a fragrance of cloves as a bonus.
↕ 18 in (45 cm) ↔ 16 in (40 cm) ☼ ◊ ❊❊❊

Echinops ritro 'Veitch's Blue'
Round, purplish-blue flowers resembling those of thistles are borne on tall stems in summer, with architectural interest provided by the spiny gray-green leaves.
↕ 4 ft (1.2 m) ↔ 30 in (75 cm) ☼ ◊ ❊❊❊

SUMMER AND FALL PERENNIALS *CONTINUED*

Echinacea purpurea 'Magnus'
The purple-pink flowers of 'Magnus' have orange centers with the raised shape that gives the common name of coneflower to this genus of late-summer perennials.
↕↔ 24 in (60 cm) ☼ ◊ ◐ ✿✿✿

Eryngium x *oliverianum*
Large, rounded, thistlelike heads in lavender blue are borne in late summer, a striking sight against the jagged-edged, mid-green leaves.
↕ 3 ft (1 m) ↔ 2 ft (60 cm) ☼ ◊ ✿✿✿

Geranium 'Nimbus'
This hardy geranium is prolific in flower with large, violet-blue, saucer-shaped blooms produced all summer. It is compact with finely divided foliage.
↕ 3 ft (1 m) ↔ 18 in (45 cm) ☼ ☀ ◊ ✿✿✿

Helenium 'Moerheim Beauty'
The rich coppery-red daisy flowers of this plant appear in late summer, a time when the garden may begin to lack color. Deadhead to prolong flowering.
↕ 3 ft (1 m) ↔ 2 ft (60 cm) ☼ ◊ ✿✿✿

Hemerocallis 'Buzz Bomb'
This lovely daylily has broad-petaled, tawny flowers with yellow throats, appearing throughout the summer. The foliage is thick and strap-like.
↕↔ 24 in (60 cm) ☼ ◊ ◐ ✿✿✿

Kniphofia 'Bees' Sunset'
Tall spires of pale orange, tubular flowers rising from arching foliage bloom over a long season, making this an excellent plant for a hot-colored border.
↕ 3 ft (1 m) ↔ 2 ft (60 cm) ☼ ☀ ◊ ◐ ✿✿✿

Monarda 'Cambridge Scarlet'
Like all bergamots, 'Cambridge Scarlet' is attractive to bees. It has spidery, vivid red flowers and aromatic toothed foliage; with the right conditions it spreads fast.
↕ 3 ft (1 m) ↔ 18 in (45 cm) ☼ ◐ ✿✿✿

Papaver orientale 'Cedric Morris'
This Oriental poppy bears large, soft pink flowers with black centers above the gray divided leaves in May or June; many bloom again later in the summer.
↕↔ 36 in (90 cm) ☼ ◊ ✿✿✿

Penstemon 'Stapleford Gem'
One of the hardiest penstemons, this has multicolored flowers in pastel shades of pink, mauve, and purple, blooming from midsummer through early fall.
↕ 24 in (60 cm) ↔ 18 in (45 cm) ☼ ☀ ◊ ✿✿

❋❋❋ FULLY HARDY	❋❋ HARDY IN MILD REGIONS/SHELTERED SITES	❋ PROTECT FROM FROST IN THE WINTER	❆ NO TOLERANCE TO FROST
☼ FULL SUN	☼ PARTIAL SUN	❋ FULL SHADE　◊ WELL-DRAINED SOIL	◐ MOIST SOIL　● WET SOIL

Perovskia 'Blue Spire'
With profuse spires of violet-blue flowers on white stems and aromatic, gray-green foliage, this is a beautiful subshrub that can find a place in many color schemes.
‡ 4 ft (1.2 m)　↔ 3 ft (1 m)　☼　◊　❋❋❋

Persicaria bistorta 'Superba'
This vigorous, rapidly spreading plant produces tall spikes of small, tightly massed, soft pink flowers, standing above clumps of broad green leaves.
‡ 30 in (75 cm)　↔ 24 in (60 cm)　☼　☼　◊　◐　❋❋❋

Phlox paniculata 'Eva Cullum'
Dense clusters of bright pink flowers with magenta eyes are produced on upright stems in midsummer; their strong fragrance is an added attraction.
‡ 4 ft (1.2 m)　↔ 2 ft (60 cm)　☼　☼　◊　◐　❋❋❋

Rudbeckia fulgida var. sullivantii 'Goldsturm' Bearing golden flower heads with conical black centers on tall stems in late summer and fall, 'Goldsturm' provides valuable color in a border.
‡ 30 in (75 cm)　↔ 12 in (30 cm)　☼　☼　◊　◐　❋❋❋

Salvia x jamensis 'Hot Lips'
The showy red and white flowers of this variety provide bright color through the summer. The small, oval foliage is aromatic and may turn red in the fall.
‡↔ 30 in (75 cm)　☼　◊　❋❋

Verbascum 'Cotswold Queen'
This is a short-lived perennial that has rosettes of gray-green foliage; tall stems bear soft apricot-buff flowers with a purplish eye throughout the summer.
‡ 4 ft (1.2 m)　↔ 12 in (30 cm)　☼　◊　❋❋❋

Verbena bonariensis
Though this is tall, the minimal presence of its slender stems and tiny blue-purple flowers make it ideal for the front of a border, framing smaller plants behind.
‡ 5 ft (1.5 m)　↔ 24 in (60 cm)　☼　◊　❋❋

ALSO RECOMMENDED

Actaea simplex 'James Compton'

Agapanthus inapertus subsp. *pendulus* 'Graskop'

Anaphalis triplinervis 'Sommerschnee'

Aster x *frikartii* 'Mönch'

Centaurea pulcherrima

Cosmos atrosanguineus (Chocolate cosmos)

Galega x *hartlandii* 'Lady Wilson'

Gaura lindheimeri

Helianthus 'Lemon Queen'

Impatiens tinctoria

Kniphofia 'Percy's Pride'

Kniphofia 'Royal Standard'

Ligularia 'The Rocket'

Linaria triornithophora (Three birds toadflax)

Lobelia cardinalis 'Queen Victoria'

Persicaria amplexicaulis 'Firetail'

Potentilla 'Arc-en-ciel'

Romneya coulteri (Tree poppy)

Salvia patens

Thalictrum delavayi 'Hewitt's Double'

PERENNIALS FOR WINTER INTEREST

Anaphalis triplinervis
Pearly everlasting bears clusters of tiny flowers in midsummer with papery white bracts. The flowers and foliage persist into winter and are good for drying.
‡ 36in (90cm) ↔ 24in (60cm) ☼ ☀ ◊ ◗ ❋❋❋

Arum italicum 'Marmoratum'
A truly exotic-looking plant whether in leaf, flower, or fruit. The glossy green leaves are veined with white, and spears of red berries appear in late fall.
‡ 10in (25cm) ↔ 12in (30cm) ☀ ◊ ◗ ❋❋

Bergenia 'Ballawley'
This vigorous evergreen has large, dark green leaves flushed with red in winter. In spring clusters of bright crimson flowers appear at the top of strong stems.
‡↔ 24in (60cm) ☼ ☀ ◊ ◗ ❋❋❋

Bergenia cordifolia 'Purpurea'
During late winter this bergenia bears magenta flowers. Its round, green leaves turn reddish-purple in winter; the color is most intense in very cold weather.
‡↔ 20in (50cm) ☼ ☀ ◊ ◗ ❋❋❋

Cynara cardunculus
The cardoon's silver, thistlelike foliage and purple flower heads add a theatrical touch to the border; leave them on the plant as a structural feature over winter.
‡ 6ft (2m) ↔ 3ft (1m) ☼ ◊ ❋❋❋

Dianthus gratianopolitanus
A delightful perennial for the rock garden that forms evergreen mats of narrow, gray-green leaves. Fragrant pink flowers appear in early summer.
‡ 6in (15cm) ↔ 12in (30cm) ☼ ◊ ❋❋❋

Eryngium giganteum
Miss Willmott's ghost makes a dramatic addition to a sunny border with its ruffs of silver bracts. Its architectural flower heads remain attractive into early winter.
‡ 4ft (1.2m) ↔ 12in (30cm) ☼ ◊ ❋❋❋

Helleborus niger
The Christmas rose has leathery, dark green leaves that remain green over winter. Large, white flowers appear in early winter and remain until early spring.
‡↔ 12in (30cm) ☀ ◊ ❋❋❋

Heuchera 'Plum Pudding'
Evergreen heucheras are useful for year-round foliage interest. This cultivar has purple leaves, and its small white flowers are held aloft on thin stems in late spring.
‡ 20in (50cm) ↔ 12in (30cm) ☀ ◊ ❋❋❋

❀❀❀ FULLY HARDY | ❀❀ HARDY IN MILD REGIONS/SHELTERED SITES | ❀ PROTECT FROM FROST OVER THE WINTER | ❀ NO TOLERANCE TO FROST

☼ FULL SUN | ◐ PARTIAL SUN | ❂ FULL SHADE | ◊ WELL-DRAINED SOIL | ◖ MOIST SOIL | ◗ WET SOIL

Iris foetidissima
This iris really comes into its own when the seed pods ripen in the fall and split to reveal glistening orange seeds that remain in place until winter.
‡ 36in (90cm) ↔ indefinite ☼ ❂ ◊ ❀❀❀

Liriope muscari
Lily turf is a neat, spreading perennial that flowers from late summer to late fall. The evergreen foliage makes good ground cover that endures the winter.
‡ 12in (30cm) ↔ 18in (45cm) ◐ ❂ ◊ ◖ ❀❀❀

Miscanthus sinensis 'Gracillimus'
This elegant grass has narrow, arching leaves and silky flower heads that turn from white to purple-brown; it retains a graceful presence throughout winter.
‡ 4ft (1.2m) ↔ 1½ft (45cm) ☼ ◊ ❀❀

Monarda 'Beauty of Cobham'
Flowering during late summer and early fall, this lovely plant bears crowded heads of pink flowers with purple bracts that turn a warm brown in winter.
‡ 36in (90cm) ↔ 18in (45cm) ◐ ❂ ◊ ◖ ❀❀❀

Ophiopogon planiscapus 'Nigrescens'
Few plants are as deeply colored as this small evergreen, black-leaf perennial. It provides a useful contrast in designs where grasses are predominant.
‡ 9in (23cm) ↔ 12in (30cm) ☼ ❂ ◊ ◖ ❀❀❀

Phlomis russeliana
The pale yellow, hooded flowers of this sage-like plant appear throughout summer. During winter the tall stems carry dense brown, spherical seed heads.
‡ 3ft (1m) ↔ 2ft (60cm) ☼ ◊ ❀❀❀

Sedum 'Matrona'
Purple leaves and dark red stems form a backdrop to the flattened heads of tiny pink flowers in summer. The dried flower-heads add structure to the winter garden.
‡ 30in (75cm) ↔ 18in (45cm) ☼ ◊ ❀❀❀

Viola x wittrockiana Universal Series
Winter pansies are among the most prolific of all winter-flowering plants. The color range includes yellow, blue, mauve, maroon, red, and white.
‡ ↔ 8in (20cm) ☼ ◊ ◖ ❀❀❀

ALSO RECOMMENDED

Achillea filipendulina
　(Fern-leaf yarrow)
Chasmanthium latifolium
　(Northern sea oats)
Dianella caerulea Cassa Blue
Echinops ritro (Globe thistle)
Helleborus x *hybridus*
　(Lenten Rose)
Helleborus odorus
Iris unguicularis
Ophiopogon japonicus (Lily turf)
Stipa tenuissima (Feather grass)

WATER AND BOG PLANTS

Astilbe 'Willie Buchanan'
This cultivar produces a haze of pink in
midsummer when its tiny white flowers with
red stamens are borne on fine, branching
flower stems.
‡ 12in (30cm) ↔ 8in (20cm) ☼ ❊ ❋❋❋ ∼

Butomus umbellatus
The flowering rush has narrow leaves that
are bronze when young. Pink, fragrant late-
summer flowers are borne on long stems.
‡ 3ft (1m) ↔ indefinite ☼ ❋❋❋ ≈
♦ 2–6in (5–15cm)

Caltha palustris
Marsh marigolds bring color to pond margins
with intense yellow, cup-shaped blooms in
late spring. Grow in baskets.
‡ 24in (60cm) ↔ 18in (45cm) ☼ ❊ ❋❋❋ ≈
⊥ at water level

Darmera peltata
The umbrella plant bears heads of white to
pink flowers on long stems in late spring. The
large, round leaves gradually turn red in fall
before dying down.
‡ 4ft (1.2m) ↔ indefinite ☼ ❊ ❋❋❋ ∼

Euphorbia palustris
This spurge is an unusual waterside plant.
Strong stems are covered with narrow,
lime-green leaves, topped in early summer
by clusters of light green flowers.
‡↔ 36in (90cm) ☼ ❋❋❋ ∼

Filipendula rubra 'Venusta'
The meadowsweet needs space to spread.
Green jagged leaves sit below wiry stems
bearing a frothy display of deep rose-
pink flowers in summer.
‡ 8ft (2.5m) ↔ 4ft (1.2m) ☼ ❊ ❋❋❋ ∼

Glyceria maxima var. variegata
A handsome perennial grass, suitable
for the water's edge, with strap-shaped,
cream-striped leaves that are tinged shades
of pink in spring and fall.
‡ 30in (80cm) ↔ indefinite ☼ ❋❋❋ ∼

Iris sibirica 'Perry's Blue'
The mid-blue flowers with rust-colored veins
of this traditional cultivar appear in early
summer and brighten the edges of small
ponds and damp borders.
‡ 3ft (1m) ↔ 24in (60cm) ☼ ❋❋ ∼

Ligularia 'The Rocket'
A plant of contrasts with jet black flower
stems and bright yellow flowers that emerge
through a carpet of leaves in late summer; a
must for larger gardens.
‡ 6ft (2m) ↔ 3½ft (1.1m) ☼ ❊ ❋❋❋ ∼

❀❀❀ FULLY HARDY	❀❀ HARDY IN MILD REGIONS/SHELTERED SITES	❀ PROTECT FROM FROST OVER THE WINTER	❀ NO TOLERANCE TO FROST
☼ FULL SUN	☀ PARTIAL SUN	☀ FULL SHADE	~ BOG PLANT	≈ MARGINAL PLANT	≋ AQUATIC PLANT	⊥ PLANTING DEPTH

Myosotis scorpioides
The tiny blooms of the water forget-me-not have white, pink, or yellow eyes and appear in early summer.
↕ 18 in (45 cm) ↔ indefinite ☼ ☀ ❀❀❀
⊥ at water level

Nymphaea 'Froebelii'
Tiny burgundy-red flowers with golden stamens open amid dark green leaves; a perfect water lily for small ponds.
↔ 30 in (75 cm) ☼ ❀❀❀ ≋
⊥ 12–18 in (30–45 cm)

Pontederia cordata
The pickerel weed is a pretty plant with bright green, lance-shaped leaves and spikes of starry blue flowers in summer.
↕ 3–4½ ft (0.9–1.3 m) ↔ 24–30 in (60–75 cm)
☼ ❀❀❀ ≈ ⊥ 12 in (30 cm)

Primula beesiana
A semi-evergreen candelabra primula with vivid magenta, spherical flower heads that appear at intervals up the light green stems during the summer.
↕↔ 24 in (60 cm) ☀ ❀❀❀ ~

Rodgersia pinnata 'Superba'
The young bronze leaves of this plant mature to dark green with distinctive veins. In late summer clusters of bright pink flowers reach above the foliage.
↕ 4 ft (1.2 m) ↔ 30 in (75 cm) ☼ ☀ ❀❀❀ ~

ALSO RECOMMENDED

Actaea simplex
  (Atropurpurea Group) 'Brunette'
Aruncus dioicus 'Kneiffii'
  (Goatsbeard)
Astilbe 'Fanal'
Cardamine pratensis
  (Lady's smock)
Eupatorium purpureum
  (Joe Pye weed)
Gunnera manicata
Hottonia palustris (Water violet)
Hydrocharis morsus-ranae
  (Frogbit)
Iris sibirica 'Butter and Sugar'
Kirengeshoma palmata
Matteuccia struthiopteris
  (Ostrich fern)
Nymphaea 'Gonnère' (Water lily)
Nymphaea 'Marliacea
  Chromatella' (Water lily)
Nymphoides peltata (Water fringe)
Primula alpicola
Primula 'Inverewe'
Rheum palmatum
  'Atrosanguineum'
Sanguisorba canadensis
  (Canadian burnet)

Typha minima
Ideal for small ponds, this perennial has narrow leaves, which are joined in late summer by cylindrical flower spikes.
↕ 30 in (75 cm) ↔ 18 in (45 cm) ☼ ❀❀❀
⊥ 12 in (30 cm)

Zantedeschia aethiopica
The arum lily brings style to bog gardens. Large, pure white flowers, which gleam against the green foliage, open from late spring through to midsummer.
↕↔ 36 in (90 cm) ☼ ❀❀ ≈ ⊥ 6 in (15 cm)

PLANTS FOR SCENT

Cosmos atrosanguineus
The chocolate cosmos is a beautiful spreading perennial that bears cup-shaped, chocolate-scented, dark maroon, velvety flowers in late summer.
‡ 24 in (60 cm) ↔ 18 in (45 cm) ☀ ◊ ◐ ❀❀

***Daphne* x *burkwoodii* 'Somerset'**
A small semi-evergreen shrub, this daphne bears clusters of highly scented, white and pink flowers in late spring, and sometimes again in fall.
‡↔ 5 ft (1.5 m) ☀ ◊ ❀❀❀

***Dianthus* 'Becky Robinson'**
This modern pink bears clove-scented, red-bordered, rose-pink double blooms above strappy, gray-green foliage in summer. Deadhead regularly to promote flowering.
‡ to 18 in (5 cm) ↔ 16 in (40 cm) ☀ ◊ ❀❀❀

***Erysimum cheiri* 'Orange Bedder'**
A small evergreen perennial with green, lance-shaped leaves. From late spring to midsummer it bears dense clusters of brilliant orange, scented flowers.
‡↔ 12 in (30 cm) ☀ ◊ ❀❀❀

***Hamamelis* x *intermedia* 'Arnold Promise'**
In late winter this witch hazel is a welcome sight with a profusion of spidery, yellow, fragrant flowers blooming on its bare, upright branches.
‡↔ 12 ft (4 m) ☀ ✷ ◊ ◐ ❀❀❀

***Jasminum officinale* 'Argenteovariegatum'**
This climbing jasmine has cream-edged, green leaves. The sweetly scented, pure white flowers appear in clusters throughout the summer.
‡ 40 ft (12 m) ☀ ✷ ◊ ❀❀

***Lavandula angustifolia* 'Hidcote'**
This compact lavender with thin, silvery-green leaves and spikes of dark purple, fragrant flowers in summer is an evergreen shrub that is useful for edging.
‡ 24 in (60 cm) ↔ 30 in (75 cm) ☀ ◊ ❀❀❀

***Lilium* 'Star Gazer'**
Both the color and the perfume of this Asian lily attract attention. The upward-facing, pink and white flowers with speckled petals appear in summer.
‡ 3–5 ft (1–1.5 m) ↔ 10 in (25 cm) ☀ ◊ ❀❀❀

***Lonicera periclymenum* 'Belgica'**
Early Dutch honeysuckle is a vigorous climber that bears fragrant, tubular flowers in spring and again in summer, followed by bright red berries in fall.
‡ 22 ft (7 m) ☀ ✷ ◊ ◐ ❀❀❀

Mahonia x media 'Charity'

A beautiful architectural shrub with spiny, dark green leaves. From late fall to early spring it bears spikes of strongly fragrant, lemon yellow flowers.

‡ 15 ft (5 m) ↔ 12 ft (4 m) ☼ ◊ ❋❋

Melissa officinalis 'Aurea'

Lemon balm is a perennial with small white flowers, which attract bees. The leaves are splashed with gold and smell strongly of lemons when crushed.

‡ 48 in (1.2 m) ↔ 18 in (45 cm) ☼ ◊ ❋❋❋

Philadelphus x lemoinei

The arching shoots of this mock orange are smothered in small, deliciously fragrant, creamy-white flowers from early to midsummer.

‡ 5 ft (1.5 m) ↔ 10 ft (3 m) ☼ ◊ ❋❋❋

Rosa 'Gertrude Jekyll'

This hardy shrub rose is grown for its deep pink flowers, which are extremely fragrant and start to appear in early summer. Deadhead regularly.

‡ 6 ft (2 m) ↔ 4 ft (1.2 m) ☼ ◊ ◆ ❋❋❋

Sarcococca hookeriana var. digyna

This robust winter-flowering evergreen has slender, dark green leaves and is prized for its honey-scented, white flowers, followed by black fruit.

‡ 2½ ft (75 cm) ↔ 5 ft (1.5 m) ☼ ◊ ◆ ❋❋

Syringa vulgaris 'Madame Florent Stepman'

An upright lilac with heart-shaped, dark green leaves, it bears spikes of large, sweetly scented, single white flowers in late spring.

‡↔ 20 ft (6 m) ☼ ◊ ❋❋❋

Viburnum x burkwoodii 'Anne Russell'

This semi-evergreen shrub bears clusters of intensely fragrant white flowers from mid- to late spring. Plant it near a pathway to make the most of its scent.

‡↔ 5 ft (1.5 m) ☼ ❋ ◊ ◆ ❋❋❋

ALSO RECOMMENDED

Azara microphylla

Chimonanthus praecox (Wintersweet)

Galium odoratum (Sweet woodruff)

Hemerocallis lilioasphodelus (Daylily)

Hyacinthus orientalis

Jasminum humile (Yellow jasmine)

Lathyrus odoratus (Sweet pea)

Lavandula stoechas subsp. stoechas f. rosea 'Kew Red' (French lavender)

Lonicera etrusca 'Michael Rosse' (Etruscan honeysuckle)

Matthiola incana (Gilliflower)

Mentha suaveolens 'Variegata' (Pineapple mint)

Narcissus tazetta

Nicotiana sylvestris

Nymphaea 'Blue Beauty' (Water lily)

Ornithogalum arabicum

Rosa The Pilgrim ('Auswalker')

Salvia officinalis (Common sage)

Salvia rosmarinus (Rosemary)

Wisteria sinensis 'Prolific'

SHRUBS FOR WALLS

Abelia x grandiflora
A semi-evergreen shrub with glossy, dark green leaves and an abundance of pink-flushed white flowers in summer. Best against a sunny wall in colder areas.
‡ 10ft (3m) ↔ 12ft (4m) ☼ ◊ ◐ ❀❀

Acacia dealbata
Silver wattle is a fast-growing tree with bright yellow, scented flowers that bring a bit of Australian sunshine into the garden in early spring.
‡↔ 50ft (15m) ☼ ◊ ❀❀

Buddleja crispa
The sweetly scented lilac summer flowers of this bushy shrub are highly attractive to bees and butterflies. It has white woolly shoots and grayish-green leaves.
‡↔ 10ft (3m) ☼ ◊ ◐ ❀❀

Carpenteria californica
The tree anemone is an evergreen shrub with glossy, dark green leaves that bears large, fragrant white flowers with showy yellow stamens in the summer.
‡↔ 6ft (2m) ☼ ◊ ❀❀

Ceanothus 'Concha'
A dense, evergreen, glossy-leaf shrub. Masses of purple buds appear in late spring and open up to dark blue flowers. A good choice for a sunny wall or fence.
‡↔ 10ft (3m) ☼ ◊ ◐ ❀❀

Chaenomeles speciosa 'Moerloosei'
Ornamental quinces can be trained against a shaded wall or fence. This variety bears clusters of white flowers, flushed pink, in early summer.
‡ 8ft (2.5m) ↔ 15ft (5m) ☼ ☀ ◊ ◐ ❀❀❀

Crinodendron hookerianum
The lantern tree is an upright, evergreen shrub, so called because of its large, scarlet to crimson-red flowers, which hang from upright shoots in late spring.
‡ 20ft (6m) ↔ 15ft (5m) ☀ ◊ ◐ ❀❀

Cytisus battandieri
The pineapple broom bears bright yellow, upright, pineapple-scented flowers from early to midsummer, above grayish-green leaves. It does best against a warm wall.
‡↔ 15ft (5m) ☼ ◊ ❀❀

Daphne odora 'Aureomarginata'
This evergreen shrub bears clusters of purple-pink and white fragrant flowers from midwinter to early spring among yellow-edged green leaves.
‡↔ 5ft (1.5m) ☼ ◊ ◐ ❀❀

❁❁❁ FULLY HARDY ❁❁ HARDY IN MILD REGIONS/SHELTERED SITES ❁ PROTECT FROM FROST OVER THE WINTER ❁ NO TOLERANCE TO FROST

☼ FULL SUN ☼ PARTIAL SUN ❋ FULL SHADE ◊ WELL-DRAINED SOIL ◖ MOIST SOIL ◗ WET SOIL

Fremontodendron 'California Glory'
This vigorous shrub grows best against a warm, south-facing wall. It bears an abundance of bright yellow flowers between late spring and fall.
‡ 20ft (6m) ↔ 12ft (4m) ☼ ◊ ◖ ❁❁

Garrya elliptica
The silk tassel bush bears waxy, dark green leaves, and between midwinter and late spring, male plants bear dangling gray catkins up to 8in (20cm) long.
‡↔ 12ft (4m) ☼ ❋ ◊ ◖ ❁❁

Jasminum humile
Yellow jasmine is a bushy, evergreen shrub that has bright yellow flowers between early spring and late fall. It flowers best against a warm wall.
‡ 8ft (2.5m) ↔ 10ft (3m) ☼ ❋ ◊ ◖ ❁❁❁

Myrtus communis subsp. tarentina
Ideal for hedging, this evergreen shrub has a long season of interest: its fragrant white flowers, borne between spring and summer, are followed by white berries.
‡↔ 5ft (1.5m) ☼ ◊ ◖ ❁❁

Pyracantha 'Golden Charmer'
The bright orange berries of this spiny shrub provide striking fall interest and are a useful food source for birds. It also bears white flowers in summer.
‡↔ 10ft (3m) ☼ ❋ ❋ ◊ ◖ ❁❁❁

ALSO RECOMMENDED

Abutilon megapotamicum

Acca sellowiana (Pineapple guava)

Acradenia frankliniae

Azara serrata

Ceanothus arboreus 'Trewithen Blue'

Cestrum elegans

Chaenomeles x *superba* 'Crimson and Gold' (Japanese quince)

Dendromecon rigida

Desfontainia spinosa

Drimys lanceolata (Mountain pepper)

Eriobotrya japonica (Loquat)

Fabiana imbricata f. *violacea*

Forsythia suspensa (Golden bells)

Grevillea 'Canberra Gem'

Hydrangea anomala subsp. *petiolaris*

Itea ilicifolia

Piptanthus nepalensis (Evergreen laburnum)

Prostanthera cuneata (Alpine mint bush)

Prostanthera rotundifolia 'Rosea'

Pyracantha 'Mohave'

Ribes speciosum

Stachyurus chinensis 'Joy Forever'
In spring, this deciduous shrub bears dangling clusters of yellow flowers; the leaves that later develop are gold-variegated. It prefers an acid soil.
‡ 6ft (2m) ↔ 12ft (4m) ☼ ❋ ◊ ◖ ❁❁❁

Vestia foetida
From mid-spring to midsummer this upright, evergreen shrub bears hanging clusters of pale yellow flowers. Its glossy dark green leaves are also attractive.
‡ 6ft (2m) ↔ 5ft (1.5m) ☼ ◊ ❁❁

CLIMBERS FOR SHADE

Climbers suitable for cold or shady north- or east-facing walls are those that naturally grow in shade or semi-shade—many of these can become "stressed" and vulnerable to pests if they receive too much hot midday sun. It is important to select suitable plants—the flowers and foliage will suffer in the wrong conditions. Shade-tolerant plants prefer moist soils, so when planting, dig in plenty of organic matter, such as leaf mold, to improve the soil structure. Position young plants at least 18 in (45 cm) from the base of the wall to avoid the driest soil.

CLIMBING PLANTS

Aconitum hemsleyanum

Asteranthera ovata

Celastrus orbiculatus
   (Oriental bittersweet)

Celastrus scandens
   (American bittersweet)

Clematis 'Carnaby'

Clematis 'Helsingborg'

Clematis 'Henryi'

Clematis 'Minuet'

Clematis montana

Clematis 'Niobe'

Clematis 'Venosa Violacea'

Codonopsis clematidea

Codonopsis convolvulacea

Dactylicapnos scandens

Ercilla volubilis

Forsythia suspensa (Golden bells)

Hedera algeriensis
   'Gloire de Marengo'
   (Algerian ivy)

Hedera colchica 'Dentata' (Bullock's heart ivy)

Hedera colchica 'Sulphur Heart'
   (Sulfur heart ivy)

Hedera helix 'Goldheart'

Hydrangea anomala subsp.
   petiolaris (Climbing hydrangea)

Itea ilicifolia

Lapageria rosea (Chilean bellflower)

Lonicera japonica 'Aureoreticulata'

Lonicera japonica 'Halliana'
   (Japanese honeysuckle)

Muehlenbeckia complexa

Parthenocissus henryana
   (Chinese Virginia creeper)

Rosa 'Albéric Barbier'

Rosa 'Danse du Feu'

Rosa 'Händel'

Rosa 'Mermaid'

Schisandra chinensis

Schizophragma hydrangeoides

Vitis amurensis (Amur grape)

***Akebia quinata* (Chocolate vine)**

Ampelopsis brevipedunculata

***Berberidopsis corallina* (Coral plant)**

Clematis montana* var. *rubens

Clematis 'Nelly Moser'

Hydrangea petiolaris
(Climbing hydrangea)

Lonicera periclymenum 'Serotina'
(Honeysuckle)

Parthenocissus tricuspidata
(Boston ivy)

Pileostegia viburnoides

Schisandra rubriflora

Schizophragma integrifolium

Trachelospermum jasminoides
(Star jasmine)

Vitis coignetiae

CLIMBERS FOR SUN

Sun-loving climbers will thrive in the warm, sheltered conditions provided by south- and west-facing walls or fences. Many marginally hardy climbers will fruit or flower better if grown in these conditions, since the wall will absorb the sun's heat during the day and store it, acting like a radiator. However, walls that face the sun are often at risk of producing very dry conditions, so plant climbers at least 18 in (45 cm) from the base of the wall to avoid the driest soil, and dig in organic matter to encourage the soil to retain as much moisture as possible.

CLIMBING PLANTS

Akebia trifoliata
Clematis 'Bill MacKenzie'
Clematis cirrhosa var.
 purpurascens 'Freckles'
Clematis 'Étoile Violette'
Clematis 'Jackmanii'
Clematis 'Lasurstern'
Clematis rehderiana
Clematis 'The President'
Jasminum officinale
 'Argenteovariegatum'
 (Common jasmine)
Jasminum x *stephanense*
Hardenbergia violacea
 (Purple coral pea)
Lonicera x *italica* (Honeysuckle)
Lonicera x *tellmanniana*
 (Honeysuckle)
Parthenocissus tricuspidata
 'Veitchii' (Virginia creeper)
Passiflora caerulea
 'Constance Eliot' (Blue passion flower)

Rosa 'Compassion'
Rosa filipes 'Kiftsgate'
Rosa 'Gloire de Dijon'
Rosa 'Golden Showers'
Rosa 'Madame Alfred Carrière'
Rosa 'Maigold'
Solanum laxum (Potato vine)
Tecoma capensis
 (Cape honeysuckle)
Thunbergia alata
 (Black-eyed Susan)
Trachelospermum asiaticum
Vitis 'Brant'
Vitis davidii
Vitis vinifera 'Purpurea'
Wisteria floribunda 'Alba'
 (Japanese wisteria)
Wisteria sinensis 'Prolific'
 (Chinese wisteria)

Actinidia kolomikta

Campsis x tagliabuana
'Madame Galen'

Clematis armandii

Eccremocarpus scaber
(Chilean glory flower)

Humulus lupulus '**Aureus**'
(Golden hop)

Ipomoea purpurea **(Common morning glory)**

Parthenocissus quinquefolia
(Virginia creeper)

Passiflora caerulea
(Blue passion flower)

Rhodochiton atrosanguineus

Rosa banksiae '**Lutea**'

Solanum crispum '**Glasnevin**'
(Potato tree)

Tropaeolum speciosum **(Flame creeper)**

Wisteria brachybotrys '**Shiro-kapitan**'

SCREENING AND HEDGING PLANTS

Hedges and plant screens can be used to define the garden or areas within it and also to provide wind protection or shelter. The plants you choose for screening or hedging need to fit your garden's design, and be resilient enough to withstand the forces of wind and weather—check to see if they will grow tall enough to do the job. Fast-growing types are useful because they can provide quick results but will result in a hedge that needs frequent clipping. Bamboos and grasses are worth considering since they make an attractive alternative to a traditional hedge.

TREES
Arbutus unedo (Strawberry tree)
Chamaecyparis lawsoniana (Lawson's cypress)
Juniperus communis (Common juniper)
Nothofagus dombeyi
Olea europaea (Olive)
Populus x *canadensis* 'Robusta' (Canadian poplar)
Prunus lusitanica (Laurel)
Umbellularia californica (California laurel)

SHRUBS
Berberis thunbergii f. *atropurpurea* 'Rose Glow'
Buxus sempervirens 'Suffruticosa' (Dwarf boxwood)
Cotoneaster salicifolius
Elaeagnus umbellata
Escallonia 'Donard Beauty'
Euonymus japonicus 'Macrophyllus' (Japanese euonymus)
Forsythia x *intermedia*

Griselinia littoralis (Broadleaf)
Hibiscus rosa-sinensis (Chinese hibiscus)
Leptospermum scoparium (Manuka)
Ligustrum ovalifolium
Pyracantha 'Watereri'
Rhododendron 'Loderi King George'
Rhododendron 'Furnivall's Daughter'
Rosa gallica 'Versicolor'
Tamarix ramosissima
Viburnum tinus 'Eve Price'

GRASSES AND BAMBOOS
Arundo donax (Giant reed)
Chimonobambusa tumidissinoda
Cortaderia selloana 'Sunningdale Silver' (Pampas grass)
Fargesia nitida (Fountain bamboo)
Miscanthus sinensis
Phyllostachys flexuosa
Pseudosasa japonica
Semiarundinaria fastuosa (Narihira bamboo)

SHRUB: *Aucuba japonica* **'Gold Dust'** **(Spotted laurel)**

SHRUB: *Berberis darwinii*

TREE: *Carpinus betulus* **(Common hornbeam)**

SHRUB: *Cotoneaster lacteus*

TREE: *Crataegus laevigata* **'Paul's Scarlet' (Hawthorn)**

SHRUB: *Hydrangea paniculata* 'Floribunda'

SHRUB: *Ilex aquifolium* 'Madame Briot' (Holly)

TREE: *Laurus nobilis* (Bay laurel)

SHRUB: *Ligustrum obtusifolium* (Privet)

SHRUB: *Lonicera nitida* 'Baggesen's Gold' (Honeysuckle)

SHRUB: *Photinia* x *fraseri* 'Red Robin'

TREE: *Taxus baccata* (Yew)

SHRUB: *Pittosporum tenuifolium* 'Abbotsbury Gold' (Kohuhu)

SHRUB: *Rhododendron* 'Hydon Dawn'

ROCK PLANTS

Campanula cochlearifolia
Masses of pale blue or white bell-shaped flowers adorn this dwarf campanula in midsummer—the toothed, bright green leaves form rosettes beneath them.
↕ 3 in (8 cm) ↔ indefinite ☼ ☀ ◊ ❀❀❀

Convolvulus sabatius
This trailing plant produces its trumpet-shaped, bright lavender-blue flowers from summer to fall, set against small, mid-green oval leaves.
↕ 8 in (20 cm) ↔ 12 in (30 cm) ☼ ◊ ❀❀

Dianthus 'Pike's Pink'
Fragrant, pink, double flowers are produced in summer; the evergreen foliage is gray-green and spiky, forming compact cushions.
↕↔ 4 in (10 cm) ☼ ◊ ❀❀❀

Diascia 'Salmon Supreme'
This trailing herbaceous perennial bears spikes of salmon-pink tubular flowers rising from heart-shaped green foliage in summer and through to fall.
↕ 6 in (15 cm) ↔ 20 in (50 cm) ☼ ◊ ❀❀

Erigeron karvinskianus
A carpeting perennial with gray-green foliage and daisylike summer flowers in white or pink, aging to purple, this plant spreads freely once it is established.
↕ 4–6 in (10–15 cm) ↔ indefinite ☼ ◊ ❀❀❀

Erinus alpinus
In late spring and summer, small purple or pink flowers are profusely borne on this semi-evergreen perennial. It is short lived but self-seeds freely.
↕↔ 2–3 in (5–8 cm) ☼ ◊ ❀❀❀

Erysimum 'Bredon'
Clusters of bright yellow flowers, highly attractive to beneficial insects, are produced from spring to summer on a bushy, semi-evergreen perennial plant.
↕↔ 18 in (45 cm) ☼ ◊ ❀❀❀

Gentiana verna
This evergreen perennial produces small rosettes of dark green leaves. In early spring bright blue flowers with white centers are borne on short stems.
↕↔ 2 in (5 cm) ☼ ◊ ❀❀❀

Hebe pinguifolia 'Pagei'
Evergreen, oval blue-green leaves are carried on purple stems, against which the abundant clusters of white flowers stand out in summer.
↕ 12 in (30 cm) ↔ 36 in (90 cm) ☼ ☀ ◊ ◑ ❀❀❀

❀❀❀ FULLY HARDY ❀❀ HARDY IN MILD REGIONS/SHELTERED SITES ❀ PROTECT FROM FROST OVER THE WINTER ❀ NO TOLERANCE TO FROST

☼ FULL SUN ☼ PARTIAL SUN ❀ FULL SHADE ◊ WELL-DRAINED SOIL ◐ MOIST SOIL ● WET SOIL

Helianthemum apenninum
Saucer-shaped white flowers with bright
yellow stamens are borne on this shrub
in midsummer. The stems and evergreen
leaves are covered with white down.
↕↔ 18 in (45 cm) ☼ ◊ ❀❀❀

Phlox bifida
Masses of slender-petaled, star-shaped,
lilac or white flowers appear in summer,
smothering the mound-forming stems
and evergreen leaves.
↕ 4–6 in (10–15 cm) ↔ 6 in (15 cm) ☼ ◊ ❀❀❀

Saponaria ocymoides
Soapwort forms a sprawling carpet of
soft, hairy leaves, above which masses of
tiny pale pink flowers appear in summer.
Excellent for a dry bank.
↕ to 3 in (8 cm) ↔ 16 in (40 cm) ☼ ◊ ❀❀❀

Saxifraga 'Hindhead Seedling'
This low-growing evergreen perennial has
slender, spiky, blue-green foliage; in spring it
bears open, cup-shaped pale yellow flowers
with bright yellow stamens.
↕ 1 in (2.5 cm) ↔ 3 in (8 cm) ☼ ◊ ❀❀❀

Scabiosa lucida
A clump-forming dwarf perennial with
finely cut gray-green leaves, *S. lucida*
bears lavender-blue pincushion
flowers from late spring to summer.
↕ 8 in (20 cm) ↔ 6 in (15 cm) ☼ ◊ ❀❀❀

ALSO RECOMMENDED

Anchusa caespitosa

Androsace sempervivoides

Aquilegia alpina
(Alpine columbine)

Armeria maritima 'Vindictive'
(Sea thrift)

Aster alpinus

Aubrieta 'Purple Charm'

Calceolaria arachnoidea

Crambe maritima (Sea kale)

Daphne jasminea

Daphne petraea 'Grandiflora'

Dianthus alpinus (Alpine pink)

Draba mollissima

Draba rigida

Gentiana acaulis
(Stemless gentian)

Geranium orientalitibeticum

Lewisia 'George Henley'

Lithodora oleifolia

Osteospermum jucundum

Penstemon newberryi f. *humilior*

Potentilla 'Gibson's Scarlet'

Saxifraga 'Jenkinsiae'

Saxifraga scardica

Sisyrinchium 'E.K. Balls'

Vitaliana primuliflora

Sempervivum tectorum
Rosettes of broad, pointed leaves are tipped
with purple, sometimes turning purple-red
in summer. The star-shaped, reddish-purple
flowers bloom in summer.
↕ 4–6 in (10–15 cm) ↔ 8 in (20 cm) ☼ ◊ ❀❀❀

Thymus 'Bressingham'
A compact, carpeting, scented thyme,
'Bressingham' has small, hairy, gray-green
leaves and bears clear pink flowers from
early to midsummer.
↕ 1¼ in (3 cm) ↔ 5 in (12 cm) ☼ ◊ ❀❀❀

SPRING-FLOWERING SHRUBS

Abeliophyllum distichum
The white forsythia bears clusters of white, fragrant flowers in early spring; it flowers more freely grown against a sunny wall. Its dark green leaves turn purple in the fall.
↕↔ 4 ft (1.5 m) ☼ ◊ ❀❀❀

Berberis julianae
Ideal as a screen, this evergreen shrub has glossy, deep green leaves. From spring to summer clusters of scented yellow flowers appear, followed by blue-black fruits.
↕↔ 10 ft (3 m) ☼ ☀ ◊ ❀❀❀

Camellia x williamsii 'Donation'
This evergreen, shade-loving shrub bears semi-double, rich pink blooms through mid- and late spring. It requires acid soil and is suitable for growing in a large pot.
↕ 15 ft (5 m) ↔ 8 ft (2.5 m) ☀ ◊ ◑ ❀❀❀

Ceanothus thyrsiflorus 'Skylark'
This bushy shrub with glossy green leaves bears a profusion of deep blue flowers in late spring. In cold areas it benefits from the protection of a warm wall.
↕ 6 ft (2 m) ↔ 5 ft (1.5 m) ☼ ◊ ❀❀

Chaenomeles x superba 'Pink Lady'
In early spring clusters of deep, rose-pink flowers appear on the bare branches of this showy Japanese quince, followed in fall by apple-shaped, yellow fruits.
↕ 5 ft (1.5 m) ↔ 6 ft (2 m) ☼ ☀ ◊ ❀❀❀

Corylopsis sinensis var. sinensis 'Spring Purple'
This shrub bears hanging clusters of yellow flowers that will brighten up the garden in spring. It produces purple foliage that develops to green with age.
↕↔ 12 ft (4 m) ☀ ◑ ◊ ❀❀❀

Cytisus x praecox 'Allgold'
This ornamental broom is smothered by a mass of pealike, golden-yellow flowers from mid- to late spring. Its tiny, silky, gray-green leaves are borne on arching stems.
↕ 4 ft (1.2 m) ↔ 5 ft (1.5 m) ☼ ◊ ❀❀

Daphne cneorum
A low-growing, trailing shrub with clusters of scented, rose-pink flowers in late spring; position to make the most of its fragrance. The leaves are leathery and dark green.
↕ 9 in (23 cm) ↔ 6 ft (2 m) ☼ ◊ ❀❀❀

Erica arborea var. alpina
This tree heath is an upright shrub, densely covered with honey-scented, white flowers from late winter to late spring. The dark green, needlelike leaves are evergreen.
↕ 6 ft (2 m) ↔ 34 in (85 cm) ☼ ◊ ❀❀❀

❀❀❀ FULLY HARDY ❀❀ HARDY IN MILD REGIONS/SHELTERED SITES ❀ PROTECT FROM FROST OVER THE WINTER ❀ NO TOLERANCE TO FROST

☼ FULL SUN ☀ PARTIAL SUN ☀ FULL SHADE ◊ WELL-DRAINED SOIL ◐ MOIST SOIL ● WET SOIL

Exochorda x macrantha 'The Bride'
Pure white, showy, saucer-shaped flowers on arching branches cover this spreading evergreen shrub in late spring. It is ideal for growing as a specimen plant.
‡ 6ft (2m) ↔ 10ft (3m) ☼ ☀ ◊ ◐ ❀❀❀

Forsythia x intermedia 'Lynwood'
A vigorous, deciduous shrub with upright stems that arch slightly at the tips. An abundance of bright golden-yellow flowers appear on bare branches in early spring.
‡↔ 10ft (3m) ☼ ☀ ◊ ❀❀❀

Fothergilla major
Bearing spikes of bottlebrush-like, fragrant white flowers in late spring, this slow-growing shrub is also valued for its blaze of orange, yellow, and red fall leaves.
‡↔ 20ft (6m) ☀ ◐ ❀❀❀

Kolkwitzia amabilis 'Pink Cloud'
The beauty bush is a deciduous shrub with an arching style. Bell-shaped, pink flowers with yellow flushed throats are borne in profusion from late spring to early summer.
‡ 10ft (3m) ↔ 12ft (4m) ☼ ◊ ❀❀❀

Magnolia stellata
The star magnolia bears pure white or pink-flushed, star-shaped flowers in early spring, before the leaves emerge. Spring frosts may damage early blooms.
‡ 10ft (3m) ↔ 12ft (4m) ☼ ☀ ◊ ◐ ❀❀❀

Osmanthus x burkwoodii
This evergreen shrub is grown for its glossy leaves and clusters of tiny, creamy-white, trumpet-shaped flowers, which are sweetly scented and appear in mid-spring.
‡↔ 10ft (3m) ☼ ☀ ◊ ❀❀

Paeonia delavayi var. ludlowii
In late spring the nodding, glossy, bright yellow flowers of this vigorous tree peony open among its deeply cut, bright green leaves. The flowers are attractive to bees.
‡ 6ft (2m) ↔ 9ft (3m) ☼ ☀ ◊ ◐ ❀❀❀

Philadelphus 'Belle Etoile'
This mock orange is an arching, deciduous shrub with tapering leaves. Its fragrant, single white flowers have a maroon center and are freely borne in late spring.
‡ 4ft (1.2m) ↔ 8ft (2.5m) ☼ ☀ ◊ ❀❀❀

Prunus laurocerasus 'Zabeliana'
The evergreen cherry laurel looks its best in spring when long spikes of fragrant white flowers appear. 'Zabeliana' has a low, spreading style, ideal for ground cover.
‡ 3ft (1m) ↔ 8ft (2.5m) ☼ ☀ ◊ ◐ ❀❀❀

SPRING-FLOWERING SHRUBS CONTINUED

Prunus x cistena
A slow-growing, ornamental cherry with glossy oval leaves that are red when young, maturing to purple. Delicate white flowers appear in late spring.
‡↔ 5 ft (1.5 m) ☼ ◊ ❋❋❋

Rhododendron 'Hotspur'
Azaleas are unsurpassed for vivid spring color, and 'Hotspur' is no exception with its clusters of flame-red flowers. It also has brightly colored fall foliage.
‡↔ 6 ft (2 m) ☼ ☀ ◊ ❋❋❋

Ribes sanguineum 'Pulborough Scarlet'
This flowering currant has aromatic leaves and bears clusters of dark red, white-centered, tubular flowers in spring, followed by blue-black berries.
‡ 6 ft (2 m) ↔ 8 ft (2.5 m) ☼ ◊ ❋❋❋

Spiraea 'Arguta'
At its peak in late spring, bridal wreath presents a marvelous display, with masses of white flowers carried all along the upper sides of its arching stems.
‡ 6 ft (2 m) ↔ 5 ft (1.5 m) ☼ ◊ ◊ ❋❋❋

Syringa meyeri 'Palibin'
This dwarf lilac has a neat, rounded shape and small, dark green oval leaves. It bears abundant clusters of fragrant, lavender-pink flowers in late spring.
‡↔ 5 ft (1.5 m) ☼ ◊ ❋❋❋

ALSO RECOMMENDED

Berberis darwinii
  (Darwin's barberry)

Berberis valdiviana

Chaenomeles speciosa 'Snow'

Corylopsis glabrescens

Deutzia x rosea

Dipelta floribunda

Edgeworthia chrysantha

Enkianthus cernuus f. *rubens*

Genista tinctoria
  (Dyer's greenweed)

Hamamelis x intermedia
  'Barmstedt Gold' (Witch hazel)

Hamamelis x intermedia 'Jelena'
  (Witch hazel)

Leptospermum scoparium
  'Red Damask' (Manuka)

Lindera benzoin (Spicebush)

Malus toringo

Pieris japonica

Rhododendron 'Percy Wiseman'

Ribes sanguineum 'King Edward VII'
  (Flowering currant)

Staphylea pinnata (Bladdernut)

Telopea truncata
  (Tasmanian waratah)

Viburnum bitchiuense

Viburnum plicatum f. tomentosum 'Mariesii' With its horizontal branches this shrub creates a striking architectural effect. The flowers are white, and the dark green leaves turn red-purple in the fall.
‡ 10 ft (3 m) ↔ 12 ft (4 m) ☼ ◊ ❋❋❋

Weigela florida 'Foliis Purpureis'
Funnel-shaped flowers, deep pink on the outside and white inside, appear in spring and look striking against the bronze-green foliage of this dark-leaf cultivar.
‡ 3 ft (1 m) ↔ 5 ft (1.5 m) ☼ ◊ ❋❋❋

SUMMER-FLOWERING SHRUBS

Buddleja globosa
This eye-catching shrub bears bright, orange-yellow balls of honey-scented flowers above its handsome, dark green leaves in early summer.
↕↔ 15 ft (5 m) ☼ ◊ ❄❄

Caryopteris x clandonensis 'Worcester Gold'
The small but vivid, lavender-blue flowers of this pretty shrub appear in late summer and stand out against the warm yellow, deciduous foliage.
↕ 3 ft (1 m) ↔ 5 ft (1.5 m) ☼ ◊ ❄❄❄

Ceanothus x delilenus 'Gloire de Versailles'
A fast-growing, evergreen bushy shrub with glossy foliage and large, pale blue flowers in mid- to late summer. A good choice for a sunny wall.
↕↔ 5 ft (1.5 m) ☼ ◊ ❄❄

Ceratostigma willmottianum
The hardy plumbago bears pale to mid-blue flowers in late summer, and its dark green, purple-margined leaves turn shades of red in the fall.
↕ 3 ft (1 m) ↔ 5 ft (1.5 m) ☼ ◊ ◑ ❄❄❄

Choisya x dewitteana 'Aztec Pearl'
An elegant Mexican orange blossom with slim dark green leaves. Fragrant clusters of white, star-shaped flowers emerge from pink buds in late spring to early summer.
↕↔ 8 ft (2.5 m) ☼ ◊ ❄❄❄

Convolvulus cneorum
With its silky, silvery leaves this shrub is an asset even when not in bloom. The delicate, funnel-shaped white flowers appear from late spring to summer.
↕ 2 ft (60 cm) ↔ 3 ft (1 m) ☼ ◊ ❄❄

Deutzia x elegantissima 'Rosealind'
Stunning when grown in the border or as a specimen plant, this sun-loving shrub bears thousands of star-shaped, pale pink flowers in early summer.
↕ 4 ft (1.2 m) ↔ 5 ft (1.5 m) ☼ ◊ ❄❄❄

Hebe 'Midsummer Beauty'
This adaptable, evergreen shrub, with purplish-brown stems and bright green leaves, bears tapering plumes of lilac flowers from midsummer to fall.
↕ 6 ft (2 m) ↔ 5 ft (1.5 m) ☼ ☀ ◊ ◑ ❄❄❄

Helianthemum 'Wisley Primrose'
A sun-loving rock rose that forms low mounds of evergreen, gray-green foliage and bears plenty of saucer-shaped, pale yellow flowers throughout summer.
↕ 9 in (23 cm) ↔ 12 in (30 cm) ☼ ◊ ❄❄❄

SUMMER-FLOWERING SHRUBS CONTINUED

Hibiscus syriacus 'Woodbridge'
Exotic flowers are the main allure of hibiscus cultivars. In late summer 'Woodbridge' produces a succession of large, pink flowers with deep red centers.
↕↔ 10ft (3m) ☼ ◊ ❀❀❀

Hydrangea macrophylla 'Mariesii Lilacina'
A handsome, free-standing hydrangea grown for its showy, mauve-pink to blue, lacecap flowers, which appear in midsummer.
↕ 6ft (2m) ↔ 8ft (2.5m) ☼ ☀ ◊ ◔ ❀❀❀

Hydrangea paniculata 'Unique'
In midsummer this beautiful cultivar bears large, creamy-white flower heads that develop pink tints as they age, and its leaves turn yellow before falling.
↕ 22ft (7m) ↔ 8ft (2.5m) ☼ ☀ ◊ ◔ ❀❀❀

Hypericum 'Hidcote'
The arching branches of 'Hidcote' are covered with lance-shaped leaves, and throughout summer clusters of golden yellow flowers are borne in profusion.
↕ 4ft (1.2m) ↔ 5ft (1.5m) ☼ ◊ ❀❀❀

Lavandula stoechas
In early summer French lavender bears dense spikes of fragrant, dark purple flowers, topped by rose-purple bracts, on long stalks above silvery-gray leaves.
↕↔ 24in (60cm) ☼ ◊ ❀❀

Magnolia liliiflora 'Nigra'
One of the most reliable magnolias, this beautiful cultivar produces large, dark purple-red upright flowers in early summer and intermittently into fall.
↕ 10ft (3m) ↔ 8ft (2.5m) ☼ ☀ ◊ ◔ ❀❀❀

Myrtus communis 'Flore Pleno'
Myrtle is a sun-loving, evergreen Mediterranean shrub with aromatic foliage. Masses of pretty, fragrant white pom-pom flowers appear in late summer.
↕↔ 10ft (3m) ☼ ◊ ◔ ❀❀

Nandina domestica
The leaves of this evergreen shrub have red tints in spring and fall, and small, star-shaped white flowers emerge in midsummer, followed by red berries.
↕ 6ft (2m) ↔ 5ft (1.5m) ☼ ◊ ◔ ❀❀❀

Paeonia delavayi
In early summer this magnificent tree peony produces single, dark crimson flowers on long, lax stems. The dark green leaves are tinged burgundy in spring.
↕↔ 6ft (2m) ☼ ◊ ❀❀❀

Phygelius x rectus 'African Queen'
This evergreen shrub has graceful upward-curving branches. The long, tubular flowers, produced in midsummer, are soft red with yellow inside.
‡ 3 ft (1 m) ↔ 4 ft (1.2 m) ☼ ◊ ◔ ❀❀

Potentilla fruticosa 'Red Ace'
This shrub-like cinquefoil bears orange-red, single flowers, which contrast well with the small, divided leaves. It blooms from late spring to early fall.
‡ 3 ft (1 m) ↔ 5 ft (1.5 m) ☀ ◊ ❀❀❀

Rosa 'Geranium'
A spectacular shrub rose with arching branches and dark green leaves. Masses of scarlet flowers appear in early summer, followed by orange-red hips in fall.
‡ 8 ft (2.5 m) ↔ 5 ft (1.5 m) ☼ ◊ ◔ ❀❀❀

Rosa glauca
This delicate shrub has striking, deep purple stems and elegant gray-purple foliage. Clusters of clear pink flowers in early summer are followed by red hips.
‡ 6 ft (2 m) ↔ 5 ft (1.5 m) ☼ ◊ ❀❀❀

Rosa 'Roseraie de l'Hay'
A hardy rugosa shrub rose with attractive light green foliage that produces richly scented, velvety, purple-red flowers throughout summer.
‡ 7 ft (2.2 m) ↔ 6 ft (2 m) ☼ ◊ ❀❀❀

ALSO RECOMMENDED

Abutilon vitifolium 'Veronica Tennant'

Cistus x *cyprius*

Clethra delavayi

Crinodendron patagua

Cuphea cyanea

Escallonia 'Apple Blossom'

Fuchsia magellanica 'Thompsonii'

Genista cinerea

Hebe 'Bowles' Variety'

Hypericum x *inodorum* 'Elstead'

Hyssopus officinalis (Hyssop)

Indigofera dielsiana

Kalmia latifolia (Calico bush)

Lavatera x *clementii* 'Rosea'

Olearia ilicifolia (Mountain holly)

Penstemon isophyllus

Philadelphus 'Beauclerk' (Mock orange)

Potentilla fruticosa 'Abbotswood'

Spartium junceum (Spanish broom)

Spiraea japonica 'Goldflame'

Syringa vulgaris 'Katherine Havemeyer'

Tamarix ramosissima

Sambucus nigra f. porphyrophylla 'Eva'
This graceful elder's dark purple, lacy foliage provides color contrast in a mixed border. Showy, pale pink, flattened flower heads appear in early summer.
‡ 10 ft (3 m) ↔ 6 ft (2 m) ☼ ☀ ◊ ◔ ❀❀❀

Spiraea nipponica 'Snowmound'
At its peak in early summer this spirea gives a marvelous display, with clusters of white flowers carried all along the upper sides of the arching stems.
‡↔ 8 ft (2.5 m) ☼ ◊ ◔ ❀❀❀

SHRUBS FOR FALL INTEREST

***Acer palmatum* 'Atropurpureum'**
The leaves of this small, elegant tree open
crimson in spring, mature to purple-red,
and then turn a fiery red that blazes in the
fall garden.
‡ 25 ft (8 m) ↔ 30 ft (10 m) ☼ ◊ ✹✹✹

Berberis* x *ottawensis* f. *purpurea
'Superba' With graceful arching branches
this large shrub has an attractive look and
also offers red berries and purplish leaves
that turn bright crimson in fall.
‡↔ 8 ft (2.5 m) ☼ ☀ ◊ ✹✹✹

Callicarpa bodinieri* var. *giraldii
'Profusion' An upright shrub providing
interest from bronze-green leaves in spring,
pink flowers in summer, and long-lasting
violet berries in fall.
‡ 10 ft (3 m) ↔ 8 ft (2.5 m) ☼ ☀ ◊ ◊ ✹✹

***Calluna vulgaris* 'Robert Chapman'**
A heather with a spreading style, bearing
mauve-pink flowers. It has dense, golden-
yellow foliage that turns orange in fall then
red in winter and spring.
‡ 10 in (25 cm) ↔ 26 in (65 cm) ☼ ◊ ✹✹✹

Clerodendrum trichotomum
From late summer to mid-fall this
treelike, large-leaf shrub produces
fragrant white flowers, followed by
attractive blue berries.
‡↔ 15–20 ft (5–6 m) ☼ ◊ ◊ ✹✹✹

***Cotinus* 'Grace'**
The purple foliage of *C*. 'Grace' turns a
brilliant translucent red in fall. A fast-growing
shrub or small tree, it bears tiny pink-purple
flowers in summer.
‡ 20 ft (6 m) ↔ 15 ft (5 m) ☼ ☀ ◊ ◊ ✹✹✹

***Cotoneaster salicifolius* 'Gnom'**
The profusion of berries this dwarf shrub
bears mature to red in fall and last into
winter, when the slender, glossy, dark
green leaves take on a bronze tinge.
‡ 1 ft (30 cm) ↔ 6 ft (2 m) ☼ ◊ ✹✹✹

Disanthus cercidifolius
This rounded, deciduous shrub produces
dark red flowers in fall, when the heart-
shaped leaves turn shades of yellow,
orange, purple, and red.
‡↔ 10 ft (3 m) ☀ ◊ ✹✹

Euonymus alatus
A dense, bushy, deciduous shrub, *E. alatus*
puts on a spectacular fall display of purple
and red fruits as the dark green leaves turn
to scarlet.
‡ 6 ft (2 m) ↔ 10 ft (3 m) ☼ ☀ ◊ ✹✹✹

❀❀❀ FULLY HARDY　　❀❀ HARDY IN MILD REGIONS/SHELTERED SITES　　❀ PROTECT FROM FROST OVER THE WINTER　❀ NO TOLERANCE TO FROST

☼ FULL SUN　　☼ PARTIAL SUN　　☀ FULL SHADE　　◊ WELL-DRAINED SOIL　　◊ MOIST SOIL　　◆ WET SOIL

Fothergilla major
In spring this upright, slow-growing shrub produces bottlebrush-like white flower heads; fall turns the dark green leaves orange, yellow, and red.
‡ 8 ft (2.5 m)　↔ 6 ft (2 m)　☼ ◊ ❀❀❀

Hydrangea quercifolia **'Snow Queen'**
The large, oak leaf–shaped foliage of this shrub turns from green to striking shades of coral and red in fall while the white flowers fade through pink to brown.
‡ 6 ft (2 m)　↔ 8 ft (2.5 m)　☼ ☼ ◊ ◊ ❀❀❀

Itea ilicifolia
Tiny, greenish-white flowers open in long, catkin-like plumes from summer through to fall, standing out against the glossy dark green leaves.
‡ 10–15 ft (3–5 m)　↔ 10 ft (3 m)　☼ ◊ ❀❀❀

Rhus glabra
From the reddish-purple stems of this bushy shrub grow slender, deep blue-green leaves that turn red in fall. Female plants bear red fruits.
‡ 8 ft (2.5 m)　↔ 6 ft (2 m)　☼ ◊ ❀❀❀

Sambucus racemosa **'Plumosa Aurea'**
Deeply cut leaves, bronzed when young, mature to golden yellow and take on a red tinge in fall. The creamy flowers are followed by red berries in summer.
‡↔ 10 ft (3 m)　☼ ☼ ◊ ◊ ❀❀❀

ALSO RECOMMENDED

Acer palmatum var. *heptalobum* (Japanese maple)

Berberis x *carminea* 'Barbarossa'

Berberis thunbergii f. *atropurpurea* 'Rose Glow'

Callicarpa bodinieri var. *giraldii* (Beautyberry)

Cornus alba 'Sibirica Variegata'

Cotinus 'Flame' (Smoke bush)

Decaisnea fargesii

Euonymus hamiltonianus 'Red Elf'

Euonymus oxyphyllus

Fothergilla gardenii (Witch alder)

Gaultheria tasmanica

Hamamelis virginiana (Witch hazel)

Hippophae rhamnoides (Sea buckthorn)

Leonotis leonurus (Lion's tail)

Rhus typhina 'Dissecta' (Stag's horn sumac)

Rosa 'Geranium'

Ruscus aculeatus (Butcher's broom)

Vaccinium angustifolium var. *laevifolium* (Low-bush blueberry)

Vaccinium parvifolium (Red bilberry)

Sorbus reducta
This deciduous shrub forms a low thicket of dense, upright branches, carrying finely divided gray-green leaves that turn to shades of red and purple in fall.
‡↔ 12 in (30 cm)　☼ ◊ ❀❀❀

Viburnum opulus
The guelder rose bears flattened heads of white flowers in spring and summer, followed by bright red fruits and reddening leaves in fall.
‡ 15 ft (5 m)　↔ 12 ft (4 m)　☼ ☼ ◊ ◊ ❀❀❀

SHRUBS FOR WINTER INTEREST

Azara microphylla
This upright, shrubby evergreen tree has attractively glossy dark green oval leaves; from late winter to spring it produces clusters of vanilla-scented yellow flowers.
↕ 30ft (10m) ↔ 12ft (4m) ☼ ◊ ❀❀

Chimonanthus praecox 'Grandiflorus'
An upright, deciduous shrub with lance-shaped green leaves, this plant is prized for the very fragrant, deep yellow flowers borne on bare winter stems.
↕ 12ft (4m) ↔ 10ft (3m) ☼ ◊ ❀❀❀

Cornus alba 'Sibirica'
The main attraction here is the bright coral-red stems that are exposed in winter; cutting back hard in spring produces the best results.
↕↔ 10ft (3m) ☼ ◊ ❀❀❀

Cornus mas
A vigorous shrub or small tree, *C. mas* offers red fall foliage and fruits but is most notable in winter, when its bare branches are adorned with yellow flowers.
↕↔ 15ft (5m) ☼ ☀ ◊ ❀❀❀

Corylus avellana 'Contorta'
Its twisted shoots give the corkscrew hazel its name, and in winter, when they are free of leaves, long pale yellow catkins dangle from them.
↕↔ 20ft (6m) ☼ ◊ ❀❀❀

Cotoneaster lacteus
This evergreen shrub has handsome dark green leaves; white flowers in summer are succeeded by large clusters of bright red berries that last into winter.
↕↔ 12ft (4m) ☼ ◊ ❀❀❀

Daphne bholua 'Jacqueline Postill'
The midwinter flowers of this evergreen *Daphne* are pink to purple with white or pale pink centers; their intense fragrance is a delight in colder months.
↕ 6ft (2m) ↔ 5ft (1.5m) ☼ ◊ ❀❀❀

Elaeagnus x ebbingei 'Gilt Edge'
Broad, rich golden margins on the evergreen leaves make 'Gilt Edge' a cheerful sight in winter; the fall flowers are small but very fragrant.
↕↔ 12ft (4m) ☼ ◊ ❀❀❀

Hamamelis x intermedia 'Pallida'
Fall leaf shades of yellow, orange, and red are followed by strongly scented sulfur-yellow flowers on bare branches, growing in graceful arched tiers.
↕↔ 12ft (4m) ☼ ☀ ◊ ♦ ❀❀❀

❋❋❋ FULLY HARDY   ❋❋ HARDY IN MILD REGIONS/SHELTERED SITES   ❋ PROTECT FROM FROST OVER THE WINTER   ❋ NO TOLERANCE TO FROST

☼ FULL SUN   ☀ PARTIAL SUN   ❋ FULL SHADE   ◊ WELL-DRAINED SOIL   ◊ MOIST SOIL   ◊ WET SOIL

Jasminum nudiflorum
Winter jasmine has arching green stems, covered with dark green leaves in the growing season; they are replaced by bright yellow flowers in midwinter.
↕↔ 10ft (3m) ☼ ☀ ◊ ❋❋❋

Mahonia japonica
The dark green, spiny leaves of this upright shrub are complemented by long sprays of fragrant yellow flowers from late fall to early spring.
↕ 6ft (2m) ↔ 10ft (3m) ☀ ◊ ◊ ❋❋❋

Salix hastata 'Wehrhahnii'
In winter the bare purple-brown stems of this small, slow-growing, upright willow contrast beautifully with soft silvery-gray catkins.
↕↔ 3ft (1m) ☼ ◊ ❋❋❋

Sarcococca hookeriana var. digyna
A dense, spreading shrub with slender evergreen leaves, this plant produces tiny, fragrant, white flowers with prominent pink anthers in winter.
↕ 30ft (10m) ↔ 12ft (4m) ☼ ☀ ◊ ◊ ❋❋❋

Skimmia japonica 'Nymans'
Fragrant white flowers are borne in spring, and if a male variety is planted nearby, they will be followed by long-lasting bright red berries in fall.
↕ 3ft (1m) ☀ ❋ ◊ ◊ ❋❋❋

Viburnum x bodnantense
Fragrant flowers are borne on the bare stems of this deciduous shrub. Cultivars with flowers ranging from almost white through pale to dark pink are available.
↕ 10ft (3m) ↔ 6ft (2m) ☼ ☀ ◊ ◊ ❋❋❋

Viburnum tinus 'Eve Price'
From winter to spring, flat clusters of small, star-shaped white flowers develop from pink buds amid dark green leaves; they are followed by blue berries.
↕↔ 10ft (3m) ☼ ☀ ◊ ◊ ❋❋❋

ALSO RECOMMENDED

Correa pulchella

Cotoneaster scrotinus

Daphne mezereum (Mezereon)

Daphne odora 'Aureomarginata'

Erica carnea 'Challenger'
(Alpine heath)

Erica x darleyensis 'Furzey'
(Darley Dale heath)

Hamamelis x intermedia
'Aphrodite' (Witch hazel)

Hamamelis japonica 'Sulphurea'
(Witch hazel)

Lonicera x purpusii
(Honeysuckle)

Mahonia x media 'Charity'

Nandina domestica 'Fire Power'
(Heavenly bamboo)

Pyracantha atalantioides 'Aurea'

Pyracantha 'Golden Dome'

Rubus biflorus

Rubus thibetanus

Sarcococca confusa

Sarcococca humilis
(Sweet box)

Stachyurus praecox

Symphoricarpos x doorenbosii
'White Hedge'

Viburnum farreri

GROUND-COVER PLANTS FOR SUN

Ground-cover plants are a useful addition to the garden because their dense, light-excluding canopies can help suppress weeds, often requiring little maintenance, but with colorful and striking effects. Not all of the plants classed as "ground cover" are low-growing, so it can be easy to create a varied and visually stimulating design. Consider using the plant suggestions on these pages to fill sunny "problem areas," such as a steep, sloping bank, where access for planting, sodding, or mowing may be difficult.

SHRUBS

Ceanothus thyrsiflorus var. *repens* (Blue blossom)

Cotoneaster cashmiriensis

Erica x *darleyensis* 'Jenny Porter' (Darley Dale heath)

Genista hispanica (Spanish gorse)

Hypericum calycinum (Aaron's beard)

Salvia rosmarinus 'Severn Sea' (Rosemary)

Thymus pulegioides 'Bertram Anderson' (Thyme)

PERENNIALS

Artemisia stelleriana 'Boughton Silver'

Campanula glomerata 'Superba' (Clustered bellflower)

Cerastium tomentosum (Snow-in-summer)

Dicentra 'Stuart Boothman'

Geranium x *oxonianum* 'Wargrave Pink'

Gypsophila repens 'Dorothy Teacher'

Hosta fortunei var. *aureomarginata*

Juniperus squamata 'Blue Carpet' (Flaky juniper)

Lamium maculatum 'White Nancy'

Mentha suaveolens 'Variegata' (Pineapple mint)

Persicaria vacciniifolia

Phalaris arundinacea var. *picta* (Gardener's garters)

Phlomis russeliana

Potentilla megalantha

Saponaria ocymoides (Soapwort)

Scutellaria orientalis

Silene schafta

Veronica gentianoides

Viola 'Nellie Britton'

ROCK PLANTS

Phlox subulata 'McDaniel's Cushion' (Moss phlox)

Sempervivum ciliosum

PERENNIAL: *Alchemilla mollis*

PERENNIAL: *Aubrieta* 'Joy'

SHRUB: *Erica carnea* f. *alba* 'Springwood White' (Alpine heath)

SHRUB: *Euonymus fortunei* 'Emerald 'n' Gold'

PERENNIAL: *Euphorbia polychroma*

PERENNIAL: *Geranium* 'Johnson's Blue'

ROCK PLANT: *Hebe pinguifolia* 'Pagei'

PERENNIAL: *Osteospermum jucundum*

PERENNIAL: *Lysimachia nummularia* 'Aurea' (Golden creeping Jenny)

PERENNIAL: *Origanum vulgare* 'Aureum' (Golden wild marjoram)

PERENNIAL: *Persicaria bistorta* (Bistort)

SHRUB: *Santolina pinnata* subsp. *neapolitana* 'Sulphurea'

PERENNIAL: *Stachys byzantina* (Lamb's ears)

PERENNIAL: *Veronica prostrata* (Prostrate speedwell)

SHRUB: *Vinca minor* 'La Grave' (Lesser periwinkle)

GROUND-COVER PLANTS FOR SHADE

Many of the plants suggested on these pages are woodland natives and depend on the absence of bleaching sunlight to produce their lush foliage. They provide ground cover in shady "problem areas" that do not receive a lot of light, such as the base of walls or fences, or beneath trees or shrubs. To encourage strong, healthy growth, remove any weeds before planting, since these will compete with your plants for moisture and nutrients. Improve the soil structure by digging in plenty of well-rotted manure, compost, or leaf mold before planting.

SHRUBS
Cotoneaster dammeri
Euonymus fortunei 'Emerald Gaiety'
Gaultheria procumbens
Leucothoe Scarletta (Switch ivy)
Mahonia repens 'Rotundifolia'
Vinca difformis

PERENNIALS
Aegopodium podagraria 'Variegatum'
  (Variegated ground elder)
Anemone x *lipsiensis*
Bergenia 'Silberlicht'
Cardamine trifolia
  (Trifoliate bitter cress)
Chelidonium majus 'Flore Pleno'
  (Greater celandine)
Cornus canadensis
  (Creeping dogwood)
Cyclamen hederifolium
Epimedium x *perralchicum*
Euphorbia amygdaloides var. *robbiae*
  (Mrs. Robb's bonnet)

Galax urceolata
Galium odoratum
  (Sweet woodruff)
Geranium sylvaticum 'Album'
  (Wood cranesbill)
Heuchera 'Red Spangles'
Hosta 'Frances Williams'
Polypodium vulgare
  (Common polypody)
Sanguinaria canadensis f. *multiplex* 'Plena'
  (Bloodroot)
Saxifraga x *urbium* (London pride)
Symphytum 'Goldsmith'
Tolmiea menziesii 'Taff's Gold'
  (Thousand mothers)
Tradescantia
  (Andersoniana Group) 'Osprey'
Vinca minor 'Argenteovariegata'
  (Lesser periwinkle)

CLIMBERS
Hedera helix 'Glacier' (English ivy)
Hedera hibernica (Irish ivy)

PERENNIAL: *Ajuga reptans*

PERENNIAL: *Asarum europaeum*
(Asarabacca)

PERENNIAL: *Brunnera*
macrophylla

PERENNIAL: *Convallaria majalis*
(Lily of the valley)

PERENNIAL: *Epimedium* x *rubrum*

PERENNIAL: *Geranium macrorrhizum*

PERENNIAL: *Hosta* 'Francee'

PERENNIAL: *Lamium maculatum* 'White Nancy'

PERENNIAL: *Luzula sylvatica* 'Aurea' (Greater wood-rush)

PERENNIAL: *Omphalodes cappadocica*

PERENNIAL: *Pachysandra terminalis*

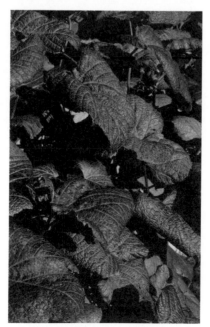

PERENNIAL: *Tiarella cordifolia* (Foam flower)

PERENNIAL: *Pulmonaria rubra* 'Redstart'

PERENNIAL: *Tellima grandiflora* Rubra Group

SHRUB: *Vinca major* 'Variegata' (Greater periwinkle)

GRASSES, SEDGES, AND BAMBOOS

Anemanthele lessoniana
Fine-leaf pheasant's tail grass has an arching style. In summer it produces purplish flower spikes; in winter the evergreen leaves turn orange-brown.
↕ 3 ft (1 m) ↔ 4 ft (1.2 m) ☼ ☼ ◊ ◊ ❀❀

Briza maxima
One of the most attractive of the annual grasses, quaking grass has nodding flower-heads that rattle in the slightest breeze. Stems dry well for flower arranging.
↕ 1 ft (30 cm) ↔ 9 in (23 cm) ☼ ◊ ◊ ❀❀❀

Calamagrostis x acutiflora 'Overdam'
The striped feather reed makes a strong vertical accent in the border. As the leaves emerge in spring, there is a pink tinge to the green and white variegation.
↕ 3 ft (1 m) ↔ 4 ft (1.2 m) ☼ ◊ ❀❀❀

Carex buchananii
This striking evergreen sedge has slender, coppery-brown leaves with a hint of a curl. It is upright when young, becoming more arching with age.
↕↔ 2 ft (60 cm) ☼ ☼ ◊ ◊ ❀❀

Carex elata 'Aurea'
Bowles' golden sedge produces a broad spray of vibrant yellow leaves, edged in green. In summer there is the added bonus of feathery brown flower spikes.
↕ 30 in (75 cm) ↔ 3 ft (1 m) ☼ ☼ ◊ ◊ ❀❀❀

Cortaderia selloana 'Pumila'
Ideal for smaller gardens, this dwarf pampas is half the size of the parent species. Golden-brown plumes are produced in summer on stout stems.
↕↔ 6 ft (2 m) ☼ ◊ ◊ ❀❀❀

Elymus magellanicus
Blue wheatgrass is a wonderful blue steel color that looks stunning against gravel. It bears herringbone flower heads that look like ears of wheat.
↕↔ 18 in (45 cm) ☼ ◊ ◊ ❀❀❀

Fargesia murielae
A tough plant for tough situations, this evergreen bamboo copes well with dry soils and exposed sites and makes an effective windbreak or screen.
↕↔ 12 ft (4 m) ☼ ☼ ◊ ◊ ❀❀❀

Festuca glauca 'Elijah Blue'
One of those useful plants that look good all year. The silvery-blue, needlelike leaves of this little fescue form neat, round mounds.
↕ 12 in (30 cm) ↔ 24 in (60 cm) ☼ ☼ ◊ ◊ ❀❀❀

❀❀❀ FULLY HARDY ❀❀ HARDY IN MILD REGIONS/SHELTERED SITES ❀ PROTECT FROM FROST OVER THE WINTER ❀ NO TOLERANCE TO FROST

☼ FULL SUN ☀ PARTIAL SUN ✲ FULL SHADE ◊ WELL-DRAINED SOIL ◔ MOIST SOIL ● WET SOIL

Imperata cylindrica 'Rubra'
Japanese blood grass has fluffy white flower spikes in summer. Its crimson-tipped, upright leaves glow in the sun. It is an invasive species in some places, so check before planting.
↕ 18 in (45 cm) ↔ 6 ft (1.8 m) ☼ ☀ ◔ ❀❀

Lagurus ovatus
Hare's tail grass is a popular annual that can be grown easily from seed. The soft, hairy spikelets are pale green at first, maturing to pale cream.
↕ 20 in (50 cm) ↔ 12 in (30 cm) ☼ ◊ ❀❀❀

Miscanthus sinensis 'Kleine Silberspinne'
An attractive ornamental grass that produces silky white and red flower spikes in late summer. These turn silver as they age and last all winter.
↕↔ 4 ft (1.2 m) ☼ ◊ ◔ ❀❀❀

Pennisetum alopecuroides 'Hameln'
This compact fountain grass has narrow leaves that tumble from the center of the plant, joined in summer and fall by flowing, bristly, decorative flower heads.
↕ to 5 ft (1.5 m) ↔ to 4 ft (1.2 m) ☼ ◊ ❀❀❀

Phyllostachys nigra
Black bamboo is a popular plant for contemporary gardens, grown for its distinctive tall stems, which are initially green and then turn a glossy black.
↕ to 15 ft (5 m) ↔ 10 ft (3 m) ☼ ✲ ◊ ◔ ❀❀❀

Phyllostachys vivax f. aureocaulis
This slow-growing bamboo has striking, bright lemon yellow canes that are flecked with green and slim arching foliage. Control its spread with a root guard.
↕ to 20 ft (6 m) ↔ 12 ft (4 m) ☼ ✲ ◊ ◔ ❀❀❀

Stipa gigantea
Giant feather grass is a fabulous plant for a sunny border. Tall, fluttering plumes of flowers emerge above the narrow evergreen foliage in summer.
↕ 8 ft (2.5 m) ↔ 3 ft (1 m) ☼ ◊ ◔ ❀❀❀

ALSO RECOMMENDED

Calamagrostis brachytricha

Carex flagellifera

Chimonobambusa tumidissinoda

Chionochloa rubra

Chusquea culeou
(Chilean bamboo)

Cortaderia richardii (Toe toe)

Cortaderia selloana 'Sunningdale Silver'
(Pampas grass)

Elegia capensis

Eragrostis curvula
'Totnes Burgundy'

Juncus effusus f. *spiralis*
(Corkscrew rush)

Luzula nivea (Snowy wood-rush)

Miscanthus sinensis var.
condensatus 'Cosmopolitan'

Miscanthus sinensis 'Zebrinus'
(Zebra grass)

Molinia caerulea subsp. *caerulea*
'Heidebraut' (Purple moor grass)

Panicum virgatum 'Northwind'
(Switch grass)

Pleioblastus variegatus
(Dwarf white-striped bamboo)

Sasa veitchii

Thamnocalamus crassinodus
'Kew Beauty'

CONIFERS FOR SMALL GARDENS

Abies cephalonica 'Meyer's Dwarf'
Broad, nearly horizontal growth makes
'Meyer's Dwarf' a good conifer for a rock
garden. The short branches have dark
green, sturdy needles.
‡20in (50cm) ↔ 5ft (1.5m) ☼ ☀ ◊ ♦ ❀❀❀

Cedrus deodara 'Aurea'
This evergreen conifer has a drooping look
at first, developing a broad crown with age.
The foliage is golden yellow, becoming
greenish in late summer.
‡↔ 15ft (5m) ☼ ◊ ❀❀❀

Chamaecyparis obtusa 'Nana Gracilis'
The glossy, bright green foliage of this
bushy Hinoki cypress makes it an asset
to any garden; it is ideal grown in a rock
garden or in a large container.
‡6ft (2m) ↔ 5–6ft (1.5–2m) ☼ ◊ ❀❀❀

Cupressus macrocarpa 'Goldcrest'
A narrow, columnar tree, 'Goldcrest' has
aromatic golden yellow foliage held in
graceful sprays. It makes a good hedge,
needing only minor trimming in summer.
‡30ft (10m) ↔ 15ft (5m) ☼ ◊ ❀❀

Juniperus communis 'Compressa'
A dwarf juniper forming a slim column,
'Compressa' has dense, aromatic, dark
green foliage. It produces small fruits
that ripen over three years.
‡30in (75cm) ↔ 6in (15cm) ☼ ◊ ❀❀❀

Juniperus × pfitzeriana 'Pfitzeriana Aurea'
This low-growing, spreading
plant bears graceful tiers of golden foliage,
drooping slightly at the tips. In winter the
foliage takes on a greener hue.
‡↔ 5ft (1.5m) ☼ ◊ ❀❀❀

Juniperus squamata 'Blue Carpet'
Light steel-blue, prickly foliage and a low,
spreading style distinguish this juniper. It is
fast-growing and makes excellent ground
cover, forming a dense mat.
‡1ft (30cm) ↔ 6–10ft (2–3m) ☼ ◊ ❀❀❀

Picea abies 'Reflexa'
While this Norway spruce variety is a
sprawling ground-cover plant, it is also
possible to train it up a stake to provide
an attractive mound of weeping foliage.
‡1ft (30cm) ↔ 15ft (5m) ☼ ◊ ❀❀❀

Pinus heldreichii 'Smidtii'
This slow-growing dwarf plant is a neat,
dense mound of upward-thrusting long
bright green needles, making it an excellent
choice for a rock garden.
‡1½ft (50cm) ↔ 3ft (1m) ☼ ◊ ❀❀❀

❋❋❋ FULLY HARDY ❋❋ HARDY IN MILD REGIONS/SHELTERED SITES ❋ PROTECT FROM FROST OVER THE WINTER ❋ NO TOLERANCE TO FROST

☼ FULL SUN ❋ PARTIAL SUN ❋ FULL SHADE ◊ WELL-DRAINED SOIL ◊ MOIST SOIL ◉ WET SOIL

Pinus mugo 'Mops'
This slow-growing dwarf plant forms an almost spherical shape of thick upright branches, which are covered with long, bright to dark green needles.
↕ 3ft (1m) ↔ 6ft (2m) ☼ ◊ ❋❋❋

Pinus sylvestris Aurea Group
This is a slow-growing group of Scots pines, suitable for smaller gardens. The long needles are blue-green, turning golden-yellow in winter.
↕ 30ft (10m) ↔ 15ft (5m) ❋ ◊ ❋❋❋

Platycladus orientalis 'Aurea Nana'
The shape of this conifer varies from nearly spherical to columnar, with dense foliage held in flat sprays. It is golden yellow, sometimes bronzing in winter.
↕↔ 24in (60cm) ☼ ◊ ❋❋❋

Taxus baccata 'Dovastonii Aurea'
A spreading, slow-growing yew with horizontally tiered branches weeping at the tips, this has yellow-margined or wholly golden-yellow foliage.
↕ 30ft (10m) ↔ 15ft (5m) ❋ ◊ ❋❋❋

Taxus cuspidata
This bushy, spreading dwarf yew is covered with flattened needlelike foliage that is deep golden yellow in the first year and then matures to dark green.
↕↔ 15ft (5m) ❋ ◊ ❋❋❋

Thuja plicata 'Stoneham Gold'
With bright golden aromatic foliage held in irregular sprays that form an overall conical shape, this slow-growing dwarf conifer is ideal for a rock garden.
↕ 3–6ft (1–2m) ↔ 3ft (1m) ☼ ◊ ◉ ❋❋❋

Tsuga canadensis 'Jeddeloh'
The arching branches of this plant form a spreading mound of dark green foliage, developing from the crown and leaving a hollow like a bird's nest at the center.
↕ 2ft (60cm) ↔ 4ft (1.2m) ❋ ◉ ❋❋❋

ALSO RECOMMENDED

Abies balsamea Hudsonia Group (Balsam fir)

Abies concolor 'Compacta' (White fir)

Abies koreana (Korean fir)

Chamaecyparis lawsoniana 'Columnaris' (Lawson cypress)

Chamaecyparis pisifera 'Filifera Aurea' (Sawara cypress)

Cryptomeria japonica 'Cristata' (Japanese cedar)

Juniperus chinensis 'Obelisk' (Chinese juniper)

Juniperus x pfitzeriana 'Old Gold'

Juniperus squamata 'Holger' (Flaky juniper)

Microbiota decussata

Picea abies 'Ohlendorffii' (Norway spruce)

Picea glauca var. *albertiana* 'Conica' (White spruce)

Picea pungens 'Globosa'

Pinus cembroides (Mexican stone pine)

Pinus sylvestris 'Beuvronensis' (Scots pine)

Taxus baccata 'Repens Aurea'

Thuja occidentalis 'Holmstrup'

STRUCTURAL PLANTS

Aralia elata 'Variegata'
Sparse, stout, prickly stems are carried in tiers, bearing dark green leaflets with broad yellow margins. Clusters of small white flowers appear in late summer.
↕↔ 15 ft (5 m) ☀ ◐ ◑ ✽✽✽

Buxus sempervirens 'Suffruticosa'
Very dense and slow-growing with small, glossy, bright green leaves, this evergreen boxwood is ideal for use as low hedging around beds or for topiary.
↕ 3 ft (1 m) ↔ 5 ft (1.5 m) ☀ ◐ ✽✽✽

Chamaerops humilis
A slow-growing evergreen palm bearing dramatic fanlike leaves with sharply pointed, slender leaflets, *C. humilis* will need winter cover in colder areas.
↕↔ 5 ft (1.5 m) ☼ ◐ ✽

Cordyline 'Red Star'
This dramatic foliage plant has long, swordlike, stiffly arching leaves colored a deep bronze-red. When mature, it bears scented white flowers.
↕ 10–30 ft (3–10 m) ↔ 3–12 ft (1–4 m) ☼ ☀ ◐ ✽✽

Cornus sericea 'Flaviramea'
Bright yellow, slender stems lift the mood of any winter garden; in summer, small white flowers appear, followed by white fruit and attractive fall leaf color.
↕ 6 ft (2 m) ↔ 12 ft (4 m) ☼ ☀ ◐ ✽✽✽

Dicksonia antarctica
This tree fern is ideal for adding height to a fern planting, producing its arching, spreading fronds at the top of a sturdy trunk covered with brown fibers.
↕ 20 ft (6 m) ↔ 12 ft (4 m) ☀ ☼ ◐ ◑ ✽✽

Dryopteris wallichiana
With upright fronds forming a shuttlecock shape, this fern makes a dramatic statement. The fronds are yellow-green in spring and mature to dark green.
↕ 36 in (90 cm) ↔ 30 in (75 cm) ☀ ◑ ✽✽✽

Echinops bannaticus
The globe thistle has woolly gray stems and impressive spiny, hairy, gray-green leaves up to 10 in (25 cm) long. Spherical, blue, thistle flowers appear in summer.
↕ 1½–4 ft (0.5–1.2 m) ↔ 30 in (75 cm) ☼ ◐ ✽✽✽

Ensete ventricosum
The sword-shaped, glossy, dark green leaves of this perennial can reach up to 20 ft (6 m) long. Overlapping leaf sheaths form the "stem." Min. temp. 45°F (7°C).
↕ 20 ft (6 m) ↔ 15 ft (5 m) ☼ ☀ ◑ ❀

❋❋❋ FULLY HARDY   ❋❋ HARDY IN MILD REGIONS/SHELTERED SITES   ❋ PROTECT FROM FROST OVER THE WINTER   ❋ NO TOLERANCE TO FROST

☼ FULL SUN   ☼ PARTIAL SUN   ❋ FULL SHADE   ◊ WELL-DRAINED SOIL   ◊ MOIST SOIL   ◊ WET SOIL

Eriobotrya japonica
The large, glossy, deep green leaves of this bushy shrub or tree have a whitish furry underside. Clusters of white flowers in fall are followed by yellow fruits.
↕↔ 25 ft (8 m) ☼ ◊ ❋❋

Euphorbia characias
Upright stems bearing evergreen, narrow, gray-green leaves are joined in spring by domes of cup-shaped lime-green flowers with maroon eyes.
↕↔ 4 ft (1.2 m) ☼ ◊ ❋❋

Fatsia japonica
Huge, palm-shaped, glossy green leaves make a stunning display, which is complemented in summer by large heads of creamy-white flowers.
↕↔ 5–12 ft (1.5–4 m) ☼ ❋ ◊ ◊ ❋❋

Melianthus major
This sprawling evergreen shrub has leaves up to 18 in (45 cm) long with feathery, jagged-edged, blue-gray leaflets. It bears brown-red flowers in summer.
↕ 6–10 ft (2–3 m) ↔ 3–10 ft (1–3 m) ☼ ◊ ◊ ❋

Musa basjoo
The Japanese banana has spectacular arching leaves up to 3 ft (1 m) long. Drooping, pale yellow flowers are borne in summer, followed by green fruits.
↕ 15 ft (5 m) ↔ 12 ft (4 m) ☼ ◊ ❋❋

Woodwardia radicans
This strong-growing fern has large, broad, lance-shaped, arching fronds, mid-green in color; it spreads by producing new little ferns at their tips.
↕ 6 ft (2 m) ↔ 10 ft (3 m) ❋ ◊ ❋❋

Yucca filamentosa 'Bright Edge'
The stiff, lance-shaped leaves of this yucca are dark green with striking broad yellow margins. In summer tall spikes of white flowers tower above them.
↕ 30 in (75 cm) ↔ 5 ft (1.5 m) ☼ ◊ ❋❋❋

ALSO RECOMMENDED

Trees
Ailanthus altissima
  (Tree of heaven)
Araucaria heterophylla
  (Norfolk island pine)
Betula pendula 'Youngii'
  (Young's weeping birch)
Fagus sylvatica 'Pendula'
Prunus 'Kiku-shidare-zakura'

Shrubs
Aesculus parviflora
  (Bottlebrush buckeye)
Corylus avellana 'Contorta'
Paeonia delavayi
Viburnum plicatum f.
  tomentosum 'Pink Beauty'

Perennials
Acanthus spinosus
Kniphofia caulescens
  (Red hot poker)
Gunnera manicata
Phormium tenax Purpureum Group
  (New Zealand flax)
Phyllostachys nigra
  (Black bamboo)

TREES FOR SMALL GARDENS

Acacia baileyana 'Purpurea'
This small tree or shrub has finely divided purple-flushed leaves that are deep red-purple when young. Yellow flowers are borne from winter to spring.
↕ 25 ft (8m) ↔ 20 ft (6m) ☼ ◊ ✾

Acer japonicum 'Vitifolium'
A vigorous deciduous tree or large shrub, this maple has large, rounded, mid-green leaves that turn vivid colors of red, orange, and purple in fall.
↕↔ 30 ft (10m) ☼ ☀ ◊ ◖ ✾✾✾

Amelanchier lamarckii
In spring, bronze young leaves are accompanied by abundant star-shaped white flowers. The leaves mature to dark green, turning red and orange in fall.
↕ 30 ft (10m) ↔ 40 ft (12m) ☼ ☀ ◊ ◖ ✾✾✾

Cercis canadensis 'Forest Pansy'
This tree or multi-stemmed shrub has heart-shaped red-purple leaves held on spreading stems. In fall, they turn briefly yellow and orange before falling.
↕↔ 30 ft (10m) ☼ ☀ ◊ ◖ ✾✾✾

Cornus controversa 'Variegata'
The spreading branches of this deciduous tree are layered to lovely effect, bearing bright green leaves margined creamy white. White flowers appear in summer.
↕↔ 25 ft (8m) ☼ ◊ ✾✾✾

Crataegus persimilis 'Prunifolia'
This variety of hawthorn is a small, rounded tree with green, oval leaves that turn vivid red or orange in fall, accompanied by dark red fruits.
↕ 25 ft (8m) ↔ 30 ft (10m) ☼ ☀ ◊ ◖ ✾✾✾

Ficus carica 'Brown Turkey'
The large, lobed, bright green leaves are the main attraction of this fig tree, though fruit may ripen in long, hot summers, especially if it is trained on a sunny wall.
↕ 10 ft (3m) ↔ 12 ft (4m) ☼ ◊ ◖ ✾✾

Laburnum x watereri 'Vossii'
Long clusters of yellow pea flowers hang from the branches of this tree in spring and early summer; they look particularly striking when trained over an arch.
↕↔ 25 ft (8m) ☼ ◊ ✾✾✾

Malus 'Evereste'
This crab apple puts on a magnificent display of blossoms in spring, with white flowers opening from pink buds. The small apples that follow last into winter.
↕ 22 ft (7m) ↔ 20 ft (6m) ☼ ☀ ◊ ◖ ✾✾✾

✽✽✽ FULLY HARDY	✽✽ HARDY IN MILD REGIONS/SHELTERED SITES	✽ PROTECT FROM FROST OVER THE WINTER	✽ NO TOLERANCE TO FROST
☼ FULL SUN	☀ PARTIAL SUN	✲ FULL SHADE	◊ WELL-DRAINED SOIL	◐ MOIST SOIL	● WET SOIL

Olea europaea
A slow-growing evergreen tree, the European olive has attractive silvery gray-green leaves. Small white flowers are followed by fruits that ripen to black.
‡↔ 30 ft (10 m) ☼ ◊ ✽✽

Prunus 'Kiku-shidare-zakura'
Large, clear pink, double flowers are borne in dense clusters on weeping branches in mid- to late spring; the young leaves are flushed bronze.
‡↔ 10 ft (3 m) ☼ ◊ ◐ ✽✽✽

Pyrus salicifolia 'Pendula'
Silvery-gray oval leaves cover the weeping branches of this attractive ornamental pear. In spring it produces dense clusters of white flowers.
‡ 15 ft (5 m) ↔ 12 ft (4 m) ☼ ◊ ✽✽✽

Robinia x slavinii 'Hillieri'
In early summer, trusses of lilac-pink flowers similar to wisteria are profusely borne on this rounded tree. The foliage is mid-green, formed of feathery leaflets.
‡↔ 15 ft (5 m) ☼ ◊ ✽✽✽

Salix caprea 'Kilmarnock'
This beautiful weeping willow is densely branched with dark green foliage, gray-green beneath. In spring it bears gray catkins that later turn yellow.
‡↔ 6 ft (2 m) ☼ ◊ ◐ ✽✽✽

ALSO RECOMMENDED

Acer davidii 'Ernest Wilson' (Snakebark maple)

Acer palmatum 'Atropurpureum' (Japanese maple)

Amelanchier x *grandiflora* 'Ballerina'

Betula utilis var. *jacquemontii* (Himalayan birch)

Cercis siliquastrum (Judas tree)

Cornus kousa

Crataegus laevigata 'Paul's Scarlet'

Cydonia oblonga 'Vranja' (Common quince)

Gleditsia triacanthos 'Rubylace' (Honey locust)

Hoheria angustifolia

Magnolia x *loebneri* 'Leonard Messel'

Malus tschonoskii

Prunus incisa (Fuji cherry)

Prunus persica 'Prince Charming'

Pyrus calleryana 'Chanticleer'

Salix 'Erythroflexuosa'

Sorbus 'Joseph Rock'

Styrax japonicus

Sorbus aria 'Lutescens'
The foliage of this upright tree opens silvery, maturing to gray-green. It bears white flowers in spring and early summer; orange-red fruits follow in fall.
‡ 30 ft (10 m) ↔ 25 ft (8 m) ☼ ☀ ◊ ◐ ✽✽✽

Tsuga canadensis 'Aurea'
This conifer has a broad, conical shape. The gray shoots are spirally held, with flattened needlelike leaves that are golden when young and mature to green.
‡ 25 ft (8 m) ↔ 12 ft (4 m) ☼ ☀ ◊ ◐ ✽✽✽

MULTI-INTEREST TREES

Acer griseum
Peeling orange-brown bark is a major attraction of the Paperbark maple; it also has yellow flowers in spring, then brown winged fruit and blazing fall color.
↕↔ 30ft (10m) ☀ ☀ ◌ ◌ ✿✿✿

Acer palmatum 'Sango-kaku'
The lobed leaves of the coral bark maple open pink-green, maturing to dark green and then yellow and orange in fall. In winter the bark is bright coral red.
↕ 20ft (6m) ↔ 15ft (5m) ☀ ☀ ◌ ◌ ✿✿✿

Acer pensylvanicum 'Erythrocladum'
The moosewood's bright green leaves turn yellow in fall; in winter, the young shoots turn orange-red, developing white stripes as they mature.
↕ 40ft (12m) ↔ 30ft (10m) ☀ ☀ ◌ ◌ ✿✿✿

Arbutus unedo
The bark of the spreading strawberry tree is attractively red-brown and rough. White flowers open in fall as fruits from the previous season ripen to red.
↕↔ 25ft (8m) ☀ ◌ ◌ ✿✿✿

Betula utilis var. jacquemontii
In winter this tree's smooth, peeling white bark is seen at its best; spring brings catkins, while in fall the dark green foliage turns buttery yellow.
↕ 60ft (18m) ↔ 30ft (10m) ☀ ◌ ◌ ✿✿✿

Cornus kousa var. chinensis 'China Girl'
Flower heads with large white bracts are profusely borne in late spring and early summer; fall brings deep red-purple leaf color and raspberrylike fruits.
↕ 22ft (7m) ↔ 15ft (5m) ☀ ☀ ◌ ◌ ✿✿✿

Eucalyptus pauciflora subsp. niphophila
The evergreen snow gum tree has open, spreading branches covered in peeling gray and white bark, complemented by deep blue-green lance-shaped leaves.
↕↔ 20ft (6m) ☀ ◌ ◌ ✿✿✿

Ilex aquifolium 'Handsworth New Silver'
This dense, column-shaped holly is a female variety bearing dark green leaves with cream margins. It produces a generous crop of bright red berries.
↕ 25ft (8m) ↔ 15ft (5m) ☀ ☀ ◌ ◌ ✿✿✿

Malus x purpurea 'Lemoinei'
The leaves of this tree are reddish-purple when young, bronzing when mature. In spring dark red flowers appear; red-purple crab apples are borne in fall.
↕↔ 30ft (10m) ☀ ◌ ◌ ✿✿✿

※※※ FULLY HARDY　　※※ HARDY IN MILD REGIONS/SHELTERED SITES　　※ PROTECT FROM FROST OVER THE WINTER　　◊ NO TOLERANCE TO FROST

☼ FULL SUN　　☀ PARTIAL SUN　　✳ FULL SHADE　　◊ WELL-DRAINED SOIL　　◐ MOIST SOIL　　● WET SOIL

Malus tschonoskii
Pink-tinged, single white flowers are borne
in spring, followed by red-flushed crab
apples. In fall the green foliage turns to
brilliant oranges and reds.
‡ 40ft (12m) ↔ 22ft (7m) ☼ ☀ ◊ ◐ ※※※

Parrotia persica
This tree has flaking gray and fawn bark and
is still bare of foliage in spring when the small
red flowers appear. In fall the leaves turn
orange, red, and purple.
‡ 25ft (8m) ↔ 30ft (10m) ☼ ☀ ◊ ◐ ※※※

Prunus serrula
Coppery-colored peeling bark is the
prettiest feature here; backlit by winter
sun, the trailing bark is golden. Single
white flowers appear in spring.
‡↔ 30ft (10m) ☼ ◊ ◐ ※※※

Rhus typhina
The velvety shoots of this spreading tree
are clad in dark green, leafleted foliage that
turns brilliant red in fall; female plants bear
deep red fruits, too.
‡ 15ft (5m) ↔ 20ft (6m) ☼ ◊ ● ※※※

Sorbus commixta 'Embley'
A vigorous, spreading tree, 'Embley' has
glossy dark green leaves with slender leaflets,
which turn orange and red in fall with bright
red fruit among them.
‡ 30ft (10m) ↔ 22ft (7m) ☼ ☀ ◊ ◐ ※※※

ALSO RECOMMENDED

Acer campestre (Field maple)

Acer palmatum 'Osakazuki'
  (Japanese maple)

Acer rubrum 'October Glory'
  (Red maple)

Betula nigra (Black birch)

Cercidiphyllum japonicum
  (Katsura tree)

Crataegus persimilis 'Prunifolia'
  (Hawthorn)

Fraxinus excelsior 'Pendula'
  (Weeping ash)

Gleditsia triacanthos 'Sunburst'
  (Honey locust)

Malus 'Royalty' (Crab apple)

Nyssa sinensis (Chinese tupelo)

Prunus padus 'Watereri'
  (Bird cherry)

Prunus 'Shirotae'
  (Ornamental cherry)

Prunus 'Spire'
  (Ornamental cherry)

Prunus x *subhirtella* 'Fallalis
  Rosea' (Rosebud cherry)

Robinia pseudoacacia 'Frisia'
  (False acacia)

Sorbus sargentiana
  (Sargent's rowan)

Stewartia sinensis
Dark green leaves provide contrast with the
peeling reddish-brown bark before turning
to blazing fall colors. In summer fragrant
white flowers appear.
‡ 20ft (6m) ↔ 10ft (3m) ☼ ☀ ◊ ◐ ※※※

Styrax hemsleyanus
In early summer this tree bears long plumes
of bell-shaped, white flowers on graceful
branches. The large, pointed leaves turn
a buttery yellow in fall.
‡ 15ft (5m) ↔ 12ft (4m) ☼ ☀ ◊ ※※※

PLANTS FOR ACID SOIL

Although many plants will tolerate a slight variation in soil pH, some plants, such as rhododendrons, camellias, and most heathers, which are native to woodlands, specifically require an acidic pH to thrive. Dig in lime-free compost before planting, and mulch plants regularly. If conditions become too acidic, dig in some organic matter. If your soil is not acidic but you want to grow any of the plants suggested on these pages, consider growing them in a container, where they can be grown in special ericaceous potting mix.

TREES
Acer davidii (Snakebark maple)
Acer pensylvanicum 'Erythrocladum' (Moosewood)
Amelanchier lamarckii (Juneberry)
Arbutus unedo (Strawberry tree)
Cercis canadensis 'Forest Pansy' (Eastern redbud)
Halesia carolina (Snowdrop tree)
Stewartia monadelpha

SHRUBS
Acer palmatum var. *dissectum* (Japanese maple)
Andromeda polifolia 'Compacta' (Bog rosemary)
Camellia species
Cassiope 'Edinburgh'
Chamaedaphne calyculata
Disanthus cercidifolius
Embothrium coccineum (Chilean firebush)
Erica cinerea and cultivars (Heather)
Fothergilla major

Hamamelis species (Witch hazel)
Kalmia angustifolia (Sheep laurel)
Myrica gale (Bog myrtle)
Physocarpus opulifolius 'Dart's Gold'
Pieris 'Forest Flame'
Rhododendron species

CLIMBERS
Berberidopsis corallina
Crinodendron hookerianum
Desfontainia spinosa

PERENNIALS
Cirsium rivulare
Gentiana sino-ornata (Gentian)
Smilacina racemosa
Trillium erectum (Stinking Benjamin)
Uvularia grandiflora (Bellwort)

WATER AND BOG PLANTS
Osmunda regalis (Royal fern)
Sarracenia flava

SHRUB: *Calluna vulgaris* **'County Wicklow' (Heather)**

SHRUB: *Camellia* **'Leonard Messel'**

SHRUB: *Daboecia cantabrica* **'Bicolor' (Cantabrian heath)**

SHRUB: *Enkianthus campanulatus*

SHRUB: *Fothergilla gardenii* **(Witch alder)**

PERENNIAL: *Gillenia trifoliata*
(Bowman's root)

SHRUB: *Kalmia latifolia*
(Mountain laurel)

TREE: *Liquidambar styraciflua*
(Sweet gum)

SHRUB: *Pieris japonica* 'Blush'

SHRUB: *Lithodora diffusa*
'Heavenly Blue'

SHRUB: *Rhododendron*
Blue Tit Group

SHRUB: *Sorbus vilmorinii*

TREE: *Styrax japonicus*
(Japanese snowball)

SHRUB: *Vaccinium parvifolium*
(Red bilberry)

PLANTS FOR CHALKY AND LIME-RICH SOILS

There is a vast number of plants to choose from if you can provide chalky or lime-rich soil conditions—the list given on these pages only contains a relatively small number. Chalky soils are often quite light and free-draining, so you may need to dig in well-rotted manure or compost to improve the soil structure and encourage water retention. Consider the fertility of your soil when selecting your plants: some will need a rich, fertile soil in order to flower well, while others, such as wildflowers, often do best on poorer soils. Feed plants accordingly.

TREES
Acer negundo 'Variegatum' (Variegated box elder)
Catalpa bignonioides 'Aurea' (Indian bean tree)
Cercis siliquastrum (Judas tree)
Fraxinus ornus (Manna ash)
Ilex species (Holly)
Laurus nobilis (Bay laurel)
Malus species (Crab apple)
Morus nigra (Black mulberry)
Prunus 'Pink Perfection' (Ornamental cherry)

SHRUBS
Abutilon 'Kentish Belle'
Berberis darwinii (Barberry)
Chaenomeles speciosa 'Nivalis' (Japanese quince)
Ceanothus impressus
Cistus species (Rock rose)
Cornus mas (Cornelian cherry)
Cotoneaster conspicuus 'Decorus'
Escallonia 'Donard Beauty'
Euonymus hamiltonianus
Fuchsia 'Prosperity'
Genista tenera 'Golden Shower' (Broom)
Helianthemum 'Jubilee' (Sun rose)
Magnolia salicifolia (Willowleaf magnolia)
Potentilla fruticosa (Cinquefoil)

CLIMBERS
Campsis radicans (Trumpet vine)
Clematis 'Miss Bateman'
Fremontodendron 'California Glory'
Parthenocissus henryana (Chinese Virginia creeper)

PERENNIALS
Doronicum 'Miss Mason' (Leopard's bane)
Helenium 'Butterpat' (Helen's flower)
Knautia macedonica
Pulsatilla vulgaris (Pasqueflower)
Verbascum 'Cotswold Beauty'

SHRUB: *Buddleja* 'Lochinch'

PERENNIAL: *Campanula punctata*

TREE: *Cotinus coggygria*
Purpureus Group (Smoke bush)

SHRUB: *Hibiscus syriacus* 'Oiseau Bleu'

SHRUB: *Indigofera heterantha*

PERENNIAL: *Knautia macedonia*

PERENNIAL: *Malva moschata*
(Musk mallow)

SHRUB: *Osmanthus delavayi*

SHRUB: *Prunus tenella*
(Dwarf Russian almond)

SHRUB: *Philadelphus* 'Boule d'Argent'

PERENNIAL: *Rudbeckia laciniata*
'Herbstsonne'

SHRUB: *Syringa x persica*
(Persian lilac)

SHRUB: *Rubus* 'Benenden'

PLANTS FOR HEAVY CLAY

Clay soils can provide a hostile growing environment for plants: they are slow to warm in spring, sticky when wet, slow to drain, and quick to become solid when dry. However, given the right care and attention, clay soils can provide a rich, fertile growing medium because their structure makes them excellent at retaining nutrients and therefore ideal for any of the plants listed here. Where possible, improve soils by turning them over in fall and then again in spring, incorporating organic matter, coarse sand, or lime to improve the structure.

TREES

Acer palmatum 'Bloodgood' (Japanese maple)

Alnus glutinosa (Common alder)

Cornus kousa var. *chinensis* (Kousa dogwood)

Magnolia virginiana (Sweet bay)

Populus tremula 'Pendula' (Aspen)

Prunus maackii (Manchurian cherry)

Sorbus cashmiriana (Kashmir rowan)

SHRUBS

Aronia arbutifolia (Red chokeberry)

Berberis thunbergii f. *purpurea* 'Rose Glow' (Barberry)

Cotoneaster x *watereri* 'John Waterer'

Euonymus europaeus 'Red Cascade'

Ribes sanguineum 'King Edward VII' (Flowering currant)

Sambucus racemosa 'Plumosa Aurea' (Elder)

Viburnum opulus (Guelder rose)

CLIMBERS

Garrya elliptica 'James Roof' (Silk tassel bush)

Humulus lupulus 'Aureus' (Golden hop)

Rosa filipes 'Kiftsgate'

Vitis coignetiae (Vine)

PERENNIALS

Anemone x *hybrida* (Japanese anemone)

Bergenia species (Elephant's ears)

Campanula latiloba 'Hidcote Amethyst' (Bellflower)

Geranium Rozanne 'Gerwat'

Geum 'Bell Bank'

Heliopsis helianthoides var. *scabra* 'Sommersonne' (Ox-eye)

Hyacinthoides non-scripta (Bluebell)

Monarda 'Mahogany' (Bergamot)

Polygonatum hirtum (Solomon's seal)

Pulmonaria 'Sissinghurst White'

Symphyotrichum novi-belgii 'Jenny' (Michaelmas daisy)

PERENNIAL: *Astrantia major* 'Claret'

SHRUB: *Ceanothus* 'Joyce Coulter'

SHRUB: *Chaenomeles* x *superba* 'Crimson and Gold'

PERENNIAL: *Filipendula purpurea*

SHRUB: *Hydrangea arborescens* 'Grandiflora'

SHRUB: *Philadelphus* 'Manteau d'Hermine'

SHRUB: *Potentilla fruticosa* 'Abbotswood'

SHRUB: *Pyracantha* 'Mohave'

SHRUB: *Sinocalycanthus chinensis*

SHRUB: *Skimmia japonica* 'Rubella'

SHRUB: *Spiraea japonica* 'Anthony Waterer'

SHRUB: *Syringa vulgaris* 'Katherine Havemeyer' (Common lilac)

SHRUB: *Viburnum davidii*

PLANTS FOR HOT, DRY SITES

Plants that are native to very hot, dry climates have developed a range of methods for coping. Many gray-, silver-, or blue-leaf plants are covered in fine hair or have a waxy surface, which deflects the sun's rays. Scented plants emit a haze of aromatic oils that create a barrier against the sun, while succulent plants store water in their fleshy leaves to prevent dehydration. Many heat-loving plants will suffer if grown in soil that is too fertile, so dig in leaf mold to improve the soil structure, since it does not add as many nutrients as other organic matter.

TREES

Arbutus unedo (Strawberry tree)

Eucalyptus dalrympleana

Ficus carica (Common fig)

Gleditsia triacanthos 'Rubylace' (Honey locust)

Maackia amurensis

Pinus aristata (Bristlecone pine)

Rhus typhina (Stag's horn sumac)

SHRUBS

Abutilon vitifolium 'Veronica Tennant'

Ceanothus 'Cascade'

Convolvulus cneorum

Cytisus battandieri

Erysimum 'Bowles's Mauve'

x *Halimiocistus wintonensis*

Halimium lasianthum

Hebe macrantha

Lavandula pedunculata subsp. *pedunculata*

Parahebe perfoliata

Perovskia 'Blue Spire'

PERENNIALS

Agapanthus 'Loch Hope'

Agave victoriae-reginae

Amsonia orientalis Artemisia 'Powis Castle'

Dianthus 'Haytor White'

Dictamnus albus var. *purpureus*

Dierama pulcherrimum

Eryngium bourgatii

Euphorbia characias subsp. *wulfenii* 'John Tomlinson'

Festuca glauca 'Blaufuchs' (Blue fescue)

Gaura lindheimeri

Geranium maderense

Verbascum 'Gainsborough'

BULBS

Allium hollandicum

Amaryllis belladonna

Cyclamen coum Pewter Group

Triteleia laxa

Tulipa tarda

SHRUB: *Ballota acetabulosa*

SHRUB: *Callistemon pallidus* (Lemon bottlebrush)

SHRUB: *Cistus x dansereaui* 'Decumbens'

SHRUB: *Coronilla valentina* subsp. *glauca*

SHRUB: *Genista hispanica* (Spanish gorse)

SHRUB: *Helichrysum italicum* subsp. *serotinum* (Curry plant)

SHRUB: *Hibiscus syriacus* 'Diana'

SHRUB: *Kerria japonica* 'Golden Guinea'

SHRUB: *Lavandula angustifolia* 'Munstead' (Lavender)

SHRUB: *Lavatera* x *clementii* 'Barnsley'

SHRUB: *Leptospermum scoparium* 'Kiwi' (Manuka)

SHRUB: *Phlomis fruticosa* (Jerusalem sage)

SHRUB: *Romneya coulteri* (Tree poppy)

SHRUB: *Salvia rosmarinus* 'Sissinghurst Blue' (Rosemary)

PLANTS FOR EXPOSED SITES

The biggest problem facing plants in exposed sites is likely to be high winds, which can loosen roots, break stems and branches, and scorch foliage by removing water from the leaves faster than the plant can replenish it. Choosing resilient plants, or those that will bend with the wind rather than resist it, will ensure that your garden can withstand even very tough conditions. Remember that even in exposed sites, sheltered areas can be created for more delicate plants by arranging sturdy shrubs or trees to act as protective screens or windbreaks.

TREES
Acer platanoides (Norway maple)

Betula utilis var. *jacquemontii* (Himalayan birch)

Chamaecyparis pisifera 'Filifera Aurea' (Sawara cypress)

Crataegus laevigata 'Paul's Scarlet' *Fagus sylvatica* (European beech)

Fraxinus excelsior 'Jaspidea' (Ash)

Juniperus communis 'Hibernica' (Irish juniper)

Laburnum x watereri 'Vossii'

Picea breweriana (Brewer's spruce)

Taxus baccata (Yew)

Tsuga canadensis (Eastern hemlock)

SHRUBS
Berberis thunbergii f. *atropurpurea* 'Golden Ring'

Calluna vulgaris 'Kinlochruel' (Scots heather)

Corylus maxima 'Purpurea' (Filbert)

Cotinus coggygria Golden Spirit (Smoke bush)

Cotoneaster salicifolius

Elaeagnus umbellata

Erica carnea 'Vivellii' (Alpine heath)

Hypericum olympicum

Lonicera pileata (Honeysuckle)

Philadelphus 'Virginal'

Potentilla fruticosa 'Abbotswood'

Pyracantha 'Watereri'

Sambucus nigra f. *porphyrophylla* 'Guincho Purple' (Black elder)

Spiraea nipponica 'Snowmound'

Tamarix tetrandra

Viburnum opulus 'Roseum' (Snowball tree)

PERENNIALS
Aster alpinus

Brunnera macrophylla (Siberian bugloss)

Dianthus gratianopolitanus (Cheddar pink)

Euphorbia cyparissias (Cypress spurge)

TREE: *Cupressus macrocarpa* **'Goldcrest' (Monterey cypress)**

SHRUB: *Deutzia gracilis*

SHRUB: *Dryas octopetala* **(Mountain avens)**

SHRUB: *Escallonia* **'Apple Blossom'**

SHRUB: *Euonymus fortunei*
'Emerald Gaiety'

SHRUB: *Euphorbia mellifera*
(Canary spurge)

SHRUB: *Fuchsia magellanica*

PERENNIAL: *Helianthemum*
'Fire Dragon'

SHRUB: *Hippophae rhamnoides*
(Sea buckthorn)

SHRUB: *Lupinus arboreus*
(Tree lupine)

SHRUB: *Olearia macrodonta*
(New Zealand holly)

SHRUB: *Salix reticulata*

SHRUB: *Spartium junceum*

SHRUB: *Tamarix ramosissima*
'Pink Cascade'

INDEX

Page numbers that appear in italics in this index indicate an illustration.

A

Abelia 113, *392*
Abeliophyllum distichum 402
Abies 155, *418*
Abutilon 146
Acacia 392, 422
Acanthus spinosus 301, *383*
access to garden 61, 74, 79
Acer 108, 113
    A. griseum 424
    A. japonicum 422
    A. negundo 315
    A. palmatum 22, 108, 123, *408*, 424
    A. pensylvanicum *111*, 424
Achillea 105, 134, *135*, *140*, 157, 333
    A. 'Moonshine' *139*
    A. 'Paprika' *383*
acid soil 66, 105, 128, 130, 285, 426–7
Actaea simplex 117, *131*
aeoniums 109
Agapanthus *374*, 383
agaves 10
Ageratum 374
Agrostemma githago 169, 170, 341
Ajania pacifica 137
Ajuga reptans 175, 333
Alchemilla mollis 106, 117, *131*, 138
alkaline soil 66, 128, 428
All-America Selections Award (AAS) 199
Allium 105, 111, 160, *161*, *378*
aloes 10
alpine mint bush
    see *Prostanthera cuneata*
alpines 53, 56, 109, 138, 400–1
Alstroemeria 160, *378*
Alyssum 138, 170, 293
    sweet see *Lobularia maritima*
Amelanchier 422
Amur grape see *Vitis amurensis*
Anchusa *139*
Anemanthele *157*, 416
Anemone
    A. blanda *158*, *376*
    A. ranunculoides 380
    A. x *hybrida* 332, *383*, 385
annuals 12, 102, 166–73
    choosing/planting 168–71
    grasses 157
    herbs 248–9
    for insects 170
    maintenance 170, 306–7
    plant directory 372–3
    self-seeding 169
    transplanting seedlings 288
    weeds 352–3
    wildflowers 341

Anthemis arvensis 341
Antirrhinum majus 372
aphids 133, 199, 226, 360, 361, 362, 363, 367, 369
Aponogeton distachyos 177, 345
apples 36, 257, 262–3
    see also *Malus*
    crop planner 185, 260
    harvesting 294
    pests and diseases 294, 361, 364, 365, 366, 368
    storing 258, 259, 263
apricots 257, 260, *271*, 365
aquatic plants 103, 174–5
    choosing/planting 55, 97, 176–9, 345, 347
    maintenance 344–5
    plant directory 388–9
Aquilegia 137, *380*, 382
Arabis 138
Aralia 333, *420*
arbors 106, 119, *133*
Arbutus unedo 424
arches
    climbers 16, 52, 115, 143, 149
    English gardens 106, 115
    making 94–5
    vegetables 37
architectural plants 108, 109, 308, 420–1
Arctostaphylos *128*
Argyranthemum 374
arrowhead see *Sagittaria*
Artemisia 138
artichokes
    globe 189, 196, 203, 246, 290
    Jerusalem 204, 246
Arum italicum 'Marmoratum' *386*
arum lily see *Zantedeschia*
Arundo donax 152
ash see *Fraxinus*
Asian plants 224
asparagus 202, *247*, 360
astelias 109, 140
asters
    conditions preferred 168
    as cut flowers 170
    dividing 333
    fall interest 113, 137
    maintenance 138
    planting ideas 129
    wildlife garden 108
    A. amellus 'King George' *383*
    A. amellus 'Rosa Erfullung' *137*
    A. novae-angliae 138
Astilbe 123, *175*, *388*
Astrantia 135, 157, *383*
Atriplex *129*, 341
Begonia 162, 168, *171*
Aubretia 138

Aucuba 109, 321
autumn snowflake *(Acis)* 379
awnings 32
azaleas 22, 105
Azara 410
Azolla filiculoides 177

B

baby blue-eyes 373
bacterial canker 364
balconies, planting 115
bamboo 102
    calming retreat 44, 45, 47
    choosing/planting 58, 152–5, 416–17
    effective use 16, 107, 150–1
    maintenance 154
    planting ideas 108, 155, 421
    winter interest 112
bananas *11*, 54, *134*, 308, 309
barberry see *Berberis darwinii*
bare root plants 19, 296
bark
    as mulch 23, 350
    ornamental *111*, 118, 119, *124*, 424–5
barrel pool 175, 180
basil *248–249*
bats 51
bay *251*, 324, 325
bean chocolate spot 364
bean halo blight 238
beans
    crop rotation 198
    fava 202, *237*, 364
    green 200, 202, *238*, 364
    intercropping 200
    pests and diseases 363, 364
    preserving 201
    runner 36–7, 202, *239*, 364
bear's breeches 301, *383*
beauty bush *(Kolkwitzia)* 313, *403*
bedding plants 12, 22, 291, 293, 372–3
beds
    see also raised beds
    bulbs 160, 162
    fruit/vegetables 186–7, 189
    grasses 151
    mixed planting 189, 252, 356
    mulches 301
    perennials 134–5
    preparing 192–3, 196
    reshaping 63
    watering 299
beech 322, 323
beets 195, 200, 201, 202, *225*, 329, 367
Begonia 162, 168, *171*
bellflower see *Campanula*

bells of Ireland *170*
benjamin see *Trillium*
berberis *126*, 323
    B. julianae 402
    B. x *ottawensis* 408
bergamot see *Monarda*
Bergenia 138, *140*, *179*
    B. 'Ballawley' *386*
    B. ciliata 380
    B. cordifolia 'Purpurea' *386*
berries
    fruit 276–85
    ornamental climbers 146
    preserving 259
    texture and color 111
    on trees/shrubs 113, 143, *393*, 408–11, 424–5
    wildlife garden 48, 51
Betula
    B. utilis var. *jacquemontii* 117, 424
Bidens 169
biennials 12, 102, 166–7
    choosing/planting 168–71
    for insects 170
    self-seeding 169
    sowing 169
    transplanting seedlings 288
Billardiera longiflora 146
bindweed 352
biological controls 199
birch
    Himalayan 112, 117, *118*, 424
birds
    attracting 293, 297, 343
    deterring 346
    fruit damage 199, 264, 269, 283, 285, 360
    as pest deterrents 357
    wildlife garden 30, 48, 49, 51, 175
bistort *(Persicaria)* *385*
bitter pit 364
black-eyed Susan 147
blackberries *280–1*
    maintenance 256, 257, 260
    ornamental 314, 315
    pests and diseases 362, 364
    preserving 259
    as weeds 352
black currants 256, 257, 259, 260, *282*, 361, 368
black currant reversion disease 364
blackfly see aphids
bleeding hearts see *Dicentra*
blight 228, 229, 324, 367, 369
block planting 105, 108
blossom problems 364, 365
blue flax *(Linum)* 341
blueberries 36, 253, 257, 260, *285*, 364

bog gardens
  acid soil 426
  family gardens 40, 41
  perennials 141
  plant directory 388–9
  plants 10, 31, 55, 103, 175–6, 178–9, *381*
  wildlife garden 49
bok choy 200, *207*
borders
  adding height 150, 151, 156
  annuals/biennials 166
  bulbs 160, 161, 162
  calming retreat 44, 47
  edging shrubs 130
  enthusiast's garden 52
  grasses 151, 155, 156–7
  herbs 250–1
  mulches 301
  perennials 134–5, 139
  planting plan 116–17
  potted plants in gaps 52
  seasonal effects 112–13
  shrubs 129, 131
  sunflowers 173
  traditional 105
  trees 123, 125
  watering 299
Borinda 152
botanical names 14–15
botrytis 275, 277, 366, 369
bottlebrush *126*, 309
boundaries 40, 42, 44, *70–1*
boxwood *420*
  alkaline soil *128*
  contemporary gardens 105
  edging plants 37, 130
  fertilizers 22–3
  hedges 115, *127*
  potager 38
  taking cuttings 331
  topiary 54, 108, 129, *131*, 324–5
  trimming 291, 325
  winter 112
boxwood blight 324, 365
boysenberry 281
Brachyscome iberidifolia 374
Bracteantha bracteata 170
brassicas, pests/diseases 198, 361, 362, 365, 369
Briza 154, 157, 416
broccoli 198, 202, *244*
broom
  ornamental *392*, *402*
Brunnera 137, 138, *140*, 380
Brussels sprouts 198, 200, 202, *243*
bubble plans 82
Buddleja 108, 312, 313, 331
  B. alternifolia 313
  B. crispa 392
  B. davidii 297, 313
  B. globosa 405
budgetary considerations 60
bugle (*Ajuga*) 175, 333
bulbils *13*
bulbs 102, 158–9, 163

acid soil 426
choosing/planting 116, 160–3
dividing 307, 333
hot/dry sites 432
in lawns *16*, 58, 158, 162
pests and diseases 362, 365
restricted spaces 115
spring-flowering 112, 158, 159, 161, 162, 376–7
summer/fall flowering 55, 113, 158, 161, 162, 378–9
under trees 125
winter protection 309
bullaces 266, 267, 367
bulrush 175
bunny tails 157
busy lizzie see *Impatiens*
Butomus 176, *388*
buttercup see *Ranunculus*
butterflies and moths 108, 170, 360, 361
butterfly bush see *Buddleja*
Buxus see boxwood
buying plants 18–19

C

cabbage 36, 39, 202, *240–1*
  pests/diseases 198, 199, 360, 361, 362, 365, 369
  preserving 201
cacti 10, 53
calabrese 200, 202, 244
Calamagrostis 105, *117*, 157, 416
Calendula 166, 168, 169, 170, 372
Calibrachoa 374
California poppy see *Eschscholzia californica*
Callicarpa bodinieri 113, 408
Callistemon (bottlebrush) *126*, 309
Callistephus chinensis 170
Calluna vulgaris 408
calming retreat 29, 44–7
Caltha palustris (marsh marigold) *175*, 176, 344, *388*
Camassia leichtlinii 376
camellias 105, 111, *128*, 321, 333
  C. x williamsii 402
Campanula
  C. cochleariifolia 400
  C. lactiflora 147
  C. poscharskyana 136
campion see *Silene*
Canadian burnet 389
Canadian pondweed 345
candytuft see *Iberis*
canes 191
canker 364, 365
Canna 54, 159, 160, 309
  C. indica 179
  C. 'Striata' 378
Canterbury bells see *Campanula medium*
capsid bug 360
Cardamine 14
cardoon (*Cynara*) 386
Carex 152

C. buchananii 416
C. comans 150, 179
C. elata 'Aurea' *151*, 416
Carpenteria californica 146, 392
Carpinus betulus (hornbeam) 115, *118*, 322, 323, 324, 325
carrots 226
  pests/diseases 356, 360, 363
  sowing 195, *196*, 198, 199, 200, 203
  storing 201
  wild 341
Caryopteris clandonensis 313, 405
Catalpa bignonioides 315, 332
catch cropping 200
caterpillars 360–1
catnip (*Nepeta*) 135
cauliflower 198, 200, 203, 245
Ceanothus 128
  C. 'Concha' 146
  C. 'Gloire de Versailles' *392*, 405
  C. 'Skylark' 402
Cedrus deodara 'Aurea' *418*
celeriac 198, 200, 203, *230–1*
celery 203, *219*, 290, 360
Centaurea 14, 136, 169, 170, 341
Cerastium 138
Ceratophyllum demersum 177, 344, 345
Ceratostigma willmottianum 405
Cercis 111, 315, 422
Cerinthe major 169, 170
Cestrum 308
Chaenomeles 146, 331, 361
  C. speciosa 392
  C. x superba 402
chalky soil 21, 428–9
Chamaecyparis 418
Chamaerops humilis 420
chamomile 341
chard 36, 39, 189, 205, *209*
cheddar pink see *Dianthus gratianopolitanus*
Chelsea chop 138
chemicals
  avoiding 357, 358
  fungicides/pesticides 359
  rooting hormones 331
  storing 359
  weed killer 64, 351
cherries
  see also *Prunus*
  edible 36, 257, 259–61, *268–9*
  fall interest 113
  frost protection 256, 289
  ornamental *119*, 124–5, *404*, 423, 425
  pests and diseases 360, 361, 364, 365, 368
  spring bulbs 163
  wall-trained 253
cherry and pear slug worm 360
cherry laurel 321
chickens 36, 39
chickweed 352
children 29, 40
Chilean potato tree see *Solanum crispum*
chiles *212*

Chimonanthus praecox 410
China aster 170
Chinese houses (*Collinsia*) 169
Chinese cabbage 202, *209*
chives *251*
chlorosis 303
Choisya x *dewitteana* 405
Christmas rose see *Helleborus*
Chrysanthemum 166
Chusquea 152
cider gum (*Eucalyptus gunnii*) 315, 321
cilantro 249
cinquefoil see *Potentilla*
Cirsium rivulare 108
Cistus 107, *128*, 301
clamping 201
Clarkia amoena 169
clay soil 20, *21*, 66, 430–1
Clematis 148–9
  English-style gardens 106
  layering 333
  pests and diseases 365
  pruning 149, 317
  with roses 133, *143*, 149
  shearing 149
  supports 114, 144, 147
  in trees *143*, 148
  C. 'Comtesse de Bouchard' *147*
  C. montana 16
Clerodendrum 308, *309*, 408
climbers 103
  see also clematis; roses
  acid soil 426
  chalky/lime-rich soils 428
  choosing/planting 144–7
  clay soil 430
  effective use 114–15, 142–3
  fruit and vegetables 37, 189, 238–9
  ground-cover 414
  layering 333
  lighting 77
  pruning/training 197, 316–17
  for shade 414
  supports 94–5, 196, 292
  in trees 143
  urban gardens 107
  winter protection 308
cloches 37, 191, 193, 195, 257, 288, 308, 327
clubroot 365
Cobaea scandens 143
codling moth 358, 360
Colchicum 160, 161, *378*
cold frames 37, 53, 189, 195, 326–7, 329
coleus (*Solenostemon*) 166, 168, 331
Collinsia bicolor 169
color 110–11, 119, 158, 314
columbine see *Aquilegia*
comfrey see *Symphytum*
common sorel (*Rumex acetosa*) 341
companion planting 189
compost heaps 22, 39, 42, 48, 303, 337
coneflower see *Rudbeckia*
conifers 13, 112, 115, 123, 127, 410–19

Consolida ajacis 170
containers
  annuals/biennials 167–8, 170
  bamboo/grasses 150, *151*, 155
  boxwood hedge 115
  bulbs 159, 161, 162
  climbers 143, 148
  designing displays 109
  feeding 141, 196, 256, 303, 304, 305
  focal points 44, 45, 57, 59, 79, 109,
    305
  fruit trees 125, 188, 253, 257, 264,
    270, 271, 273
  grasses 153
  herbs 109, 248, 249
  lavender 107
  perennials 141
  planting 304–5
  potting media 21
  preparing to plant 193
  recycled 38
  roof gardens 107
  roses 127, 133
  shrubs 127, 129, 130
  soft fruit 37, 188, 253, 255, 259, 276,
    277, 282, 285
  summer plants 374–5
  sunflowers 173
  vegetables 36, *38*, 185, 188, 207–8,
    211, 215, 225–6, 229
  water garden 175, 177, *180*
  watering 38, 56, 299, 301
  winter protection 308–9
Contemporary designs 105, 108, 109,
  115
Convallaria majalis 376
Convolvulus 400, 405
cooking areas 28, *33, 34*, 35
coppicing 314, 315
coral spot 365
cordials 259
cordons 197, 211, 255, 263, 275
Cordyline 130, 309, *420*
Coreopsis 341
corkscrew rush 176
corms 102, 160, 378–9
corn chamomile (*Anthemis*) 341
corn cockle (*Agrostemma*) 169, 170, 341
corn lily (*Ixia*) 162, 377
corn salad 207
cornflower *14*, 168, 169, 170
Cornus (dogwood)
  ground-cover 414
  pruning 314, 315, 321
  taking cuttings 331
  winter color 112, 123, *314*, 321
  C. alba 123, *410*
  C. controversa 129, *422*
  C. kousa 424
  C. mas 410
  C. sericea 'Flaviramea' *420*
Cortaderia 416
Corylopsis 402
Corylus 410
Cosmos 169, *171, 372, 390*

Cotinus 113, 313, 315
  C. 'Grace' 131, *408*
Cotoneaster 113, *131*, 146, 323, 329
  C. horizontalis 393
  C. lacteus 410
  C. salicifolius 408
cotton lavender see *Santolina*
courtyards 36, 59, 108, 115, 143
cowslip 382
crab apple see *Malus*
Crassula helmsii 177
Crataegus 122, 361, *422*
creeping Jenny see *Lysimachia*
Crinodendron 392
Crinum x *powellii* 378
Crocosmia 113, *378*
Crocus 160, 161, 162
  C. chrysanthus 'E. A. Bowles' *376*
  fall 113, *378*
crop rotation 197, 198
crown rot 365
Cryptomeria japonica 325
cucumber 201, 203, *214–15*, 365
cultivars 13, 15, 132, 140, 146, 150, 156,
  172, 180, 211, 229, 426
cup and saucer vine 143
Cupressus macrocarpa 418
curled pondweed 177
curly waterweed 177
currant blister aphid 361
curry plant see *Helichrysum italicum*
cut-and-come-again *207*
cut flowers 170
cut worms 361
cuttings 326, 330–1, 332
Cyclamen 160, 161, *376, 378*
Cydonia oblonga 146, 260, 272
  see also quince
Cynara cardunculus 386
cypress
  Leyland 322
Cytisus 128, 392, 402

D

Dactylicapnos scandens 394
Dahlia 164–5, 309, *378*
  annuals 169, *171*
  in containers 55, *159*
  lifting/storing 162, 309
  planting 161, 169
  tubers *160*
  winter protection 309
Dame's violet (*Hesperis*) 169
damp conditions 17, 138
  see also bog plants
damping off 329, 365
damsons 257, 260, 266, 267, 367
dandelion 352
Daphne 126, *390, 392, 402, 410*
Darmera peltata 388
Daucus carota 341
Davidia involucrata 315
daylilies see *Hemerocallis*
deadheading 12, 257, 293, 306, 319

deadnettle 141
debris disposal 61, 64
decks
  design 72, 73, 76
  laying 90–1
  uses 32, 40, 43, 57
Delphinium 12, 106, *135*, 136, 138, 290,
  341, *383*
Deschampsia 139, 156, 157
design
  see also structural elements
  achieving targets 60–1
  assessing needs 28–31, 60
  calming retreat 44–7
  color and texture 110–11
  creating a style 31, 106–9
  drawing plans 79, 80–3
  easy-care gardens 56–9
  entertaining areas 32–5
  enthusiast's garden 52–5
  family gardens 40–3
  fruit/vegetables 36–9
  garden rooms 114–15
  inspiration 31
  lighting 76–7
  new gardens 65
  planning restrictions 65
  planting plans 62, 80–1, 104–5, 300
  redesigning gardens 62–4
  surveying site 66–7
  weed prevention 350
  wildlife garden 48–51
Deutzia 128, 313, *405*
Dianthus 138, 363
  D. barbatus 170
  D. 'Becky Robinson' *374, 390*
  D. 'Bovey Belle' *383*
  D. gratianopolitanus 386
  D. 'Pike's Pink' *400*
Diascia 400
dibble 191
Dicentra 141, 412
Dichelostemma 162
Dicksonia antarctica (tree fern) 54, 123,
  308–9, *420*
Dierama pulcherrimum 136, *379*
digging 21, 24, 192, 430
Digitalis 12, 167
  conditions preferred 168
  D. grandiflora 380
  D. purpurea 169, *372*
dill *249*
dining area 28, 32, 34–5, 70, 114
Disanthus cercidifolius 408
diseases see pests and diseases
dividing plants 154, 162, 307, 326, 332–3, 344
divisions 32, 35, 70–1, 77, *121*
dogs 40
dog's-tooth violet 376
dogwoods see *Cornus*
Doronicum 111
drainage 60, 65, 66, 69, 72
Drimys 391
dry conditions 56, 135, 301
  ground-cover plants 412

hot/dry spots 17, 140, 141, 412, 432–3
Mediterranean plants 17, 23, 53, 107
perennials 135, 138, 141
shrubs for 126
Dryopteris 105, 123, *179, 420*

E

earthworms *20*, 21, 23
eastern redbud *422*
easy-care gardens 30, 56–9, 103, 107
Echinacea 138, *139, 384*
Echinops 173, *383, 420*
eelworms 362
eggplant 187, 194, 202, *213*
Eichhornia crassipes (Water hyacinth) 177
Elaeagnus 109, 301, 321, *410*
elder see *Sambucus*
elephant's ears see *Bergenia*
Elodea canadensis 345
Elodea nuttallii (Nutall's waterweed) 177
Elymus magellanicus 416
endive 203, *209*
English-style garden 106
  climbers 115, 143, *149*
  containers 109
  grouping plants 105
  ornamental vegetables 39
  perennials 135
  roses 115, 133, *143*
  scented plants 142, *143*
Enkianthus 128
Ensete ventricosum 420
entertaining outdoors 28, 32–5
enthusiast's garden 52–5
environmental factors 38, 109, 298, 300–1
  see also wildlife
Epimedium 117, 137
equipment see tools and equipment
Equisetum hyemale 179
Eragrostis 150
Eranthis hyemalis 380
Erica
  see also heather; heaths
  E. arborea var. *alpina* 402
  E. carnea 123, 155
Erigeron karvinskianus 400
Erinus alpinus 400
Eriobotrya japonica 421
Eryngium 111, 301, *384, 386*
Erysimum 169, *390, 400*
Erythronium dens-canis 376
Escallonia 321, 323
Eschscholzia californica 169, 170, 341, *372*
espaliers 16, 36, 115, 264, 265
Eucalyptus 315, 321, *424*
Eucomis 309
Euonymus 109, 329
  E. alatus 408
  E. fortunei 130, 146, 317, 333
Eupatorium 105, 136, *139*, 157
Euphorbia 111, *140, 156*
  E. characias 421
  E. griffithii 'Fireglow' *163*
  E. hypericifolia 373

E. marginata 166
E. myrsinites 301
E. palustris 388
E. polychroma 380
E. rigida 138
evening primrose 169
evergreen laburnum 393
evergreens
see also conifers
climbers/wall shrubs 143, 146, 149, 317, 392, 393
easy-care gardens 56, 58, 59
frost pockets 67
grasses 150, 156
perennials 137, 138, 140
pruning 311, 321
scented 142, 390, 391
shrubs 126, 127, 311
topiary 324
trees 119, 393
urban gardens 107
wildlife garden 48
winter interest 112
everlasting flower 170
Exochorda 313, 403
exotic plants
bulbs 159
in containers 109, 290
garden design 31, 52–4, 61, 134
protecting 10, 308–9
tree ferns 54, 123, 308, 309, 420
exposed sites 60–1, 67, 434–5
exposure of garden 61, 67
eyesores 16, 52, 55, 398

F

F1/F2 hybrids 329–30
fall
bulbs/corms/tubers 158, 161, 378–9
perennials 112, 113, 383–5
shrubs 113, 146, 408–9, 422
tasks 197, 257, 294–7, 309, 341
falling stars (*Campanula*) 375
false acacia see *Robinia*
false spikenard 382
family gardens 29, 40–3, 109
Fargesia 152, 155, 416
fat hen 353
Fatsia 111, 421
feather grass see *Stipa tenuissima*
feeding 23, 302–3, 355, 356
Felicia amelloides 372
fences
climbers 142, 143, 149
design 70–1, 85
fruit/vegetables 188, 189, 264, 274
putting up 84–5
renovating 63
fennel 203, 217, 301
ferns 22, 123, 141, 159
acid soil 426
near water 179, 389
for shade 17, 105, 138
structural plants 420–1

tree ferns 54, 123, 308, 309, 420
fertilizers 22–3, 302–3
before planting 192, 193
lawns 336, 337
natural 22, 197, 199, 303
nutrient deficiencies 355
Festuca 333, 416
feverfew see *Tanacetum*
figs (*Ficus*) 256, 260, 273, 422
Filipendula 388
fir see *Abies*
fire pit 28, 32, 33
fire blight 366
fish 97, 174, 288, 342, 346–7
flag see *Iris*
flannel bush 146, 393
flea beetles 361
flowers
edible 37, 39, 220, 292
feeding 23
pollination 13, 254, 256
with vegetables 36, 38, 39
focal points
calm retreat 29, 44–7
containers 44, 45, 57, 59, 79, 109, 305
easy-care garden 57, 59
lighting 71
plants 104, 131, 143, 153, 164
redesigning gardens 63
trees 108, 119, 121, 125
Foeniculum vulgare 301
foliage plants
see also evergreens
annuals/biennials 166
bamboo/grasses 150, 156–7
in containers 109
fall 113, 408–9, 427
perennials 140–1, 386
pests and diseases 361, 366
pruning 315, 317
shrubs 126, 129
structural 420–1
texture and color 111
trees 119, 124, 424–5
variegated 315
forget-me-nots see *Myosotis*
forks 190
formal gardens 37, 106, 115, 133
Forsythia 311, 313, 323
F. x *intermedia* 403
white 402
Fothergilla 403, 409
fountains 33, 40, 44–5, 56, 58, 77, 343
foxglove tree 315, 332
foxgloves see *Digitalis*
Frankenia 138
freezing produce 201, 259
Fremontodendron 146, 393
French marigolds see *Tagetes*
Fritillaria 162, 362, 376, 378
frogbit (*Hydrocharis*) 389
frost 37, 53, 274, 288, 300–9
frost-hardy plants 10
frost pockets 67
fruit

in beds 186–7
berries/currants 274–85
choosing/planting 254–5
in containers/small spaces 188–9, 253, 257
crop planner 260–1
feeding 23, 257
flower pollination 13, 254
growing 36–9, 183–9, 252–3
harvesting 257, 258–9, 291
mixed planting 252, 356
pests and diseases 198–9, 294, 356, 358, 360–1, 365, 368
planting trees 289, 296
preparing site 192–3
protection 37, 289, 309, 358
reproduction 13
seasonal planner 256–8
storing/preserving 258–9
texture and color 111
tools 190–1
trees 36, 188, 252–7, 262–73
under cover 187
watering 299, 300
Fuchsia 22, 167, 307
pruning 312, 313, 325
taking cuttings 331
F. 'Celia Smedley' 374
fungal diseases 364, 365–9
fungicides 359
furniture 32, 33, 45, 57
fusarium wilt 366

G

gages 261, 266–7, 367
Galanthus (snowdrops) 159, 160, 161, 162, 376
Gallium verum 341
Galtonia 309
garden buildings
climbers 16, 143
design 74–5, 77, 82
green roofs 48
play areas 41, 43, 75
renovating 63
for storage 25, 41, 43, 57
summerhouse 34, 43
garden fabric 93, 191, 193, 196, 199, 256, 257, 288, 308, 334
garden rooms 32, 70–1, 114–15
gardening year
fall 294–5, 296–7
spring 288–9, 290–1
summer 290–1, 292–3, 294–5
winter 296–7
garlic 201, 203, 234
Garrya elliptica 146, 317, 393
gates 71
Gaura lindheimeri 159
Gazania 374
Gentiana 400
Geranium
hardy 12, 138, 380
roof gardens 107

tender 12
white 131
G. cinereum 'Ballerina' 380
G. 'Nimbus' 384
germination 194, 329
Geum 137, 381
gherkins 215
giant lily (*Cardiocrinum*) 379
gillyflower (*Matthiola*) 375, 391
ginger lily (*Hedychium*) 209
Gladiolus 160, 161, 162, 309, 379
glasshouse red spider mite 212, 223, 270, 361–3
glasshouse whitefly 213, 242, 356, 358, 361, 363
globe artichokes 189, 203, 246, 290
globe thistle see *Echinops*
glory flower see *Clerodendrum*; *Eccremocarpus*
Glyceria maxima 388
goatsbeard (*Aruncus*) 389
golden bell (*Forsythia suspensa*) 393
golden club (*Orontium*) 177, 345
golden sedge 151
gooseberries 256, 257, 258, 260, 282, 284
gooseberry sawfly 361
preserving 259
grape hyacinths see *Muscari*
grapes 253, 256, 257, 258, 261, 274–5
grasses 102
see also lawns
balconies/roofs 107, 115
blue 156, 416
borders 105, 126, 156–7, 173
with bulbs 159
choosing/planting 152–5, 157, 416–17
dark leaves 140
dry conditions 135
effective use 150–1
fall/winter 112, 113, 387
family gardens 109
maintenance 154
natural planting 55, 105, 135
planting ideas 155
pollination 13
rustling sound 44
screening/hedging 398
seed heads 112, 113, 154, 296
shelterbelts 67
with shrubs 129
water plants 388
as weeds 352
wildlife garden 49, 50, 108
gravel 55, 56, 59, 72–3, 107, 135, 157
gravel board 85
gray mold see botrytis
green manures 23
green onions 200, 205, 233
green roofs 48, 115
greenfly see aphids
greenhouse 75
exotic plants 53, 309
hardening off 195

maintenance 196
pollination 256
propagation 326, 327
using 75, 187, 189, 197, 211
ground elder 353
ground-cover plants
  garden design 16, 56, 104
  perennials 134, 382, 387
  for shade 414–15
  for sun 412–13
  weed prevention 351
groundsel 353
growing bags 36, 188, 193, 211
Guelder rose see *Viburnum opulus*
Gunnera manicata 10, 111, 141

H

hairy bitter cress 353
Hakonechloa macra 157
Hamamelis (*witch hazel*) 112, 127, *128*, 390
  H. x intermedia *390, 410*
hammock 32, 46
hand sprayers 191
handkerchief tree 315
hanging baskets
  annuals/biennials 167
  fruit/vegetables 36, 37, 188, 211, 276
  planting 305
  watering 293, 298, 299
hard surfaces 32, 40, 45, 57, 63, 72–3
hardening off 10, 195, 196, 329
hardy plants 10, 12
hawthorn 323, 345, 361, 422
hazel, corkscrew 410
heather 123, *128*, 130
  see also *Calluna; Erica*
heaths 130, 402
heavenly bamboo (*Nandina*) 406
Hebe 127, *128*
  H. 'Midsummer Beauty' *405*
  H. pinguifolia *400*
hedges
  Contemporary styles 108
  cutting 60, 291, 311, 322–3
  design 70–1
  formal 106, 322–3
  garden rooms 114
  plants 130, 133, 142, 151, 398–9
  renovating 323
  topiary 83, 324–5
  wildlife 50
Hedychium 309
Helenium 138, *159, 384*
Helianthemum *401, 405*
Helianthus *172–3, 385*
Helichrysum 171
Helictotrichon 156, 157
heliotrope 168
Helleborus 112, 134, *137,* 159
  H. argutifolius *381*
  H. foetidus 117
  H. niger *386*
  H. x ericsmithii *382*

Hemerocallis (day lilies) 39, 107, 147, 307, 332–3, *384*
herbs
  annual 248–9
  bringing indoors 296
  in containers *37,* 109, 188
  deadheading 257
  formal garden 36, 37
  freezing 201
  ground-cover 351, *413*
  in lawns 341
  perennial 196, 250–1
  potagers *38*
  in raised beds 43
Hesperis matronalis 169
Heuchera 107, 137, *140,* 386
Hibiscus 111
  H. rosa-sinensis 14
  H. syriacus 313, *406,*
  H. trionum *372*
Himalayacalamus 152
hoes 190, 351
Holcus 152
holly 322, 323, 324, 325
honesty (*Lunaria*) 169, *373*
honey bush (*Melianthus*) 141, 309, *421*
honey fungus 366
honeysuckle see *Lonicera*
hop (*Humulus*) 131
hornbeam 115, *118,* 322, 323, 324, 325
hornwort (*Ceratophyllum*) 177, 344, 345
horsetails 179
hoses 25, 154, 299
hostas 140, 141, *175,* 290, 333
  planting 137, 138
  H. 'Francee' *138*
hot/dry spots 17, 134, 140, 141, 412, 432–3
Hottonia palustris 345
house leek see *Sempervivum*
Humulus 131
Hyacinthus 163, *376*
hydrangeas
  climbing 142
  pruning 311, 313
  shady spots *128*
  taking cuttings 331
  texture and color *111,* 113
  H. macrophylla *406*
  H. paniculata 313, *406*
  H. quercifolia *409*
  H. serrata 'Blue Deckle' *127*
Hydrocotyle ranunculoides 177
Hylotelephium 137, 138
  H.'Herbstfreude' *157*
  H. spectabile (Ice plant) *139, 307*
  H. telephium *141*
Hypericum *406*

I

Iberis 12, 169, 170, 341
ice plant see *Sedum*
Ilex (holly) 322, 323, 324, 325
  I. aquifolium *424*
  I. crenata 325

Impatiens 167, 168, *374*
Imperata cylindrica 155, *417*
Indian bean tree see *Catalpa bignonioides*
Indian shot plant see *Canna*
Indocalamus 152, *155*
insects
  attracting 108, 170, 357
  flower pollination 13, 254
  pests 360–3
  preventing 191
  removing 199, 358, 359
  wildlife garden 30, 48, 49, 51, 175
intercropping 185, 200
Ipomoea (morning glory) 147, 149, 329, *375*
Iris
  by water 10, 176, *178,* 180
  contemporary plots 105, 108
  dividing/planting 307, 344
  rhizomes 160
  I. foetidissima *387*
  I. 'George' *377*
  I. laevigata *175, 178, 179*
  I. pallida 'Variegata' *379*
  I. pseudacorus *175,* 345
  I. sibirica *381, 388*
  I. unguicularis 301
  I. versicolor *181,* 345
Itea ilicifolia *409*
ivy 114, 123, 144, 316
Ixia viridiflora *162*

J

Japanese anemone
  see Anemone × hybrida
Japanese blood grass *417*
Japanese knotweed 353
Japanese maple see *Acer palmatum*
Japanese onions 233
Japanese quince see *Chaenomeles*
Japanese rush 344
Japanese wineberry 281
Japanese-style gardens 46, 155
jasmine 114, 115, 149
  layering 333
  star jasmine 115, *142*
  winter *411*
  J. humile *393*
  J. nudiflorum *411*
  J. officinale *390*
Jerusalem artichokes 204, 246
Joe pye weed see *Eupatorium*
Judas tree 315
Juncus effusus 176
juneberry (*Amelanchier*) *422*
Juniperus 325, *418*

K

kale 198, 204, *242*
  mixed planting 36, 39, 189
Kerria 313, 333
Knautia 51
Kniphofia 55, 111, 135, 173
  K. 'Bees' Sunset' *384*

K. 'Percy's Pride' *155*
kohlrabi 200, 204, 227
Kolkwitzia 313, *403*

L

laburnum 329, *422*
lady's smock 389
Lagarosiphon major 177
Lagurus ovatus 157, *417*
lamb's ears (*Stachys*) 111, *140,* 141, 301
lamb's lettuce 207
Lamium 138, 141
Lamprocapnos 137
land cress 207
Lantana camara 'Radiation' *372*
lantern tree (*Crinodendron*) *392*
larkspur *170,* 341
Lathyrus odoratus 143
Latin names 14–15
laurel
  bay *251,* 324, 325
  cherry 322
  Portuguese 324, 325
Lavandula (lavender) 106, 107, 108, 130, 133, 323
  drought tolerance 301
  pruning 295, 313
  taking cuttings 331
  L. angustifolia *390*
  L. stoechas *406*
Lavatera 113, 313, 331
lawns 334–41
  see also meadows
  alternatives 56, 73, 334, 341
  with bulbs *16,* 58, 158, 162
  buying turf 334
  caring for 23, 25, 73, 289, 334–9, 341
  Contemporary style 108
  dead leaves 295, 337
  edges 99, 335, 336, 338
  family gardens 40
  herb lawns 341
  pests/diseases 361, 369
  renovating 335, 338–9
  reshaping 63, 335, 336
  sowing/laying 92–3, 299, 334, 335
  tools and equipment 25, 335
  watering/feeding 336–7
layering 332–3
leaf crops 208–9, 227
leaf miners 361
leaf spots 366
leaf mold 22, 295
leatherjackets 361
LED light 76–7
leeks 204, *235,* 290, 366
legumes 198
lemon balm *391*
lemon verbena (*Aloysia*) *375*
Lenten rose see *Helleborus × hybridus*
Leonotis leonurus 309
leopard's bane (*Doronicum*) *111*
lettuces 188, 200, 204, *206, 363*

Leucanthemum 137, *156*, *171*, 341
Leucojum aestivum 'Gravetye Giant' *377*
Leucothoe 128
Leycesteria 313
Libertia 115, 137, 140
lifestyle 60, 103, 185
lighting 32, 57, 76–7
Ligularia 388
lilac see *Syringa*
lilies 160, *173*, 309, 362
    L. 'Golden Splendor' *158*
    L. regale 379
    L. 'Stargazer' *390*
lily turf see *Liriope*; *Ophiopogon*
lily-of-the-valley (*Convallaria*) *376*, 382
lime trees, pleached 60
lime-rich soil 21, 428–9
Limnathes douglasii (poached egg plant)
    170, 200, *375*
Linum perenne 341
lion's ear (*Leonotis*) 309
Liriope muscari 387
Lobelia 167, *178*, 375
Lobularia maritima 170
log piles 48
loganberries 256, 257, 260, 281, 362,
    364, 367
Lonicera (honeysuckle) 115, 142, 144, 145,
    316, 333
    L. nitida 129
    L. periclymenum 390
loquat (*Eriobotrya*) *393, 421*
Lotus maculatus 173
love-in-the-mist see *Nigella*
Ludwigia spp. (Water primrose) *177*
Lunaria annua 169
Lupine see *Lupinus*
Lupinus 106, 136, *139*, *381*
Lysimachia 131, 138, *176*, *179*
Lythrum 139, 176, 177

M

Magnolia 14, 112, 333
    M. liliiflora 'Nigra' *406*
    M. stellata 403
Mahonia 108, 321
    M. japonica 112, *411*
    M. x media 391, 393
maintenance, design 56, 58, 60, 103
Malcolmia 169
Malus 113, 163
    M. 'Evereste' *422*
    M. 'Lemoinei' *424*
    M. tschonoskii 425
maple see *Acer*
marginal plants 103
    choosing 55, *175*, 176, 178, 179
    maintenance 178, 344
    plant directory 388–9
marguerites 167
marigolds
    corn 341
    French see *Tagetes*
    marsh see *Caltha palustris*

pot see *Calendula*
marrows 203, 220, 290
marsh marigold see *Caltha palustris*
meadow clary (*Salvia*) 341
meadows
    annuals/biennials 167, 168
    easy-care garden 56, 57, 334
    grasses 151
    mowing 341
    sowing 340–1
    wildlife garden 50, 51
mealybugs 362
Mediterranean plants 23, 53, 107
Melianthus major 141, 309, *421*
Melissa officinalis 391
melons 256
mesh 144, 230, 231
    insect-proof 191, 226, 358, 360, 361
    wire 233, 234, 306
mice 362
Michaelmas daisies (*Symphyotrichum*) 113,
    138, 157, 430, 440
microclimates 17, 52, 61
mildew 359, 366, 367
Milium 152
millet, annual *173*
Mimulus 178
mint *251*, 344, 391
mirrors 45
Miscanthus 105, *156*, 157, *173*, 296
    M. sinensis 387, 417
mizuna 207
mock orange see *Philadelphus*
Modernist designs 105, 108
Moluccella laevis 170
Monarda 384, 387
monkey flower (*Mimulus*) *178*
morning glory see *Ipomoea*
mosaic virus 366, 369
moths 362
mountain pepper (*Drimys*) *393*
mulberry 365
mulches 23, 56, 300–1, 350
mullein see *Verbascum*
Musa basjoo (banana) 54, *134*, 308, 309, *421*
Muscari 159, 161, *163*, *377*, 391
musk mallow (*Malva moschata*) 341
mustard, white 207
Myosotis 168, 169, *389*
Myriophyllum 177, 344, 345
Myrtus communis (myrtle) 324, 325, *393*,
    406

N

Nandina domestica 406
Narcissus 158
nasturtium see *Tropaeolum*
native plants 48
natural planting 55, 105, 135
nectarines 253, 256, 257, 261, 270–1, 289
    diseases 367, 368
Nectaroscordum siculum 379
nematode 199, 229, 247, 248, 277, 289,
    290, 362

Nemesia 171, 293, *373*, 391
Nepeta racemosa 135
Nerine 113, 160, 161, *379*
netting 191, 199, 224, 257
nettles 353
new gardens 64–5, 66–7
New Zealand cabbage palm 309
New Zealand flax see *phormiums*
Nicotiana 167, *373*
Nigella 167, 168, 169, 341, *373*
north-facing walls 394
northern sea oats (*Chasmanthium*) 387
nutrition 11, 355
Nymphaea 174, 179, 180, 344, 391
    N. 'Aurora' 345
    N. 'Froebelli' *389*
    N. 'James Brydon' 345

O

oak, holm 325
obelisks 95
Oenothera biennis 169
offsets 13
Olea europaea (olive) 107, *423*
oleander 375
olive (*Olea*) 107, *423*
onions 232–3
    bulbils *13*
    crop rotation 198
    intercropping 200
    pests and diseases 362, 366
    planting/harvesting 204, 295
    spring 200, *233*
Ophiopogon 140, 333, 387
orache, red (*Atriplex*) 129
oregano *251*
organic gardening 184, 199
Orontium aquaticum 177, 345
Osmanthus 403
Osteospermum 171, *373*
ostrich fern (*Matteuccia*) *389*
ox-eye daisy (*Leucanthemum*) 341
oxalis 353
oxygenating plants 103, 176, 177, 344,
    345, 347

P

Pachysandra 138
Paeonia 307, *381, 403, 406*, 421
palms 53, *420*
Pampas grass (*Cortaderia*) *416*
Panicum 157, *173*
pansies see *Viola*
Papaver (poppies) 168, 170
    meadows *167*, 168, 341
    Mediterranean gardens 107
    P. orientalis 136, 332, *384*
    P. rhoeas 341, *373*
Parrotia persica 425
parrot's feather (*Myriophyllum*) *177*, 345
parsley *249*, 360
parsnips 198, 200, 201, 204, *230–1*

pests/diseases 360, 363, 366
parterres 133, 173
Parthenocissus
    P. quinquefolia 144
    P. tricuspidata 142
pasqueflower (*Pulsatilla*) *381*
Passiflora (passion flower) 144
paths
    calming retreat 45
    design 68–9, 72–3, 79, 80
    easy-care garden 30
    family gardens 40, 41, 43
    in lawns 338, 339, 341
    laying 60, 86–7
    renovating 63
    tree-lined 119
patios
    containers 109, 304
    design 40, 67
    fruit/vegetables 36, 38, 188, 253
    laying 88–9
    Mediterranean style 107
    paving feature 57
    plants 143, 148, 149
    secluded 34, 35
    upgrading 63
Paulownia tomentosa 315, 332
paving 57, 60, 86–9, 138
pea sticks 191
peaches 253, 256, 257, 260, 270–1, 289
    pests/diseases 365, 367, 368
pearly everlasting (*Anaphalis*) 385, *386*
pears 253, 257, 258, 260, *264–5*, 294
    pests and diseases 294, 361, 362, 364,
        365, 366, 368
peas 198, 200, 204, 236, 292
pebble fountain 40, 56, 58
pebbles, decorative 57, 59
Pelargonium 167, *171*, 331, *375*
Pennisetum 156, 157
    P. alopecuroides 154, 155, *417*
    P. orientale 159
Penstemon 171, *384*
peony see *Paeonia*
peppers 189, 194, 201, 204, *212*, 364
perennials 12, 102
    acid soil 426
    with bulbs *163*
    chalky/lime-rich soils 428
    Chelsea chop 138
    choosing 18, 136–9
    clay soil 430
    in containers 109
    cuttings 330–1, 332
    diseases 365, 366
    easy-care gardens 56, 58
    exposed sites 434
    fall 112, 113, 383–5
    family gardens 109
    foliage effects 140–1
    ground-cover 351, 412, 414
    herbs 250–1
    hot/dry sites 432
    lifting/dividing 307, 332–3
    maintenance 306–7

planting plans 104, 105, 134–5, 139
planting/aftercare 137–8
restricted spaces 115
with shrubs 129, 131
spring 112, 163, 380–2
staking 306
structural plants 421
summer 380–2, 380–5
weeds 64, 352–3
wildlife garden 48
winter 386–7
pergolas
climbers 52, 143, 149
entertaining areas 32, 35
fruit/vegetables 37, 189, 274
making 94–5
for privacy 44
wiring up posts 145
periwinkle see Vinca
Perovskia 312, 313, *385*
Persian buttercup see *Ranunculus asiaticus*
Persicaria 106, *179*, *385*
Peruvian lilies (Alstroemeria) 160, *378*, 379
pests and diseases
apples 263, 294
avoiding 198–9
barriers and traps 199, 358
biological controls 358, 361, 362, 363
blackberries 280
blueberries 285
cherries 269
common diseases 364–9
common pests 360–3
crop rotation 198
currants 283
dealing with 198–9, 356–9
fungicides 359
grapes 275
hedge trimming 323, 324
identification 62, 360–9
insecticides 359, 360, 361, 362, 363
peaches/nectarines 270
pears 264
plants to deter 200
plums/gages 267
quinces 272
raspberries 279
resistant varieties 184, 199
roses 133
slugs and snails 178, 199, 228, 289, 290, 357, 358, 363
strawberries 277
Petunia
containers 167
deadheading 293
feeding 22
planting out 12, 168, 293
sowing 169
P. surfinia 'Pink Vein' *375*
Phacelia tanacetifolia 170, 341
Philadelphus 313, 331
P. 'Belle Etoile' *403*
P. 'Lemoinei' *391*

Phillyrea latifolia 324, 325
Phlomis 157, *387*
Phlox 385, *401*
phormiums 67, 107, 109, *140*, 141, 421
Photinia 313
Phygelius × *rectus* *407*
Phyllostachys 152
P. aureosulcata *150*
P. bambusoides 155
P. nigra *150*, 417
P. vivax f. *aureocaulis* *417*
phytophthora 367
Picea 418
pickerelweed (*Pontederia*) 180, 345, *389*
Pieris 66, 105, *128*
pinching off 306–7
pineapple lily (*Eucomis*) 309
pineapple mint 391
pinks see *Dianthus*
Pinus 155, 418, 419
Pistia stratiotes 345
Pittosporum 129, *139*, 399
plant directory 370–93
planting plans
design 62, 83, 104–5
drawing up 116–17
fruit 185, 258, 260–1
gardening year 196–7
lifestyle impact 103
vegetables 185, 200, 202–5
plants
calculating quantities 116
choosing healthy 18–19
classification 14–15, 102–3
cuttings 330–1, 332
diagnosing problems 354–5
dividing 326, 332–3, 344
drought tolerant 56
enthusiast's garden 52–5
exposure considerations 61, 67
functions 104
grouping 105
hardening off 10, 195–6, 329
identifying mystery 62
Latin names 14–15
layering 161
life cycles 12
low-maintenance 30, 56, 58, 103
natural planting 53, 105, 135
positioning 16–17, 52–5, 105, 354
reproduction 13
requirements 10–11
restricted spaces 115
sculptural 58
seasonal effects 112–13
Platycladus orientalis 419
play areas 40, 41, 42, 43
Pleioblastus 152, *155*
plug plants 168, 195
plums 257, 259, 261, *266–7*
pests/diseases 361, 365, 367, 368
poached egg plant (*Limnanthes*) 170, 200, *372*, *375*
pollarding 315, 321
pollination 13, 254, 256

Polygonatum 163, *381*
polytunnels 37, 187, 308
pomegranate (*Punica*) 309
ponds/pools 342–7
see also aquatic; marginal; oxygenating plants
barrel pool 177, 343
calming retreat 29, 44, 47
chemical spraying 359
dead leaves 295, 342
entertaining areas 34
fish 97, 174, 288, 342, 346–7
frogs/toads 357
invasive plants 152, 345
lighting 76
maintenance 342–5, 347
making 96–7
pebble pool 343
plants near 123, 176, 179
weeds 176, 177, 178, 342–3
wildlife 30, 47, 48, 49, 51, 108, 293, 342, 347
Pontederia cordata 180, 345, *389*
poppies
see also *Papaver*
blue see *Meconopsis grandis*
California see *Eschscholzia californica*
oriental see *Papaver orientalis*
tree see *Romneya coulteri*
Portuguese laurel (*Prunus lusitanica*) 324, 325
positioning plants 16–17, 52–5, 105, 354
pot marigolds see *Calendula*
potagers 36, 38, 130
Potamogeton crispus 177
potato vine 145, 396
potatoes 188, 196, 198, 204, *228–9*
pests/diseases 361, 362, 367, 369
Potentilla fruticosa 407
pots
see also containers
feeding 303, 304
plant displays 52, 54, 109
preparing 193, 304–5
restricted spaces 115
sowing seed 326
to fill border gaps 52, 55
watering 299, 301
potting media 21, 304–5, 327
water-retaining crystals 301
prairie cord grass (*Spartina*) 152
prairie planting 55, 105, 135, 139, 156
preserving produce 201, 259
pricking out 194, 196
Primula 163
near ponds 176, 179, 389
P. beesiana 389
P. pulverulenta Bartley hybrids *179*
P. × *bulleesiana* *381*
privacy 32, 34–5, 40–3, 44, 70, 107, 118
privet 322
problems 349
see also shade
acid soil 66, 105, 128, 130, 285, 426–7
chalky/lime-rich soil 21, 428–9

diagnosing 354–5
eyesores *16*, 52, 55, 398
heavy clay soil 66, 430–1
hot/dry spots 17, 134, 140, 141, 412, 432–3
lawns 338–9
pests and diseases 356–69
screening/hedging plants 16, 398–9
weeds 350–3
windy/exposed spots 60, 61, 67, 434–5
professional help 60, 64, 83
propagation 326–33
blackberries 280
cuttings 326, 330–1, 332
dividing plants 326, 332–3, 344
growing from seed 12, 194–5, 196, 197, 326, 328–9
layering 332–3
materials 327
strawberries 277
protecting plants 37, 53, 288, 308–9
pruners 190
pruning 257, 310–11
apples 263
blackberries 281
black currants 282
blueberries 285
cherries 269
clematis 149
climbers 316–17
disease prevention 356
fans/cordons 256, 263, 265, 267, 269, 271
figs 273
for foliage 315
gooseberries 284
grapevines 275
peaches/nectarines 271
pears 265
pinching off 310
plums 267
quinces 272
raspberries 279
red/white currants 283
renovating plants 320–1
roses 318–19
shrubs 312–15
tools 24, 25, 190, 311, 320
wall shrubs 317
Prunus
see also cherries
pests/diseases 360–1, 364, 368
P. 'Kiku-shidare-zakura' *423*
P. laurocerasus 321, *403*
P. lusitanica 324, 325
P. serrula 112, *425*
P. × *cistena* *404*
Pseudosasa 152
Pulmonaria 140, 141, 333, *381*
Pulsatilla vulgaris *381*
pumpkin 205, *222*
Punica granatum 309
Puschkinia scilloides 377

Pyracantha 143, 146, 323, 331, 366
  P. 'Golden Charmer' *393*
Pyrus salicifolia 'Pendula' *423*

Q

Quercus ilex 325
quinces 146, 261, *272*, 331, *392*, 393
  Japanese see *Chaenomeles*
  pests and diseases 361, 367

R

radicchio 209
radish 198, 200, 205, *224*, 367
raised beds
  design 35, 55, 60
  easy-care gardens 56, 59
  family gardens 40, 43
  fruit and vegetables 36, *37*, 39, 187
  making 98–9, 192
  preparing to plant 193
  wildlife garden 50
rakes 190
ramps 69
Ranunculus 176, 177, 344, 345
raspberries 256, 257, 259, 261, *278–9*, 292
  pests/diseases 360, 362, 367
recycling 38, 109
red cabbage *241*
red currants *283*
  crop planner 260
  maintenance 256, 257
  mixed planting 36, 252
  pests and diseases 361
  preserving 259
red hot poker see *Kniphofia*
reed
  giant 398
  miniature 181, 344, 345, *389*
replant disease 368
reproduction process 13
restricted spaces 115
  color 110
  family space 42, 43
  fruit/vegetables 185, 188–9
  planting 115
  trees 115, 418–19, 422–3
rhizomes *13*, 102, 154, *160*
Rhodanthemum hosmariense 382
Rhododendron 105, *128*, 333
  R. 'Hotspur' *404*
  R. mucronulatum 127
rhubarb 205, *218*
Rhus 333, *409*, 425
Ribes 313, 331, 404
Ribwort plantain (*Plantago lanceolata*) 341
Ricinus communis 166, 375
Robinia 423
rock plants see *alpines*
rock rose see *Cistus*
Rodgersia 141, *389*
Romneya coulteri 332
roof gardens 107, 115

roofs, green 48, 115
root aphids 363
root cuttings 332
rootstocks 262, 266, 268, 272
rose bay (*Nerium*) 375
rosemary *250–251*, 301, 325, 391, 412
roses
  with clematis 133, *143*, 149
  climbers 16, 132, 133, 142, *143*, 319, 394, 398
  in containers 127, 133
  deadheading 293, 319
  edible petals 39, 292
  English gardens 106, *135*
  feeding 23
  floribunda 132, 318–19
  hybrid tea 132, 318
  miniature 132, 319
  old 132
  patio 22, 109, 127, 132, 318, 319
  pests and diseases 363, 368
  planting 105, 133
  planting ideas 131
  pruning 295, *310*, 312, 318–19
  ramblers 16, 132, 133, 142, *147*, 295, 319
  rose hips *146*
  for shade 394
  shrub 132, 133, *407*
  suckers 319, 333
  for sun 396
  supports 114, 144, 145, 147
  texture and color 111
  Rosa 'Gertrude Jekyll' *391*
  R. glauca 407
  R. 'Minnehaha' *147*
  R. 'Rose of Picardy' *139*
  R. 'Roseriaie de l'Hay' *407*
  R. 'The Fairy' *11*
  R. 'Winchester Cathedral' *131*
rowan see *Sorbus*
Rubus (ornamental bramble) 315
Rudbeckia 105, 137, 138, *159*, 307
  R. fulgida 385
runners *13*, 333
rust 239, 366, 368
rutabaga 185, 200, 201, 205, *230–1*, 367

S

safety 40, 76, 108, 336, 359
sage 39, *251*, 301, 331, 391
Sagittaria 176, 180, 345
salad burnet (*Sanguisorba minor*) 341
salads
  leaves 200, 203, 207
  lettuces 188, 204, *206*, 363
  loose-leaf crops *208–9*, 225
Salix 123, 314, 315, 321, 331
  S. caprea 'Kilmarnock' *423*
  S. hastata 'Wehrhahnii' *411*
Salvia 12, *111*, 135, 173, 331
  S. officinalis 251, 301
  S. pratensis 341
  S. rosmarinus 325, *395*, 412, *433*

S. x jamensis 'Hot Lips' *385*
Sambucus 315, 331, *407, 409*
Santolina 107, 325
Saponaria ocymoides 401
Sarcococca 112, *391, 411*
Sasa 152
Sasaella 152
satin flower (Clarkia) 169
sawfly 363
Saxifraga 159, *163*, 332
  S. 'Hindhead Seedling' *401*
  S. 'Southside Seedling' *382*
scab 364, 367, 368
scale insects 363
scented plants *390–1*
  bulbs 158
  calming retreat 45
  climbers 142
  water lilies 181
  wildlife gardens 51
  winter shrubs 410, 411
Scilla bifolia 377
sclerotinia rot 368–9
screening plants 398–9
  bamboo/grasses 16, 151, 153
  calming retreat 44, 45, 46
  climbers 16, 147, 149
  eyesores 63
  garden rooms 114
  restricted spaces 115
  shrubs 127
sculptural plants 58, 77
sculptures 31, 44, 45, 57, 59, 77
sea holly see *Eryngium*
seaside sites 67, 434–5
seasons
  assessing new gardens 62
  bulbs 159
  fruit/vegetables 200, 258
  planting effects 104, 112–13
  shrubs 127
seating 28, 60, 61
  calming retreat 29, 45
  courtyard garden 59
  entertaining areas 32, 34–5
  family gardens 29, 41, 42, 43
security 70, 76
sedges 102, 129, 151, 152, 153, 154, 416–17
Sedum 103, 105, 113, 137, 138, 332, 333
  Hylotelephium spectabile 139, 157
  S. 'Matrona' *387*
  S. telephium 141
seed
  bed 235
  collecting/storing 326, 329
  growing from 12, 194–5, 196, 197, 326, 328–9
  inducing germination 329
  preparing site 192–3
seed trays 191
self heal (*Prunella vulgaris*) *341*
Semiarundinaria 152
Sempervivum 109, 301, 332, *401*
Setaria macrostachya 157

shade 17, 67
  annuals/biennials 167, 168
  climbers for 394–5
  damp 17, 138
  grasses/bamboos 152
  ground-cover plants 414–15
  perennials for 105, 117, 134, 138, 140, 141
  seating areas *32, 35*
  shrubs for 126, 128
shallots 197, 201, 205, *232–3*, 366
Shasta daisies see *Leucanthemum*
sheds *74*
shelter 61, 67, 434
shepherd's purse 353
shrubs 102, 126–7
  see also wall shrubs
  acid soil 105, 128, 130, 426–7
  berries 113
  in borders 129
  chalky/lime-rich soils 428
  choosing 18, 128–31
  clay soil 430
  climbers through 143, 148
  in containers 129
  creating shade pockets 61
  easy-care gardens 56, 58
  edging plants 130
  evergreens 126, 127, 290, 311, 321, 351
  exotic planting 123
  exposed sites 434
  for fall 113, 408–9
  family gardens 109
  ground-cover 412, 414
  hot/dry sites 432
  pests and diseases 365, 367
  planting combinations 131
  planting/caring for 129–30, 306–7, 355
  propagation 330–1, 332, 333
  protection 308
  pruning 63, 297, 310–15, 320–1
  roses 132–3, *407*
  screening/hedging 398
  spring-flowering 402–4
  structural plants 421
  summer-flowering 297, 405–7
  wildlife garden 48, 50
  winter 112, 123, 297, 314, 410–11
Siberian bugloss see *Brunnera*
Siberian squill (*Scilla*) 377
Silene armeria 169, 341
silk tassel bush (*Garrya*) 146, 317, *393*
silver leaf 268
silver wattle 392
Sisyrinchium 137
site
  assessing 62, 66–7
  constraints 61
  measuring 80–1
  new gardens 65
  revamping 64
Skimmia 126, *411*
sloping gardens 60, 68–9, 412

slugs and snails 178, 199, 289, 290, 357, 358, 363
Smilacina racemosa 382
smoke bush see *Cotinus*
snake's head fritillary see *Fritillaria*
snapdragons (*Antirrhinum*) 372
snowdrops see *Galanthus*
soapwort (*Saponaria*) 401
soil
  acid 66, 105, 128, 130, 285, 426–7
  alkaline 23, 66, 128, 428
  analyzing 65, 66
  annual upkeep 57, 63, 341
  chalky/lime-rich 21, 428–9
  clay 20, *21*, 66, 430–1
  compaction *65*
  design impact 61, 66, 105
  digging 21, 24, 192, 430
  enriching 22–3, 51, 129, 139
  improving problem 21
  loam 20, 21
  mulching 23
  nitrogen 22–3
  pH 65, 66
  preparing site 192–3, 195
  sandy 20, 21, 66, 135
  structure 20–1, 65, 66
Solanum 145, 396, 397
Solenostemon 166, 168, 331
Solomon's seal see *Polygonatum*
sooty mold 369
Sorbus 113, 361
  S. aria 'Lutescens' *423*
  S. commixta 'Embley' *425*
  S. reducta 409
  S. vilmorinii 527
sound 44, 46
south-facing walls 396–7
spades 190
Sparaxis 162
Spartina 152
special collections 52
specimen plants 53
spinach 195, 200, 205, *209*
spindle 323
Spiraea 313, *404,* 407
spiritual features 44, 47
spotted wing drosophila 269
spring
  annual tasks 196, 256
  blossoms 112, 119, 124–5, 264, 272
  bulbs 125, 158–9, 161–3, 376–7
  early-mid 288–9
  late 290–1
  plants for 112, 380–2, 402–4
sprinklers 299
spruce *418*
spurge see *Euphorbia*
squash
  growing 37, *39,* 200, 205
  storing 297
  summer *221*
  winter *223*
Stachys 111, *135, 140,* 141, 301
Stachyurus 393

staking 306
steps 68–9, 76, 77
Stewartia 425
Stipa 105, 173
  S. calamagrostis 154
  S. gigantea 151, 155, 157, *417*
  S. tenuissima 150, 157, 301
stooling 315
storage
  apples and pears 258, 263, 265
  chemicals 359
  outdoors 41, 43, 57, 74–5
  tools 25
  vegetables 201, 297
Stratiotes aloides 345
strawberries 36, 276–7
  in containers 188, 252
  crop planning 258, 261
  grown with flowers 39
  harvesting 291
  maintenance 256, 257, 261
  pests and diseases 360, 368
  preserving 259
  runners *13,* 333
strawberry tree (*Arbutus*) *424*
structural elements
  boundaries/divisions 70–1
  fences 70–1, 84–5
  garden buildings 74–5
  lawn 73, 92–3
  lighting 76–7
  patios 67, 88–9
  pergolas/archways 94–5
  raised beds 98–9
  slopes 60, 68–9
  surfaces 72–3
  water features 96–7
structural plants 104, 106, 108, 127, 420–1
Styrax 425
succulents 52, 53, 56, 135, 141
suckers 319, 333
sumac (*Rhus*) 333, *425*
summer cabbages 200
summer 113
  annual tasks 197, 257
  annuals/biennials 166, 171
  bulbs/corms/tubers *158, 159,* 161, 162, 378–9
  containers 374–5
  early 290–1, 380–2
  late *159,* 294–5, 383–5
  midsummer 164, 292–3
  perennials 112, 113, 135, 139, 163, 380–5
  shrubs for 405–7
  wall shrubs 146
sun rose see *Helianthemum*
sunflowers see *Helianthus*
sunlight 11
sunny conditions 16
  annuals/biennials 168, 171
  climbers for 147, 396–7
  grasses/bamboos 152, 153
  ground-cover plants 412–13

hot/dry spots 17, 134, 140, 141, 396, 412, 432–3
  perennials 138, 139
  shrubs 128
sunroom 53
Swan River daisy 374
sweet box (*Sarcococca*) 128, *391*
sweet corn 13, 200, 201, 205, *216*
sweet peas (*Lathyrus*) 143, 391
sweet rocket (*Hesperis*) 169
sweet Williams (*Dianthus*) 170
sweet woodruff (*Galium*) 391
Symphytum 382
Syringa 313, *391, 404*

T

Tagetes 169, 170, *171,* 351, 356
Tanacetum parthenium 382
tansy, purple (*Phacelia*) 170, 341
tarragon *251*
Taxus
  exposed sites 434
  T. baccata (yew) 105, 115, 322, 323, 324, 325, *419*
  T. cuspidata 419
tayberries 256, 281
  pests/diseases 362, 364, 367
temperature 10, 17
tender plants
  annuals/biennials 167
  bulbs 159
  choosing 31, 52, 53, 54
  fruit trees 256, 257
  moving outside 290
  needs 10, 12, 61, 67
  perennials 134
  protecting 37, 53, 308–9
  shrubs 130
  water lilies 181
terraces 35, 63, 68–9
Tetrapanax 333
texture 111, 119, 150, 156, 158
Thalictrum 333, *382*
Thamnocalamus 152
Three Sisters method 200
Thuja 419
Thunbergia alata (black-eyed Susan) 147
thyme 108, 130, *251,* 341, 401
tickseed (*Coreopsis*) 341
Tigridia (tiger flower) 309
tiles 32, 72
tobacco plant see *Nicotiana*
tomatoes 197, *210–11*
  in containers 188
  crop rotation 198
  feeding 23, 294, 302
  grown with flowers 39
  pests/diseases 362, 364, 367, 369
  sowing/harvesting 205, 294
  under cover 187, 189, 194
tools and equipment
  basic 24–5
  family gardens 40
  fruit/vegetable growing 190–1

lawn-care 335, 336, 337
  ponds 343
  propagation 327
  pruning 311, 322, 325
  sterilizing 324
  winter maintenance 297
topiary
  basic techniques 324–5
  in containers 44, 109
  Contemporary gardens 108
  entertaining areas 32
  enthusiast's garden 52–3
  formal gardens 37, 106
  pruning 311
  shrubs 83, 129
  time available 60
  trees/focal points 119
Trachelospermum 115, *142*
traditional designs 105, 109
training, basic principles 26
Trapa natans 345
tree anemone (*Carpenteria*) 146, *392*
tree ferns 54, 123, 308, 309, *420*
tree poppy (*Romneya*) 332, 385
trees 102
  acid soil 426, 427
  chalky/lime-rich soils 428
  choosing healthy 18
  clay soil 430
  climbers through 143, 148
  conifers 13, 112, 115, 123, 127, 418–19
  in containers 125, 127, 188
  cordons 263, 264
  diseases 364, 365, 366, 367, 368
  dwarf 253
  effective use 118–19
  espalier 36, 115, 264–5, 266
  exposed sites 434
  family gardens 109
  fans 36, 255, 263, 264, 265, 269, 271
  focal points 111, 119
  frost protection 309
  fruit 36, 188, 252–7, 262–73, 275–85
  hot/dry sites 432
  multi-interest 424–5
  near ponds 176, 295
  new gardens 61, 63, 65
  ornamental 120–2, 124–5, 252
  planting ideas 123, 129
  planting plans 117
  planting under 105, 134, 141, 162, 163, 167
  planting/maintaining 121–2, 256, 257, 289, 296
  pleached 60, 107, 118
  pruning *310,* 315
  removing 64
  renovating 62, 320–1
  rootstocks 262, 266, 268, 272
  screening/hedging 398
  seasonal interest 112, 113
  small spaces 115, 422–3
  staking 122, 257
  structural plants 421
  topiary 106, 324–5

wildlife 122
wire supports 145, 255
trellis
climbers 52, 145, 147
dividing spaces 70, 71, 114
in fence panel 85
as screen 55
vegetables 36, 37
Triteleia 162
Trollius x *cultorum* 382
Tropaeolum
edible flowers 39, 292
growing 12, 143, 168, 169, *173*
intercropping 200
pest deterrent 356
weed prevention 351
T. majus 169, *375*
T. speciosum 379
troubleshooting see problems
trowels 190
Tsuga canadensis 419, *423*
tubers 102, *160*, 164–5, 309, 363, 378–9
tulips *159*, 160, 161, 163
T. 'Spring Green' *377*
turf red thread 369
turnips 195, 198, 201, 205, *230–1*, 367
Typha 175, 181, 344, 345, *389*

U

umbrella plant (*Darmera*) *388*
underwatering 11
urban-style gardens 107

V

variegated plants 140
vegetables
in beds 186–7
in containers/small spaces 185, 188–9
crop planner 200, 202–5
crop rotation 198
disease resistance 184, 199
family gardens 42, 43
freezing/preserving 201
gardening year 196–7
harvesting 294
heritage varieties 184
homegrown 28, 36–9, 183–9
inter-/catch-cropping 185, 200
mixed planting 36, *39*, 189, 356
pests/diseases 198–9, 356, 358
planting out 290
preparing site 192–3
protection *37*, 356
reproduction 13
storing 201
tools 190–1
under cover 187
watering 299, 300
Venus's Navelwort 373
veranda 35
Verbascum 137, 140, 169, *332*
V. bombyciferum 111
V. 'Cotswold Queen' *385*

V. 'Gainsborough' *139*
Verbena 113, 136, 157, *375*, *385*
lemon see *Aloysia triphylla*
Veronica 131
Veronicastrum virginicum 173
vertical planting 52, 115
verticillium wilt 369
Vestia foetida 393
Viburnum 331
V. burkwoodii 391
V. opulus 113, *409*
V. plicatum 404
V. tinus 128, 321, 325, *411*
V. x *bodnantense* 411
views 71, 82
Vinca 138
vine weevil 363
vines, grapes 274–5
Viola 37, 124, *159*, 167, 169, 293
edible flowers 292
white 131
V. 'Bowles's Black' *373*
V. x *wittrockiana* 382, 387
violet root rot 369
Virginia creeper see *Parthenocissus*
viruses 369
Vitis
grapevines 274–5

W

wake-robin (*Trillium*) 382
wall shrubs 77, 142–3, 146, 317, 392–3
wallflowers (*Erysimum*) 169, 390
walls
annuals 171
boundaries 70–1
climbers 114–15, 145, 149, 189, 394, 396
fruit trees 36, 189, 253, 255, 264–5, 268, 270–1, 273
fruit and vegetables 188, 189, 253
grapes 274
lighting 77
planting by 105, 299, 396, 414
renovating 63
retaining 68–9
urban gardens 107
vertical planting 52, 115
wildlife garden 48, 50
water barrels 300
water chestnut (*Trapa*) 345
water crowfoot (*Ranunculus*) 176, 177, 344, 345
water features 342–3
see also ponds/pools
bubble pool 97
calm retreat 29, 44–5, 47
in containers 175, *180*
easy-care garden 56, 58
entertaining areas 33
family gardens 40, 42
lighting 77
plants 10, 103, 174–5, 388–9
wildlife 47, 48, 49, 51

water fringe (*Nymphoides*) 389
water lettuce (*Pistia*) 345
water lilies see *Nymphaea*
water plants see aquatic; bog; marginal plants
water soldier (*Stratiotes*) 345
water violet (*Hottonia*) 345, 389
watering 298–301
automatic 56, 59, 299
bags 122
cans 25
conservation 300–1
containers 38
feeding techniques 302–3
fruit 256, 257
gray water 300
lawns 336–7
plant requirements 10
spring/summer 291
vegetables 196, 197
weeds
in bought plants 19
in lawns 335, 339
perennial 64, 352–3
ponds 342–3
prevention and control 196, 197, 198, 257, 350–1
spring 289
tools 24
troublesome 352–3
weed killers 351
Weigela 313, *404*
west-facing walls 396–7
whirled milfoil (*Myriophyllum*) 344, 345
white blister 369
white currants 257, 260, *283*, 361
wildflowers 16, 41, 46, 334, 340–1
see also meadows
wildlife gardens
calming sounds 44, 46
design 30, 48–51
family gardens 41
hedge trimming 323
pest deterrents 357
plants 108, 133, 173
ponds 177, 178, 343, 347
trees 122
water features 175, 346–7
willow herb 353
willows (*Salix*) 123, 314, 315, 321, 331, *411*
wind-chimes 44
window boxes 36, 115, 159, 188
windowsills 327
windy spots 61, 67, 434–5
winter
annual tasks 197, 257
bulbs 161
caring for garden 296–7, 337
perennials 386–7
plants for 112, 123
ponds 347
shrubs for 410–11
wall shrubs 146
winter aconite see *Eranthis*

winter box 112
winter's bark (*Drimys*) 391
wire supports 145, 255
wireworms 363
Wisteria 142, 144, 317, 333
witch hazel see *Hamamelis*
wood betony (*Stachys*) 135
wood cranesbill see *Geranium sylvaticum*
woodland 49, 105, 118, 134, 159, 167
Woodwardia radicans 421

Y

yarrow *135*, 307, 335, 383, 387
yellow mariposa (*Calochortus*) 377
yew 105, 114, 115, 322, 323, 324, 325
Yucca filamentosa 421

Z

Zantedeschia 175, *178*, 179, 379, *389*
zebra grass (*Miscanthus sinensis*) 387
Zinnia 169, 170, 373
creeping see *Sanvitalia procumbens*
zucchini 37, 39, 201, 203, *220*, 290

PICTURE CREDITS

The publisher would like to thank the following for their kind permission to reproduce their photographs.
(Key: a-above; b-below/bottom; c-center; f-far; l-left; r-right; t-top)

Every effort has been made to trace the copyright holders. Dorling Kindersley apologizes for any unintentional omissions and would be pleased, in such cases, to add an acknowledgment in future editions.

Majerus Garden Images: Marianne Majerus (tr). **176 GAP Photos:** Michael King / Design: Marianne Krogh Ali (tr). **179 Harpur Garden Library:** Jerry Harpur / Design: Ian and Morag Hughes, Essex (tr, cla). **180-181 GAP Photos:** Lynn Keddie / Design: Michael Littlewood - Ecodesignscape (t). **180 Marianne Majerus Garden Images:** Marianne Majerus / Sir Seewoosagur Ramgoolam Botanical Gardens, Pamplemousses, Mauritius (bl). **Photolibrary:** John Glover / Garden Picture Library (tr); Dan Kloeg / Garden Picture Library (br). **181 GAP Photos:** Lynn Keddie (clb); Jenny Lilly (br). **182-183 GAP Photos:** Elke Borkowski. **185 GAP Photos:** Geoff Kidd (bl). **Photolibrary:** JS. Sira / Garden Picture Library (r). **186 GAP Photos:** Elke Borkowski (l); Juliette Wade (r). **187 GAP Photos:** Elke Borkowski (tr, bl). **188 GAP Photos:** Friedrich Strauss (tr); Graham Strong (bl). **189 GAP Photos:** Elke Borkowski (bl, r); Jonathan Buckley (tl). **192 Alamy Images:** Julian Marshall (tr). **GAP Photos:** Maxine Adcock (bl). **Photolibrary:** Mark Winwood (br). **194 Dorling Kindersley:** Alan Buckingham (br). **195 GAP Photos:** FhF Greenmedia (tl). **196 Photolibrary:** Gary k Smith / Garden Picture Library. **197 GAP Photos:** Michael Howes (l). **198 GAP Photos:** Hanneke Reijbroek (l). **207 GAP Photos:** Elke Borkowski (cb). **208 Dorling Kindersley:** Alan Buckingham (tr). **209 Photolibrary:** Cora Niele / Garden Picture Library (crb). **213 GAP**

Photos: Graham Strong (tr). **214 GAP Photos:** Juliette Wade (bl). **215 GAP Photos:** Maxine Adcock (crb); Juliette Wade (tc). **221 Alamy Images:** Steffan Hauser / botanikfoto (br). **Photolibrary:** FoodCollection (bl). **223 Dorling Kindersley:** Alan Buckingham (tr, bl, br). **224 Alamy Images:** Clive Sawyer (bc). **Photolibrary:** Alexandre Petzold / Bios (br). **230 GAP Photos:** Fiona Lea (bc); Mark Winwood (br). **231 GAP Photos:** BIOS / Gilles Le Scanff & Joelle-Caroline Mayer (crb). **233 Dorling Kindersley:** Alan Buckingham (tl). **234 GAP Photos:** Dave Bevan (bc); Sharon Pearson (bl); Tommy Tonsberg (br). **236 Dorling Kindersley:** Alan Buckingham (bl). **238 Dorling Kindersley:** Alan Buckingham (tr). **241 GAP Photos:** Geoff Kidd (tr); S & O (crb). **242 Dorling Kindersley:** Alan Buckingham (br). **243 Dorling Kindersley:** Alan Buckingham (bl). **244 GAP Photos:** Maxine Adcock (tr); Martin Hughes-Jones (bl); Michael Howes (br). **249 GAP Photos:** Mark Winwood (bl). **250 GAP Photos:** Rob Whitworth / Design: Claudia de Yong (tr). **252 GAP Photos:** Elke Borkowski (t); Lynn Keddie (br). **252-253 Photolibrary:** Jonathan Buckley / Practical Pictures (t). **253 GAP Photos:** Janet Johnson (b). **Photolibrary:** Christopher Gallagher / Garden Picture Library (br). **254 Dorling Kindersley:** Alan Buckingham (tr). **256 GAP Photos:** Pernilla Bergdahl. **257 The Garden Collection:** Derek St Romaine (r). **262 Blackmoor Nurseries:** (b). **271 GAP**

Photos: Mark Winwood (tr). **276 GAP Photos:** John Glover (br). **281 Photolibrary:** Claire Higgins (cra). **286-287 GAP Photos:** Maayke de Ridder / Design: James Towillis. **290 FLPA:** Gary K. Smith (clb). **Garden World Images:** Sarah Lee (br). **291 The Garden Collection:** Liz Eddison (clb). **293 Photolibrary:** Leroy Alfonse (r). **299 Alamy Images:** Brian Hoffman (cr); Holmes Garden Photos (c). **GAP Photos:** BBC Magazines Ltd (cl). **300 Alamy Images:** Mark Boulton (bl). **301 GAP Photos:** (bc). **308 GAP Photos:** Lynn Keddie (tl). **309 Alamy Images:** Pete Thomas (clb). **327 Garden World Images:** Liz Cole (bc). **329 Garden World Images:** John Swithinbank (br). **336 Alamy Images:** Steven May (bl). **343 Alamy Images:** gardeningpix (br). **345 Photolibrary:** JS. Sira (br). **346 GAP Photos:** Fiona Lea (bl). **347 Alamy Images:** Steve Welsh (tc). **GAP Photos:** Anne Green-Armytage (cr). **348-349 Photolibrary:** Stephen Hamilton. **351 GAP Photos:** Zara Napier (tl). **352 GAP Photos:** Martin Hughes-Jones (tl). **353 Photolibrary:** Bob Gibbons (tr); John Miller (tl). **Dorling Kindersley:** Neil Fletcher (cr). **354 GAP Photos:** Adrian Bloom (bl); Geoff Kidd (cr). **Photolibrary:** Carole Drake (br). **355 Dorling Kindersley:** Alan Buckingham (tr, bl). **FLPA:** Nigel Cattlin (tl). **GAP Photos:** J S Sira (br). **356 GAP Photos:** Christina Bollen (tl). **357 Dorling Kindersley:** Josef Hlasek (br); Kim Taylor (cr). **GAP Photos:**

Fiona Lea (cl). **NatureSpot:** Graham Calow (bc). **358 FLPA:** Nigel Cattlin (br). **GAP Photos:** Dave Bevan (t). **359 Alamy Images:** Grant Heilman Photography (t). **GAP Photos:** Simon Colmer (cb). **360 Dorling Kindersley:** Alan Buckingham (cb). **362 Dorling Kindersley:** Alan Buckingham (bl). **363 Dorling Kindersley:** Alan Buckingham (cb, br). **364 Dorling Kindersley:** Alan Buckingham (br). **GAP Photos:** Dave Bevan (bl). **366 Dorling Kindersley:** Alan Buckingham (br). **GAP Photos:** Dave Bevan (bl). **369 Alamy Images:** Nigel Cattlin (bc). **Dorling Kindersley:** Alan Buckingham (br). **372 Dorling Kindersley:** Courtesy of Unwins (tr). **373 Dorling Kindersley:** Mark Winwood / Ball Colegrave (br). **374 Dorling Kindersley:** Courtesy of the Lechlade Garden and Fuchsia Centre, Gloucestershire (bl). **377 Clive Nichols:** (c). **380 Photolibrary:** Jacqui Hurst (br). **381 Dorling Kindersley:** Emma Firth (tr). **Science Photo Library:** (bc). **390 Garden World Images:** MAP / Arnaud Descat (bc). **418 GAP Photos:** Adrian Bloom (br). **419 GAP Photos:** Adrian Bloom (cl). **423 GAP Photos:** Martin Staffler (tc). **427 Photos Horticultural:** Michael Warren (cb). **433 Photos Horticultural:** Michael Warren / Photoshot (br).

All other images © Dorling Kindersley. For further information see: www.dkimages.com

ACKNOWLEDGMENTS

Author acknowledgments:

Zia Allaway would like to thank the teams at the RHS and Dorling Kindersley, in particular Sarah Ruddick who steered the project so well, and Alison Donovan and Becky Tennant for their unfailing design expertise.

Helena Caldon would like to thank the team at DK for staying calm and friendly, and Nick, Tomas and Millie for bearing with her through the process.

Jenny Hendy would like to thank the book's editorial and design team at DK for their endless good humor, professionalism, and attention to detail.

Martyn Cox would like to thank his mum and dad.

Publisher acknowledgments:

Dorling Kindersley would like to thank Sarah Ruddick, Chauney Dunford, Caroline Reed, Becky Shackleton, Diana Vowles, Helena Caldon, Vicky Read, Alison Shackleton, Rebecca Tennant, Joanne Doran, Elaine Hewson, Mark Cavanagh, Joanna Byrne, Lucy Claxton, Sarah Hopper, Esther Ripley, Alison Donovan, Liz Wheeler, Jonathan Metcalf, and Peter Luff for their work on the first edition, along with Fiona Wild and Ingrid Lock. Thanks also to Simon Maughan, Rae Spencer-Jones, Guy Barter, and Andrew Halstead at the RHS for their invaluable help and expertise.

For their work on this edition, Dorling Kindersley would like to thank Zia Allaway, Simon Akeroyd, and Martyn Cox for supplying updates, Myriam Megharbi for picture research, Andrew Salisbury and Leigh Hunt for reviewing pest and disease guidance, and Simon Maughan and Guy Barter for all their help.

US consultants Lori Spencer (first edition) and John Tullock (this edition)

Illustrations Vanessa Hamilton except p.78 by Peter Thomas; and pp.84, 86, 88, 90, 94, 96, and 98 by Richard Lee.

Additional photography Peter Anderson

SECOND EDITION
Project Editor Amy Slack
Senior Designer Glenda Fisher
Editor Jane Simmonds
Designer Jessica Tapolcai
Editorial Assistant Lucy Philpott
US Editor Megan Douglass
Senior Jacket Designer Nicola Powling
Jackets Coordinator Lucy Philpott
Pre-production Producer David Almond
Senior Producer Samantha Cross
Managing Editor Ruth O'Rourke
Managing Art Editor Christine Keilty
Art Director Maxine Pedliham
Publishing Director Mary-Clare Jerram

DK DELHI
Senior Editor Janashree Singha
Assistant Editor Ankita Gupta
Managing Editor Soma B. Chowdhury
Senior DTP Designer Pushpak Tyagi
DTP Designers Manish Upreti, Anurag Trivedi,
Satish Gaur
Pre-production Manager Sunil Sharma

ROYAL HORTICULTURAL SOCIETY
Consultant Guy Barter
Editor Simon Maughan
Publisher Rae Spencer-Jones
Head of Editorial Chris Young

This American Edition, 2020
First American Edition, 2011
Published in the United States by DK Publishing
1450 Broadway, Suite 801, New York, NY 10018

21 22 23 24 10 9 8 7 6 5 4 3
005–318175–Oct/2020

A catalog record for this book is available from the Library of Congress.
ISBN 978-1-4654-9940-0

DK books are available at special discounts when purchased in bulk for sales
promotions, premiums, fund-raising, or educational use. For details, contact:
DK Publishing Special Markets,
1450 Broadway, Suite 801, New York, NY 10018
SpecialSales@dk.com

Printed and bound in China

For the curious

www.dk.com